W9-DIH-216

THE FACTS ON FILE DICTIONARY OF

Proverbs

Second Edition

MARTIN H. MANSER

Associate Editors:

Rosalind Fergusson
David Pickering

Facts On File

An imprint of Infobase Publishing

The Facts On File Dictionary of Proverbs

Copyright © 2002, 2007 by Martin H. Manser

Facts On File, Inc.
An imprint of Infobase Publishing
132 West 31st Street
New York NY 10001

ISBN-10: 0-8160-6673-6
ISBN-13: 978-0-8160-6673-5

Library of Congress Cataloging-in-Publication Data

Manser, Martin H.
 The Facts On File dictionary of proverbs/Martin Manser; associate editor,
 Rosalind Fergusson. David Pickering.
  p.   cm.
 Includes index.
 ISBN 0-8160-6673-6
 1. Proverbs, English. I. Title: Dictionary of proverbs. II. Fergusson, Rosalind.
 III. Title.
 PN6421 .M36 2002
 082—dc21   2002067832

Text design by Sandy Watanabe

Cover design by Cathy Rincon

Printed in the United States of America

MP Hermitage 10 9 8 7 6 5 4 3 2 1

This book is printed on acid-free paper.

To Hannah and Ben

Contents

Preface to the New Edition

The text of this second edition of the dictionary has been expanded to include more familiar, long-established proverbs (e.g., **it takes one to know one**; **worse things happen at sea**) as well as a selection of more modern proverbial sayings (e.g., **you snooze, you lose**; **men are from Mars, women are from Venus**). As in the first edition, care has been taken not to confuse idiomatic sayings with true proverbs and to include details of variant forms by which proverbs might be known to different readers. Existing entries have also been updated to include modern variants, e.g., *the email of the species is more deadly than the mail*, as a variant of **the female of the species is deadlier than the male**; and *the geek shall inherit the earth*, as a variant of **the meek shall inherit the earth**. The indexes have been similarly expanded.

Boxes

In addition, this text of this new edition has been embellished with boxes containing selections of interesting proverbs from a number of other languages and cultures. The aim of these is to provide a glimpse of other proverbial traditions. Many of these examples are foreign-language equivalents of familiar English sayings, while others are unique to their particular cultural background. Further boxes group proverbs that are related through their biblical or literary origins. Most of the proverbs included in the boxes are not covered elsewhere in the main text.

Introduction

A proverb is a saying, usually short, that expresses a general truth about life. Proverbs give advice, make an observation, or present a teaching in a succinct and memorable way. This dictionary covers the main English-language proverbs that are widely recognized today.

We use proverbs or allude to them quite often in everyday speech: *Better safe than sorry; The grass is always greener on the other side of the fence; If at first you don't succeed, try, try again; Let sleeping dogs lie; A trouble shared is a trouble halved.*

Arrangement of proverbs

In this dictionary the proverbs are listed by strict letter-by-letter alphabetical order of the proverb, excluding only at the beginning of a proverb, *A, An,* and *The:*

> **big fish eat little fish**
>
> **the bigger they are, the harder they fall**
>
> **a bird in the hand is worth two in the bush**
>
> **a bird never flew on one wing**
>
> **too much of a good thing is worse than none at all**
>
> **toot your own horn lest the same be never tooted**
>
> **to the pure all things are pure**

Proverbs can also be found using the keyword index, which lists all the main nouns, adjectives, and verbs.

Definitions

After the proverb itself comes an explanation of the meaning of the proverb:

> **pride goes before a fall**

Arrogance and overconfidence often lead to humiliation or disaster; often used as a warning . . .

uneasy lies the head that wears a crown

Those in power are weighed down by responsibilities, feelings of insecurity, or fears of losing their position and can never rest easy . . .

Examples

Examples have been chosen to demonstrate the use of a proverb. They come from English literature or have been specially compiled for this text:

boys will be boys

Boys must be forgiven for their bad or boisterous behavior; also used ironically when grown men behave in an irresponsible or childish manner: "Aunt Sally was a good deal uneasy; but Uncle Silas he said there warn't no occasion to be—boys will be boys, he said, and you'll see this one turn up in the morning all sound and right" (Mark Twain, *Huckleberry Finn,* 1884).

a good name is sooner lost than won

It takes a lot of time and effort to earn a good name for yourself, but you can lose it in an instant with a single foolish act: *Think carefully before you get involved in anything that is not strictly legal—remember that a good name is sooner lost than won.*

Origins

Many proverbs have been in use for many years:

every man is his own worst enemy

. . . The proverb was first recorded in Thomas Browne's *Religio Medici* (1643).

every man is the architect of his own fortune

. . . The proverb is attributed to the Roman politician Appius Claudius Caecus, who held the post of censor from 312 B.C. to 308 B.C.

Sometimes, proverbs are quotations:

the leopard can't change its spots

. . . The proverb is of biblical origin: "Can the Ethiopian change his skin, or the leopard his spots?" (Jeremiah 13:23).

a rose by any other name would smell as sweet

. . . The proverb comes from Shakespeare's play *Romeo and Juliet* (2:2): "What's in a name? that which we call a rose/By any other name would smell as sweet."

Some proverbs have come into use in contemporary times. These include:

garbage in, garbage out

. . . First recorded in 1964, the proverb originally referred to computer input and output, and is still used in that context, often in the form of the acronym *GIGO.*

if it ain't broke, don't fix it

. . . The proverb was first recorded in 1977, popularized by Bert Lance, director of the Office of Management and Budget in President Jimmy Carter's administration.

it takes a village to raise a child

. . . Of African origin, the proverb was popularized by Hillary Clinton, wife of President Bill Clinton, in the mid-1990s.

The "first recorded" date given is not the date of origin—most proverbs originated in spoken language, and this is simply the first known written record of the proverb:

first impressions are the most lasting

. . . The proverb was first recorded in William Congreve's play *The Way of the World* (1700) in the form "There is a great deal in the first impression."

Where an early form of a proverb or other quotation is taken from a named source, the spellings of the original have been retained; in other cases spellings have been modernized for the convenience of the user:

nature abhors a vacuum

. . . Of ancient origin, the proverb was first recorded in English in 1551, in Thomas Cranmer's *Answer to Gardiner:* "Naturall reason abhorreth vacuum."

a cat has nine lives

. . . The proverb was first recorded in 1546 in the form "A woman has nine lives like a cat."

Variants and use of proverbs

Variants on the proverb are given after the main entry:

a word to the wise is sufficient

Variant of this proverb: a word is enough to the wise.

Alterations to the words of the proverb, shorter expressions of the proverb, or humorous applications are also shown:

once a thief always a thief

. . . Other words may be substituted for *thief,* such as *crook, drunkard, fool,* or *whore,* and the proverb is occasionally applied to those with enduring virtues rather than persistent vices, as in "Once a lady, always a lady."

to err is human, to forgive divine

. . . A modern facetious variant is "To err is human, but to really foul things up requires a computer."

Cross-references

Cross-references are given from all variant entries that are not alphabetically adjacent to the main form:

A word is enough to the wise   *See* A WORD TO THE WISE IS SUFFICIENT.

Proverbs with similar or opposite meanings

Proverbs that express similar or opposite meanings are listed at the end of entries:

actions speak louder than words

Proverb expressing similar meaning: DEEDS ARE FRUITS, WORDS ARE BUT LEAVES.

absence makes the heart grow fonder

Proverb expressing opposite meaning: OUT OF SIGHT, OUT OF MIND.

Indexes

Two indexes are included at the back of this dictionary:

Index of themes—a listing of proverbs under thematic headings.

Index of keywords—a listing of the nouns, adjectives, and verbs of the proverbs.

Martin H. Manser
Rosalind Fergusson
David Pickering

a

absence is the mother of disillusion A period of separation may enable you to consider people or things more objectively and see them in a truer but less favorable light: *While her boyfriend was away she became increasingly aware of all his little faults, which she had ignored when they were together—absence is the mother of disillusion.* The proverb is recorded as a regional expression in the United States.

absence makes the heart grow fonder Your affection for those close to you— family and friends—increases when you are parted from them: ". . . meantime he exhorts me to the exercise of patience, 'that first of woman's virtues,' and desires me to remember the saying, 'Absence makes the heart grow fonder,' and comfort myself with the assurance that the longer he stays away the better he shall love me when he returns" (Anne Brontë, *Tenant of Wildfell Hall,* 1848). The proverb was first recorded c. 1850, but the sentiment is expressed in earlier literature— for example, by James Howell (1593?–1666), who wrote "Distance sometimes endears friendship, and absence sweeteneth it." Compare Sextus Propertius (c. 54 B.C.–A.D. 2), "*semper in absentes felicior aestus amantes* [passion is always warmer toward absent lovers]."

Proverb expressing opposite meaning: OUT OF SIGHT, OUT OF MIND.

the absent are always in the wrong *See* HE WHO IS ABSENT IS ALWAYS IN THE WRONG.

the absent are never without fault nor the present without excuse *See* HE WHO IS ABSENT IS ALWAYS IN THE WRONG.

accidents will happen in the best-regulated families No matter how careful you are, you may still do something by accident or mistake; often used to console somebody who has done such a thing: "'Copperfield,' said Mr. Micawber, 'accidents will occur in the best-regulated families; and in families not regulated by . . . the influence of Woman, in the lofty character of Wife, they must be expected with confidence, and must be borne with philosophy'" (Charles Dickens, *David Copperfield,* 1850). The proverb was first recorded in George Colman's play *Deuce Is in Him* (1763) in the shorter form "accidents will happen."

Variant of this proverb: accidents will happen in the best of families.

accusing the times is but excusing ourselves People who seek to blame the times or conditions they live in are really trying to avoid taking the blame themselves: *It strikes me that the prime minister needs to be reminded that those who accuse the times are but excusing themselves.* The proverb was first recorded in 1732 by Thomas Fuller in *Gnomologia.*

Proverb expressing similar meanings: HE WHO EXCUSES HIMSELF ACCUSES HIMSELF.

action is worry's worst enemy You can banish anxiety by keeping busy and active, or by taking action to solve the problem that is worrying you: *Action is worry's worst enemy, so don't just sit there brooding—do something!*

actions speak louder than words What you do is more important than what you say, or what you promise to do: "The gallant foreigner, who could not tell them how he sympathized with them, but whose actions spoke louder than words" (F. McCullagh, *With the Cossacks,* 1906). The first recorded use of the proverb, in the form "actions are more precious than words," was in a speech by the English politician John Pym in 1628. Its current form is of U.S. origin.

Proverb expressing similar meaning: DEEDS ARE FRUITS, WORDS ARE BUT LEAVES.

action without thought is like shooting without aim Think before you act in order to achieve the best results: *Disregarding the proverb that action without thought is like shooting without aim, he went straight out and bought a computer that proved to be totally unsuitable for his needs.*

Proverb expressing similar meaning: LOOK BEFORE YOU LEAP.

admiration is the daughter of ignorance People often admire others about whom they only have incomplete knowledge: *The president's current popularity only proves the rule that admiration is the daughter of ignorance.* This U.S. proverb was first recorded in 1733–58 by Benjamin Franklin in *Poor Richard's Almanack.*

Proverb expressing similar meaning: WHAT THE EYE DOESN'T SEE, THE HEART DOESN'T GRIEVE OVER.

Proverb expressing opposite meaning: PREJUDICE IS THE DAUGHTER OF IGNORANCE.

adventures are to the adventurous Those who are not bold, and who take no risks, will not have exciting lives or achieve spectacular things: "He told himself that adventure was to the adventurous. . . . If he could not make the effort for the small he would miss the big adventure" (Thomas Hinde, *Mr. Nicholas,* 1952). The proverb was first recorded in Benjamin Disraeli's *Coningsby* (1844).

adversity makes strange bedfellows In times of hardship or misfortune people often befriend or form alliances with those whose company they would normally avoid: *The merger of the two companies surprised everybody, but these are hard times for the industry and adversity makes strange bedfellows.* The proverb was first recorded in Shakespeare's play *The Tempest* (2:2) in the form "Misery acquaints a man with strange bedfellows."

Variants of this proverb: misery makes strange bedfellows; poverty makes strange bedfellows.

after a storm comes a calm A period of anger or trouble is usually followed by a period of relative peace: "After a

AFRICAN PROVERBS

Every African country has its heritage of sayings and proverbs. Some are known throughout the continent, while others are unique to particular countries. The following list includes some of the most colorful examples, many of them inspired by the wildlife and landscape of Africa.

The best trees grow on the steepest hills

By trying often, the monkey learns to jump from the tree

Do not blame God for having created the tiger, but thank him for not giving it wings

Even if the elephant is thin he is still the lord of the jungle

Even the best cooking pot will not produce food

Every beast roars in its own den

Fear is no obstacle to death

Goats cannot live in a herd of leopards

He on whose head we would break a coconut never stands still

The horizon will not disappear as you run towards it

Hunt in every jungle, for there is wisdom and good hunting in all of them

If there were no elephants in the jungle, the buffalo would be big

If they are offered winged ants, people will eat them

If you have escaped the jaws of the crocodile while bathing in the river, you will surely meet a leopard on the way

If you have five wives, then you have five tongues

Rain does not fall on one roof alone

The smaller the lizard the greater the hope of becoming a crocodile

The viper assumes the colors of his surroundings

When you chop off a snake's head all you are left with is a piece of rope

Where the cattle stand together, the lion lies down hungry

Where there is no wealth there is no poverty

storm comes a calm. Wearied with a former blustering they began now to repose themselves in a sad silence" (Thomas Fuller, *Church History of Britain,* 1655). The proverb was first recorded in this form in 1582, but the sentiment it expresses is found in writing more than 200 years earlier. It has given rise to the cliché *the calm before the storm,* which reverses the order of things and describes a period of peace before an upheaval.

Proverbs expressing similar meaning: THE DARKEST HOUR IS JUST BEFORE DAWN; WHEN THINGS ARE AT THE WORST THEY BEGIN TO MEND.

after death the doctor Help sometimes comes too late: "All his tricks founder, and he brings his physic/After his patient's death: the King already/Hath married the fair lady" (William Shakespeare, *Henry VIII,* 3:2). The proverb was first recorded c. 1385–90 by Geoffrey Chaucer in *Troilus and Criseyde.*

after dinner rest awhile, after supper walk a mile It is best for the digestion

3

to rest after a heavy meal and take some exercise after a light meal: "As the proverb says, for health sake, after dinner, or rather after supper, willingly then I'll walk a mile to hear thee" (Philip Massinger, *The Unnatural Combat,* 1639). The proverb was first recorded in 1582 in a slightly different form, with *talk* in place of *rest.*

Variant of this proverb: after dinner sit awhile, after supper walk a mile.

age before beauty Older people have precedence over those who are younger and more attractive; said when standing back to let another person go first or when pushing in ahead of somebody: *"Age before beauty," she said as she stepped in front of the young woman at the head of the line.* The proverb was first recorded in 1843. Facetious retorts or extensions to the proverb include "Beauty before the beast," "Grace before meat," and "Pearls before swine."

the age of miracles is past Miracles no longer happen; used when some desirable occurrence seems highly unlikely: *I didn't expect the authorities to take any action in response to my complaint—the age of miracles is past.* The proverb occurs in Shakespeare's play *All's Well that Ends Well* (2:3) in the form "They say miracles are past," which implies that it is of earlier origin.

Proverb expressing opposite meaning: WONDERS WILL NEVER CEASE!

agree, for the law is costly It is expensive to settle disputes in court because of the legal costs involved: "Come, agree, agree; the law's costly" (Jonathan Swift, *A Complete Collection of Polite and Ingenious Conversation*, 1738). The proverb was first recorded in 1605 by William Camden in *Remains Concerning Britain.*

alcohol will preserve anything but a secret People have a tendency to talk too freely and become indiscreet when they are drunk: *I hoped that he would not have too much to drink at the reception—I had told him about Kate's pregnancy in confidence, and it's well known that alcohol will preserve anything but a secret.* The proverb is recorded as a regional expression in the United States.

Proverbs expressing similar meaning: DRUNKENNESS REVEALS WHAT SOBERNESS CONCEALS; THERE'S TRUTH IN WINE.

all animals are equal, but some are more equal than others In a society or organization where all are supposedly equal, it is often the case that some have special privileges, or greater power than others: "Thus, even on the night of such personal triumph, Jason Gilbert was once again reminded that although all Harvard undergraduates are equal, some are more equal than others" (Erich Segal, *The Class,* 1985). Other words may be substituted for *animals,* as in the above quotation. The proverb comes from George Orwell's novel *Animal Farm* (1945), where it is the ultimate slogan of a supposedly egalitarian regime set up by the animals of a farm, which gradually becomes as tyrannical as the human one it replaced.

Proverb expressing similar meaning: ALL MEN ARE CREATED EQUAL.

all arts are brothers, each is a light to the other The arts should not be considered as separate entities but as parts of one whole, each complementing and leading to a better understanding and appreciation of the others: *Looking at a great painting can move me in the same way as listening to a fine piece of music—they say all arts are brothers.* The proverb was first recorded in 1847.

Variant of this proverb: all arts are one, all branches on one tree.

all bad things come in threes *See* THINGS COME IN THREES.

all cats are gray in the dark People have no distinguishing features, and their appearance becomes unimportant, in the dark; sometimes used with reference to a person's choice of sexual partner: "You forgot that all cats are grey in the dark and so are uniformed policemen" (Jonathan Ross, *Dark Blue and Dangerous,* 1981). The proverb was first recorded in this form in 1596. It was used with sexual connotations in a letter written by Benjamin Franklin in 1745: "And as in the dark all Cats are grey, the Pleasure of corporal Enjoyment with an old Woman is at least equal, and frequently superior."

Variants of this proverb: all cats are black at night; at night all cats are gray.

all chiefs and no Indians *See* TOO MANY CHIEFS AND NOT ENOUGH INDIANS.

all commend patience, but none can endure to suffer It is far easier to tell somebody else to be patient than to be patient yourself: *She said I should wait and see, but it was difficult to take her advice—all commend patience, but none can endure to suffer.* The proverb was first recorded in 1948 in a U.S. proverb collection.

all fish are not caught with flies In some circumstances different methods must be employed to achieve a desired end: *The old man grinned and said something about all fish not being caught with flies.* The proverb was first recorded in 1580 by John Lyly in *Euphues and his England.*

all good things come in threes *See* THINGS COME IN THREES.

all good things come to those who wait *See* ALL THINGS COME TO THOSE WHO WAIT.

all good things must come to an end Nothing lasts forever; often said resignedly when a pleasant experience or sequence of events finally ends: *We had had a wonderful vacation, but all good things must come to an end.* The proverb was first recorded c. 1440: "Ye wote wele of all thing moste be an ende" (*Partonope of Blois*). The word *good* was probably not added until the 19th or early 20th century.

all is fish that comes to the net Anything that comes along is accepted and turned to advantage: "I don't know that she cares for one more than the other. There are a couple of young Air Force chaps too. I fancy all's fish that comes to her net at present" (Agatha Christie, *Murder in Mesopotamia,* 1936). First recorded c. 1520, the proverb is sometimes applied to a particular person by substituting *my, his, her,* and so on for *the,* as in this example.

Proverb expressing similar meaning: ALL IS GRIST THAT COMES TO THE MILL.

all is grist that comes to the mill Everything, no matter how small or unpromising, can be put to use: *She carried a notebook and pencil with her wherever she went—for a writer, all is grist that comes to the mill.* The proverb was first recorded, with slightly different wording, in 1655. It also occurs with *my, his, her,* and so on in place of *the* and in the figurative phrase *grist to the mill,* as in Charles Dickens's novel *A Tale of Two*

5

Cities (1859): "The clearance was effected at last; the Stryver arrears were handsomely fetched up; everything was got rid of until November should come with its fogs atmospheric, and fogs legal, and bring grist to the mill again." *Grist* is grain brought to a mill to be ground.

Variant of this proverb: it's all grist for the mill.

Proverb expressing similar meaning: ALL IS FISH THAT COMES TO THE NET.

all is not gold that glitters   *See* ALL THAT GLITTERS IS NOT GOLD.

all lay loads on the willing horse   *See* THE WILLING HORSE CARRIES THE LOAD.

all men are created equal   No person is born superior or inferior to another, so all should have equal rights: "Colonel Cathcart was infused with the democratic spirit: he believed that all men were created equal, and therefore spurned all men outside Group Headquarters with equal fervor" (Joseph Heller, *Catch-22*, 1955). The proverb comes from the Declaration of Independence (1776), in which Thomas Jefferson wrote: "We hold these truths to be self-evident, that all men are created equal, that they are endowed by their Creator with certain unalienable Rights, that among these are Life, Liberty, and the pursuit of Happiness."

Proverbs expressing similar meaning: JACK'S AS GOOD AS HIS MASTER; ALL ANIMALS ARE EQUAL, BUT SOME ARE MORE EQUAL THAN OTHERS.

Proverb expressing opposite meaning: EQUALITY BEGINS IN THE GRAVE.

all roads lead to Rome   There are many different ways to achieve the same result, or to come to the same conclusion: "All roads lead to Rome: and even animal individuality throws a ray on human problems" (J. S. Huxley, *The Individual in the Animal Kingdom*, 1912). The proverb was first recorded, with different wording, in Chaucer's *Prologue to Astrolabe* (c. 1391). Compare the medieval Latin proverb "*Mille vie ducunt hominem per secula Romam* [A thousand roads lead man forever toward Rome]." In modern use other place-names are sometimes substituted for *Rome*.

Proverbs expressing similar meaning: THERE ARE MORE WAYS OF KILLING A CAT THAN CHOKING IT WITH CREAM; THERE'S MORE THAN ONE WAY TO SKIN A CAT.

all's fair in love and war   Any action, however mean or unscrupulous, is permissible in certain situations; often used to justify cheating or deception: "'You opened the letter!' . . . 'How was I to read it if I hadn't? All's . . . fair in love and war, you know'" (Francis Edward Smedley, *Frank Fairleigh*, 1850). The proverb was first recorded, with different wording, in 1620. In modern use an extra word is often added to or substituted for part of the proverb, as in "All's fair in love—an' war—an' politics" (George Ade, *County Chairman*, 1903).

all's for the best in the best of all possible worlds   Everything that happens does so for a good reason, and things in general cannot be any better; generally used to present an optimistic worldview: "The administrative departments were consuming miles of red tape in the correctest forms of activity, and everything was for the best in the best of all possible worlds" (George Bernard Shaw, *The Shew-ing-up of Blanco Posnet,* 1911). The proverb is a translation of a line from the French writer Voltaire's philosophical tale *Candide* (1759). In *The Silver Stallion* (1926), James Branch Cabell made the more cynical observation: "The optimist proclaims that we live in the best of all possible worlds; and the pessimist fears this is true."

all's well that ends well Problems and misfortunes along the way can be forgotten when everything ends satisfactorily: "When the books were signed the vicar congratulated the husband and wife on having performed a noble, and righteous, and mutually forgiving act. 'All's well that ends well,' he said smiling" (Thomas Hardy, *Jude the Obscure,* 1895). First recorded in this form c. 1530, the proverb is perhaps best known as the title of one of Shakespeare's plays.

all that glitters is not gold People and things are not always as attractive or valuable as they seem: "'I do wish I hadn't a penny in the world, then I should know who my true friends were.' 'Poor little lass! She has found out that all that glitters is not gold, and the disillusion has begun,' said the doctor to himself" (Louisa May Alcott, *Rose in Bloom,* 1876). The proverb occurs in Shakespeare's play *The Merchant of Venice* (2:7) in the form "All that glisters is not gold," but the sentiment it expresses was first recorded c. 1220.

Variant of this proverb: all is not gold that glitters.

Proverb expressing similar meaning: APPEARANCES ARE DECEIVING.

all the world's a stage Everybody goes through life acting out the roles that they have to play: "Jackie [Onassis] never lets down in public. The whole world is a stage and she's its leading lady" (*New York Post,* 1994). The proverb was popularized in this form in Shakespeare's play *As You Like It* (2:7): "All the world's a stage, / And all the men and women merely players: / They have their exits and their entrances; / And one man in his time plays many parts."

Variant of this proverb: the world is a stage and all the people in it actors.

all things are easy to industry, all things difficult to sloth Anything can be achieved by those who are prepared to work hard: *You'll never find a job if you sit in front of the television all day—all things are easy to industry, all things difficult to sloth.* The proverb was first recorded in 1734, in Benjamin Franklin's *Poor Richard's Almanack.*

Variant of this proverb: sloth makes all things difficult, but industry makes all things easy.

all things are possible with God Nothing is impossible to the divine will; often used more generally to imply that anything might happen: *He seemed an unlikely candidate for the priesthood, but all things are possible with God.* The proverb is of biblical origin in its current form: "With men this is impossible; but with God all things are possible" (Matthew 19:26), but the sentiment it expressed is found much earlier, in Homer's *Odyssey* (c. eighth century B.C.): "with the gods all things can be done."

all things come to an end *See* EVERYTHING HAS AN END.

all things come to those who wait If you are patient, you will have what you desire: *Remember that all things come to those who wait, and don't be too disappointed if you miss promotion this time.* First recorded in 1530 with different wording, the proverb occurs in Henry Wadsworth Longfellow's *Tales of a Wayside Inn* (1863): *"All things come to him who will but wait."*

Variants of this proverb: all good things come to those who wait; everything comes to those who wait.

all things will pass   See THIS, TOO, SHALL PASS.

all words are pegs to hang ideas on Words are simply tools for the formulation and communication of ideas: *It doesn't matter which terminology you use—all words are pegs to hang ideas on.* The proverb originated in 1887, in Henry Ward Beecher's *Proverbs from Plymouth Pulpit.*

all work and no play makes Jack a dull boy People who do not make time for leisure activities risk damaging their health, the quality of their work, or their personal relationships; often used to justify a break from work or to persuade somebody to take one: *You're doing far too much overtime—all work and no play makes Jack a dull boy.* The proverb was first recorded in 1659. It may be applied to people of either sex, often with the person's name in place of *Jack* (and *girl* in place of *boy,* if appropriate).

always a bridesmaid, never a bride If you are often asked to be a bridesmaid—traditionally, three or more times—you will never marry yourself; also used more generally as a lament by a young woman who receives many invitations to be bridesmaid but no proposals of marriage: *I've been bridesmaid to three of my old schoolfriends—when will it be my turn to get married? Always a bridesmaid, never a bride.* The proverb was first recorded in 1882 in E. M. Ingraham's *Bond & Free* in the form "Always a maiden, never a wife," the word *maiden* meaning "bridal attendant" in this context.

Variant of this proverb: three times a bridesmaid, never a bride.

always in a hurry, always behind When you try to do things too quickly you work less efficiently and ultimately take longer: *Bearing in mind the saying "Always in a hurry, always behind," I made an effort to slow down and work more methodically.* The proverb was first recorded in 1948 in a U.S. proverb collection.

Proverbs expressing similar meaning: MORE HASTE, LESS SPEED; HASTE MAKES WASTE.

always look on the bright side You should always take the optimistic or positive view, especially when things are going badly: "I was walking the ridgepole and I fell off. I expect I have sprained my ankle. But . . . I might have broken my neck. Let us look on the bright side of things" (Lucy Maud Montgomery, *Anne of Green Gables,* 1908). The proverb was first recorded in 1726, in a sermon by John Wesley. According to a less well-known saying, "If you try to make some people see the bright side, they will complain that it hurts their eyes."

Variant of this proverb: look on the bright side, or polish up the dark one.

always something new out of Africa Africa is an endless source of novelty and interest: *The story just goes to prove that there is always something new out of Africa.*

The proverb was recorded as early as the fourth century B.C. by Aristotle in *De Anima*. It became more familiar in more modern times through the release of the film entitled *Out of Africa* in 1985.

always take the bitter with the better *See* YOU HAVE TO TAKE THE BITTER WITH THE SWEET.

America is a tune: it must be sung together There is a need for unity and harmony among and within the states of America: *America is a tune, it must be sung together, and we must strive to achieve consensus on this issue.* The proverb is recorded as a regional expression in the United States.

anger improves nothing but the arch of a cat's back There is nothing to be gained by losing your temper: *It's no use shouting at them when they make a mistake—anger improves nothing but the arch of a cat's back.* The proverb is recorded as a regional expression in the United States.

anger without power is folly It is futile to get angry about things you can do nothing about: *He is in no position to do anything and might as well as calm down: as they say, anger without power is folly.* The proverb is thought to have been ultimately of German origin.

another day, another dollar However hard or tedious paid work may be, at least there is some financial reward; often said with relief at the end of the working day or, more generally, in the hope of a better day tomorrow: *I get little job satisfaction from the work, but my philosophy is "Another day, another dollar."* The proverb was first recorded in 1957, in D. Erskine's *Pink Hotel,* but may have originated earlier in the 20th century.

Variant of this proverb: a new day, a new dollar.

any port in a storm In desperate circumstances people will accept help from any source, including those they would normally shun: "'I have understood that there is a little feeling between you and Mr. Hand and the other gentlemen I have mentioned. But . . . I'm in a corner, and it's any port in a storm. If you want to help me I'll make the best terms I can, and won't forget the favor'" (Theodore Dreiser, *The Titan,* 1914). The proverb was first recorded in 1749, in John Cleland's *Memoirs of a Woman of Pleasure,* better known as *Fanny Hill.*

any publicity is good publicity Even bad publicity draws attention to a person or product and may therefore serve a useful purpose: *The show was panned in the popular press, but ticket sales have soared—it seems that any publicity is good publicity!* The proverb probably originated in the 20th century.

any stick will serve to beat a dog with *See* IT'S EASY TO FIND A STICK TO BEAT A DOG.

anything worth doing is worth doing well *See* IF A THING'S WORTH DOING, IT'S WORTH DOING WELL.

an ape's an ape, a varlet's a varlet, though they be clad in silk or scarlet The true nature of a person or thing may be hidden by outside appearance but cannot be changed: "The naked ape is in danger of

. . . forgetting that beneath the surface gloss he is still very much a primate. ('An ape's an ape, a varlet's a varlet, though they be clad in silk or scarlet')" (Desmond Morris, *The Naked Ape,* 1967). The proverb is of ancient origin in the form "An ape is an ape, even if it has gold insignia," which occurs in the works of the Greek writer Lucian (c. 125–c. 200). The word *varlet* may mean "servant" or "rogue," and silk and scarlet are traditionally worn by holders of high office, such as in the legal profession, at whom the proverb is often directed.

Proverb expressing similar meaning: CLOTHES DON'T MAKE THE MAN.

Proverb expressing opposite meaning: CLOTHES MAKE THE MAN.

appearances are deceiving Things are not always as they seem, and you cannot necessarily trust the evidence of your eyes: "Ahem—nothing of this, eh, Selden? As one of the family, I know I may count on you—appearances are deceptive—and Fifth Avenue is so imperfectly lighted" (Edith Wharton, *The House of Mirth,* 1905). The proverb was first recorded in 1666, in an Italian proverb collection, but the sentiment it expresses can be found in one of the fables of Aesop (sixth century B.C.), which also gave rise to the figurative phrase *a wolf in sheep's clothing.*

Variant of this proverb: appearances are deceptive.

Proverbs expressing similar meaning: ALL THAT GLITTERS IS NOT GOLD; A GOOD HORSE CANNOT BE OF A BAD COLOR.

Proverbs expressing opposite meaning: IF IT LOOKS LIKE A DUCK, WALKS LIKE A DUCK, AND QUACKS LIKE A DUCK, IT'S A DUCK; WHAT YOU SEE IS WHAT YOU GET.

appetite comes with eating Desire or enthusiasm for something often increases as you do it: *They say that appetite comes with eating, and it seemed that the killer grew more hungry for blood after each successive murder.* The proverb was first recorded in Rabelais's *Gargantua* (1534), in the French form *"l'appétit vient en mangeant."* In *Hamlet* (1:2), Shakespeare wrote (of Gertrude's love for Hamlet's father): "Why, she would hang on him, / As if increase of appetite had grown / By what it fed on."

Variant of this proverb: the appetite grows on what it feeds on.

an apple a day keeps the doctor away Fruit is an important part of a healthy diet: "An apple a day keeps the doctor away. But wait! Has the apple been treated with Alar?" (*Washington Post,* 1991). The proverb was first recorded in 1866 in the form "Eat an apple on going to bed, / And you'll keep the doctor from earning his bread."

the apple never falls far from the tree Children resemble their parents in character and nature: "Forbes has a lively sense of fun (his motorcycling, balloon-riding father, Malcolm, certainly had one, and the apple does not fall far from the tree)" (*Washington Post,* 1996). The proverb is also sometimes used with reference to children who choose to live close to their parents or their place of birth, as in a letter by Ralph Waldo Emerson (1839): "As men say the apple never falls far from the stem, I shall hope that another year will draw your eyes and steps to this old dear odious haunt of the race." Compare the 16th-century German proverb "*Der Apfel fellt nicht gerne weit vom Baume* [The apple does not usually fall far from the tree].”

Variant of this proverb: an apple doesn’t roll far from the tree.

Proverbs expressing similar meaning: LIKE FATHER, LIKE SON; LIKE MOTHER, LIKE DAUGHTER.

April showers bring May flowers Something unpleasant often leads to something more desirable: *We have had a difficult few months setting up the project, but April showers bring May flowers, and we’re optimistic about the future.* First recorded c. 1560, with different wording, the proverb is often used with its literal meaning as one of the many sayings quoted by amateur weather forecasters.

Variant of this proverb: March winds and April showers always bring May flowers.

Proverb expressing similar meaning: EVERY CLOUD HAS A SILVER LINING.

ARABIAN PROVERBS

Arabic culture places great importance upon the qualities of courage and honor, and this is reflected in numerous proverbs of Arabian origin. Others are clearly rooted in the desolate desert wastes in which that culture evolved.

Better a thousand enemies outside the tent than one within

Better to be a free dog than a caged lion

Death rides a fast camel

Don’t pour away your water on the strength of a mirage

Fate loves a rebel

A good deed dies when it is spoken about

He who has been bitten by a snake is scared of a rope on the ground

If we are both masters, then who shall lead the mules?

It is better to cut off the head that has no pride

It is not the bullet that kills you, it is fate

Kiss the hand of your enemy if you cannot chop it off

Men fear, but time fears the pyramids

The monkey looks into the mirror and sees a gazelle

A mule can go to Mecca, but it will not come back as a pilgrim

Never trust a fool with a sword

Peace is only possible after war

Talent without skill is like a desert without an oasis

A thousand curses never tore a shirt

Trust in Allah, but tie up your camel

Two scorpions living in the same hole will get along better than two sisters in the same house

Whoever knew you when you were small will not respect you when you are big

You know a man by the sweat of his brow and the strength of his word

an army marches on its stomach You must eat well if you want to work effectively or achieve great things: "'We should go,' one of the sergeants said, eating his cheese and drinking a cup of wine. . . . 'An army travels on its stomach,' I said" (Ernest Hemingway, *A Farewell to Arms*, 1929). The proverb has been attributed to Frederick the Great (1712–86) and Napoleon Bonaparte (1769–1821).

Variant of this proverb: an army travels on its stomach.

art consists in concealing art *See* THE BEST ART CONCEALS ART.

art is long and life is short Works of art are far more enduring than human lives: *He used the works of the great artists of the Italian Renaissance to illustrate the saying "Art is long and life is short."* The proverb originated in the writings of the Greek physician Hippocrates (fourth century B.C.), where it was used with the meaning that life is too short to become fully versed in an art, specifically the profession of medicine. Chaucer translated this c. 1380 as "The lyf so short, the craft so long to lerne." The proverb is still sometimes used with its ancient interpretation, as in Charles Dickens's novel *Martin Chuzzlewit* (1843–44): "This . . . is my chamber. I read here when the family suppose I have retired to rest. Sometimes I injure my health rather more than I can quite justify to myself, by doing so; but art is long and time is short." The proverb is also quoted in the Latin form *"Ars longa, vita brevis."*

Proverb expressing similar meaning: THE DAY IS SHORT AND THE WORK IS LONG.

art is power The arts, and those who work with them, are powerful agents of influence: *We should remember that art is power, and treat our young artists accordingly.* The proverb was first recorded in 1839, in Henry Wadsworth Longfellow's prose romance *Hyperion*.

the art of being a parent consists of sleeping when the baby isn't looking The parents of a young baby must take whatever opportunity they can to catch up on lost sleep; a facetious comment on parenthood, implying that babies delight in keeping their parents awake: *Jack's first child was born three weeks ago, and he's been coming to work with dark rings under his eyes—I had to remind him that the art of being a parent consists of sleeping while the baby isn't looking!* This proverb is recorded as a regional expression in the United States.

as a tree falls, so shall it lie People should not attempt to change their beliefs or opinions just because they are about to die: "She sent a message . . . to the old father to come and see her before she died. . . . His answer was, 'As a tree falls so shall it lie'" (W. H. Hudson, *Traveller in Little Things*, 1921). The proverb is of biblical origin: "in the place where the tree falleth, there it shall be" (Ecclesiastes 11:3). It was first recorded in its current form in a proverb collection of 1678.

Variant of this proverb: where the tree falls, there it shall lie.

as good be an addled egg as an idle bird Somebody who tries and fails has achieved no less than somebody who does nothing at all; used as a reprimand for idleness or inaction: *You could at least go out and try to fix the gate—as good be an addled egg as an idle bird.* The proverb was first recorded in 1578: "If I had not bene gathered from the tree in the budde, I should beeing blowne haue proued a blast, and as good as it is to bee an addle egge as an idle bird" (John Lyly, *Euphues*).

as is the father, so is the son   *See* LIKE FATHER, LIKE SON.

as is the mother, so is the daughter   *See* LIKE MOTHER, LIKE DAUGHTER.

ask, and it shall be given to you; seek, and ye shall find; knock, and it shall be opened unto you   If you want something, take positive action to get it: *Ask, and it shall be given you—don't just sit there hoping that something will turn up.* The proverb is of biblical origin, from Matthew 7:7.

Variant of this proverb: them as asks, gits; them as don't ask, don't git.

ask advice, but use your own common sense   It is wise to ask for the advice of others when you need it, but foolish to follow that advice if your common sense suggests otherwise: *Everybody says I should resign, but I think this is a bit rash—my policy is "Ask advice, but use your own common sense."*

ask a silly question and you get a silly answer   If you ask a question that cannot be answered, or to which the answer is obvious, you are likely to receive a facetious or nonsensical reply: *I asked her what time I should expect her and she said, "When I arrive." Ask a silly question and you get a silly answer!* The proverb is based on a biblical quotation, "Answer a fool according to his folly, lest he be wise in his own conceit" (Proverbs 26:5). Its current form is

relatively recent; in earlier versions other words (such as *foolish* or *strange*) were used in place of *silly*.

Variant of this proverb: silly question, silly answer.

ask me no questions and I'll tell you no lies   It is better not to ask questions that somebody is likely to be unwilling to answer truthfully; used in response to such a question or simply to discourage an inquisitive person: "—Did she fall or was she pushed? he asked her. She answered, slighting:—Ask no questions and you'll hear no lies" (James Joyce, *Ulysses*, 1922). The proverb originated in 1773, in Oliver Goldsmith's *She Stoops to Conquer:* "Ask me no questions and I'll tell you no fibs."

Variant of this proverb: ask no questions and hear no lies.

Proverb expressing similar meaning: CURIOSITY KILLED THE CAT.

as Maine goes, so goes the nation   The members of a large group will follow the lead of an influential part of the group: *They are worried that this crisis in the computer industry may be just the beginning—as Maine goes, so goes the nation.* The proverb originated in the late 19th or early 20th centuries, referring to state elections in Maine that were thought to predict how the subsequent national elections would go. Other words or place-names are sometimes substituted for *Maine* and *nation,* as in *Crain's New York Business* (1994): "As Wall Street goes, so goes the New York office market."

Variant of this proverb: so goes Maine, so goes the nation.

as many men, as many opinions   *See* SO MANY MEN, SO MANY OPINIONS.

as the day lengthens, so the cold strengthens The coldest part of the winter often occurs in the period following the shortest day, as the hours of daylight begin to grow longer: *We usually get our worst frosts in January and February, proving the old saying "As the day lengthens, so the cold strengthens."* The proverb was first recorded in 1631: "The New Year now begun, as the Days began to lengthen, so the Cold began to strengthen" (E. Pellham, *God's Power*).

as the twig is bent, so is the tree inclined A child's early education and training are of great importance in determining the way he or she will grow up: *It is never too soon to teach your children right from wrong—as the twig is bent, so is the tree inclined.* The proverb originated in 1732, in Alexander Pope's *Epistles to Several Persons:* "'Tis Education forms the common mind,/Just as the Twig is bent, the Tree's inclined."

Variant of this proverb: as the twig is bent, the child will grow.

Proverb expressing opposite meaning: NATURE PASSES NURTURE.

as you bake, so shall you brew The way you begin determines whether you will do badly or well: *As you bake, so shall you brew, and if you had worked harder at college you would have got a better job at the end of it.* The proverb was first recorded c. 1577: "As thou bakst, so shat brewe" (*Misogonus*).

Proverb expressing similar meaning: AS YOU SOW, SO SHALL YOU REAP.

as you brew, so shall you drink People have to face the consequences of their actions: *He built up his business by exploiting his workforce, and now they have turned against him—as you brew, so shall you drink.* The proverb occurs in a collection of 13th-century poetry in the form "Let him habbe [have] as he brew, bale [misery] to dryng [drink]." From the 16th century onward the variant form became more frequent.

Variant of this proverb: as you brew, so shall you bake.

Proverb expressing similar meaning: AS YOU MAKE YOUR BED, SO YOU MUST LIE IN IT.

as you make your bed, so you must lie in it You must put up with the unpleasant results of a foolish action or decision: *We disapprove of the young man our daughter is living with, and I told her not to come running home to us if he treats her badly. "As you make your bed, so you must lie in it,"* I said. The proverb was first recorded, with different wording, c. 1590. A similar proverb was recorded in French a century earlier: "*Comme on faict son lict, on le treuve* [As one makes one's bed, so one finds it]."

Variant of this proverb: you've made your bed, now lie in it.

Proverb expressing similar meaning: AS YOU BREW, SO SHALL YOU DRINK.

as you sow, so shall you reap The way you behave—badly or well—determines what will happen to you in the future: *Her article offended a lot of important people, and now she finds herself ostracized—as you sow, so shall you reap.* The proverb is of biblical origin: "whatsoever a man soweth, that shall he also reap. For he that soweth to his flesh shall of the flesh reap corruption; but he that soweth to the Spirit shall of the Spirit reap life everlasting" (Galatians 6:7–8).

Proverb expressing similar meaning: AS YOU BAKE, SO SHALL YOU BREW.

at night all cats are gray *See* ALL CATS ARE GRAY IN THE DARK.

attack is the best form of defense *See* THE BEST DEFENSE IS A GOOD OFFENSE.

avoidance is the only remedy Sometimes the only solution to a problem is to avoid it in the first place: *As we have no cure for the disease, avoidance is the only remedy.* The proverb was first recorded c. 1380 by Geoffrey Chaucer in *Minor Poems*.

Proverb expressing opposite meaning: THERE'S A REMEDY FOR EVERYTHING EXCEPT DEATH.

away goes the devil when he finds the door shut against him Evil will never triumph if all temptations are rejected: *The old lady prevented her daughter receiving male visitors, firmly believing that the devil goes away when he finds the door shut against him.* The proverb was first recorded in 1659 by James Howell in *Paroemiographia*.

the back door robs the house *See* A POSTERN DOOR MAKES A THIEF.

a bad excuse is better than none It is better to give a poor or implausible excuse—which may, in fact, be believed—than to have no explanation or justification at all: *On the basis that a bad excuse is better than none, I told him that I had accidentally put my essay in the mailbox.* The proverb was first recorded in 1551: "This is as thei saie in English, better a badde excuse, then none at all" (Thomas Wilson, *The Rule of Reason*).

Variant of this proverb: a poor excuse is better than none.

a bad husband makes a bad wife *See* A GOOD HUSBAND MAKES A GOOD WIFE.

bad money drives out good The existence or availability of something inferior or worthless—whether it be money, music, literature, or whatever—has a tendency to make things of better quality or greater value more scarce: "bad politics tends to drive out good politics just as bad money drives out good money" (Aldous Huxley, letter dated November 18, 1933). Known as Gresham's Law, this principle was suggested by the English financier Sir Thomas Gresham (c. 1519–79), who observed that the circu-

lation of coins made of low-value metal caused people to hoard those made of precious metal and thus remove them from circulation. Although Gresham may not have originated the idea, the principle was formulated as a theory and named in his honor by the Scottish economist H. D. MacLeod in 1858. The proverb was first recorded in its current form in 1902 in *The New English Dictionary.*

bad news always comes too soon *See* HE COMES TOO EARLY WHO BRINGS BAD NEWS.

bad news travels fast Bad news, or unfavorable gossip, tends to be disseminated far more quickly than good news, the implication being that people delight in talking or hearing about the misfortunes of others: *I know bad news travels fast, but I had only just got home from work when my sister phoned to ask if it was true that I had been fired.* The proverb was first recorded in 1592 ("Euill newes flie faster still than good" [Thomas Kyd, *Spanish Tragedy*]) but is probably of ancient origin.

Variant of this proverb: ill news comes apace.

a bad penny always turns up Undesirable people will always return; often used when somebody who has left in disgrace reappears after a long absence: *I hear her ex-husband's back in town—a bad penny always turns up.* First recorded in 1766 as a simile, in a letter written by Abigail Adams, it subsequently occurred in Sir Walter Scott's *Redgauntlet* (1824) in the form "the bad shilling is sure enough to come back again."

Variant of this proverb: a bad penny always comes back.

a bad workman quarrels with his tools Workers who lack skill or competence blame their tools or equipment when things go wrong: *He apologized for the rough edges on some of the panels, saying that his saw was blunt—a bad workman always quarrels with his tools.* The proverb was first recorded in English, with different wording, in 1611. However, the French had a similar proverb in the late 13th century: "*Mauvés ovriers ne trovera ja bon hostill* [A bad workman will never find a good tool]." The U.S. writer Ambrose Bierce parodied the proverb in his *Devil's Dictionary* (1911): "A bad workman quarrels with the man who calls him that."

Variant of this proverb: a bad workman blames his tools.

a barking dog never bites People who make the most or the loudest threats are the least likely to take action: "'*De la poigne et des formes,*' cried the stout general, '*de la poigne surtout.*' And to translate into Russian; be civil, but don't spare your fists." "'Ah, you're a rascal, an incorrigible rascal,' interposed the condescending general. 'Mesdames, don't listen to him, please. A barking dog does not bite'" (Ivan Turgenev, *Smoke,* 1867). First recorded in French in the

13th century, the proverb features in a popular 20th-century joke about a man who is reluctant to enter premises where a dog is barking loudly. On being assured that "A barking never bites," he replies, "I know that and you know that, but does the dog know that?"

Variants of this proverb: dogs that bark don't always bite; barking dogs seldom bite.

a bawling cow soon forgets her own calf *See* A BELLOWING COW SOON FORGETS HER CALF.

a bayonet is a weapon with a worker at each end The weapons of war are used by ordinary people against ordinary people: *Although I knew I was fighting the enemies of my country, my conscience kept reminding me of the saying that a bayonet is a weapon with a worker at each end.* The proverb originated in 1940 as a British pacifist slogan.

bear and forbear Patience, tolerance, endurance, and forgiveness are valuable qualities in all walks of life: "'Davie, ye'll have to try and forgive me.' 'O man, let's say no more about it! . . . We're neither one of us to mend the other—that's the truth! We must just bear and forbear'" (Robert Louis Stevenson, *Kidnapped,* 1886). First recorded in this form in 1573, the proverb is probably of ancient origin: the Greek philosopher Epictetus (first century A.D.) wrote "be patient and endure." In its early use the proverb was often put forward as a formula for harmonious married life.

Variant of this proverb: you must take two bears to live with you—bear and forbear.

17

beauty and honesty seldom agree   It is rare for a person to be both good-looking and honest: "Beawtie and honesty seldome agree, for of beautie comes temptation, of temptation dishonour (John Florio, *Second Frutes*, 1591). The proverb was first recorded in 1580 by John Lyly in *Euphues and his England*.

Proverb expressing similar meaning: BEAUTY IS ONLY SKIN DEEP.

Proverb expressing opposite meaning: BEAUTY IS TRUTH, TRUTH BEAUTY.

beauty draws with a single hair   A beautiful woman has great powers of attraction: "Fair tresses man's imperial race insnare, / And beauty draws us with a single hair" (Alexander Pope, *The Rape of the Lock*, 1714). The proverb was first recorded in 1591, in John Florio's *Second Fruits:* "Ten teems of oxen draw much less, / Than doth one haire of Helens tresse."

Variant of this proverb: beauty draws more than oxen.

beauty is a good letter of introduction   Beautiful people make a better first impression on strangers than ugly people do: *She doesn't know anybody in the town, but if it's true that beauty is a good letter of introduction, then she'll have no difficulty making friends.* This proverb is recorded as a regional expression in the USA.

beauty is but a blossom   Good looks do not last: "As there is no true cuckold but calamity, so beauty's a flower" (William Shakespeare, *Twelfth Night*, 1:5). The proverb was first recorded in 1616 by T. Draxe in *Bibliotheca Scholastica*.

Proverb expressing opposite meaning: A THING OF BEAUTY IS A JOY FOREVER.

beauty is in the eye of the beholder   The perception of beauty is subjective, and not everybody finds the same people or things attractive: "'Answer, O my Gul-Bahar, more beautiful growing as the days multiply!' 'Thou flatterer! Do I not know beauty is altogether in the eye of the beholder, and that all persons do not see alike?'" (Lewis Wallace, *Prince of India*, 1893). The proverb was first recorded in this form in the late 18th century, but the sentiment it expresses is of much earlier origin. Compare Theocritus (c. 308–c. 240 B.C.), "in the eyes of love that which is not beautiful often seems beautiful."

beauty is no inheritance   Good looks are not necessarily passed on from generation to generation: *It took only one look at mother and daughter to confirm the truth behind the saying "beauty is no inheritance."* The proverb was first recorded in 1633 by T. Draxe in *Bibliotheca Scholastica*, in the variant form "beauty is no heritage."

Proverbs expressing opposite meaning: LIKE FATHER, LIKE SON; LIKE MOTHER, LIKE DAUGHTER.

beauty is only skin deep   Beauty is only a superficial quality, and may conceal an unpleasant character or nature: *He was one of the many men who forget that beauty is only skin deep and find themselves filing for divorce after a couple of years of marriage.* The proverb was first recorded in 1613. In 1960 Jean Kerr wrote, in *The Snake Has All the Lines*, "I'm tired of all this nonsense about beauty being only skin deep. That's deep enough. What do you want—an adorable pancreas?"

Variant of this proverb: beauty is only skin deep, but goodness goes to the bone.

Proverb expressing similar meaning: BEAUTY AND HONESTY SELDOM AGREE.

beauty is truth, truth beauty The qualities of beauty and truth are, or should be, inseparable and interlinked; often used when real life falls short of this ideal: *"Beauty is truth, truth beauty," but there is nothing beautiful about the truths that have been exposed in this sordid affair.* The proverb originated in 1819, in John Keats's poem *Ode on a Grecian Urn:* "'Beauty is truth, truth beauty,'—that is all/Ye know on earth, and all ye need to know."

be careful what you wish for: you might get it *See* DON'T WISH TOO HARD; YOU MIGHT JUST GET WHAT YOU WISHED FOR.

because a man is born in a stable that does not make him a horse *See* THE MAN WHO IS BORN IN A STABLE IS NOT A HORSE.

beggars can't be choosers We must accept with gratitude and without complaint what we are given when we do not have the means or opportunity to provide ourselves with something better: ". . . it's a shame we got to entertain you in such a cramped place. And there ain't any water except that ole iron sink outside in the hall, but . . . beggars can't be choosers" (Sinclair Lewis, *Main Street,* 1920). First recorded in 1546, the proverb formerly had *must not* or *should not* in place of *can't.*

Proverbs expressing similar meaning: NEVER LOOK A GIFT HORSE IN THE MOUTH; WHEN ALL FRUIT FAILS, WELCOME HAWS.

be happy while you're living, for you're a long time dead Make the most of life during the relatively short period that it lasts: *My philosophy is "Be happy while you're living, for you're a long time dead," and I try not to let things get me down.* The origin of this proverb is the Scottish motto for a house: "Be happy while y'er leevin,/For y'er a lang time deid."

behind every great man is a great woman Important or successful men often owe their status or success to the support of a female partner or colleague: *They say that behind every great man there is a great woman, but the new head of the corporation—a confirmed bachelor—seems to be an exception to that rule.*

be just before you're generous You should make sure all your debts are paid and other obligations met before you start giving money away or living extravagantly: "I owe every farthing of my money. . . . There's an old proverb—be just before you're generous" (Captain Marryat, *Peter Simple,* 1834). The proverb was first recorded in 1745, but with the implication that it was already in general use.

be kind to your friends; if it weren't for them, you would be a total stranger You cannot afford to lose your friends by treating them badly, because without them you would be alone in society: *I think you should invite her to stay with you for a few days—be kind to your friends; if it weren't for them, you would be a total stranger.*

believe only half of what you see and nothing you hear Do not be too ready to believe all the evidence of your eyes and ears; used as a warning to beware of false appearances and rumors: "Diplomats arriving in Haiti are told to believe 'nothing you hear and only half of what you see'" (*New York Times,* 1994). The proverb was first recorded in 1845, but the sentiment it expresses dates from c. 1300 or earlier. The verb *read* is sometimes substituted for *see* or *hear.*

Variant of this proverb: believe nothing of what you hear, and only half of what you see.

a believer is a songless bird in a cage Religious belief restricts a person's freedom of action and expression: *When asked why she never went to church, my aunt would always reply with the saying "A believer is a songless bird in a cage."* The proverb originated in a speech made in 1873 by the U.S. lawyer, orator, and agnostic Robert Green Ingersoll.

believing has a core of unbelieving Belief and unbelief are closely related, and sometimes you need to start from a position of skepticism to arrive at the truth: *Believing has a core of unbelieving, and they eventually accepted what had first appeared to be an incredible explanation of the phenomenon.* The proverb originated in Robert Buchanan's *Songs of Seeking* (c. 1866).

a bellowing cow soon forgets her calf The loudest laments or complaints are often the first to subside; used specifically of those whose mourning seems excessive: "When a woman, newly widowed, had tried to throw herself into her husband's grave . . . someone . . . said . . . 'Ah, you wait. The bellowing cow's always the first to forget its calf'" (Flora Thompson, *Lark Rise to Candleford,* 1945). The proverb was first recorded in 1895, but with the implication that it had long been in regional use.

Variant of this proverb: a bawling cow soon forgets her own calf.

be longing   *See* AN IDLE YOUTH, A NEEDY AGE.

be nice to people on your way up because you'll meet them on your way down Try to avoid making enemies as you rise in your chosen career, because you may need the help of the same people if you find yourself descending through the ranks again: "The man whose posture is servile in the presence of his superiors and rude or off-hand with his subordinates has forgotten the old chestnut 'Be nice to the little man on your way up, you might meet him on your way down'" (Milla Alihan, *Corporate Etiquette,* 1974). Of U.S. origin, the proverb is believed to have been coined by either Wilson Mizner (1876–1933) or Jimmy Durante (1893–1980).

be not idle and you shall not be longing   *See* AN IDLE YOUTH, A NEEDY AGE.

the best art conceals art Artistic excellence lies in making something that is subtle or intricate in construction appear simple and streamlined: "In oratory the greatest art is to hide art" (Jonathan Swift, *Faculty of Mind,* 1707). The proverb was first recorded in English c. 1583, with different wording, but is obviously of earlier origin. It also exists in the Latin form "*Ars est celare artem.*"

Variant of this proverb: art consists in concealing art.

the best defense is a good offense You are more likely to win if you take the initiative and make an attack rather than preparing to defend yourself; used in sport, politics, business, and the like: "The reigning corporate strategy these days is that the best defense is a good offense" (*Washington Post,* 1997). The proverb was first recorded in the late 18th century, and the sentiment it expresses is found in the writings of George Washington (1799): "Make them believe, that offensive operations, often times, is the surest . . . means of defense."

Variant of this proverb: attack is the best form of defense.

the best doctors are Dr. Diet, Dr. Quiet, and Dr. Merryman The best recipe for good health consists of eating and drinking sensibly and having plenty of rest and recreation: *Many modern ills are caused by the junk food we eat and the hectic pace of our working lives. We should follow the advice of our great-grandparents, who believed that the best doctors are Dr. Diet, Dr. Quiet, and Dr. Merryman.* The proverb was first recorded in 1558. "I should not staye my selfe vpon the opinion of any one phisicion, but rather vpon three. . . . The first was called doctor diet, the seconde doctor quiet, the thirde doctor mery man" (W. Bullein, *Government of Health*).

Variant of this proverb: the three doctors Diet, Quiet, and Temperance are the best physicians.

Proverb expressing similar meaning: DIET CURES MORE THAN DOCTORS.

the best is the enemy of the good By constantly striving for the best we risk destroying, or failing to produce, something good: "To maintain that all that a school provides must be provided free makes the best the enemy of the good"

(*London Times,* 1981). First recorded in English in 1861, the proverb may be of French, Italian, or Spanish origin.

Proverbs expressing opposite meaning: THE GOOD IS THE ENEMY OF THE BEST; IF A THING'S WORTH DOING, IT'S WORTH DOING WELL.

the best is yet to be No matter how good or bad the present may seem, something better lies ahead in the future: *Long-term economic forecasts suggest that the best is yet to be.* The proverb originated in 1864, in Robert Browning's poem *Rabbi Ben Ezra:* "Grow old along with me! / The best is yet to be, / The last of life, for which the first was made: / Our times are in His hand."

Proverb expressing opposite meaning: THE WORST IS YET TO COME.

the best-laid schemes of mice and men gang aft a-gley There is always the possibility that things will go wrong, no matter how carefully you make your plans: *I thought I had everything organized for the party, but the best-laid schemes of mice and men gang aft a-gley—the caterers delivered the food to the wrong address!* The proverb comes from Robert Burns's poem *To a Mouse* (1786). The Scottish phrase *gang aft a-gley* means "often go awry." In general use, the proverb is often shortened, and *plans* may be substituted for *schemes.*

Variant of this proverb: the best-laid schemes of mice and men oft go astray.

the best of friends must part Friends cannot always be together, and not all friendships last a lifetime: "'Aren't there going to be any more lessons?' . . . 'The best of friends must part'" (William

Golding, *Darkness Visible,* 1979). The proverb was first recorded in 1611, but a similar sentiment was expressed by Chaucer in *Troilus and Criseyde* (c. 1385). It features in the traditional song "There is a Tavern in the Town": "Fare thee well, for I must leave thee,/Do not let this parting grieve thee,/And remember that the best of friends must part."

Variant of this proverb: even the best of friends must part.

the best of men are but men at best   Even the greatest people have their failings and limitations: *Although it is said that the best of men are but men at best, the nation has a right to expect greater integrity from its head of state.* The proverb was first recorded in John Aubrey's *Brief Lives* (1877), as a saying of General John Lambert (1619–84).

Variant of this proverb: the best of men are but men after all.

the best place for criticism is in front of your mirror   Before you criticize others, you should first take a close look at yourself: *If she starts harping on again about the faults of her sister, I shall be tempted to remind her that the best place for criticism is in front of your own mirror.*

Proverb expressing similar meaning: THE POT CALLS THE KETTLE BLACK.

the best things come in small packages Size has no bearing on quality, and a small container may hold something of great value; often said by or to a short person: *When teased about her height, she would always reply, "The best things come in small packages."* The proverb was first recorded in 1877 in a letter by B. Farjeon, but with the implication that it was already in general use. Other words and phrases may be substituted for *the best things,* including *diamonds* and *dynamite.*

Variant of this proverb: good things come in small packages.

Proverb expressing similar meaning: SMALL IS BEAUTIFUL.

Proverb expressing opposite meaning: THE LARGER THE BODY, THE BIGGER THE HEART.

the best things in life are free   The most rewarding or satisfying experiences in life are often those that cost nothing; also used of the wonders of nature or of abstract qualities such as health and friendship: *The best things in life are free, and what could be better than a brisk walk across the hill on a sunny winter's morning?* The proverb originated in 1927 as the title of a song, which contains the following lines: "The moon belongs to everyone,/The best things in life are free,/The stars belong to everyone,/They gleam there for you and me."

Proverb expressing similar meaning: MONEY ISN'T EVERYTHING.

the best way to get even is to forget   It can be more effective to suggest an insult or injury has had no lasting impact than it would be to retaliate: "She thought about writing him a dismissive letter about disloyalty, but then remembered that the best way to get even is to forget." Though a relatively recent introduction in this form, similar sentiments have been expressed for centuries.

Variant of this proverb: to forget a wrong is the best revenge.

Proverb expressing opposite meaning: NEGLECT WILL KILL AN INJURY SOONER THAN REVENGE.

be the day weary or be the day long, at last it ringeth to evensong No matter how tiring or stressful a day you are having, you can console yourself with the fact that it will eventually be over; also used more generally to recommend perseverance or endurance in a trying situation: *Whenever she felt things were getting me down, my mother would remind me that "be the day weary or be the day long, at last it ringeth to evensong."* The proverb was first recorded in 1509. "For thoughe the day, be neuer so longe, At last the belles ryngeth to euensonge" (Stephen Hawes, *Pastime of Pleasure*).

Proverbs expressing similar meaning: IT'S A LONG ROAD THAT HAS NO TURNING; THE LONGEST DAY MUST HAVE AN END.

better a big fish in a little pond than a little fish in a big pond It is better to have a position of importance in a small organization than to be an unimportant member of a large group: *She turned down the offer of a job with one of the largest multinationals in the industry, on the basis that it is better to be a big fish in a little pond than a little fish in a big pond.* The proverb is recorded as a regional expression in the United States.

Variant of this proverb: better a big fish in a little puddle than a little fish in a big puddle.

Proverb expressing similar meaning: BETTER BE THE HEAD OF A DOG THAN THE TAIL OF A LION.

better a dinner of herbs where love is than a stalled ox where hate is It is better to be poor or dine badly in a loving environment than to eat well or have a wealthy lifestyle in an atmosphere of discord or hatred: "Lunch was a silent affair. . . . I said, 'Better a dinner of herbs than a stalled ox where hate is'" (J. Drummond, *I Saw Him Die,* 1979). The proverb is of biblical origin: "Better is a dinner of herbs where love is, than a stalled ox and hatred therewith" (Proverbs 15:17).

better a good cow than a cow of a good kind A person's character is of more importance than his or her family background: *He was afraid his parents might be disappointed in his fiancée, an ordinary girl who had worked to support her unemployed parents since her mid-teens, but his mother later voiced her approval—in private—with the remark, "Better a good cow than a cow of a good kind."* The proverb was first recorded in 1922, but with the implication that it was already in general use.

Proverb expressing similar meaning: KIND HEARTS ARE MORE THAN CORONETS.

better a little fire to warm us than a big one to burn us Sometimes it is more desirable to have only a small amount of something: *We must not be too dissatisfied with the size of our inheritance—better a little fire to warm us than a big one to burn us.* The proverb was first recorded c. 1510. "Then better is small fire one easyly to warme Then is a great fire to do one hurt or harme" (Alexander Barclay, *Eclogues*).

better be an old man's darling than a young man's slave It is better to marry an older man who will cherish you than to choose a younger husband who may treat you badly: "Let defeated rivals snarling,/ Talk of one foot in the grave,/ Better be an old man's darling,/ Than become a young man's slave" (James Robinson Planché, *Love and Fortune,* 1859). The proverb was first recorded in 1546, but with the implication that it was of much earlier origin.

At this time it had the rhyming words *derlyng* in place of *darling* and *werlyng* (meaning "object of scorn") in place of *slave*.

Variant of this proverb: better be a poor man's darling than a rich man's slave.

better be dead than out of fashion   *See* BETTER BE OUT OF THE WORLD THAN OUT OF THE FASHION.

better be envied than pitied   It is preferable to have possessions or attributes that arouse envy in others than to be pitied for having little or nothing: *I was aware that my good fortune might provoke resentment among my friends, but "Better be envied than pitied," I always say.* The proverb was first recorded in English in 1546, but the sentiment it expresses is probably of ancient Greek origin. Compare Pindar (c. 522–443 B.C.), "envy is stronger than pity," and Herodotus (c. 480–c. 425 B.C.), "it is better to be envied than to be pitied."

better be first in a village than second at Rome   It is better to be in charge in a small community or company than it is to be in a secondary position in a larger concern: "I should like Caesar . . . and choose rather to be the first man of the village, than second at Rome" (Abraham Cowley, *Essays*, 1668). The proverb was first recorded in English in 1542 by Nicholas Udall in *Apothegms of Erasmus*, but was originally a Roman saying, supposedly quoted by Julius Caesar in relation to his post as ruler of Gaul.

Proverbs expressing opposite meaning: THE HIGHEST BRANCH IS NOT THE SAFEST ROOST; UNEASY LIES THE HEAD THAT WEARS THE CROWN.

better be out of the world than out of the fashion   Some people are so intent on following fashion that it seems they would rather die than do otherwise; also used with the implication that something that is not fashionable might as well not exist: "Women seem seldom hindered by lack of money when it is a case of follow-my-leader. 'Better be out of the world than out of the fashion'" (E. F. Maitland, *From Window in Chelsea*, 1903). The proverb was first recorded in 1639.

Variant of this proverb: better be dead than out of fashion.

better be the head of a dog than the tail of a lion   It is preferable to lead a relatively minor group of people than to have an inferior position in a more important body: "The ancient . . . spirit of Englishmen was once expressed by our proverb, 'Better be the head of a dog than the tail of a lion'; i.e. the first of the yeomanry rather than the last of the gentry" (Isaac D'Israeli, *Curiosities of Literature*, 1791–1834). The proverb was first recorded in 1599. The earliest versions of the proverb had *fox, mouse,* or *lizard* in place of *dog.*

Variant of this proverb: better be the head of an ass than the tail of a horse.

Proverb expressing similar meaning: BETTER A BIG FISH IN A LITTLE POND THAN A LITTLE FISH IN A BIG POND.

better death than dishonor   People should be prepared to give up their lives to avoid dishonor; used specifically in warfare and also more generally, as when the collapse of a business seems more desirable than a loss of integrity: "'What was the old soldier's code?' Cortez asked himself. 'Death before dishonor'" (Tom Clancy, *Clear and Present Danger*, 1989).

The first recorded reference to the proverb is in P. Wylie's *Murderer Invisible* (1931), but it is probably of earlier origin.

Variant of this proverb: death before dishonor.

better late than never It is better that somebody arrives or something happens later than expected or desired, than not at all: "I'm sick of these disgusting women I've spent my life with . . . and I'm rather anxious to settle down. A bit late in the day, perhaps, but better late than never" (George Orwell, *A Clergyman's Daughter*, 1935). First recorded in English c. 1330, the proverb is probably of ancient Roman origin. The phrase "but better never late" is often added or said in response to the proverb.

better luck next time Hopefully things will go better for you next time: *"Better luck next time," said the dealer as he scooped up the chips*. The proverb was first recorded in 1834 by Captain Frederick Marryat in *Jacob Faithful*.

better one house spoiled than two It is a good thing for two bad, foolish, or otherwise undesirable people to become husband and wife and thus avoid causing trouble in two separate marriages: *I was pleased to hear that our neighbor's awful son is marrying that dreadful girl from the florist's—better one house spoiled than two!* The proverb was first recorded, with different wording, in 1586.

better safe than sorry It is wiser to take precautions—even if they seem unnecessary or excessive—than to risk disaster: *I went around the building one last time to check that all the doors and windows were locked—better safe than sorry.* The proverb was first recorded in 1837, in Samuel Lover's novel *Rory O'More*, with *sure* in place of *safe*.

Proverb expressing similar meaning: IT'S BETTER TO BE ON THE SAFE SIDE.

better something than nothing See SOMETHING IS BETTER THAN NOTHING.

the better the day, the better the deed An action is of greater value because it is performed on a holy day; often used to justify working on Sunday, Good Friday, or Christmas Day: "The better the day, the better the deed . . . It was only the Pharisees who objected to any necessary work being done on the Sabbath" (J. C. Hutcheson, *Crown and Anchor*, 1896). The proverb was first recorded in English in 1607. A similar proverb was recorded in French three centuries earlier: "*A bon jour bone euvre* [For a good day, a good deed]."

better the devil you know than the devil you don't know It is often preferable to choose or stay with people or things you know, despite their faults, than to risk replacing them with somebody or something new but possibly less desirable: *She was surprised that I was using the same builders again, after the problems I'd had with them last time, but better the devil you know than the devil you don't know.* The proverb was first recorded in this form in 1857, in Anthony Trollope's novel *Barchester Towers*: "'Better the d— you know than the d— you don't know,' is an old saying . . . but the bishop had not yet realised the truth of it." Compare the ancient Latin proverb "*nota res mala, optima* [an evil thing known is best]."

better three hours too soon than a minute too late *See* IT'S BETTER TO BE AN HOUR TOO EARLY THAN A MINUTE TOO LATE.

better to wear out than to rust out It is better to be exhausted by hard work than to remain idle; used by people accused of working too hard, especially old people who choose to remain active: *Our gardener is in his eighties but has no plans to retire just yet—"Better to wear out than to rust out," he says.* The proverb was first recorded in this form in 1820, but the sentiment it expresses is of much earlier origin. In Shakespeare's play *Henry IV, Part 2* (1:2), Sir John Falstaff presents the opposite viewpoint: "I were better to be eaten to death with a rust than to be scoured to nothing with perpetual motion."

between two stools one falls to the ground Failure to choose between alternative courses of action, or to align yourself with one of two opposing groups, may lead to disastrous consequences: *You must make up your mind which job to accept, or they will both go to other people—between two stools one falls to the ground.* The proverb was first recorded in 1390, with different wording, a version c. 1530 being closer to the modern form: "Between two stools, the arse goes to ground." A similar sentiment is expressed in the medieval Latin proverb "*labitur enitens sellis herere duabus* [he falls trying to sit on two seats]." In modern times the proverb is more frequently used in the form of the figurative phrase *to fall between two stools.*

Variant of this proverb: between two stools we come to the ground.

Proverb expressing opposite meaning: WHEN IN DOUBT, DO NOTHING.

beware of an oak, it draws the stroke; avoid an ash, it counts the flash; creep under the thorn, it can save you from harm It is dangerous to shelter from lightning under the oak, ash, or other trees: *At the first sound of thunder I made for the shelter of the hut, remembering my mother's warning: "Beware of an oak, it draws the stroke; avoid an ash, it counts the flash."* This is a piece of ancient folklore that was first recorded in 1878.

beware of Greeks bearing gifts It is wise to be suspicious of offers or friendly gestures made by enemies or opponents: *Remembering the saying "Beware of Greeks bearing gifts," I decided to reject the invitation of my professional rival, even at the risk of offending him.* The proverb comes from Virgil's *Aeneid* (first century B.C.), "*timeo Danaos, et dona ferentes* [I fear the Greeks, even when bringing gifts]," a warning given to the Trojans when a large wooden horse (filled with Greek soldiers) was delivered to the gates of their city. An early reference to the proverb in English occurs in Anthony Trollope's novel *Phineas Redux* (1873): "He would remind the right honourable gentleman that presents from Greeks had ever been considered dangerous."

Variant of this proverb: fear the Greeks bearing gifts.

Proverb expressing opposite meaning: NEVER LOOK A GIFT HORSE IN THE MOUTH.

be what you would seem to be Your appearance should reflect your true nature, and vice versa: "It's a vegetable. It doesn't look like one, but it is. . . . The moral of that is—'Be what you would seem to be'" (Lewis Carroll, *Alice's*

BIBLICAL PROVERBS

Many proverbs in common use today began as quotations from the Bible. The following list includes a selection of some of the best-known of these.

As a dog returns to his vomit, so a fool returns to his folly (Proverbs)

The borrower is servant to the lender (Proverbs)

Faith moves mountains (1 Corinthians)

A good name is better than precious ointment (Ecclesiastes)

It is more blessed to give than to receive (Acts)

The labourer is worthy of his hire (Luke)

Many are called but few are chosen (Matthew)

No man can serve two masters (Matthew)

Render therefore unto Caesar the things which are Caesar's; and unto God the things that are God's (Matthew)

Seek and ye shall find (Matthew)

A soft answer turneth away wrath (Proverbs)

Sow the wind and reap the whirlwind (Hosea)

Spare the rod and spoil the child (Proverbs)

Stolen waters are sweet, and bread eaten in secret is pleasant (Proverbs)

There is nothing new under the sun (Ecclesiastes)

The spirit is willing but the flesh is weak (Matthew)

The wages of sin is death (Romans)

The wind bloweth where it listeth (John)

Wisdom is more precious than rubies (Proverbs)

You cannot make bricks without straw (Exodus)

You cannot serve God and Mammon (Matthew)

Adventures in Wonderland, 1865). An early example is "Suche as thow semest in syghte, be in assay [trial] y-founde" (William Langland, *Piers Plowman,* c. 1377), although the sentiment is found in classical sources such as Aeschylus.

Variant of this proverb: be what you appear to be.

big fish eat little fish Small organizations or insignificant people tend to be swallowed up or destroyed by those that are greater and more powerful: *Only a handful of independent companies have survived in this competitive industry, where the big fish eat the little fish.* The proverb was first recorded in a text dating from before 1200. In Shakespeare's play *Pericles* (2:1), the following exchange occurs between two fishermen: "'Master, I marvel how the fishes live in the sea.' 'Why, as men do a-land—the great ones eat up the little ones.'"

big fleas have little fleas upon their backs to bite 'em, and little fleas have lesser fleas, and so ad infinitum In a hierarchy of size or importance, every member is affected by or dependent on the one above or below, and the hierarchy stretches to infinity in both directions: *Even a company of this size risks financial disaster if one of its suppliers has problems—big fleas have little fleas, and so on.* The proverb was first recorded in 1733, with different wording, in the satirical advice to a poet *On Poetry, A Rhapsody* by Jonathan Swift. Its current form comes from a 19th-century rhyme that continues: "And the great fleas themselves, in turn, have greater fleas to go on;/While these again have greater still, and greater still, and so on."

the bigger they are, the harder they fall The downfall of a great or important person is more painful and catastrophic than that of a lesser person: "'You are just a youth,' he observed at last, 'and he has been a great man of war from his boyhood. . . .' 'The bigger they are,' I replied, 'the harder they fall'" (Joseph Heller, *God Knows,* 1984). The proverb in its current form is attributed to the heavyweight boxer Robert Fitzsimmons (1858–1917), but the sentiment it expresses was first recorded in English as early as 1493. Compare the Roman poet Claudian (fourth century A.D.), "*Tolluntur in altum/Ut lapsu graviore ruant* [men are raised on high in order that they may fall more heavily]."

Variant of this proverb: the bigger they come, the harder they fall.

big is beautiful There are advantages to large size: *The success of this huge conglomerate only goes to prove that big is beautiful.* A U.S. proverb that became current from the 1960s, it is commonly applied in discussions of economies of scale in commercial contexts.

Proverb expressing opposite meaning: SMALL IS BEAUTIFUL.

a bird in the hand is worth two in the bush Something you have for certain now is of more value than something better you may get, especially if you risk losing what you have in order to get it: "More money might be obtained by selling the packages, but there was risk in this. Besides, it would take time, and they decided that a bird in the hand was worth two in the bush" (Horatio Alger, *Paul the Peddler,* 1871). The proverb was first recorded in English c. 1450, with different wording, but the sentiment it expresses can be found in the fables of Aesop in the sixth century B.C. The current form dates from no later than 1581. The U.S. actress Mae West parodied the proverb when she said, "A man in the house is worth two in the street," in the movie *Belle of the Nineties* (1934).

Variant of this proverb: a bird in the hand is worth a hundred flying.

a bird never flew on one wing Something extra or additional is required; often used to hint that another drink or some more money would be welcome: *Let's have another drop of whiskey before we go—a bird never flew on one wing.* The proverb was first recorded in 1721, with different wording, in a collection of Scottish proverbs. It is found in the writings of 20th-century Irish writers, notably Sean O'Casey.

Variant of this proverb: you can't fly with one wing.

birds in their little nests agree People who live or work together should try to do so in harmony; often used to stop children from arguing: "'I detest rude, unladylike girls!' 'I hate affected, niminy-piminy chits!' 'Birds in their little nests agree,' sang Beth, the peacemaker, with such a funny face that both sharp voices softened to a laugh, and the 'pecking' ended for that time" (Louisa May Alcott, *Little Women,* 1868). The proverb originated in Isaac Watts's *Divine Songs for Children* (1715): "Birds in their little Nests agree;/And 'tis a shameful Sight,/When Children of one Family/Fall out, and chide, and fight."

birds of a feather flock together   People tend to associate with those of similar character, interests, or opinions; often used with derogatory implications: "Who are the guys that mostly get asked to the clubs? Preppies from St. Paul's, Mark's, Groton. It's kind of a common bond. You know, birds of a feather flocking together and so forth" (Erich Segal, *The Class,* 1985). The proverb dates from the 16th century or earlier in this form, but the sentiment it expresses is found in the Apocrypha "The birds will resort unto their like" (Ecclesiasticus 27:9). It also occurs in a translation of Plato's dialogues by Benjamin Jowett, published in 1871: "The old proverb says that 'birds of a feather flock together'; I suppose that equality of years inclines them to the same pleasures, and similarity begets friendship; yet you may have more than enough even of this." Some writers have substituted other verbs for *flock,* as in "birds of a feather laugh together" (James Joyce, *Ulysses,* 1922) and "birds of a feather fight together [that is, on the same side]" (Leo Tolstoy, *War and Peace,* 1863–69).

Variant of this proverb: birds of a feather fly together.

Proverbs expressing similar meaning: LIKE ATTRACTS LIKE; A MAN IS KNOWN BY THE COMPANY HE KEEPS.

the bird that can sing and won't sing should be made to sing   *See* LITTLE BIRDS THAT CAN SING AND WON'T SING MUST BE MADE TO SING.

birth is much but breeding more   A person's upbringing counts for more in the long run than the traits of character he or she was born with: *If it is true that birth is much but breeding more then even such an unpromising beginning as this should not have any lasting effect upon the child's prospects.* The proverb was first recorded in 1639 by John Clarke in *Paroemiologia Anglo-Latina.*

Proverb expressing opposite meaning: NATURE PASSES NURTURE.

the biter is sometimes bit   Those who criticize or otherwise set about others are not immune from criticism or other attack themselves: "The biter was bit: the fox . . . was caught" (Charles Reade, *Hard Cash,* 1863). Quoted by Lucian, it was first recorded in English in 1693 by Thomas D'Urfey in *The Richmond Duchess.*

a bleating sheep loses a bite   Those who talk too much may miss an important opportunity: "He said something about a bleating sheep losing a bite; but I should think this young man is not much of a talker" (Ted Hughes, *Tom Brown at Oxford,* 1861). The proverb was first recorded in 1599, with wording closer to that of the variant form.

Variant of this proverb: the sheep that bleats loses a mouthful.

blessed are the dead that the rain rains on   According to popular superstition, rainfall during a funeral is a blessing on the corpse: *The old saying "Blessed are the dead that the rain rains on" was of little consolation to the mourners caught out by the* *downpour as they crossed the graveyard.* The proverb was first recorded in 1607.

blessed are they who expect nothing, for they shall not be disappointed It is better to have no expectations of happiness or good fortune if you want to avoid suffering the pangs of disappointment: "'Oh, Marilla, looking forward to things is half the pleasure of them,' exclaimed Anne. '. . . Mrs. Lynde says, "Blessed are they who expect nothing for they shall not be disappointed." But I think it would be worse to expect nothing than to be disappointed'" (Lucy Maud Montgomery, *Anne of Green Gables,* 1908). The proverb dates from the 1720s, when it was quoted by the writer Alexander Pope as "a ninth Beatitude" in some of his letters.

Variant of this proverb: expect nothing and you won't be disappointed.

blessed is the bride that the sun shines on *See* HAPPY IS THE BRIDE THAT THE SUN SHINES ON.

blessings brighten as they take their flight People often fail to appreciate the good things that they have until they lose them: "Blessings brighten as they take their flight. Katy began to appreciate for the first time how much she had learned to rely on her aunt" (Susan Coolidge, *What Katy Did,* 1873). The proverb comes from the poem "Night Thoughts" (1742) by Edward Young.

Proverbs expressing similar meaning: THE COW KNOWS NOT THE VALUE OF HER TAIL TILL SHE HAS LOST IT; YOU NEVER MISS THE WATER TILL THE WELL RUNS DRY.

blind chance sweeps the world along Life is governed by chance rather than by destiny: *She believed in the saying "Blind chance sweeps the world along," and was confident that her luck would change one of these days.* The proverb was first recorded in 1948 in a U.S. proverb collection.

a blind man's wife needs no paint Attempts to improve the appearance of somebody or something are superfluous when it is the true nature of the person or thing that is of value, or when the improvements will not be appreciated: *The cosmetics industry would founder if every woman took on board the adage that a blind man's wife needs no paint.* The proverb was first recorded in 1659 in James Howell's collection of proverbs.

blood is thicker than water Bonds of loyalty and affection between members of the same family are much stronger than any other relationship: "Blood is thicker than water, my dear; and I know no earthly ties that can bind people together if those of family connection will not do so" (Anthony Trollope, *Can You Forgive Her?,* 1864). The proverb was first recorded in this form in 1813, but the sentiment it expresses is of much earlier origin. Compare the 12th-century German saying "*sippebluot von wassere niht verdirbet* [kin-blood is not spoiled by water]."

Variant of this proverb: blood is thicker than water, but sometimes it runs mighty thin.

the blood of the martyrs is the seed of the church The martyrdom of early members of the Christian Church helped the religion to flourish and spread; also used more generally to point out that persecution and oppression often have the opposite effect to that intended: *Bearing in* mind that the blood of the martyrs is the seed of the church, the government has adopted a less confrontational approach to the problem of eco-terrorism. The proverb was first recorded in 1560, but with the implication that it was of earlier origin. The Christian theologian Tertullian (c. A.D. 160–c. 220) wrote, "*semen est sanguis Christianorum* [the blood of Christians is seed]."

blood will have blood One act of violence provokes another, by way of revenge: *Blood will have blood, and the parents of the murdered child swore to hunt down and kill the man convicted of the crime if he was ever released from prison.* The proverb was first recorded in this form in 1559, but the sentiment it expresses is of biblical origin: "Whoso sheddeth man's blood, by man shall his blood be shed" (Genesis 9:6). It occurs in Shakespeare's play *Macbeth* (3:4): "It will have blood; they say blood will have blood."

blood will tell Inherited characteristics—whether good or bad—cannot be hidden forever: *He launched himself into the attack with all the fighting instincts of his military forebears—as they say, blood will tell.* The proverb was first recorded in this form in 1850 in *World a Mask* by the American poet, playwright, and diplomat George Henry Boker.

Proverb expressing similar meaning: WHAT'S BRED IN THE BONE WILL COME OUT IN THE FLESH.

blue are the hills that are far away Distant places or things seem more desirable than they are in reality; also applied to past or future events: *When I hear my grandparents reminiscing about the carefree days of their youth, I am tempted to remind*

them of the saying "Blue are the hills that are far away." The proverb was first recorded in this form in 1902, but with the implication that it was already in common use.

Variant of this proverb: far away the hills are green.

Proverb expressing similar meaning: DISTANCE LENDS ENCHANTMENT TO THE VIEW.

blushing is a sign of grace A person's blushes may be interpreted as a proof of a good, sensitive character: "However, blushing is some sign of grace" (Jonathan Swift, *A Complete Collection of Polite and Ingenious Conversation*, 1738). The proverb was first recorded in 1595 in *A Quest of Enquirie*.

Variant of this proverb: blushing is virtue's color.

a book is like a garden carried in the pocket A book can bring as much pleasure and contain as much variety as a garden, with the advantage that it can be carried with you wherever you go: *"A book is like a garden carried in the pocket," my uncle used to say as he took me to the local bookstore to choose my birthday present.* The proverb is recorded as a regional expression in the United States.

books and friends should be few and good It is best to be selective both in your choice of reading and of friends: *Those who ignore the maxim that books and friends should be few and good will find they have neither the time nor the inclination to give proper attention to either.* The proverb is thought to be of Spanish origin.

the boot is on the other foot *See* THE SHOE IS ON THE OTHER FOOT.

borrowing brings sorrowing   *See* HE THAT GOES A-BORROWING, GOES A-SORROWING.

both poverty and prosperity come from spending money — prosperity from spending it wisely   Spending money recklessly will make you poor, but spending it on things that are bound to yield a profit or rise in value will make you rich: *The two brothers inherited equal shares of their parents' wealth, but one died penniless while the other amassed a considerable fortune. When asked the secret of his success, he would reply, "Both poverty and prosperity come from spending money—prosperity from spending it wisely."* The proverb is recorded as a regional expression in the United States.

boys seldom make passes at girls who wear glasses   It is popularly believed that girls who wear glasses are less attractive to the opposite sex: *She began to wonder whether the saying "Boys seldom make passes for girls who wear glasses" had been invented by the male sex so that their own physical shortcomings would not be observed too clearly by the nearsighted young women they met.* The proverb occurs in a verse "News Item" by the journalist Dorothy Parker (1893–1967), "Men seldom make passes/At girls who wear glasses." It has also been associated with the humorist Ogden Nash (1902–1971).

boys will be boys   Boys must be forgiven for their bad or boisterous behavior; also used ironically when grown men behave in an irresponsible or childish manner: "Aunt Sally was a good deal uneasy; but Uncle Silas he said there warn't no occasion to be—boys will be boys, he said, and you'll see this one turn up in the morning all sound and right" (Mark Twain, *Huckleberry Finn,* 1884). The proverb was first recorded in 1601 in the form "Youth will be youthful." Other words, such as *girls* or *kids,* may be used in place of *boys.*

brave men lived before Agamemnon   People whose brave or noble exploits are not recorded in history or literature tend to be forgotten over the course of time: "Brave men were living before Agamemnon/And since, exceeding valorous and sage" (Lord Byron, "Don Juan," 1819). The proverb originated in the writings of the Roman poet Horace (65–8 B.C.): "Many brave men lived before Agamemnon's time; but they are all, unmourned and unknown, covered by the long night, because they lack their sacred poet."

bread always falls buttered side down   In any situation, the least desirable of two or more possible outcomes is the one that will occur: *Bread always falls buttered side down, so it seemed inevitable that the train would be delayed on the one day I had to get to work on time.* First recorded in the mid-19th century, the proverb appears in a rhyme written by James Payn (as a parody of a more serious poem) and published in 1884: "I never had a piece of toast/Particularly long and wide,/But fell upon the sanded floor,/And always on the buttered side." The diplomat Henry Kissinger is said to have remarked, "If you drop a piece of buttered bread on the carpet, the chances of its falling with the buttered side down are in direct relationship with the cost of the carpet." The proverb—or the phenomenon it describes—is popularly regarded as an illustration of Murphy's Law, "If anything can go wrong, it will."

Variant of this proverb: the bread always falls on its buttered side.

Proverb expressing similar meaning: IF ANYTHING CAN GO WRONG, IT WILL.

bread is the staff of life Food is essential for survival: *We must at least ensure that these people have enough money to buy basic food items—bread is the staff of life.* The proverb was first recorded in 1638 in Penkethman, *Artachthos.*

brevity is the soul of wit When you tell a joke or make a speech, you are most likely to please or impress your listeners if you keep it as short as possible; used to discourage long-windedness or encourage conciseness of expression: "Clinton is . . . given to garrulousness while brevity, they say, is the soul of wit" (*Washington Post,* 1996). The proverb was first recorded in Shakespeare's play *Hamlet* (2:2), where it is used by Polonius, a character known for his verbosity. In this early instance the word *wit* means "wisdom," but in modern usage it usually means "humor." Dorothy Parker parodied the proverb when she wrote, in a caption for *Vogue* (1916), "Brevity is the soul of lingerie."

Proverb expressing similar meaning: LENGTH BEGETS LOATHING.

a bribe will enter without knocking The use of money enables access where it would otherwise be denied: *He planned to use the money to buy his way into the great man's presence, knowing that he would be refused admittance if he came empty-handed but also that a bribe will enter without knocking.* The proverb was first recorded in 1619 by B. Rich in *Irish Hubbub:* "Honesty stands at the gate and knockes, and bribery enters in."

Proverb expressing similar meaning: A GOLDEN KEY CAN OPEN ANY DOOR.

a bully is always a coward Bullies only pick on those who are weaker than themselves and cannot fight back—they are afraid of everybody else: *A bully is always a coward, and the girls stopped teasing her when they discovered that she was the principal's niece.* The proverb was first recorded in this form in Charles Lamb, *Essays of Elia* (1820–23).

burn not your house to scare away the mice Do not try to solve a minor problem by taking action that will cause much greater harm: *Such a drastic step could destroy your whole business, and all because of one dissatisfied customer—don't burn your house to scare away the mice.* The proverb was first recorded, with different wording, in 1615 in T. Adams, *England's Sickness.*

Variant of this proverb: burn not your house to fright the mouse away.

a burnt child dreads the fire Somebody who has had an unpleasant experience thereafter shrinks from the cause of that experience: "In his savage taunting, he flared the candle so close at me, that I turned my face aside, to save it from the flame. 'Ah!' he cried, laughing, after doing it again, 'the burnt child dreads the fire!'" (Charles Dickens, *Great Expectations,* 1860–61). First recorded c. 1250 with slightly different wording, the proverb was used in its current form in John Lyly's *Euphues and His England* (1580).

Proverbs expressing similar meaning: ONCE BITTEN, TWICE SHY.

the busiest men have the most leisure People who are industrious by nature always seem to have the most spare time, either because they accomplish their work more quickly and efficiently or because they cram so much into their busy lives: "The busiest men have always the most leisure; and while discharging the multifarious duties of a parish priest and a guardian he found time for travelling" (*London Times Literary Supplement,* 1911). The proverb was first recorded in 1884, but the sentiment it expresses is of earlier origin.

Proverbs expressing similar meaning: IF YOU WANT SOMETHING DONE, ASK A BUSY PERSON; IDLE PEOPLE HAVE THE LEAST LEISURE.

business before pleasure   It is best to get work or business matters out of the way before turning your attention to more pleasurable things: "Much as I adore your company, there is still business to attend to . . . and . . . business must come before pleasure" (James Jones, *From Here to Eternity,* 1951). The proverb was first recorded in 1767, in the form "Pleasure should always give way to business," in Thomas Hutchinson's *Diary and Letters.*

Variant of this proverb: pleasure first and business after.

Proverb expressing similar meaning: WORK BEFORE PLAY.

business is business   There is no room for sentiment in business: "Business is business, my dear young sir" (William Thackeray, *The Virginians,* 1857). The proverb was first recorded in 1797 by George Colman in *The Heir at Law.*

Proverb expressing similar meaning: NEVER MIX BUSINESS AND PLEASURE.

business is like a car, it will not run by itself except downhill   You must take an active part in the day-to-day running of your business, or employ a competent person to do this for you, if you want it to be a success: *He had only himself to blame for the failure of his company. Having used his inheritance to set it up, he then turned his attention to other things, forgetting the adage that business is like a car—it will not run by itself except downhill.* The proverb is recorded as a regional expression in the United States.

business neglected is business lost   In the world of commerce, you cannot afford to neglect any opportunity to do business: *I have had a number of inquiries from potential customers, which must be followed up as soon as possible—business neglected is business lost.*

the business of America is business   Commercial activity is essential for America—or any other nation—to thrive and develop: *The business of America is business, and even small companies such as these have an important place in our society.* The proverb originated in a speech made in 1925 by President Calvin Coolidge: "After all, the chief business of the American people is business."

busy folks are always meddling   It is in the nature of busy people to interfere in the affairs of others: *Her tireless efforts to improve the morality of her neighbors led to dark mutterings to the effect that "busy folks are always meddling."* The proverb was first recorded in 1721 by James Kelly in *A Complete Collection of Scotish Proverbs.*

the buyer needs a thousand eyes, the seller wants but one   A buyer must exercise great caution, and examine the goods thoroughly, to avoid being exploited by an unscrupulous seller: *Tourists looking for bargains in the local markets would do well to remember the proverb "The buyer needs a thousand eyes, the seller wants but one."* The proverb was first recorded in 1640 in George Herbert's *Outlandish Proverbs.*

Variant of this proverb: the buyer has need of a hundred eyes, the seller of but one.

Proverb expressing similar meaning: LET THE BUYER BEWARE.

buy in the cheapest market and sell in the dearest The golden rule of commerce is to buy a commodity for as little as possible and sell it for as much as possible: "'To buy in the cheapest market and sell in the dearest' was Mr. Badman's common rule in business. . . . In Bunyan's opinion it was knavery in disguise" (J. A. Froude, *Bunyan,* 1880). The proverb was first recorded in Thomas Lodge's *A Fig for Momus* (1595): "Buy cheape, sell deare."

by learning to obey, you will know how to command *See* HE THAT CANNOT OBEY CANNOT COMMAND.

C

Caesar's wife must be above suspicion Those in positions of importance—and their associates—must lead blameless lives and have spotless reputations: *The president surrounded himself with aides and advisers of irreproachable character, knowing that Caesar's wife must be above suspicion.* Julius Caesar is said to have made this remark when asked why he had divorced his wife (who was suspected of having been indirectly involved in a scandal).

calamity is the touchstone of a brave mind It is at times of crisis that you find out who the truly strong, courageous, or great people are: *When the fire broke out she immediately took charge of the situation, glad of a chance to prove her worth at last—calamity is the touchstone of a brave mind.* The proverb was first recorded, with different wording, in 1602: "Calamity gives man a steddy heart" (John Marston, *Antonio's Revenge*).

Proverb expressing similar meaning: WHEN THE GOING GETS TOUGH, THE TOUGH GET GOING.

call a man a thief and he will steal Give a person a bad reputation and he or she may start to justify it. The proverb was first recorded in 1838 by Thomas Carlyle in *Sartor Resartus*: "In a very plain sense the proverb says, Call one a thief, and he will steal."

call a spade a spade Identify things by their real names; do not prevaricate about awkward truths; say what you mean: *He was never afraid to call a spade a spade.* The proverb was recorded in 1519 by William Rastell in *The Four Elements*, though it was also quoted by Erasmus.

call no man happy till he dies However happy somebody seems to be, there is always the risk that he or she will be struck by sorrow or misfortune: *"'Call no man happy until he is dead.' . . . He was seventy-two, and yet there was still time for this dream . . . to change to a nightmare"* (C. S. Forester, *Hornblower and the Crisis*, 1967). Of ancient origin, the proverb has been attributed to the Athenian statesman Solon (c. 638–559 B.C.), who told the wealthy King Croesus, "Call no man happy before he dies, he is at best but fortunate." Compare Sophocles (c. 496–405 B.C.), "Deem no man happy until he passes the end of his life without suffering grief."

Variant of this proverb: call no man happy till he is dead.

can't live with 'em, can't live without 'em Some alternatives are equally impossible (usually applied to a person's male or female partner): *That's the trouble with women, can't live with 'em, can't live without 'em.* The origins of the proverb are obscure, though it is thought to be of 20th-century U.S. coinage.

cards are the devil's tools   Card games—specifically those played for money—lead to trouble or evil: *Hearing that a poker game was in progress, she burst into the room and knocked over the table where the players sat, exclaiming, "Cards are the devil's tools!"* The proverb was first recorded in 1676 in *Poor Robin's Almanac* in the form "Cards and dice . . . are the devil's books and the devil's bones."

   Variant of this proverb: cards are the devil's books.

care is no cure   Worrying about something does nothing to put it right. The proverb was first recorded c. 1590 by William Shakespeare in *Henry VI Part 1* (3:3): "Care is no cure, but rather corrosive, for things that are not to be remedied."

   Proverbs expressing similar meaning: CARE KILLED THE CAT; IT'S NOT WORK THAT KILLS, BUT WORRY.

care killed the cat   Too much worrying can be injurious to your health: *Relax and enjoy your holiday—care killed the cat!* The proverb was first recorded in Shakespeare's play *Much Ado About Nothing* (5:1), "Though care killed a cat, thou hast mettle enough in thee to kill care." It is also used with the word *care* in the sense of "caution" or "loving attention."

   Proverbs expressing similar meaning: CARE IS NO CURE; IT'S NOT WORK THAT KILLS, BUT WORRY.

a cat can look at a king   Even the lowliest people have the right to look at, or show an interest in, those of higher status or prestige; often used by somebody accused of staring insolently: "'Don't be impertinent,' said the King, 'and don't look at me like that!' He got behind Alice as he spoke. 'A cat may look at a king,' said Alice. 'I've read that in some book, but I don't remember where'" (Lewis Carroll, *Alice's Adventures in Wonderland,* 1865). The proverb was first recorded in John Heywood's *Dialogue of Proverbs* in 1546. The French equivalent is "*Un chien regarde bien un évêque* [A dog can look at a bishop]."

   Variant of this proverb: a cat may look at a king.

catching's before hanging   Offenders can only be punished when or if they are caught: *We all know what we would like to do to the culprit, but first we have to find out who it is—catching's before hanging.* The proverb was first recorded in 1818 in A. N. Royall's *Letters from Alabama.*

catch not at the shadow and lose the substance   Do not allow yourself to be distracted from your main purpose by irrelevancies: "Like the dog in the fable, to throw away the substance in catching at the shadow" (Thomas Love Peacock, *Nightmare Abbey*, 1818). The proverb was first recorded in 1578 by John Lyly in *Euphues: The Anatomy of Wit.*

a cat has nine lives   Cats seem to be incredibly lucky or skillful at surviving or avoiding accidents: *They say that a cat has nine lives, but if the one next door makes a habit of dozing off under my car it could find itself using them up rather quickly.* The proverb was first recorded in 1546 in the form "A woman has nine lives like a cat." In 1894 two writers compared the lives of a cat with those of a lie: R. D. Blackmore wrote "If a cat has nine lives . . . a lie has ninety-nine," and Mark Twain wrote "One of the most striking differences between a cat and a lie is that a cat has only nine lives."

a cat in gloves catches no mice It is sometimes necessary to be bold or ruthless, or to do unpleasant things, in order to achieve one's ends: "Handle your Tools without Mittens; remember that the Cat in Gloves catches no Mice" (Benjamin Franklin, *Poor Richard's Almanack,* 1758). The proverb was first recorded in French in the 14th century and in English in 1573.

a cat may look at a king *See* A CAT CAN LOOK AT A KING.

the cat would eat fish, but would not wet her feet You must be prepared to put up with personal inconvenience, discomfort, or risk in order to get what you want; often used when somebody is hesitant about doing something for this reason: *Many people deny themselves their dream vacations because of a fear of flying—the cat would eat fish, but would not wet her feet.* The proverb was first recorded in English c. 1225. It is alluded to in Shakespeare's play *Macbeth* (1:7), "Wouldst thou . . . live a coward in thine own esteem, / Letting 'I dare not' wait upon 'I would,' / Like the poor cat i' the adage?"

Proverb expressing similar meaning: HE THAT WOULD HAVE EGGS MUST ENDURE THE CACKLING OF HENS.

caution is the parent of safety You must proceed with care, and take all the necessary precautions, if you want to avoid harm or injury: *After listening to the weather forecast, we decided to postpone our sailing trip—caution is the parent of safety.* This proverb is first recorded in Benjamin Franklin's *Poor Richard's Almanack* (1733).

a chain is no stronger than its weakest link A weak part or member will affect the success or effectiveness of the whole: "To begin with, how can things so insecure as the successful experiences of this world afford a stable anchorage? A chain is no stronger than its weakest link, and life is after all a chain" (William James, *The Varieties of Religious Experience,* 1902). The proverb was used in 1856 in a letter by Charles Kingsley in the form "nothing is stronger than its weakest part." The first recorded occurrence of the current form dates from 1868.

Proverb expressing similar meaning: THE THREAD BREAKS WHERE IT IS WEAKEST.

a change is as good as a rest Doing something different for a time can be just as refreshing as taking a break from work; also used more generally of any change in routine: *A change is as good as a rest, and after a couple of hours spent weeding the garden I returned to my desk with renewed inspiration.* The proverb was first recorded in 1890: "One of our greatest statesmen has said that a change of work is the best rest. So it is" (Sir Arthur Conan Doyle, *Lippincott's Monthly Magazine*).

Variant of this proverb: a change of work is a rest.

Proverb expressing similar meaning: VARIETY IS THE SPICE OF LIFE.

change not a clout till May be out   *See* NE'ER CAST A CLOUT TILL MAY BE OUT.

character is destiny   A person's character determines the way that his or her life will develop: "'Character'—says Novalis, in one of his questionable aphorisms—'character is destiny.' But not the whole of our destiny" (George Eliot, *The Mill on the Floss,* 1860). In this quotation, and elsewhere, the proverb is attributed to the German writer Friedrich Leopold von Hardenberg (1772–1801), whose pen-name was Novalis. Others, however, have traced it back to the Greek philosopher Heraclitus (fifth century B.C.).

charity begins at home   You should look after those nearest and dearest to you before you turn your attention to others further afield: "And hard it is upon the part of the law that it should be so confoundedly down upon us unfortunate victims; when it takes such amazing good interest for itself from all its clients. But charity begins at home, and justice begins next door" (Charles Dickens, *Martin Chuzzlewit,* 1843–44). The proverb was first recorded in this form in Beaumont and Fletcher's play *Wit Without Money* (c. 1625), but the sentiment it expresses is of earlier origin: in the late 14th century John Wycliffe wrote, "Charity should begin at himself."

Variant of this proverb: charity begins at home but should not end there.

charity covers a multitude of sins   A kind and loving person is prepared to forgive a great deal of wrongdoing; also used to imply that acts of charity may be used to cover up sinful behavior or ease a guilty conscience: "A cloak (on a woman's back) is an emblem of charity—it cov-ers a multitude of sins" (Wilkie Collins, *The Moonstone,* 1868). The proverb is of biblical origin: "And above all things have fervent charity among yourselves: for charity shall cover the multitude of sins" (1 Peter 4:8). Other words may be used in place of *charity:* Louisa May Alcott wrote "beauty always covers a multitude of sins in a man's eyes."

charity is not a bone you throw to a dog but a bone you share with a dog   There should be more to charity than simply giving money or other material goods—it is better to establish a relationship with those in need and to work with them for the benefit of all concerned: *She spends much of her spare time working with the homeless, firmly believing that charity is not a bone you throw to a dog but a bone you share with a dog.*

cheaters never prosper   Those who cheat—whether at school, at sports and games, or in business—may be initially successful but will ultimately suffer for their wrongdoing: *He set out to disprove the saying "Cheaters never prosper," and made a fortune selling fake works of art, but lost everything when his deception was discovered.* The proverb was first recorded in 1805, in R. Parkinson, *Tour in America* in the form "Cheating never thrives," but with the implication that it was already in general use.

Variants of this proverb: cheats never prosper; cheaters never win and winners never cheat.

Proverbs expressing similar meaning: HONESTY IS THE BEST POLICY; HONESTY PAYS.

cheerful company shortens the miles   *See* GOOD COMPANY ON THE ROAD IS THE SHORTEST CUT.

cheese digests all things but itself   Eating cheese at the end of a meal helps to digest what has gone before, but the cheese itself may prove to be indigestible: *I couldn't resist helping myself to another slice of cheese, though I knew I would regret it later—cheese digests all things but itself.* Of Latin origin, the proverb was first recorded in English in the 16th century: "Cheese . . . digesteth all things except itselfe" (John Lyly, *Sappho & Phao*).

chickens always come home to roost   *See* CURSES, LIKE CHICKENS, COME HOME TO ROOST.

the child is father of the man   A child's character is an indication of the type of adult he or she will become—human nature does not change from youth to maturity: "The lady who is my opponent is very persuasive, but what of her past? . . . They say the child is the father of the man" (Howard Fast, *The Immigrant's Daughter,* 1985). The proverb originated in this form in William Wordsworth's poem "My Heart Leaps Up" (1807), but it echoes a sentiment expressed by John Milton in *Paradise Regained* (1671): "The childhood shews the man."

Proverb expressing similar meaning: GIVE ME A CHILD FOR THE FIRST SEVEN YEARS AND HE IS MINE FOR LIFE.

a child on a giant's shoulders sees further of the two   *See* A DWARF ON A GIANT'S SHOULDERS SEES FURTHER OF THE TWO.

children, fools, and drunkards tell the truth   *See* CHILDREN AND FOOLS SPEAK THE TRUTH.

children and fools speak the truth   Children and foolish people have a tendency to say what is true, because they have not learned that it may be advantageous or diplomatic to do otherwise: *Children and fools tell the truth, and Matthew learned the hard way that it is sometimes expedient to lie.* The proverb was first recorded, in *Letters & Papers of Reign of Henry VIII* (1537), but with the implication that it was of much earlier origin.

Variant of this proverb: children, fools, and drunkards tell the truth.

Proverb expressing similar meaning: OUT OF THE MOUTHS OF BABES AND SUCKLINGS COME GREAT TRUTHS.

children are certain cares, but uncertain comforts   Children are bound to cause their parents anxiety, and may or may not also bring them joy: *Those contemplating parenthood should bear in mind the saying "Children are certain cares, but uncertain comforts"—the pleasure I gain from having my kids around me is obliterated by the horrors I imagine when they don't come home on time.* The proverb was first recorded in 1639 in John Clarke, *Parœmiologia Anglo-Latina.*

Proverb expressing opposite meaning: HAPPY IS HE THAT IS HAPPY IN HIS CHILDREN.

children should be seen and not heard   In the company of adults, children should not speak until they are spoken to: "When he asks questions I can't answer I'll just tell him children should be seen and not heard" (Lucy Maud Montgomery, *Anne of Avonlea,* 1909). The proverb was first recorded c. 1400 in the form "A maid [young woman] should be seen but not heard." It was applied to children from the early 19th century onward,

CHINESE PROVERBS

The Chinese have hundreds of proverbs on which to draw for advice in their everyday lives. Western tradition often attributes such sayings to the Chinese philosopher Confucius, though in reality most are of unknown authorship.

All things seem difficult at first

Almond nuts come to those who have no teeth

Always leave a little room for a mistake

Before you prepare to improve the world, look around your own house three times

Do not climb a tree to catch a fish

Do not remove a fly from your friend's forehead with a hatchet

Drunkards talk to the gods

Every book must be chewed to get out its juice

The first time you cheat me, be ashamed. The second time it is I who must be ashamed

He who is not friendly towards a good guest will never have one

He who rides a tiger can never get off

If no one comes, the dog does not bark

If you are not a fish, how can you know if the fish are happy?

If you don't climb the mountain, you can't view the plain

If you wish to succeed, consult three old people

It is better to light a candle than to curse the darkness

A journey of a thousand miles must begin with a single step

Love your neighbors but don't pull down the fence

One bamboo does not make a forest

One joy scatters a hundred griefs

Only one who can swallow an insult is a man

Pain is easier to endure than an itch

A picture is worth ten thousand words

Procrastination is the thief of time

Rivalry between scholars improves science

A thousand workers, a thousand plans

A tiger cannot beat a crowd of monkeys

A wise man will not rebuke a fool

but it is now considered to be a rather old-fashioned notion.

the child that is born on the Sabbath day is bonny and blithe and good and gay Children born on a Sunday are supposed to be happy, healthy, good-looking, and well-behaved: *I can't believe that such a miserable, sickly little boy could have been born on a Sunday—I thought that children born on the Sabbath day were supposed to be "bonny and blithe and good and gay."* The proverb is the last line of a traditional rhyme beginning "Monday's child is fair of face." See entries at the days of the week for other proverbs from this rhyme.

choose neither a woman nor linen by candlelight   See NEVER CHOOSE YOUR WOMEN OR LINEN BY CANDLELIGHT.

choose the lesser of two evils   If you are forced to choose between two options, both of which are undesirable, all you can do is choose the one that is less undesirable than the other: *Choose the lesser of two evils—if you tell her the truth she'll be upset, but if she finds out later that you lied to her you could lose a friend for life.* The proverb occurs in the writings of Aristotle and Cicero, and was first recorded in English in Chaucer's *Troilus and Criseyde* (c. 1385). The U.S. actress Mae West parodied the proverb when she said, "Between two evils, I always pick the one I never tried before," in the movie *Klondike Annie* (1936).

Variant of this proverb: of two evils choose the less.

Christmas comes but once a year   Extravagance and self-indulgence at Christmas—or any other annual celebration—can be justified by the fact that it is a relatively infrequent occurrence: *All over the country, people will be eating and drinking to excess, telling themselves that Christmas comes but once a year.* The proverb was first recorded in 1557 in Thomas Tusser, *A Hundreth good pointes of husbandrie.*

the church is an anvil that has worn out many hammers   The Christian Church has proved strong enough in the past to resist criticism, attack, and persecution, and will continue to do so in the future: "The Church is an anvil which has worn

out many hammers and the story of the first collision is, in essentials, the story of all" (Alexander MacLaren, *The Acts of the Apostles,* 1908). The proverb is attributed to the theologian Theodore Beza, who made this remark in response to a massacre of Huguenots in 1562.

a church is God between four walls   A church is more than just a building—its inner space is filled with the divine presence: *If a church is God between four walls, then this building, with its atmosphere of spirituality and devotion, must once have been a place of worship.* The proverb was first recorded in 1948 in a U.S. proverb collection.

circumstances alter cases   The same general principle cannot be applied to every individual case, and what is right, good, or appropriate in one set of circumstances may be wrong in another: "On a table of immense size lay the budget, piles of the Chamber records, open volumes of the 'Moniteur,' with passages carefully marked, to throw at the head of a Minister his forgotten words and force him to recant them, under the jeering plaudits of a foolish crowd incapable of perceiving how circumstances alter cases" (Honoré de Balzac, *The Rise and Fall of César Birotteau,* 1837). The proverb was first recorded in 1678.

civility costs nothing   You have nothing to lose by being polite: "'You wretch' (she says), 'how did you come by this?' I made her a low bow. I said, 'Civility costs nothing, ma'am; and sometimes buys a great deal'" (Wilkie Collins, *Jezebel's Daughter,* 1880). The proverb was first recorded in 1706 in J. Stevens' *A New Spanish and English Dictionary* in the form "Civility is worth much and costs little," echoing the sentiment expressed in a French proverb of the late 15th century.

Variants of this proverb: courtesy costs nothing; politeness costs nothing and gains everything.

Proverb expressing similar meaning: THERE'S NOTHING LOST BY CIVILITY.

a civil question deserves a civil answer If somebody asks you something politely, you should respond in the same manner: *I was tempted to tell her to mind her own business, but a civil question deserves a civil answer and I replied as politely as I could.* The proverb was first recorded, in its variant form, in 1853.

Variant of this proverb: give a civil answer to a civil question.

cleanliness is next to godliness Personal hygiene indicates a pious or virtuous nature; also used more generally to emphasize the importance of cleanness: *Having been brought up to believe that cleanliness is next to godliness, she was seriously concerned for the spiritual well-being of her roommate, who bathed only once a week.* The proverb was first recorded in this form in a sermon given by John Wesley in 1788, but the sentiment it expresses is of ancient Egyptian or Hebrew origin. In *The Advancement of Learning* (1605), Francis Bacon wrote, "Cleanness of body was ever esteemed to proceed from a due reverence to God."

Variant of this proverb: cleanliness is akin to godliness.

a clear conscience can bear any trouble People who have done no wrong find it easier to face the demands of the world than those who have guilty consciences:

A clear conscience can bear any trouble, but there are limits even for the most guiltless. The proverb was first recorded in 1732 by Thomas Fuller in *Gnomologia.*

Proverb expressing similar meaning: DO RIGHT AND FEAR NO MAN.

clergymen's sons always turn out badly It might be expected that the children of ministers of religion should lead exemplary lives in adulthood, but the opposite is often the case—perhaps as a reaction against their early upbringing: "An Eton boy . . . when asked why the sons of Eli turned out badly, replied 'The sons of clergymen always turn out badly'" (W. R. Inge, *Outspoken Essays,* 1922). The proverb was first recorded in 1885.

Variant of this proverb: a preacher's son is often bad.

the clock goes as it pleases the clerk It is up to civil servants and other bureaucrats how time is governed and spent: *They were kept waiting in reception for two hours, but the clock goes as it pleases the clerk, as they say.* The proverb was first recorded in 1678 by John Ray in *A Collection of English Proverbs.*

a closed mouth catches no flies *See* A SHUT MOUTH CATCHES NO FLIES.

the closer to the bone, the sweeter the meat *See* THE NEARER THE BONE, THE SWEETER THE FLESH.

close sits my shirt, but closer my skin *See* NEAR IS MY SHIRT, BUT NEARER IS MY SKIN.

clothes don't make the man You should not judge a person by the way he or she is dressed: *He was such a smartly dressed, well-groomed young man that I trusted him instantly—unlike some of the scruffy individuals who knock at our door offering their services. However, I was wrong—he cheated us out of all our savings, which just goes to prove that clothes don't make the man.*

Proverb expressing similar meaning: AN APE'S AN APE, A VARLET'S A VARLET, THOUGH THEY BE CLAD IN SILK OR SCARLET.

Proverbs expressing opposite meaning: CLOTHES MAKE THE MAN; FINE FEATHERS MAKE FINE BIRDS.

clothes make the man The style or quality of people's clothing is often an indicator of their character, and also has a tendency to affect both the way that others judge them and the way that they behave: "It is truly miserable to behold how our youth even now is subjected to a fashion madness which helps to reverse the sense of the old saying: 'Clothes make the man' into something truly catastrophic" (Adolf Hitler, *Mein Kampf*, 1925). First recorded in English c. 1400, the proverb is of ancient origin and is echoed in other languages. The sentiment it expresses occurs frequently in literature, notably in Shakespeare's play *Hamlet* (1:3): "the apparel oft proclaims the man."

Proverbs expressing similar meaning: FINE FEATHERS MAKE FINE BIRDS; THE TAILOR MAKES THE MAN.

Proverbs expressing opposite meaning: AN APE'S AN APE, A VARLET'S A VARLET, THOUGH THEY BE CLAD IN SILK OR SCARLET; CLOTHES DON'T MAKE THE MAN.

the cobbler's children go barefoot *See* THE SHOEMAKER'S CHILD ALWAYS GOES BAREFOOT.

the cobbler should stick to his last *See* LET THE COBBLER STICK TO HIS LAST.

the cobbler to his last and the gunner to his linstock *See* LET THE COBBLER STICK TO HIS LAST.

a cock is mighty in his own backyard *See* EVERY COCK WILL CROW UPON HIS OWN DUNGHILL.

cold hands, warm heart According to traditional belief, people whose hands feel cold to the touch are kind and affectionate by nature: *He touched my cheek with his hand and I was reassured to feel the coolness of his fingers, despite the heat of the night—"cold hands, warm heart," as my mother always says.* The proverb was first recorded in 1903 in V.S. Lean, *Collectanea.*

come live with me and you'll know me Nobody truly knows another person until they have spent some time living together: *"Come live with me and you'll know me," they say, and how right they are! Sharing an apartment with my friend for six months showed me what a selfish, moody person she really is, and now I understand why her parents threw her out of their house.* The proverb was first recorded in 1925 in Sean O'Casey's *Juno and the Paycock,* but is probably of much earlier origin.

Proverb expressing similar meaning: YOU NEVER KNOW A MAN UNTIL YOU LIVE WITH HIM.

coming events cast their shadows before Future events, especially those of some significance, can often be predicted from the warning signs that precede them: "Everything in the world is in agitation. The signs of the times are ominous. Coming events cast their shadows before. The Spirit of God is withdrawing from the earth, and calamity follows calamity by sea and by land" (Ellen G. White, *The Desire of Ages*, 1898). The proverb originated in this form in Thomas Campbell's poem "Lochiel's Warning" (1803), but the sentiment it expresses is of ancient origin.

a common danger causes common action People are more willing to work together to avert danger when they all feel similarly threatened: *We had little support for our campaign against the new legislation until it was discovered that every employee in the state would be adversely affected—a common danger causes common action.* The proverb is recorded as a regional expression in the United States.

common fame is seldom to blame Rumors are rarely without substance, and if unpleasant things are being said about somebody, then that person has probably done something to deserve them: *Common fame is seldom to blame, and nobody gets a reputation for lying if he or she has always told the truth.* The proverb was first recorded in 1639 in J. Clarke, *Paroemiologia Anglo-Latina.*

Proverbs expressing similar meaning: THERE'S NO SMOKE WITHOUT FIRE; WHAT EVERYBODY SAYS MUST BE TRUE.

the company makes the feast You will enjoy a meal or celebration far more if you are among cheerful friendly people, and the quality of the food and drink—or of the surroundings—is of lesser importance: *As impoverished students we couldn't afford to eat out anywhere better than the local burger bar, but I enjoyed those get-togethers far more than the business lunches I now have at the most expensive restaurant in town—the company makes the feast.* The proverb was first recorded in 1653, in Izaak Walton's *The Compleat Angler.*

comparisons are odious People and things should be judged on the individual qualities they possess, rather than by comparing one with another: "Comparisons are odious; but I think that by the side of German English generally has the advantage in expressiveness" (W. R. Inge, *More Lay Thoughts*, 1931). The proverb was first recorded in English c. 1440, but a similar French proverb, translated as "Comparisons are hateful," dates from a hundred years earlier. The malapropism "Comparisons are odorous" comes from Shakespeare's play *Much Ado about Nothing* (3:5).

confess and be hanged There is little incentive for confession when punishment is the inevitable result; used as justification for not owning up to wrongdoing: "It is so easy, and apparently so natural, to deny what you cannot be easily convicted of, that a savage as well as a child lies to excuse himself, almost as instinctively as he raises his hand to protect his head. The old saying, 'confess and be hanged,' carries much argument in it" (Sir Walter Scott, *Chronicles of the Canongate*, 1827). The proverb was first recorded in 1589 in "Misophonus," *De Caede Gallorum Regis*, but with the implication that it was already in general use.

Proverb expressing opposite meaning: CONFESSION IS GOOD FOR THE SOUL.

confession is good for the soul Owning up to wrongdoing will ease your conscience and make you feel better:

They say that confession is good for the soul, but I was reluctant to put my job on the line by admitting to such an egregious mistake. The proverb was first recorded c. 1641 in David Fergusson's *Scottish Proverbs.*

Variant of this proverb: open confession is good for the soul.

Proverb expressing opposite meaning: CONFESS AND BE HANGED.

conscience does make cowards of us all People troubled by their conscience often reveal their guilt by acting in an uncharacteristically fearful manner: *Her reluctance to testify in court made me suspicious. Conscience does make cowards of us all, and I began to wonder if the whole story was just a figment of her imagination.* The proverb originated in this form in Shakespeare's play *Hamlet* (3:1), and is sometimes still used in a way that is closer to the original meaning, namely, that people often use scruples of conscience as an excuse for not taking bold action that may have unpleasant results.

Variant of this proverb: conscience makes cowards of us all.

conscience gets a lot of credit that belongs to cold feet Something commended as an act of conscience may be simply due to cowardice or loss of nerve: *Everybody thought the governor had decided to keep the school open because it was the right thing to do, but it seems he was just afraid of the political backlash if he closed it—conscience gets a lot of credit that belongs to cold feet.* The proverb is recorded as a regional expression in the United States.

conscience makes cowards of us all *See* CONSCIENCE DOES MAKE COWARDS OF US ALL.

consistency is the hobgoblin of little minds *See* A FOOLISH CONSISTENCY IS THE HOBGOBLIN OF LITTLE MINDS.

constant dropping wears away a stone It is often possible to achieve a major purpose—for example, persuading people or breaking down their resistance—by a series of small but persistent actions or remarks: ". . . notwithstanding the proverb that constant dropping will wear away a stone, you may set your mind at rest that these people never will—never would, in a hundred years—impair your ground with Miss Havisham, in any particular, great or small" (Charles Dickens, *Great Expectations,* 1860–61). The proverb was first recorded in the 13th century, with different wording, but the sentiment it expresses is of ancient origin. Compare Tibullus (c. 48–19 B.C.), "*longa dies molli saxa peredit aqua* [length of time eats away stones with soft water]."

Variant of this proverb: constant dripping wears away a stone.

Proverb expressing similar meaning: LITTLE STROKES FELL GREAT OAKS.

a constant guest is never welcome Visitors who turn up too frequently will find they are no longer welcome: *They appeared to have forgotten the old warning that a constant guest is never welcome.* The proverb was first recorded in 1732 by Thomas Fuller in *Gnomologia.*

Proverbs expressing similar meaning: FISH AND GUESTS STINK AFTER THREE DAYS; SHORT VISITS MAKE LONG FRIENDS.

a contented mind is a continual feast Those who are satisfied with their lot in life are far happier than those who are constantly striving for something better: "'. . . although I take fifty pounds a year here after taking above two hundred elsewhere, I prefer it to running the risk of having my old domestic experiences raked up against me, as I should do if I tried to make a move.' 'Right you are. A contented mind is a continual feast'" (Thomas Hardy, *Jude the Obscure,* 1895). The proverb was first recorded in 1535 in the form "A quiet heart is a continual feast" (Miles Coverdale, *Bible Proverbs* [15:15]).

Variant of this proverb: a contented mind is a perpetual feast.

Proverb expressing similar meaning: CONTENT IS MORE THAN A KINGDOM.

content is more than a kingdom Contentment is more valuable than material riches: *To those who face a friendless and lonely death content must surely be worth more than a kingdom.* The proverb was first recorded in 1591 in the works of Robert Greene.

Proverb expressing similar meaning: A CONTENTED MIND IS A CONTINUAL FEAST.

corporations have neither bodies to be punished nor souls to be damned Large organizations are accountable to nobody—unlike individual people, who can be made to suffer physically or mentally for their unjust or immoral behavior: *The company acted unethically, but stayed within the law, so there was nothing that anybody could do about it—corporations have neither bodies to be punished nor souls to be damned.* The proverb is attributed to Lord Chancellor Thurlow, who is said to have made this or a similar remark c. 1775—a variant of the original quotation is "Did you ever expect a corporation to have a conscience, when it has no soul to be damned, and no body to be

kicked." This sentiment was, however first expressed c. 1580 or earlier.

corruption will find a dozen alibis for its evil deeds Those who are guilty of corruption are so lacking in integrity that they will not hesitate to make excuses for or lie about what they have done: *We knew that the officials had been accepting bribes, but we could not impeach them without more concrete evidence—corruption will find a dozen alibis for its evil deeds.* The proverb is recorded as a regional expression in the United States.

councils of war never fight When a number of people get together to discuss something important, they rarely decide on a drastic course of action: *As soon as I heard that a committee had been set up to discuss the issue, I knew I could rest assured that no action would be taken—it's well known that councils of war never fight.* The proverb was first recorded in 1863, in H. W. Halleck, *Telegram,* but with the implication that it was already in general use.

courage is fear that has said its prayers A brave person is not necessarily fearless, but has drawn strength from religion or some other source: *I admired her bravery in facing up to the bullies.* "I'm not really brave," she replied, "courage is simply fear that has said its prayers." The proverb is recorded as a regional expression in the United States.

the course of true love never did run smooth Even the most loving relationship has its ups and downs; usually said when lovers have a minor quarrel or face a temporary obstacle to their happiness: "Ralph's letter was a long, involved . . . document, beginning with another string of apologies, repeating most of what he had said, and going over all their past. Quite a valuable essay on the theme of the course of true love never did run smooth, Etta thought sardonically" (Richard Aldington, *Women Must Work,* 1934). The proverb comes from Shakespeare's play *A Midsummer Night's Dream* (1:1).

Variant of this proverb: the path of true love never runs smooth.

courtesy costs nothing See CIVILITY COSTS NOTHING.

courtesy is contagious If you are polite to other people, then they will be polite to you: *Courtesy is contagious, and if you start treating your staff with a bit more respect you may be pleasantly surprised by the results.* The proverb is recorded as a regional expression in the United States.

cowards die many times before their death Cowards who repeatedly fear for their lives are constantly suffering an experience similar to death itself; also used figuratively of the ignominy of cowardly behavior: *His courage failed him when he saw the size of the boat—cowards die many times before their death, but he found that prospect infinitely preferable to the possible consequences of setting sail on the ocean in such a frail craft.* The proverb comes from Shakespeare's play *Julius Caesar* (2:2), "Cowards die many times before their deaths;/The valiant never taste of death but once."

Variant of this proverb: the coward dies a thousand deaths, the brave but one.

the cow knows not the value of her tail till she has lost it People often fail to appreciate the value of their attributes or possessions until they have them no more; also used when the kindness of friends is spurned or taken for granted: *You may live to regret responding so ungraciously to their offers of help—the cow knows not the value of her tail till she has lost it.* The proverb was first recorded, in Randle Cotgrave, *A Dictionary of the French and English Tongues* with different wording, in the early 17th century.

Proverbs expressing similar meaning: BLESSINGS BRIGHTEN AS THEY TAKE THEIR FLIGHT; YOU NEVER MISS THE WATER TILL THE WELL RUNS DRY.

the cowl does not make the monk Do not judge a person's character by his or her outward appearance or behavior: "Such impostures are sure of support from the sort of people . . . who think that it is the cowl that makes the monk" (George Bernard Shaw, *Music in London,* 1932). Of medieval Latin origin, the proverb was first recorded in English in Thomas Usk's *Testament of Love* (1387), in the form "For habit maketh no monk; ne weringe of gilte spurres maketh no knight."

Variant of this proverb: the habit does not make the monk.

Proverbs expressing similar meaning: DON'T JUDGE A BOOK BY ITS COVER; JUDGE NOT ACCORDING TO APPEARANCES.

a creaking door hangs longest Those who have many minor ailments and infirmities often outlive those who don't: *Facing the prospect of yet another operation—this time to replace an arthritic knee—she consoled herself with the saying that a creaking door hangs longest.* The proverb was first recorded in 1776 in T. Cogan, *John Buncle, Junior.*

Variants of this proverb: a creaking door never falls from its hinges; a creaking gate hangs longest.

cream always comes to the top　People of great worth or quality will ultimately enjoy high achievement or public recognition: "Never mind the cream: it will always rise to the top. It's the skim milk that needs good teachers" (Bel Kaufman, *Up the Down Staircase,* 1964). The proverb was first recorded in 1841, in an essay by Ralph Waldo Emerson.

Variant of this proverb: cream always rises to the top.

crime doesn't pay　Criminal activity may seem to be profitable, at least in the short term, but it ultimately leads to far greater loss—of liberty, or even of life; used as a deterrent slogan: *It's hard to believe that crime doesn't pay when you read of the luxurious lives some of these criminals lead in exile.* The proverb was first recorded in the early 20th century. The proverb's first citation is 1927 in N. Martin's *Mosaic.* The expression was a slogan of the FBI and the cartoon detective Dick Tracy.

crime must be concealed by crime　One crime often leads to another, committed to avoid detection of the first: *Crime must be concealed by crime, and after embezzling the funds he had to construct an elaborate network of lies to explain where the money had gone.* The proverb was first recorded in 1948 in a U.S. proverb collection.

criticism is something you can avoid by saying nothing, doing nothing, and being nothing　Whatever you say or do, somebody is bound to criticize you for it: *If you want to achieve anything in life, you must learn how to handle criticism, because it is virtually impossible to avoid it—criticism is something you can avoid only by saying nothing, doing nothing, and being nothing.* The proverb is recorded as a regional expression in the United States.

crosses are ladders that lead to heaven　Suffering and misfortune often bring out the best in a person's character: "If there be real worth in the character . . . it will give forth its finest fragrance when pressed. 'Crosses' says the old proverb, 'are ladders that lead to heaven'" (Samuel Smiles, *Self-Help,* 1859). The proverb was first recorded in 1616, in Thomas Draxe's *Adages.*

cross the stream where it is shallowest　Always take the easiest possible approach to doing something: *Why do you have to make things so difficult for yourself? "Cross the stream where it is shallowest," as my mother used to say.* The proverb was first recorded in 1603, but with the implication that it was already in regional use in England.

a crow doesn't pick out the eye of another crow　*See* HAWKS WILL NOT PICK OUT HAWKS' EYES.

the cure may be worse than the disease　*See* THE REMEDY MAY BE WORSE THAN THE DISEASE.

curiosity killed the cat　Inquisitiveness—or a desire to find out about something—can lead you into trouble; usually said in response to an importunate question: "The townspeople had learned the hard way that curiosity killed the cat—you stayed indoors if there was trouble"

(Timothy Mo, *The Redundancy of Courage,* 1991). The proverb seems to be of comparatively recent origin, having been first recorded in 1909 in Henry, *Schools and Schools.*

Proverb expressing similar meaning: ASK ME NO QUESTIONS AND I'LL TELL YOU NO LIES.

curses, like chickens, come home to roost Wrongdoers ultimately have to suffer the consequences of their bad deeds; also used when those who have wished evil on others are struck by misfortune themselves: "Their injustice will return upon them. Curses, like chickens, come home to roost" (Samuel Smiles, *Duty,* 1880). The proverb was first recorded, with different wording, in Chaucer's *Canterbury Tales* (c. 1390). In the play *The Tragedy of Mr Arden of Feversham* (1592), of unknown authorship, a different simile is used: curses are compared to "arrowes shot upright," which come back down on the shooter's head.

Variant of this proverb: chickens always come home to roost.

Proverb expressing similar meaning: WHAT GOES AROUND, COMES AROUND.

the customer is always right In order to maintain goodwill in business, you should always do what your customers want and give them the benefit of the doubt in any dispute: *The company gained its position as market leader by observing the principle that the customer is always right.* The proverb was first recorded in English in 1917 as a translation of the French proverb "*Le patron n'a jamais tort* [The customer is never wrong]." It has been attributed to various businessmen, including César Ritz (1850–1918) and H. Gordon Selfridge (1864–1947).

cut your coat according to your cloth Match your actions to your resources, and do not try to live beyond your means; also used as in the following quotation: "We must cut our coat according to our cloth and adapt ourselves to changing circumstances" (W. R. Inge, *Lay Thoughts of a Dean,* 1926). The proverb was first recorded in 1546.

Proverbs expressing similar meaning: EVERYBODY STRETCHES HIS LEGS ACCORDING TO THE LENGTH OF HIS COVERLET; STRETCH YOUR ARM NO FURTHER THAN YOUR SLEEVE WILL REACH.

the danger past and God forgotten People are prone to calling on God in times of trouble, only to forget all about their newly found religious faith as soon as the crisis is past: "The danger past, both are alike requited;/God is forgotten, and the soldier slighted" (T. Jordan, *Epigram*, 1685). The proverb was first recorded in 1611 by Randle Cotgrave in *A Dictionary of the French and English Tongues*.

Variant of this proverb: the danger past God is forgotten; the river past and God forgotten.

Proverb expressing similar meaning: MAN'S EXTREMITY IS GOD'S OPPORTUNITY.

the darkest cloud has a silver lining *See* EVERY CLOUD HAS A SILVER LINING.

the darkest hour is just before dawn Things are often at their worst just before they begin to improve: *When my fellow-campaigners began to lose heart, I reminded them of the proverb, "The darkest hour is just before dawn," confident that victory was now within our grasp.* The proverb was first recorded in 1650 in Thomas Fuller's *Pisgah Sight.*

Variant of this proverb: it's always darkest before dawn.

Proverbs expressing similar meaning: AFTER A STORM COMES A CALM; WHEN THINGS ARE AT THE WORST THEY BEGIN TO MEND.

the day is short and the work is long Life is short and there is little time in which to get work done: *We must apply ourselves to our labour, for the day is short and the work is long.* The proverb was first recorded c. 1400 in *Beryn.*

Proverb expressing similar meaning: ART IS LONG AND LIFE IS SHORT.

a dead dog tells no tales *See* DEAD MEN TELL NO TALES.

dead men don't bite A dead person can no longer do others any harm; often used to justify murder: "Then, with a pistol in either hand, I addressed him. 'One more step, Mr. Hands,' said I, 'and I'll blow your brains out! Dead men don't bite, you know,' I added with a chuckle" (Robert Louis Stevenson, *Treasure Island*, 1883). The proverb is of ancient origin: according to Plutarch, the Egyptians were advised to kill Pompey for this reason in 48 B.C. It was first recorded in English c. 1547 in the form "A dead man does no harm." In 1587 Lord Gray is said to have advocated the execution of Mary Queen of Scots with the words, "A dead woman bites not."

51

dead men tell no tales It may be expedient to kill somebody who could betray a secret or give information about the criminal activities of others: ". . . in five minutes' time the yacht will be scuttled, and the cabin hatch will be nailed down on you. Dead men tell no tales; and the sailing-master's notion is to leave proofs afloat that the vessel has foundered with all on board" (Wilkie Collins, *Armadale*, 1866). The proverb was first recorded in 1664 in J. Wilson *Andronicus Comnenius*.

Variant of this proverb: a dead dog tells no tales.

a deaf husband and a blind wife are always a happy couple A recipe for a successful marriage is one in which the husband is deaf to his wife's constant chatter or nagging and the wife is blind to her husband's physical shortcomings or misdeeds: *Conjugal harmony requires tolerance on both sides—there is some truth in the old saying that "A deaf husband and a blind wife are always a happy couple."* The proverb was first recorded with wording close to the current form in 1637: "Then marriage may be said to be past in all quietnesse, When the wife is blind, and the husband deafe" (T. Heywood, *Pleasant Dialogues*). An earlier citation (1578) recommends that the man be blind and the woman deaf.

death before dishonor *See* BETTER DEATH THAN DISHONOR.

death defies the doctor All patients will eventually die, whatever the doctors do: *We can keep the old lady alive for months, but not indefinitely: in the end death always defies the doctor.* The proverb was first recorded in 1721 in James Kelly's *A Complete Collection of Scottish Proverbs*.

Proverbs expressing similar meaning: MEDICINE CAN PROLONG LIFE, BUT DEATH WILL SEIZE THE DOCTOR, TOO; THERE'S A REMEDY FOR EVERYTHING EXCEPT DEATH.

death is the great leveler People of all ranks and classes are equal in death, and nobody is exempt from dying: *The list of those who perished in the hotel fire—everybody from visiting dignitaries and film stars to porters and cleaning staff—provided a sobering illustration of the adage "Death is the great leveler."* The proverb was first recorded in English in 1732, but the sentiment it expresses is of ancient origin. Compare Claudian (A.D. 340–410), "*omnia mors aequat* [death levels all things]." Other words have been substituted for *death,* such as *religion, golf, AIDS,* or *the Internet.*

Variant of this proverb: death is a great leveler.

Proverb expressing similar meaning: EQUALITY BEGINS IN THE GRAVE.

death keeps no calendar Death can strike at any time: *Death keeps no calendar, which is why many people follow the philosophy of living every day as if it were their last.* The proverb was first recorded in 1640 in George Herbert's *Outlandish Proverbs.*

death pays all debts The dead no longer have any obligations, financial or otherwise, to the living: "'It must be sorely answered,' said the peace-officer. 'Never you mind that—death pays all debts; it will pay that too'" (Sir Walter Scott, *Chronicles of the Canongate*, 1827). The proverb occurs in Shakespeare's play *The*

Tempest (3:3) in the form "He that dies pays all debts" (1597–98).

deeds, not words   What a person does is more important than—and may be quite different from—what he or she says: *My boss has an infuriating habit of interrupting my lengthy excuses and explanations with the curt remark, "Deeds, not words."* The proverb originated in the Latin form *"Facta, non verba."* It occurs in various forms in Shakespeare's plays, such as these lines from *Henry VIII* (3:2): *"'Tis a kind of good deed to say well:/And yet words are no deeds."*

deeds are fruits, words are but leaves   Mere words have no value unless they are followed by positive action: *The new governor would do well to remember the proverb "Deeds are fruits, words are but leaves"—his predecessor promised to tackle the problem of juvenile crime, but nothing was ever done.* The proverb was first recorded in 1616 in Thomas Draxe's *Adages.*

Proverb expressing similar meaning: ACTIONS SPEAK LOUDER THAN WORDS.

delays are dangerous   Hesitation or procrastination may lead to trouble or disaster: *"'My dear fellow, delays are dangerous. Let us have done with suspense, and risk it, the day after to-morrow'"* (Wilkie Collins, *Queen of Hearts,* 1859). The proverb was first recorded in 1578 in the form "Delays breed dangers" (John Lyly, *Euphues*).

Proverb expressing similar meaning: HE WHO HESITATES IS LOST.

Proverb expressing opposite meaning: THERE'S LUCK IN LEISURE.

deny self for self's sake   You can do yourself a favor by not satisfying your every desire or indulging your every whim—self-denial and unselfishness can be beneficial to the body and soul: *A recent survey seemed to suggest that those who occasionally "deny self for self's sake" live longer, happier lives.* The proverb was first recorded in 1735, in Benjamin Franklin's *Poor Richard's Almanack.*

desert and reward seldom keep company   People are often not rewarded for their good deeds or meritorious behavior; conversely, those who do receive rewards have often done nothing to deserve them: *You will find that in this organization desert and reward seldom keep company, so do not expect your efforts to be recognized or appreciated by those in high places.* The proverb was first recorded in this form in 1670 in John Ray's *A Collection of English Proverbs.*

desires are nourished by delays   A wish or desire becomes stronger if it is not satisfied immediately: *I had hoped that he would lose interest in going on the expedition if I made him wait until the end of the school year, but desires are nourished by delays and he is now more enthusiastic than ever.* The proverb was first recorded in 1601, in *Love's Metamorphosis* by John Lyly.

desperate diseases must have desperate remedies   Drastic action is called for—and justified—when you find yourself in a particularly difficult situation: *"and there the King . . . asked him how he could have the heart to intend to destroy so many innocent people? 'Because,' said Guy Fawkes, 'desperate diseases need desperate remedies'"* (Charles Dickens, *A Child's History of England,* 1851–53). Of ancient origin, the proverb was first recorded in English in 1539 in Richard Taverner's

Proverbs in the form "A strong disease requires a strong medicine." Compare the Latin proverb *"extremis malis extrema remedia* [extreme remedies for extreme ills]." The substitution of *desperate* for *strong* or *extreme* may have been influenced by a quotation from Shakespeare's play *Hamlet* (4:3): "Diseases desperate grown/By desperate appliance are relieved,/Or not at all."

Proverb expressing similar meaning: KILLING NO MURDER.

the devil always leaves a stink behind him Evil always leaves its taint behind: *He exerted a baleful influence on everyone he knew and, like the devil, always left a stink behind him.* The proverb was first recorded in 1591 in Henry Smith's *Sermons.*

the devil can cite scripture for his purpose Passages from the Bible are sometimes quoted to support a bad idea, to justify wrongdoing, or simply as a hypocritical show of piety; used in response to, or as a warning against, people who do this: *Her argument was very persuasive, and she reminded me of a remark on the subject that Jesus made to his disciples in the New Testament, but I remained wary—the devil can cite scripture for his purpose.* The proverb comes from Shakespeare's play *The Merchant of Venice* (1:3). It alludes to Jesus' temptation in the wilderness (Matthew 4:6), when the devil quotes Psalm 91:11–12: "If thou be the Son of God, cast thyself down: for it is written, He shall give His angels charge concerning thee: and in their hands they shall bear thee up, lest at any time thou dash thy foot against a stone."

Variant of this proverb: the devil can quote scripture to his own advantage.

the devil dances in an empty pocket The poor are easily tempted to do evil. The proverb was first recorded in 1412 by Thomas Hoccleve in *The Regiment of Princes.* The fuller version of the proverb runs "the devil dances in an empty pocket because it contains no cross" (a reference to the cross that adorned the coinage in past centuries): "No devil so frightful as that which dances in the pocket where there is no cross to keep him out" (Walter Scott, *Woodstock,* 1826).

Proverb expressing a similar meaning: THE DEVIL FINDS WORK FOR IDLE HANDS TO DO.

the devil finds work for idle hands to do Idle people may find themselves tempted into wrongdoing: "There is a risk that youngsters will leave school and college to find themselves unwanted, with the devil finding work for idle hands to do" (*London Times,* 1980). The proverb comes from a poem by Isaac Watts, published in his *Divine Songs for Children* (1715): "In works of labour, or of skill,/I would be busy too;/For Satan finds some mischief still/For idle hands to do." In Charles Dickens's novel *David Copperfield* (1850), the character Mr. Wickfield observes, "if Doctor Watts knew mankind, he might have written, with as much truth, 'Satan finds some mischief still, for busy hands to do.' The busy people achieve their full share of mischief in the world, you may rely upon it."

Proverbs expressing similar meaning: THE DEVIL DANCES IN AN EMPTY POCKET; AN IDLE BRAIN IS THE DEVIL'S WORKSHOP; IDLENESS IS THE ROOT OF ALL EVIL.

the devil gets up to the belfry by the vicar's skirts Wicked people may operate among good people in order to enact their schemes. The proverb was first recorded in 1659 in J. Howell's *Paroemiographia*: "By the skirts of the Vicar the Devil climes up to the Steeple."

Variant of this proverb: the devil lurks behind the cross.

the devil is in the details The details of something are of paramount importance, and you should always examine or pay attention to them in any proposition you are considering or any project you undertake: *Read the contract very carefully before you sign. Remember that the devil is in the details, and there may be hidden drawbacks or unacceptable conditions that are not immediately apparent.* The proverb was first recorded in English as recently as the 1970s, and it may be of German, French, or Italian origin. It has been attributed to the Renaissance artist Michelangelo (1475–1564) and the French writer Gustave Flaubert (1821–80), among others.

Variant of this proverb: God is in the details.

the devil is not as black as he is painted People are rarely as bad as others say they are; often used in defense of a specific person: "Again, it cannot be gainsaid that the greater number of those who hold high places in our poetical literature are absolute nincompoops—fellows alike innocent of reason and of rhyme. But neither are we all brainless, nor is the devil himself so black as he is painted" (Edgar Allan Poe, *The Quacks of Helicon,* 1850). The proverb was first recorded in 1534, but with the implication that it was already in general use.

the devil looks after his own Bad or undeserving people often prosper and thrive; said in response to the success or good fortune of such a person: *She lied and cheated her way through college, and now she has risen to the very pinnacle of her profession—the devil looks after his own!* The proverb was first recorded in 1721, with slightly different wording, in James Kelly's collection of Scottish proverbs.

Variant of this proverb: the devil takes care of his own.

Proverb expressing similar meaning: THE DEVIL'S CHILDREN HAVE THE DEVIL'S LUCK.

the devil lurks behind the cross See THE DEVIL GETS UP TO THE BELFRY BY THE VICAR'S SKIRTS.

the devil makes his Christmas pies of lawyers' tongues and clerks' fingers Beware of unscrupulous lawyers and their assistants: *In commercial disputes my father was always anxious to steer clear of litigation, on the basis of the saying "The devil makes his Christmas pies of lawyers' tongues and clerks' fingers."* The proverb was first recorded in 1591, in John Florio's conversation manual *Second Fruits,* with the implication that a third ingredient of the devil's pie is women.

the devil's children have the devil's luck Bad people often have good luck; usually said with envy rather than malice on hearing of somebody's good fortune: *I might have guessed that Richard would win the jackpot—the devil's children have the devil's luck!* The proverb was first recorded in 1678 in John Ray's *A Collection of English Proverbs.*

Proverb expressing similar meaning: THE DEVIL LOOKS AFTER HIS OWN.

the devil takes care of his own   *See* THE DEVIL LOOKS AFTER HIS OWN.

the devil was sick, the devil a saint would be; the devil was well, the devil a saint was he   People often turn to religion or promise to reform when they are ill or in trouble, only to revert to their former ways as soon as the crisis is over: *The prisoner's remorse seemed genuine, but the authorities were reluctant to release him, on the grounds that "the devil was sick, the devil a saint would be."* The word *monk* is used in place of *saint* in a medieval Latin form of the proverb and in its earliest English citation in 1629 in a sermon by Thomas Adams. The closing phrase "the devil a saint was he" means "he was not a saint at all."

diamond cuts diamond   The only match for a very sharp-witted or cunning person is somebody of equally sharp wit or great cunning: *She thought she had outwitted me, but diamond cuts diamond, and I still had a few tricks up my sleeve.* The proverb was first recorded in 1604 in John Marston *The Malcontent.*

diet cures more than doctors   A sensible diet does more for the health than medical intervention: *Her grandfather always insisted that diet cures more than doctors and never entered a hospital in his life.* The proverb was first recorded in 1875 by A. B. Cheales in *Proverbs.*

Proverb expressing similar meaning: THE BEST DOCTORS ARE DR. DIET, DR. QUIET, AND DR. MERRYMAN.

different strokes for different folks   Different people have different habits, methods, and tastes; also (and perhaps originally) used to suggest that different people must be approached or dealt with in different ways: "He dictates everything he writes. . . . I write out everything. Different strokes for different folks" (Alexandra Stoddard, *Gift of a Letter,* 1990). The proverb is of U.S. origin, dating from the mid-20th century or earlier.

the difficult is done at once, the impossible takes a little longer   Difficult tasks present no problem, and even those that seem impossible will ultimately be accomplished; used as a motto or policy statement, as in commerce: *Our company has an excellent record of success in tracking down rare or out-of-print books, but we urge our customers to be patient—"The difficult is done at once, the impossible takes a little longer."* Used as a slogan of the armed forces, the proverb is attributed to Louis XVI's finance minister Charles Alexandre de Calonne (1734–1802). It was first recorded in English in 1873.

dig the well before you are thirsty   Do not wait until it is too late to prepare for future necessities: *He had worked out a possible escape route in case things went wrong, on the principle that it is better to dig the well before you are thirsty.* The proverb was first recorded in 1948 in a U.S. proverb collection, but it is believed to be of ancient origin. The Roman dramatist Plautus (c. 254–184 B.C.) is said to have remarked, "It's a wretched business to be digging a well just as thirst is overcoming you."

Variant of this proverb: dig a well before it rains.

diligence is the mother of good luck   Those who work hardest are most likely to enjoy good fortune: "Diligence is the mother of good luck. . . . A man's success in life will be proportionate to his efforts" (Samuel Smiles, *Thrift,* 1875). The proverb was first recorded in 1591 in W. Stepney's *Spanish Schoolmaster.*

dirty water will quench fire   You cannot afford to be too fastidious at a time of great necessity; often used with specific reference to the satisfaction of sexual desire with a partner of ugly appearance or loose morals: "'How could anyone go with her?' Dewi shrugged. 'They do say dirty water puts out fire just as well'" (Alison G. Taylor, *Simeon's Bride,* 1995). The proverb was first recorded in 1546 in the form "Foul water as soon as fair, will quench hot fire."

discretion is the better part of valor   It is often wiser to avoid taking an unnecessary risk than to be recklessly courageous: "You have shown the discretion which is the better part of valour . . . had you attacked Sir Richard, you would now be lying senseless on the greensward, quite unable to undertake the journey that lies before you tomorrow" (L. P. Hartley, *Eustace and Hilda,* 1947). The proverb comes from Shakespeare's play *Henry IV, Part 1* (5:4): "The better part of valour is discretion; in the which better part, I have saved my life" (1597–98). The sentiment it expresses, however, is of earlier origin.

Proverb expressing similar meaning: HE WHO FIGHTS AND RUNS AWAY MAY LIVE TO FIGHT ANOTHER DAY.

distance lends enchantment to the view   Distance in space or time makes things seem better than they are—or were—in reality: *I remember college life as a happy, carefree existence, but distance lends enchantment to the view, and reading the diaries I wrote during those years has brought back* *many painful memories.* The proverb comes from Thomas Campbell's poem "Pleasures of Hope" (1799): "'Tis distance lends enchantment to the view, / And robes the mountain in its azure hue."

Proverb expressing similar meaning: BLUE ARE THE HILLS THAT ARE FAR AWAY.

divide and conquer   The best way to conquer or control a group of people is by encouraging them to fight among themselves rather than allowing them to unite in opposition to the ruling authority: "This Republican Administration treats us as if we were pieces of a puzzle that can't fit together. They've tried to put us into compartments and separate us from each other. Their political theory is 'divide and conquer'" (transcript of speech by Ann Richards, *New York Times,* 1988). Of Latin origin, the proverb was first recorded in English in 1605. It has been the maxim of many rulers and authorities throughout history.

Variant of this proverb: divide and rule.

Proverbs expressing similar meaning: A HOUSE DIVIDED AGAINST ITSELF CANNOT STAND; UNITED WE STAND, DIVIDED WE FALL.

do as I say, not as I do   Do what somebody tells or advises you to do rather than what that person actually does himself or herself: *This was a classic case of "Do as I say, not as I do"—she had appeared on television urging mothers to have their babies vaccinated, but subsequently admitted that she had refused the vaccine for her own child.* The proverb was first recorded in an Anglo-Saxon text dating from before the 12th century.

Proverbs expressing opposite meaning: EXAMPLE IS BETTER THAN PRECEPT; A GOOD EXAMPLE IS THE BEST SERMON.

do as you would be done by Treat other people in the way that you would like to be treated: *Do as you would be done by—you can't expect people to be honest with you if you persist in lying to them.* The proverb was first recorded in this form in c. 1596. It was used in a letter written by Lord Chesterfield in 1747,—"'Do as you would be done by,' is the surest method that I know of pleasing"—and was further popularized as the name of a good fairy, Mrs. Doasyouwouldbedoneby, in Charles Kingsley's *The Water Babies* (1863).

Proverb expressing similar meaning: DO UNTO OTHERS AS YOU WOULD THEY SHOULD DO UNTO YOU.

the doctor is often more to be feared than the disease Some courses of medical treatment are worse than the disease they aim to cure: *In years gone by there was a deal of truth in the saying "the doctor is often more to be feared than the disease."* The proverb was first recorded in 1621 by Robert Burton in his *Anatomy of Melancholy*.

the dog always returns to his vomit People always return to the scene of their crime or wrongdoing: *The police kept a 24-hour watch on the building where the body was found, hoping that as a dog returns to its vomit, the murderer would eventually reappear.* The proverb is of biblical origin: "As a dog returneth to his vomit, so a fool returneth to his folly" (Proverbs 26:11); "The dog is turned to his own vomit again; and the sow that was washed to her wallowing in the mire" (2 Peter 2:22). It also occurs in Chaucer's *Canterbury Tales* (c. 1390): "the hound . . . retourneth to eten his spewing."

dog does not eat dog A member of a particular group of people will not—or should not—take action that will harm another member of the same group: "Except where I felt it to be absolutely essential . . . I have avoided any discussion of criticism and critics: dog should not eat dog" (J. B. Priestley, *Literature and Western Man,* 1960). Of Latin origin, the proverb was first recorded in English in 1543. It has given rise to the cliché *dog eat dog,* referring to ruthless competition in industry, politics, etc.

Variant of this proverb: dog will not eat dog.

Proverbs expressing similar meaning: HAWKS WILL NOT PICK OUT HAWKS' EYES; THERE'S HONOR AMONG THIEVES.

a dog is man's best friend Dogs are more faithful than any human companion: "'A dog is man's best friend' is an old adage which the defendants have either forgotten or decided to ignore" (Transcript of judgment in a case involving laboratory animals, *New York Times,* 1993). The proverb was first recorded in a letter written by the English poet Alexander Pope in 1709.

Variant of this proverb: man's best friend is his dog.

the dogs bark, but the caravan goes on The warnings or protests of those in lowly positions are often ignored by those in power and are not allowed to stand in the way of progress: *Disregarding public opinion, they went ahead with their plan—the dogs bark, but the caravan goes on.* Of Asian origin, the proverb was first recorded in English in 1891 in John Lockwood Kipling's *Beast and Man in India.*

dogs that bark don't always bite *See* A BARKING DOG NEVER BITES.

a dog that will fetch a bone will carry a bone Beware of people who bring you gossip about others, because they are equally likely to pass on gossip about you: *She came rushing over to tell me that Julia had left Peter, but I gave her no hint that my own marriage was heading the same way. A dog that will fetch a bone will carry a bone, and I didn't want the whole town to know.* The proverb was first recorded in 1830 in R. Forby's *Vocabulary of East Anglia,* but with the implication that it was already in use.

dog will not eat dog *See* DOG DOES NOT EAT DOG.

don't air your dirty linen in public *See* DON'T WASH YOUR DIRTY LINEN IN PUBLIC.

don't bite off more than you can chew Do not take on a task that is larger or more difficult than you can manage: *Don't bite off more than you can chew—this project is far too complex to be tackled by a single person.*

Proverbs expressing similar meaning: DON'T GO NEAR THE WATER UNTIL YOU LEARN HOW TO SWIM; DON'T START ANYTHING YOU CAN'T FINISH.

don't bite the hand that feeds you Do not behave unkindly or ungratefully toward those on whom you depend for financial or other support: "And having looked to government for bread, on the very first scarcity they will turn and bite the hand that fed them" (Edmund Burke, *Thoughts and Details on Scarcity,* 1797). The proverb was first recorded in 1711. The producer Sam Goldwyn apparently confused this proverb with another when he remarked, "That's the way with these directors, they're always biting the hand that lays the golden egg" (Alva Johnston, *The Great Goldwyn,* 1937).

don't burn your bridges behind you Think carefully before taking any step that is irrevocable, because you cannot be sure what the future holds: *You might want to return to this town some day, so try to leave it on good terms with everybody and don't burn your bridges behind you.* The proverb was first recorded in 1923 in A. Crowley, *Confessions.* It refers to the military practice of burning bridges as an army advances, making retreat impossible. The figurative phrase *to burn one's boats* has the same meaning.

Variant of this proverb: don't burn your bridges before you.

don't carry all your eggs in one basket *See* DON'T PUT ALL YOUR EGGS IN ONE BASKET.

don't cast your pearls before swine It is pointless to waste fine or beautiful things on people who are incapable of appreciating them: *Ignoring advice not to cast pearls before swine, he signed up some of the greatest classical musicians in the country to perform at the concert.* The proverb is of biblical origin: "Give not that which is holy unto the dogs, neither cast ye your pearls before swine, lest they trample them under their feet, and turn again and rend you" (Matthew 7:6).

Variant of this proverb: don't throw pearls to swine.

don't change horses in the middle of the stream *See* DON'T SWAP HORSES IN MIDSTREAM.

don't change the rules in the middle of the game It is wrong or unfair to change the rules, terms, or conditions relating to something once it is in progress, or after people have become involved in it: *It is an unwritten law of business that you don't change the rules in the middle of the game, which is precisely what our customers have done by reducing the tolerances on their specifications.*

don't count your chickens before they are hatched Do not act on the optimistic assumption that you will get or achieve something until you actually have it or are absolutely certain of success: "The experts, you know, the big dealers—we don't want any publicity just yet. . . . And we don't want to count our purely putative chickens before they're hatched" (William Plomer, *Museum Pieces,* 1950). The proverb was first recorded c. 1570 in the form "Count not thy chickens that unhatched be."

Proverbs expressing similar meaning: FIRST CATCH YOUR HARE; THERE'S MANY A SLIP BETWEEN CUP AND LIP.

don't cross the bridge till you come to it Do not anticipate trouble or worry about future problems that may or may not arise: *The case may not even come to court, so there's no point in worrying whether or not you will have to give evidence—don't cross the bridge till you come to it.* The proverb was first recorded in 1850, in the American poet Henry Wadsworth Longfellow's *Journal,* and reappeared the following year in his poem "The Golden Legend": "Don't cross the bridge till you come to it,/Is a proverb old, and of excellent wit."

Proverbs expressing similar meaning: DON'T MEET TROUBLES HALFWAY; SUFFICIENT UNTO THE DAY IS THE EVIL THEREOF; TAKE THINGS AS THEY COME.

don't cry before you're hurt There is no point in upsetting yourself about something bad that may or may not happen: *They probably have no intention of dismissing you, so don't cry before you're hurt.* The proverb was first recorded in English in 1548, in *Reliq. Antiquae,* in the form "I cry not before I am pricked," but a similar proverb existed in French more than 200 years earlier.

don't cry over spilled milk *See* IT'S NO USE CRYING OVER SPILLED MILK.

don't cut off your nose to spite your face Do not take action to spite others that will harm you more than them: "For that money and your own infernal vanity you are willing to deliberately turn out bad work. You'll do quite enough bad work without knowing it. And . . . I am not going to let you cut off your nose to spite your face for all the gold in England" (Rudyard Kipling, *The Light That Failed,* 1890). The proverb was first recorded in English c. 1560, in *Deceit of Women,* in the form "He that bites his nose off, shames his face," but similar proverbs existed in medieval Latin and 14th-century French.

don't get into deep water until you learn how to swim *See* DON'T GO NEAR THE WATER UNTIL YOU LEARN HOW TO SWIM.

don't get mad, get even Take positive action to retaliate for a wrong that has been done to you, rather than wasting your time and energy in angry recriminations: *"Don't get mad, get even" was her watchword, so when one of the other students in the art class laughed at her painting she calmly picked up his sculpture and dashed it to the ground.* The proverb is of comparatively recent origin; it was first recorded in 1975: "Some of the reasons have their roots in that wonderful law of the Boston Irish political jungle: 'Don't get mad; get even'" (Ben Bradlee, *Conversations with Kennedy*).

don't give up the ship Never stop fighting and do not surrender: *My wife encouraged me to stand up to the bullies at work, and when I talked of resigning she always said, "Don't give up the ship."* The proverb has been attributed to James Lawrence, commander of the U.S. frigate "Chesapeake," when he was fatally wounded in 1813. It first appeared in print the following year in *The Diary of F. Palmer, Privateersman*.

Proverb expressing similar meaning: NEVER SAY DIE.

don't go near the water until you learn how to swim Do not put yourself in a difficult or dangerous situation until you are capable of handling it: *You should not have agreed to take part in this mission with the little experience that you have. Have you never heard the proverb "Don't go near the water until you learn how to swim"?* The proverb was first recorded in 1855 in the form "Never venture out of your depth till you can swim."

Variant of this proverb: don't get into deep water until you learn how to swim.

Proverbs expressing similar meaning: DON'T BITE OFF MORE THAN YOU CAN CHEW; DON'T START ANYTHING YOU CAN'T FINISH.

don't halloo till you are out of the woods *See* DON'T SHOUT UNTIL YOU ARE OUT OF THE WOODS.

don't hide your light under a bushel If you have special skills or talents, do not conceal them through modesty and prevent others from appreciating or benefiting from them: "It ain't that I am vain, but that you don't like to put your own light under a bushel. What's the worth of your reputation, if you can't convey the reason for it to the person you most wish to value it?" (Charles Dickens, *Doctor Marigold*, 1865). The proverb is of biblical origin: "Neither do men light a candle, and put it under a bushel, but on a candlestick; and it giveth light unto all that are in the house" (Matthew 5:15).

don't hit a man when he's down It is unkind and unsportsmanlike to cause further physical or mental harm to somebody who is already suffering: ". . . while it did Tom's heart good to see the cordial respect paid to his father, it tried his patience . . . to hear . . . 'That's the son; it's hard on him. Wild fellow, do him good.' 'Granted; but you needn't hit a man when he's down,' muttered Tom to himself, feeling every moment a stronger desire to do something that should silence everybody" (Louisa May Alcott, *An Old-Fashioned Girl*, 1870). The proverb was first recorded in 1551 in the writings of the English archbishop Thomas Cranmer.

don't judge a book by its cover Do not form an opinion about something or somebody based solely on outward appearance: "Appreciate your allowing me to participate, but you should be less trusting, Ellie—can't always judge a book by its cover" (Dorothy Cannell, *Thin Woman*, 1984). The proverb was first recorded in 1929 in the form "You can't

61

judge a book by its binding" in the periodical *American Speech.*

Variant of this proverb: you can't tell a book by its cover.

Proverbs expressing similar meaning: THE COWL DOES NOT MAKE THE MONK; JUDGE NOT ACCORDING TO APPEARANCES; THERE'S MANY A GOOD COCK COME OUT OF A TATTERED BAG.

don't judge a man until you have walked a mile in his boots Do not criticize or pass judgment on somebody until you have been in the same situation, undergone the same experiences, or tried to do the same thing: *I was sure that I would never have made such a fundamental mistake if I had been in his position, but I made no comment, remembering the old adage "Don't judge a man until you have walked a mile in his boots."*

don't jump from the frying pan into the fire Do not go from a bad situation to a worse one: "If it is decided that the religious fundamentalism of Iran is a danger to all the nations of the Middle East . . . then Israelis will have to ask themselves: Are we jumping from the frying pan into the fire?" (*New York Times,* 1989). The proverb was first recorded in English in 1528, in the works of the English statesman Sir Thomas More, but it is of ancient origin. It is perhaps more frequently used in the form of the figurative phrase *out of the frying pan into the fire.*

Variant of this proverb: don't jump out of the frying pan into the fire.

don't kill the goose that lays the golden eggs Take care not to destroy something valuable, such as a source of steady income, through greed, impatience, or a desire for instant gain: "All these turns

which he was making through the streets seemed to indicate that he was not a simple and honest man. To arrest him too hastily would be 'to kill the hen that laid the golden eggs.' Where was the inconvenience in waiting? Javert was very sure that he would not escape" (Victor Hugo, *Les Misérables,* 1862). The proverb comes from one of the fables of Aesop (sixth century B.C.), in which a farmer has a goose that lays golden eggs. Instead of being content with receiving one golden egg every day for the foreseeable future, he kills the goose in the hope of gaining instant access to all the gold inside. Needless to say, he finds nothing.

Variant of this proverb: don't kill the goose that laid the golden egg.

don't let the fox guard the henhouse Do not put somebody in a position where he or she will be tempted to wrongdoing: *There was widespread outrage when it was discovered that a known pedophile had been given a job at the school. "You don't let the fox guard the henhouse," said one of the protesters.* The proverb was first recorded in *Contre-League* in 1589.

Variant of this proverb: don't set a wolf to watch the sheep.

don't make the same mistake twice You should learn from your mistakes rather than repeating them: *You can't expect to get everything right first time, but try to put past experience to good use and don't make the same mistake twice.*

Proverb expressing similar meaning: EXPERIENCE IS THE BEST TEACHER.

don't marry for money, but don't marry without money *See* NEVER MARRY FOR MONEY, BUT MARRY WHERE MONEY IS.

don't meet troubles halfway Do not worry about problems before they actually happen: "Do not meet troubles halfway. . . . When need arises we will see what can be done" (Michael Sadleir, *Fanny by Gaslight,* 1940). The proverb was first recorded in this form in 1896, but the sentiment it expresses is of ancient origin. Compare Seneca (c. 4 B.C.–A.D. 65), *"quid iuvat dolori sui occurrere?* [what help is it to run out to meet your troubles?]."

Proverbs expressing similar meaning: DON'T CROSS THE BRIDGE TILL YOU COME TO IT; NEVER TROUBLE TROUBLE TILL TROUBLE TROUBLES YOU; TAKE THINGS AS THEY COME.

don't overload gratitude; if you do, she'll kick When people are grateful to you, do not take excessive advantage of the situation, because any sense of obligation has its limits: *You seem to think that just because you once did me a great favor, I should be forever in your debt—haven't you heard the proverb "Don't overload gratitude; if you do, she'll kick"?* The proverb was first recorded in 1741, in Benjamin Franklin's *Poor Richard's Almanack.*

don't play with edged tools *See* IT'S ILL JESTING WITH EDGED TOOLS.

don't play with fire *See* IF YOU PLAY WITH FIRE, YOU GET BURNED.

don't put all your eggs in one basket Spread your risks or investments so that if one enterprise fails you will not lose everything: *When my aunt died, she left us some money, which we invested in a wide range of companies, not wanting to put all our eggs into one basket.* The proverb was first recorded in English in the 17th century in Giovanni Torriano's *A Common Place of Italian Proverbs and Proverbial Phrases,* and it is probably of Spanish or Italian origin. The earlier English proverb "Venture not all in one bottom [ship]," of Latin origin, expresses the same sentiment. Mark Twain, in *Pudd'nhead Wilson* (1894), gives a piece of alternative advice: "Put all your eggs in the one basket, and—*watch that basket.*"

Variant of this proverb: don't carry all your eggs in one basket.

Proverb expressing similar meaning: THE MOUSE THAT HAS BUT ONE HOLE IS QUICKLY TAKEN.

don't put new wine in old bottles *See* YOU CAN'T PUT NEW WINE IN OLD BOTTLES.

don't put the cart before the horse It is important to do things in the right or natural order; also used when people confuse cause and effect: *Don't put the cart before the horse—it's pointless to start advertising for staff until you have raised the money to set up the business.* The proverb was first recorded in this form c. 1520, but the sentiment it expresses is of earlier origin.

Proverb expressing similar meaning: FIRST THINGS FIRST.

don't rock the boat It is often wise to avoid taking action or making suggestions that will cause upset or trouble: *There are some who will always speak out when they think things should be changed, and there are others who remain silent, preferring not to rock the boat.* The proverb dates from the 1920s and was popularized by the song "Sit Down, You're Rocking the Boat" in the musical *Guys and Dolls* (1950).

Proverb expressing similar meaning: LET SLEEPING DOGS LIE.

don't rush the cattle   *See* HURRY NO MAN'S CATTLE.

don't set a wolf to watch the sheep   *See* DON'T LET THE FOX GUARD THE HEN-HOUSE.

don't shoot the messenger   When you receive bad news, do not vent your anger or distress on the person who brings it: *Enraged by a report from one of his financial advisers, the president called for the man's dismissal. He was warned against such a drastic step by somebody who reminded him, "The man only wrote the report—don't shoot the messenger."* The sentiment expressed by this proverb is of ancient origin: Sophocles wrote c. 442 B.C., "Nobody likes the man who brings bad news." Its current form, however, is relatively recent.

don't shoot the pianist, he's doing his best   Don't criticize somebody who is not to blame, or who is doing the best he or she can in difficult circumstances: *I heard that the new temporary lecturer could barely control the rowdy students—but on the basis of "Don't shoot the pianist, he's doing his best" I decided that the best policy was to remain silent.* The proverb was first recorded in 1883, in Oscar Wilde's *Personal Impressions of America,* "Over the piano was printed a notice: Please do not shoot the pianist. He is doing his best" referring to a saloon in Leadville, Colorado.

don't shout until you are out of the woods   Avoid any show of triumph or relief until you are sure that a period of difficulty or danger is over: "Don't holla till you are out of the wood. This is a night for praying rather than boasting" (Charles Kingsley, *Hereward the Wake,* 1866). The proverb was first recorded in 1770. It has given rise to the figurative phrase *out of the woods,* meaning "out of danger or trouble."

Variant of this proverb: don't halloo till you are out of the woods.

don't shut the barn door after the horse is stolen   It is too late to take action to prevent an undesirable event after it has already occurred: "'The union has to act now if it is to affect events,' said Harley Shaiken, a former auto worker . . . 'If they wait until the national contract expires in September 1993, it will be like closing the barn door after the horse has gotten out'" (*New York Times,* 1994). The proverb was first recorded c. 1350 in *Douce MS.*

Variant of this proverb: it's too late to shut the stable door after the horse has bolted.

Proverb expressing similar meaning: IT'S EASY TO BE WISE AFTER THE EVENT.

don't spoil the ship for half a penny's worth of tar   Do not make petty economies that will adversely affect the final result of something, especially if you have already spent a lot of money on it or put a lot of effort into it: "Mrs. Owen . . . had recommended a doctor, and Mildred saw him once a week. He was to charge fifteen guineas. 'Of course I could have got it done cheaper, but Mrs. Owen strongly recommended him, and I thought it wasn't worth while to spoil the ship for a coat of tar'" (W. Somerset Maugham, *Of Human Bondage,* 1915). The proverb was first recorded in 1623 in the form "A man will not lose a hog, for a halfpennyworth of tar." (Tar was used to treat sores and wounds on farm animals.) The word *hog* was subsequently replaced by *sheep,* and through a misunderstanding of rural pronunciation it ultimately became *ship.*

Variant of this proverb: don't spoil the ship for a ha'porth of tar.

don't start anything you can't finish Do not begin something unless you are sure that you have sufficient strength, courage, etc. to see it through to the end: *Ignoring the advice "Don't start anything you can't finish," he embarked on a costly lawsuit against his former employers.* The proverb was first recorded in 1477 in *Dictes and Sayenges of Philosophirs.*

Proverbs expressing similar meaning: DON'T BITE OFF MORE THAN YOU CAN CHEW; DON'T GO NEAR THE WATER UNTIL YOU LEARN HOW TO SWIM.

don't swallow the cow and worry with the tail *See* IT'S IDLE TO SWALLOW THE COW AND CHOKE ON THE TAIL.

don't swap horses in midstream Once you have embarked on a course of action or an undertaking, it is better not to change your tactics or methods along the way: "'If ours is the true religion why do you not become a Catholic?' . . . 'Reverend father, we have a proverb in England never to swap horses while crossing a stream'" (Robert Graves, *Goodbye to All That,* 1929). The proverb was first recorded in 1864, in the works of Abraham Lincoln: "I am reminded . . . of a story of an old Dutch farmer, who remarked to a companion once that 'it was best not to swap horses when crossing streams.'"

Variant of this proverb: don't change horses in the middle of the stream.

don't take down a fence unless you are sure why it was put up Most things were constructed or established for a purpose, and it is unwise to destroy or dismantle them unless you are certain that they are not longer required: *The law seemed outdated, but the legislators were reluctant to repeal it, on the basis that you shouldn't take down a fence unless you are sure why it was put up.*

Variant of this proverb: don't tear down a wall unless you are sure why it was put up.

don't talk the talk if you can't walk the walk Don't boast of something if you are unwilling or unable to back it up by your actions: *It's all very well to say you can climb that tree, but don't talk the talk if you can't walk the walk.* The proverb first became familiar in the USA toward the end of the 20th century. A more concise variant is "walk the talk."

don't teach your grandmother to suck eggs Do not presume to give advice or instruction to those who are older and more experienced than you: "Why, if you knew how many tens of thousands of women, especially in New York, say just what you do, you'd lose all the fun of thinking you're a lone genius. . . . There's always about a million young women just out of college who want to teach their grandmothers how to suck eggs" (Sinclair Lewis, *Main Street,* 1920). The proverb was first recorded in 1707.

Proverb expressing similar meaning: THEY THAT LIVE LONGEST SEE MOST.

don't tear down a wall unless you are sure why it was put up *See* DON'T TAKE DOWN A FENCE UNLESS YOU ARE SURE WHY IT WAS PUT UP.

don't throw away your dirty water until you get clean It is advisable to keep what you have, however unacceptable it has become, until you are sure that you can replace it with something better: "I'm keeping him on for the present. . . . It's no good throwing away dirty water until one's got clean" (Victor Bridges, *Greensea Island,* 1922). The proverb was first recorded, with different wording, c. 1475. Its current form occurs in a proverb collection of 1710.

don't throw good money after bad If you have already spent money on a venture that seems likely to fail, do not waste any further money on it. *The repairs to the boat cost me a fortune, and it's still not seaworthy, so I've decided not to throw good money after bad—I'm going to save up for a new boat instead.* The proverb was first recorded in J. Stevens's *A New Spanish and English Dictionary,* 1706.

don't throw out the baby with the bathwater Do not take the drastic step of abolishing or discarding something in its entirety when only part of it is unacceptable: *Let's not throw the baby out with the bathwater—the law as it stands is basically sound, and just needs a few amendments to close up the loopholes.* First recorded in English in 1853 in Thomas Carlyle, *Nigger Question,* the proverb is of German origin, dating from the 16th century or earlier.

don't throw pearls to swine *See* DON'T CAST YOUR PEARLS BEFORE SWINE.

don't wash your dirty linen in public Do not discuss private disputes or family scandals in public: *The chat-show format in which ordinary people air their personal grievances against friends and family in front of a nationwide audience was obviously dreamed up by somebody unacquainted with the saying "Don't wash your dirty linen in public."* The proverb was first recorded in 1809 in T. G. Fessenden's *Pills.*

Variant of this proverb: don't air your dirty linen in public.

don't wish too hard; you might just get what you wished for Beware of wishing for something too much, because you might not like it when you get it: *Don't wish too hard; you might just get what you wished for. Many who strive for fame and fortune—and achieve it—long to return to their former lives of humble obscurity.* The sentiment expressed by this proverb is of ancient origin. Its variant form is associated with Oscar Wilde, and is the moral of his novel *The Picture of Dorian Gray* (1891).

Variant of this proverb: be careful what you wish for: you might get it.

a door must be either shut or open You must choose between two alternatives, one of which excludes the other: *You must decide whether you are going to accept or refuse their offer—there is no middle way. A door must be either shut or open.* The proverb was first recorded in 1762, in Oliver Goldsmith's *The Citizen of the World.*

Proverb expressing similar meaning: YOU CAN'T HAVE IT BOTH WAYS.

do right and fear no man Take courage from a clear conscience: *Her motto was "Do right and fear no man," so she had no qualms about exposing the corrupt practices of the* *organization, and facing the inevitable repercussions.* The proverb was first recorded in c. 1450. In modern use it sometimes has a punning extension, "don't write and fear no woman."

Proverbs expressing similar meaning: A CLEAR CONSCIENCE CAN BEAR ANY TROUBLE; EVIL DOERS ARE EVIL DREADERS.

a dose of adversity is often as needful as a dose of medicine Hardship and misfortune may be unpleasant, but they can sometimes have a beneficial effect on the character, especially when people fail to appreciate the good things they have: *Life has always been easy for him, and this spell of ill luck has hit him hard. But it may be all for the best—they say that a dose of adversity is often as needful as a dose of medicine.* The proverb is recorded as a regional expression in the United States.

do unto others as you would have them do unto you Treat other people as you would wish them to treat you: "He turned the other cheek on every occasion and always did unto others exactly as he would have had others do unto him" (Joseph Heller, *Catch-22*, 1961). The proverb is of biblical origin: "Therefore all things whatsoever ye would that men should do to you, do ye even so to them" (Matthew 7:12), "And as ye would that men should do to you, do ye also to them likewise" (Luke 6:31), and is known as the Golden Rule. Charles Dickens produced a cynical parody of the proverb, "Do other men, for they would do you," in *Martin Chuzzlewit* (1843), and George Bernard Shaw wrote in *Man and Superman* (1903), "Do not do unto others as you would that they should do unto you. Their tastes may not be the same."

Variant of this proverb: do unto others as you would they should do unto you.

Proverb expressing similar meaning: DO AS YOU WOULD BE DONE BY.

do well and have well *See* NEVER DO THINGS BY HALVES.

dream of a funeral and you hear of a marriage According to popular superstition, if you dream about a funeral you will shortly receive news that somebody of your acquaintance is to be married: *Last night I dreamed I was at the funeral of some famous person I'd never heard of, so I'm expecting a wedding invitation in the mail today—dream of a funeral and you hear of a marriage.* The proverb was first recorded in J. Clarke's *Parœmiologia Anglo-Latina,* 1639 in the opposite form, "After a dream of weddings comes a corpse."

Proverb expressing similar meaning: DREAMS GO BY CONTRARIES.

dreams go by contraries What happens in your dreams is usually the opposite of what is going to happen in reality: *Don't upset yourself—everybody has nightmares sometimes, and they never come true. Haven't you heard the saying "Dreams go by contraries"?* The proverb was first recorded in c. 1400 in *Tale of Beryn.*

Proverb expressing similar meaning: dream of a funeral and you hear of a marriage.

dreams retain the infirmities of our character Our weaknesses are often revealed—usually in symbolic disguise—in our dreams: *If it's true that dreams retain the infirmities of our character, then I hate to think what some of my dreams say about* *me!* The proverb was first recorded in Emerson's *Demonology,* 1877.

a dripping June sets all in tune   A rainy June means there will be a good harvest of crops and flowers later in the summer: *The thought that a dripping June sets all in tune was of little comfort as we sheltered from the downpour under a tarpaulin.* The proverb was first recorded in 1742 in the *Agreeable Companion.*

Variant of this proverb: a dry May and a dripping June bringeth all things into tune.

drive gently over the stones   Take a cautious and delicate approach to any problems or difficulties you encounter in life: *Newlyweds should not expect their happy, carefree state to last forever, but if they learn to drive gently over the stones, they can look forward to a long and successful marriage.* The proverb was first recorded in 1711, in Jonathan Swift's *Journal to Stella:* "A gallop: sit fast, sirrah, and don't ride hard upon the stones."

drive nature out of the door and it will return by the window   See YOU CAN DRIVE OUT NATURE WITH A PITCHFORK BUT SHE KEEPS ON COMING BACK.

drought never bred dearth in England Because of its notoriously damp climate, England has never suffered famine as a result of lack of rainfall: *Complain as much as you like about the weather, but drought never bred dearth in England.* The proverb was first recorded in 1533 by John Heywood in *Play of Weather.*

a drowning man will catch at a straw Desperate people will seize any opportunity to save themselves, however small:

"His gratitude caught at those words, as the drowning man is said to catch at the proverbial straw." (Wilkie Collins, *My Lady's Money,* 1877). The proverb was first recorded in 1534 in Sir Thomas More's *Dialogue of Comfort* in the form "Lyke a man that in peril of drowning catcheth whatsoever cometh next to hand . . . be it never so simple a sticke."

Variant of this proverb: a drowning man will clutch at a straw.

drunkenness reveals what soberness conceals   People who have had too much to drink tend to reveal things they would otherwise keep to themselves: "It is an old proverbe, whatsoever is in the heart of the sober man, is in the mouth of the drunkarde" (John Lyly, *Euphues: The Anatomy of Wit,* 1578). The proverb was first recorded in English c. 1387 by Geoffrey Chaucer in *The Canterbury Tales* but was also quoted much earlier by Horace.

Proverbs expressing similar meaning: ALCOHOL WILL PRESERVE ANYTHING BUT A SECRET; THERE'S TRUTH IN WINE.

a dry cough is the trumpeter of death A dry cough often heralds death in the chronically ill: *I don't want to alarm you, but some will tell you that a dry cough is the trumpeter of death.* The proverb was first recorded in 1670 by John Ray in *A Collection of English Proverbs.*

a dry May and a dripping June bringeth all things in tune   See A DRIPPING JUNE SETS ALL IN TUNE.

a dwarf on a giant's shoulders sees further of the two   Those who build on the breakthroughs of their predecessors surpass their achievements: *Modern scien-*

DUTCH PROVERBS

The Dutch have long been famous for their achievements in commerce and trade, and so their stock of proverbs includes, among other subjects, a rich choice of proverbs relevant to commercial transactions and the transport of goods.

The best goods are the cheapest

Better lose the anchor than the whole ship

Better poor on land than rich at sea

A crown is no cure for the headache

Everyone is a thief in his own craft

Froth is not beer

Good-looking apples are sometimes sour

Great boast, little roast

A handful of patience is worth more than a bushel of brains

He that has a choice has trouble

A man overboard, one mouth less to feed

A man without money is like a ship without sails

Poverty is the reward of idleness

The rich have many friends

Set your expense according to your trade

A usurer, a miller, a banker, and a publican are the four evangelists of Lucifer

What costs nothing is worth nothing

Who watches not catches not

The world likes to be cheated

Your friend lends and your enemy asks for payment

tists are not necessarily more brilliant than those who have gone before, but by standing on giants' shoulders they see further than their predecessors could. The proverb was first recorded in 1621 by Robert Burton in his *Anatomy of Melancholy.*

Variant of this proverb: a child on a giant's shoulders sees further of the two.

eagles don't catch flies People of high rank are considered—or consider themselves—too important to deal with trivial things or lowly folk: "'Eagles don't catch flies.' 'What do you mean?' 'Inspectors of Police don't trail urchins'" (H. C. Bailey, *Nobody's Vineyard,* 1942). First recorded in English in 1563, the proverb is of Latin origin: "*Aquila non captat muscas* [The eagle does not catch flies]."

the early bird catches the worm Those who are late to act, arrive, or get up tend to miss opportunities already seized by those who came earlier: *To be sure of getting the best-quality produce, you need to be among the first to arrive at the market—remember that the early bird catches the worm.* The proverb was first recorded in William Camden, *Remaines Concerning Britaine,* 1636. It features in a joke about a father who tries to get his son out of bed in the morning by reminding him, "The early bird catches the worm." "Being early didn't do the worm much good, did it?" replies the boy.

Proverb expressing similar meaning: FIRST COME, FIRST SERVED.

the early man never borrows from the late man Farmers who sow their crops in good time have a plentiful harvest and do not need to borrow food or money from others; also used in other walks of life: *The old agricultural saying "The early man never borrows from the late man" could be applied to pensions—the sooner you start saving for your retirement, the more you will have to live on.* The proverb was first recorded in 1659.

early ripe, early rotten *See* SOON RIPE, SOON ROTTEN.

early to bed and early to rise, makes a man healthy, wealthy, and wise A lifestyle that involves neither staying up late nor sleeping late is good for body and mind and leads to financial success: "'Early to bed and early to rise.' Makes a man healthy, wealthy, and wise, McGuffin replied to himself. But in Ben Volper's case it was perhaps two out of three at best" (Robert Upton, *Fade Out,* 1984). The proverb was first recorded, with different wording, in 1496: "As the olde englysshe prouerbe sayth in this wyse. Who soo woll ryse erly shall be holy helthy and zely" (*Treatise of Fishing with Angle*). The current form dates from 1639. The U.S. humorist James Thurber parodied the proverb in "The Shrike and the Chipmunks" (1939): "Early to rise and early to bed makes a male healthy and wealthy and dead."

Proverb expressing similar meaning: ONE HOUR'S SLEEP BEFORE MIDNIGHT IS WORTH TWO AFTER.

easier said than done It is usually far easier to advise, suggest, or talk about doing something than actually to do it: "'Why don't some one kill him?' was Joe's sharp question. 'Easier said than done, lad'" (Zane Grey, *Spirit of the Border,* 1905). The proverb was first recorded in 1483 in the form "It is easier to say than to do."

Variant of this proverb: sooner said than done.

east, west, home's best No matter how far you travel, you will never find a place that is better than your own home; usually said by a returning traveler: "'You're soon returned, my dear,' said Agathya Mikhailovna. 'I grew homesick, Agathya Mikhailovna. East or West, home is best,' he answered, and went into his study" (Leo Tolstoy, *Anna Karenina,* 1873–77). Of German origin, the proverb was first recorded in English in 1859.

Variant of this proverb: travel east and travel west, a man's own home is still the best.

Proverbs expressing similar meaning: HOME IS HOME, BE IT EVER SO HOMELY; THERE'S NO PLACE LIKE HOME.

East is East and West is West and never the twain shall meet People who are very different in background or outlook are likely never to agree: *Please try to keep off politics at the dinner party tonight—you know that you will never bring Matt around to your way of thinking. East is East and West is West and never the twain shall meet!* The proverb comes from Rudyard Kipling's poem "The Ballad of East and West" (1889).

easy come, easy go Things that are easily acquired, especially money, are just as easily lost or spent: "I doubt the ability of any of them to keep money more than five years at the rate they're spending. Easy come, easy go" (Margaret Mitchell, *Gone with the Wind,* 1936). The proverb was first recorded in this form in 1832, but the sentiment it expresses is of much earlier origin, occurring in Chaucer's *Canterbury Tales* (c. 1390): "And lightly as it comth, so wol we spende."

Variant of this proverb: light come, light go.

Proverb expressing similar meaning: QUICKLY COME, QUICKLY GO.

easy does it A cautious or gentle approach, such as to a difficult task or an awkward person, is often best: *Easy does it. It's best to be very careful when dealing with your Uncle Jack—he's old and ill and doesn't take kindly to being disturbed.* The proverb was first recorded in 1863 in T. Taylor's *Ticket-of-Leave Man.*

Variant of this proverb: gently does it.

Proverb expressing similar meaning: SOFTLY, SOFTLY, CATCHEE MONKEY.

eat, drink, and be merry, for tomorrow we die Live life to the full every day, because death could strike at any time: *The latest government health campaign warns that those who live their lives too literally according to the proverb "Eat, drink, and be merry, for tomorrow we die" may actually be hastening their own deaths by overindulgence.* The proverb is of biblical origin—it occurs in four passages in the Old and New Testaments, none of which exactly mirrors its current form: "a man hath no better thing under the sun, than to eat, and to drink, and to be merry" (Ecclesiastes 8:15); "let us eat and drink;

for to morrow we shall die" (Isaiah 22:13); "eat, drink, and be merry" (Luke 12:19); "let us eat and drink; for to morrow we die" (1 Corinthians 15:32).

Proverbs expressing similar meaning: GATHER YE ROSEBUDS WHILE YE MAY; LIVE EVERY DAY AS THOUGH IT WERE YOUR LAST; SEIZE THE DAY.

eat to live, do not live to eat   The main purpose of eating is to stay fit and healthy—it should not be regarded solely as a source of pleasure, which inevitably leads to excessive consumption of the wrong types of food: *As children we hated taking tea with our grandmother, whose motto was "Eat to live, do not live to eat" and whose table was accordingly bare of cookies, pastries, and all the other things that would have made these visits bearable.* The proverb is attributed to the ancient Greek philosopher Socrates (469–399 B.C.). An article in the *New York Times* (1982) made the telling observation, "Until recently the world was divided into those who eat to live and those who live to eat."

eavesdroppers hear no good of themselves   *See* LISTENERS NEVER HEAR ANY GOOD OF THEMSELVES.

education doesn't come by bumping your head against the schoolhouse   Education can only be acquired by studying, and by listening and talking to teachers: *Children must learn to read with understanding, and to ask questions in class when they do not understand. Education doesn't come by bumping your head against the schoolhouse.* The proverb is recorded as a regional expression in the United States.

an elephant never forgets   Some people have an extraordinary ability to remember things, especially wrongs done to them; used by or of such a person: *You may live to regret insulting my brother—an elephant never forgets.* It has been suggested that this is a variant of an ancient Greek proverb, "The camel never forgets an injury," but other authorities interpret it more favorably as a tribute to the elephant's apparent intelligence and ability to remember acts of kindness. The proverb was first recorded in English in W. Martyn, *Blue Ridge* (1937).

an empty bag cannot stand   *See* AN EMPTY SACK CANNOT STAND UPRIGHT.

an empty barrel makes the most noise   *See* EMPTY VESSELS MAKE THE MOST SOUND.

an empty sack cannot stand upright   People who are poor or hungry cannot survive, work effectively, or remain honest: *You'd better have a good breakfast before you set off—an empty sack cannot stand upright.* The proverb was first recorded in 1642 in a collection of Italian proverbs, with the note "Applied to such as either pinch themselves, or are pincht by hard fortune."

Variant of this proverb: an empty bag cannot stand.

empty vessels make the most sound   Foolish people are the most talkative; often used as a put-down to somebody who chatters incessantly: *Don't be deceived by his glib patter—remember that empty vessels make the most sound.* The proverb was first recorded before 1430. It occurs in Shakespeare's *Henry V* (4:4), "I did never know so full a voice issue from so empty a heart: but the saying is true—The empty vessel makes the greatest sound." In *Ulysses* (1922), James Joyce toys with the literal meaning of the proverb: "Chamber music. Could make a kind of pun on that. . . . Tinkling. Empty vessels make most noise. Because the acoustics, the resonance changes according as the weight of the water is equal to the law of falling water."

Variant of this proverb: an empty barrel makes the most noise.

the end crowns the work The outcome or conclusion of an enterprise is the basis on which it is judged: "'But proof, sir, proof must be built up stone by stone,' said the Mayor. 'As I say, the end crowns the work'" (Charles Dickens, *The Mystery of Edwin Drood,* 1870). Of Latin origin, the proverb was first recorded in English in the 16th century. It occurs in Shakespeare's play *Troilus and Cressida* (4:5) "The end crowns all, / And that old common arbitrator, Time, / Will one day end it."

Variant of this proverb: the end crowns all.

the end justifies the means Any course of action, however immoral or unscrupulous, is justifiable if it achieves a worthy objective: "It was a fundamental principle of the order that the end justifies the means. By this code, lying, theft, perjury, assassination, were not only pardonable but commendable, when they served the interests of the church" (Ellen G. White, *The Great Controversy between Christ and Satan,* 1888). The proverb has been traced back to the works of the Roman poet Ovid (43 B.C.–A.D. 18): "*exitus acta probat* [the outcome justifies the deeds]." It was first recorded in English in 1583.

Proverb expressing opposite meaning: NEVER DO EVIL THAT GOOD MAY COME OF IT.

the enemy of my enemy is my friend Those who dislike or oppose the same person or thing are bound to be friends or allies: "While the government of Iran had no great sympathy for Communism, they apparently believed that the Sandinistas qualified for that old Middle Eastern proverb: the enemy of my enemy is my friend" (Oliver L. North, *Under Fire,* 1991). The proverb is of ancient Arab origin.

the English are a nation of shopkeepers It is in the national character of the English to be preoccupied with commercial, middle-class concerns: "Americans . . . are a nation of salesmen just as the English are a nation of small shopkeepers" (Ruth Rendell, *Put on by Cunning*, 1981). The proverb began as a quotation from Adam Smith's *The Wealth of Nations*, published in 1776, but is usually associated with Napoleon.

an Englishman's home is his castle *See* A MAN'S HOME IS HIS CASTLE.

enough is as good as a feast A moderate amount is sufficient; often said by somebody who does not want any more: "'Fighting? . . . what have you seen but a skirmish or two?—Ah! if you saw war on the grand scale—sixty or a hundred thousand men in the field on each side!' 'I am not at all curious, Colonel.—"Enough," says our homely proverb, "is as good as a feast'" (Sir Walter Scott, *Waverly,* 1814). The proverb was first recorded in this form c. 1470 in Sir Thomas Malory's *Le Morte d'Arthur.* In *The Picture of Dorian Gray* (1891), Oscar Wilde presented the opposite view: "Moderation is a fatal thing. Enough is as bad as a meal. More than enough is as good as a feast."

Proverbs expressing similar meaning: ENOUGH IS ENOUGH; MODERATION IN ALL THINGS; THERE'S MEASURE IN ALL THINGS.

enough is enough Enough of something is sufficient: *I could have stayed all night but enough is enough.* The proverb was first recorded in 1546 by John Heywood in *A Dialogue containing ... the Proverbs in the English Tongue,* but it is ultimately of Roman origin and is common to several European languages. Today it is usually employed when calling for an end to something irritating or something threatening to get out of control.

Proverb expressing similar meaning: ENOUGH IS AS GOOD AS A FEAST.

envy never dies Envy does not fade with passing time: "Hatred hath an end, envy never ceaseth" (Robert Burton, *Anatomy of Melancholy,* 1624). The proverb was first recorded in 1523–25 by John Berners in *Froissart* but is of older, possibly Roman, origin.

equality begins in the grave Only in death are all people truly equal: *Don't talk to me about equality—discrimination and injustice are rife in modern society, and equality begins in the grave.*

Proverb expressing similar meaning: DEATH IS THE GREAT LEVELER.

Proverb expressing opposite meaning: ALL MEN ARE CREATED EQUAL.

even a blind pig occasionally picks up an acorn An incompetent person or an unsystematic approach is bound to succeed every now and then by chance: *I was the worst basketball player in the school, so I was almost as surprised as everybody else when my shot went through the hoop. I guess it's true that even a blind pig occasionally picks up an acorn.*

even a worm will turn Even the most humble or submissive person will ultimately respond in anger to excessive harassment or exploitation: "If he intended to be sullen with her to the end, and to show his contempt for her, she would turn against him. 'The worm will turn,' she said to herself. And yet she did not think herself a worm" (Anthony Trollope, *The Eustace Diamonds,* 1873). The proverb was first recorded in 1546 in the form "Tread a worm on the tail, and it must turn again." It occurs in Shakespeare's play *Henry VI, Part 3* (2:2), "The smallest worm will turn being trodden on."

Variant of this proverb: the worm will turn.

even Homer sometimes nods *See* HOMER SOMETIMES NODS.

even the best of friends must part *See* THE BEST OF FRIENDS MUST PART.

everybody has his fifteen minutes of fame Most people will find themselves briefly in the public eye at least once in their lives: *Everybody has his fifteen minutes of fame, and my turn came when I found myself hailed as a hero for diving into the lake to rescue the drowning child.* The proverb is associated with the U.S. artist Andy Warhol, who prophetically remarked in the 1960s, "In the future everyone will be famous for fifteen minutes."

Proverb expressing similar meaning: EVERY DOG HAS HIS DAY.

everybody loves a lord Members of the aristocracy, and other wealthy or influential people, are never short of admirers or flatterers among the general public: "All the human race loves a lord—that is, loves to look upon or be noticed by the possessor of Power or Conspicuousness" (Mark Twain, *The $30,000 Bequest,* 1906). The proverb was first recorded in 1869 by F. J. Furnivall in *Queen Elizabeth's Academy.*

everybody's business is nobody's business Matters that are of general concern, but are the responsibility of nobody in particular, tend to get neglected because everybody thinks that somebody else should deal with them: *It was a classic case of "Everybody's business is nobody's business"—the document had been passed from one department to another, but no action had been taken.* The proverb was first recorded in 1611, but the sentiment it expresses occurs in the writings of Aristotle: "A matter common to most men receives least attention."

everybody speaks well of the bridge that carries him over *See* PRAISE THE BRIDGE THAT CARRIES YOU OVER.

everybody's queer but you and me, and even you are a little queer There are times when it seems that you are the only normal or sane person in the world: *I'm amazed that such a crazy proposal should have such widespread public support—it just goes to prove the old saying, "Everybody's queer but you and me, and even you are a little queer."* The proverb has been attributed to the social reformer Robert Owen (1771–1858).

everybody stretches his legs according to the length of his coverlet People must adapt themselves to their circumstances and live within their means: *We had to make some drastic changes to our lifestyle when my husband lost his job, but we coped—everybody stretches his legs according to the length of his coverlet.* The proverb was first recorded in this form in 1550 in W. Harrys's *Market or Fair of Usurers.*

Proverbs expressing similar meaning: CUT YOUR COAT ACCORDING TO YOUR CLOTH; STRETCH YOUR ARM NO FURTHER THAN YOUR SLEEVE WILL REACH.

everybody talks about the weather, but nobody does anything about it People are always ready to complain about a problem but never willing to solve it: *Successive administrations have expressed their concern about the rise in juvenile crime, but no positive steps have been taken to curtail it—everybody talks about the weather, but nobody does anything about it.* The proverb is attributed to Mark Twain or his friend Charles Dudley Warner.

everybody to whom much is given, of him will much be required More is expected of those who have received more—that is, those who have had good fortune, are naturally gifted, or have been shown special favor: "'Throughout my professional career, I have been privileged to assist people with their vocational aspirations. I have done so for two reasons. First, I stand on the shoulders of many individuals who have helped me. Second, I believe "to whom much is given much is required" so I have tried to lend a helping hand'" (Vernon Jordan's statement quoted in Bill Clinton's response to the Starr Report, 1998). The proverb is of biblical origin: "For unto whomsoever much is given, of him shall be much required: and to whom men have committed much, of him they will ask the more" (Luke 12:48).

every bullet has its billet In a life-threatening situation, destiny decides who will die and who will survive: "'Why run risks, Captain? You should dismount,' he said. 'Oh, every bullet has its billet,' answered Vaska Denisov, turning in his saddle" (Leo Tolstoy, *War and Peace,* 1863–69). The proverb was first recorded in 1575 in George Gascoigne's *Fruits of War:* "every bullet hath a lighting place." Its current form has been attributed to King William III (1650–1702). The military superstition that every bullet has somebody's name on it is a modern variant of this proverb.

Proverb expressing similar meaning: IF YOU'RE BORN TO BE HANGED, THEN YOU'LL NEVER BE DROWNED.

every cloud has a silver lining Even the most unpleasant experience or depressing situation may have a consoling aspect or hopeful prospect; used to raise somebody's spirits, or said by those who discover a hidden advantage in their misfortune: *I was devastated when the accident put an end to my sporting career, but in the idle days that followed I discovered I had a talent for writing. Every cloud has a silver lining, so they say.* The proverb was first recorded in 1863. Noël Coward was less optimistic when he wrote the song "There are Bad Times Just Around the Corner" (1953), which says "it's no good whining/About a silver lining" in the approaching dark clouds.

Variant of this proverb: the darkest cloud has a silver lining.

Proverb expressing similar meaning: APRIL SHOWERS BRING MAY FLOWERS.

every cock will crow upon his own dunghill People are always at their bravest or most self-assured when they are on their own home territory: *Every cock will crow upon his own dunghill, but by the time they had crossed to the other side of town, where a rival gang held sway, they were looking distinctly ill at ease.* The proverb is of ancient origin, and has been traced back to the writings of Seneca (c. 4 B.C.–A.D. 65): "*gallum in suo sterquilinio plurimum posse* [the cock is most powerful on his own dunghill]."

Variants of this proverb: a cock is mighty in his own backyard; every dog is a lion at home.

every cook praises his own broth People tend to sing the praises of their own work. The proverb was first recorded in 1663 in Gerbier's *Counsel:* "Every cook commends his own sauce."

every country has its own customs *See* SO MANY COUNTRIES, SO MANY CUSTOMS.

every dog has his day Everybody has a spell of good fortune, success, or fame at least once in his or her life: *Don't begrudge him his moment of triumph—every dog has his day.* The proverb was first recorded in 1545. It occurs in Shakespeare's play *Hamlet* (5:1): "The cat will mew, and dog will have his day."

Proverb expressing similar meaning: EVERYBODY HAS HIS FIFTEEN MINUTES OF FAME.

every dog is a lion at home *See* EVERY COCK WILL CROW UPON HIS OWN DUNGHILL.

every dog is allowed one bite Somebody may be forgiven for a single misdemeanor, provided that it does not happen again: *First offenders are usually let off with a warning, on the basis that every dog is allowed* one bite. The proverb was first recorded in 1902, but the law on which it based dates from at least the 17th century, according to which the owner of a domestic animal was not responsible for injury caused by the animal unless the owner knew of the animal's ferocious tendencies.

every door may be shut but death's door Death comes to us all, and is the only thing in life over which we have no control: *She knew that she had only a few days left to live, and seemed to be facing the prospect with uncharacteristic acquiescence. "Every door may be shut but death's door," she explained.* The proverb was first recorded in 1666, in an Italian proverb collection.

every elm has its man Elm trees are notorious for causing death or serious injury: "Owing to the frequency with which this tree sheds its branches, or is uprooted in a storm, it has earned for itself a sinister reputation. 'Every elm has its man' is an old country saying" (*London Times,* 1928).

every employee tends to rise to his level of incompetence People in a hierarchical organization are promoted until they reach a position that is just beyond their capabilities; this cynical observation implies that nobody is fit to do the work he or she is employed to do: *The monthly meeting of departmental managers did nothing to destroy my belief in the theory that every employee tends to rise to his level of incompetence.* This proverb is known as "The Peter Principle," having been coined by Dr. Laurence J. Peter in a book of that name (1969).

every family has a skeleton in the closet
See THERE'S A SKELETON IN EVERY CLOSET.

every herring must hang by its own gill Everybody must take responsibility for his or her own actions: *If you get into trouble, don't expect me to come and bail you out—every herring must hang by its own gill.* The proverb was first recorded in 1609 by Simon Harward, with *tail* in place of *gill.*

every horse thinks its own pack heaviest Everybody thinks that he or she has harder work, greater misfortune, or more problems than others: *I tend to ignore her when she starts moaning about her troubles. Every horse thinks its own pack heaviest, and I don't believe she is any worse off than the rest of us.* The proverb was first recorded in this form in 1732, but the sentiment it expresses is of earlier origin: in 1573 George Gascoigne wrote, "Every body thinketh their own greif greatest."

every Jack has his Jill Everybody will ultimately find a suitable person to share his or her life with: "Every Jack has his Jill;/If one won't, the other will" (H. W. Thompson, *Body, Boots and Britches,* 1940). The proverb was first recorded in 1611 in Randle Cotgrave's *A Dictionary of the French and English Tongues.*

Variant of this proverb: there's a Jack for every Jill.

every land has its own law Each nation, region, class, or profession has its own rules and customs, which must be respected by outsiders: *The traveler must learn to be tolerant of the ways of others, remembering that every land has its own law.* Of Scottish origin, the proverb dates from before 1628.

Proverb expressing similar meaning: SO MANY COUNTRIES, SO MANY CUSTOMS.

every little helps All contributions, however small, are of use: "'The Petition for the Branch Bill is in the coffee-room. Would you put your name to it? Every little helps'" (Charles Dickens, *The Uncommercial Traveller,* 1861). The proverb was first recorded in this form in 1787, but the sentiment it expresses is of earlier origin. In 1623 William Camden wrote, "Euery thing helpes, quoth the Wren when she pist i' the sea," echoing a French saying of the 16th century that featured an ant making a similar contribution to the waters of the ocean.

Variant of this proverb: every little bit helps.

Proverbs expressing similar meaning: LITTLE DROPS OF WATER, LITTLE GRAINS OF SAND, MAKE A MIGHTY OCEAN AND A PLEASANT LAND; MANY A LITTLE MAKES A MICKLE.

every man after his fashion Every individual must follow his or her own inclination: *When it came to what to do with their free time it was a case of every man after his fashion.* The proverb was first recorded in 1546 by John Heywood in *A Dialogue containing ... the Proverbs in the English Tongue.*

Variant of this proverb: every one after his fashion.

every man for himself and God for us all At times of crisis or great danger, each must take responsibility for his or her own personal survival and hope for divine protection for everybody: "'Every man for himself, and God for us all!' was the cool answer of the refractory seaman" (Captain Marryat, *The King's Own,* 1830). The proverb was first recorded in 1546. In the shorter form "Every man for himself" it is of earlier origin, occurring in Chaucer's *Canterbury Tales*

(c. 1390): "Ech man for hymself, ther is noon oother."

Proverb expressing similar meaning: EVERY MAN FOR HIMSELF AND THE DEVIL TAKE THE HINDMOST.

every man for himself and the devil take the hindmost In highly competitive or dangerous situations, you must guard or pursue your own interests with ruthless disregard for those who are falling behind or struggling to cope: "The result was a bear-garden, a den of prize-fighters, liars, cut-throats and thieves in which every man was for himself openly and avowedly and the devil take the hindmost" (Theodore Dreiser, *The Genius,* 1915). The proverb was first recorded in this form in 1858, but it is of earlier origin. Either of its two parts may be used independently: "The devil take the hindmost" occurs in Francis Beaumont and John Fletcher's play *Philaster* (1620) and expresses a sentiment found in the writings of the Roman poet Horace (65–8 B.C.), "*occupet extremum scabies* [may the itch take the one who is last]."

Proverbs expressing similar meaning: EVERY MAN FOR HIMSELF AND GOD FOR US ALL; SELF-PRESERVATION IS THE FIRST LAW OF NATURE.

every man has his price It is possible to bribe anybody, as long as you offer him or her enough money: "'You can do nothing with Mowle. He never took a penny in his life.' 'Oh, every man has his price'" (G. P. R. James, *The Smuggler,* 1845). The proverb was first recorded in 1734, but with the implication that it was already in general use.

every man is his own worst enemy People often suffer most as a result of their own behavior, attitudes, or nature: *They say that every man is his own worst enemy, and if you weren't so tactless and insensitive you might find it easier to keep your friends!* The proverb was first recorded in Thomas Browne's *Religio Medici* (1643).

every man is the architect of his own fortune Everybody is responsible for his or her own success or failure in life: *Every man is the architect of his own fortune, and nobody else can be blamed for the foolish decisions that brought you to this crisis.* The proverb is attributed to the Roman politician Appius Claudius Caecus, who held the post of censor from 312 B.C. to 308 B.C.

Proverbs expressing similar meaning: LIFE IS WHAT YOU MAKE IT; PADDLE YOUR OWN CANOE.

every man must skin his own skunk People should be self-reliant and not depend on others to do things—especially unpleasant tasks—for them: *She raised her children to be independent and responsible members of society, one of her favorite sayings being "Every man must skin his own skunk."* Of U.S. origin, the proverb was first recorded in *Dictionary of Americanisms,* 1813.

every man thinks his own geese swans Everybody tends to rate his or her own children, possessions, or achievements more highly than others would do: *We are up against that age-old problem: the parents of our students will not accept that their offspring are anything but perfect. As the saying goes, "Every man thinks his own geese swans."* The proverb was first recorded in 1526 in the play *Magnyfycence* by John Skelton.

every man to his taste Different things appeal to different people, and taste is a highly subjective quality: *I wouldn't want a picture like that hanging in my house, but every man to his taste.* The proverb was first recorded, with different wording, in 1580. It is sometimes quoted in its French form, "*Chacun à son goût,*" or with the facetious extension ". . . as the old woman said when she kissed the cow."

Proverbs expressing similar meaning: ONE MAN'S MEAT IS ANOTHER MAN'S POISON; TASTES DIFFER; TO EACH HIS OWN.

every man to his trade People should remain within their own line of work or range of knowledge: ". . . one man showed me a young oak which he had transplanted from behind the town, thinking it an apple-tree. But every man to his trade. Though he had little woodcraft, he was not the less weatherwise, and gave us one piece of information; viz. he had observed that when a thunder-cloud came up with a flood-tide it did not rain" (Henry David Thoreau, *Cape Cod,* 1865). The proverb occurs in Shakespeare's play *Henry IV, Part 1* (2:2) in the form: "Every man to his business." The sentiment it expresses is of biblical origin: "Let every man abide in the same calling wherein he was called" (1 Corinthians 7:20).

Proverb expressing similar meaning: LET THE COBBLER STICK TO HIS LAST.

every one after his fashion *See* EVERY MAN AFTER HIS FASHION.

every picture tells a story Meaning is often conveyed by people's actions, movements, gestures, or facial expressions without the need for words: *Nobody* actually passed comment on the food, but every picture tells a story, and the row of empty plates told me all I needed to know. First recorded in 1847, the proverb was popularized in the early 20th century in an advertisement for a backache remedy featuring a picture of a person bent double in pain.

every rose has a thorn *See* THERE'S NO ROSE WITHOUT A THORN.

every soldier has the baton of a field-marshal in his knapsack A common soldier, or any other worker, may aspire to senior rank: *He entered the business as a lowly sales assistant, but every soldier has the baton of a field-marshal in his knapsack and five years later he owned the company.* First recorded in English in 1840, the proverb is commonly ascribed to Napoleon, in whose army many senior officers rose from the ranks.

everything comes to those who wait *See* ALL THINGS COME TO HIM WHO WAITS.

everything has an end Nothing lasts forever; often used of something unpleasant: "They devoured the food, and I did likewise. . . . everything has an end, everything passes away, even the hunger of people who have not eaten for fifteen hours" (Jules Verne, *20,000 Leagues Under the Sea,* 1869). The proverb was first recorded c. 1385 in Chaucer's *Troilus and Criseyde.*

Variant of this proverb: all things come to an end.

Proverb expressing similar meaning: TIME ENDS ALL THINGS.

everything is good in its season Foodstuffs and other items are best enjoyed when at their prime: *Everything is good in its season, but few vegetables are at their best all year round.* The proverb was first recorded in 1591 by W. Stepney in *The Spanish Schoolmaster.*

everything old is new again Old ideas, fashions, or methods often return to popularity after a long absence, and are sometimes perceived or presented as innovations: "Like so many products on the market today, fruit butters prove the adage, 'What's old is new again'" (*New York Times,* 1991). The proverb was first recorded in this form in 1824, but the sentiment it expresses is of much earlier origin.

Proverb expressing similar meaning: THERE'S NOTHING NEW UNDER THE SUN.

every tub must stand on its own bottom People should be self-sufficient and not dependent on others, financially or otherwise: "She would have had me support the old man in idleness, but I am not one of that kind. Every tub should stand on its own bottom" (Horatio Alger, *Driven from Home,* 1889). The proverb was first recorded in 1564 in W. Bullein's *Dialogue Against Fever.* The word *stand* may be replaced by *sit* or *rest.*

every why hath its wherefore Everything has an underlying reason: "For they say every why hath a wherefore" (William Shakespeare, *The Comedy of Errors*). The proverb was first recorded in 1566 by George Gascoigne in *Supposes.*

Proverb expressing similar meaning: THERE'S REASON IN ALL THINGS.

evil be to him who thinks it Those who wish ill upon others deserve ill luck themselves. The proverb was first recorded c. 1387 by Geoffrey Chaucer in *The Canterbury Tales*: "Now the evyl which men wysshe to other cometh to hym which wyssheth it."

evil communications corrupt good manners   Good people can be led astray by listening to bad ideas, associating with bad people, or following a bad example: *His parents did their best to steer him away from potentially harmful influences during his formative years, on the basis that evil communications corrupt good manners.* The proverb is of biblical origin: "Be not deceived: evil communications corrupt good manners" (1 Corinthians 15:33).

evil doers are evil dreaders   Criminals and other wrongdoers have a tendency to fear and suspect all those around them; sometimes used to imply that a distrustful person has something on his or her conscience: "Put me not to quote the old saw, that evil doers are evil dreaders.—It is your suspicion, not your knowledge, which speaks" (Sir Walter Scott, *The Fair Maid of Perth,* 1828). The proverb dates from before 1568 in the form "Ill doings, breed ill thinkings" (R. Ascham, *Schoolmaster*).

Variant of this proverb: Ill doers are ill dreaders.

Proverb expressing similar meaning: DO RIGHT AND FEAR NO MAN.

example is better than precept   It is better to teach somebody what to do by doing it yourself rather than by giving advice or instructions; usually applied to correct behavior, but equally applicable in other contexts: *Example is better than precept, and if more parents could be persuaded to adopt a healthy lifestyle, then perhaps their*

children would follow suit. The proverb was first recorded, with different wording, c. 1400.

Proverb expressing similar meaning: A GOOD EXAMPLE IS THE BEST SERMON.

Proverb expressing opposite meaning: DO AS I SAY, NOT AS I DO.

the exception proves the rule   The existence of an exception to a rule shows that the rule itself exists and is applicable in other cases; often used loosely to explain away any such inconsistency: "You will find no such unimaginative people anywhere as you find in Italy, Spain, Greece, and the other Southern countries. . . . Now and then, in the course of centuries, a great genius springs up among them; and he is the exception which proves the rule" (Wilkie Collins, *The Haunted Hotel,* 1878). First recorded in this form in 1664, the proverb is of Latin origin: *"exceptio probat regulam in casibus non exceptis* [the exception confirms the rule in cases not excepted]." In his *Devil's Dictionary* (1911), the U.S. writer Ambrose Bierce observed: "'The exception proves the rule' is an expression constantly upon the lips of the ignorant, who parrot it from one another with never a thought of its absurdity."

Proverb expressing similar meaning: THERE'S AN EXCEPTION TO EVERY RULE.

expect nothing and you won't be disappointed   See BLESSED ARE THEY WHO EXPECT NOTHING, FOR THEY SHALL NOT BE DISAPPOINTED.

experience is a comb that fate gives a man when his hair is all gone   Experience often comes too late to be of any use: *It was only after working in the industry for* *many years that I realized what a foolish investment I had made at the outset. As they say, experience is a comb which fate gives a man when his hair is all gone.* The proverb is recorded as a regional expression in the United States.

experience is the best teacher   The best way to learn is by doing things yourself, and by having the good sense not to repeat any mistakes you make along the way: *Experience is the best teacher, and I soon learned to approach the larger animals in my care with a mixture of caution and respect.* First recorded in this form in 1803, the proverb is of Latin origin: "*experientia docet* [experience teaches]."

Proverbs expressing similar meaning: DON'T MAKE THE SAME MISTAKE TWICE; AN OUNCE OF PRACTICE IS WORTH A POUND OF PRECEPT; YEARS KNOW MORE THAN BOOKS.

Proverb expressing opposite meaning: EXPERIENCE IS THE TEACHER OF FOOLS.

experience is the mother of wisdom   You cannot attain great wisdom or knowledge other than by practical experience and learning from your mistakes: "If it be true, that experience is the mother of wisdom, history must be an improving teacher" (*American Museum*, 1788). First recorded in the 16th century, the proverb is of ancient Greek origin.

Variants of this proverb: experience is the father of wisdom; experience is the mother of knowledge.

Proverbs expressing similar meaning: LIVE AND LEARN; THE OLDER THE WISER.

experience is the teacher of fools   It is foolish to learn—or to expect other people to learn—solely by making mistakes; also used with the implication that

wise people learn from others' mistakes rather than their own: *How many more patients must be killed by inadequately trained medical staff before the government will accept the fact that experience is the teacher of fools?* The proverb dates from before 1568 in the form "Experience is the common schoolhouse of fools."

Proverb expressing similar meaning: LEARN FROM THE MISTAKES OF OTHERS.

Proverb expressing opposite meaning: EXPERIENCE IS THE BEST TEACHER.

experience keeps a dear school   Learning by your mistakes is often a costly exercise: *Experience keeps a dear school, and the armed forces are now counting the cost of this ill-fated mission.* The proverb was first recorded in 1743, in Benjamin Franklin's *Poor Richard's Almanack.*

Variant of this proverb: experience keeps a dear school, but fools will learn in no other.

extremes meet   People and things that seem to be diametrically opposed are often found to have a point of contact: ". . . the contrast could not be much greater between . . . a meek sheep and the rough-coated keen-eyed dog, its guardian. He had spoken of Mr. Rochester as an old friend. A curious friendship theirs must have been: a pointed illustration, indeed, of the old adage that 'extremes meet'" (Charlotte Brontë, *Jane Eyre*, 1847). The proverb comes from the French mathematician and writer Pascal's *Pensées* (1669): "*les extrèmes se touchent* [extremes meet]."

Proverb expressing similar meaning: OPPOSITES ATTRACT.

an eye for an eye, and a tooth for a tooth   Retaliation or punishment should take the same form as the original offense or crime: *In a country where the justice system is based on the principle of "An eye for an eye, and a tooth for a tooth," the death penalty is the only appropriate punishment for the crime of murder.* The proverb is of biblical origin: "Eye for eye, tooth for tooth, hand for hand, foot for foot" (Exodus 21:24).

the eye is bigger than the belly   Greed persuades a person to take more than he or she can manage: *He had to concede, as he pushed his plate away, that his eye was bigger than his belly.* The proverb was first recorded in 1580 by John Lyly in *Euphues and his England.* The proverb is usually quoted in relation to food but may also be applied in other contexts, such as money.

the eye of a master does more work than both his hands   Constant super-vision is the key to getting the best performance from your employees or domestic staff: *If you want to increase productivity, get out of your cozy little office and spend more time in the factory—the eye of the master does more work than both his hands.* The proverb was first recorded in 1744, in Benjamin Franklin's *Poor Richard's Almanack.*

the eyes are the mirrors of the soul   A person's eyes will often reveal his or her inmost thoughts, feelings, or character: *Aware that the eyes are the mirrors of the soul, and anxious to keep her true feelings from him, she turned her face away before she spoke.* First recorded in English in 1545 in T. Phaer's *Regiment of Life,* the proverb is of Latin origin.

Variants of this proverb: the eyes are the windows of the soul; the face is the index of the mind.

the face is the index of the mind *See*
THE EYES ARE THE MIRRORS OF THE SOUL.

fact is stranger than fiction Things
that happen in real life are often far more
unlikely than those dreamed up by writers: *If the events of that day had been put
forward as the plot of a TV drama, the idea
would have been rejected as utterly implausible.
But fact is stranger than fiction.* The proverb was first recorded in 1853 in T. C.
Haliburton's *Sam Slick's Wise Saws.*

Proverb expressing similar meaning:
TRUTH IS STRANGER THAN FICTION.

facts are stubborn things The truth
cannot be disputed, disproved, or ignored:
"'Well, you get your money easy. . . . All
you have to do is to sit there and hear lessons.' I used to argue the matter at first,
but I'm wiser now. Facts are stubborn
things, but as some one has wisely said,
not half so stubborn as fallacies." (Lucy
Maud Montgomery, *Anne of the Island,*
1915). The proverb was first recorded in
1732 in E. Budgell's *Liberty & Progress.*

faint heart never won fair lady It is
necessary to be bold and courageous to
win the heart of a woman—or to achieve
any other cherished objective: "Of course
there would be difficulty. But was it not

the business of his life to overcome difficulties? Had he not already overcome
one difficulty almost as great; and why
should he be afraid of this other? Faint
heart never won fair lady!" (Anthony Trollope, *Phineas Finn,* 1869). The proverb was
first recorded, with different wording, in
1545, but it is probably of ancient origin.
The current form dates from 1614 or earlier, and occurs in Gilbert and Sullivan's
comic opera *Iolanthe* (1882).

Proverb expressing similar meaning:
NONE BUT THE BRAVE DESERVE THE FAIR.

fair and softly goes far in a day If you
proceed with care, or at a gentle pace,
you will achieve far more than if you
rush; also used to recommend a tactful approach when dealing with people:
*Don't try to do too much too soon—remember
the proverb, "Fair and softly goes far in a day."*
The proverb was first recorded c. 1350 in
Douce MS 52.

Proverb expressing similar meaning:
SLOW AND STEADY WINS THE RACE.

a fair exchange is no robbery Exchanging things of equivalent worth is a fair
transaction; also used to justify taking
something from somebody who has taken
something from you: *He gave me his leather
jacket, which had a tear in the sleeve, and I*

gave him my CD player with its broken head-phones—a fair exchange is no robbery! The proverb was first recorded in 1546 in John Heywood's *Dialogue of Proverbs.*

fair feathers make fair fowl *See* FINE FEATHERS MAKE FINE BIRDS.

fair play's a jewel Sportsmanlike behavior is of the utmost importance in any competitive situation: *Let's start again, and this time there's to be no cheating. Fair play's a jewel.* The proverb was first recorded in 1809, in Washington Irving's *A History of New York,* but with the implication that it was already in general use.

fair words butter no cabbage *See* FINE WORDS BUTTER NO PARSNIPS.

faith will move mountains Nothing is impossible to those who have sufficient faith; applied not only to religious faith, but to any strong belief in a cause or objective: *She firmly believes that she can make him change his ways, and faith will move mountains, so she may yet succeed.* The proverb is of biblical origin: "If ye have faith as a grain of mustard seed, ye shall say unto this mountain, Remove hence to yonder place; and it shall remove; and nothing shall be impossible unto you" (Matthew 17:20).

Variant of this proverb: FAITH CAN MOVE MOUNTAINS.

the falling out of lovers is the renewing of love *See* THE QUARREL OF LOVERS IS THE RENEWAL OF LOVE.

familiarity breeds contempt We tend to lose respect for people or things as we become better acquainted with them; also used in a wide range of other contexts, such as when somebody develops a dangerously blasé approach to a task that has become routine: ". . . he sat himself down to ruminate upon his prospects, which, like the prospect outside his window, were sufficiently confined and dingy. As they by no means improved on better acquaintance, and as familiarity breeds contempt, he resolved to banish them from his thoughts by dint of hard walking" (Charles Dickens, *Nicholas Nickleby,* 1838–39). The proverb is of ancient origin, and has been traced back to the writings of Publilius Syrus (first century B.C.). The sentiment it expresses can be found in one of the fables of Aesop (sixth century B.C.), in which a fox gradually loses its fear of a lion. The facetious variant "Familiarity breeds contempt—and children" is attributed to Mark Twain.

Proverb expressing similar meaning: NO MAN IS A HERO TO HIS VALET.

the family that prays together stays together Families that share the same religious faith remain united: "Mother Teresa opined . . . 'The family that prays together stays together; and if you stay together, you will love one another with the same love with which God loves each one of us'" (*Washington Post,* 1996). The proverb was coined in the 1940s as a slogan of the Roman Catholic Family Rosary Crusade. In modern usage other words are sometimes substituted for *prays*—notably *plays,* encouraging families to engage in leisure activities together.

fancy passes beauty It is more important that a potential partner is likeable than good-looking: *The duke's friends were initially surprised at his choice of wife, who* was far from the first flush of youth, but fancy passes beauty. The proverb was first recorded in 1678 by John Ray in *A Collection of English Proverbs*.

far away the hills are green   *See* BLUE ARE THE HILLS THAT ARE FAR AWAY.

far-fetched and dear-bought is good for ladies   Women like expensive things from exotic places: *Browsing through a catalog of Christmas gifts that arrived in the mail this morning, it occurred to me that the old proverb "Far-fetched and dear-bought is good for ladies" still has some relevance in modern times.* The proverb was first recorded c. 1350 in *Douce MS 52.*

the farthest way about is the nearest way home   *See* THE LONGEST WAY AROUND IS THE SHORTEST WAY HOME.

a fat kitchen makes a lean will   Those who eat well all their lives will have little money left when they die: *Their lavish dinner parties were a legend in the neighborhood, but a fat kitchen makes a lean will, and nobody was surprised when the deplorable state of their financial affairs came to light.* The proverb was first recorded in 1948 in a U.S. proverb collection.

Variant of this proverb: a fat kitchen makes a lean purse.

a fault confessed is half redressed   The act of confessing that you have done something wrong goes some way toward making amends for your offense or error: "A fault confessed is half redressed, so I hope he will forgive us" (Peter O'Donnell, *The Xanadu Talisman,* 1981). The proverb was first recorded, with different wording, in 1558.

faults are thick where love is thin   People are quick to find faults in those they do not like: *She had little good to say about her husband, but faults are thick where love is thin.* This Welsh proverb was first recorded in 1616 by T. Draxe in *Bibliotheca Scholastica.*

fear lends wings   Fear inspires extra speed in those attempting to escape whatever threatens them: "Therto fear gave her wings" (Edmund Spenser, *The Faerie Queene,* 1590). This French proverb was first recorded in English in 1580 by Philip Sidney in *Arcadia.*

fear the Greeks bearing gifts   *See* BEWARE OF GREEKS BEARING GIFTS.

feed a cold and starve a fever   You should eat well when you have a cold but fast when you have a fever: "'Forget about feeding a cold and starving a fever,' Dr. Edelman said, adding there is no medical reason for diet changes" (*Washington Times,* 1997). The proverb is sometimes interpreted as a warning that eating well during a cold will bring on a fever, or if you feed a cold now you will have to starve a fever later. Other conflicting explanations interpret *starve* as "prevent" or even "die of." The proverb was first recorded in 1832, but fasting has been recommended as a remedy for fever since the 16th century or earlier.

Variant of this proverb: stuff a cold and starve a fever.

the female of the species is deadlier than the male   Women often prove to be more dangerous than men, when roused to anger; the proverb also is used literally in natural history contexts: *The female of the species is deadlier than the male, and they don't* come much deadlier than the mother who thinks her child has been wrongly accused. The proverb comes from Rudyard Kipling's poem *The Female of the Species* (1911): "When the Himalayan peasant meets the he-bear in his pride,/He shouts to scare the monster, who will often turn aside./But the she-bear thus accosted rends the peasant tooth and nail/For the female of the species is more deadly than the male." A jocular modern variant of the proverb reported among computer users runs: "The email of the species is more deadly than the mail."

few words are best It is best to communicate meaning in as few words as possible: "Wherefore, few words are best, wench" (Walter Scott, *The Fair Maid of Perth*, 1828). The proverb was first recorded c. 1600 in *Roxburghe Ballads*.

fields have eyes and woods have ears There are very few places where you can do or say something without the risk of being seen or overheard: *Although they were careful never to meet in public places, their affair did not remain a secret for long—fields have eyes and woods have ears.* First recorded c. 1225, the proverb occurs in Chaucer's *Canterbury Tales* (c. 1390).

Proverb expressing similar meaning: WALLS HAVE EARS.

fight fire with fire The best way to deal with an opponent or an attack is to fight back with similar weapons or tactics: *Fight fire with fire—if they resort to underhand methods to win over your customers, then you must not be afraid to do likewise.* The proverb was first recorded in this form in 1869, but the sentiment it expresses is of much earlier origin. Shakespeare's play *Coriolanus* (4:7) contains the line "One fire drives

out one fire," and a 14th-century French proverb translates as "One fire must put out another."

Proverb expressing similar meaning: LIKE CURES LIKE.

find a penny, pick it up, all day long you'll have good luck *See* SEE A PIN AND PICK IT UP, ALL THE DAY YOU'LL HAVE GOOD LUCK.

finders keepers, losers weepers If you lose something and it is found by another, you have no right to reclaim it and must bear your loss as best you can: *The boy found his sister's missing watch and carried it off triumphantly to his room. "Finders keepers, losers weepers," he jeered.* The proverb was first recorded in 1825 in J. T. Brockett's *Glossary of North Country Words*.

Proverb expressing similar meaning: FINDING IS KEEPING.

finding is keeping The person who finds something is entitled to keep it: *In this country the principle of "finding is keeping" is not enshrined in law, and whoever found and kept the missing money is no better than a thief.* The proverb was first recorded in 1863 in John Hanning Speke's *Journal of the Discovery of the Source of the Nile*.

Proverb expressing similar meaning: FINDERS KEEPERS, LOSERS WEEPERS.

fine feathers make fine birds By dressing in elegant or good-quality clothing, people create a favorable impression on others, often appearing to be of better breeding or higher class than they are: "Mrs. Joe . . . essayed to pick her to pieces, intimating that she was much indebted to her dress—that fine feathers made fine birds" (Robert Smith Surtees, *Ask Mamma,*

1858). Of French origin, the proverb was first recorded in English in the late 16th century. It is also used in the opposite form, "Fine feathers don't make fine birds."

Variant of this proverb: fair feathers make fair fowl.

Proverb expressing similar meaning: CLOTHES MAKE THE MAN.

Proverb expressing opposite meaning: CLOTHES DON'T MAKE THE MAN.

fine words butter no parsnips   Promises or compliments are pleasant to hear but serve no practical purpose unless they are backed up by action: "'Ye speak reasonably, my lord,' said Dalgetty, 'and, *ceteris paribus,* I might be induced to see the matter in the same light. But, my lord, there is a southern proverb,—fine words butter no parsnips'" (Sir Walter Scott, *A Legend of Montrose,* 1819). The proverb was first recorded in 1639.

Variant of this proverb: fair words butter no cabbage.

fingers were made before forks   People ate with their hands before cutlery was invented; used as an excuse for picking up food with your fingers at table: *After several attempts to spear an onion she gave up and removed one from the pot by hand.* "Fingers were made before forks," *she said apologetically.* The proverb was first recorded in 1567 in the form "God made hands before knives." The current form occurs in Jonathan Swift's *Polite Conversation* (1738): "Fingers were made before Forks, and Hands before Knives."

Variant of this proverb: fingers were made before knives and forks.

fire is a good servant but a bad master   Fire is very useful when it is under control, but highly dangerous when it takes control: *Many forest fires are caused by some careless person who has dropped a match after lighting a cigarette, or failed to extinguish a campfire, having forgotten—or never heard—the saying* "Fire is a good servant but a bad master." The proverb was first recorded in 1615 in T. Adams's *England's Sickness.* Other words are sometimes substituted for *fire,* such as *money* or *alcohol.*

Variant of this proverb: fire and water are good servants but bad masters.

first catch your hare   Do not act in anticipation of something that is yet to be achieved: "A modern cookery-book, in giving a recipe for cooking a hare, says, 'first catch your hare, and then kill it'; a maxim of indisputable wisdom. The Christian chiefs on this occasion had not so much sagacity, for they began a violent dispute among themselves for the possession of a city which was still unconquered" (Charles MacKay, *Memoirs of Extraordinary Popular Delusions and the Madness of Crowds,* 1841). The proverb is popularly and erroneously believed to be the opening line of a recipe in an 18th- or 19th-century cookbook. It is actually of much earlier origin, and was first recorded c. 1300 in Latin, with *deer* in place of *hare:* "*vulgariter dicitur, quod primo opporte cervum capere* [it is commonly said that one must first catch the deer]."

Variant of this proverb: first catch your rabbit and then make your stew.

Proverb expressing similar meaning: DON'T COUNT YOUR CHICKENS BEFORE THEY ARE HATCHED.

first come, first served   Those who arrive or apply earliest are most likely to get what they want from a limited supply of things, such as tickets, discounted goods, or refreshments: "I have little doubt of procuring a remission for you, provided we can keep you out of the claws of justice till she has selected and gorged upon her victims; for in this, as in other cases, it will be according to the vulgar proverb, 'First come, first served'" (Sir Walter Scott, *Waverly,* 1814). The proverb was first recorded in this form in 1548, but the sentiment it expresses is of earlier origin. The 13th-century French proverb *"qui ainçois vient au molin ainçois doit moldre* [he who comes first to the mill may grind first]" recurs 100 years later in Chaucer's *Canterbury Tales* (c. 1390).

Variant of this proverb: first there, first served.

Proverb expressing similar meaning: THE EARLY BIRD CATCHES THE WORM.

the first duty of a soldier is obedience
No army can be an efficient fighting force unless its members are prepared to obey orders without question: *I was aware that this action would cause the death of hundreds of innocent civilians, but I had to follow the instructions of my commanding officer—the first duty of a soldier is obedience.* The proverb was first recorded in 1872, but earlier evidence suggests that it had long been in general use.

the first hundred years are the hardest
Life will always be difficult; said jocularly or ironically to those who complain about their problems, sometimes with the implication that things will improve eventually: *We had a rocky time during the early months of our marriage, and the only words of consolation I got from my mother were, "Don't worry—the first hundred years are the hardest!"* The proverb was first recorded in 1928. Other periods may be substituted

for *hundred years,* such as *nine months* (for a pregnant woman) or *four years* (for a college student).

first impressions are the most lasting
An initial opinion formed of somebody or something at the first encounter lingers in the mind and is difficult to efface: *When approaching a potential new customer, whether in person, by phone or mail, or through advertising, always remember that first impressions are the most lasting.* The proverb was first recorded in William Congreve's play *The Way of the World* (1700) in the form "There is a great deal in the first impression."

the first seven years are the hardest The first stage in any enterprise is the hardest: *"Never mind," the older man said as he helped his young apprentice up from the floor, "the first seven years are the hardest."* The origins of this proverb are obscure, but it probably made its first appearance during World War I, when soldiers signed up for seven years' service. It is commonly applied to marriage or new jobs.

Proverb expressing similar meaning: THE FIRST STEP IS THE HARDEST.

the first step is the hardest   Making a start is often the most difficult part of an undertaking: *If only I could pluck up courage to speak to her, I know that the rest would be easy—the first step is always the hardest.* The proverb was first recorded c. 1596 in the form "The first stretch [of a journey] is the worst." It is popularly associated with the story that Saint Denis, patron saint of France, walked several miles with his head in his hands after being executed, and that on learning of this, a French noblewoman remarked,

"*Ce n'est que le premier pas qui coûte* [It's only the first step that counts]."

Variant of this proverb: it's the first step that is difficult.

Proverbs expressing similar meaning: THE FIRST SEVEN YEARS ARE THE HARDEST; A JOURNEY OF A THOUSAND MILES BEGINS WITH ONE STEP.

first there, first served   *See* FIRST COME, FIRST SERVED.

first things first   It is important to do things in the proper order, and not to omit a basic first step: *First things first, before we come to look at the product's new features, how much does it cost?* The proverb comes from the title of a book published in 1894.

Variant of this proverb: put first things first.

Proverb expressing similar meaning: DON'T PUT THE CART BEFORE THE HORSE.

first think, and then speak   *See* THINK BEFORE YOU SPEAK.

first thrive and then wive   It is sensible to get established in a career before getting married. The proverb was first recorded in 1608–09 by William Shakespeare in *Pericles* (5,2): "So he thriv'd that he is promis'd to be wiv'd to fair Marina."

first try and then trust   Before relying upon something (or someone), it is best to test it first: *The safest principle when it comes to old bridges is first try and then trust.* The proverb was first recorded in 1639 by J. Clarke in *Paroemiographia Anglo-Latina.*

Variant of this proverb: try before you trust.

Proverb expressing similar meaning: TRUST NOT ONE NIGHT'S ICE.

the fish always stinks from the head downward   *See* A FISH STINKS FROM THE HEAD.

fish and guests stink after three days   Guests who stay for longer than three days risk becoming a burden or an irritation to their hosts: "How long should she stay? She remembered the universal truth that fish and guests smell after three days" (J. S. Borthwick, *Down East Murders,* 1985). The proverb was first recorded in 1580, but the sentiment it expresses occurs in *Miles Gloriosus* by the Roman dramatist Plautus (c. 254–184 B.C.).

Variant of this proverb: FISH AND VISITORS SMELL IN THREE DAYS.

Proverbs expressing a similar meaning: A CONSTANT GUEST IS NEVER WELCOME; SHORT VISITS MAKE LONG FRIENDS.

fish begin to stink at the head   *See* A FISH STINKS FROM THE HEAD.

fish or cut bait   The time has come to choose between two courses of action—either get on with what you have to do, or go away and let somebody else do it: *It's fish or cut bait—if you're not prepared to give this job the 100% commitment it requires, then clear your desk and make way for somebody who will.* Of U.S. origin, the proverb was first recorded in 1876, in the record of a debate in the House of Representatives. The phrase *cut bait* means "stop fishing."

Proverb expressing similar meaning: PISS OR GET OFF THE POT.

a fish stinks from the head   A corrupting influence often spreads from a leader to the rest of the organization or group: *The moral decline in this country can be traced back to the questionable behavior of those in high office—a* *fish stinks from the head.* First recorded in English in 1581, the proverb is of ancient origin. It refers to the fact that fish tend to rot from the head toward the tail.

Variants of this proverb: the fish always stinks from the head downward; fish begin to stink at the head.

fish where the fish are If you want to obtain or achieve something, you must concentrate your efforts and attention on the places, people, or activities that are most likely to bring success: "Metro-North and its agency . . . are putting a new twist on the marketing adage to 'fish where the fish are.' The commuter railroad is sponsoring outdoor advertisements, situated where it believes potential customers—frustrated drivers who might prefer taking the train—are sure to see it" (*New York Times,* 1992). The proverb is thought to be of recent origin.

Proverb expressing similar meaning: GO HUNTING WHERE THE DUCKS ARE.

flattery, like perfume, should be smelled but not swallowed There is no harm in taking pleasure from flattery, but do not make the mistake of believing it: *He acknowledged the compliment with a gracious smile, but I could see that he was not going to let it affect his decision.* Somebody had obviously told him that flattery, like perfume, should be smelled but not swallowed. The proverb was first recorded in 1858 in H. W. Shaw's *Josh Billings' Philosophy.*

fling dirt enough, and some will stick *See* THROW DIRT ENOUGH, AND SOME WILL STICK.

flowers leave fragrance in the hand that bestows them A person who gives usu-

ally derives some benefit from the act of giving: "As artists find joy in giving beauty to others, so anyone who masters the art of praising will find that it blesses the giver as much as the receiver. There is truth in the saying, 'Flowers leave part of their fragrance in the hand that bestows them'" (*Reader's Digest,* 1991). The proverb is recorded as a regional expression in the United States.

food without hospitality is medicine It is hard to enjoy refreshments that are offered with ill grace, or without friendly companionship: *Although she arrived much later than expected and I was longing to go to bed, I stayed up to chat while she ate the sandwiches I had prepared for her. I know from experience that food without hospitality is medicine.* The proverb is recorded as a regional expression in the United States.

a fool and his money are soon parted Foolish people are easily swindled or persuaded to waste their money: *Thousands of people bought the expensive potion, which claimed to reverse the aging process, proving that a fool and his money are soon parted.* The proverb was first recorded in this form in 1587 in J. Bridges's *Defence of Government in Church of England.*

a fool at forty is a fool indeed People who have not gained the wisdom of experience by the time they reach middle age are likely to remain fools for the rest of their lives: *You might expect a man of his age to have a bit more common sense, but I've given up hope of changing him now—a fool at forty is a fool indeed!* The current form of the proverb comes from Edward Young's *The Universal Passion* (1725): "Be wise with speed;/A fool at forty is a fool indeed," but the sentiment it expresses is of earlier origin.

Variant of this proverb: A fool over forty is a fool indeed.

Proverb expressing similar meaning: THERE'S NO FOOL LIKE AN OLD FOOL.

a fool can ask more questions in an hour than a wise man can answer in seven years See FOOLS ASK QUESTIONS THAT WISE MEN CANNOT ANSWER.

a foolish consistency is the hobgoblin of little minds A lack of flexibility in making judgments is regarded as a sign of petty narrow-mindedness: "'You can say consistency is the hobgoblin of small minds and accuse me of having a small mind; I'll take it,' he told reporters . . ., referring to his opposition to capital punishment and his support for tax cuts. 'But I have been consistent. Maybe consistently wrong in your book. But consistent'" (*New York Times*, 1994). The proverb comes from Ralph Waldo Emerson's essay "Self-Reliance" (1841): "A foolish consistency is the hobgoblin of little minds, adored by little statesmen and philosophers and divines."

Variant of this proverb: consistency is the hobgoblin of little minds.

a fool may give a wise man counsel People are often able to give good advice to those who are considered to be intellectually superior; sometimes said apologetically by the giver of such advice, or used as a warning against disregarding it: *If a fool may give a wise man counsel, I would suggest you make further inquiries before signing the contract.* The proverb was first recorded in this form in 1641, but the sentiment it expresses is found in the romance *Ywain and Gawain* (c. 1350).

fool me once, shame on you; fool me twice, shame on me Somebody who is taken in by a hoax or swindle on one occasion may justifiably blame the perpetrator, but those who fall victim a second time have only themselves to blame: *I believed her story last time, to my cost, but I won't be caught out if she tries the same trick again. As they say, "Fool me once, shame on you; fool me twice, shame on me."* The proverb was first recorded as recently as 1980, but with the implication that it was a well-established saying. It was probably originally used by children.

a fool over forty is a fool indeed See A FOOL AT FORTY IS A FOOL INDEED.

fools and children should never see half-done work You should not judge the quality of a piece of work until it is complete, because it often appears unpromising in its unfinished form; sometimes said in response to criticism, or as a reason for not letting such work be seen: "No stage of the manufacture was incredible by itself, but the result was incredible . . . authenticating the adage that fools and children should never see anything till it is done" (Arnold Bennett, *Anna of the Five Towns*, 1902). The proverb was first recorded in 1721 in James Kelly's *Scottish Proverbs*.

fools ask questions that wise men cannot answer It is often better not to ask too many questions, or to avoid showing your ignorance; sometimes said to those who disregard this advice: *I longed to ask him to translate what had just been said, but remembering the proverb "Fools ask questions that wise men cannot answer," I decided to hold my tongue.* The proverb was first recorded in 1666, in an Italian proverb collection.

Variant of this proverb: a fool can ask more questions in an hour than a wise man can answer in seven years.

a fool's bolt is soon shot Foolish people act hastily and thus waste their efforts: "'Your bolt is soon shot, according to the old proverb,' said she" (Tobias Smollett, *Roderick Random*, 1748). The proverb was first recorded c. 1320 in *Proverbs of Alfred*. The allusion is to a crossbow bolt, which is likely to miss its target if fired too quickly.

Proverb expressing similar meaning: HASTY CLIMBERS HAVE SUDDEN FALLS.

fools build houses and wise men live in them The cost of building property is such that those who build houses cannot afford to live in them, and have to sell them to recoup their losses; also applied to other things that are expensive to produce: *They borrowed a huge sum of money to build their dream home, and were forced to sell it for a price that barely covered the interest on the loan, a classic illustration of the adage "Fools build houses and wise men live in them."* The proverb was first recorded, in its variant form, in 1670.

Variant of this proverb: fools build houses and wise men buy them.

fools rush in where angels fear to tread Foolish people often act recklessly or impetuously in situations that others would approach with caution or avoid altogether: *Fools rush in where angels fear to tread—he must be either very brave or very foolish to enter into negotiations with terrorists like these.* The proverb comes from Alexander Pope's *Essay on Criticism* (1711): "No place so Sacred from such Fops is barr'd, Nor is Paul's Church more safe than Paul's Church-yard: Nay, fly to Altars; there they'll talk you dead; For Fools rush in where Angels fear to tread."

footprints on the sands of time are not made by sitting down People who idle their lives away will not make a lasting impression on history or be remembered for their great achievements; used as a spur to action and industry: *Her motto was "Footprints on the sands of time are not made by sitting down," and her energy and commitment to the cause was an example to us all.* The phrase *footprints on the sands of time* comes from Henry Wadsworth Longfellow's poem *A Psalm of Life* (1839): "Lives of great men all remind us / We can make our lives sublime, / And, departing, leave behind us / Footprints on the sands of time."

forbidden fruit is sweet Things that you must not have or do are always the most desirable: "There are many portals forbidden to me, as there are many forbidden to all men; and forbidden fruit, they say, is sweet; but my lips have watered after no other fruit but that which grows so high, within the sweep of that great policeman's truncheon" (Anthony Trollope, *Can You Forgive Her?*, 1864). The proverb was first recorded, with different wording, in Chaucer's *Canterbury Tales* (c. 1390). The phrase *forbidden fruit* alludes to the fruit of the tree of the knowledge of good and evil in the Garden of Eden, which Adam and Eve were forbidden to eat.

Variants of this proverb: forbidden fruit is the sweetest; stolen fruit is sweet.

Proverb expressing similar meaning: STOLEN WATER IS SWEET.

forewarned is forearmed Advance warning of something gives you the opportunity to prepare for it: "'You think,' continued Max, smiling at Goddet's speech, 'that I intend to marry Flore when Père Rouget dies, and so this sister and her son, of whom I hear to-night for the first time, will endanger my future?' 'That's just it,' cried François. . . . 'Well, don't be uneasy, friends,' answered Max. 'Forewarned is forearmed!'" (Honoré de Balzac, *Two Brothers,* 1843). The proverb was first recorded in English, with different wording c. 1425. Compare the Latin saying *"praemonitus, praemunitus* [forewarned, forearmed]."

to forget a wrong is the best revenge   *See* THE BEST WAY TO GET EVEN IS TO FORGET.

forgive and forget   Do not bear grudges—forgive those who have wronged you and forget the wrong: "He spoke suddenly, as if concluding a discussion. 'The best thing for us is to forget all this.' She started a little and shut the fan with a click. 'Yes, forgive—and forget,' he repeated, as if to himself'" (Joseph Conrad, *Tales of Unrest,* 1898). The proverb was first recorded c. 1377 in William Langland's *Piers Plowman.* It occurs in Shakespeare's play *King Lear* (4:7) in the form "forget and forgive."

Variant of this proverb: good to forgive, best to forget.

Proverb expressing similar meaning: LET BYGONES BE BYGONES.

fortune favors fools   Foolish people often have good luck, or succeed by chance: ". . . fortune favours fools and his very stupidity served him well at the end" (Eden Phillpotts, *Red Redmaynes,* 1922). Of Latin origin, the proverb was first recorded in English in 1546 in the form "God sends fortune to fools."

fortune favors the brave   Those who act boldly or courageously are most likely to succeed: *They say that fortune favors the brave, and I hope they are right, because it's too late to turn back now!* Of ancient origin, the proverb occurs in Virgil's *Aeneid* (first century B.C.): *"audentes fortuna iuvat* [fortune aids the bold]."

Variant of this proverb: fortune favors the bold.

for want of a nail the shoe was lost, for want of a shoe the horse was lost, and for want of a horse the rider was lost   Do not neglect minor details that seem insignificant in themselves: *We must check and double-check everything—even the smallest error or omission may have disastrous consequences. Remember the proverb "For want of a nail the shoe was lost, for want of a shoe the horse was lost, and for want of a horse the rider was lost."* First recorded in this form in George Herbert's *Outlandish Proverbs* (1640) the proverb may be of French origin.

Variant of this proverb: for want of a nail the kingdom was lost.

four eyes see more than two   Two people keeping watch, supervising, or searching have a better chance of noticing or finding something: *I've read the essay over, but I'd be grateful if you would have a look at it too, in case I've missed any errors—four eyes see more than two.* The proverb was first recorded, in its variant form, in 1591.

Variant of this proverb: two eyes see more than one.

Proverb expressing similar meaning: TWO HEADS ARE BETTER THAN ONE.

the fox preys furthest from his hole   Criminals and other persons engaged in illicit activity operate away from their

FRENCH PROVERBS

The French are renowned for their love of life and in particular that of food and wine. The French stock of proverbs includes many that deal with the good things that life has to offer.

A day is lost if one has not laughed

The best herbs are in the smallest bags

The best soup is made of old meat

Eat with pleasure, drink with measure

The friends of our friends are our friends

A good meal ought to begin with hunger

He who has much, wants more

It is only the first bottle that is expensive

Life is an onion that you peel crying

A living dog is better than a dead lion

No saint was ever popular in his own parish

Nothing dries so fast as tears

Patience is bitter but its fruits are sweet

Ridicule kills

Tasty is the chicken that is fed by someone else

There are more old drunkards than old doctors

We are all a long time dead

Where love sets the table food tastes at its best

Where the hostess is beautiful the wine is delicious

Young saints, old devils

home territory, where they may be recognized: *In robbing the local newsagent he ignored the old saw that the fox preys furthest from his hole.* The proverb was first recorded in 1629 in the *Sermons* of T. Adams.

Friday's child is loving and giving Children born on a Friday are supposed to have an affectionate, generous nature: *My mother tells me that my cantankerous, miserly uncle was born on Good Friday, which disproves the saying "Friday's child is loving and giving."* The proverb is the fifth line of a traditional rhyme beginning "Monday's child is fair of face." See entries at the days of the week for other proverbs from this rhyme.

a friend in need is a friend indeed True friends are those who stand by you in times of hardship: "You came to my side when I was in trouble. . . . A friend in need is a friend indeed" (Charles Reade, *Griffith Gaunt,* 1866). First recorded in this form in 1678, the proverb is of ancient origin: compare Euripides (fifth century B.C.), "in adversity good friends are most clearly seen" and Ennius (c. 239–169 B.C.), "a sure friend is known in unsure times."

a friend to all is a friend to none A person who tries to be friends with everyone will end up being friends with no one.

The proverb was first recorded in English in 1623 in Wodroephe's *Spares Houres*, but is of much older origin and is usually attributed to Aristotle.

Proverb expressing similar meaning: YOU CAN'T BE ALL THINGS TO ALL MEN.

from nothing, nothing is made *See* NOTHING COMES OF NOTHING.

from shirtsleeves to shirtsleeves is only three generations A family may pass from poverty to wealth in one generation, through effort and enterprise, but return from wealth to poverty in the next generation, through extravagance or bad management: *The youngest child of poor parents, he taught himself to read and write and built up a thriving manufacturing business, which has just gone bankrupt in the hands of his son—yet another illustration of the proverb "From shirtsleeves to shirtsleeves is only three generations."* The proverb was first recorded, in its variant form, in 1871, and is said to have originated in Lancashire, an industrial county of England. Its current form has also been attributed to the U.S. industrialist Andrew Carnegie (1835–1919).

Variant of this proverb: from clogs to clogs is only three generations.

from the day you were born till you ride in a hearse, there's nothing so bad but it might have been worse *See* NOTHING SO BAD BUT IT MIGHT HAVE BEEN WORSE.

from the mouths of babes come words of wisdom *See* OUT OF THE MOUTHS OF BABES AND SUCKLINGS COME GREAT TRUTHS.

from the sublime to the ridiculous is only one step Somebody or something that commands great respect or admiration can very quickly become the object of scorn or derision: "They also raised such foolish questions as, whether God might not have become an ass or a cucumber as well as a man, and what effect the sacrament would have upon a dog or a mouse. From reverence to profanity, as from the sublime to the ridiculous, there is only one step" (Philip Schaff, *History of the Christian Church, 1883–1893*). The proverb was first recorded in 1795 in Tom Paine's *The Age of Reason:* "The sublime and the ridiculous are often so nearly related that it is difficult to class them separately. One step above the sublime makes the ridiculous; and one step above the ridiculous makes the sublime again." In its current more concise form, the proverb is usually attributed to Napoleon Bonaparte, referring to his retreat from Moscow in 1812. It has given rise to the cliché *from the sublime to the ridiculous,* used with reference to any sudden transition or sharp contrast between the grand and the contemptible.

Variant of this proverb: from the sublime to the ridiculous is but a step.

from the sweetest wine, the tartest vinegar Great love may turn to the intense hatred; also used of other changes of feeling or nature from one extreme to the other: *She loved him blindly and passionately for a time, but from the sweetest wine comes the tartest vinegar, and now she swears she would dance on his grave.* The proverb was first recorded in 1578.

Variant of this proverb: the sweetest wine makes the sharpest vinegar.

full cup, steady hand Those who enjoy great power, wealth, or happiness must behave with caution to avoid losing what they have: "Poor things! They were so happy—so open-hearted. I did long to caution them. 'Full cup, steady hand'" (Charlotte M. Yonge, *The Monthly Packet,* 1889). The proverb was first recorded c. 1025.

Variant of this proverb: a full cup needs a steady hand.

the future ain't what it used to be In modern times people are less optimistic than they were in the past; also used more generally when making adverse comparisons with the past: *I remember leaving college full of expectations and ambition, but my daughter has a far more downbeat—and perhaps more realistic—view of her prospects. As they say, "The future ain't what it used to be."* The proverb is of uncertain origin, having been attributed to the baseball player Yogi Berra (1925–) and the writer Arthur C. Clarke (1917–), among others.

gambling is getting nothing for something Gambling is not a wise use of money, as you are very likely to receive no return whatsoever for your financial outlay: *The saying "Gambling is getting nothing for something" may be disproved by a few lucky winners, but its truth is acknowledged by the majority of the population—who carry on squandering their money on lottery tickets regardless.* The proverb is recorded as a regional expression in the United States.

the game is not worth the candle It is not worth persisting in an enterprise that is unlikely to yield enough profit or benefit to compensate for the effort or expense involved, or that carries a risk of actual harm or loss: *"Your brain may, as you say, be roused and excited, but it is a pathological and morbid process which involves increased tissue-change and may at least leave a permanent weakness. . . . Surely the game is hardly worth the candle. Why should you, for a mere passing pleasure, risk the loss of those great powers with which you have been endowed?"* (Sir Arthur Conan Doyle, *The Sign of Four,* 1890). The proverb was first recorded in the writings of the French essayist Michel de Montaigne (1533–92).

garbage in, garbage out A person or machine provided with inferior source material, faulty instructions, or erroneous information can produce only poor-quality work or rubbish: *The poor quality of the teaching at the school is reflected in the examination results, which are way below the national average. As they say in computing, "Garbage in, garbage out."* First recorded in 1964, the proverb originally referred to computer input and output, and is still used in that context, often in the form of the acronym *GIGO.*

Proverb expressing similar meaning: YOU CAN'T MAKE A SILK PURSE OUT OF A SOW'S EAR.

gasoline and whiskey don't mix *See* WHISKEY AND GASOLINE DON'T MIX.

gather ye rosebuds while ye may Live life to the full while you are still young enough to enjoy it: *My friends thought I was crazy to give up my job and sell my home to join the round-the-world voyage, but my motto is "Gather ye rosebuds while ye may."* The current form of the proverb comes from Robert Herrick's poem "To the Virgins, to Make Much of Time" (1648), but the sentiment it expresses is of earlier origin. In 1578 the French poet Pierre de Ronsard wrote, "Gather the roses of life today," and Edmund Spenser's *The Faerie Queene* (1590) contains the lines, "Gather therefore the Rose, whilst yet is prime,/For soon comes age, that will her pride deflower."

Proverbs expressing similar meaning: EAT, DRINK, AND BE MERRY, FOR TOMORROW WE DIE; SEIZE THE DAY.

genius is an infinite capacity for taking pains What appears to be a product of superior intellectual power is often simply the result of great assiduity and meticulous attention to detail: "Finally, he examined with his glass the word upon the wall, going over every letter of it with the most minute exactness. This done, he appeared to be satisfied, for he replaced his tape and his glass in his pocket. 'They say that genius is an infinite capacity for taking pains,' he remarked with a smile. 'It's a very bad definition, but it does apply to detective work'" (Sir Arthur Conan Doyle, *A Study in Scarlet,* 1887). The proverb was first recorded, with different wording, in 1858, but the sentiment it expresses is of earlier origin. The comte de Buffon (1707–88) is said to have remarked, "*Le génie n'est qu'une plus grande aptitude à la patience* [Genius is only a greater aptitude for patience]."

genius is one percent inspiration and ninety-nine percent perspiration Great achievements or innovations require some intellectual input but are largely due to hard work: *She received numerous awards for her work, and was hailed as one of the greatest minds of her generation, but in newspaper interviews she always remained modest, quoting the proverb* "Genius is one percent inspiration and ninety-nine percent perspiration." The proverb is traditionally attributed

to the U.S. inventor Thomas Alva Edison (1847–1931).

Variant of this proverb: genius is ten percent inspiration and ninety percent perspiration.

genius without education is like silver in the mine Superior intellectual power is a wasted resource unless it is nurtured by education: *The school was set up to feed the minds of exceptionally gifted students, on the principle that genius without education is like silver in the mine.*

a gentleman's word is his bond *See* A MAN'S WORD IS AS GOOD AS HIS BOND.

gently does it *See* EASY DOES IT.

give a beggar a horse and he'll ride it to death People who suddenly acquire wealth or power are likely to misuse it: *Give a beggar a horse and he'll ride it to death—within six months he had squandered all his winnings, and had to go cap in hand to his former employer to ask for his old job back.* The proverb was first recorded, with different wording, in 1576. It occurs in Shakespeare's play *Henry VI, Part 3* (1:4): "Unless the adage must be verified,/ That beggars mounted run their horse to death."

Proverb expressing similar meaning: SET A BEGGAR ON HORSEBACK, AND HE'LL RIDE TO THE DEVIL.

give a civil answer to a civil question *See* A CIVIL QUESTION DESERVES A CIVIL ANSWER.

give a dog a bad name and hang him Once somebody's reputation has been damaged—for example, by rumor or

GERMAN PROVERBS

German proverbs include many wise warnings against the perils of daily existence. These range from self-deception and physical temptation to the hazards of love.

Beauty is the eye's food but the soul's sorrow

Begged bread has a hard crust

Better a good hanging than a bad marriage

Birds of prey do not sing

Boredom is the father of all sins

Don't throw away your old shoes until you have a new pair

Even the devil's grandmother was a nice girl when she was young

Fire in the heart sends smoke to the head

He who does not punish evil invites it

He who has no enemies has no friends either

He who has not tasted bitter things, knows not what sweet is

Howling makes the wolf bigger than he really is

High climbers and deep swimmers never grow old

A lie becomes true when one believes it

More people drown in glasses than in rivers

Never give advice unless asked

Never tickle the nose of a sleeping bear

No bed is big enough to hold three

The silent dog is the first to bite

Time is anger's medicine

Two is an army against one

What little Hans did not learn, big Hans does not know

When an old man marries, death laughs

Where there is no jealousy there is no love

slander—it will never recover: "The Liberal impulse is almost always to give a dog a bad name and hang him: that is, to denounce the menaced proprietors as enemies of mankind, and ruin them in a transport of virtuous indignation" (George Bernard Shaw, *The Intelligent Woman's Guide to Socialism,* 1928). The proverb was first recorded, with different wording, in 1706.

Variant of this proverb: he that has an ill name is half hanged.

Proverbs expressing similar meaning: HE THAT WOULD HANG HIS DOG GIVES OUT FIRST THAT HE IS MAD; THROW DIRT ENOUGH, AND SOME WILL STICK.

give a loaf and beg a slice People who are too generous risk having to beg themselves: *Her generosity was such that it was a case of give a loaf and beg a slice herself.* The proverb was first recorded in 1678 by John Ray in *A Collection of English Proverbs.* Sometimes found with *slice* replaced by the archaic word *shive*, meaning the same thing.

give a man a fish and you feed him for a day; show him how to fish and you feed him for a lifetime Many of the problems of the needy are better solved by education than by charitable handouts: *Our organization believes in the principle that if you give a man a fish, you feed him for a day, whereas if you show him how to fish, you feed him for a lifetime. In projects all over the Third World, our volunteers are actively involved in teaching local people the skills they need to farm their land more efficiently.* The proverb is of ancient Chinese origin.

give a man an inch and he'll take a mile People are inclined to take excessive advantage of the tolerance or generosity of others; often used to warn against making even the smallest concession: *He came to us once for an evening meal and now he expects us to put up his wife and children for three weeks! Talk about giving him an inch and he'll take a mile!* The proverb was first recorded in 1546 in the form "When I gave you an inch you took an ell." An *ell* is an obsolete measure of length, varying according to locality: in England it is approximately 45 inches, in Scotland, 37 inches.

Variants of this proverb: give a man an inch and he'll take an ell; an inch is as good as a mile.

give a man enough rope and he'll hang himself People who are given complete freedom of action will ultimately bring about their own downfall, for example by inadvertently revealing their guilt: *Rather than accuse her without any firm evidence, I suggest we let things take their course. Give a man enough rope and he'll hang himself— sooner or later we'll catch her red-handed.* The proverb was first recorded in 1639 in Thomas Fuller's *Holy War.*

give and take is fair play Exchanging like for like—whether it be a blow, an insult, a favor, or a pardon—is a fair and legitimate way to proceed: "Give and take is fair play. All I say is, let it be a fair stand-up fight" (Captain Marryat, *Newton Forster,* 1832). The proverb was first recorded in 1778, in Fanny Burney's novel *Evelina,* in the form "Give and Take is fair in all nations." It is also used with *give and take* in the sense of "mutual concession or compromise."

give a thing, and take a thing, to wear the devil's gold ring It is wrong to take back a gift: *He subsequently regretted his generosity, and asked his sister to return the CD. "Give a thing, and take a thing, to wear the devil's gold ring," came her reply.* Mainly used by children, the proverb was first recorded in 1571, but the sentiment it expresses is of ancient origin. Compare Plato (c. 428–348 B.C.), "as with children, there is no taking away of what has been rightly given."

give credit where credit is due Do not neglect to give people the praise they deserve, or to acknowledge the good things they do; often used when such credit is given grudgingly: "Yes, yes! let us be tenderly conscientious in giving credit where credit is due; let us never forget that the citizen Maurice contributed something to the cure of the interesting invalid, as well as the victuals and drink from the Piebald Horse" (Wilkie Collins, *After Dark,* 1856). The proverb was first recorded in 1777, in the form "May honor be given to whom honor may be due." It may be of biblical origin: "Render therefore to all their dues . . . honour to whom honour" (Romans 13:7). The word *credit* replaced *honor* in the 19th century.

give me a child for the first seven years and he is mine for life A child's future is determined by what it learns in its first seven years: *The emperor watched the child leave and murmured to his secretary "give me a child for the first seven years and he is mine for life."* The proverb was recorded in 1902–04 by V. S. Lean in *Collecteana* but is much older, being particularly associated with Saint Ignatius Loyola, the founder of the Jesuits in the 16th century.

Variant of this proverb: give me a child for the first seven years, and you may do what you like with him afterwards.

Proverb expressing similar meaning: THE CHILD IS THE FATHER OF THE MAN.

give the devil his due People deserve recognition for their skills and contributions even if they are otherwise unworthy or unlikable: *I can't stand the man, on a purely personal level, but—give the devil his due—he has done a fantastic job in getting the company back on its feet.* The proverb was first recorded in 1589 in John Lyly's *Pappe with an Hatchet.*

the glass is either half empty or half full Many situations can be viewed negatively or positively—a negative thinker with half a glass of beer would say that the glass was half empty, whereas a positive thinker would say it was half full: *Some employees equate redundancy with being thrown on the scrap heap, others see it as a golden opportunity for a change of career—the glass is either half empty or half full.*

Variant of this proverb: the optimist's cup is half full; the pessimist's cup is half empty.

gluttony kills more than the sword Overeating, or overindulgence in the wrong kind of food, may lead to an early death: *Whenever he was offered a second helping, my grandfather would shake his head and say, "Gluttony kills more than the sword." I was often tempted to ask him how many people actually died by the sword in this day and age.* The proverb dates from before 1384 in John Wycliffe's *Works.*

go abroad and you'll hear news of home People often remain ignorant of matters concerning their family and friends, or events in their own neighborhood, until they go traveling, when they hear about them at second hand: "What is the meaning of this silly story that people are circulating about Thomasin and Mr. Wildeve? . . . It is said that one should go abroad to hear news of home, and I appear to have done it" (Thomas Hardy, *Return of the Native,* 1878). The proverb was first recorded, with different wording, in 1678.

God fits the back to the burden *See* GOD MAKES THE BACK TO THE BURDEN.

God helps those who help themselves Those who are self-reliant and make an effort are more likely to get what they want than those who sit back and wait for divine assistance: "I wish you all success, Paul, and I thank you for wishing me to share in your good fortune. God helps those who help themselves, and he will help you if you only deserve it" (Horatio Alger, *Paul Prescott's*

Charge, 1865). The proverb is of ancient origin. It is sometimes used facetiously as a justification for stealing, or in the extended form "God helps those who help themselves, but God help those who are caught helping themselves."

Variants of this proverb: God helps them that help themselves; heaven helps those who help themselves.

God is always on the side of the big battalions *See* PROVIDENCE IS ALWAYS ON THE SIDE OF THE BIG BATTALIONS.

God is in the details *See* THE DEVIL IS IN THE DETAILS.

God made the country and man made the town The urban environment, constructed by human hands, is inferior to the natural countryside, which is the work of divine creation: "The miserable routinists who keep repeating invidiously Cowper's 'God made the country and man made the town,' as if the town were a place to kill out the race in, do not know what they are talking about" (Oliver Wendell Holmes, *Elsie Venner,* 1861). In its current form, the proverb comes from William Cowper's poem *The Task* (1785). The sentiment it expresses, however, is of ancient origin: in the first century B.C. the Roman scholar Varro wrote, "*divina natura dedit agros, ars humana aedificavit urbes* [divine nature gave us the fields, human art built the cities]."

God makes the back to the burden Nobody has to endure more than his or her body or spirit can bear; used to imply that the strongest are destined to suffer the greatest adversity, or that at times of great adversity we are given extra strength: *She*

certainly seems to have had more than her fair share of grief in recent years—more than most of us could stand—but God makes the back to the burden, as they say. The proverb was first recorded in 1822.

Variant of this proverb: God fits the back to the burden.

Proverb expressing similar meaning: GOD TEMPERS THE WIND TO THE SHORN LAMB.

God moves in mysterious ways Strange or unpleasant things that happen are meant to be, and often turn out for the best: *God moves in a mysterious way, and Jenkins's knee injury, which everybody thought would spell disaster for the team, had the opposite effect—his replacement scored a record number of goals, giving the team its best season ever.* The proverb comes from William Cowper's hymn "Light Shining Out of Darkness" (1779): "God moves in a mysterious way/His wonders to perform;/He plants his footsteps in the sea/And rides upon the storm."

Variant of this proverb: the Lord moves in mysterious ways.

God never sends mouths but he sends meat God can be relied upon to provide for everybody: "God never sends mouths . . . but he sends meat, and any man who has sense enough to be honest, will never want wit to know how to live" (John Pendleton Kennedy, *Swallow Barn,* 1832). The proverb was first recorded in this form in 1546.

Variant of this proverb: God never sends a mouth but he feeds it.

God protect me from my friends—I can protect myself from my enemies *See* SAVE US FROM OUR FRIENDS.

God sends meat, but the devil sends cooks Good food can be ruined by a bad cook: *The brochure for the hotel boasted that only the best local produce was used in its kitchens, but our first meal there was a big disappointment. "God sends meat, but the devil sends cooks," remarked my wife.* The proverb was first recorded in 1542 (A. Borde, *Dietary of Health*), but with the implication that it was already in general use.

God's in his heaven; all's right with the world All is well at this moment in time; used as a general expression of happiness or contentment: "Let us then resolutely turn our backs on the once-born and their sky-blue optimistic gospel; let us not simply cry out, in spite of all appearances, 'Hurrah for the Universe!—God's in his Heaven, all's right with the world'" (William James, *Varieties of Religious Experience,* 1902). In its current form, the proverb comes from Robert Browning's poem "Pippa Passes" (1841). It replaces an earlier proverb, "God is where he was," first recorded in 1530 and used to console or encourage those in trouble or despair.

the gods send nuts to those who have no teeth Opportunities or good fortune often come too late in life for people to enjoy them or take full advantage of them; also applied more generally to people of any age who are unable to use or benefit from good things that come their way: *The gods send nuts to those who have no teeth—if only I had won a holiday like this while I was still young and fit enough to make the most of it!* The proverb was first recorded in 1929 in the periodical *American Speech.*

God takes soonest those he loves best God's favorites die young, because he longs to have them by his side again; often said in consolation, for example to bereaved parents: *God takes soonest those he loves best, and little Bethany, who brought such happiness to so many people in the five short years of her life, lost her battle with leukemia yesterday.*

Proverbs expressing similar meaning: WHOM THE GODS LOVE DIE YOUNG; THE GOOD DIE YOUNG.

God tempers the wind to the shorn lamb Weak or vulnerable people have divine protection from the worst misfortunes; also used when such people are treated with compassion by their fellow human beings: "There is an unduly optimistic proverb which declares that God tempers the wind to the shorn lamb. My subsequent history was hardly to justify such naive faith in the Deity" (Vera Brittain, *Testament of Youth,* 1933). The proverb was first recorded in 1594 in the French form *"Dieu mesure le froid à la brebis tondue* [God measures the cold to the shorn sheep]."

Proverb expressing similar meaning: GOD MAKES THE BACK TO THE BURDEN.

go farther and fare worse If you reject something acceptable in the hope of finding something better, you may end up having to settle for something worse: "She's just as rich as most of the girls who came out of India. I might go farther and fare worse" (William Makepeace Thackeray, *Vanity Fair,* 1848). The proverb was first recorded in 1546.

go hunting where the ducks are If you want to find or accomplish something, you must go to the right places, make contact with the right people, and do the right things: "The cold facts of 1988 do suggest that if in 1992 the Democrats—in Barry Goldwater's phrase—are to 'go hunting where the ducks are,' the most ducks are likely to be found outside of Dixie" (*New York Times*, 1991).

Proverb expressing similar meaning: FISH WHERE THE FISH ARE.

the golden age was never the present age

The past and the future always seem infinitely preferable to the present time: *People have fond memories of the past and great hopes for the future, forgetting that today is yesterday's future and tomorrow's past—the golden age was never the present age.* The proverb was first recorded in 1732 in Thomas Fuller's *Gnomologia: Adagies and Proverbs*.

a golden key can open any door

With money you can gain access to anything you want; used specifically of bribery, or more generally of the power and influence of wealth: "Their better-educated neighbours . . . did not call on the newly rich family. That was before the days when a golden key could open any door" (Flora Thompson, *Lark Rise to Candleford*, 1945). The proverb was first recorded in 1580, in John Lyly's *Euphues and his England*: "Who is so ignorant that knoweth not, gold be a key for every locke."

Proverbs expressing similar meaning: A BRIBE WILL ENTER WITHOUT KNOCKING; MONEY IS POWER; MONEY TALKS.

gold may be bought too dear

Wealth is not worth having if there is too great a risk or sacrifice involved in acquiring it: *Gold may be bought too dear, and in his ruthless pursuit of financial gain he has lost most of his friends, destroyed his marriage,* and damaged his health. The proverb was first recorded in 1546 in John Heywood's *Dialogue of Proverbs*.

good Americans, when they die, go to Paris

Paris is regarded as a kind of paradise by certain Americans, especially the literati, many of whom have taken up residence there over the years: *If it is true that good Americans, when they die, go to Paris, then they must not expect to have the city to themselves—the French capital has become a mecca for tourists from all nations.* The proverb was coined by the poet and artist Thomas Gold Appleton (1812–84) and recorded in Oliver Wendell Holmes's *The Autocrat of the Breakfast-Table* (1858). It occurs in Oscar Wilde's play *A Woman of No Importance* (1894), followed by the observation that "when bad Americans die . . . they go to America."

a good beginning is half the battle

If you make a good start to a project or enterprise, you are halfway to making a success of it: *We were very pleased to have made such excellent progress on the first day—a good beginning is half the battle.* The proverb was first recorded in Oliver Goldsmith's play *She Stoops to Conquer* (1773) in the form "The first blow is half the battle." The sentiment it expresses, however, is of much earlier origin. In modern times it is most frequently encountered in the form of the cliché *half the battle*.

Proverb expressing similar meaning: WELL BEGUN IS HALF DONE.

a good beginning makes a good ending

Something that is well planned and well executed from the start is likely to end in success: *A good beginning makes a good ending, and if you don't measure out the ingredients accurately your loaf may be a disaster.* The proverb was first recorded c. 1300.

good company on the road is the shortest cut A journey seems much shorter when you have pleasant people to talk to along the way: *My friends went with me to the station, and what is usually a long and tedious walk seemed to be over in no time at all. As they say, "Good company on the road is the shortest cut."* The proverb was first recorded in 1653, in Izaak Walton's *The Compleat Angler.*

Variant of this proverb: cheerful company shortens the miles.

Proverb expressing opposite meaning: HE TRAVELS FASTEST WHO TRAVELS ALONE.

the good die young It often seems that good people are more likely to meet a premature death than bad people; also used to console those who have lost a young friend or relative: "The good do die young. That's why people like you and me are left to grow old" (James Leasor, *Love and the Land Beyond,* 1979). The proverb was first recorded in 1697 in Daniel Defoe's *Character of the Late Dr. S. Annesley:* "The best of men cannot suspend their fate; / The good die early, and the bad die late."

Proverb expressing similar meaning: WHOM THE GODS LOVE DIE YOUNG.

a good dog deserves a good bone A loyal servant or employee deserves his reward: "A good dog deserves, sir, a good bone" (Ben Jonson, *A Tale of a Tub,* 1633). The proverb was first recorded in 1611 by Randle Cotgrave in *A Dictionary of the French and English Tongues.*

Proverb expressing similar meaning: THE LABORER IS WORTHY OF HIS HIRE.

a good example is the best sermon It is better to show people how to behave by setting a good example instead of just telling them: *The priest was famous locally for his active role in the community and clearly believed that a good example was the best sermon.* The proverb was first recorded in 1732 by Thomas Fuller in *Gnomologia.*

Proverb expressing similar meaning: EXAMPLE IS BETTER THAN PRECEPT.

Proverb expressing opposite meaning: DO AS I SAY, NOT AS I DO.

a good face is a letter of recommendation An honest demeanor may be interpreted as a sign of a person's integrity: "His honest countenance was a good letter of recommendation" (Tobias Smollett, *Humphrey Clinker,* 1771). The proverb was first recorded in English in 1620 by T. Shelton in his translation of *Don Quixote,* but is much older and appeared in the writings of Publius Syrus.

good fences make good neighbors A good relationship between neighbors depends on each respecting the other's privacy and not entering his or her property uninvited; also used more broadly of international relations and the need to maintain trade barriers and border controls: *The saying "Good fences make good neighbors" is equally relevant in the workplace, and you should make every effort not to encroach on a colleague's personal space.* First recorded in 1640, in the form "A good fence helps to keep peace between neighbors," the proverb is often associated with Robert Frost, who used it in his poem "Mending Wall" (1914).

Proverb expressing similar meaning: A HEDGE BETWEEN KEEPS FRIENDSHIP GREEN.

good health is more to be desired than wealth *See* HEALTH IS WEALTH.

a good horse cannot be of a bad color
Superficial appearances do not affect the essential worth of something: "It is observed by some, that there is no good horse of a bad colour" (Isaac Walton, *The Compleat Angler*, 1653). The proverb was first recorded in 1628 by J. Carmichaell in *Proverbs in Scots*.

Proverbs expressing similar meaning: APPEARANCES ARE DECEIVING; JUDGE NOT ACCORDING TO APPEARANCES.

a good husband makes a good wife A husband who treats his family with respect, and carries out his duties as he should, will find that his wife does likewise: *He complains if his shirts aren't ironed, or if the dinner's late, but when I ask him to do something around the house he always manages to put it off. I told him, "A good husband makes a good wife."* The proverb was first recorded in 1492 in *Salomon & Marcolphus*.

Variant of this proverb: A BAD HUSBAND MAKES A BAD WIFE.

Proverb expressing similar meaning: A GOOD JACK MAKES A GOOD JILL.

the good is the enemy of the best If you are content with producing what is merely good you will never achieve excellence: *In this company we believe that the good is the enemy of the best—our products are not just of an acceptable standard, they are of the highest possible quality.* The proverb was first recorded in 1912, but with the implication that it was already in general use.

Proverb expressing similar meaning: IF A THING'S WORTH DOING, IT'S WORTH DOING WELL.

Proverb expressing opposite meaning: THE BEST IS THE ENEMY OF THE GOOD.

a good Jack makes a good Jill People who live or work together should set a good example to each other—a good husband will have a good wife, a good master will have a good servant, and so on: *You cannot expect your secretary to be punctual if you are regularly late for work—a good Jack makes a good Jill.* The proverb was first recorded in 1623 in William Painter's *Palace of Pleasure*.

Proverb expressing similar meaning: A GOOD HUSBAND MAKES A GOOD WIFE.

a good leader is also a good follower
Those best suited to leadership are those who have shown a willingness to follow the commands of others: *Before you cast your vote, remember that a good leader is also a good follower, and consider the way that the candidates have behaved in their previous roles.* The proverb is recorded as a regional expression in the United States.

Proverb expressing similar meaning: HE THAT CANNOT OBEY CANNOT COMMAND.

good men are scarce It is often difficult to find a talented or suitably qualified person when you need one; also used literally as a comment on the dearth of decent people—or eligible bachelors in the modern world: *He's an excellent worker, and we're anxious not to lose him—good men are scarce.* The proverb was first recorded in 1609 in D. Tuvill's *Essays Moral and Theological*.

Variant of this proverb: a good man is hard to find.

a good name is better than precious ointment Your good name should be your most cherished possession: "Let me tell you something straight from the shoulder: good name in man or woman is the immediate jewel of their soul. A good name is better than precious ointment" (Joseph Heller, *God Knows*, 1984). The proverb is of biblical origin: "A good name is better than precious ointment; and the day of death than the day of one's birth" (Ecclesiastes 7:1). The words *precious ointment* are sometimes replaced by *precious stones, fine jewels, rubies, great riches,* or *gold.*

Proverb expressing similar meaning: A GOOD REPUTATION IS MORE VALUABLE THAN MONEY.

a good name is sooner lost than won   It takes a lot of time and effort to earn a good name for yourself, but you can lose it in an instant with a single foolish act: *Think carefully before you get involved in anything that is not strictly legal—remember that a good name is sooner lost than won.* The proverb was first recorded in 1727 in John Gay's "Fox at Point of Death," in *Fables.*

a good reputation is more valuable than money   A good reputation is worth more than anything else: *It is reassuring to learn that are still a few incorruptible individuals in public office, who are aware that a good reputation is more valuable than money.* The proverb is of ancient origin, and has been traced back to the writings of Publilius Syrus (first century B.C.).

Proverb expressing similar meaning: A GOOD NAME IS BETTER THAN PRECIOUS OINTMENT.

good riddance to bad rubbish   We are better off without worthless people or things; usually said on the departure of such a person or the loss of such a thing: "'I have been in this house waiting on my young lady a dozen year and I won't stop in it one hour under notice from a person owning to the name of Pipchin trust me, Mrs P.' 'A good riddance of bad rubbish!' said that wrathful old lady. 'Get along with you, or I'll have you carried out!'" (Charles Dickens, *Dombey and Son*, 1847–48). The proverb was first recorded in 1771 in *Essex Gazette.*

the good seaman is known in bad weather   Those who are truly able or skillful prove their worth at times of crisis or when major problems are encountered; also used literally with specific application to sailing: *She seems competent enough, but she has not yet been put to the test—a good seaman is known in bad weather.* The proverb was first recorded in 1767 in *Papers of Benjamin Franklin.*

good seed makes a good crop   The quality of a product depends on the quality of the raw materials or ingredients: "Seed-time's pretty sure to come around . . . And good seed makes a good crop" (Laura Ingalls Wilder, *The Long Winter*, 1940). The proverb was first recorded in 1569 in the form "Of good seed proceeds good corn," with reference to parents and their offspring.

a good tale is not the worse for being told twice   There is no harm in telling a good joke or anecdote—or a story with a moral—a second time; often used by way of apology or justification for such repetition: *You may have heard this story before, but a good tale is not the worse for being told twice.* The proverb was first recorded in 1577 in the form "A good tale may be twice told." In the 18th century it was used when grace was accidentally said twice before a meal.

the good that men do lives after them People are remembered after their deaths for the good things that they did during their lives: *He was a tyrannical ruler, and had many innocent people put to death, but he was also a great patron of the arts, and the good that men do lives after them—he has gone down in history as one of the founders of modern civilization.* The proverb was first recorded in this form in 1942, but the sentiment it expresses is found in the writings of Euripides (fifth century B.C.): "When good men die their goodness does not perish,/But lives though they are gone." The opposite sentiment is expressed in Shakespeare's play *Julius Caesar* (3:2), "The evil that men do lives after them, /The good is oft interred with their bones."

good things come in small packages *See* THE BEST THINGS COME IN SMALL PACKAGES.

good to forgive, best to forget *See* FORGIVE AND FORGET.

good wine needs no bush A good product does not need advertising: *In the competitive marketplace of the modern world, few companies are prepared to trust the wisdom of the age-old proverb, "Good wine needs no bush."* Of ancient origin, the proverb occurs in the epilogue of Shakespeare's play *As You Like It*: "If it be true that good wine needs no bush, 'tis true that a good play needs no epilogue." The word *bush* refers to a bunch of ivy that was formerly hung outside a wine merchant's premises.

a goose quill is more dangerous than a lion's claw Written words of criticism or defamation can do more harm or cause more pain than a physical attack: *The color drained from her face as she read the letter, with its vile accusations, and she collapsed before she reached the end—a goose quill is indeed more dangerous than a lion's claw.*

Proverb expressing similar meaning: THE PEN IS MIGHTIER THAN THE SWORD.

gossip is the lifeblood of society Social intercourse thrives on gossip—if people stopped talking *about* each other they might stop talking *to* each other: *Gossip is the lifeblood of society—how dull our parties would be if we were driven to discussing politics or sport all the time.* The proverb was first recorded in 1941 in David Kent's *Jason Burr's First Case.*

gossip is vice enjoyed vicariously People feel they can innocently participate in the illicit pleasures of other people's immoral behavior by talking about it with their friends or reading about it in the newspaper: *They say that gossip is vice enjoyed vicariously, and women who would never dream of being unfaithful to their husbands always seem eager to hear about those who are.* The proverb was first recorded in 1904 in E. Hubbard, *The Philistine.*

governments have long arms *See* KINGS HAVE LONG ARMS.

grace will last, beauty will blast A good character will outlive superficial physical attractiveness: *She may be the more beautiful of the two sisters, but remember how the old adage goes, "grace will last, beauty will blast."* The proverb was first recorded c. 1450 in *Proverbis of Wysdom.*

Variant of this proverb: grace will last, favor will blast.

grasp no more than the hand will hold Do not be greedy or overambitious:

People who ignore the proverb "Grasp no more than the hand will hold" often end up losing everything they have in an attempt to gain just a little more. The proverb was first recorded in 1732 in Thomas Fuller's *Gnomologia: Adagies and Proverbs.*

the grass is always greener on the other side of the fence   A different place, situation, job, or lifestyle always seems more attractive or appealing than your own: *She is one of those people for whom the grass is always greener on the other side of the fence, and who are never satisfied with what they have if they think their friends have something better.* In its current form the proverb is of relatively recent origin, but the sentiment it expresses dates back to ancient times. Compare Ovid (43 B.C.–A.D. 18): *"fertilior seges est alienis semper in agris* [the harvest is always more fruitful in another man's fields]."

Variant of this proverb: the grass is always greener in somebody else's backyard.

the gray mare is the better horse   A woman is often more competent or powerful than a man; used specifically of wives who have the upper hand over their husbands: "She did not wish it to seem, to quote an old fashioned expression, that the grey mare was the better horse. . . . She strove to avoid prejudicing her husband's position" (Violet Powell, *Flora Annie Steel,* 1981). The proverb was first recorded in 1529.

great boats may venture more, but little boats should keep near shore   See LITTLE BOATS SHOULD STAY CLOSE TO SHORE.

a great book is a great evil   A long book is a bad book—good writers know how to express themselves concisely: "If there is any truth in the old Greek maxim that a large book is a great evil, English dictionaries have been steadily growing worse ever since their inception more than three centuries ago" (*Oxford English Dictionary,* Preface, 1933). The proverb originated in the writings of the poet Callimachus (third century B.C.).

a great city, a great solitude   People often feel more lonely in a large city, among thousands of strangers, than they would do if they were actually alone: *It was on the crowded streets of Los Angeles that I learned the meaning of the proverb "A great city, a great solitude," and I longed to be back in my cozy apartment, with just the television for company.* The proverb is of ancient Greek origin.

great cry but little wool   See MUCH CRY AND LITTLE WOOL.

the greater the truth, the greater the libel   Some people will take greater offense at a true accusation of wrongdoing than at a false one: *The vehemence with which he denied any involvement in the scandal aroused my suspicions—the greater the truth, the greater the libel.* The proverb is associated with the English judge Lord Mansfield (1705–93).

great men have great faults   Remarkable people tend to have serious character flaws: "Great men's faults are never small" (John Clarke, *Paroemiologia Anglo-Latina,* 1639). The proverb was first recorded in 1616 by T. Draxe in his *Bibliotheca Scholastica.*

great minds think alike   People often say or do the same thing, or make the same decision, coincidentally; said when such a

coincidence occurs, with no more than a jocular reference to the size of the intellect: *"I was planning to buy them an espresso machine." "So was I. Great minds think alike!"* The proverb was first recorded in 1618. In early occurrences it had the form "Great minds [or wits] jump," the word *jump* being used in the now archaic sense of "agree."

Variant of this proverb: great minds run in the same channels.

great oaks from little acorns grow Things of great size or importance may develop from a relatively small or insig-nificant beginning: "A curfew, I admit, is not the end of civilization, nor even a steep imposition. But mighty oaks, as they say, from little acorns grow" (*Washington Times,* 1995). The proverb was first recorded c. 1385, in Chaucer's *Troilus and Criseyde.* The word *great* is sometimes replaced by *big, mighty, tall,* or some other synonym.

great trees keep down little ones The predominance of a particular person, company, nation, etc., results in lesser rivals being kept in the shade: *In the*

GREEK PROVERBS

Many Greek proverbs are of ancient origin, but most remain as relevant today as when first coined. In particular, the Greeks have many proverbs offering guidance in the conduct of personal relationships, both with friends and enemies.

Don't forget to distrust
Greeks only agree with each other about going to the toilet
The heart that loves is always young
He who eats and drinks with the rich leaves the table hungry
He who thinks the worst usually is right
He who wants to be happy must stay at home
Listen to that which is well said, even if it from the mouth of an enemy
My donkey is dead; let no more grass grow
An old enemy never becomes a friend
Observe your enemies, for they first find your faults
One minute of patience can mean ten years of peace
One word spoken in anger may spoil an entire life
The people make the town
Remorse is worse than a beating
Success has many friends
Time is the soul of the world
Under every stone sleeps a scorpion
Where there is a sea there are pirates
Whoever feeds the wolf in the winter will be eaten by him in the spring
Women are as changeable as the sea

competitive world of politics it is a sad but unavoidable fact that great trees keep down little ones. The proverb was first recorded in 1642 by Thomas Fuller in *The Holy State and the Profane State*.

a green winter makes a fat churchyard More deaths occur during mild winters than they do in cold winters: *Scientists agree that "a green winter makes a fat churchyard," as milder winters encourage the development of a variety of epidemics*. The proverb was first recorded in 1635 by J. Swan in *Speculum Mundi*.

Variant of this proverb: a green Yule makes a fat churchyard.

a growing youth has a wolf in his stomach Adolescent boys are perpetually hungry: *I'd better fill up the freezer—a growing youth has a wolf in his stomach, and my teenage son has invited three of his friends for the weekend!* The proverb was first recorded in 1611 in Randle Cotgrave's *A Dictionary of the French and English Tongues*.

Variant of this proverb: A growing youth has a wolf in his belly.

a guilty conscience needs no accuser People who know they have done wrong reveal their guilt by the things they say or the way they interpret what other people say: "Then I knew he was speaking of Hinckman's murder and must be the murderer—'a guilty conscience needs no accuser.'" (*Ellery Queen's Mystery Magazine*, 1952). The proverb was first recorded in its current form in 1744, but a similar sentiment was expressed in a proverb recorded by Dionysius Cato (fourth century A.D.): "the man with something on his conscience thinks he is always the subject of talk."

the habit does not make the monk   *See* THE COWL DOES NOT MAKE THE MONK.

the hair of the dog is good for the bite   *See* TAKE A HAIR OF THE DOG THAT BIT YOU.

half a loaf is better than no bread   We must be grateful for what we get, even if it is less than we desire—it is better to have a small amount than nothing at all: *I was disappointed not to find all the information I required, but half a loaf is better than no bread, and at least I have enough to start writing my article.* The proverb was first recorded in 1546.

Variants of this proverb: half a loaf is better than none; half an egg is better than an empty shell.

Proverb expressing similar meaning: SOMETHING IS BETTER THAN NOTHING.

the half is better than the whole   A restrained approach to something is often the most effective; used to warn against excess: "It is true of conversation as of many other things, that the half is better than the whole. People who are fond of talking ought to beware of being lengthy" (A. C. Benson, *From a College Window,* 1906). The proverb comes from the Greek poet Hesiod's *Works and Days* (eighth century B.C.)

"The half is greater than the whole." It was first recorded in English in 1550.

Variant of this proverb: half is more than the whole.

Proverb expressing similar meaning: LESS IS MORE.

half the truth is often a whole lie   Not telling the whole truth, or saying something that is only partly true, is tantamount to lying: *What she said was not entirely untrue, but she omitted to mention a number of significant details, and half the truth is often a whole lie.* The proverb was first recorded in Benjamin Franklin's *Poor Richard's Almanack* (1758) in the form "Half the truth is often a great lie." It occurs in Alfred, Lord Tennyson's poem *The Grandmother* (1847): That a lie which is half a truth is ever the blackest of lies, / That a lie which is all a lie may be met and fought with outright, / But a lie which is part a truth is a harder matter to fight."

Variant of this proverb: a half-truth is often a great lie.

half the world knows not how the other half lives   *See* ONE HALF OF THE WORLD DOESN'T KNOW HOW THE OTHER HALF LIVES.

handsome is as handsome does   People should be valued for their good deeds,

not their good looks; also occasionally used of things, or as a warning not to be misled by an attractive appearance: "'Such a handsome young man.' 'Handsome is as handsome does. Much too fond of poking fun at people'" (Agatha Christie, *A Murder Is Announced,* 1950). The proverb was first recorded in this form in 1659, but the sentiment it expresses is of much earlier origin.

Proverb expressing similar meaning: THE TREE IS KNOWN BY ITS FRUIT.

the hand that rocks the cradle rules the world Mothers have a powerful influence—if indirectly—on world affairs, because it is they who mold the characters of future leaders: "The habits of the home in one generation become the morals of society in the next. As the old adage says: 'The hand that rocks the cradle rules the world'" (*Washington Times,* 1996). The proverb comes from William Ross Wallace's poem "What Rules the World" (1865).

hanging and wiving go by destiny Some people are fated to marry each other, just as some are fated to be hanged: *Hanging and wiving go by destiny, and if I am meant to have him, then he will be mine!* The proverb was first recorded in 1546, and occurs in Shakespeare's play *The Merchant of Venice* (2:9): "The ancient saying is no heresy:/ Hanging and wiving goes by destiny."

Proverb expressing similar meaning: MARRIAGES ARE MADE IN HEAVEN.

happy is he that is happy in his children Parents derive much pleasure from their children, if they happen to be happy and well-behaved: *The bishop patted the infant on the head and murmured wistfully "happy is he that is happy in his children."* The proverb was first recorded in 1732 in Thomas Fuller's *Gnomologia.*

Proverb expressing opposite meaning: CHILDREN ARE CERTAIN CARES, BUT UNCERTAIN COMFORTS.

happy is the bride that the sun shines on According to popular superstition, a woman who has a sunny wedding day will have a happy marriage: "Monday came, a cloudless lovely day . . . the clerk ascending the church steps, quoted the old proverb to the pew-opener, meeting him under the porch: 'Happy is the bride on whom the sun shines!'" (Wilkie Collins, *No Name,* 1862). The proverb was first recorded in Robert Herrick's *Hesperides* (1648) in the form "Blest is the Bride, on whom the Sun doth shine."

Variants of this proverb: blessed is the bride that the sun shines on; happy is the bride that the sun shines on, blessed is the corpse that the rain falls on; happy is the bride that the sun shines on, sorry is the bride that the rain rains on.

happy is the country that has no history It is a happy or fortunate country that has no unpleasant events worth recording in its past: "Quoting the familiar dictum: 'Happy is the country which has no history,' I remarked that I belonged . . . to a generation which was still on the early side of middle age but had already seen almost more history than any generation could bear" (Vera Brittain, *Testament of Experience,* 1957). The proverb has been attributed to the French philosopher Montesquieu (1689–1755) in the form "Happy the people whose annals are blank in history-books!" A similar sentiment occurs in Benjamin Franklin's *Poor*

Richard's Almanack (1740): "Happy that nation, fortunate that age, whose history is not diverting."

happy's the wooing that's not long a-doing   It is best to have only a short period of courtship before marriage: *Happy's the wooing that's not long a-doing, says the proverb, but many couples who marry in haste soon discover that it is not a recipe for wedded bliss.* The proverb was first recorded in 1576 in *Parade of Devil's Devices.*

Proverb expressing opposite meaning: MARRY IN HASTE, REPENT AT LEISURE.

hard cases make bad law   Cases that are complex or difficult to decide often cause the true meaning of the law to be distorted or obscured and sometimes lead to what is perceived as a miscarriage of justice: *The saying "Hard cases make bad law" should never be used to vindicate incompetent members of the legal profession.* The proverb was first recorded in 1854 by G. Hayes in W. S. Holdsworth's *History of English Law* (1926).

the harder the storm, the sooner it's over   *See* THE SHARPER THE STORM, THE SOONER IT'S OVER.

hard words break no bones   Adverse criticism or verbal abuse may be unpleasant, but it does no physical harm: *She called me every name under the sun, and told me never to go near any member of her family again, but hard words break no bones.* The proverb was first recorded in 1697 in G. Meriton's *Yorkshire Ale.*

Proverb expressing similar meaning: STICKS AND STONES MAY BREAK MY BONES, BUT WORDS WILL NEVER HURT ME.

Proverb expressing opposite meaning: THE TONGUE IS NOT STEEL, BUT IT CUTS.

hard work never hurt anybody   *See* WORK NEVER HURT ANYBODY.

haste is from the devil   Never be tempted to act in haste—you are bound to regret it: "Listening patiently to the views . . . he knew that for an Intelligence officer 'haste is from the devil'" (*London Times,* 1929). The proverb was first recorded in 1633, and may have originated in Eastern Europe or Asia.

haste makes waste   By acting too hastily or doing things too hurriedly you risk causing damage or making mistakes that subsequently have to be put right, resulting in a loss of time, money, and materials: *Haste makes waste—I broke at least four of the glasses in my rush to get them washed and dried before the guests started arriving.* The proverb was first recorded in this form in 1546 by John Heywood in his *Dialogue of Proverbs.*

Variant of this proverb: haste makes waste, and waste makes want, and want makes strife between a good man and his wife.

Proverb expressing similar meaning: THE HASTY BITCH BRINGETH FORTH BLIND WHELPS.

the hasty bitch bringeth forth blind whelps   Things done in haste tend to produce poor results: *The foreman had forgotten the age-old warning that "the hasty bitch bringeth forth blind whelps."* The proverb appeared in R. Robinson's 1556 translation of Thomas More's *Utopia* but is of much older origin, being quoted by Livy, Aristotle, and Galen. The word *whelps* may sometimes be replaced by *puppies.*

Proverb expressing similar meaning: HASTE MAKES WASTE.

hasty climbers have sudden falls Unduly rapid progress in a person's career, or in some other sphere of activity, often leads to an abrupt and ignominious downfall or failure: *The speed with which he rose through the ranks caused his parents some concern, for hasty climbers have sudden falls.* The proverb dates from before 1439 in J. Lydgate's *Fall of Princes.*

Proverb expressing similar meaning: A FOOL'S BOLT IS SOON SHOT.

hawks will not pick out hawks' eyes People who belong to the same group will not—or should not—harm one another: "I have heard that hawks should not pick out hawks' eyes. What do you propose to gain?" (John Buchan, *Salute to Adventurers,* 1915). The proverb was first recorded in 1573 in the form "One crow never pulls out another's eyes."

Variant of this proverb: a crow doesn't pick out the eye of another crow.

Proverbs expressing similar meaning: DOG DOES NOT EAT DOG; THERE'S HONOR AMONG THIEVES.

heads I win, tails you lose In some situations it is impossible for one person not to be a winner—or impossible for another person not to be a loser—whatever the outcome: *It's heads I win, tails you lose—if they keep me on they'll have to start paying me the going rate, and if they don't, I'll sue them for wrongful dismissal.* The proverb was first recorded in 1846 by John Wilson Croker in *The Croker Papers.*

health is not valued till sickness comes People often fail to appreciate the good situation that they are in until circumstances change for the worse: *Health is not valued till sickness comes—he* took his home comforts for granted until his family's fortunes changed, and he found himself begging on the streets. The proverb was first recorded in 1553 in the form "Health after sickness is sweeter evermore."

health is wealth Good health is a valuable asset, worth more than any amount of money: *Remember that health is wealth, and there's no point in working yourself into an early grave just so that you can afford a better house or a bigger car.* The proverb was first recorded in the 16th century.

Variant of this proverb: good health is more to be desired than wealth.

hear all, see all, say nowt It is sometimes prudent to listen and watch carefully, but say nothing: *She remembered her grandmother's advice to hear all, see all, say nowt.* The proverb was first recorded in 1400 in *Proverbs of Wisdom.* A fuller version of the proverb runs "hear all, see all, say nowt, tak' all, keep all, gie nowt, and if tha ever does owt for nowt do it for thysen."

Proverb expressing similar meaning: KEEP YOUR MOUTH SHUT AND YOUR EYES OPEN.

heated arguments do not warm the fireside See THE ONLY THING A HEATED ARGUMENT EVER PRODUCED IS COOLNESS.

heaven helps those who help themselves See GOD HELPS THOSE WHO HELP THEMSELVES.

heaven protects children, sailors, and drunken men Certain types of people seem to enjoy divine protection; said when a child, sailor, or other person has a miraculous escape from injury or death: "Heaven, they say, protects children, sailors, and drunken men; and whatever answers to Heaven in the academical system protects freshmen" (Thomas Hughes, *Tom Brown at Oxford,* 1861). The quotation is the first recorded use of the proverb.

a heavy purse makes a light heart Those who have plenty of money are happy and carefree: *If only I could sell another of my paintings, all our troubles would be over—a heavy purse makes a light heart.* The proverb was first recorded in 1521 in A. Barclay's *Eclogues.*

Proverb expressing similar meaning: A LIGHT PURSE MAKES A HEAVY HEART.

Proverbs expressing opposite meaning: MONEY CAN'T BUY HAPPINESS; MUCH COIN, MUCH CARE.

he comes too early who brings bad news People are never in a hurry to hear bad news: *I knew they would be less pleased to see me when they heard what I had to say to them—he comes too early who brings bad news.*

Variant of this proverb: bad news always comes too soon.

a hedge between keeps friendship green It is advisable not to become too intimate with friends or neighbors, and to respect each other's privacy, if you want to maintain a good relationship with them: *We meet up for coffee once a month, and phone each other now and then, but most of the time we just get on with living our own lives—a hedge between keeps friendship green.* The proverb was first recorded in 1707 in John Mapletoft's *Select Proverbs.*

Variant of this proverb: a hedge between keeps fellowship green.

Proverb expressing similar meaning: GOOD FENCES MAKE GOOD NEIGHBORS.

he gives twice who gives quickly A prompt response to a request for something, such as money or help, is of greater value than a more generous offering given late: "'He gives twice who gives quickly.' . . . We have everything to gain by generous action at once" (*London Times,* 1980). Of ancient origin, the proverb is sometimes quoted in its Latin form, "*Bis dat qui cito dat.*" Other words, such as *promptly* or *happily,* may be substituted for *quickly.*

he laughs best who laughs last *See* HE WHO LAUGHS LAST, LAUGHS LONGEST.

he lives long who lives well Provided that you live a good life, its actual length is of no significance, whereas a bad life is worthless and wasted; also interpreted literally, with the implication that living well will extend your life span: "He liveth long who liveth well! / All other life is short and vain" (Horatio Bonar, *Hymns of Faith and Hope,* 1861). The proverb was first recorded in 1553 in the form "They lived long enough, that have lived well enough."

Variant of this proverb: he lives longest who lives best.

hell hath no fury like a woman scorned A woman who is rejected by the man she loves has an immense capacity for ferocious or malicious revenge: *Hell hath no fury like a woman scorned—he arrived home from his so-called business trip to find that his jealous wife had burned all his books, poured his vintage wine over the garden, smashed his computer, and emptied their joint account to buy herself a new wardrobe and a one-way ticket to her sister's in England.* In its current form, the proverb comes from William Congreve's play *The Mourning*

Bride (1697): "Heav'n has no rage, like love to hatred turn'd;/Nor Hell a fury, like a woman scorn'd." The sentiment it expresses, however, is of ancient origin: compare Euripides (fifth century B.C.), "a woman . . . when she has been wronged in a matter of sex, there is no other heart more bloodthirsty." The proverb is also applied to other situations where somebody—not necessarily a woman—is treated with disrespect or contempt, as in "Hell hath no fury like a rock star scorned."

Variant of this proverb: hell knows no wrath like a woman scorned.

hell is full of good meanings, but heaven is full of good works *See* THE ROAD TO HELL IS PAVED WITH GOOD INTENTIONS.

help you to salt, help you to sorrow According to popular superstition, it is unlucky to add salt to another person's food at table: "No one would at table spoon salt on to another person's plate, for 'Help you to salt, help you to sorrow'" (Flora Thompson, *Lark Rise to Candleford,* 1945). The proverb was first recorded in 1666, in an Italian proverb collection.

he must have a long spoon who sups with the devil *See* HE WHO SUPS WITH THE DEVIL SHOULD HAVE A LONG SPOON.

he that cannot obey cannot command Those who are unwilling or unable to obey orders are not fit to hold a position of leadership or authority: *His insubordinate behavior made him an unlikely candidate for promotion—his superiors were firmly of the belief that he who cannot obey cannot command.* The proverb was first recorded in this form in 1734, in Benjamin Franklin's *Poor Richard's Almanack,* but the sentiment it expresses is of ancient origin. Compare Seneca (c. 4 B.C.–A.D. 65), "*nemo regere potest nisi qui et regi* [nobody can rule unless he can also be ruled]."

Variant of this proverb: by learning to obey, you will know how to command.

Proverb expressing similar meaning: A GOOD LEADER IS ALSO A GOOD FOLLOWER.

he that complies against his will is of his own opinion still By forcing somebody to do something, or to admit that something is true, you have not actually succeeded in changing that person's mind: *They tried to brainwash me into believing that terrorism was the only possible course of action, and I knew that my life depended on at least pretending to agree with them, but he that complies against his will is of his own opinion still.* The proverb comes from Samuel Butler's poem *Hudibras* (1680): "He that complies against his will,/Is of his own opinion still;/Which he may adhere to, yet disown,/For reasons to himself best known."

he that drinks beer, thinks beer Drinking alcohol affects the way you think and the way you behave; often used with specific reference to the effects of drinking beer as opposed to other alcoholic liquor: *He that drinks beer, thinks beer, and by the end of the fifth pint our conversation had begun to deteriorate accordingly.* The proverb was first recorded in 1820 in W. Irving's *Sketch Book of Geoffrey Crayon.*

he that goes a-borrowing, goes a-sorrowing Borrowing inevitably leads to trouble, as when you find yourself unable to repay a loan; also used to imply that those who try to borrow from others will be disappointed: "Who goes a-borrowing goes a-sorrowing. Yes, the balanced-budget amendment is sort of a dumb idea, because it can so easily be evaded by cunning congressional accounting" (*American Spectator*, 1995). The proverb was first recorded in this form in 1545, but the sentiment it expresses is of earlier origin.

Variant of this proverb: borrowing brings sorrowing.

he that has a choice has trouble   Making a choice is fraught with difficulties—not only do you risk making the wrong decision, but you may also offend somebody by what you reject: *The saying "He that has a choice has trouble" is never more true than when you are faced with two equally undesirable alternatives.*

he that has a full purse never wanted a friend   Wealthy people never lack friends—or those who claim to be their friends until their money runs out: *I soon discovered that he who has a full purse never wanted a friend, and there were plenty of people who were only too anxious to help me, once they knew that they would be amply rewarded for their efforts.*

Proverbs expressing similar meaning: A RICH MAN'S JOKE IS ALWAYS FUNNY; WEALTH MAKES MANY FRIENDS.

he that has an ill name is half hanged   *See* GIVE A DOG A BAD NAME AND HANG HIM.

he that has a wife and children has given hostages to fortune   Family responsibilities can hold a man back in life, for example by discouraging him from taking risks: *It was a tempting opportunity, and one that I would have seized with both hands in my bachelor days, but he that has a wife and children has given hostages to fortune—if the venture failed, all our lives would be ruined.* In its current form, the proverb comes from Francis Bacon's essay "Of Marriage and Single Life" (1612): "He that hath wife and children hath given hostages to fortune; for they are impediments to great enterprises, either of virtue or mischief." A similar sentiment, however, occurs in the writings of the Roman poet Lucan (A.D. 39–65): "*Coniunx est mihi, sunt nati: dedimus tot pignora fatis* [I have a wife, I have sons: all of them hostages given to fate]."

Proverb expressing similar meaning: HE TRAVELS FASTEST THAT TRAVELS ALONE.

he that is born to be hanged shall never be drowned   *See* IF YOU'RE BORN TO BE HANGED, THEN YOU'LL NEVER BE DROWNED.

he that is down need fear no fall   Those in lowly positions, or who have already fallen from lofty positions, have no need to worry about failure: *I had already lost everything I valued—my job, my marriage, my self-respect—so I was prepared to take the risk. He that is down need fear no fall.* The proverb was first recorded in Richard Taverner's *Proverbs* (1539).

he that is too secure is not safe   Beware of complacency—you must remain alert and watchful if you want to avoid danger: *The old proverb "He that is too secure is not safe" has been quoted by critics of the modern trend toward increasingly sophisticated home-security systems and car-safety devices.* The proverb was first recorded in this form in 1732, but the sentiment it expresses is of earlier origin.

Variant of this proverb: the way to be safe is never to feel secure.

he that lives in hope dances to an ill tune It is unwise to let your future happiness or well-being depend on expectations that may not be realized: *She talked excitedly of the bright prospects that lay ahead of her if she passed the audition, but he that lives in hope dances to an ill tune, and I was afraid that she was heading for a major disappointment.* The proverb was first recorded in 1591, in John Florio's *Second Fruits,* in the form "He that dooth liue in hope, dooth dance in narrowe scope."

Variant of this proverb: he that lives in hope dances without music.

he that lives on hope will die fasting Do not pin all your hopes on something you may not attain, because you could end up with nothing: *It's no good just hoping that business will improve—he that lives on hope will die fasting, and you must take action now, by going out and finding some new customers.* The proverb was first recorded in 1616 in the form "Hope will make a man neither eat nor drink."

Variant of this proverb: he that lives on hope has a slender diet.

he that repairs not a part, builds all *See* WHO REPAIRS NOT HIS GUTTERS REPAIRS HIS WHOLE HOUSE.

he that touches pitch shall be defiled If you get involved with wicked people or illegal activities, you cannot avoid becoming corrupted yourself: *I would advise you to steer clear of these people and their dubious affairs, if you want to maintain your spotless reputation—he that touches pitch shall be defiled.* The proverb comes from the Apocrypha: "He that toucheth pitch shall be defiled therewith" (Ecclesiasticus 13:1).

Proverb expressing similar meaning: IF YOU LIE DOWN WITH DOGS, YOU'LL GET UP WITH FLEAS.

Proverb expressing opposite meaning: THE SUN LOSES NOTHING BY SHINING INTO A PUDDLE.

he that waits for dead men's shoes may go a long time barefoot *See* IT'S ILL WAITING FOR DEAD MEN'S SHOES.

he that will not when he may, when he will he may have nay Take advantage of an opportunity when it presents itself, even if you do not want or need it at the time, because it may no longer be available when you do: "'It was a rather pretty little box, just the kind of thing you like. . . .' 'I know,' I said. 'If you will not when you may, when you will you shall have nay'" (Barbara Pym, *A Glass of Blessings,* 1958). The proverb dates from before 1000: W. W. Skeat quotes *Anglo-Saxon Homily* in his *Early English Proverbs.*

Proverb expressing similar meaning: OPPORTUNITY KNOCKS BUT ONCE.

he that will thrive must first ask his wife A married man's financial situation, his success or failure in business, and the like often depend on the behavior and disposition of his wife: "He that would thrive, must ask his wife. It was lucky for me that I had one as much dispos'd to industry and frugality as myself" (Benjamin Franklin, *Autobiography,* 1790). The proverb dates from before 1500: *Songs and Carols* (c. 1470) has: "Fore he that cast hym for to thryve, he must ask off his wiffe leve."

he that would eat the fruit must climb the tree Nothing is achieved without effort: *It takes many years of study and training to become a brain surgeon—there is no easy way. He that would eat the fruit must climb the tree.* The proverb was first recorded in 1721 in James Kelly's *Scottish Proverbs.*

Variant of this proverb: he that would eat the kernel must crack the nut.

he that would go to sea for pleasure would go to hell for a pastime A sailor's life can be so unpleasant and dangerous, it seems that those who choose spend their leisure hours at sea must be either masochistic or insane: "'What made you come to sea anyway?' 'Search me. . . . To amuse myself, I suppose.' 'Well, a man who'd go to sea for fun'd go to hell for a pastime'" (Malcolm Lowry, *Ultramarine*, 1933). The proverb was first recorded in 1899 in A. J. Boyd's *Shellback.*

he that would hang his dog gives out first that he is mad Those who are planning some action that might attract criticism first seek to justify it in advance: *The prime minister's attack on his underling suggests that he plans a reshuffle in the near future, for we all know that he that would hang his dog gives out first that he is mad.* The proverb was first recorded in 1530 in J. Palsgrave's *L'Éclaircissement de la langue française.*

Proverb expressing similar meaning: GIVE A DOG A BAD NAME AND HANG HIM.

he that would have eggs must endure the cackling of hens You must be prepared to put up with something unpleasant or annoying in order to get what you want; also used of an undesirable aspect or drawback that accompanies something you like or enjoy: *I hate my job at the burger bar—the hours are long, the customers are rude, and the pay is lousy—but I need to go on working there if I want to save enough money to go on vacation. As my mother always says, he that would have eggs must endure the cackling of hens.* The proverb was first recorded in 1659.

Proverbs expressing similar meaning: THE CAT WOULD EAT FISH, BUT WOULD NOT WET HER FEET; YOU HAVE TO TAKE THE ROUGH WITH THE SMOOTH.

he that would learn to pray, let him go to sea Sailors face many dangers and life-threatening experiences at sea: *We ran into what was later described as one of the worst storms in living memory, and the proverb "He that would learn to pray, let him go to sea" never seemed more appropriate than in the fifteen terrifying hours that followed.* The proverb was first recorded in this form in 1640 in George Herbert's *Outlandish Proverbs,* but the sentiment it expresses is of earlier origin.

he that would the daughter win, must with the mother first begin If you want to win the affections of a young woman, or persuade her to marry you, it is important to make a favorable impression on her mother: *Her mother likes you, and that's half the battle—mothers have a way of influencing their daughters' choices, directly or indirectly. As the saying goes, "He that would the daughter win, must with the mother first begin."* The proverb was first recorded, with different wording, in 1578 in *Courtly Controversy.*

he travels fastest who travels alone Those who go through life without the encumbrance of family responsibilities make the best progress; also used more literally of companions on a journey: "The reason I can 'do what I do' is because I've never married. He travels fastest who travels alone, and that goes double for she" (Florence King, *Reflections in a Jaundiced Eye,* 1989). The proverb comes from Rudyard Kipling's poem *The Winners* (1888): "Down to Gehenna or up to the Throne, / He travels the fastest who travels alone."

Proverb expressing similar meaning: HE THAT HAS A WIFE AND CHILDREN HAS GIVEN HOSTAGES TO FORTUNE.

Proverb expressing opposite meaning: GOOD COMPANY ON THE ROAD IS THE SHORTEST CUT.

he who begins many things, finishes but few Do not try to work on too many different projects at the same time, or you will end up achieving nothing: *His life's work consists of three great novels, and more than a hundred plot summaries for books that were never written—he who begins many things, finishes but few.* The proverb's first use is recorded in Giovanni Torriano's *A Common Place of Italian Proverbs and Proverbial Phrases* (1666).

he who chases two hares catches neither See IF YOU RUN AFTER TWO HARES, YOU WILL CATCH NEITHER.

he who dances must pay the fiddler See THEY THAT DANCE MUST PAY THE FIDDLER.

he who does not work, neither should he eat Idle people do not deserve to receive charitable handouts—everybody should earn his or her own living: "Conservatives like to cite that ancient Puritan teaching: 'He who does not work, neither should he eat.' But the flip side of that

stern motto should be written in the social contract too: 'He who *does* work, *does* deserve a decent break'" (Barbara Ehrenreich, *Time,* 1991). The proverb is of biblical origin: "Neither did we eat any man's bread for nought; but wrought with labour and travail night and day. . . . For even when we were with you, this we commanded you, that if any would not work, neither should he eat" (2 Thessalonians 3:8–10). It is sometimes quoted in its more succinct Latin form, *"Qui non laborat non manducet."*

Variant of this proverb: if you won't work, you shan't eat.

he who excuses himself accuses himself By making an apology for something, or trying to justify it, or even denying it, you are actually making a confession of guilt: "The tests would be underground, every precaution taken, impossible to contaminate anything. One had heard these pleas before. . . . Who excuses himself accuses himself" (Geoffrey Wagner, *Elegy for Corsica,* 1968). The proverb was first recorded in 1611. It is sometimes quoted in its French form, *"Qui s'excuse, s'accuse."*

Variant of this proverb: who excuses himself accuses himself.

Proverbs expressing similar meaning: ACCUSING THE TIMES IS BUT EXCUSING OURSELVES; NEVER ASK PARDON BEFORE YOU ARE ACCUSED.

he who fights and runs away may live to fight another day It is wiser to withdraw from a situation that you cannot win than to go on fighting and lose—by a strategic retreat you can return to the battle or argument with renewed energy at a later date: *I conceded defeat at that point,* on the basis that *he who fights and runs away may live to fight another day*, but I have every intention of mounting a fresh challenge as soon as I have gathered enough evidence to be sure of success. The proverb was first recorded in 1542, but the sentiment it expresses is of ancient origin: the Greek poet and dramatist Menander (c. 342–292 B.C.) wrote, "A man who flees will fight again." It has given rise to the figurative phrase *to live to fight another day*.

Variant of this proverb: he who fights and runs away may live to fight another day, but he that is in battle slain will never rise to fight again.

Proverbs expressing similar meaning: DISCRETION IS THE BETTER PART OF VALOR; A LIVE DOG IS BETTER THAN A DEAD LION.

he who has a mind to beat a dog will easily find a stick *See* IT'S EASY TO FIND A STICK TO BEAT A DOG.

he who has a tiger by the tail dare not let go *See* HE WHO RIDES A TIGER IS AFRAID TO DISMOUNT.

he who hesitates is lost Do not be too slow to make a decision or take advantage of an opportunity: *You don't have forever to make up your mind—he who hesitates is lost, and if you don't put in an offer for the house soon, somebody else will buy it.* The proverb was first recorded in 1713 in the form "The woman that deliberates is lost" in Joseph Addison's *Cato.*

Proverb expressing similar meaning: DELAYS ARE DANGEROUS.

Proverb expressing opposite meaning: LOOK BEFORE YOU LEAP.

he who is absent is always in the wrong It is easy to accuse or attack those who are not present to defend themselves or their rights or arguments: "I will quote first that fine old French saying—which covers any claim Charlie may or may not have on that cake—'he who is absent is always in the wrong'" (Anthony Price, *Soldier No More,* 1981). The French saying referred to in this quotation is *"Les absents ont toujours tort."* The proverb was first recorded in English in 1640 in the form "The absent party is still faulty."

Variants of this proverb: the absent are always in the wrong; the absent are never without fault nor the present without excuse.

he who is good at making excuses is seldom good at anything else Worthless or incapable people are constantly making excuses to cover up for their shortcomings: *They always have a plausible explanation for their failure to deliver, but I put it down to sheer incompetence—he who is good at making excuses is seldom good at anything else.*

he who laughs last, laughs longest Minor successes or failures along the way are of no significance—the person who is ultimately triumphant is the only real winner; often used when somebody turns the tables with a final act of retaliation: *Their celebrations are somewhat premature—I still have one more trick up my sleeve, and he who laughs last, laughs longest.* The proverb was first recorded c. 1607 in the form "Hee laugheth best that laugheth to the end" (*The Christmas Prince*). Facetious variants include "He who laughs last didn't get the point anyway" and "He who laughs last is probably an Englishman." The proverb has given rise to the figurative phrase *to have the last laugh.*

Variants of this proverb: he who laughs last, laughs best; he laughs best who laughs last.

Proverb expressing similar meaning: LET THEM LAUGH THAT WIN.

he who lives by the sword dies by the sword Those who engage in aggression or violence will meet their death in a similar way. The proverb is of biblical origin: "Put up again thy sword into his place: for all they that take the sword shall perish with the sword" (Matthew 26:52). Other words may be substituted for *sword,* as in the following quotations: "When you live by the gun you die by the gun" (*Washington Post,* 1997) and "Live by the torch, die by the torch" (Stephen King, *The Stand,* 1978).

Variants of this proverb: he who lives by the sword shall perish by the sword; live by the sword, die by the sword.

he who never made a mistake never made anything *See* IF YOU DON'T MAKE MISTAKES YOU DON'T MAKE ANYTHING.

he who pays the piper calls the tune The person who pays for a service or finances a project has the right to say how it should be done: *The kitchen layout that our customers had specified did not—in our professional opinion—make best use of the space, but he that pays the piper calls the tune, so we gave them what they wanted.* First recorded in 1779 in *Diary of Grace Galloway,* the proverb has given rise to the figurative phrase *to call the tune,* meaning "to be in control."

Proverb expressing similar meaning: WHOSE BREAD I EAT, HIS SONG I SING.

he who rides a tiger is afraid to dismount When you are in a dangerous situation, or have embarked on a dangerous course of action, it is often safer to continue than to try to stop or withdraw: *I knew that what I was doing was illegal, but he who rides a tiger is afraid to dismount, and the possible consequences of pulling out of the deal at this late stage didn't bear thinking about.* Of Chinese origin, the proverb was first recorded in English in 1875 in W. Scarborough's *Collection of Chinese Proverbs.*

Variants of this proverb: he who rides the tiger can never dismount; He who has a tiger by the tail dare not let go.

he who sups with the devil should have a long spoon Those who have dealings with wicked, dangerous, or dishonest people should remain on their guard and try not to become too intimately involved: "Hindenburg and the army thought they could use [Hitler]. . . . Who sups with the devil needs a long spoon" (Evelyn Anthony, *The Grave of Truth,* 1979). The proverb was first recorded, with different wording, in Chaucer's *Canterbury Tales* (c. 1390). It occurs in Shakespeare's play *The Comedy of Errors* (4:3), "He must have a long spoon that must eat with the devil."

Variant of this proverb: he must have a long spoon who sups with the devil.

he who wills the end, wills the means Those who are determined to achieve something are equally determined to find a way of achieving it: *Finding his daughter in the vast and unfamiliar city seemed an impossible task, but somehow he succeeded—he who wills the end, wills the means.* The proverb was first recorded in 1692, but with the implication that it was already in general use.

Proverb expressing similar meaning: WHERE THERE'S A WILL THERE'S A WAY.

he who would climb the ladder must begin at the bottom You must start from a lowly position and rise through the ranks if you want to attain a position of high status or authority: "I was the lowest of the four in rank—but what then?—he that climbs a ladder must begin at the first round" (Sir Walter Scott, *Kenilworth,* 1821). The proverb was first recorded in 1710 in S. Palmer's *Moral Essays on some of the most Curious and Significant English, Scotch and Foreign Proverbs.*

he who would wish to thrive, must let spiders run alive *See* IF YOU WANT TO LIVE AND THRIVE, LET THE SPIDER RUN ALIVE.

he who would write and can't write can surely review People who become critics are those who lack the talent to be novelists, dramatists, or other kinds of artists in their own right; used in response to a bad review: *Asked to comment on the damning criticism of her book in the press, she simply shrugged her shoulders and said, "He who would write and can't write can surely review."* The proverb was first recorded in 1848, in James Russell Lowell's *A Fable for Critics.* Similar sentiments have been expressed by others: in 1870, Benjamin Disraeli wrote, "You know who the critics are? The men who have failed in literature and art."

the higher the monkey climbs the more he shows his tail People's faults and shortcomings become increasingly obvious as they advance to positions of high office: *He was patently unsuited to such a responsible post, but was promoted nonetheless, and the current debacle in his department is proof of the saying that the higher the monkey* climbs the more he shows his tail. The proverb was first recorded, in rather more graphic form, as an explanatory note in John Wycliffe's translation of the Bible (c. 1395): "the filthe of the hynd partis of an ape aperith more, whanne he stieth [climbs] on high." In modern usage the word *ass* is sometimes substituted for *tail.*

the higher the tree, the sweeter the plum The best fruit is found at the top of the tree: *The salaries are biggest at the top of the ladder; as the saying goes, the higher the tree, the sweeter the plum.* The proverb was first recorded in 1659 in J. Howell's *Paroemiographia.*

the highest branch is not the safest roost Those in the highest positions of power or authority are, in some respects, the most vulnerable, because there will always be plenty of others eager to take their place or cause their downfall: *I am happy in my work, and have no ambitions for further advancement—the highest branch is not the safest roost.* The proverb was first recorded, with different wording, in 1563 in *Mirror for Magistrates.*

Proverbs expressing similar meaning: THE POST OF HONOR IS THE POST OF DANGER; UNEASY LIES THE HEAD THAT WEARS A CROWN.

Proverb expressing opposite meaning: BETTER BE FIRST IN A VILLAGE THAN SECOND AT ROME.

history doesn't repeat itself—historians do *See* HISTORY REPEATS ITSELF.

history is a fable agreed upon History represents the traditionally accepted interpretation of what actually happened in the past: *It is said that history is a fable agreed upon, but there seems to be a distinct lack of agreement among modern historians on some of the more controversial issues and events of the 20th century.* The proverb was first recorded in 1948 in a U.S. proverb collection.

history repeats itself   Similar events tend to recur in different periods of history—for example, when rulers or governments fail to learn from the mistakes of those who have gone before; also used when some more trivial or personal incident recurs: "That age has passed away for ever. History repeats itself, it is true, but history will not bear mimicry" (Augustus Jessopp, *The Coming of the Friars,* 1885). The proverb was first recorded in this form in George Eliot's *Scenes of Clerical Life* (1858), but the sentiment it expresses is of ancient origin, occurring in the writings of the Greek historian Thucydides (fifth century B.C.). In 1852, in *The Eighteenth Brumaire of Louis Bonaparte,* Karl Marx wrote, "Hegel says somewhere that all great events and personalities in world history reappear in one fashion or another. He forgot to add: the first time as tragedy, the second as farce."

Variant of this proverb: history doesn't repeat itself—historians do.

Proverb expressing similar meaning: THE MORE THINGS CHANGE, THE MORE THEY STAY THE SAME.

hitch your wagon to a star   You must be ambitious, and aim to achieve the highest possible goal; also used as advice to cultivate the acquaintance of powerful, successful, or influential people who can help to advance your interests: *"Hitch your wagon to a star" is one of the unofficial mottoes of the college, which has a reputation for* encouraging students of all abilities to fulfill their potential. The proverb comes from Ralph Waldo Emerson's essay "Civilization," in *Society and Solitude* (1870).

hoist your sail when the wind is fair   Take advantage of favorable conditions or circumstances while they last: *The market is very volatile, and things could change at any moment, so hoist your sail when the wind is fair and buy now!* The proverb was first recorded in 1583 in Melbancke's *Philotimus.*

Variant of this proverb: hoist up the sail while the gale does last.

Proverbs expressing similar meaning: MAKE HAY WHILE THE SUN SHINES; STRIKE WHILE THE IRON IS HOT.

the hole calls the thief   Criminals and other wrong-doers will go where opportunity presents itself: *The police knew very well that the hole calls the thief and that was the place to lay their trap.* The proverb was first recorded in 1640 by George Herbert in *Outlandish Proverbs.*

Proverb expressing similar meaning: OPPORTUNITY MAKES A THIEF.

home is home, be it ever so homely However simple or lowly a person's abode may be, it is still his or her home and therefore the best place to be: *On international business trips I've stayed in some of the best hotels in the world, but I'm always glad to get back to my own little apartment—home is home, be it ever so homely.* The proverb was first recorded in 1546 in the form "Home is homely, though it be poor in sight." A similar sentiment is expressed in the song "Home, Sweet Home" (1823) by J. H. Payne: "Be it ever so humble, there's no place like home."

Variant of this proverb: home is home though it's never so homely.

Proverbs expressing similar meaning: EAST, WEST, HOME'S BEST; THERE'S NO PLACE LIKE HOME.

home is where the heart is   Home is the place where you are happiest, or where the people you love are: "They entertained several times a year, they went out to departmental parties from time to time, but these things did not interest Sulka much. Home was where her heart was" (Colette Dowling, *The Cinderella Complex,* 1981). The proverb was first recorded in 1870, but the sentiment it expresses is of ancient origin. Other words may be substituted for *heart,* and a facetious variant of the proverb is "Home is where the mortgage is."

home is where you hang your hat   Home is the place where you are currently living, to which you return at the end of the working day: *People keep asking me if I'm going home for Thanksgiving—meaning back to my parent's house in the country. As far as I'm concerned, home is where you hang your hat, and for me that's New York City.* The proverb was first recorded in 1930 in Fletcher's *Green Rope.*

Homer sometimes nods   Even the greatest minds have lapses of attention, leading to mistakes; often used as an excuse for error: "Scientific reason, like Homer, sometimes nods" (T. H. Huxley, *Nineteenth Century,* 1887). The proverb originated in the writings of the Roman poet Horace (65–8 B.C.): "*Indignor quandoque bonus dormitat Homerus* [I am indignant when the worthy Homer nods]."

Variant of this proverb: even Homer sometimes nods.

Proverbs expressing similar meaning: NOBODY IS INFALLIBLE; TO ERR IS HUMAN, TO FORGIVE DIVINE.

an honest look covereth many faults   An innocent demeanor may hide much guilt: *No one suspected that such a guileless child could have done such a thing, but an honest look covereth many faults.* The proverb was first recorded in 1642 in G. Torriano's *Select Italian Proverbs.*

Variant of this proverb: an honest good look covereth many faults.

an honest man's word is as good as his bond   *See* A MAN'S WORD IS AS GOOD AS HIS BOND.

honest men marry quickly, wise men not at all   Honest men marry without hesitation, seeing no threat in a wife, but wise men know better. The proverb was first recorded by James Howell in his 1645–55 publication *Epistolae Ho-Elianae: or Familiar Letters:* "Honest men use to marry, but wise men not."

honesty is more praised than practiced   Many people say that honesty is important, but few are always scrupulously honest themselves: *The latest revelations from the White House suggest that the saying "Honesty is more praised than practiced" is nowhere more applicable than in the world of politics.*

honesty is the best policy   Being honest or telling the truth is always the wisest course of action, although it is often not the easiest or most attractive option: "I am afraid we must make the world honest before we can honestly say to our children that honesty is the best policy" (Radio address by George Bernard Shaw, 1932). The proverb was first recorded in 1605. In his *Apophthegms* (1854), the English politician, philosopher, and theologian Richard Whately wrote, "Honesty is the best policy; but he who is governed by that maxim is not an honest man."

Variant of this proverb: honesty is the best policy, though it may not pay the largest dividends.

Proverbs expressing similar meaning: CHEATERS NEVER PROSPER; HONESTY PAYS.

honesty pays You will ultimately reap the benefits of being honest, although these are not always immediately obvious: *It took a lot of courage to own up to my mistake, but honesty pays—if only by relieving the burden of guilt that I have been carrying around for the past few days.* The proverb was first recorded in 1876 in W. G. Nash *New England Life.*

Proverbs expressing similar meaning: CHEATERS NEVER PROSPER; HONESTY IS THE BEST POLICY.

honey catches more flies than vinegar *See* YOU CAN CATCH MORE FLIES WITH HONEY THAN WITH VINEGAR.

honors change manners People who improve their status in society all too often become arrogant: "How I have offended the Lord of Lindesay I know not, unless honours have changed manners" (Walter Scott, *The Abbot*, 1820). The proverb was first recorded in English c. 1430 by John Lydgate in *Chaucer* but is Roman in origin.

Scottish variant of this proverb: lordships change manners.

the hook without bait catches no fish If you want to tempt or persuade people, you need to offer them something attractive as an incentive: *The company believes that the hook without bait catches no fish, and the first thousand customers to sign up for a loan will enjoy significantly reduced interest rates for the first twelve months.* The proverb is recorded as a regional expression in the United States.

hope and have If a person wants something badly enough he or she is likely to achieve it: "Hope and have, in time a man may gaine any woman" (A. Fraunce in *English Parnassus*, 1913). The proverb was first recorded 1540 in J. Palsgrave's *Acolastus*.

Variant of this proverb: hope well and have well.

Proverb expressing opposite meaning: HOPE FOR THE BEST AND PREPARE FOR THE WORST.

hope deferred makes the heart sick Delay in getting what you desire, or in learning whether or not your hopes are to be realized, is a cause of great anxiety and distress: *Hope deferred makes the heart sick, and after waiting in vain for promotion for more than ten years he finally left the army, a bitter and disillusioned man.* The proverb is of biblical origin: "Hope deferred maketh the heart sick: but when the desire cometh, it is a tree of life" (Proverbs 13:12).

hope for the best and prepare for the worst Remain optimistic, but make sure that you are mentally or physically prepared to cope with failure or disaster: "The youngest of us cannot always escape—hoping, trusting, relying on the best, we should be prepared for the worst" (Edward Howard, *Rattlin the Reefer,* 1836). The proverb was first recorded, with different wording, in 1565.

Proverb expressing similar meaning: PUT YOUR TRUST IN GOD, AND KEEP YOUR POWDER DRY.

Proverb expressing opposite meaning: HOPE AND HAVE.

hope is a good breakfast but a bad supper   There is no harm in being optimistic at the beginning of something, but beware of being left with nothing but unrealized expectations at the end: *Hope is a good breakfast but a bad supper, and when darkness forced them to abandon their efforts to find the missing child, the morale of the search party was at its lowest ebb.* The proverb was first recorded in 1625 in Francis Bacon's *Apophthegms.*

hope keeps the heart from breaking   *See* IF IT WERE NOT FOR HOPE, THE HEART WOULD BREAK.

hope springs eternal in the human breast   It is human nature to remain optimistic—even after a setback, or despite evidence to the contrary: "Night after night his disappointment is acute, but hope springs eternal in the scholastic breast" (Charles Dickens, *Our Mutual Friend,* 1865). The proverb comes from Alexander Pope's *Essay on Man* (1732): "Hope springs eternal in the human breast: / Man never Is, but always To be blest." It is often shortened to "Hope springs eternal."

hope well and have well   *See* HOPE AND HAVE.

a horse can't pull while kicking   People engaged in acts of insubordination or protest cannot work efficiently or productively: *There is no room in this organization for anybody who refuses to toe the line—a horse can't pull while kicking.* The proverb is recorded as a regional expression in the United States.

horses for courses   Different people have different strengths and talents, and each person should be assigned to the task or job that is best suited to that particular individual: "Horses for courses is a sound adage in motoring as well as the turf, and few British motorists would look to Czechoslovakia for their car" (*Daily Telegraph,* 1972). The proverb was first recorded in 1891 (A. E. T. Watson, *Turf*) in a horse-racing context, with the implication that it was already in frequent use in that context.

hot love is soon cold   Passions that arise suddenly are liable to subside equally quickly: "I hope that such hot love cannot be so soone colde" (John Lyly, *Euphues: The Anatomy of Wit,* 1578). The proverb was first recorded in 1537 in R. Whitford's *Werke for Householders.*

an hour in the morning is worth two in the evening   People are at their most efficient early in the day, when they are refreshed by sleep: *When it comes to preparing for exams, students would do well to remember the saying "An hour in the morning is worth two in the evening."* The proverb was first recorded in 1827 in William Hone's *Every-Day Book.*

Variant of this proverb: an hour before breakfast is worth two the rest of the day.

Proverb expressing similar meaning: LOSE AND HOUR IN THE MORNING, CHASE IT ALL DAY.

a house divided against itself cannot stand   The members of a group must remain united if the group is to succeed or survive; sometimes used to warn against dissension: "'A house divided against itself cannot stand.' I believe this government cannot endure, permanently half slave and half free" (Speech by Abraham Lincoln, 1858). The proverb is of biblical origin: "Every kingdom divided against itself is brought to desolation; and every city or house divided against itself shall not stand" (Matthew 12:25); "If a house be divided against itself, that house cannot stand" (Mark 3:25).

Proverbs expressing similar meaning: DIVIDE AND CONQUER; UNITED WE STAND, DIVIDED WE FALL.

the house shows the owner A person's character is revealed by the state of his or her house: *The house was disturbingly tidy, but, as they say, the house shows the owner.* The proverb was first recorded in 1611 by Randle Cotgrave in *A Dictionary of the French and English Tongues.*

a house without books is like a room without windows Books brighten and enlighten our daily lives in the same way that windows brighten and illuminate a room: *If it is true that a house without books is like a room without windows, then my uncle's house must be the darkest place on earth—the only reading matter to be found there was on the cans and boxes in the pantry!*

humble hearts have humble desires People with timid characters tend to have modest ambitions: *Humble hearts have humble desires, but surely no one could be content with such meagre rewards.* The proverb was first recorded in 1640 by George Herbert in *Outlandish Proverbs.*

hunger drives the wolf out of the wood People in dire need are forced to do things that would be unwise or undesirable in other circumstances: "'He says he doesn't want anything to eat,' answered Nanon; 'that's not good for him.' 'So much saved,' retorted her master. 'That's so,' she said. 'Bah! he won't cry long. Hunger drives the wolves out of the woods'" (Honoré de Balzac, *Eugenie Grandet,* 1833). The proverb was first recorded in English in the late 15th century, but there is evidence of a French version in the early 14th century.

hunger is the best sauce Hunger makes all food taste good, regardless of its quality or the way it is served: *We were starving after our long walk, and nobody complained about my cooking that night—hunger is the best sauce!* The proverb was first recorded in 1530, but the sentiment it expresses is of ancient origin. Compare Cicero (106–43 B.C.): "*cibi condimentum esse famem* [hunger is the spice of food]."

Variant of this proverb: hunger is the best pickle.

hungry bellies have no ears *See* A HUNGRY STOMACH HAS NO EARS.

a hungry man is an angry man Hunger makes people angry, often dangerously so: *The strikers and their families were starving, and a hungry man is an angry man, so we took care not to provoke them.* The proverb was first recorded c. 1641 in David Fergusson's *Scottish Proverbs.*

a hungry stomach has no ears There is no point in talking to or reasoning with hungry people, or those who are greedily devouring their food: *You're wasting* *your breath—these people are starving, and a hungry stomach has no ears.* The proverb was first recorded c. 1770 in W. Hubbard's *General History of New England.*

Variant of this proverb: hungry bellies have no ears.

hurry no man's cattle Do not try to make others hurry or rush because you are impatient: "I knew that in due time he would tell me the result of these mental exercises; in the meantime I stood by the old adage—hurry no man's cattle" (J. S. Fletcher, *Murder of the Ninth Baronet,* 1932). The proverb was first recorded in 1822 in Sir Walter Scott's *The Pirate.*

Variant of this proverb: don't rush the cattle.

the husband is always the last to know When a wife is unfaithful to her husband, he is always the last person to find out about it; also used in other similar situations: *He was devastated to learn that his wife was having an affair, and even more upset when he discovered that most of their friends had known about it for months—as they say, the husband is always the last to know.* The proverb was first recorded in 1604. The word *wife* may be substituted for *husband,* as in Margaret Mitchell's *Gone with the Wind* (1936): "'I thought surely the whole town knew by now. Perhaps they all do, except you. You know the old adage: 'The wife is always the last one to find out.'"

Variant of this proverb: the husband is always the last to find out.

i

an idle brain is the devil's work-shop Those who do not have worth-while or constructive things to think about may turn their minds to mischief or crime: "Steady employment . . . keeps one out of mischief, for truly an idle brain is the devil's workshop" (Samuel Smiles, *Self-Help,* 1859). The proverb dates from before 1602 in W. Perkins's *Treatise of Callings.*

Proverbs expressing similar mean-ing: THE DEVIL FINDS WORK FOR IDLE HANDS TO DO; IDLENESS IS THE ROOT OF ALL EVIL.

idleness is the root of all evil A lack of useful things to do is the cause of much crime and wrongdoing: "'The boy will be idle there,' said Miss Murdstone . . . 'and idleness is the root of all evil'" (Charles Dickens, *David Copperfield,* 1850). The proverb was first recorded in 1422, in the form "Idleness is the root of vices," but the sentiment it expresses is of earlier origin, and has been attributed to Saint Bernard (1090–1153). Its current form first occurs in George Farquhar's play *The Beaux' Strata-gem* (1707), and it was probably influenced by the biblical quotation "the love of money is the root of all evil" (1 Timothy 6:10).

Variant of this proverb: idleness is the mother of all the vices.

Proverbs expressing similar mean-ing: THE DEVIL FINDS WORK FOR IDLE HANDS TO DO; AN IDLE BRAIN IS THE DEVIL'S WORKSHOP.

idle people have the least leisure Peo-ple who are naturally disinclined to work always claim to be far too busy to do what is requested of them; also interpreted more literally, with the implication that those who are slow and lazy in their work have little or no spare time for leisure: *He sits in his office all day—doing very little, as far as we can tell—but when the shop gets busy he says he has no time to help. As they say, idle people have the least leisure.* The proverb was first recorded in 1678 in the form "Idle folks have the most labor."

Variant of this proverb: idle people lack no excuses.

Proverb expressing similar mean-ing: THE BUSIEST MEN HAVE THE MOST LEISURE.

an idle youth, a needy age People who do not work hard when they are young will have nothing set aside for when they are old. The proverb was first recorded in 1611 in Randle Cotgrave's *A Dictionary of the French and English Tongues.*

Variant of this proverb: be not idle and you shall not be longing.

if a job's worth doing, it's worth doing well *See* IF A THING'S WORTH DOING, IT'S WORTH DOING WELL.

if and an spoils many a good charter Excellent plans may be doomed to failure because of the conditions that come with them: "Then he came with his If's and And's" (Samuel Richardson, *Clarissa*, 1748). The proverb was recorded, c. 1535, by Sir Thomas More: "what quod the protectour thou servest me I wene with iffes and with andes."

if anything can go wrong, it will If there is the remotest possibility of failure or disaster, you can be sure that it will happen; often used of a minor detail, overlooked in planning, that has a major detrimental effect: *If anything can go wrong, it will—as the bride walked down the hall, ready to set off for the church, the dog bounded in from the garden, leaped up to greet her, and planted its muddy paws on the bodice of her snow-white wedding dress.* First recorded in this form in 1956, the proverb is popularly known as Murphy's Law, allegedly named for the aircraft engineer Captain Edward E. Murphy and coined by one of his colleagues in 1949. It has a number of facetious corollaries—for example, "Of the things that can't go wrong, some will" and "If two or more things can go wrong, the one that will go wrong first is the one that will cause the most damage."

Proverb expressing similar meaning: BREAD ALWAYS FALLS BUTTERED SIDE DOWN.

if a pig had wings, it might fly Some things are not just improbable, but downright impossible; said to somebody who puts forward such a suggestion: "'So, except for the crew, we'd keep her [the submarine] . . .' 'Yes, if we could hide her. And if a pig had wings, it could fly'" (Tom Clancy, *The Hunt for Red October,* 1984). The proverb was first recorded, with different wording, in 1862, by A. Hislop in *The Proverbs of Scotland.*

Variants of this proverb: pigs may fly, but they are very unlikely birds; if frogs had wings, they wouldn't bump their tails on rocks.

Proverbs expressing similar meaning: IF IFS AND ANS WERE POTS AND PANS, THERE'D BE NO WORK FOR TINKERS; IF WISHES WERE HORSES, BEGGARS WOULD RIDE; IF THE SKY FALLS, WE SHALL CATCH LARKS.

if at first you don't succeed, try, try again Do not be discouraged by failure, and never give up—if you keep trying you will ultimately enjoy success: *Their motto is "If at first you don't succeed, try, try again"—this is their third attempt to break the record for nonstop circumnavigation of the globe.* The proverb comes from a rhyme first recorded in Thomas H. Palmer's *Teacher's Manual* (1840): "'Tis a lesson you should heed,/Try, try again./If at first you don't succeed,/Try, try again."

Proverb expressing similar meaning: THE THIRD TIME IS THE CHARM.

if a thing's worth doing, it's worth doing well Always make your best effort, and do not be content with what is merely adequate: *"If a thing's worth doing, it's worth doing well" is certainly Bob's motto—and you've never seen such a thorough and meticulous young man.* The proverb comes from a letter written by Lord Chesterfield in 1746: "In truth, whatever is worth doing at all is worth doing well."

Variants of this proverb: anything worth doing is worth doing well; if a job's worth doing, it's worth doing well.

Proverbs expressing similar meaning: THE GOOD IS THE ENEMY OF THE BEST; NEVER DO THINGS BY HALVES.

Proverb expressing opposite meaning: THE BEST IS THE ENEMY OF THE GOOD.

if every man would sweep his own doorstep, the city would soon be clean If people made an effort to improve their own behavior, instead of criticizing other people's, the world would be a better place: "It appears to be hard to draw a clear distinction between deciding a question of right and wrong for one's self and deciding it for others. . . . 'If every man would sweep his own doorstep the city would soon be clean'" (*London Times*, 1930). The proverb was first recorded in this form in 1666, in an Italian proverb collection, but the sentiment it expresses is of earlier origin.

Proverb expressing similar meaning: SWEEP YOUR OWN DOORSTEP CLEAN.

if frogs had wings, they wouldn't bump their tails on rocks *See* IF A PIG HAD WINGS, IT MIGHT FLY.

if God did not exist, it would be necessary to invent him People have an innate need to believe in a divine creator who controls their destinies: *Any attempt to abolish religion is doomed to failure—if God did not exist, it would be necessary to invent him.* In its current form, the proverb comes from the writings of the French philosopher Voltaire (1694–1778): "*Si Dieu n'existait pas, il faudrait l'inventer.*" The sentiment it expresses, however, is of ancient origin:

compare Ovid (43 B.C.–A.D. 18), "*Expedit esse deos, et, ut expedit, esse putemus* [It is convenient that there be gods, and, as it is convenient, let us believe that there are]." In modern usage of the proverb, the name of some other indispensable person or thing is often substituted for *God.*

Variant of this proverb: if there were no God, it would be necessary to invent him.

if ifs and ans were pots and pans, there'd be no work for tinkers We must be realistic, and not talk about things—however desirable—that are unlikely to happen; said to somebody who makes a statement prefaced by "if": *"If the weather clears up before lunchtime, and if Jack has managed to fix my car by then, we could drive to the coast this afternoon." "If ifs and ans were pots and pans, there'd be no work for tinkers."* The word *ans* (or *ands*) is an archaic word meaning "ifs."

Proverbs expressing similar meaning: IF A PIG HAD WINGS, IT MIGHT FLY; IF WISHES WERE HORSES, BEGGARS WOULD RIDE; IF THE SKY FALLS, WE SHALL CATCH LARKS.

if it ain't broke, don't fix it Do not try to improve on something that is already working well: "If your version of Windows 98 works fine and does what you want then there is no real reason to upgrade. . . . The . . . adage applies: If it ain't broke, don't fix it" (*Guardian,* 2001). The proverb was first recorded in 1977, popularized by Bert Lance, director of the Office of Management and Budget in President Jimmy Carter's administration.

Proverb expressing similar meaning: LEAVE WELL ENOUGH ALONE.

if it looks like a duck, walks like a duck, and quacks like a duck, it's a duck It is usually safe to identify somebody as a particular type of person when his or her appearance, behavior, and words all point to the same conclusion: *If it looks like a duck, walks like a duck, and quacks like a duck, it's a duck—everything about my son's new girlfriend suggested that she was not the innocent, chaste young lady she claimed to be.* Of U.S. origin, the proverb dates from the 1950s and was originally applied to suspected communists.

Proverb expressing opposite meaning: APPEARANCES ARE DECEIVING.

if it takes two to make a bargain, it takes two to break it *See* IT TAKES TWO TO MAKE A BARGAIN.

if it were not for hope, the heart would break You must cling to hope when you have nothing else, because the alternative is despair: "No harm in hoping, Jack! My uncle says, Were it not for hope, the heart would break" (Samuel Richardson, *Clarissa,* 1748). The proverb dates from before 1250.

Variant of this proverb: hope keeps the heart from breaking.

if one sheep leaps over the ditch, all the rest will follow Where one person sets an example by doing something risky or dangerous others are likely to follow: "One sheep will leap the ditch when another goes first" (Walter Scott, *Old Mortality,* 1816).

if the blind lead the blind, both shall fall into the ditch When ignorant or inexperienced people are guided by those no more knowledgeable than themselves, the result is disaster: *The instructors were unfamiliar with some of the equipment they were training us to use, so accidents seemed inevitable—if the blind lead the blind, both shall fall into the ditch.* The proverb is of biblical origin: "Let them alone: they be blind leaders of the blind. And if the blind lead the blind, both shall fall into the ditch" (Matthew 15:14). It has given rise to the cliché *the blind leading the blind.*

if the cap fits, wear it *See* IF THE SHOE FITS, WEAR IT.

if the mountain will not come to Mohammed, Mohammed must go to the mountain If you cannot get what you want, you must adjust yourself to the circumstances or adopt a different approach: *They ignored our petition, and refused to send a representative to our protest meeting, so we marched en masse to their headquarters to put our case against the proposed development—if the mountain will not come to Mohammed, Mohammed must go to the mountain.* The proverb comes from a story about the prophet Mohammed, the founder of Islam, related in Francis Bacon's essay "Of Boldnesse" (1597).

if there were no clouds, we shouldn't enjoy the sun We cannot fully appreciate the good things in life unless they are interspersed with bad times: *Life could be better at the moment, but I mustn't grumble—if there were no clouds, we shouldn't enjoy the sun.*

if there were no God, it would be necessary to invent him *See* IF GOD DID NOT EXIST, IT WOULD BE NECESSARY TO INVENT HIM.

135

if there were no receivers, there would be no thieves Those who assist wrong-doers indirectly by enabling them to profit from their crimes are equally guilty: *Readers are hungry for stories about other people's private lives, however unscrupulously they may be obtained, so the editors of these publications should not take all the blame—if there were no receivers, there would be no thieves.* The proverb was first recorded in 1546, but the sentiment it expresses is of earlier origin, occurring in Chaucer's *Canterbury Tales* (c. 1390).

Variant of this proverb: the receiver is as bad as the thief.

if the shoe fits, wear it If it seems that a critical remark applies to you, then you must accept it; often said when somebody's response to a general remark suggests that it is appropriate to that particular person: "'You mean me? Are you callin me a son of a bitch?' 'If the shoe fits, friend, you wear it'" (James Jones, *From Here to Eternity*, 1951). The proverb was first recorded in this form in 1773. A facetious variant is "If the shoe fits, it isn't on sale."

Variant of this proverb: if the cap fits, wear it.

if the sky falls, we shall catch larks Do not make plans based on things that cannot possibly happen: *"If I could convince the committee that the project has educational value, they might give us the funding we need." "And if the sky falls, we shall catch larks."* The proverb was first recorded in c. 1445.

Proverbs expressing similar meaning: IF A PIG HAD WINGS, IT MIGHT FLY; IF IFS AND ANS WERE POTS AND PANS, THERE'D BE NO WORK FOR TINKERS; IF WISHES WERE HORSES, BEGGARS WOULD RIDE.

if two ride on a horse, one must ride behind When two people undertake a joint activity or enterprise, one of them invariably takes the lead and the other has to be content with a more subordinate role; also used of a fight or argument, where only one can win and the other must lose or surrender: "Collaboration on a book is an awkward business. If two people ride one horse, one of them must ride behind" (Anna Clarke, *The Mystery Lady,* 1986). The proverb was first recorded in Shakespeare's play *Much Ado about Nothing* (3:5), "An two men ride of a horse, one must ride behind."

Variant of this proverb: when two ride one horse, one must sit behind.

if wind blows on you through a hole, say your prayers and mind your soul It is not good for your health to be in a drafty place: *My aunt liked to sit in the corner of the room, far from any half-open doors or windows. "If wind blows on you through a hole, say your prayers and mind your soul,"* she used to say. The proverb was first recorded in 1736 in *Papers of Benjamin Franklin.*

if wishes were horses, beggars would ride There is no point in indulging in wishful thinking: "I agree that she'd be an ideal wife . . . but if wishes were horses, then beggars would ride" (Mary Scott, *The White Elephant,* 1959). The proverb dates from before 1628 in the form "If wishes were horses, poor men would ride."

Proverbs expressing similar meaning: IF A PIG HAD WINGS, IT MIGHT FLY; IF IFS AND ANS WERE POTS AND PANS, THERE'D BE NO WORK FOR TINKERS; IF THE SKY FALLS, WE SHALL CATCH LARKS; WISHES WON'T WASH DISHES.

if you can't beat 'em, join 'em   If you cannot defeat your rivals or opponents, it may be expedient to form an alliance with them; alternatively, if you can't stop people doing something you object to, you might as well start doing it yourself: *Our competitors initially condemned our business methods as unscrupulous, but when we began to dominate the market they were forced to follow suit, on the basis of the saying "If you can't beat 'em, join 'em."* The proverb was first recorded, in its variant form, in 1941, but with the implication that it had long been in use as a political adage.

Variant of this proverb: if you can't lick 'em, join 'em.

if you can't be good, be careful   If you are tempted to do something immoral or illegal, take care not to land yourself in trouble by being caught or found out—specifically, if you are going to engage in casual sex, use a contraceptive. It is said jocularly as part of a good-bye: "Always bear in mind what the country mother said to her daughter who was coming up to town to be apprenticed to the Bond Street milliner, 'For heaven's sake be good; but if you can't be good, be careful'" (Arthur M. Binstead, *Pitcher in Paradise,* 1903). The quotation is the first recorded use of the proverb. The sentiment it expresses, however, is of ancient origin: compare the 11th-century Latin proverb "*Si non caste, tamen caute* [If not chastely, nevertheless cautiously]."

if you can't bite, never show your teeth   Do not make empty threats; also used to warn against making a show of aggression when you unable to defend yourself: *If you can't bite, never show your teeth—they know you have no legal grounds*

for evicting them, and they will laugh in your face if you threaten to do so. The proverb was first recorded in 1615 by J. Chamberlain.

Variant of this proverb: never show your teeth unless you can bite.

if you can't lick 'em, join 'em   *See* IF YOU CAN'T BEAT 'EM, JOIN 'EM.

if you can't run with the big dogs, stay under the porch   If you lack the strength, courage, skill, or experience to compete with the major players—in politics, business, or any other field—then it is better not to try at all: "Signaling that he was primed for battle, Mr. Bush closed with these words: 'So you tell Governor Clinton and that Congress, "If you can't run with the big dogs, stay under the porch"'" (*New York Times,* 1992).

if you can't stand the heat, get out of the kitchen   If you cannot cope with the pace or stress, as in a competitive industry or in a position of high office, then you should leave or resign: "If you can't stand the heat, get out of the kitchen. That's what tough-talking politicians say, making it sound as though only a wimp would head for the exit" (*Washington Post,* 1990). The proverb was popularized by President Harry S. Truman (1884–1972), who attributed it to his friend General Harry Vaughan.

Variant of this proverb: if you don't like the heat, get out of the kitchen.

if you desire peace, prepare for war   *See* IF YOU WANT PEACE, PREPARE FOR WAR.

if you don't like it, you can lump it   Whether or not you like what is offered or approve of what is proposed, you will have to put up with it: *I'm inviting Jack and Sarah* *for Thanksgiving, and if you don't like it you can lump it.* The proverb was first recorded in 1828. The phrase *lump it,* which means "put up with it," is sometimes replaced by a more vulgar alternative.

if you don't like the heat, get out of the kitchen *See* IF YOU CAN'T STAND THE HEAT, GET OUT OF THE KITCHEN.

if you don't make mistakes, you don't make anything Do not be afraid of making mistakes—the only way to avoid them is to do nothing at all: *Errors like these can easily be put right, so don't worry—if you don't make mistakes, you don't make anything.* The proverb was first recorded in a speech by Edward John Phelps (1822–1900) at the Mansion House, London, England, in January 1889: "The man who makes no mistakes does not usually make anything."

Variant of this proverb: he who never made a mistake never made anything.

if you don't speculate, you can't accumulate You will not succeed or get rich unless you are prepared to take risks and spend money: *I was uneasy at first about putting money into the venture, but if you don't speculate you can't accumulate, and it could prove to be a very profitable investment if all goes well.* The proverb was first recorded, in its variant form, in 1941 in D. Dodge's *Death and Taxes.*

Variant of this proverb: you never accumulate if you don't speculate.

if you don't toot your own horn, nobody else will *See* TOOT YOUR OWN HORN LEST THE SAME BE NEVER TOOTED.

if you lie down with dogs, you'll get up with fleas If you associate with dishon-est or disreputable people, you are likely to acquire their undesirable qualities: "If you lie down with dogs, you'll get up with fleas, and that's the fruits of travelling with a fool" (Charles Lever, *Jack Hinton,* 1842). The proverb was first recorded in 1573 in the form "He that goes to bed with dogs arises with fleas."

Proverb expressing similar meaning: HE THAT TOUCHES PITCH SHALL BE DEFILED.

Proverb expressing opposite meaning: THE SUN LOSES NOTHING BY SHINING INTO A PUDDLE.

if you pay peanuts, you get monkeys Competent and highly qualified people will not work for derisory fees or wages: *She complained about the caliber of applicants for the post, but when she told me what they would be earning, I was not surprised. "If you pay peanuts, you get monkeys," I said.* The proverb was first recorded in 1966 by L. Coulthard in *Director.*

if you play with fire, you get burned If you engage in dangerous activities, mix with dangerous people, and the like, you are likely to suffer harm: *I warned her that it was a risky enterprise, but she wouldn't listen, so I've no sympathy for her—if you play with fire, you get burned.* The proverb was first recorded in this form in 1884, but the figurative phrase *to play with fire* is of earlier origin. It occurs in Henry Vaughan's poem "The Garland" (1655): "I played with fire, did counsell spurn. . . . But never thought that fire would burn."

Variant of this proverb: don't play with fire.

Proverb expressing similar meaning: IT'S ILL JESTING WITH EDGED TOOLS.

if you're born to be hanged, then you'll never be drowned Everybody is destined to die in a particular way at a particular moment and is therefore not in mortal danger at any other time; said by those who risk death and of those who miraculously escape it: *His friends urged him not to set sail until the weather improved, but he simply shrugged his shoulders and replied, "If you're born to be hanged, then you'll never be drowned."* The proverb was first recorded in this form in 1593, but the sentiment it expresses is of earlier origin. Compare the 14th-century French proverb "*Noyer ne peut, cil qui doit pendre* [He cannot drown who must hang]."

Variant of this proverb: he that is born to be hanged shall never be drowned.

Proverb expressing similar meaning: EVERY BULLET HAS ITS BILLET.

if you're not part of the solution, you're part of the problem Those who cannot or will not help to solve a problem or improve a situation are a positive hindrance: "We must fight 'hunger,' but never Communism, even when Communism itself is the direct cause of hunger. Well, as our radicals used to say, if you're not part of the solution, you're part of the problem" (*National Review*, 1985). The proverb is attributed to the U.S. activist Eldridge Cleaver (1935–98), who used the words "you're either part of the solution or you're part of the problem" in a speech in 1968, but it may be of earlier origin.

if you run after two hares, you will catch neither If you try to do two things at once you will fail at both: "Let's take things a step at a time. You know what they say. If you run after two hares you will catch neither" (Peter O'Donnell, *The*

Xanadu Talisman, 1981). The proverb is probably of ancient origin; in his *Adagia* (1500) the Dutch humanist Desiderius Erasmus quotes the Latin proverb "*Duos insequens lepores, neutrum capit* [He who chases two hares catches neither]."

Variant of this proverb: he who chases two hares catches neither.

if you sing before breakfast, you'll cry before supper *See* SING BEFORE BREAKFAST, CRY BEFORE NIGHT.

if you've got it, flaunt it Those who have wealth, beauty, or talent should not be ashamed to show it off; used as an excuse for ostentation: "Old money's motto was, *If you have it, hide it.* New money's motto was, *If you have it, flaunt it*" (Sidney Sheldon, *The Master of the Game,* 1982).

if you want a thing done well, do it yourself The only way to be sure that something is done properly is to do it yourself—you cannot rely on other people to do exactly what you want: *I told you to slice the meat, not hack it into chunks. Give me the knife—if you want a thing well done, do it yourself!* The proverb was first recorded, with different wording, in 1541. Its current form may date from 1858, when it was used in a poem by Henry Wadsworth Longfellow: "That's what I always say; if you want a thing to be well done, / You must do it yourself."

Variant of this proverb: if you want something done right, do it yourself.

Proverb expressing similar meaning: IF YOU WOULD BE WELL SERVED, SERVE YOURSELF.

if you want peace, prepare for war A nation that is seen to be ready and able to defend itself—for example, with strong armed forces and powerful weapons—is less likely to be attacked: "As always, the success of diplomacy rests on the latent availability of force. If you seek peace, prepare for war" (*Washington Times,* 1990). The proverb occurs in the work of the Roman military writer Flavius Vegetius (fourth century A.D.): "*qui desiderat pacem, praeparet bellum* [he who desires peace must prepare for war]," but it is probably of earlier origin.

Variant of this proverb: if you desire peace, prepare for war.

Proverb expressing similar meaning: ONE SWORD KEEPS ANOTHER IN ITS SCABBARD.

if you want something done, ask a busy person Busy people are reliable and efficient workers who get things done quickly and are adept at reorganizing their time to slot in extra work: *It's the usual story: if you want something done, ask a busy person. At least you know they will deliver the goods.*

Proverb expressing similar meaning: THE BUSIEST MEN HAVE THE MOST LEISURE.

if you want something done right, do it yourself *See* IF YOU WANT A THING DONE WELL, DO IT YOURSELF.

if you want to live and thrive, let the spider run alive According to popular superstition, it is unlucky to kill a spider: *I'm terrified of these eight-legged beasts, but every time I reach for a newspaper to squash one, or turn on the faucet to drown one, I recall a rhyme learned in childhood, "If you want to live and thrive, let the spider run alive."* The proverb was first recorded in 1867, but with the implication that it was already in regional use in England.

Variant of this proverb: he who would wish to thrive, must let spiders run alive.

if you won't work, you shan't eat *See* HE WHO DOES NOT WORK, NEITHER SHOULD HE EAT.

if you would be happy for a week take a wife, if you would be happy for a month kill a pig, but if you would be happy all your life plant a garden The pleasures of marriage, good food and so on are ephemeral, but a garden is a lasting source of joy: *I had a bachelor uncle who used to say, "If you would be happy for a week take a wife, if you would be happy for a month kill a pig, but if you would be happy all your life plant a garden." My recent divorce has proved the first part of the saying to be accurate, and I am now seriously considering the horticultural option.* The proverb exists in numerous forms, dating from before 1661. Most versions include the opening clause, but other suggestions for lifetime happiness are "be an honest man" and "turn priest."

if you would be well served, serve yourself The work of hired staff may fall below the standard you require, so the only way to be sure of satisfaction is to do the work yourself: "'If you would be well served, serve yourself.' Some gentlemen took pleasure in being their own gardeners" (J. E. Austen-Leigh, *A Memoir of Jane Austen,* 1871). The proverb was first recorded in 1706.

Proverb expressing similar meaning: IF YOU WANT A THING DONE WELL, DO IT YOURSELF.

Proverb expressing opposite meaning: WHY KEEP A DOG AND BARK YOURSELF?

ignorance is a voluntary misfortune Everybody has the opportunity to acquire knowledge, so you have only yourself to blame if you remain ignorant: *My grandfather was a self-taught scholar, whose motto was "Ignorance is a voluntary misfortune."* The proverb is recorded as a regional expression in the United States.

ignorance is bliss It is often better not to have knowledge that would alarm or distress you: *Ignorance is bliss, and we drove off without a care in the world, unaware of the disaster that lay ahead.* The proverb comes from Thomas Gray's poem "Ode on a Distant Prospect of Eton College" (1742): "Yet ah! why should they know their fate? . . . Thought would destroy their paradise./No more; where ignorance is bliss,/'Tis folly to be wise." It has given rise to the clichés *blissful ignorance* and *blissfully ignorant.*

Variant of this proverb: where ignorance is bliss, 'tis folly to be wise.

Proverb expressing similar meaning: WHAT YOU DON'T KNOW CAN'T HURT YOU.

ignorance of the law is no excuse You cannot argue that you are not guilty of a crime because you were unaware that you were doing anything illegal: *I had no idea that drinking alcohol in public places was banned, but ignorance of the law is no excuse in this or any other country.* The proverb is of Latin origin: "*Ignorantia iuris neminem excusat* [Ignorance of the law excuses nobody]."

Variant of this proverb: ignorance of the law is no excuse for breaking it.

an ill agreement is better than a good judgment It is better to reach an out-of-court settlement than to pursue a case in court: *The old man was disappointed with the compensation his rival agreed but reminded himself that "an ill agreement is better than a good judgment."* The proverb was first recorded in 1640 in George Herbert's *Outlandish Proverbs.*

an ill beginning makes an ill ending Something that is badly planned or that starts badly is unlikely to end well: *We had problems with transportation and supplies in the early stages of the expedition, which did not bode well for us—an ill beginning makes an ill ending.* The proverb was first recorded in 1562 in A. Broke's *Romeus and Juliet.*

an ill bird lays an ill egg Good things rarely result from bad origins: *I had hoped for a better offer, but the man's a gangster and as they say, "an ill bird lays an ill egg."* The proverb was first recorded in 1581 in G. Pettie's *Guazzo's Civil Conversation.*

ill doers are ill dreaders *See* EVIL DOERS ARE EVIL DREADERS.

ill-gotten goods never thrive Something acquired by dishonest, illegitimate, or underhand means—specifically, stolen money or property—will not bring good fortune to the person who acquires it: "That ill-gotten gain never prospers . . . is the trite consolation administered to the easy dupe, when he has been tricked out of his money or estate" (Charles Lamb, *Elia's Last Essays*, 1826). The proverb was first recorded in the 16th century, but the sentiment it expresses is of ancient origin. Compare Cicero (106–43 B.C.): "*male parta, male dilabuntur* [things ill gotten slip away in evil ways]."

Variant of this proverb: ill-gotten goods seldom prosper.

an ill master makes an ill servant *See* LIKE MASTER, LIKE MAN.

ill news comes apace *See* BAD NEWS TRAVELS FAST.

ill weeds grow apace Worthless people or evil things have a tendency to flourish where better ones fail: *Ill weeds grow apace, and our efforts to stamp out these corrupt practices were of no avail.* The proverb was first recorded c. 1470 in *Anglia,* "Wyl[d] weed ys sone y-growe" (Wild weed is soon grown), but the sentiment it expresses is of earlier origin. Compare the 14th-century French proverb "*Male herbe croist* [Bad grass thrives]."

an ill wind blows no good *See* IT'S AN ILL WIND THAT BLOWS NOBODY ANY GOOD.

INDIAN PROVERBS

Indian proverbs range from telling observations on such everyday realities as hunger and poverty to thought-provoking wise utterances on spiritual and philosophical themes. They include some of the most poetic proverbs to be found anywhere in the world.

Every dog is a tiger in his own street

The heart at rest sees a feast in everything

He who answers is inferior to the one who asks the question

Hunger drives good taste away

If you live on the river, befriend the crocodile

It's easy to throw something into the river but hard to get it out again

A man laughs at others and weeps for himself

Never stand in front of a judge or behind a donkey

Never use a dwarf to measure the depth of water

No sin is hidden to the soul

One and one sometimes make eleven

One man's beard is burning, and another warms his hands by it

Only the nightingale understands the rose

Pearls are of no value in a desert

Poverty destroys all virtues

Poverty makes thieves, like love makes poets

Theologians, dogs, and singers always disagree

The voice of the poor has no echo

Turkeys, parrots, and hares don't know what gratitude is

We admire what we do not understand

What does the blind man know of the beauty of the tulip?

When the bed breaks, there is the ground to lie on

The world flatters the elephant and tramples on the ant

You do not stumble over a mountain, but you do over a stone

imitation is the sincerest form of flattery Somebody who copies something is paying an indirect compliment, by showing that he or she considers the original worthy of imitation: *On the basis that imitation is the sincerest form of flattery, the supermarket should pay extra money to the original brand-name owners for the similar goods they are selling.* The proverb was first recorded in 1820 without the word *form,* which was not added until the 20th century.

Variant of this proverb: imitation is the highest form of flattery.

in a calm sea every man is a pilot When times are easy, everyone wants to be in charge: "When winds are steady and skies are clear, every hand the ship must steer" (D'Arcy Wentworth Thompson). The implication is that when things get difficult these same volunteers will not be so eager.

an inch is as good as a mile *See* GIVE A MAN AN INCH AND HE'LL TAKE A MILE.

in for a penny, in for a pound Once you have committed yourself to something, you might as well do it wholeheartedly and see it through to the end: *I began to doubt the wisdom of my chosen course of action, but in for a penny, in for a pound. Besides, it was probably more dangerous to turn back than to go on.* The proverb was first recorded in 1695 in Edward Ravenscroft's *Canterbury Guests.*

Proverb expressing similar meaning: ONE MIGHT AS WELL BE HANGED FOR A SHEEP AS FOR A LAMB.

in politics a man must learn to rise above principle A successful politician cannot afford to have too many scruples; a cynical observation: *They say that in politics a man must learn to rise above principle, and by his second year of office the president had left the principles on which he was elected far behind.*

interest will not lie People will do more than they would otherwise do if they pursue something in which they have an interest. The proverb was first recorded in 1688 in John Bunyan's *Work of Jesus Christ*: "Our English proverb is, Interest will not lie; interest will make a man do what which otherwise he would not do."

in the country of the blind, the one-eyed man is king People of only limited ability can succeed when surrounded by those who are even less able than themselves: *I had few of the skills required for survival in the wild, but my fellow castaways had even fewer, and in the country of the blind the one-eyed man is king.* The proverb is probably of ancient origin; in his *Adagia* (1500) the Dutch humanist Desiderius Erasmus quotes the Latin proverb "*In regione caecorum rex est luscus* [In the kingdom of the blind the one-eyed man is king]." H. G. Wells wrote a short story, *The Country of the Blind* (1911), in which a man tries and fails to prove the literal truth of the proverb in a land populated by sightless people.

Variant of this proverb: in the land of the blind, the one-eyed are kings.

in the spring a young man's fancy lightly turns to thoughts of love Spring is traditionally considered to be the time when the desire for romance or sex is strongest: *We often see a distinct increase in our sales of contraceptives at this time of year—perhaps there is some truth in the saying that in the* *spring a young man's fancy lightly turns to thoughts of love!* The proverb comes from Alfred, Lord Tennyson's poem "Locksley Hall" (1842). Facetious modern variants have other words in place of *love,* such as *baseball.*

into every life a little rain must fall Everybody must have his or her share of misfortune; often said in consolation, with the implication that such misfortune it is only temporary: "Into every life a little rain must fall;/ And, for sure, it poured down on you." (Ralph McTell, *Weather the Storm,* 1976). The proverb was first recorded in 1935.

Variant of this proverb: into each life some rain must fall.

in unity there is strength *See* UNION IS STRENGTH.

in vain the net is spread in the sight of the bird Nobody will fall into a trap if he or she is in a position to watch it being laid—to catch people out you must be both discreet and well-prepared: "'If they come, we shall be ready,' said Bessas. 'In vain the net is spread in the sight of the bird'" (L. Sprague De Camp, *The Dragon of the Ishtar Gate,* 1961). The proverb is of biblical origin: "Surely in vain the net is spread in the sight of any bird" (Proverbs 1:17).

in war there is no substitute for victory A war is only truly won by total defeat of the enemy, not by diplomatic negotiations or compromise: *The debate was evenly divided between those who believed that in war there is no substitute for victory, and those who favored a less belligerent approach.* The proverb was first recorded in General Dwight D. Eisenhower's *Letters to Mamie* (1944), but it is popularly associated with General Douglas MacArthur, who used it in a speech in 1951.

in wine there is truth *See* THERE'S TRUTH IN WINE.

iron not used soon rusts *See* THE USED KEY IS ALWAYS BRIGHT.

IRISH PROVERBS

The Irish are famed for their hospitality and a good number of their proverbs accordingly reflect a love of generosity, good drink, and entertaining company.

Age is honourable and youth is noble

Both your friend and your enemy think you will never die

The day will come when the cow will have use for her tail

A drink precedes a story

Falling is easier than rising

God's help is nearer than the door

Good as drink is, it ends in thirst

He who comes with a story to you brings two away from you

If you hit my dog you hit myself

It is sweet to drink but bitter to pay for

The light heart lives long

There is no fireside like your own fireside

There is no need like the lack of a friend

This is better than the thing we never had

Time is a great story teller

Two shorten the road

When the drop is inside, the sense is outside

When you are right no one remembers; when you are wrong no one forgets

Wine divulges truth

Women do not drink liquor, but it disappears when they are present

ITALIAN PROVERBS

The Italian national character is widely linked with passionate enjoyment of life, and it is thus perhaps not surprising that many of their proverbs focus on the subjects of food and love.

Absence is the enemy of love

A cask of wine works more miracles than a church full of saints

Adam must have an Eve to blame for his faults

All are not saints who go to church

Bed is the poor man's opera

Better one true friend than a hundred relatives

By asking the impossible you will get the best

The end of the pig is the beginning of the sausage

Every excuse is good, if it works

Failures are but mileposts on the road to success

He that is afraid of the devil does not grow rich

If it rained macaroni, what a fine time for gluttons!

If you would succeed, you must not be too good

It may be quieter to sleep alone, but not warmer

A kiss without a moustache is like beef without mustard

A meal without wine is like a day without sunshine

Virginity is noted only by its absence

What worth has beauty if it is not seen?

Whoever stays awake longest must blow out the candle

Who has no courage must have legs

You must marry a widow while she is still mourning

it'll all be the same in a hundred years Trivial problems or mistakes of the present moment have no lasting significance or effect, so there is no point in worrying about them; also used to imply that there will always be similar problems as there are now: "'It doesn't matter,' she answered quietly, out of the darkness. 'I am strong enough to suffer, and live. . . . It doesn't matter; it will all be the same a hundred years hence'" (Wilkie Collins, *No Name,* 1862). The proverb was first recorded in 1611 in the form "All will be one at the latter day."

Variant of this proverb: it'll all be the same a hundred years hence.

it'll all come out in the wash All will ultimately be satisfactorily resolved: *I'm up to my ears in debt, my job is hanging by a thread, and my wife has just left me, so please don't tell me "It'll all come out in the wash"—how can it?* The proverb was first recorded, with different wording, in 1612 in Cervantes's *Don Quixote.*

Variant of this proverb: it'll all come right in the wash.

it never rains but it pours One setback, misfortune, or other undesirable occurrence is inevitably followed by many more; also occasionally used of pleasant things, such as a run of good luck: *Talk*

145

about it never rains but it pours. *The children have all been ill this week and then the washing machine and the drier have both broken down.* The proverb was first recorded in 1726 in the form "It cannot rain but it pours," the title of a book by the Scottish physician John Arbuthnot.

Proverb expressing similar meaning: MISFORTUNES NEVER COME SINGLY.

I today, you tomorrow   See TODAY YOU, TOMORROW ME.

it's a foolish sheep that makes the wolf his confessor   Do not confide in somebody unless you are certain that he or she can be trusted: *I can't believe that you told Maggie, of all people, about the missing money—you should have guessed she'd go straight to the boss and try to get you fired. It's a foolish sheep that makes the wolf his confessor.* The proverb was first recorded in 1642 in a collection of Italian proverbs.

it's a good horse that never stumbles   See A STUMBLE MAY PREVENT A FALL.

it's all grist for the mill   See ALL IS GRIST THAT COMES TO THE MILL.

it's all in a day's work   Unpleasant things have to be accepted as part of the daily routine; also used to play down a major achievement or a heroic act by implying that it is just part of your job: "The mules merely shook themselves and then stared stonily ahead, as if it were all in the day's work" (Francis Edward Younghusband, *The Heart of a Continent*, 1896). The proverb was first recorded in 1738 in Jonathan Swift's *A Complete Collection of Polite and Ingenious Conversation*.

it's a long road that has no turning   An undesirable situation, or a run of bad luck, cannot last forever—things are bound to improve eventually: *They say that it's a long road that has no turning, but the end of our problems was not yet in sight.* The proverb was first recorded in the 17th century in the form "It's a long run that never turns."

Variant of this proverb: it's a long lane that has no turning.

Proverbs expressing similar meaning: BE THE DAY WEARY OR BE THE DAY LONG, AT LAST IT RINGETH TO EVENSONG; THE LONGEST DAY MUST HAVE AN END.

it's always darkest before dawn   See THE DARKEST HOUR IS JUST BEFORE DAWN.

it's always fair weather when good friends get together   The company of good friends is a constant source of pleasure and happiness: *I meet up with a group of my old college friends every two or three months, and we have a great time. If any of us has problems, they're soon forgotten—it's always fair weather when good friends get together.*

it's always the unexpected that happens   See THE UNEXPECTED ALWAYS HAPPENS.

it's an ill bird that fouls its own nest   You should not say or do anything that will bring discredit or harm to your own family or country: "Nothing . . . can excuse the bad taste of Samuel Butler's virulent attack upon his defenceless family. . . . It's an ill bird that fouls its own nest" (*London Times*, 1926). The proverb dates from before 1250.

it's an ill wind that blows nobody any good   There is usually somebody who benefits from an unfavorable set of circumstances: *The collapse of the company was a major disaster for employees and stockholders alike, but it's an ill wind that blows nobody any good, and some of its competitors were quick to take advantage of its demise.* The proverb was first recorded in 1546. It occurs in Shakespeare's play *Henry VI, Part 3* (2:5) in the form "Ill blows the wind that profits nobody."

Variant of this proverb: an ill wind blows no good.

Proverb expressing similar meaning: ONE MAN'S LOSS IS ANOTHER MAN'S GAIN.

it's a poor dog that's not worth whistling for Everybody has some value, or some redeeming feature: *It's a poor dog that's not worth whistling for, and I was prepared to give him the opportunity to prove himself.* The proverb was first recorded in 1546.

Variant of this proverb: it's a poor dog that deserves not a crust.

it's a poor heart that never rejoices Nobody can be miserable or gloomy all the time: "'Well,' continued he, 'it's a poor heart that never rejoiceth.' He then poured out half a tumbler of rum" (Captain Marryat, *Peter Simple*, 1834). The quotation is the first recorded use of the proverb.

Variant of this proverb: it's a sad heart that never rejoices.

it's a sad house where the hen crows louder than the cock No home can be happy where the woman has more influence than the man: "They are sory houses, where the hennes crowe, and the cock holdes his peace" (John Florio, *First Fruites*, 1578). The proverb was first recorded in 1573 in J. Sandford's *The Garden Pleasure*.

it's as cheap sitting as standing You might as well sit down and be comfortable, if you have the opportunity, rather than standing up: "He returned to Tommie Redhill's car. 'Jump in, Inspector,' Tommie suggested, opening the door at his side. 'It's as cheap sitting as standing'" (J. J. Connington, *The Sweepstake Murders*, 1932). The proverb was first recorded in 1666.

it's a sin to steal a pin Theft is a crime, regardless of the size or value of what is stolen: *It's a sin to steal a pin, and salesclerks who help themselves to candy bars without paying for them are just as guilty as one who takes a handful of cash from the till.* The proverb was first recorded in 1875, but with the implication that it was already in general use, especially as an admonition to children.

it's a small world It is amazing how often you meet somebody you know—or somebody who knows one of your friends or relatives, comes from your home town, or went to your school—in a distant or unexpected place; said when such a coincidence occurs: *I was chatting with the guy in the next seat on the airplane, and it turned out he'd gone to college with my best friend—it's a small world.* The proverb was first recorded, with different wording, in the late 19th century: "Mr. Ardale and I have met in London. . . . They say the world's very small, don't they" (A. W. Pinero, *The Second Mrs. Tanqueray*, 1893).

it's as well to know which way the wind blows *See* STRAWS SHOW WHICH WAY THE WIND BLOWS.

it's a wise child that knows its own father People cannot always be certain—

147

but sometimes instinctively know—who their natural father is: *I was devastated to learn that my mother's husband—the man who had raised me—had played no part in my conception.* As they say, *it's a wise child that knows its own father.* The proverb was first recorded in 1584 in the form "Wise sons they be in very deed, that know their parents who did them breed." It occurs in Shakespeare's play *The Merchant of Venice* (2:2) with the wording reversed: "It is a wise father that knows his own child."

it's best to be off with the old love before you are on with the new   Do not embark on a new relationship until your old one is over: *Remembering the proverb "It's best to be off with the old love before you are on with the new," I decided to make a clean break with Laura that evening.* The proverb was first recorded in 1801, but with the implication that it was of earlier origin.

it's best to be on the safe side   *See* IT's BETTER TO BE ON THE SAFE SIDE.

it's better to be an hour too early than a minute too late   If you arrive far too early, as for an appointment or a flight you can easily fill the intervening time, but if you arrive just a moment too late, you may miss it altogether: *"Surely we don't have to go yet—it's only twenty miles to the coast, and the boat doesn't leave till midday." "It's better to be an hour too early than a minute too late."*

Variant of this proverb: better three hours too soon than a minute too late.

it's better to be born lucky than rich   Rich people may lose their money and have nothing, but lucky people will always be able to get what they want: *Within six months he had squandered his entire inheritance in the casinos of Europe, and was forced to acknowledge the truth of the saying "It's better to be born lucky than rich."* The proverb was first recorded in 1639 in the form "Better to have good fortune than be a rich man's child."

it's better to be happy than wise   Happiness is more important than wisdom, knowledge, or learning: *Don't put pressure on your children to continue their education if they are not academically inclined—it's better to be happy than wise.* The proverb was first recorded in 1546 in John Heywood, *Dialogue of Proverbs.*

it's better to be on the safe side   It is advisable to err on the side of caution and avoid unnecessary risk: *The wound is unlikely to be infected, but I'll prescribe a course of antibiotics, just in case—it's better to be on the safe side.* The proverb was first recorded, with different wording, in 1668 in John Dryden and William Cavendish Newcastle's, *Sir Martin Mar-all.*

Variant of this proverb: it's best to be on the safe side.

Proverb expressing similar meaning: BETTER SAFE THAN SORRY.

it's better to be right than in the majority   Do not follow or side with the majority, just for the sake of conformity, if you believe them to be wrong: *I was the only member of the committee to vote in favor of the proposal, but I am convinced that it is a good thing, and it's better to be right than in the majority.* The proverb was first recorded in 1691 in John Norris's *Practical Discourses.*

it's better to die on your feet than live on your knees   It is better to be killed in active resistance, or while fighting for a cause, than to surrender and condemn yourself to a life of servitude: "'Why don't you use some sense and try to be more like me? . . .' 'Because it's better to die on one's feet than to live on one's knees,' Nately retorted with triumphant and lofty conviction" (Joseph Heller, *Catch-22,* 1961). In its current form the proverb is generally associated with the Spanish communist politician Dolores Ibarruri, who used it in a speech in 1936, at the beginning of the Spanish Civil War, urging the people to resist the fascist forces. The sentiment expressed by the proverb, however, is of much earlier origin.

Proverb expressing opposite meaning: A LIVE DOG IS BETTER THAN A DEAD LION.

it's better to give than to receive The act of giving is more worthy, noble, and spiritually satisfying than the act of receiving: "'Tis better to Give than to Receive, but yet 'tis Madness to give so much Charity to Others, as to become the Subject of it our Selves" (Samuel Palmer, *Moral Essays on Some of the Most Curious and Significant English, Scotch, and Foreign Proverbs,* 1710). The proverb is of biblical origin: "It is more blessed to give than to receive" (Acts 20:35).

Variant of this proverb: it's more blessed to give than to receive.

it's better to laugh than to cry It is better to see the funny side of an unfortunate situation than to distress yourself about it: *I hurt my shoulder when I fell off the stage, but it's better to laugh than to cry, and the audience thought it was all part of the show.*

it's better to light one candle than curse the darkness Any positive action, how-ever small, that helps to improve an unde-sirable state of affairs is infinitely better than simply bemoaning or complaining about it: *The charity does what little it can to help the victims of persecution and oppression around the world, on the basis that it's better to light a candle than curse the darkness.* Probably of Chinese origin, the proverb is the motto of the Christophers, a U.S. religious organization founded in 1945. In a tribute to Eleanor Roosevelt, after her death in 1962, the American politician Adlai Stevenson said, "She would rather light a candle than curse the darkness, and her glow has warmed the world."

Variant of this proverb: it's better to light one little candle than curse the darkness.

it's better to lose the battle and win the war It is sometimes prudent or expedient to concede a minor point in an argument or dispute in order to gain the overall victory: *The protesters were content to admit defeat in this particular campaign, knowing that their action had forced the government to rethink the whole road-build-ing program statewide. "It's better to lose the battle and win the war," said a spokesperson for the protest group.* It is unclear when this proverb was first used, but the sentiment was expressed by Charles de Gaulle on June 18, 1940, when he announced a few days after the fall of Paris to the Ger-mans, *"La France a perdu une bataille! Mais la France n'a pas perdu la guerre"* (France has lost a battle, but France has not lost the war).

it's better to travel hopefully than to arrive The expectation of success, or the process of working toward this end, is often more enjoyable or satisfying than the actual result: "As much as it was bet-ter to travel hopefully than to arrive, as much as I believed that and had lived by it, once you've arrived, you've arrived, and there's not much to be done about it" (Mark Vonnegut, *The Eden Express,* 1975). The proverb comes from Robert Louis Stevenson's *Virginibus Puerisque* (1881): "To travel hopefully is a better thing than to arrive, and the true success is to labour."

it's dogged as does it　Anything can be done with determination and persever-ance: "There ain't nowt a man can't bear if he'll only be dogged. . . . It's dogged as does it. It's not thinking about it" (Anthony Trollope, *The Last Chronicle of Barset,* 1867). The proverb was first recorded in 1864 in M. B. Chesnut's *Diary.*

it's easier to tear down than to build up　It is easier to destroy something, such as a building or an idea, than it is to construct or restore it: *The overthrow of the monarchy was accomplished with ease, and relatively little bloodshed, but the creation of the new republic proved to be rather more difficult. As the revolutionaries discovered, it's always far easier to tear down than to build up.* The proverb was first recorded in 1577 in the form "It is easy to raze, but hard to build."

Proverb expressing similar mean-ing: A JACKASS CAN KICK A BARN DOOR DOWN, BUT IT TAKES A CARPENTER TO BUILD ONE.

it's easy to be wise after the event　With hindsight it is easy to see why something went wrong or what should have been done, but this is of no practical purpose: "It is easy to be wise after the event, but it does certainly appear that . . . the action

at Paardeberg was as unnecessary as it was expensive" (Sir Arthur Conan Doyle, *The Great Boer War,* 1900). The proverb was first recorded in 1616, but the sentiment it expresses is of earlier origin.

Proverb expressing similar meaning: DON'T SHUT THE BARN DOOR AFTER THE HORSE IS STOLEN.

it's easy to find a stick to beat a dog　It is easy to find some reason or excuse to justify a critical attack or a harsh punish-ment: "Excuses were abundant. . . . It is easy to find a stick to beat a sick dog" (Samuel Smiles, *Thrift,* 1875). The proverb was first recorded in 1564. The English popular historian Philip Guedalla wrote punningly in *Masters and Men* (1923), "Any stigma, as the old saying is, will serve to beat a dogma."

Variants of this proverb: any stick will serve to beat a dog with; he who has a mind to beat a dog will easily find a stick.

it's good fishing in troubled waters　It is sometimes possible to take advantage of other people's difficulties in times of conflict: "Thinking it (as the proverb saith) best fishing in troubled waters" (Sir John Harington, *Orlando Furioso,* 1591). The proverb was first recorded in 1568 in Richard Grafton's *Chronicles.*

it's good to make a bridge of gold to a flying enemy　Retreating enemies will kill or destroy anybody or anything that stands in their way, so it is advisable to give them free passage: *Countless lives could have been spared if the general had paid heed to the military saying "It's good to make a bridge of gold to a flying enemy."* The proverb was first recorded in this form in

1576, but the sentiment it expresses is of ancient origin.

it's hard to live in Rome and strive against the Pope   *See* IT'S ILL SITTING AT ROME AND STRIVING WITH THE POPE.

it's idle to swallow the cow and choke on the tail   Once you have completed the major part of an enterprise or undertaking, it is foolish not to see it through to the end: "We had gone too far to turn back, and as our proverb says, 'It is idle to swallow the cow and choke on the tail'" (John Buchan, *Salute to Adventurers,* 1915). The proverb was first recorded in 1659 in James Howell's *Proverbs.*

Variant of this proverb: don't swallow the cow and worry with the tail.

it's ill jesting with edged tools   Do not trifle with dangerous things or people: *Taking drugs like these for "recreational" purposes is a risky business—it's ill jesting with edged tools.* The proverb was first recorded in 1588 in Robert Greene's *Pandosto.*

Variant of this proverb: don't play with edged tools.

Proverb expressing similar meaning: IF YOU PLAY WITH FIRE, YOU GET BURNED.

it's ill sitting at Rome and striving with the Pope   It is foolish or pointless to quarrel or fight with somebody who has supreme power in the place where you are: "'It is ill sitting at Rome and striving with the Pope.' Nebuchadnezzar's palace was not precisely the place to dispute with Nebuchadnezzar" (Alexander MacLaren, *Ezekiel,* 1908). The proverb dates from before 1628.

Variant of this proverb: it's hard to live in Rome and strive against the Pope.

it's ill speaking between a full man and a fasting   Hungry people are not on the best of terms with those who have eaten their fill: "It's ill speaking between a full man and a fasting, but two fasting men are worse at a crack" (John Buchan, *The Free Fishers,* 1934). The proverb dates from before 1641.

it's ill striving against the stream   *See* STRIVE NOT AGAINST THE STREAM.

it's ill waiting for dead men's shoes   It is not good to be impatiently awaiting somebody's death or retirement to get what you want, such as an inheritance or promotion: *She's first in line for Jack Mitchell's job at the head of the New York office, but he's still eight years from retirement, and it's ill waiting for dead men's shoes.* The proverb was first recorded in 1530.

Variant of this proverb: he that waits for dead men's shoes may go a long time barefoot.

it's merry in hall when beards wag all   A social gathering with many people talking together is a happy, convivial affair: *It's merry in hall when beards wag all, and the noise in the room had reached such a pitch that I had to bang loudly on the table to gain everybody's attention.* The proverb was first recorded c. 1300.

it's more blessed to give than to receive   *See* IT'S BETTER TO GIVE THAN TO RECEIVE.

it's never too late to learn   Nobody is too old to acquire knowledge or experience: "'It is never too late to learn,' cried he. 'I will make a fisherman of you in no time, if you will only attend to my directions'" (Wilkie Collins, *After Dark*, 1856). The proverb was first recorded in 1678 in the form "It is never too late to learn what it is always necessary to know." Its variant form is of earlier origin.

Variant of this proverb: never too old to learn.

Proverb expressing opposite meaning: YOU CAN'T TEACH AN OLD DOG NEW TRICKS.

it's never too late to mend People or things can be reformed or improved at any time: *The Church's message to habitual criminals is "It's never too late to mend."* The proverb was first recorded in 1590 as the title of a pamphlet by the English dramatist Robert Greene.

it's not over till it's over Do not anticipate the end of something; specifically, do not give up hope until you have actually lost or failed: "Beré won't say whether the company is better off than if it had never done the LBO [leveraged buyout]. Nor will he declare that the company's problems are behind it: 'It isn't over until it's over'" (*Fortune*, 1991). The proverb is attributed to the baseball player Yogi Berra (1925–), referring to a baseball game.

Proverb expressing similar meaning: THE OPERA AIN'T OVER TILL THE FAT LADY SINGS.

it's not spring until you can plant your foot upon twelve daisies According to country lore, spring has not arrived until there are so many daisies in flower that you can tread on twelve at once: *Today is officially the first day of spring, but I won't be putting my winter clothes away just yet—my* grandmother used to say, "It's not spring until you can plant your foot upon twelve daisies," and there's not a daisy to be seen on any of my neighbors' lawns. The proverb was first recorded in 1863, but with the implication that it was already in general use. Different versions have different numbers of daisies, such as nine or six, but the type of flower remains the same.

it's not the end of the world Things are not as disastrous as they seem; said in reassurance, such as after a minor mishap: *It looks as though we're going to miss our flight, but it's not the end of the world.*

it's not the size of the dog in the fight, it's the size of the fight in the dog In any combat or dispute, strength and determination to win are more important than physical size or number: *It's not the size of the dog in the fight, it's the size of the fight in the dog—the protesters were in the minority, but they conducted such a powerful and persistent campaign that they eventually won their case.* The proverb is recorded as a regional expression in the United States.

it's not what you know but who you know Influential contacts can be more useful than qualifications or experience; often said cynically by those who fail to get a job, assignment, or promotion for this reason: *The other candidate had never worked in marketing before, but her uncle is president of one of the company's biggest customers, so of course she got the job—it's not what you know, but who you know.*

it's not what you say but how you say it Phraseology and style are often more important than the actual content of speech or writing: "As one . . . researcher explains: 'It's not just what they say, it's how they say it. When people talk about "change," what words do they use?'" (*New York Times Magazine*, 1992).

it's not whether you win or lose, but how you play the game In any contest, playing well and fairly is more important than winning: "Exactly what is sportsmanship these days? Is it the age-old admonishment that 'It's not whether you win or lose but how you play the game?' Or is it Vince Lombardi's rubric that winning isn't everything, it's the only thing?" (*New York Times*, 1991). The proverb comes from "Alumnus Football" (1941), by the U.S. sportswriter Grantland Rice: "For when the One Great Scorer comes to mark against your name,/He writes— not that you won or lost—but how you played the game."

Proverb expressing opposite meaning: WINNING ISN'T EVERYTHING, IT'S THE ONLY THING.

it's not work that kills, but worry Anxiety is more injurious to your health than overwork: *It's not work that kills, but worry, so those who have lost their jobs and can't afford to feed their families are theoretically more at risk than those who are working a 60-hour week to hang on to the jobs they have.* The proverb was first recorded in 1879.

Variant of this proverb: worry kills more men than work.

Proverbs expressing similar meaning: CARE IS NO CURE; CARE KILLED THE CAT.

it's no use crying over spilled milk Do not distress yourself about mistakes or misfortunes that cannot be put right: "I wish now I'd thought about the implications, but it's no good crying over spilt milk" (Jonathan Gash, *The Gondola Scam,* 1984). The proverb was first recorded in 1659 in the form "No weeping for shed milk."

Variant of this proverb: don't cry over spilled milk.

Proverb expressing similar meaning: WHAT'S DONE CANNOT BE UNDONE.

it's six of one and half a dozen of the other There is no difference between two options or parties: *Tom blamed Sarah for starting the fight, but as far as I could tell it was six of one and half a dozen of the other.* The proverb was first recorded in 1836, in Captain Marryat's novel *The Pirate:* "I never know the children. It's just six of one and half-a-dozen of the other."

it's the first step that is difficult See THE FIRST STEP IS THE HARDEST.

it's the last straw that breaks the camel's back When somebody is close to his or her limit of patience or endurance, it takes only one little extra thing to make the whole load too much to bear: "As the last straw breaks the laden camel's back, this piece of underground information crushed the sinking spirits of Mr. Dombey" (Charles Dickens, *Dombey and Son,* 1848). The proverb was first recorded in 1655 in the form "The last feather may be said to break a horse's back." In modern times it is most frequently encountered in the form of the cliché *the last straw.*

Variant of this proverb: the last straw will break the camel's back.

Proverb expressing similar meaning: THE LAST DROP MAKES THE CUP RUN OVER.

it's the pace that kills Do not try to do too much too quickly: *If you want to enjoy a long and happy life, you must learn to slow down and relax more. Remember, it's the pace that kills!* The proverb was first recorded in 1855, with the implication that it was already well known in the sporting world.

it's too late to shut the stable door after the horse has bolted *See* DON'T SHUT THE BARN DOOR AFTER THE HORSE IS STOLEN.

it takes a heap of living to make a house a home A house or apartment does not feel like home until you lived there happily and comfortably for some time: *It takes a heap of living to make a house a home—an interior designer can make it look good, but only you and your family can make it feel good.* The proverb comes from the poem "Home" (1916) by Edgar Guest.

Variant of this proverb: it takes a heap of living to make a home.

it takes all kinds of people to make a world Other people have different ways, tastes, and so on—we must practice tolerance and respect their individuality: "'Hines was not exactly a weak sister, but he was sort of nondescript. I can't imagine his appealing to your wife.' 'It takes all sorts of people to make a world. You can never tell who is going to appeal to whom'" (Erle Stanley Gardner, *The Case of the Borrowed Brunette,* 1946). The proverb was first recorded in 1620, in a translation of Cervantes's *Don Quixote.*

Variant of this proverb: it takes all sorts to make a world.

Proverb expressing similar meaning: LIVE AND LET LIVE.

it takes a thief to catch a thief *See* SET A THIEF TO CATCH A THIEF.

it takes a village to raise a child The whole community plays a part in the upbringing of the children that live there: *It takes a village to raise a child, and parents cannot take all the blame—or all the credit—for the way their kids turn out.* Of African origin, the proverb was popularized by Hillary Clinton, wife of President Bill Clinton, in the mid-1990s.

it takes money to make money Any moneymaking scheme requires some capital investment: *I'd like to set up in business on my own, but it takes money to make money, and I don't have any.*

Proverb expressing similar meaning: MONEY BEGETS MONEY.

it takes one to know one Only those with similar flaws are capable of spotting them in others: "I told him he was a liar and a cheat. He said it took one to know one" (Abigail Van Buren, *The Best of Dear Abby,* 1981). The proverb was first recorded around the end of the 19th century.

Proverb expressing similar meaning: SET A THIEF TO CATCH A THIEF.

it takes three generations to make a gentleman You cannot consider yourself a member of the gentry if your parents or grandparents were members of the common people: "You will find it no easy matter to make a gentleman of him. The old proverb says, that 'it takes three generations to make a gentleman'" (James Fenimore Cooper, *The Pioneers,* 1823). The quotation is the first recorded use of the proverb, but the sentiment it expresses is of much earlier origin.

it takes two to make a bargain A deal or treaty cannot stand unless both parties are—and remain—in agreement: *"I thought we'd agreed that I'd pay for the gasoline and you'd pay for the food." "No—you suggested it, but I didn't say yes. It takes two to make a bargain."* The proverb was first recorded in 1597 in the form "The second word makes the bargain."

Variant of this proverb: if it takes two to make a bargain, it takes two to break it.

it takes two to make a quarrel Neither party to an argument or dispute can be held individually responsible for causing it: *Don't let her provoke you—remember, it takes two to make a quarrel.* The proverb was first recorded in 1706 in J. Stevens's *A New Spanish and English Dictionary.*

Variant of this proverb: it takes two to make a quarrel, but one can end it.

it takes two to tango In a situation involving cooperation or joint action, both participants must work together and share the responsibility for what happens: "Despite all the problems I had had with Imlach, and believe it or not I realize it takes two to tango, I wouldn't have missed playing in the best league in the world" (B. Conacher, *Hockey in Canada,* 1972). The proverb was popularized as the title of a song written by Al Hoffman and Dick Manning in 1952.

a jackass can kick a barn door down, but it takes a carpenter to build one Something that has taken time, skill, and effort to put together can be quickly ruined or destroyed by a foolish person: ". . . 'any jackass can kick a barn door down, but it takes a carpenter to build one.' Maybe the only sure answer to this sort of irresponsibility . . . is for those who run the media to insure that there are more carpenters among today's political commentators" (*New York Times,* 1994). The proverb was coined by Sam Rayburn (1882–1961), Speaker of the House of Representatives, in 1953.

Proverb expressing similar meaning: IT'S EASIER TO TEAR DOWN THAN TO BUILD UP.

a jack of all trades is master of none Somebody who has a very wide range of abilities or skills usually does not excel at any of them: *We encourage our students to specialize at an early age, on the basis that a jack of all trades is master of none.* The proverb was first recorded in 1732 in the form "A jack of all trades is of no trade." It is perhaps most frequently encountered in the form of the cliché *a jack of all trades.*

Jack's as good as his master All people are fundamentally equal, and having a higher rank or status does not make one person better than another: "She was far from thinking Jack as good as his master and explained failure in plebeian upstarts by saying with suave contempt: 'Well, what can you expect? Wasn't bred to power'" (Winifred Holtby, *South Riding,* 1936). The proverb was first recorded in 1706, in a Spanish/English dictionary, in the form "Peter is as good as his master."

Proverbs expressing similar meaning: ALL MEN ARE CREATED EQUAL; WHEN ADAM DELVED AND EVE SPAN, WHO WAS THEN THE GENTLEMAN?

jam tomorrow and jam yesterday, but never jam today Good times always seem to belong to the past or to the future, but never to the present: *She promised us she would pay us more when things improved, but with her it's always "jam tomorrow."* The proverb appears to have made its first appearance in *Through the Looking-Glass* (1871) by Lewis Carroll: "'The rule is, jam to-morrow and jam yesterday—but never jam to-day.' 'It *must* come sometimes to "jam to-day,"' Alice objected. 'No, it can't,' said the Queen."

jesters do oft prove prophets A prediction made in jest often comes true: *I was only joking when I said that Tom and Jenny, who never*

JAPANESE PROVERBS

Many Japanese proverbs convey mystical notions about personal character and happiness, although others are firmly rooted in a more pragmatic world, in which hunger and mothers-in-law are two misfortunes to be approached with proverbial caution.

Advertising is the mother of trade

A bath refreshes the body, tea refreshes the mind

Better to wash an old kimono than borrow a new one

Character can be built on daily routine

The character of a man lies not in his body but in his soul

Flattery is the best persuader of people

Growing rice gives you more than poetry will

The lotus flower blooms in the mud

The most beautiful flowers flourish in the shade

Never rely on the glory of the morning or the smiles of your mother-in-law

One joy can drive away a hundred sorrows

One moment of intense happiness prolongs life by a thousand years

A pig used to dirt turns its nose up at rice

The prettiest of shoes makes a sorry hat

Time spent laughing is time spent with the gods

Too much politeness is impertinent

To the starving man the beauty of Fujiyama has no meaning

Truthful words are seldom pleasant

Unhappiness can be a bridge to happiness

Unspoken words are the flowers of silence

You have to bow a few times before you can stand upright

You should climb Mount Fujiyama once in your life. Climb it twice and you're a fool

---

stopped arguing, were bound to end up marrying each other, but jesters do oft prove prophets, and I've just received an invitation to their wedding. The proverb comes from Shakespeare's play *King Lear* (5:3) in the words of Regan: "Jesters do oft prove prophets."

Proverb expressing similar meaning: MANY A TRUE WORD IS SPOKEN IN JEST.

a journey of a thousand miles begins with one step Do not be put off by the magnitude of the task ahead of you—the important thing is to make a start: *As they*

set out from home on their round-the-world trip they recalled the proverb "A journey of a thousand miles begins with one step." The proverb is attributed to the Chinese philosopher Lao-tzu (c. 604–c. 531 B.C.), founder of Taoism.

Variant of this proverb: the longest journey begins with a single step.

Proverb expressing similar meaning: THE FIRST STEP IS THE HARDEST.

Jove but laughs at lovers' perjury The breaking of oaths and promises made by lovers is so commonplace that it is not regarded as a serious matter: "Perjury in the Divorce Court has been openly permitted to the upper classes for many years, following the maxim . . . that 'Jove but laughs at lovers' perjury'" (*London Evening Standard,* 1922). Of ancient origin, the proverb occurs in the writings of the Roman poet Tibullus (c. 48–19 B.C.): "*periuria ridet amantum Iuppiter* [Jupiter laughs at lovers' perjuries]." It is also found in Shakespeare's play *Romeo and Juliet* (2:2) "At lovers' perjuries,/They say, Jove laughs" and in John Dryden's poem *Palamon and Arcite* (1700): "Fool, not to know that love endures no tie,/And Jove but laughs at lovers' perjury."

the joy of the heart makes the face fair *See* A MERRY HEART MAKES A CHEERFUL COUNTENANCE.

judge and you shall be judged *See* JUDGE NOT, THAT YE BE NOT JUDGED.

judge not, that ye be not judged If you make a habit of judging and criticizing others, they will subject you to the same treatment in return: *She's not the best player in the team, but we all have our faults. "Judge not, that ye be not judged," is my motto.* The proverb is of biblical origin: "Judge not, that ye be not judged. For with what judgment ye judge, ye shall be judged: and with what measure ye mete, it shall

be measured to you again" (Matthew 7:1–2).

Variant of this proverb: judge and you shall be judged.

Proverb expressing similar meaning: PEOPLE WHO LIVE IN GLASS HOUSES SHOULDN'T THROW STONES.

judge not according to appearances Do not make a judgment about something or somebody on the basis of outward appearance alone: "She wore . . . every appearance of innocence, but in her person she illustrated the truth of the old adage that one should not judge by appearances" (M. Williams, *Leaves of a Life,* 1890). The proverb is of biblical origin: "Judge not according to the appearance, but judge righteous judgment" (John 7:24).

Variant of this proverb: never judge by appearances.

Proverbs expressing similar meaning: APPEARANCES ARE DECEIVING; THE COWL DOES NOT MAKE THE MONK; DON'T JUDGE A BOOK BY ITS COVER; A GOOD HORSE CANNOT BE OF A BAD COLOR.

justice is blind Justice must be dispensed with objectivity and without regard to irrelevant details or circumstances: "Justice is supposed to be blind; the color of a person's skin should not determine their guilt or innocence" (Oliver L. North, *Under Fire,* 1991). The proverb was first recorded in 1663 in John Dryden's *The Wild Gallant.*

keep a thing seven years and you'll find a use for it An object that seems useless now may be just what you need at some future time, so do not discard it: *I have a drawer full of odds and ends that I cannot bring myself to throw away, on the basis that if you keep a thing seven years you'll find a use for it.* The proverb was first recorded, with different wording, in 1566 in William Painter's *Palace of Pleasure.*

Variant of this proverb: keep a thing seven years and it's bound to come in handy.

keep no more cats than will catch mice Do not support any members of your family or household who cannot earn their keep: *The new president's policy is to keep no more cats than will catch mice, so some of the less productive members of staff are likely to lose their jobs.* The proverb was first recorded in 1673 in J. Dare's *Counsellor Manners.*

keep your eyes wide open before marriage, half shut afterward You should choose your husband or wife with care, but be prepared to overlook his or her faults after the wedding day: *They say that you should keep your eyes wide open before marriage and half shut afterward, but there are limits to what even the most tolerant wife will put up with.* The proverb was first recorded in 1738, in Benjamin Franklin's *Poor Richard's Almanack.*

keep your mouth shut and your eyes open A recipe for success in many walks of life is to speak only when necessary and to remain alert, observant, and watchful at all times: *On your first day at work, remember the proverb "Keep your mouth shut and your eyes open"—don't say anything that could land you in trouble, and pay attention to everything that's going on around you.* The proverb was first recorded, in its variant form, in 1581.

Variant of this proverb: keep your mouth shut and your ears open.

Proverb expressing similar meaning: HEAR ALL, SEE ALL, SAY NOWT.

keep your shop and your shop will keep you If you run a business efficiently, the profits will provide you with a comfortable income: *Whenever anybody accused him of paying more attention to his business than to his family, my uncle would argue that he had his family's interests at heart, on the basis of the saying "Keep your shop and your shop will keep you."* The proverb was first recorded in 1605. The U.S. actress Mae West parodied the proverb when she said "Keep a diary and some day it'll keep you" in the movie *Every Day's a Holiday* (1937).

killing no murder Sometimes circumstances make extreme actions forgivable: *Her grandfather appeared to be of the opinion that when it came to politicians and journalists it was a case of "killing no murder."* The proverb first appeared as the title of the Royalist pamphlet *Killing Noë Murder* (1657), which called for the assassination of the Lord Protector, Oliver Cromwell.

Proverb expressing similar meaning: DESPERATE DISEASES MUST HAVE DESPERATE REMEDIES.

kind hearts are more than coronets Kindness and compassion are of greater value than noble birth: *She discovered a number of aristocratic ancestors in her genealogical research, but her husband was not impressed. "Kind hearts are more than coronets," he said.* The proverb comes from Alfred, Lord Tennyson's poem "Lady Clara Vere de Vere" (1833): "Howe'er it be, it seems to me, / 'Tis only noble to be good, / Kind hearts are more than coronets, / And simple faith than Norman blood."

Proverb expressing similar meaning: BETTER A GOOD COW THAN A COW OF GOOD KIND.

the king can do no wrong People in authority are not bound by the rules and regulations that apply to others; specifically, a monarch is above the law: *If one of us had made such a careless and potentially dangerous mistake, we would have faced dismissal, but he's the boss, and the king can do no wrong.* The proverb dates from before 1654 and is a translation of the Latin legal maxim *"Rex no potest peccare."* The word *king* may be replaced by *queen,* with specific reference to a female monarch, or by the name of some other person or institution considered to be exempt from punishment or criticism.

Proverb expressing opposite meaning: NOBODY IS ABOVE THE LAW.

kings have long arms Few people, places, or things are beyond the reach of those in authority, and it is not easy for an offender to escape capture or punishment: *Even if you manage to get across the border, your safety is not guaranteed—kings have long arms, you know.* The proverb was first recorded in English in 1539, but the sentiment it expresses dates back to ancient times. Compare Ovid (43 B.C.–A.D. 18): "*an nescis longas regibus esse manus?* [know you not that kings have far-reaching hands?]"

Variant of this proverb: governments have long arms.

kissing goes by favor People often bestow honors and privileges on those they like, rather than on those who are most worthy of them: *She was probably the least suitable candidate for the post, but kissing goes by favor, and nobody was surprised to hear that she had been appointed.* The proverb was first recorded in 1616 in Thomas Draxe's *Adages.*

knock on wood *See* TOUCH WOOD.

knowledge and timber shouldn't be much used until they are seasoned Knowledge is not useful until it is tempered by experience: *Newly qualified police officers can be a danger to themselves and to the general public unless they remember the saying "Knowledge and timber shouldn't be much used until they are seasoned."* The proverb comes from Oliver Wendell Holmes's *The Autocrat of the Breakfast-Table* (1858).

knowledge and wisdom are far from being one Knowledgeable people may lack the wisdom to make sound judgments: *One might expect such scholarly and learned members of society to behave with a little more common sense, but knowledge and wisdom are far from being one.* The proverb was first recorded c. 1783.

knowledge is power Those who have knowledge can control or influence those who do not; sometimes used of a specific piece of information that gives one person an advantage over others: "Of a truth, Knowledge is power, but it is a power reined by scruple, having a conscience of what must be and what may be" (George Eliot, *Daniel Deronda,* 1876). The proverb is often attributed to the English philosopher Francis Bacon, who wrote "Knowledge itself is power" in his *Religious Meditations* (1597). The sentiment it expresses, however, is of biblical origin: "A man of knowledge increaseth strength" (Proverbs 24:5).

know thyself Be aware of your own strengths and weaknesses: "Know then thyself, presume not God to scan;/The proper study of Mankind is Man" (Alexander Pope, *Essay on Man,* 1732). The proverb dates from the sixth century B.C., when it was inscribed in Greek on the temple of Apollo at Delphi. It was first recorded in English in 1387.

the laborer is worthy of his hire   Those who work for others are entitled to be paid for their efforts: "Your service will not be altogether gratuitous, my old friend—the labourer is worthy of his hire" (Sir Walter Scott, *St. Ronan's Well,* 1824). The proverb is of biblical origin: "And in the same house remain, eating and drinking such things as they give: for the labourer is worthy of his hire" (Luke 10:7).

Proverb expressing similar meaning: A GOOD DOG DESERVES A GOOD BONE.

the larger the body, the bigger the heart   Large people are reputed to be kinder and more generous than others: *He was a smiling, rosy-cheeked mountain of a man, dearly loved by all who knew him, and a walking illustration of the proverb "The larger the body, the bigger the heart."* The proverb is recorded as a regional expression in the United States.

Proverb expressing opposite meaning: THE BEST THINGS COME IN SMALL PACKAGES.

last but not least   A person or thing that is not any the less important because listed last: "Though last, not least in love" (William Shakespeare, *Julius Caesar*). The proverb was first recorded in 1580 in John Lyly's *Euphuist and his England:*

"Of these three but one can stand me in steede, the last, but not the least."

the last drop makes the cup run over   One final additional thing may push a person beyond his or her limit of tolerance or endurance: *The last drop makes the cup run over, and when they asked me to cut down the tree because it was casting a shadow on their children's play area, my patience finally snapped.* The proverb was first recorded in this form in 1855, but the sentiment it expresses is of earlier origin. In his *Church History of Britain* (1655), Thomas Fuller wrote, "When the Cup is brim full before, the last (though least) superadded drop is charged alone to be the cause of all the running over."

Proverb expressing similar meaning: IT'S THE LAST STRAW THAT BREAKS THE CAMEL'S BACK.

the last straw will break the camel's back   *See* IT'S THE LAST STRAW THAT BREAKS THE CAMEL'S BACK.

late children, early orphans   Children born to older parents run a greater risk of being orphaned before they reach adulthood: *She disapproved of our decision to have another baby, quoting the proverb "Late children, early orphans," but I pointed out that* human life expectancy had increased considerably since the saying was coined.

laugh and grow fat Cheerfulness and merrymaking are good for your health: *Those seeking a recipe for a long, happy, healthy life need look no further than the old saying "Laugh and grow fat."* The proverb was first recorded in 1596 in Sir John Harington's *Metamorphosis of Ajax.*

Proverb expressing similar meaning: LAUGHTER IS THE BEST MEDICINE.

laugh and the world laughs with you, weep and you weep alone Cheerful people never lack company, but miserable people are shunned by others: *A happy face often hides a sorrowful heart—most people learn at an early age the wisdom of the proverb "Laugh and the world laughs with you, weep and you weep alone."* The current form of the proverb comes from Ella Wheeler Wilcox's poem *Solitude* (1883): "Laugh, and the world laughs with you; / Weep, and you weep alone. / For the sad old earth must borrow its mirth, / But has trouble enough of its own." The sentiment it expresses, however, is found in the writings of the Roman poet Horace (65–8 B.C.): "*ut ridentibus arrident, ita flentibus adsunt humani voltus* [men's faces laugh on those who laugh, and correspondingly weep on those who weep]."

laugh before breakfast, cry before sunset *See* SING BEFORE BREAKFAST, CRY BEFORE NIGHT.

laughter is the best medicine Laughing is an excellent remedy for disorders of the body or mind: *She belongs to a group of performers who visit local hospitals to entertain the patients with humorous sketches, on the basis that laughter is the best medicine.*

Proverb expressing similar meaning: LAUGH AND GROW FAT.

lawmakers should not be lawbreakers Legislators should abide by the laws they make: *Lawmakers should not be lawbreakers— congressmen and congresswomen are expected to set an example to their fellow citizens.* The first recorded use is c. 1386 in Geoffrey Chaucer's *Man of Law's Tale.*

laws go as kings like Laws are made by those in power: *The opposition can complain as much as they like, but laws go as kings like.* The proverb was first recorded in 1885 in J. Ormsby's *Quixote.*

learn from the mistakes of others Observe the mistakes that other people make and try not to repeat them yourself: *The best way to succeed in this competitive world is not to do something before anybody else, but to learn from the mistakes of others and do it better than everybody else.* The sentiment expressed by the proverb is of ancient origin: the Roman dramatist Plautus (c. 254–184 B.C.) wrote, "*Feliciter is sapit qui periculo alieno sapit* [He is happy in his wisdom, who is wise at the expense of another]."

Variant of this proverb: Wise men learn by other men's mistakes, fools by their own.

Proverb expressing similar meaning: EXPERIENCE IS THE TEACHER OF FOOLS.

learning is better than house or land Education and knowledge are of greater value than property ownership: *Learning is better than house or land, and my parents saw to it that I had sufficient schooling to make up for my lack of inherited wealth.* The proverb was first recorded in 1773, in David Garrick's prologue to Oliver Goldsmith's play *She Stoops to Conquer*.

Proverb expressing similar meaning: WHEN HOUSE AND LAND ARE GONE AND SPENT, THEN LEARNING IS MOST EXCELLENT.

least said, soonest mended The less you say, the less likely you are to cause trouble; often used to discourage somebody from complaining, apologizing, arguing, or making excuses: "If you defend, you'll have to go up to London. In the box, least said is soonest mended. You'll simply say you found you were mistaken, and thought it more honourable to break off at once than to go on" (John Galsworthy, *A Feud,* 1930). The proverb was first recorded, with different wording, c. 1460. It was parodied by the U.S. writer Ambrose Bierce in his *Devil's Dictionary* (1911): "Least said is soonest disavowed."

Variant of this proverb: the least said is the easiest mended.

leave no stone unturned Leave no possibility unchecked: *The police left no stone unturned looking for evidence.* The proverb appears in the writings of Euripedes and Pliny and was first recorded in English c. 1550 in *Dice-Play*.

leave off while the play is good *See* QUIT WHILE YOU ARE AHEAD.

leave well enough alone Do not try to change or improve something that is satisfactory as it stands: "'I'm going to him,' Nicole got to her knees. 'No, you're not,' said Tommy, pulling her down firmly. 'Let well enough alone'" (F. Scott Fitzgerald, *Tender Is the Night,* 1934). The proverb is of ancient origin.

Variant of this proverb: let well alone.

Proverb expressing similar meaning: IF IT AIN'T BROKE, DON'T FIX IT.

lend your money and lose your friend You risk losing your friends by lending them money, either because they fail to repay the loan or because they resent being asked to repay it: *It's not that I don't want to help you out of your financial crisis, and it's not that I don't have the money, but I value your friendship too highly. Have you never heard the saying "Lend your money and lose your friend"?* The proverb was first recorded, with different wording, in 1474. Similar advice is to be found in Shakespeare's play *Hamlet* (1:3), "Neither a borrower not a lender be;/For loan oft loses both itself and friend."

Variant of this proverb: Lend money and you get an enemy.

length begets loathing Nobody likes a long-winded speaker or writer: *Remember that length begets loathing, and keep your opening remarks short and to the point.* The proverb was first recorded in 1742 in C. Jarvis's *Don Quixote*.

Proverb expressing similar meaning: BREVITY IS THE SOUL OF WIT.

the leopard can't change its spots A person cannot change his or her character or nature: "Although he swears he has changed, leopards don't usually change their spots, especially those who don't cooperate in counseling" (*Washington Times,* 1997). The proverb is of biblical origin: "Can the Ethiopian change his skin, or the leopard his spots?" (Jeremiah 13:23).

Variant of this proverb: The leopard does not change his spots.

Proverb expressing similar meaning: ONCE A THIEF, ALWAYS A THIEF; YOU CAN DRIVE OUT NATURE WITH A PITCHFORK BUT SHE KEEPS ON COMING BACK.

less is more   A work of art, piece of writing, or other creative endeavor can be made more elegant or effective by reducing ornamentation and avoiding excess: *Her motto was "Less is more," and the simple lines of the furniture she designed began a new trend for minimalism.* The proverb is associated with the U.S. architect Ludwig Mies van der Rohe (1886–1969) but was not coined by him: it was first recorded in English in Robert Browning's poem "Andrea del Sarto" (1855).

Proverb expressing similar meaning: THE HALF IS BETTER THAN THE WHOLE.

let bygones be bygones   Put the past behind you, make a fresh start, and do not bear grudges against those who have wronged you: "Into every real friendship a little rain must fall. . . . Let's go and get the men and drink a friendship cup and let bygones be bygones" (John Cheever, *The Wapshot Chronicle,* 1957). The proverb dates from before 1577 in the form "Bygones to be bygones."

Proverbs expressing similar meaning: FORGIVE AND FORGET.

let him who is without sin cast the first stone   Only those who are truly virtuous have the right to criticize or condemn others; used to imply that nobody has this right: *I accept that what she did was wrong, but most of us have done similar things in our time—let him who is without sin cast the first stone.* The proverb is of biblical origin: "He

that is without sin among you, let him first cast a stone at her [a woman taken in adultery]" (John 8:7).

Proverb expressing similar meaning: NOBODY IS PERFECT.

let not the sun go down on your wrath   *See* NEVER LET THE SUN GO DOWN ON YOUR ANGER.

let sleeping dogs lie   Do not cause trouble by disturbing a stable—but potentially problematic—situation: "Take my advice, and speer [ask] as little about him as he does about you. Best to let sleeping dogs lie" (Sir Walter Scott, *Redgauntlet,* 1824). The proverb was first recorded c. 1385 in Chaucer's *Troilus and Criseyde,* in the form "It is nought good a slepyng hound to wake."

Proverbs expressing similar meaning: DON'T ROCK THE BOAT; NEVER TROUBLE TROUBLE TILL TROUBLE TROUBLES YOU.

let the buyer beware   It is the buyer's responsibility to check the quality or nature of goods or services before purchasing them; a legal principle in some types of transaction, and also used as a general warning to anybody making or considering a purchase: *The streets of the old town are lined with colorful market stalls, but tourists who are tempted by the goods on display would do well to remember the saying* "Let the buyer beware." The proverb was first recorded in 1523 in J. Fitzherbert's *Husbandry.* It is often used in the Latin form *"Caveat emptor."*

Proverb expressing similar meaning: THE BUYER NEEDS A THOUSAND EYES, THE SELLER WANTS BUT ONE.

let the chips fall where they may   Pay no attention to the possible consequences of your actions, and carry on regardless: "This is one area where Mr. Jacoby admits to a certain reckless disregard for practical consequences, saying that he has, perhaps foolishly, 'let the chips fall where they may'" (*New York Times,* 1987). The proverb comes from a speech made by U.S. senator Roscoe Conkling in 1880: "He [Ulysses S. Grant] will hew to the line of right, let the chips fly where they may." Chips are small, thin pieces of wood: the woodcutter carries on with his task, disregarding any chips that are thrown up in his process of hewing.

let the cobbler stick to his last   People should not offer advice, make criticisms, or otherwise interfere in matters outside their own area of knowledge or expertise: *I'm sick and tired of accountants from the city telling me how to farm my own land—let the cobbler stick to his last.* Of ancient origin, the proverb comes from a story about the Greek painter Apelles (fourth century B.C.), who permitted a certain cobbler to point out a mistake in the way he had painted a shoe but would not tolerate his criticism of other parts of the painting. The proverb was first recorded in English in 1539, in the form "Let not the shoemaker go beyond his shoe."

Variants of this proverb: The cobbler should stick to his last; the cobbler to his last and the gunner to his linstock.

Proverb expressing similar meaning: EVERY MAN TO HIS TRADE.

let the dead bury the dead   Do not concern yourself with things that are past and gone: "Let, then, the dead bury the dead. The task for us is to rejuvenate ourselves and our subject" (J. S. Huxley, *What Dare I Think?,* 1931). The proverb is of biblical

origin: "And another of his disciples said unto him, Lord, suffer me first to go and bury my father. But Jesus said unto him, Follow me; and let the dead bury their dead" (Matthew 8:21–22).

let them laugh that win   Do not rejoice until you are certain of victory or success: *Let them laugh that win—the battle is still far from over.* The proverb was first recorded in 1546 in John Heywood's *Dialogue of Proverbs.*

Variant of this proverb: the winners laugh, the losers weep.

Proverb expressing similar meaning: HE WHO LAUGHS LAST, LAUGHS LONGEST.

let well alone   *See* LEAVE WELL ENOUGH ALONE.

let your head save your heels   You can avoid wasted journeys on foot by careful planning or forethought, such as by combining errands: *If you had put the drinks on a tray, you could have saved yourself at least two trips to the kitchen. Will you never learn to let your head save your heels?* The proverb was first recorded in 1828 in W. Carr's *Dialect of Craven.*

Variant of this proverb: use your head and save your feet.

a liar is not believed when he tells the truth   There is no way of knowing when somebody with a reputation for lying is telling the truth: *She was an attention-seeker, known for wasting police time with tall stories about muggings and burglaries. So she had only herself to blame when her genuine complaint about the stalker was not taken seriously—a liar is not believed when he tells the truth.* The proverb occurs in the writings of Aristotle and Cicero.

The sentiment it expresses can be found in one of the fables of Aesop (sixth century B.C.), about a shepherd boy who repeatedly cries "Wolf!" when his sheep are not in danger, and whose cries are therefore ignored when the wolf finally appears.

Variant of this proverb: nobody believes a liar when he speaks the truth.

a liar is worse than a thief People who lie are even less trustworthy than people who thieve: "But sure the proverbe is as true as briefe, / A lyer's ever worse then a thiefe" (John Taylor, *All the Workes of John Taylor, the Water Poet*, 1630). The proverb was first recorded in 1623 in W. Painter's *Chaucer New Painted*.

Proverb expressing similar meaning: SHOW ME A LIAR AND I WILL SHOW YOU A THIEF.

a liar should have a good memory Liars must remember the untruths they have told, to avoid contradicting themselves at some later date: "They say a liar has to have a good memory. In that case, Mr. Reagan's testimony is proof of his honesty" (*Washington Times,* 1990). The proverb occurs in the writings of Quintilian (c. A.D. 35–c. 100). It was first recorded in English, in its current form, c. 1690.

liberty is not licence [license] Freedom does not mean that a person can whatever he or she wants: *As far as his wife is concerned, he is allowed to go out and enjoy himself, but he knows very well that liberty is not licence.* The proverb is a quotation from *Sonnet* vii, written by John Milton in 1645: "Licence they mean when they cry liberty."

a lie can go around the world and back again while the truth is lacing up its boots False rumors travel with alarming speed: *A lie can go around the world and back again while the truth is lacing up its boots, and if the media get hold of the idea that you are guilty, you will have a hard job subsequently proving your innocence.* The proverb was first recorded in 1859, but with the implication that it had long been in general use. The sentiment it expresses is of ancient origin.

Variant of this proverb: a lie is halfway around the world before the truth has got its boots on.

life begins at forty Your middle years can be the best time of your life, and many people make a fresh start or take a renewed interest in life at this time: "All our age benchmarks, which used to seem solid as rocks, have turned into shifting sands. *"Life Begins at 40? More like 60"* (*New York Times,* 1991). The proverb dates from 1932, when it was used as the title of a book by the U.S. writer Walter B. Pitkin. In the text of the book Pitkin predicted its future proverbial status: "Life begins at forty. . . . Today it is half a truth. Tomorrow it will be an axiom."

life is hard by the yard, but by the inch life's a cinch Life is less overwhelming if you take it one step at a time: *A difficult time lay ahead, but I drew strength from the saying: "Life is hard by the yard, but by the inch life's a cinch."* The proverb is recorded as a regional expression the United States.

Proverb expressing similar meaning: ONE STEP AT A TIME.

life is just a bowl of cherries Life is pleasant and carefree; said when things are going well, or ironically when things are going badly: *She looked back nostalgically on the days when she was young and single, and life was just a bowl of cherries.* The proverb dates from 1931, when it was used as the title of a song by Lew Brown and Ray Henderson. In 1978 the American humorist Erma Bombeck wrote a book entitled *If Life Is Just a Bowl of Cherries, What Am I Doing in the Pits?*

Proverbs expressing opposite meaning: LIFE IS NO BED OF ROSES; LIFE ISN'T ALL BEER AND SKITTLES.

life is no bed of roses   Do not expect life to be easy and pleasant; often used of life in a particular situation or with a particular person: *Everybody knows that life is no bed of roses in the armed forces, but new recruits are often horrified to learn just how hard they are expected to work.* The proverb was first recorded in 1780.

Proverb expressing similar meaning: LIFE ISN'T ALL BEER AND SKITTLES.

Proverb expressing opposite meaning: LIFE IS JUST A BOWL OF CHERRIES.

life isn't all beer and skittles   You cannot always be enjoying yourself: "Life isn't all beer and skittles, but beer and skittles, or something better of the same sort, must form a good part of every Englishman's education" (Thomas Hughes, *Tom Brown's Schooldays,* 1857). The proverb was first recorded in the 19th century, when drinking beer and playing skittles (a bowling game) were popular leisure activities among British working men.

Proverb expressing similar meaning: LIFE IS NO BED OF ROSES.

Proverb expressing opposite meaning: LIFE IS JUST A BOWL OF CHERRIES.

life is short and sweet   Life seems all the more pleasurable for being brief in duration: *Life is short and sweet, but not for some of the aged residents of hospitals in countries where euthanasia remains illegal.* The proverb was first recorded in 1802 in *Port Folio.*

Variant of this proverb: life is sweet.

Proverb expressing opposite meaning: LIFE'S A BITCH, AND THEN YOU DIE.

life is short and time is swift   Time passes too quickly for us to waste any moment of our short lives: *He tried to cram as much as possible into his waking hours, on the basis of the proverb "Life is short and time is swift."*

Proverb expressing similar meaning: SEIZE THE DAY.

life is sweet   *See* LIFE IS SHORT AND SWEET.

life is too short   We must make the most of our short lives, and not waste time on trivial things: *I have no patience with people who fall out with their friends or relatives over some petty issue and don't speak to them for months or years on end—life is too short!*

Variant of this proverb: life is too short to be little.

life is what you make it   You have only yourself to blame if your life does not turn out as you would have liked it to: *I believe that life is what you make it, and there is no point in sitting around complaining about your lack of good fortune.* The proverb was first recorded in 1897 in the writings of the American philosopher and psychologist William James.

Proverb expressing similar meaning: EVERY MAN IS THE ARCHITECT OF HIS OWN FORTUNE.

life's a bitch, and then you die   Life is full of unpleasantness and injustice: *"It's not fair, Dad—I have to do all the hard jobs around the house, and Kate gets all the easy ones." "I know, son—life's a bitch, and then you die."*

Proverb expressing opposite meaning: LIFE IS SHORT AND SWEET.

light come, light go   *See* EASY COME, EASY GO.

light gains make heavy purses   It is possible to become rich by making small profits: *They took a tiny percentage of each item sold, but light gains make heavy purses if there are enough of them.* The proverb was first recorded in 1546 in J. Heywood's *A Dialogue containing . . . the Proverbs in the English Tongue.*

Variant of this proverb: light winnings make heavy purses.

Proverb expressing similar meaning: TAKE CARE OF THE PENNIES AND THE DOLLARS WILL TAKE CARE OF THEMSELVES.

lightning never strikes twice in the same place   The same unpleasant or unexpected phenomenon will not recur in the same place or circumstances, or happen to the same person again; a superstition that often leads to a false sense of security: *"They did not hit me at all. . . . Lightning never strikes twice in the same place, nor cannon balls either, I presume"* (P. H. Myers, *The Prisoner of the Border,* 1857). The quotation is the first recorded use of the proverb.

Variant of this proverb: lightning never strikes the same place twice.

a light purse makes a heavy heart   Those who have little money are anxious and troubled: *The careworn faces of the unemployed are a graphic illustration of the saying "A light purse makes a heavy heart."* The proverb was first recorded in 1555 by J. Heywood.

Proverb expressing similar meaning: A HEAVY PURSE MAKES A LIGHT HEART.

Proverb expressing opposite meaning: MONEY CAN'T BUY HAPPINESS.

light winnings make heavy purses   *See* LIGHT GAINS MAKE HEAVY PURSES.

like attracts like   Similar people tend to be drawn to one another: *Like attracts like, so it seemed inevitable that they would become friends.* The proverb was first recorded in English c. 1375, but with the implication that it was already in general use. The sentiment it expresses is of ancient origin, and is found in Homer's *Odyssey* (c. eighth century B.C.): "the god always brings like to like."

Variant of this proverb: like will to like.

Proverb expressing similar meaning: BIRDS OF A FEATHER FLOCK TOGETHER.

Proverb expressing opposite meaning: OPPOSITES ATTRACT.

like breeds like   People are influenced by others and tend to behave in the same way; also used to imply that one thing will lead to something similar: "Like men, like manners: / Like breeds like, they say" (Alfred, Lord Tennyson, *Poems,* 1842). The proverb was first recorded in 1557 (Roger Edgeworth, *Sermons*) in the form "Like makes like." It is sometimes interpreted with literal reference to parents and their offspring.

Variant of this proverb: like begets like.

like cures like   The best remedy for a disease or affliction is something that is capable of causing the same condition; the motto of homeopathic medicine: "On the homeopathic principle of 'like cures like,' a cigar was the best preventative against . . . smoke" (Cuthbert Bede, *Verdant Green,* 1853). The proverb is associated with the German physician Samuel Hahnemann (1755–1843), the founder of homeopathy. It also exists in the Latin form *"Similia similibus curantur."*

Proverbs expressing similar meaning: FIGHT FIRE WITH FIRE; TAKE A HAIR OF THE DOG THAT BIT YOU.

like father, like son   Sons tend to resemble their fathers in character and behavior; often used to draw attention to such a similarity: *We weren't surprised to learn that he had developed an alcohol problem—like father, like son.* The proverb was first recorded c. 1340 in the form "Ill sons follow ill fathers."

Variant of this proverb: as is the father, so is the son.

Proverbs expressing similar meaning: THE APPLE NEVER FALLS FAR FROM THE TREE; LIKE MOTHER, LIKE DAUGHTER.

Proverb expressing opposite meaning: BEAUTY IS NO INHERITANCE.

like master, like man   Servants and other workers tend to follow the good or bad example set by their employers: *I don't trust him—the person he works for is a rogue and a swindler, and like master, like man.* The proverb was first recorded in English in 1530 in the form "Such master such man." The sentiment it expresses is of ancient origin, and is found in Petronius's *Satyricon* (first century A.D.): *"qualis dominus, talis et servus* [as is the master, so is the servant]."

Variant of this proverb: an ill master makes an ill servant.

like mother, like daughter   Daughters tend to resemble their mothers in character and behavior; often used to draw attention to such a similarity: "It's a case of like mother, like daughter—they're not the kind of women who forgive and forget, I'll tell you that" (Michael Korda, *Queenie,* 1985). The proverb is of biblical origin: "Behold, every one that useth proverbs shall use this proverb against thee, saying, As is the mother, so is her daughter" (Ezekiel 16:44).

Variant of this proverb: as is the mother, so is the daughter.

Proverbs expressing similar meaning: THE APPLE NEVER FALLS FAR FROM THE TREE; LIKE FATHER, LIKE SON.

Proverb expressing opposite meaning: BEAUTY IS NO INHERITANCE.

like people, like priest   The quality of a spiritual leader can be judged by the behavior of his or her followers: "He had so deep a reverence for the clergy, that it never entered into his mind that perhaps, after all, it was 'like people, like priest'" (Richard Heath, *The English Peasant,* 1893). The proverb is of biblical origin: "And there shall be, like people, like priest: and I will punish them for their ways, and reward them their doings" (Hosea 4:9).

Variant of this proverb: like priest, like people.

like will to like   *See* LIKE ATTRACTS LIKE.

the lion is not so fierce as he is painted   Some people have reputations that far exceed their real characters: *Many of the staff were nervous about meeting the new* headteacher, but it turned out that the lion was not so fierce as he had been painted. The proverb was first recorded in 1599 in R. Percyvall's *A Spanish Grammar, now augmented . . . by J. Minsheu.*

listeners never hear any good of themselves People who eavesdrop on the conversations of others risk hearing unfavorable comments about themselves; used as a warning or reprimand: *Come away from that door—you know what they are talking about in there, and listeners never hear any good of themselves.* The proverb was first recorded in 1647 in the form "Hearkeners never hear good of themselves."

Variant of this proverb: eavesdroppers hear no good of themselves.

a little absence does much good A short period of absence can have a surprisingly beneficial effect: *It might be better, both for you and for your workforce, if you didn't visit the factory every single day. Remember the saying "A little absence does much good."* The proverb is recorded as a regional expression in the United States.

LITERARY PROVERBS

A significant number of proverbs in regular use today have their origins in the writings of a particular author. The following selection identifies just a few familiar proverbs as the contributions of specific writers.

The best is yet to be (Browning)

The best-laid schemes of mice and men gang oft aglay (Burns)

Blessed is he who expects nothing, for he shall never be disappointed (Pope)

Brevity is the soul of wit (Shakespeare)

Cowards die many times before their deaths (Shakespeare)

To err is human; to forgive, divine (Pope)

Fools rush in where angels fear to tread (Pope)

Frailty, thy name is woman! (Shakespeare)

Gather ye rosebuds while ye may (Herrick)

God's in his heaven—all's right with the world (Browning)

Hope springs eternal (Pope)

A little learning is a dangerous thing (Pope)

Neither a borrower nor a lender be (Shakespeare)

Ours not to reason why (Tennyson)

A rose by any other name would smell as sweet (Shakespeare)

Self-praise is no recommendation (Dickens)

Sweet are the uses of adversity (Shakespeare)

There is a divinity that shapes our ends (Shakespeare)

A thing of beauty is a joy for ever (Keats)

Where ignorance is bliss, 'tis folly to be wise (Gray)

little and often fills the purse   A small but regular income will provide you with all the money you need; also applied to small amounts saved regularly: *Little and often fills the purse, and by putting away just ten dollars a week I managed to accumulate a substantial nest egg.* The proverb was first recorded in 1582 in S. Gosson's *Plays Confuted.*

Proverb expressing similar meaning: MANY A LITTLE MAKES A MICKLE.

little birds that can sing and won't sing must be made to sing   Those who refuse to tell what they know must be forced to do so; also interpreted more literally: "When the disdainful oligarchs declined to join in the songs . . . the great Republican leader, with his rough humour, said the words which are written in gold upon his monument, 'Little birds that can sing and won't sing, must be made to sing'" (G. K. Chesterton, *Napoleon of Notting Hill,* 1904). The proverb was first recorded in 1678 in John Ray's *A Collection of English Proverbs.*

Variant of this proverb: the bird that can sing and won't sing should be made to sing.

little boats should stay close to shore   Do not take large risks if you have limited resources: *We are only a small company, and little boats should stay close to shore—we dare not risk investing in such an uncertain enterprise.* The proverb was first recorded in 1751, in Benjamin Franklin's *Poor Richard's Almanack.*

Variant of this proverb: great boats may venture more, but little boats should keep near shore.

little drops of water, little grains of sand, make a mighty ocean and a pleasant land   Nothing is too small to be

of value: *All contributions, however small, will be gratefully received and put to good use—little drops of water, little grains of sand, make a mighty ocean and a pleasant land.* The proverb was first recorded in 1845 in Julia A. Carney's *Little Things.*

Variant of this proverb: many drops of water make an ocean.

Proverb expressing similar meaning: EVERY LITTLE HELPS.

little fish are sweet   The smallest things are sometimes the most desirable or acceptable; used specifically of something received, bought, or otherwise acquired: "'They'll sell at a loss,' he went on, with a sigh, 'but sure, little fish is sweet!' and the rent has to be made up'" (K. F. Purdon, *The Folk of Furry Farm,* 1914). The proverb was first recorded in 1830 in R. Forby's *Vocabulary of East Anglia.*

Proverb expressing similar meaning: SMALL IS BEAUTIFUL.

a little knowledge is a dangerous thing   It is often better to have no knowledge of something than to have incomplete or inadequate knowledge, which can lead to false confidence, wrong judgments, and disastrous mistakes: *People who try to treat major injuries after a few lessons in first aid can do more harm than good—a little knowledge is a dangerous thing.* Of ancient origin, the proverb takes its current form from Alexander Pope's *Essay on Criticism* (1711): "A little learning is a dang'rous thing;/Drink deep, or taste not the Pierian spring" and is sometimes regarded as a misquotation. In his essay "Science and Culture," written in 1877, Thomas Huxley asked: "If a little knowledge is dangerous, where is the man who has so much as to be out of danger?"

Variant of this proverb: a little learning is a dangerous thing.

little leaks sink the ship   Small and apparently insignificant expenses can mount up to major sums and cause serious financial problems: *"Surely you can afford to give me a few dollars." "Maybe I can, but little leaks sink the ship, and if I gave handouts to everybody who asked for them, I'd soon be ruined."* The proverb was first recorded in 1616 in the form "It is a little leak that drowns a ship."

Variant of this proverb: small leaks sink big ships.

a little learning is a dangerous thing   *See* A LITTLE KNOWLEDGE IS A DANGEROUS THING.

a little of what you fancy does you good   It is beneficial to indulge yourself from time to time: *She popped another chocolate in her mouth, telling herself that a little of what you fancy does you good.* The proverb comes from a music hall song of the same title that became well known in the 1890s, especially as sung by Marie Lloyd. The original implication was sexual, but it may now refer to any number of more or less illicit pleasures.

little pitchers have big ears   Children miss little of what is said in their hearing; often used as a warning: *I thought the kids were engrossed in their computer game, but little pitchers have big ears, and the story was all over the school by the end of the next day.* The proverb was first recorded in 1546 in the form "Small pitchers have wide ears." It occurs in Shakespeare's play *Richard III*

(2:4): "Good madam, be not angry with the child. Pitchers have ears."

a little pot is soon hot   Small people are reputed to be more easily angered than others: *A little pot is soon hot, and the staff soon learned to stay on the right side of the diminutive Mr. Green.* First recorded in 1546, the proverb occurs in Shakespeare's play *The Taming of the Shrew* (4:1): "Now were not I a little pot and soon hot, my very lips might freeze to my teeth."

little strokes fell great oaks   Great things can be achieved in small stages, or with persistent effort: "Stick to it steadily and you will see great Effects; for . . . little Strokes fell great Oaks" (Benjamin Franklin, *Poor Richard Improved*, 1757). The proverb is probably of ancient origin; in his *Adagia* (1500) the Dutch humanist Desiderius Erasmus quotes the Latin proverb "*Multis ictibus deiicitur quercus* [The oak is felled by many blows]." It also occurs in Shakespeare's play *Henry VI, Part 3* (2:1): "And many strokes, though with a little axe, / Hews down and fells the hardest-timber'd oak."

Proverb expressing similar meaning: CONSTANT DROPPING WEARS AWAY A STONE.

little thieves are hanged, but great ones escape   It is often the case that petty criminals are brought to justice, while those involved in more serious crimes succeed in evading capture and punishment: *The man who masterminded the robbery is living a life of luxury in exile, while his accomplices rot in jail. As always, the little thieves are hanged but the great ones escape.* The proverb was first recorded in English in 1639, but the French had a similar saying in the late 14th century: "*Les petits larrons sont penduez, non pas les grands* [Little thieves are hanged, not big ones]."

little things please little minds Foolish people are easily pleased; said contemptuously to or of somebody who is amused by something childish or trivial: *She was engrossed in folding the discarded candy wrappers into different shapes—little things please little minds!* The proverb has been traced back to the works of the Roman poet Ovid (43 B.C.–A.D. 18): "*parva leves capiunt animos* [small things enthral light minds]." It was first recorded in English in 1576 in the form "A little thing pleases a fool." A person to whom the proverb is contemptuously addressed may retort, "While smaller minds look on" or "While bigger fools look on."

Variant of this proverb: small things affect light minds.

live and learn People learn by experience; often said by or to somebody who has made an error of judgment: *I thought they could be trusted, but it seems I was wrong—live and learn.* The proverb was first recorded in 1575 (in George Gascoigne, *The Glasse of Governement*) as "We live to learne."

Variant of this proverb: live and learn; die and forget.

Proverbs expressing similar meaning: EXPERIENCE IS THE MOTHER OF WISDOM; THE OLDER THE WISER.

live and let live We must be tolerant of other people, and not condemn or try to change their way of life just because it is different from our own: "If 'pragmatism' and 'pluralism' meant a new openness and tolerance, a willingness, in common parlance, 'to live and let live,' an erosion of dogmatism, and a decline in religious and racial prejudices, they also meant an often bewildering absence of certitude, a sense of confusion and even abandonment" (Page Smith, *The Rise of Industrial America,* 1984). The proverb was first recorded in 1622, and is said to be of Dutch origin.

Proverb expressing similar meaning: IT TAKES ALL KINDS OF PEOPLE TO MAKE A WORLD.

live by the sword, die by the sword See HE WHO LIVES BY THE SWORD DIES BY THE SWORD.

a live dog is better than a dead lion It is better to be alive than dead; used to justify an apparent act of cowardice in a life-threatening situation: "When the lion is shot, the dog gets the spoil. So he had come in for Katherine, Alan's lioness. A live dog is better than a dead lion" (D. H. Lawrence, *The Woman Who Rode Away,* 1928). The proverb is of biblical origin: "To him that is joined to all the living there is hope: for a living dog is better than a dead lion" (Ecclesiastes 9:4).

Variant of this proverb: a living dog is better than a dead lion.

Proverb expressing similar meaning: HE WHO FIGHTS AND RUNS AWAY MAY LIVE TO FIGHT ANOTHER DAY.

Proverb expressing opposite meaning: IT'S BETTER TO DIE ON YOUR FEET THAN LIVE ON YOUR KNEES.

live every day as though it were your last Live life to the full, and make the most of every waking moment: "He enjoyed variety. He loved adventure. 'Live each day as if it's your last'—that became his philosophy" (C. David Heymann, *A Woman Named Jackie*, 1989).

Variant of this proverb: live each day as though it were the last.

Proverb expressing similar meaning: EAT, DRINK, AND BE MERRY, FOR TOMORROW WE DIE.

a living dog is better than a dead lion   *See* A LIVE DOG IS BETTER THAN A DEAD LION.

location, location, location   It is the physical location that gives something its real value: *In the end they decided not to move the company into the center of town, forgetting the golden rule "location, location, location."* An introduction of the late 20th century, it has become partiularly associated with the selling of property.

the longest day must have an end   No bad experience lasts forever: *He hid in the shelter while the bombardment continued, telling himself over and over again that the longest day must have an end.* The proverb was first recorded in 1580 in John Lyly's *Euphues and His England*.

Variant of this proverb: the longest night will have an end.

Proverbs expressing a similar meaning: BE THE DAY WEARY OR BE THE DAY LONG, AT LAST IT RINGETH TO EVENSONG; IT'S A LONG ROAD THAT HAS NO TURNING.

the longest journey begins with a single step   *See* A JOURNEY OF A THOUSAND MILES BEGINS WITH ONE STEP.

the longest night will have an end   *See* THE LONGEST DAY MUST HAVE AN END.

the longest way around is the shortest way home   It is best to do things carefully and thoroughly rather than trying to cut corners: *There is a quicker method of doing the calculation, but people often make mistakes when they use it—in this case the longest way around is the shortest way home.* The proverb was first recorded in 1635 in the form "The next way home's the farthest way about." The sentiment it expresses, however, is of earlier origin.

Variant of this proverb: the farthest way about is the nearest way home.

long foretold, long last; short notice, soon past   A change in the weather that is predicted well in advance lasts longer than one that arrives with little warning: *If the saying "Long foretold, long last; short notice, soon past," an old piece of weather lore, can be applied to the economy, then this unexpected downturn should be of relatively brief duration.* The proverb was first recorded in 1866 (A. Steinmetz, *Manual of Weathercasts*), but with the implication that it had long been in use among amateur weather forecasters.

look after the pennies and the dollars will look after themselves   *See* TAKE CARE OF THE PENNIES AND THE DOLLARS WILL TAKE CARE OF THEMSELVES.

look before you leap   Think before you act, especially before you do something that could have serious or disastrous consequences: "When you feel tempted to marry . . . look twice before you leap" (Charlotte Brontë, *Shirley*, 1849). The proverb was first recorded c. 1350 in the form "First look and afterward leap," but the sentiment it expresses can be found in the fables of Aesop (sixth century B.C.).

Proverb expressing similar meaning: ACTION WITHOUT THOUGHT IS LIKE SHOOTING WITHOUT AIM.

Proverb expressing opposite meaning: HE WHO HESITATES IS LOST.

lookers-on see most of the game An objective observer with an overall view of a situation is often more knowledgeable, or better placed to make a judgment, than somebody who is actively involved, and whose attention is therefore focused on individual details: *Lookers-on see most of the game, and the solution was obvious to all except those who were trying to find it.* The proverb was first recorded in Francis Bacon's essay "Of Followers" (1597): "To take aduise of friends is euer honorable: For lookers on many times see more then gamesters." The sentiment it expresses, however, is of earlier origin.

Variant of this proverb: lookers-on see more than players.

look on the bright side, or polish up the dark one *See* ALWAYS LOOK ON THE BRIGHT SIDE.

look out for number one *See* TAKE CARE OF NUMBER ONE.

loose lips sink ships Careless talk can cause trouble, if it results in the wrong people gaining access to sensitive information: "Mr. Hopkins, who said he was 'appalled' when Mr. Aspin left the hearing Tuesday and talked at length with reporters waiting outside, was particularly harsh in his criticism today. 'It makes us bring back the old saying, perhaps—loose lips sink ships,' Mr. Hopkins said" (*New York Times,* 1987). The proverb originated as a security slogan of World War II.

Variant of this proverb: a slip of the lip will sink a ship.

the Lord gives and the Lord takes away God has the right to take away something that he has previously given to us: often said in consolation to, or resignedly by, somebody who has suffered a devastating loss: *We would all like to hold onto the beauty and stamina of our youth, but we must remember that the Lord gives and the Lord takes away.* The proverb is of biblical origin: "Naked came I out of my mother's womb, and naked shall I return thither: the Lord gave, and the Lord hath taken away" (Job 1:21).

Variant of this proverb: the Lord who gave can take away.

the Lord moves in mysterious ways *See* GOD MOVES IN MYSTERIOUS WAYS.

lordships change manners *See* HONORS CHANGE MANNERS.

the Lord who gave can take away *See* THE LORD GIVES AND THE LORD TAKES AWAY.

lose an hour in the morning, chase it all day Time lost in the morning is impossible to make up later in the day: *His secretary was always punctual, knowing that is she lost an hour in the morning she would chase it all day.* The proverb was first recorded in 1859 in Samuel Smiles's *Self-Help.*

Variant of this proverb: lost time is never found again.

Proverb expressing similar meaning: AN HOUR IN THE MORNING IS WORTH TWO IN THE EVENING; TIME LOST CANNOT BE RECALLED.

love and a cough cannot be hid It is impossible to conceal the fact that you are in love with somebody: *It is said that love and a cough cannot be hid, but they managed to keep their relationship secret for several months.* Of Latin origin, the proverb was first recorded in English in 1573 in J. Sandforde's *Garden of Pleasure* (1573): "Foure things cannot be kept close, Loue, the cough, fyre, and sorrowe."

Variant of this proverb: love and smoke cannot be hidden.

love begets love The best way to win somebody's affection is to treat him or her in a loving manner: "Love begets love, and . . . if a man loves God, then that glowing beam will glow whether it is turned to earth or turned to heaven" (Alexander MacLaren, *The Epistle to the Ephesians,* 1909). Of Latin origin, the proverb was first recorded in English in Robert Herrick's *Hesperides* (1648): "Love love begets, then never be/Unsoft to him who's smooth to thee."

love conquers all Love can overcome any obstacle or opposition: *Their relationship survived and flourished, despite parental disapproval and long periods of separation, proving that love does indeed conquer all.* The proverb comes from the writings of Virgil (70–19 B.C.): "*Omnia vincit Amor* [Love conquers all things]." The alternative Latin form *"Amor vincit omnia"* occurs in Chaucer's *Canterbury Tales* (c. 1390).

Proverb expressing similar meaning: LOVE WILL FIND A WAY.

love is blind People do not notice the faults of those they love: "Love is blind. It's also deaf and sometimes stupid" (*Washington Times,* 1998). Of ancient origin, the proverb occurs in the writings of the Greek poet Theocritus (c. 308–c. 240 B.C.). It

was first recorded in English in Chaucer's *Canterbury Tales* (c. 1390).

love is blind; friendship closes its eyes Lovers do not notice each other's faults, whereas friends notice but disregard them: *Love is blind; friendship closes its eyes—I know Jack's a rogue, but I still value him as a friend, whereas Molly is too infatuated with him to believe that he's anything but a saint.*

love is free People tend to fall in love regardless of the suitability of the match or other obstacles. The proverb was first recorded c. 1386 in Geoffrey Chaucer's *The Knight's Tale*: "Thynk wel that love is fre! And I wol love hire mawgree al thy myght."

Proverb expressing similar meaning: LOVE WILL FIND A WAY.

love laughs at locksmiths Nothing and nobody can keep lovers apart: *There's no point in trying to stop her seeing her boyfriend by making her a prisoner in her own home—love laughs at locksmiths.* The proverb dates from 1803, when it was used as the title of a play by George Colman. The sentiment it expresses, however, occurs in Shakespeare's poem "Venus and Adonis" (1592–93): "Were beauty under twenty locks kept fast,/Yet love breaks through and picks them all at last."

Proverb expressing similar meaning: LOVE WILL FIND A WAY.

love makes the world go round Love gives motivation and meaning to all human activity: "'Oh, 'tis love, 'tis love that makes the world go round!' 'Somebody said,' Alice whispered, 'that it's done by everybody minding their own business'" (Lewis Carroll, *Alice's Adventures in*

Wonderland, 1865). The proverb occurs in a French popular song of unknown date and authorship, and a similar observation regarding heaven was made by the Italian poets Jacopone da Todi (c. 1230–1306) and Dante Alighieri (1265–1321). In his novel *Whisky Galore* (1947), Compton Mackenzie wrote, "Love makes the world go round? Not at all. Whisky makes it go round twice as fast."

love me, love my dog If you love somebody, you must be prepared to accept or tolerate everything and everybody connected with that person—his or her failings, idiosyncrasies, friends, relatives, and so on: "'I hope, Glencora, you do not count me as your enemy?' said Mrs. Marsham, drawing herself up. 'But I shall—certainly, if you attack Alice. Love me, love my dog. I beg your pardon, Alice; but what I meant was this, Mrs. Marsham; Love me, love the best friend I have in the world'" (Anthony Trollope, *Can You Forgive Her?*, 1864). The proverb dates from the 12th century or earlier, and was used in a sermon by Saint Bernard: "*qui me amat, amat et canem meum* [who loves me, also loves my dog]."

love me little, love me long Warm affection lasts longer than burning passion: *Their relationship was far too intense to last—there is truth in the old saying "Love me little, love me long."* The proverb dates from before 1500. The sentiment it expresses occurs in Shakespeare's play *Romeo and Juliet* (2:6), "Therefore love moderately; long love doth so."

the love of money is the root of all evil Greed and avarice are the cause of many of the ills of this world: *There are*

those who condemn capitalism on the basis of the proverb "The love of money is the root of all evil." The proverb is of biblical origin: "For the love of money is the root of all evil: which while some coveted after, they have erred from the faith" (1 Timothy 6:10).

Proverb expressing similar meaning: MONEY IS THE ROOT OF ALL EVIL.

love will find a way There are no effective obstacles to or defenses against love: *The behavior of difficult children can improve dramatically after a few months in a caring foster family—love will find a way.* The proverb was first recorded in Thomas Deloney's *The Gentle Craft* (c. 1598).

Proverbs expressing similar meaning: LOVE CONQUERS ALL; LOVE IS FREE; LOVE LAUGHS AT LOCKSMITHS.

love your enemy, but don't put a gun in his hand Treat your enemies with respect and humanity, but also with caution— do not give them the opportunity to repay your kindness with an act of aggression: *Several people spoke against the proposal, warning that it could prove to be a step too far in the détente between East and West. One of them reminded the assembly of the proverb "Love your enemy, but don't put a gun in his hand."*

love your neighbor as yourself Everybody should treat everybody else with respect, kindness, and tolerance: *The world would be a better place if only people could be persuaded to follow this simple rule: "Love your neighbor as yourself."* The proverb is of biblical origin: "Thou shalt not avenge, nor bear any grudge against the children of thy people, but thou shalt love thy neighbor as thyself" (Leviticus 19:18). Extensions of the proverb include "Love your neighbor, but don't pull down the fence" and "Love your neighbor, but leave his wife alone."

lucky at cards, unlucky in love   Those who have luck at card games are less fortunate in matters of the heart; said when somebody wins or loses at cards: *After losing six games in succession, she consoled herself with the saying "Lucky at cards, unlucky in love."* The proverb was first recorded in 1866, but with the implication that it had long been in general use. The sentiment it expresses occurs in Jonathan Swift's *Polite Conversation* (1738): "Well, Miss, you'll have a sad Husband, you have such good Luck at Cards."

m

make a virtue of necessity The best way to handle an undesirable situation is to turn it to your advantage: "Welcomed as a friend of the house, I had nothing for it but to take my seat quietly, and making a virtue of necessity, endeavour to derive my share of the benefit arising from an excellent sermon" (Sir Walter Scott, *Chronicles of the Canongate,* 1827). Of ancient origin, the proverb occurs in the writings of Chaucer and Shakespeare.

make haste slowly Do not rush—you will achieve your end more quickly if you proceed with care: *In conducting an investigation of this nature, the police were well aware of the need to make haste slowly—it was far too easy to overlook a vital clue.* In its Latin form *"Festina lente,"* the proverb is attributed to the Roman emperor Augustus (63 B.C.–A.D. 14). It was first recorded in its current form in Benjamin Franklin's *Poor Richard's Almanack* (1744).

Proverb expressing similar meaning: SLOW AND STEADY WINS THE RACE.

make hay while the sun shines Take advantage of an opportunity or a favorable situation when it presents itself, because it may be short-lived: "Meanwhile . . . I was busy with my own affairs, making hay while the sun shone. So great were

the crowds of people who came up to Nodwengu that in a week I had sold everything I had to sell in the two wagons, that were mostly laden with cloth, beads, knives and so forth" (H. Rider Haggard, *Child of Storm,* 1913). The proverb was first recorded in John Heywood's *Dialogue of Proverbs* (1546).

Proverbs expressing similar meaning: HOIST YOUR SAIL WHEN THE WIND IS FAIR; STRIKE WHILE THE IRON IS HOT.

a man can only die once Death can only happen once in a lifetime: *The condemned man was sanguine about the coming ordeal, telling himself "a man can only die once."* The proverb was first recorded c. 1597 by William Shakespeare in *2 Henry IV* (3:2), in the form "A man can die but once."

man does not live by bread alone People need more than the basic necessities, such as food and shelter, to lead a full and satisfying life: "Man, we know, cannot live by bread alone but hang me if I don't believe that some women could live by love alone" (Joseph Conrad, *Chance,* 1913). The proverb is of biblical origin: "man doth not live by bread only, but by every word that proceedeth out of the mouth of the Lord" (Deuteronomy 8:3),

"It is written, Man shall not live by bread alone, but by every word that proceedeth out of the mouth of God" (Matthew 4:4).

Variant of this proverb: man cannot live by bread alone.

a man in debt is caught in a net Those who owe money are trapped by their obligations and at the mercy of their creditors: *My father once told me, "A man in debt is caught in a net," and on the basis of that advice I have never borrowed a cent from anybody.*

Proverb expressing similar meaning: OUT OF DEBT, OUT OF DANGER.

a man is a lion in his own cause People tend to exceed expectations when they have a personal interest in something: *No one thought he would put up much of a struggle in court, but men can prove lions in their own cause.* The proverb was first recorded in David Fergusson, *Scottish Proverbs,* 1641.

a man is as old as he feels, and a woman as old as she looks Chronological age is irrelevant—a man of 40 may feel 30 on a good day and 50 on a bad day, and a woman can use clothing and cosmetics to make herself look younger or older than she is: "She is always making me out so much older than I am and that's not fair, for a man is only as old as he *feels* and a woman is only as old as she *looks*" (V. Lush, *Thames Journal,* 1871). The quotation is the first recorded use of the proverb. Its two halves are often used separately, the first to encourage a youthful attitude to life, and the second to encourage women to take care of their appearance. Facetious variants include "A man is as old as the woman he feels" and "A man is as old as he feels, a woman as old as she feels like admitting."

a man is innocent until proven guilty A person accused of a crime or wrongdoing is assumed to be innocent until his or her guilt has been proved; a legal principle in many countries: "'Do you feel your "no comment" will be translated as saying you're guilty?' 'To my knowledge,' he said, 'you're innocent until proven guilty'" (*New York Times,* 1989). The proverb was first recorded in 1910, but the sentiment it expresses is of earlier origin, e.g., Junius, *Letters:* "Where the guilt is doubtful, a presumption of innocence should in general be admitted."

a man is known by the company he keeps People may base their judgment of you on the reputation or character of those you associate with, so take care in choosing your friends: "Now when you came here, I told you to make friends slowly, I told you to make sure they were the right kinds of friends. You're known by the company you keep" (Robert Anderson, *Tea and Sympathy,* 1953). First recorded in 1541 with different wording, the proverb appeared in 1591 in a book offering advice to those preparing for marriage: "If a man can be known by nothing else, then he may be known by his companions."

Proverb expressing similar meaning: BIRDS OF A FEATHER FLOCK TOGETHER.

man is the measure of all things Human beings are capable of rising to any challenge: "As of all things man is said the measure,/So your full merits measure forth a man" (George Chapman, *Caesar and Pompey,* 1631). Similar sentiments were voiced by Plato, but the earliest record of the proverb in English dates to 1547, when it appeared in W. Baldwin's *Morall Phylosophie.*

manners make the man Good manners are of the utmost importance: *Remember that manners make the man—you will be judged on how you behave, not on what you look like, where you come from, or who your parents are.* First recorded c. 1350, the proverb was the motto of the bishop of Winchester, England, William of Wykeham (1324–1404).

Variant of this proverb: manners maketh man.

man proposes, God disposes Human plans and ambitions will come to nothing unless God chooses to permit their realization: "'he will allow you an income of 50,000 livres per annum during the whole time of your stay in Paris.' 'Then in that case I shall always choose to remain there.' 'You cannot control circumstances, my dear sir; "man proposes, and God disposes"'" (Alexandre Dumas, *The Count of Monte Cristo,* 1844–45). First recorded in French in the early 14th century, the proverb occurs in its Latin form, *"homo proponit, sed Deus disponit,"* in Thomas à Kempis's *De Imitatione Christi* (c. 1420), which was translated into English c. 1450.

man's best friend is his dog *See* A DOG IS A MAN'S BEST FRIEND.

a man's best reputation for the future is his record of the past A person's record of past achievement or conduct may be used to predict his or her future performance: *A man's best reputation for the future is his record of the past, so with a résumé like this you should have no difficulty finding another job.* The proverb is recorded as a regional expression in the United States.

man's extremity is God's opportunity People often turn to religion in times of crisis, and such times give God the opportunity to demonstrate his power: "In the first winter of the war . . . we were all much 'encouraged by tales of a new thirst for religion among the majority of the men. . . . 'Man's extremity, God's opportunity'" (E. A. Burroughs, *The Valley of Decision,* 1916). The proverb was first recorded in 1629.

Proverb expressing similar meaning: THE DANGER PAST AND GOD FORGOTTEN.

a man's got to do what a man's got to do You must do what needs to be done, or what you feel ought to be done, however unpleasant it may be; sometimes used facetiously: *It won't be easy, breaking the news to them, but a man's got to do what a man's got to do.* The proverb is associated with the U.S. actor John Wayne, who used it in the movie *Stagecoach* (1939). It also occurs in John Steinbeck's novel *The Grapes of Wrath* (1939): "I know this—a man got to do what he got to do."

a man's home is his castle People have the right to privacy and freedom of action in their own home: "A man's home is his castle—he can defend it with bazookas and machine guns if he knows where to get them" (Clifford Irving, *The Campbell Murder Case,* 1988). The proverb was first recorded in 1581 and enshrines a legal maxim stated by the English jurist Sir Edward Coke (1552–1634): "For a man's house is his castle, *et domus sua cuique tutissimum refugium* [and each man's home is his safest refuge]." It is sometimes adapted to different situations by substituting another word for *home,* as in "A man's automobile is his castle."

Variant of this proverb: an Englishman's home is his castle.

a man's word is as good as his bond Honorable people do not break their promises: *I said I would repay the money before the end of the month, and I will do so—a man's word is as good as his bond.* The proverb was first recorded c. 1500 in the form "A king's word should be a king's bond."

Variants of this proverb: an honest man's word is as good as his bond; a gentleman's word is his bond.

Proverb expressing opposite meaning: PROMISES, LIKE PIECRUST, ARE MADE TO BE BROKEN.

man's work lasts till set of sun; woman's work is never done *See* A WOMAN'S WORK IS NEVER DONE.

the man who is born in a stable is not a horse A person does not necessarily have the stereotypical characteristics of the place where he or she was born: *Teased at college about his Oklahoma origins, he used to reply, "The man who is born in a stable is not a horse."* The proverb is attributed to Arthur Wellesley, Duke of Wellington (1769–1852).

Variant of this proverb: because a man is born in a stable that does not make him a horse.

a man who is his own lawyer has a fool for his client It is not wise to act as your own attorney in a court of law, or in some other legal process; also used in other fields of activity requiring professional expertise or objectivity: *She decided to represent herself, despite our warnings that a man who is his own lawyer has a fool for his client, with disastrous consequences.* The proverb was first recorded in 1809 in Philadelphia (*Port Folio*).

a man without a religion is a horse without a bridle Religion helps to guide a person through life, and control his or her behavior, just as a bridle is used to guide and control a horse: *My grandmother was fairly tolerant in matters of religion, believing that everybody should be allowed to worship their own god, but she had no time for atheists. "A man without a religion is a horse without a bridle," she used to say.* The proverb is first recorded in Robert Burton's *The Anatomy of Melancholy* (1621). The proverb is of Latin origin: *Homo sine religione, sicut equus sine freno.*

a man wrapped up in himself makes a very small bundle Self-centeredness is not a quality that is associated with greatness: *Rather than wallowing in self-pity after the death of his wife, he threw himself into voluntary work for a number of good causes, on the basis that a man wrapped up in himself makes a very small bundle.*

many a little makes a mickle Small amounts accumulate to form a large quantity; often used of small sums of money saved over a long period: "My mother used, upon all occasions, to inculcate some salutary axioms . . . and as I grew up, stored my memory with deeper observations; restrained me from the usual puerile expenses, by remarking that MANY A LITTLE MADE A MICKLE" (Samuel Johnson, *Essays*, c. 1750). The proverb was first recorded in this form in 1614, but the sentiment it expresses is of earlier origin. *Mickle* is a dialect word for a large quantity. The variant form "Many a mickle makes a muckle" is actually meaningless, as *muckle* is synonymous with *mickle.*

Variant of this proverb: many a mickle makes a muckle.

Proverbs expressing similar meaning: EVERY LITTLE HELPS; LITTLE AND OFTEN FILLS THE PURSE.

many are called, but few are chosen
Not everybody who wants to do something is selected or permitted to do it; used in any elitist situation: *Although some of the lesser-known colleges and universities are desperate for students, in the case of Harvard and similarly prestigious institutions, many are called but few are chosen.* The proverb is of biblical origin, occurring in this form in Matthew 22:14.

many a true word is spoken in jest
Something said jokingly often proves to be true: *Many a true word is spoken in jest, and the seeds of suspicion were sown in my mind when somebody flippantly remarked, regarding my wife's strange behavior, "Perhaps she's having an affair."* The proverb was first recorded in this form in 1665, but the sentiment it expresses is of earlier origin, occurring in Chaucer's *Canterbury Tales* (c.1390): "Be nat wrooth, my lord, though that I pleye./Ful ofte in game a sooth [truth] I have herd seye!"

Variant of this proverb: there's many a true word said in jest.

Proverb expressing similar meaning: JESTERS DO OFT PROVE PROPHETS.

many drops of water make an ocean *See* LITTLE DROPS OF WATER, LITTLE GRAINS OF SAND, MAKE A MIGHTY OCEAN AND A PLEASANT LAND.

many go out for wool and come home shorn Many people who set out to make their fortune, or to achieve some other aim, end up in a worse state than before: "Some go intent on repairing the ravages of Epsom or Newmarket [English horse-racing events]; and in this speculative section not a few . . . who go for wool come away shorn" (G. W. E. Russell, *Sketches and Snapshots,* 1910). The prov-erb was first recorded in 1599 in John Minsheu's *Spanish Dialogues.*

many hands make light work Work is quickly and easily done when many people help: *Come on, many hands make light work, and if we all do our bit the house will be spotless again by the time my parents get back.* Of ancient origin, the proverb was first recorded in English c. 1330.

Proverb expressing opposite meaning: TOO MANY COOKS SPOIL THE BROTH.

many kiss the hand they wish to see cut off A person's true feelings or intentions may be concealed by the mask of politeness or hypocrisy; used to warn against being deceived by such a show: *Some were surprised to see him at the ceremony, knowing his intense dislike of everything the organization stands for, but many kiss the hand they wish to see cut off.* The proverb was first recorded in 1599 in John Minsheu's *Spanish Dialogues.*

March comes in like a lion and goes out like a lamb The month of March often begins with wild, stormy weather and ends with mild, fair weather: *Those who are still repairing the damage caused by the storms that struck the region earlier this month are hoping that the saying about March coming in like a lion and going out like a lamb will prove true.* The proverb dates from before 1625 (John Fletcher, *A Wife for a Month*).

Variant of this proverb: March is in like a lion, out like a lamb.

March winds and April showers always bring May flowers *See* APRIL SHOWERS BRING MAY FLOWERS.

marriage is a lottery Whether a marriage succeeds or fails is all a matter of luck; also applied to the choice of a marriage partner: *If it's true that marriage is a lottery, then my grandparents must be one of the couples that hit the jackpot.* The proverb was first recorded in 1642 (Thomas Fuller's *Holy State*).

marriages are made in heaven Providence decides who will marry whom: "I have always liked the sound of the phrase 'a marriage has been arranged' . . . . I prefer the idea of arrangement to that other statement, that marriages are made in Heaven" (Stella Gibbons, *Cold Comfort Farm*, 1932). The proverb was first recorded in 1567, in William Painter's *Palace of Pleasure*: "True it is, that marriages be don in Heaven and performed in earth." It has given rise to the figurative phrase *a marriage made in heaven,* describing an ideal marriage or any merger or combination of two parties or elements that are in perfect harmony.

Proverb expressing similar meaning: HANGING AND WIVING GO BY DESTINY.

marry in haste, repent at leisure Those who rush into marriage, and subsequently discover that they have made a mistake, may have to live with the unpleasant consequences for a long time: "'Marry in haste and repent at leisure' is a proverb that may be borne in mind with advantage in the choice of a party as well as of a wife" (Sir William Stirling-Maxwell, *Works*, 1872). The proverb was first recorded in 1568. It is sometimes applied to other acts of rashness, with a different verb in place of *marry.*

Proverb expressing opposite meaning: HAPPY'S THE WOOING THAT'S NOT LONG A-DOING.

marry in May, rue for aye According to popular superstition, it is unlucky to marry in May: *My mother was horrified to hear that we had chosen May 15 for our wedding day. "Marry in May, rue for aye!" she cried. I wonder what she would have said if she had lived to join us at our 50th anniversary celebrations last weekend.* The proverb occurs in the writings of the Roman poet Ovid (43 B.C.–A.D. 18): "*mense malum Maio nubere volgus ait* [the common people say it is bad luck to marry in May]."

May chickens come cheeping Children born in the month of May are weak and delicate: *Born on May 20, 1902, he never had a day's illness in his life and died at the grand old age of 98. So much for the proverb "May chickens come cheeping"!* The proverb was first recorded in 1868 in A. Hislop's *The Proverbs of Scotland.*

meat and mass never hindered man You can always find time to eat and to go to church; said to somebody who claims to be too busy, or in too much of a hurry, for one or both of these: "Meat and mass never hindered man. The mass I cannot afford you, for we are all good Protestants. But the meat I press on your attention" (Robert Louis Stevenson, *Catriona,* 1893). The proverb dates from before 1628.

medicine can prolong life, but death will seize the doctor, too The power of medicine is limited, and everybody must die eventually: *Those who expect miracles of the medical profession would do well to remember the saying "Medicine can prolong life, but death will seize the doctor too."*

Proverb expressing similar meaning: DEATH DEFIES THE DOCTOR.

185

the meek shall inherit the earth Humility will ultimately be rewarded: "We have the highest authority for believing that the meek shall inherit the Earth; though I have never found any particular corroboration of this aphorism in the records of Somerset House [British registry of births, marriages, and deaths]" (F. E. Smith, Earl of Birkenhead, *Contemporary Personalities,* 1924). The proverb is of biblical origin: "Blessed are the meek: for they shall inherit the earth" (Matthew 5:5). The facetious variant "The meek shall inherit the earth, but not its mineral rights" is attributed to the U.S. oil executive J. Paul Getty (1892–1976). Equally flippant is the modern variant "The geek shall inherit the earth."

Proverb expressing similar meaning: SOFT AND FAIR GOES FAR; SOFTLY, SOFTLY, CATCHEE MONKEY.

men are blind in their own cause People cannot be objective or think rationally in matters they feel very strongly about: *It's useless trying to reason with him—men are blind in their own cause.* The proverb was first recorded in 1546 in John Heywood's *Dialogue of Proverbs.*

Proverb expressing similar meaning: NOBODY SHOULD BE JUDGE IN HIS OWN CAUSE.

men are from Mars, women are from Venus Men and women have essentially dissimilar natures: *My mother and father never agreed about anything, but then, men are from Mars and women are from Venus.* It achieved proverbial status after appearing as the title of the 1993 book *Men Are from Mars, Women Are from Venus: A Practical Guide for Improving Communication and Getting What You Want in Your Relationships* by John

Gray. A jocular variant runs: "Men are from earth, women are from earth. Deal with it."

men make houses, women make homes Although men can build or buy property, it takes a woman to turn a house into a home: *His apartment is very tastefully furnished, but it's a bit austere and unwelcoming—as they say, "Men make houses, women make homes."* The proverb was first recorded in 1938 in Selwyn Gurney Champion's *Racial Proverbs.*

Variant of this proverb: men build houses, women build homes.

a merry heart makes a cheerful countenance Inward feelings of happiness are reflected on the face: *I'm supposed to greet the customers with a happy face, but what do I have to smile about? If a merry heart makes a cheerful countenance, it's small wonder that I'm accused of looking miserable most of the time.* The proverb is of biblical origin: "A merry heart maketh a cheerful countenance: but by sorrow of the heart the spirit is broken" (Proverbs 15:13).

Variant of this proverb: the joy of the heart makes the face fair.

might makes right In any dispute or contest, the more powerful party will prevail, regardless of justice: *Might makes right, and litigation is a costly and futile exercise when the defendant is one of the largest multinational companies in the world.* First recorded in English in the early 14th century, the proverb is of ancient origin, occurring in the epic *Pharsalia* by the Roman poet Lucan (A.D. 39–65) "*mensuraque iuris vis erat* [might was the measure of right]." The sentiment it expresses occurs even earlier, in Plato's *Republic* (fourth century B.C.): "justice is nothing else than the interest of the stronger."

Variants of this proverb: might is right; might beats right.

Proverb expressing similar meaning: PROVIDENCE IS ALWAYS ON THE SIDE OF THE BIG BATTALIONS.

the mill cannot grind with the water that is past There is no point in looking back with regret on missed opportunities; used either to encourage people to take full advantage of the present or simply to discourage them from yearning for the past: "It did no good to think back. The mill cannot grind with the water that is past, as the old people in the mountains used to say" (Guy Richards, *Red Kill,* 1980). The proverb was first recorded in Thomas Draxe's *Adages* (1616).

Proverbs expressing similar meaning: SEIZE THE DAY; TAKE TIME BY THE FORELOCK.

the mills of God grind slowly, yet they grind exceedingly small Retribution may be a long time in coming, but it cannot be avoided; also loosely applied to any slow or painstaking process: *You may think you've got off scot-free, but just you wait—the mills of God grind slowly, yet they grind exceedingly small.* The proverb was first recorded in English in 1640 in the form "God's mill grinds slow, but sure." It originated in a line quoted by the Greek philosopher Sextus Empiricus (second century A.D.), which was subsequently used by the German poet Friedrich Von Logau (1604–55) in a poem ultimately translated into English by Henry Wadsworth Longfellow (1807–82): "Though the mills of God grind slowly, yet they grind exceeding small;/Though with

patience He stands waiting, with exactness grinds He all."

Variant of this proverb: the mills of God grind slowly, but they grind exceedingly fine.

a mind is a terrible thing to waste Everybody should make best use of the intellectual capacity they have: "We will launch a renaissance in education, in science and learning. A mind is a terrible thing to waste" (Walter Mondale, *New York Times,* 1984). The proverb has been the slogan of the United Negro College Fund since 1972.

Proverb expressing similar meaning: MIND UNEMPLOYED IS MIND UNENJOYED.

mind unemployed is mind unenjoyed By failing to put your mind to use you fail to take advantage of the resources and pleasures it offers you: *At his retirement party he announced that he had enrolled for a correspondence course in sociology, on the basis of the proverb "Mind unemployed is mind unenjoyed."*

Proverb expressing similar meaning: A MIND IS A TERRIBLE THING TO WASTE.

mind your own business Concentrate upon your own affairs (rather than those of others): "The Devil has got a lot of maxims which his adherents . . . are not slow to use—'Mind your own business'" (R. J. Mackenzie, *Life,* 1905). The proverb (now used more often as a rebuke to those who interfere in the business of others) was first recorded in 1639 in J. Clarke's *Paroemiologia Anglo-Latina.*

misery loves company When you are unhappy, it is good to be with others who have suffered in a similar way, or simply with people who will listen to your woes and offer sympathy; also used to imply that miserable or unfortunate people like everybody around them to be in the same situation: *Group therapy can be very effective in cases like these—misery loves company.* The proverb dates from before 1349.

Proverb expressing similar meaning: A TROUBLE SHARED IS A TROUBLE HALVED.

misery makes strange bedfellows *See* ADVERSITY MAKES STRANGE BEDFELLOWS.

misfortunes never come singly It is often the case that several misfortunes happen together, or in quick succession: "'We are now without father: we shall soon be without home and brother,' she murmured. At that moment a little accident supervened, which seemed decreed by fate purposely to prove the truth of the adage, that 'misfortunes never come singly.' . . . St. John passed the window reading a letter. He entered. 'Our uncle John is dead,' said he" (Charlotte Brontë, *Jane Eyre,* 1847). The proverb was first recorded, with different wording, c. 1300. The sentiment it expresses occurs in Shakespeare's play *Hamlet* (4:5), "When sorrows come, they come not single spies,/But in battalions." The current form of the proverb dates from the 17th or 18th century.

Variants of this proverb: misfortunes seldom come alone; troubles never come singly.

Proverb expressing similar meaning: IT NEVER RAINS BUT IT POURS.

a miss is as good as a mile If you fail, the margin of failure is irrelevant: "He was very near being a poet—but a miss is as good as a mile, and he always fell short of the mark" (Sir Walter Scott, *Journal,* 1825). The proverb was first recorded in 1614 in the form "An inch in a miss is as good as an ell."

moderation in all things Excess is to be avoided wherever possible: *Too much strenuous exercise can be as bad for you as too little—moderation in all things.* The proverb comes from the Greek poet Hesiod's *Works and Days* (eighth century B.C.) "moderation is best in all things."

Proverbs expressing similar meaning: ENOUGH IS AS GOOD AS A FEAST; ENOUGH IS ENOUGH; THERE'S MEASURE IN ALL THINGS.

Monday's child is fair of face Children born on a Monday are supposed to be good-looking: *I was born on a Monday, but I sometimes find it hard to believe the saying "Monday's child is fair of face" when I look in the mirror!* The proverb is the first line of a traditional rhyme. See entries at the days of the week for other proverbs from this rhyme.

money begets money It is easy to make more money when you already have some: "'Wish I knew something about business.' 'I can tell you all I know in one sentence. Money gets money'" (John Steinbeck, *The Winter of Our Discontent,* 1961). The proverb was first recorded in T. Wilson's *Discourse upon Usury* (1572).

Variants of this proverb: money gets money; money makes money; money loves company.

Proverb expressing similar meaning: IT TAKES MONEY TO MAKE MONEY.

money burns a hole in the pocket People are often too eager to spend their money: *Money burns a hole in the pocket—*

my grandmother used to give me some money to take on vacation, and my parents always had to restrain me from spending it all on the first day. The proverb was first recorded c. 1530 in the works of Sir Thomas More: "A little wanton money which . . . burned out the bottom of his purse."

money can't buy happiness Money cannot satisfy your emotional or spiritual needs: *Money can't buy happiness, as a number of lottery jackpot winners have discovered.* The proverb was first recorded in 1792. Other words may be substituted for *happiness,* such as *love* or *friends.*

Proverbs expressing opposite meaning: A HEAVY PURSE MAKES A LIGHT HEART; A LIGHT PURSE MAKES A HEAVY HEART.

money doesn't grow on trees Money is not easily earned or acquired; often said by a parent to a child who is constantly asking for money or who spends it unwisely: *No, I won't give you 100 dollars to buy a ticket for the concert. Money doesn't grow on trees, you know.* The proverb was first recorded in 1750. With another word in place of *money* it may be used in different situations, to indicate a scarcity of the specified thing, as in "Jobs don't grow on trees" or "Good teachers don't grow on trees."

money gets money See MONEY BEGETS MONEY.

money has no smell Money that comes from unsavory or questionable sources is no different from—and no less acceptable than—money that comes from anywhere else: "The associations of the wealth scarcely affected him. He understood in the flesh the deep wisdom of that old proverb . . . that money has no smell"

(Arnold Bennett, *Mr. Prohack,* 1922). The proverb comes from a story about the Roman emperor Vespasian, whose son objected to a tax on public lavatories. Vespasian asked him to sniff a coin thus obtained, and he was forced to admit that it did not smell offensive. The proverb is sometimes quoted in the Latin form "*Non olet* [It does not smell]."

money isn't everything Money is not the only thing that matters: "He said quite angrily that money was not everything, there was the satisfaction of knowing you'd turned out a good job" (Flora Thompson, *Still Glides the Stream,* 1948). The proverb was first recorded in 1842 in the form "Money is not all."

Proverb expressing similar meaning: THE BEST THINGS IN LIFE ARE FREE.

money is power Wealthy people can have or do what they want: "'Money is power,' Lanny said. 'Money commands respect and obedience from other people'" (Upton Sinclair, *A World to Win,* 1946). The proverb was first recorded in 1741 (N. Ames, *Almanacs*).

Proverbs expressing similar meaning: A GOLDEN KEY CAN OPEN ANY DOOR; MONEY TALKS.

money is round and rolls away Money is easily spent: *Money is round and rolls away—despite my best efforts, I never seem to have any left at the end of the week.* The proverb was first recorded in 1619 in *Helpe to Discourse.*

Proverb expressing similar meaning: RICHES HAVE WINGS.

money is the root of all evil Money is the cause of many undesirable human qualities and the motivation for many wicked or immoral acts: *He justified the low wages he paid to his workers by quoting the proverb "Money is the root of all evil."* Based on a misquotation of the biblical saying "the love of money is the root of all evil" (1 Timothy 6:10), the proverb was first recorded in its current form in 1777. The opposite view was put forward by Samuel Butler, in *Erewhon* (1872)—"The want of money is the root of all evil"—and George Bernard Shaw, in *Man and Superman* (1903): "Lack of money is the root of all evil."

Proverb expressing similar meaning: THE LOVE OF MONEY IS THE ROOT OF ALL EVIL.

money loves company   *See* MONEY BEGETS MONEY.

money makes a man   People are impressed by wealth, and have respect and admiration for those with money: "Money maketh a man; even if he was a monkey to start with" (D. H. Lawrence, letter dated May 7, 1920). The proverb dates from before 1500.

money makes money   *See* MONEY BEGETS MONEY.

money makes the mare go   Money enables things to be done, and things are done faster or more readily for those who are willing and able to pay well: *Money makes the mare go, and a not-too-subtle display of wealth can work wonders in cutting through red tape.* The proverb was first recorded in 1573 in the form "Money makes the horse to go," but the sentiment it expresses is of earlier origin.

Variant of this proverb: money makes the mare to go.

Proverb expressing similar meaning: MONEY MAKES THE WORLD GO ROUND.

money makes the world go round   Money funds most human affairs: *Idealism is all very well, but it's money makes the world go round.* This relatively modern proverb began life as a song title from the Fred Ebb and John Kander musical *Cabaret* (1966), although similar sentiments expressing virtually the same thing date back much earlier.

Proverb expressing similar meaning: MONEY MAKES THE MARE GO.

money talks   Wealthy people have great influence: "'At least I assume they are millionaires?' 'That is what they would like you to assume, certainly. And if money talks . . . they are certainly making the right amount of noise'" (Anita Brookner, *Hotel du Lac,* 1984). The proverb was first recorded in 1666, in an Italian proverb collection, in the form "Gold speaks." A facetious variant is "Money talks, but all it says is goodbye."

Proverbs expressing similar meaning: A GOLDEN KEY CAN OPEN ANY DOOR; MONEY IS POWER.

monkey see, monkey do   Foolish people mindlessly copy others: *On the basis of the saying "Monkey see, monkey do," stunts like these have to be accompanied by the warning "Don't try this at home" when shown on prime-time television.* The proverb was first recorded in 1934 in Robert Hare's *Hand of the Chimpanzee* (1934).

more die of food than famine   Excessive indulgence in the wrong type of food is a bigger killer than famine: *Posters bearing the message "More die of food than famine," part of a new campaign for healthy eating, have been criticized by some of the charitable organizations involved in overseas aid.*

more haste, less speed   If you do things hurriedly, you will make more mistakes and ultimately take longer; often used to advise somebody to act more slowly or carefully: "Ah, those advisers!" said he. "If we had listened to them all we should not have made peace with Turkey and should not have been through with that war. Everything in haste, but more haste, less speed" (Leo Tolstoy, *War and Peace*, 1863–69). The proverb was first recorded c. 1350 in the form "The more haste, the worse speed."

Variant of this proverb: more haste, worse speed.

Proverb expressing similar meaning: ALWAYS IN A HURRY, ALWAYS BEHIND.

the more said, the less done   The more things are talked about, the less likely they are to get done: *We could talk about this all night, but the more said, the less done.* The proverb was first recorded in 1760 in George Colman's *Polly Honeycombe*: "It's an old saying and a true one, The more there's said the less there's done."

the more the merrier   The more people who take part, the more fun everybody will have, so extra people are always welcome: *"Is it OK with you if Tom and Megan come along too?" "Sure, the more the merrier."* The proverb was first recorded c. 1340 in the alliterative poem *Pearl*.

the more things change, the more they stay the same   Things never change very much, and something thought to be new and different—or peculiar to the current age—is often very similar to something that has happened before: *Reading 19th-century literature, I am often struck by the truth of the proverb "The more things change, the more they stay the same."* The proverb originated in French, in Alphonse Karr's *Les Guêpes* (1849): *"Plus ça change, plus c'est la même chose,"* and the French form is sometimes used by English speakers, often abbreviated to *"Plus ça change."* The proverb was first recorded in English in George Bernard Shaw's *The Revolutionists' Handbook* (1903).

Proverbs expressing similar meaning: HISTORY REPEATS ITSELF; THERE'S NOTHING NEW UNDER THE SUN.

the more you get, the more you want   Getting what you want only leads to a desire for more: "I was averaging eighty to a hundred a week. Well, you know how it is. The more you get the more you want" (George Harmon Coxe, *The Glass Triangle*, 1940). The proverb was first recorded, with different wording, c. 1340 in R. Rolle's *Psalter*.

Variant of this proverb: the more you have, the more you want.

Proverb expressing similar meaning: MUCH WOULD HAVE MORE.

the more you stir it, the worse it stinks   The more you investigate an unsavory or dubious affair, the more unpleasant details you discover: *The more you stir it, the worse it stinks—it now appears that a number of major public figures were involved in the scandal, and the cover-up was coordinated by the president himself.* The proverb was first recorded in 1546 in John Heywood, *Dialogue of Proverbs*: "The more we stur a tourde [turd], the wours it will stynke."

Variant of this proverb: the more you stir a stink, the louder it smells.

morning dreams come true According to popular superstition, the dreams you have in the early hours of the morning, or just before waking, are the most likely to come true: *If morning dreams really do come true, then I'm in for an interesting day at work—I dreamed this morning that my boss was found wandering naked in the parking lot!* The proverb was first recorded in this form in 1813, but the sentiment it expresses is of ancient origin: in the second century B.C. the pastoral poet Moschus wrote, "at the third watch of the night, when dawn is near, . . . and when the flock of true dreams is out grazing."

most people consider thrift a fine virtue in ancestors People are generally pleased when the thrift of their ancestors enables them to live comfortably without having to be too thrifty themselves: *If it is true that most people consider thrift a fine virtue in ancestors, then the fortune amassed by his family over the generations should make him the envy of the nation.*

a mother can take care of ten children, but sometimes ten children can't take care of one mother No matter how many children she raises, a woman is often neglected or abandoned by all of them in her old age: *It's not easy, with so many mouths to feed, but I try to put a little money away each week in case I end up in a nursing home. Maybe I'm cynical, but I believe there's a lot of truth in the saying "A mother can take care of ten children, but sometimes ten children can't take care of one mother."* The proverb is of Jewish origin.

the mother of mischief is no bigger than a midge's wing A great quarrel, or other major trouble, is often caused by something trivial: *The mother of mischief is no bigger than a midge's wing, and a throwaway remark about her sister's in-laws led to a family feud that lasted for more than 20 years.* The proverb dates from before 1628.

a mouse may help a lion Small or lowly people can sometimes give valuable assistance to those who are greater or more powerful than themselves: "I only offer to show my gratitude by doing what I can. . . . A mouse may help a lion" (John Buchan, *The House of the Four Winds,* 1935). The proverb comes from one of the fables of Aesop (sixth century B.C.), in which a mouse helps a lion caught in a trap by chewing through the ropes that bind it.

the mouse that has but one hole is quickly taken Do not be dependent on one thing alone, or on a single possible course of action, but have other options in reserve: *Be sure to have an alternative plan to fall back on if the first one fails—remember that the mouse that has but one hole is quickly taken.* Of ancient origin, the proverb was first recorded in English in Chaucer's *Canterbury Tales* (c. 1390): "I holde a mouses herte nat worth a leek, / That hath but oon hole for to sterte to."

Variant of this proverb: the mouse that has but one hole is soon caught.

Proverb expressing similar meaning: DON'T PUT ALL YOUR EGGS IN ONE BASKET.

moving three times is as bad as a fire *See* THREE MOVES ARE AS BAD AS A FIRE.

much coin, much care People with a lot of money have much to worry about. The proverb was first recorded in English 1639 in J. Clarke's *Paroemiologia Anglo-Latina*, although it also appeared as far back as the *Odes* of Horace, who rendered it in the form: "Care follows increasing wealth."

Proverb expressing opposite meaning: A HEAVY PURSE MAKES A LIGHT HEART.

much cry and little wool Those who make the most noise, the loudest boasts, or the greatest promises often have the least to offer, are the least productive, or simply fail to deliver the goods: "'What noisy fellow is that in the next room?' said Joe, when he had disposed of his breakfast, and had washed and brushed himself. 'A recruiting serjeant,' replied the Lion. . . . 'And I wish . . . he was anywhere else but here. The party make noise enough, but don't call for much. There's great cry there, Mr Willet, but very little wool'" (Charles Dickens, *Barnaby Rudge,* 1841). The proverb dates from before 1475.

Variant of this proverb: great cry but little wool.

much smoke, little fire Often when there is most fuss about something, there is least cause for it: *As usual with such stories in the press it was a case of much smoke, little fire.* It was first recorded in 1639 in the *Berkeley MSS*.

Proverb expressing opposite meaning: THERE'S NO SMOKE WITHOUT FIRE.

much water goes by the mill that the miller knows not of Many things are stolen or go astray without the knowledge of the person affected: "What, man! More water glideth by the mill than wots the miller of" (William Shakespeare, *Titus Andronicus*, 2:1).

much would have more People are never satisfied with what they have: *We gave them all we could spare, but much would have more—they returned under cover of darkness and robbed us while we slept.* The proverb was first recorded c. 1350 in *Douce MS 52*.

Proverb expressing similar meaning: THE MORE YOU GET, THE MORE YOU WANT.

murder will out The crime of murder rarely goes undetected, and few murderers escape justice: "Crimes cause their own detection, do they? And murder will out . . ., will it?" (Wilkie Collins, *The Woman in White,* 1860). The proverb was first recorded in this form in Chaucer's *Canterbury Tales* (c. 1390): "Mordre wol out; that se we day by day," but the sentiment it expresses is of earlier origin, and it recurs in a number of Shakespeare's plays.

music hath charms to soothe the savage breast Music can have a calming influence on mind and spirit, or on violent people: *The principle that music hath charms to soothe the savage breast is being tested by a new experimental form of therapy for hyperactive and disruptive youngsters, which involves periods of gentle exercise accompanied by classical music.* The proverb comes from William Congreve's play *The Mourning Bride* (1697): "Music has charms to soothe a savage breast, / To soften rocks, or bend a knotted oak." The variant is a common misquotation. Shakespeare expressed a similar—but more disturbing—sentiment in his play *Measure for Measure* (4:1): "music oft hath such a charm/To make bad good, and good provoke to harm."

Variant of this proverb: music has charms to soothe the savage beast.

my son is my son till he gets him a wife, but my daughter's my daughter all the days of her life *See* A SON IS A SON TILL HE GETS HIM A WIFE, A DAUGHTER'S A DAUGHTER ALL OF HER LIFE.

nature abhors a vacuum There are no deficiencies in nature—whenever a gap or vacancy occurs, something or somebody will come along to fill it: "Whatever philosophy may determine of material nature, it is certainly true of intellectual nature, that it abhors a vacuum: our minds cannot be empty" (Samuel Johnson, letter dated June 20, 1771). Of ancient origin, the proverb was first recorded in English in 1551, in Thomas Cranmer's *Answer to Gardiner:* "Naturall reason abhorreth vacuum."

nature does nothing in vain Nothing in nature happens without a purpose: *The death of some insects immediately after laying their eggs may seem tragic, but nature does nothing in vain.* A proverb that dates back to Aristotle, it was first recorded in English c. 1580 in G. Harvey's *Marginalia.*

nature passes nurture A person's inborn character, or inherited characteristics, cannot be changed by his or her upbringing: *They worked hard to give him the best education that money could buy, but nature passes nurture, and their efforts were wasted.* The proverb was first recorded in 1492 in the form "Nature goes before learning."

Proverbs expressing similar meaning: NATURE WILL HAVE ITS COURSE; WHAT'S BRED IN THE BONE WILL COME OUT IN THE FLESH; YOU CAN DRIVE OUT NATURE WITH A PITCHFORK BUT SHE KEEPS ON COMING BACK; YOU CAN TAKE THE BOY OUT OF THE COUNTRY BUT YOU CAN'T TAKE THE COUNTRY OUT OF THE BOY.

Proverbs expressing opposite meaning: AS THE TWIG IS BENT, SO IS THE TREE INCLINED; BIRTH IS MUCH BUT BREEDING MORE; NURTURE PASSES NATURE.

nature will have its course There is no denying natural processes or impulses: *She tried to keep her doubts to herself but nature will have its course.* The proverb was first recorded c. 1400 in *Beryn.*

Proverbs expressing similar meaning: NATURE PASSES NURTURE; YOU CAN DRIVE OUT NATURE WITH A PITCHFORK BUT SHE KEEPS ON COMING BACK.

the nearer the bone, the sweeter the flesh Thin people are more attractive or desirable; also used literally of meat: *I would describe her as skinny rather than slim, but the nearer the bone, the sweeter the flesh, as my father used to say.* The proverb dates from before 1398.

Variant of this proverb: the closer to the bone, the sweeter the meat.

the nearer the church, the farther from God People who are active members or officials of a church are often the least godly in their daily lives; also applied to those who live close to a church: "I fear it was a practical comment on the truth of the uncomfortable proverb, 'The nearer the church, the farther from God,' that so bad a district should adjoin one of the great headquarters of the church" (Jane Ellice Hopkins, *Work amongst Working Men,* 1879). The proverb was first recorded in 1303.

near is my shirt, but nearer is my skin   A person's own best interests take precedence over those of his or her friends and family: *I'm not prepared to sacrifice my own chances of success for the sake of my brother— near is my shirt, but nearer is my skin.* The proverb was first recorded c. 1570, in the form "Nearer is my skin than shirt," but the sentiment it expresses occurs in the writings of the Roman dramatist Plautus (c. 250–184 B.C.): *"tunica propior palliost* [my tunic is closer than my cloak]."

Variants of this proverb: close sits my shirt, but closer my skin; near is my kirtle, but nearer is my smock.

necessity is the mother of invention   When people have an urgent need or a difficult problem, they use their creativity and imagination to devise a solution: "I soled my shoes with wood, which I cut from a tree . . . necessity is the mother of invention" (Jonathan Swift, *Gulliver's Travels,* 1726). The proverb was first recorded in its current form in 1658, but the sentiment it expresses is of earlier origin.

necessity knows no law   Rules and laws are often broken at times of emergency or urgent need: *It went against all my principles to steal the food, but necessity knows no law, and my children were starving.* The proverb was first recorded c. 1377, in William

Langland's *Piers Plowman:* "Nede . . . hath no lawe." It also exists in the Latin form *"Necessitas non habet legem* [Necessity has no law]."

necessity sharpens industry   Need makes people work harder: *With heavy rain forecast for the following day, I knew I only had a few hours left to fix the roof and I worked harder than ever before—necessity sharpens industry.*
Proverb expressing similar meaning: NEED MAKES THE OLD WIFE TROT.

need makes the old wife trot   Necessity provides a sense of urgency: "Stimulated by the spur which maketh the old woman proverbially to trot, Swertha posted down to the hamlet, with all the speed of threescore" (Sir Walter Scott, *The Pirate,* 1822). The proverb was first recorded c. 1225.
Proverb expressing similar meaning: NECESSITY SHARPENS INDUSTRY.

needs must when the devil drives   There are times when people are forced to do things that they would not do under normal circumstances: *I had never killed an animal before, and I had no desire to kill this one, but needs must when the devil drives.* The proverb was first recorded c. 1450 in the form "He must needs go that the devil drives."
Variant of this proverb: needs must when necessity drives.

ne'er cast a clout till May be out   Do not stop wearing any item of warm winter clothing before the end of May: *A sudden change in the weather made us glad that we had heeded the old proverb "Ne'er cast a clout till May be out."* The proverb was first recorded in 1706, in a Spanish/English dictionary, in the form "Do not leave off your coat till May be past." *Clout* is a British dialect word meaning "rag," and the proverb is sometimes taken to refer to old clothes, as in Robert Graves's *The White Goddess* (1948): "In ancient Greece, as in Britain, this was the month in which people went about in old clothes—a custom referred to in the proverb 'Ne'er cast a clout ere May be out,' meaning 'do not put on new clothes until the unlucky month is over.'" It is sometimes wrongly suggested that the word *May* in the proverb refers to may blossom—that is, the hawthorn or a similar shrub.

Variants of this proverb: change not a clout till May be out; what you put off and what you put on, never change till May be gone.

neglect will kill an injury sooner than revenge   Insults and other malicious acts are forgotten most quickly when the victim chooses to ignore them: "Neglect kills injuries; revenge increases them" (Benjamin Franklin, *Poor Richard's Almanack*, 1733–58). The proverb was first recorded c. 1620 in Owen Felltham's *Resolves, Divine, Morall, Politicall.*

Proverb expressing similar meaning: FORGIVE AND FORGET; LET BYGONES BE BYGONES.

neither a borrower nor a lender be   It is advisable never to borrow or lend anything, specifically money: *"Neither a borrower nor a lender be" is a lesson I learned too late, after losing $200 and the friend who borrowed it.* The proverb comes from Shakespeare's play *Hamlet* (1:3; 1600–01) and is part of Polonius's advice to his son Laertes.

neither give nor take offense   Try to avoid offending anybody, and ignore any apparent slights or insults directed at you: *The best way to avoid being drawn into an argument or fight is to follow the golden rule "Neither give nor take offense."* The proverb was first recorded in 1948 in a U.S. proverb collection.

Variant of this proverb: neither take offense nor make offense.

Nero fiddled while Rome burned   People in positions of authority sometimes behave irresponsibly during a crisis: *Nero fiddled while Rome burned, and the president was more concerned with improving his golf handicap than trying to avert a strike that would cripple the company.* The proverb refers to the legend that in A.D. 64 Emperor Nero set fire to the city of Rome and played his lyre while it burned.

never ask pardon before you are accused   If nobody knows that you have done something wrong, do not apologize and reveal your guilt—you may get away with it: *With a bit of luck he won't notice the scratch on the car where I hit the wall, so I'm saying nothing. My policy is "Never ask pardon before you are accused."*

Proverb expressing similar meaning: HE WHO EXCUSES HIMSELF ACCUSES HIMSELF.

never choose your women or linen by candlelight   Soft or inadequate lighting can give people and things a deceptively attractive appearance, or hide their faults and flaws: *The proverb "Never choose your women or linen by candlelight" may sound old-fashioned, but if you replace candlelight with the lights of a disco or nightclub, there are many young men who will vouch for its* *wisdom.* The proverb was first recorded in 1573. Other versions of the proverb advise against choosing gold or horses in this way.

Variant of this proverb: choose neither a woman nor linen by candlelight.

never do evil that good may come of it
A wicked or immoral course of action cannot be vindicated by a worthy objective: *She remained firmly opposed to animal experimentation—even for medical research into lifesaving drugs—on the basis of the proverb "Never do evil that good may come of it."* The proverb is of biblical origin: "And not rather (as we be slanderously reported, and as some affirm that we say), Let us do evil, that good may come?" (Romans 3:8).

Proverb expressing opposite meaning: THE END JUSTIFIES THE MEANS.

never do things by halves Whatever you do, do it properly, not in a half-hearted manner: *The general did not call a halt until the whole town was destroyed, but he was never one to do things by halves.* The proverb was first recorded in 1753 in Hanway's *Travels.*

Variant of this proverb: do well and have well.

Proverbs expressing similar meaning: IF A THING'S WORTH DOING, IT'S WORTH DOING WELL; IN FOR A PENNY, IN FOR A POUND; ONE MIGHT AS WELL BE HANGED FOR A SHEEP AS FOR A LAMB.

never give a sucker an even break
Foolish or gullible people are easily exploited and do not deserve a fair chance; used to justify taking advantage of such a person: "Never give a sucker an even break. . . . But your sermon has made me see that there is something higher and nobler than a code of business ethics" (P. G. Wodehouse, *Eggs, Beans and Crumpets,* 1940). Of uncertain origin, the proverb was popularized from the 1920s onward by the U.S. actor W. C. Fields (1880–1946), who wrote and starred in a film with this title in 1941.

never is a long time Think carefully before you use the word *never,* which implies a certainty about the future that you cannot possess: *He swore that he would never betray my secret, but never is a long time, and I fear that I may live to regret taking him into my confidence.* The proverb was first recorded in 1721, in the form "Never is a long term," but the sentiment it expresses occurs in Chaucer's *Canterbury Tales* (c. 1390).

Variant of this proverb: never is a long day.

Proverb expressing similar meaning: NEVER SAY NEVER.

never judge by appearances See JUDGE NOT ACCORDING TO APPEARANCES.

never let the sun go down on your anger If you have quarreled or lost your temper with somebody, make your peace before the end of the day: *I believe that you should never let the sun go down on your anger, and I always insist that the children resolve any minor differences among themselves before they go to bed.* The proverb is of biblical origin: "Be ye angry, and sin not: let not the sun go down upon your wrath" (Ephesians 4:26).

Variant of this proverb: let not the sun go down on your wrath.

never let your education interfere with your intelligence There are times when you must trust your intuition or native wit rather than what you have been taught or what you have read: *In emergencies such as these, medical professionals often have to follow their common sense rather than their textbooks, on the basis of the saying "Never let your education interfere with your intelligence."*

Proverb expressing similar meaning: AN OUNCE OF COMMON SENSE IS WORTH A POUND OF THEORY.

never look a gift horse in the mouth When you are offered something for nothing, accept it with gratitude and do not find fault with it: "Mr. Featherstone eyed him again over his spectacles and presented him with a little sheaf of notes. . . . He took them, saying, 'I am very much obliged to you, sir,' and was going to roll them up without seeming to think of their value. But this did not suit Mr. Featherstone, who was eying him intently. 'Come, don't you think it worth your while to count 'em? . . .' 'I thought I was not to look a gift-horse in the mouth, sir. But I shall be very happy to count them'" (George Eliot, *Middlemarch*, 1871–72). The proverb alludes to the practice of examining a horse's teeth to ascertain its age. It was first recorded in this form in 1546, but the sentiment it expresses dates from the fifth century A.D. or earlier.

Proverb expressing similar meaning: BEGGARS CAN'T BE CHOOSERS.

Proverb expressing opposite meaning: BEWARE OF GREEKS BEARING GIFTS.

never marry for money, but marry where money is It is good to marry somebody with sufficient means for a comfortable life, but wealth should not be your sole criterion in choosing a marriage partner: *She could do a lot worse than marry young Jack Piper, who has a promising legal career ahead of him. As my grandmother used to say, "Never marry for money, but marry where money is."* The proverb was first recorded in 1870 in Alfred, Lord Tennyson's "Northern Farmer."

Variant of this proverb: don't marry for money, but don't marry without money.

never mention a rope in the house of a man who has been hanged *See* NEVER SPEAK OF ROPE IN THE HOUSE OF A MAN WHO HAS BEEN HANGED.

never mix business with pleasure Keep your working life separate from your private affairs and leisure activities: *They say you should never mix business with pleasure, but I see no harm in doing a little networking at social functions like these.* The proverb was first recorded in 1913.

Variant of this proverb: you can't mix business and pleasure.

Proverb expressing similar meaning: BUSINESS IS BUSINESS.

never put off until tomorrow what you can do today If something needs doing—however undesirable the task may be—the sooner you do it, the better: "No idleness, no laziness, no procrastination; never put off till tomorrow what you can do today" (Lord Chesterfield, letter dated December 26, 1749). The proverb was first recorded in 1616, but the sentiment it expresses is of earlier origin. The facetious variant "Never do today what you can put off until tomorrow" dates from the 19th century.

Proverbs expressing similar meaning: PROCRASTINATION IS THE THIEF OF TIME; TODAY IS YESTERDAY'S TOMORROW.

never say A without saying B   *See* WHO
SAYS A MUST SAY B.

never say die   Do not surrender, stop
trying, or give up hope: *The first few months
will be very difficult, and you may feel that
success is beyond your grasp, but never say die.*
The proverb was first recorded in 1837 in
Charles Dickens's novel *The Pickwick Papers.*

Proverbs expressing similar meaning: DON'T GIVE UP THE SHIP; WHILE
THERE'S LIFE, THERE'S HOPE.

never say never   Nobody can look far
enough into the future to say with
certainty that something will never happen—anything is possible: "Al Marshall
did not rule out a resumption of talks,
saying 'you can never say "never" in this
business'" (*Washington Post*, 1984). First
recorded in 1977, the proverb was used
in the title of the James Bond movie
Never Say Never Again (1983), allegedly
because the actor Sean Connery had
been persuaded to make a comeback
as Agent 007, 12 years after announc-
ing that he would never play the role
again.

Proverb expressing similar meaning:
NEVER IS A LONG TIME.

never sell America short   Do not belit-
tle or underestimate the potential of
America: "Speculation ran wild, and an
orgy of boom-or-bust trading pushed the
bull markets up to dizzy peaks. 'Never sell
America short' and 'Be a bull on America'
were favorite catchwords" (Thomas A.
Bailey, *The American Pageant*, 1966). The
proverb was first recorded c. 1866.

never send a boy to do a man's job   Do
not assign a difficult task to somebody
who lacks the strength, experience, or
qualifications to do it properly; also used
of inanimate objects, such as an inadequate piece of equipment or a low card
that fails to win a trick: *I should have
known better than to put O'Connor in charge
of the investigation—never send a boy to do a
man's job.* The proverb was first recorded
in 1931.

**never show your teeth unless you can
bite**   *See* IF YOU CAN'T BITE, NEVER SHOW
YOUR TEETH.

never speak ill of the dead   You should
not make disparaging or defamatory
remarks about people after their death:
*I know that you should never speak ill of the
dead, but I'm not sure that I can think of
anything good to say about her.* Of ancient
origin, the proverb is sometimes quoted
in its Latin form, "*De mortuis nil nisi bonum*
[Say nothing but good of the dead]."

Variant of this proverb: speak well
of the dead.

**never speak of rope in the house of a
man who has been hanged**   Be tactful
and steer clear of sensitive subjects in the
company of people who might be upset or
offended by them: *I was just about to tell Bill
and Maggie a funny story about my neighbor
setting his kitchen on fire when I remembered
that Bill's sister and brother-in-law were killed
in a hotel blaze several years ago, and you
should never speak of rope in the house of a
man who has been hanged.* The proverb was
first recorded in 1599 in the form "A man
ought not to make mention of a halter in
the house of a man that was hanged."

Variant of this proverb: never mention a rope in the house of a man who has
been hanged.

never tell tales out of school   Do not pass on confidential information, secrets, or gossip to others, especially to outsiders: *New employees of the royal household are obliged to sign a confidentiality document, the content of which can be summarized by the proverb "Never tell tales out of school."* The proverb was first recorded in 1530.

never too old to learn   See IT'S NEVER TOO LATE TO LEARN.

never trouble trouble till trouble troubles you   Do not anticipate future problems—wait until something troublesome needs to be dealt with before taking any action: *It might be better to turn a blind eye to the situation unless it threatens to get out of hand—never trouble trouble till trouble troubles you.* The proverb was first recorded in 1884 in *Folk-Lore Journal.* It is sometimes quoted as part of a rhyme: "Never trouble trouble till trouble troubles you, / You only double trouble and trouble others too."

Proverbs expressing similar meaning: DON'T MEET TROUBLES HALFWAY; LET SLEEPING DOGS LIE.

never work with children or animals   The unpredictability of children and animals make them unreliable as fellow-workers (a favorite maxim of actors and other entertainers but also used in many other contexts): *He learned the hard way the truth of never working with children or animals when a small boy kicked him in the shin and he was bitten by a pet rat, both on camera.* A proverb of U.S. origin, it was popularized by (and possibly coined by) comedian W. C. Fields.

a new broom sweeps clean   When a new person takes up a position of authority in an organization, he or she is likely to make radical changes: "New brooms sweep clean. Abbot Thomas, like most of his predecessors, began with attempts at reformation" (J. A. Froude, *Short Studies,* 1877). First recorded in 1546, the proverb has given rise to the figurative phrase *new broom* meaning "somebody newly appointed to a position of authority": *Talk about a new broom! When the new principal came into school she reorganized everything— and everyone!—in her first term.*

Variant of this proverb: a new broom sweeps clean, but an old broom knows all the corners.

Proverb expressing similar meaning: NEW LORDS, NEW LAWS.

a new day, a new dollar   See ANOTHER DAY, ANOTHER DOLLAR.

new lords, new laws   When a new ruler or government comes to power—or when a new person takes control of a situation—changes are made and different rules apply: "'What's yer hurry then, Laban?' inquired Coggan. 'You used to bide as late as the latest.' 'Well, ye see, neighbours, I was lately married to a woman, and she's my vocation now. . . . ' The young man halted lamely. 'New lords new laws, as the saying is, I suppose,' remarked Coggan" (Thomas Hardy, *Far from the Madding Crowd,* 1874). The proverb was first recorded in the mid-16th century, but with the implication that it had long been in general use.

Variant of this proverb: new lairds make new laws.

Proverb expressing similar meaning: A NEW BROOM SWEEPS CLEAN.

nice guys finish last   It is sometimes necessary to be ruthless and aggressive—

even cruel or unscrupulous—to get what you want: *He's the kindest, most considerate person I've ever worked with, but he's a loser—everybody knows that nice guys finish last.* The proverb was coined in the mid-20th century by the U.S. baseball manager Leo Durocher and used in 1975 as the title of his autobiography.

night brings counsel If you have a difficult problem to solve or an important decision to make, a good night's sleep will work wonders: *Night brings counsel, and I woke up the following morning with a new plan of action that couldn't possibly fail.* The proverb was first recorded in English in 1590, in Edmund Spenser's *The Faerie Queene,* but the sentiment it expresses is of ancient origin: the Greek poet and dramatist Menander (c. 342–292 B.C.) wrote, "at night comes counsel to the wise."

nine tailors make a man A well-dressed person does not buy all his or her clothes from the same source: *They say that nine tailors make a man, so don't be afraid of sporting several different designer labels at the same time.* The proverb was first recorded in this form in 1647; its variant form was first recorded 34 years earlier. The original sense was that a gentleman should choose his garments from a wide range of tailors. The expression is also sometimes linked to bell-ringing: a *tailor* being a *teller* or "stroke" in a funeral knell: nine tailors referred to a man (six, a woman; three, a child); compare Dorothy Sayers's mystery *The Nine Tailors* (1934).

Variant of this proverb: two tailors go to a man.

nobody believes a liar when he speaks the truth *See* A LIAR IS NOT BELIEVED WHEN HE TELLS THE TRUTH.

nobody ever went broke underestimating the intelligence of the American people There is much money to be made by exploiting the gullibility or poor taste of the general public: *It should have been obvious to anybody that the devices couldn't possibly work, but they sold like hotcakes—nobody ever went broke underestimating the intelligence of the American people.* The proverb was coined in 1926 by the U.S. journalist H. L. Mencken in the form "No one in this world . . . has ever lost money by underestimating the intelligence of the great masses of the plain people." The word *intelligence* is sometimes replaced by *taste.*

nobody forgets a good teacher A good teacher is long remembered by his or her pupils: "They were surprised by the number of people who wanted to add their names to the tribute, but nobody forgets a good teacher." It appears to be a proverb of 20th-century invention. It enjoyed renewed circulation in the late 1990s as the slogan of a UK government campaign to recruit more teachers.

nobody is above the law Everybody must obey the law of the land: "Declaring that 'no one is above the law,' a federal prosecutor yesterday urged that former Pentagon official Paul Thayer be put behind bars for his part in a $3 million illegal stock trading scheme" (*Boston Globe,* 1985). The proverb comes from a speech made by President Theodore Roosevelt in 1903.

Variant of this proverb: no man is above the law, and no man is below it.

Proverb expressing opposite meaning: THE KING CAN DO NO WRONG.

nobody is born learned; bishops are made of men Education and scholarship are not innate qualities, and anybody can acquire knowledge or aspire to high office: *When students try to blame their failure or lack of ambition on a deprived family background, I remind them of the saying "Nobody is born learned; bishops are made of men."*

nobody is indispensable Nobody is so important or well qualified that he or she cannot be replaced by another: *The dismissal of the vice president was a salutary reminder that nobody is indispensable in this organization.*

Variant of this proverb: no man is necessary.

nobody is infallible Nobody can claim to be always right and never to have made a mistake: *She may be the world's greatest expert on the subject, but nobody is infallible, and in this case I am sure she is wrong.* The proverb was first recorded c. 1880.

Proverbs expressing similar meaning: HOMER SOMETIMES NODS; TO ERR IS HUMAN, TO FORGIVE DIVINE.

nobody is perfect Everybody has his or her faults; often said in response to criticism. "We ain't none of us perfect that I knows of" (L. Hollingworth, *Death Leaves Us Naked*, 1931). The proverb was first recorded in 1805, in Gouverneur Morris's *Diary of the French Revolution*.

Proverb expressing similar meaning: LET HIM WHO IS WITHOUT SIN CAST THE FIRST STONE.

nobody should be judge in his own cause People cannot be objective in matters that concern themselves: "No man is a good judge in his own cause. I believe I am tolerably impartial" (John Wesley, letter dated November 3, 1775). The prov-

erb was first recorded c. 1449 and is a translation of the Latin legal maxim *"Nemo debet esse iudex in propria causa."*

Proverb expressing similar meaning: MEN ARE BLIND IN THEIR OWN CAUSE.

a nod's as good as a wink to a blind horse In certain circumstances only the smallest hint is needed to make yourself understood; also used to imply that any kind of hint is wasted on somebody who is determined not to take it: "You needn't say no more—a nod's as good as a wink to a blind horse" (Sean O'Casey, *The Shadow of a Gunman*, 1925). The proverb was first recorded in 1794, in William Godwin's novel *Caleb Williams.*

Proverb expressing similar meaning: A WORD TO THE WISE IS SUFFICIENT.

no good deed goes unpunished When you do something kind or helpful you often get something unpleasant in return; a cynical observation: *A million dollars had been spent on a new gym for the prison earlier in the year, but no good deed goes unpunished, and the rioting prisoners found some useful makeshift weapons among the new equipment.* The proverb was first recorded in 1938 in the form "Every good deed brings its own punishment." It has been attributed to a number of people, including the writers Oscar Wilde and Clare Boothe Luce, but it is of unknown origin.

no joy without annoy Happiness is always accompanied by some sorrow or trouble: *No joy without annoy, but we were determined not to let the bad news from home spoil our honeymoon.* The proverb was first recorded, with different wording, in Chaucer's *Canterbury Tales* (c. 1390): "For evere the latter ende of joye is wo."

Variant of this proverb: no joy without alloy.

Proverbs expressing similar meaning: THERE'S NO PLEASURE WITHOUT PAIN; THERE'S NO ROSE WITHOUT A THORN.

no man can call again yesterday *See* YESTERDAY WILL NOT BE CALLED AGAIN.

no man can serve two masters Nobody can be loyal or committed to two different causes, organizations or employers simultaneously: "Men cannot serve two masters. If this cant of serving their country once takes hold of them, good-bye to the authority of the Church" (George Bernard Shaw, *Saint Joan,* 1924). The proverb is of biblical origin: "No man can serve two masters: for either he will hate the one, and love the other; or else he will hold to the one, and despise the other. Ye cannot serve God and mammon" (Matthew 6:24).

Proverbs expressing similar meaning: YOU CAN'T SERVE GOD AND MAMMON; YOU CAN'T RUN WITH THE HARE AND HUNT WITH THE HOUNDS.

no man is above the law, and no man is below it *See* NOBODY IS ABOVE THE LAW.

no man is a hero to his valet The better you know somebody, with all his or her faults and weaknesses, the less likely you are to regard that person with awe or veneration: "It has been said . . . that no man is a hero to his valet de chambre; now I am afraid when you and I grow a little more intimate . . . you will be horribly disappointed in your high expectations" (Samuel Foote, *The Patron,* 1764). The proverb is attributed to the Parisian hostess Anne-Marie Bigot de Cornuel

(1605–94), in the French form *"Il n'y a pas de héros pour son valet-de-chambre,"* but the sentiment it expresses is of earlier origin. Lord Byron turned the proverb around to express high praise in his mock-heroic poem *Beppo* (1818): "In short, he was a perfect cavaliero, / And to his very valet seem'd a hero."

Proverb expressing similar meaning: FAMILIARITY BREEDS CONTEMPT.

no man is an island Nobody can function in total isolation from the rest of society: *Those who aim for self-sufficiency—in a material or spiritual sense—eventually discover that no man is an island; we are all dependent, to a greater or lesser extent, on one another.* The proverb comes from the English poet John Donne's "Devotions upon Emergent Occasions" (1624): "No man is an Island, entire of it self; every man is a piece of the Continent, a part of the main."

no man is necessary *See* NOBODY IS INDISPENSABLE.

no moon, no man According to popular superstition, a child born at the time of the new moon—that is, when there is no moon visible in the sky—will not survive to adulthood: "'No moon, no man.' 'Tis one of the truest sayings ever spit out. The boy never comes to anything that's born at new moon" (Thomas Hardy, *The Return of the Native,* 1879). The quotation is the first recorded use of the proverb, but implies that it is already well known.

no names, no pack-drill If no names are mentioned, nobody can be punished or held responsible for something: *The report does not specify which companies are the worst offenders—no names, no pack-drill.* The proverb was first recorded in 1923 (O. Onions, *Peace in our Time*). Pack-drill is a form of military punishment that involves marching up and down with a full load of equipment.

none but the brave deserve the fair Those who lack boldness or courage do not deserve to achieve great things; also used more literally, of men courting women—or vice versa: *Firmly believing— at the tender age of ten—that none but the brave deserve the fair, she spurned the advances of any boy who couldn't hold his own in a playground battle.* The proverb comes from John Dryden's poem "Alexander's Feast" (1697), referring to Alexander the Great and the courtesan Thais: "Happy, happy, happy pair! . . . /None but the brave deserves the fair."

Proverb expressing similar meaning: FAINT HEART NEVER WON FAIR LADY.

no news is good news It is probably safe to assume that all is well if you have not heard anything to the contrary: "Everywhere, women gathered in knots, huddled in groups . . . telling each other that no news is good news, trying to comfort each other" (Margaret Mitchell, *Gone with the Wind,* 1936). The proverb was first recorded in 1616 in the form "No news is better than evil news."

no pain, no gain Nothing can be achieved without effort, suffering, or hardship; often applied specifically to physical exercise: *Some medical experts are concerned that those who follow the philosophy of "No pain, no gain" in their sports training could be doing irreparable damage to their bodies.* The proverb was first recorded in 1577 in the form "They must take pain that look for any gain." The more concise form "No pains, no gains" was used in 1648 as the title of a poem by Robert Herrick.

Variants of this proverb: there are no gains without pains; no sweat, no sweet.

no penny, no paternoster Religious services must be paid for in advance; also loosely applied to any similar business arrangement: *I accept that the church needs to raise money for essential repairs, but to me this new appeal, with the conditions attached to it, smacks of the old motto "No penny, no paternoster."* The proverb was first recorded in 1528, but with the implication that it was already in common use.

Proverb expressing similar meaning: NOTHING FOR NOTHING.

the north wind doth blow and we shall have snow Winds that blow from the north often bring cold weather with them: *Everyone in this part of the world knows that when the north wind doth blow snow is surely on the way.* The proverb has its origins in a nursery rhyme: "The north wind doth blows,/And we shall have snow,/And what will poor Robin do then? Poor thing!" (*Songs for Nursery,* 1805).

no sweat, no sweet *See* NO PAIN, NO GAIN.

nothing can bring you peace but yourself Do not rely on others for reassurance, contentment, or security: *After wasting thousands of dollars on therapists and analysts, she came to the conclusion that there is a lot of truth in the saying "Nothing can bring you peace but yourself."* The proverb comes from Ralph Waldo Emerson's essay "Self-Reliance" (1841).

nothing comes of nothing Nothing can be produced from nothing, therefore everything must originate from something; also used to imply that if you do or contribute nothing, you will get nothing in return: "You are to give me all your business. . . . If you have none, the learned gentleman here knows nothing can come of nothing" (Sir Walter Scott, *The Heart of Midlothian,* 1818). The proverb occurs in the writings of the Greek poet Alcaeus (sixth century B.C.) and also exists in the Latin form "*Ex nihilo nihil fit.*" The variant "Nothing will come of nothing" comes from Shakespeare's play *King Lear* (1:1).

Variants of this proverb: nothing will come of nothing; from nothing, nothing is made.

nothing for nothing Everything must be paid for, in money or in kind: *Nothing for nothing—you get me a seat on the next flight to Rio, and I'll give you a story that'll knock everything else off the front page.* The proverb dates from before 1704.

Variants of this proverb: you get nothing for nothing; you never get anything for nothing.

Proverbs expressing similar meaning: NO PENNY, NO PATERNOSTER; YOU DON'T GET SOMETHING FOR NOTHING.

nothing goes over the back but that comes under the belly *See* WHAT'S GOT OVER THE DEVIL'S BACK IS SPENT UNDER HIS BELLY.

nothing is certain but death and taxes Death will come to everybody and taxes must be paid, but everything else in life is unpredictable, insecure, or avoidable: "Everything's more or less a gamble. . . . Nothing is certain but death and taxes" (Laura Ingalls Wilder, *By the Shores of Silver Lake,* 1939). Although Daniel Defoe used the phrase "things as certain as death and taxes" in 1726, the proverb is generally associated with Benjamin Franklin, who wrote in a letter dated November 13, 1789, "In this world nothing can be said to be certain, except death and taxes."

nothing is certain but the unforeseen The one thing that is sure to happen is the thing that nobody expects or is prepared for; also used to imply that nothing can be predicted: *If it is true that nothing is certain but the unforeseen, then surely it is impossible to insure yourself against all eventualities.* The proverb was first recorded in 1886, but with the implication that it was already in general use.

Proverb expressing similar meaning: THE UNEXPECTED ALWAYS HAPPENS.

nothing is given so freely as advice People are at their most generous when it comes to telling others what they should and should not do: *When I asked for suggestions about tackling the problem, my friends readily offered ideas and I discovered the truth of the saying "Nothing is given so freely as advice," but when it came to getting practical or financial assistance, the phrase "like pulling teeth" was more applicable.*

nothing is impossible to a willing heart Anything can be achieved by somebody with the will to succeed: *He was one of those infuriating people who believe that there is no such word as "can't," and that nothing is impossible to a willing heart.* The proverb was first recorded in Stephen Hawes's *Passetyme of Pleasure* (1509).

Proverb expressing similar meaning: WHERE THERE'S A WILL THERE'S A WAY.

nothing should be done in haste but gripping a flea There are very few things that need to be done quickly; said by somebody urged to hurry up: *"Don't be impatient," she said, pouring herself another cup of coffee. "Nothing should be done in haste but gripping a flea."* The proverb dates from before 1655 in the form "Do nothing rashly, but catching of fleas."

nothing so bad but it might have been worse Try to take a positive view of misfortune—things are never as bad as they could be: *I broke a leg, both arms, and several ribs, but at least I'm still alive—nothing so bad but it might have been worse.* The proverb was first recorded in 1876. A more pessimistic corollary is "Nothing so good but it might have been better."

Variant of this proverb: from the day you were born till you ride in a hearse, there's nothing so bad but it might have been worse.

nothing so bold as a blind mare Those who are ignorant or unaware of danger proceed without fear or caution: *Nothing so bold as a blind mare, and those who have the least understanding of how a plane flies usually have the fewest qualms about traveling by air.* The proverb was first recorded in this form in 1721 (James Kelly, *Scottish Proverbs*) but the sentiment it expresses is of earlier origin.

nothing succeeds like success Successful people go on to ever greater things; also used to imply that people are more respected or accepted after they succeed: "Nothing succeeds like success, and if Hitler had founded his empire . . . we can well imagine how later historians would have treated him" (Hugh Trevor-Roper, *History and Imagination*, 1980). The proverb was first recorded in A. D. Richardson's *Beyond Mississippi* (1867).

Proverb expressing similar meaning: SUCCESS BREEDS SUCCESS.

nothing ventured, nothing gained You will not achieve anything unless you are prepared to make an attempt or take a risk: *I knew that my suggestion would probably be greeted with ridicule, but this did not deter me—nothing ventured, nothing gained.* The proverb was first recorded in English c. 1385, in Chaucer's *Troilus and Criseyde,* in the form: "He which that nothing under-taketh, / Nothyng n'acheveth."

Variants of this proverb: nothing venture, nothing gain; nothing venture, nothing have; nothing venture, nothing win.

nothing will come of nothing *See* NOTHING COMES OF NOTHING.

no tree takes so deep a root as prejudice Once prejudice becomes established—in a person's mind or in society as a whole—it is very difficult to eradicate it: *No tree takes so deep a root as prejudice, and neither education nor legislation can eliminate racial hatred that is handed down from generation to generation.*

nought is never in danger Persons or things of no value are at no risk of being stolen: *He never bothered to lock the house behind him, as nought is never in danger.* The proverb was first recorded in 1639 in J. Clarke's *Paroemiologia Anglo-Latina.*

nurture passes nature The way in which a person is brought up counts for more than any instinctive skills they may have been born with: *It is a fundamental principle of modern education that nurture passes nature.* The proverb was first recorded in 1611 in Randle Cotgrave's *A Dictionary of the French and English Tongues.*

Proverb expressing opposite meaning: NATURE PASSES NURTURE.

O

obey orders, if you break owners Do as you are commanded, even if this means doing something you know to be foolish or wrong: *Provided that you follow the golden rule, "Obey orders, if you break owners," nobody can hold you responsible for anything that goes wrong.* Of nautical origin, the proverb was first recorded in this form in 1823, but with the implication that it had long been in use.

the obvious choice is usually a quick regret Think carefully before you make a selection or decision: *Are you sure she is the best candidate for the job? Remember that the obvious choice is usually a quick regret.*

offenders never pardon Those who do wrong themselves are the least likely to forgive others' wrongdoing: *I was not surprised by his intolerant attitude, bearing in mind his own record—it's well known that offenders never pardon.* The proverb was first recorded in George Herbert's *Outlandish Proverbs* (1640).

of two evils choose the less *See* CHOOSE THE LESSER OF TWO EVILS.

oil and water do not mix Some people or things are incompatible by nature: *Putting people with such different temperaments in the same team is a recipe for disaster—oil and water do not mix.* The proverb was first recorded in 1783. It also occurs in the form of the simile *like oil and water,* applied to incompatible people or things.

Variant of this proverb: oil and vinegar will not mix.

an old dog will learn no tricks *See* YOU CAN'T TEACH AN OLD DOG NEW TRICKS.

the older the wiser The older a person gets, the wiser he or she becomes: *She tried to put the affair behind her and ruefully told herself "the older the wiser."* The proverb was first recorded in J. Clarke, *Paroemiologia Anglo-Latina* (1639).

Proverbs expressing similar meaning: EXPERIENCE IS THE MOTHER OF WISDOM; LIVE AND LEARN.

an old fool is the worst fool *See* THERE'S NO FOOL LIKE AN OLD FOOL.

an old fox is not easily snared A person with years of experience is unlikely to be easily fooled: *They tried to ambush him on the way home, but an old fox is not easily snared.* The proverb was first recorded in R. Taverner, *Proverbs or Adages with New Additions, gathered out of the Chiliades of Erasmus* (1539).

Variant of this proverb: old foxes want no tutors.

Proverb expressing similar meaning: WITH AGE COMES WISDOM.

old friends and old wine are best Friendships that have stood the test of time are, like old wine, the best: "Old wine and an old friend are good provisions." (G. Herbert, *Outlandish Proverbs*, 1640). The proverb was first recorded in T. Draxe, *Bibliotheca Scholastica* (1633).

Variant of this proverb: old friends and old wine and old gold are best.

old habits die hard When you have been doing a particular thing—or doing something in a particular way—for a long time, it is very difficult to change: "Old habits die hard. Police officers who were trained to pump the brakes have been crashing a lot of police cars equipped with anti-lock brakes" (*Washington Times*, 1995). The proverb was first recorded in 1758 in the form "Habits are hard to break."

old maids lead apes in hell Women who die unmarried are doomed to share the company of apes in the afterworld: "Get you to heaven, Beatrice, get you to heaven; here's no place for you maids: so deliver I up my apes" (William Shakespeare, *Much Ado about Nothing*, 2:1). The proverb was first recorded in 1575 in George Gascoigne's *Posies*.

an old poacher makes the best gamekeeper A reformed wrongdoer is good at preventing others from committing the same crime or offense, because he or she can understand their thinking and anticipate their actions: "What the Church needed, possibly, was a good leavening of sinners in its ministry, on the principle that poachers make the best gamekeepers" (Victor Canning, *The Great Affair*, 1970). The proverb was first recorded in this form in 1878, but the sentiment it expresses occurs in Chaucer's *Canterbury Tales* (c. 1390): "A theef of venysoun, that hath forlaft/His likerousnesse and al his olde craft,/Kan kepe a forest best of any man."

Proverb expressing similar meaning: SET A THIEF TO CATCH A THIEF.

old sins cast long shadows The passage of time often has the effect of making past wrongdoing seem greater or more significant than it actually was: *His sense of guilt increased as the years went by—old sins cast long shadows, as they say—and ultimately drove him to suicide.* The proverb was first recorded in 1924, but the sentiment it expresses is of earlier origin: in his play *Aglaura* (1638), Sir John Suckling wrote, "Our sins, like to our shadowes,/When our day is in its glorie scarce appear:/Towards our evening how great and monstrous they are!"

Variant of this proverb: old sins have long shadows.

old soldiers never die Those who have served in the armed forces and survived warfare often live so long that they seem indestructible: *I saw Jack Stuart in the bar the other day, regaling some of the youngsters with his army stories. He must be well into his nineties by now—I guess it's true that old soldiers never die.* The proverb comes from a popular song of World War I: "Old soldiers never die,/They simply fade away." A facetious variant is "Old soldiers never die—they just smell that way." The proverb may be applied to other classes of people or things by replacing the word *soldiers*. It has prompted numerous punning variants, such as "Old bankers never die, they just yield to maturity" and "Old insurance agents never die, it's against their policy."

old trees can't be transplanted *See* YOU CAN'T SHIFT AN OLD TREE WITHOUT IT DYING.

once a priest, always a priest People cannot change their vocation; also used to imply that people continue to behave in accordance with the habits and training of their trade or profession even after they have left it: "You must be quite sure . . . that you have a vocation because it would be terrible if you found afterwards that you had none. Once a priest always a priest, remember" (James Joyce, *A Portrait of the Artist as a Young Man,* 1916). The proverb was first recorded in this form in 1859, but the sentiment it expresses is of earlier origin. Other words may be substituted for *priest* when the proverb is used of other occupations.

once a thief, always a thief Wrongdoers cannot change their nature and can never be trusted: *However tolerant and broadminded they may be in their private lives, many employers apply the principle "Once a thief, always a thief" when it comes to considering job applications from people with criminal records.* The proverb was first recorded in 1622 in the form "Once a knave and ever a knave." Other words may be substituted for *thief,* such as *crook, drunkard, fool,* or *whore,* and the proverb is occasionally applied to those with enduring virtues rather than persistent vices, as in "Once a lady, always a lady."

Proverb expressing similar meaning: THE LEOPARD CAN'T CHANGE ITS SPOTS.

once bitten, twice shy Somebody who has had a bad experience is reluctant to do the same thing again: *She swore that she would never remarry—once bitten, twice shy.* The proverb was first recorded in this form in 1894.

Proverbs expressing similar meaning: ONCE BURNED, TWICE SHY; A BURNT CHILD DREADS THE FIRE.

once burned, twice shy People who have suffered as a result of a previous experience tend to be cautious in their approach to similar situations: "She was especially on her guard . . . because she'd been victimized in a stupid swindle herself, recently. Once burned, twice shy, you know" (Stewart Sterling, *Dead Sure,* 1949). The quotation is the first recorded use of the proverb in this form.

Proverbs expressing similar meaning: ONCE BITTEN, TWICE SHY; A BURNT CHILD DREADS THE FIRE.

one bad apple spoils the lot *See* THE ROTTEN APPLE SPOILS THE BARREL.

one business begets another When one business prospers, other businesses are likely to start up: *Within weeks the high street was full of shops selling fast food, but as they say, one business begets another.* The proverb was first recorded in 1528 in Thomas More's *Works*: "It is an olde said saw, that one busynes begetteth and bryngeth forth another."

one cannot be in two places at once Nobody can deal with two different things or attend two different events in two different places at the same time; said when conflicting demands are made on somebody, or when a choice has to be made between conflicting options: *I would love to go to the show, but I don't want to miss my evening class, and one cannot be in two places at once.* The proverb was first recorded in this form in 1611, but the sentiment it expresses is of earlier origin.

Variant of this proverb: you can't be in two places at the same time.

one cannot love and be wise People often show a lack of common sense or good judgment when they are in love: "To tax and to please, no more than to love and to be wise, is not given to men" (Edmund Burke, *On American Taxation*, 1775). The proverb has been traced back to the writings of Publilius Syrus (first century B.C.): "*amare et saper vix deo conceditur* [to love and to be wise is scarcely allowed to God]."

one courageous thought will put to flight a host of troubles A strong and positive mental attitude is the best defense against anxiety or adversity: *Keep your spirits up, and remember that one courageous thought will put to flight a host of troubles.*

one enemy is too much Having even a single enemy in the world is dangerous: "One enemy is too much for a man in a great post, and a hundred friends are too few" (H.G. Bohn, *A Hand-Book of Proverbs*, 1855). The proverb was first recorded in 1640 in George Herbert's *Outlandish Proverbs*.

one for sorrow; two for mirth; three for a wedding; four for a birth According to popular superstition, the number of magpies seen on a particular occasion portends sadness, happiness, and so on: *A magpie landed on the fence and I anxiously looked around for its mate, the old rhyme "One for sorrow, two for mirth" running through my mind.* The proverb comes from a traditional rhyme, first recorded in the nineteenth century, that continues: "five for silver; six for gold; seven for a secret not to be told; eight for heaven; nine for hell; and ten for the devil's own sel [self]."

Variant of this proverb: one for sorrow, two for joy, three for a girl, and four for a boy.

one for the mouse, one for the crow, one to rot, one to grow It is advisable not to expect a yield of more than 25 percent when sowing seed: *Don't sow the seed too thinly if you want a good crop—remember the old saying "One for the mouse, one for the crow, one to rot, and one to grow."* The proverb was first recorded in 1850.

Variant of this proverb: one for wind and one for crow, one to die and one to grow.

one funeral makes many Standing around a grave on a cold or rainy day is not good for the health, and can prove fatal for those attending a funeral: "It has been said . . . that one funeral makes many. A strong east wind . . . whistled through the crowd of mourners" (R. D. Blackmore, *Perlycross*, 1894). The quotation is the first recorded use of the proverb.

one good turn deserves another Acts of kindness or assistance should be reciprocated; often said when returning a favor: "But one good turn deserves another—in that case, you must . . . dine with me" (Sir

Walter Scott, *St. Ronan's Well,* 1824). The proverb was first recorded in English at the beginning of the 15th century, but a French equivalent was in use in the early 14th century.

Proverb expressing similar meaning: YOU SCRATCH MY BACK AND I'LL SCRATCH YOURS.

one half of the world doesn't know how the other half lives People have no conception or understanding of the problems and pleasures of everyday life for those in other social classes, occupations, or countries; chiefly used of the contrast between rich and poor: *The famous remark "Let them eat cake," allegedly made by Marie Antoinette on learning that her people had no bread, is a classic illustration of the saying "One half of the world doesn't know how the other half lives."* First recorded in English in 1607, the proverb occurs in the French satirist François Rabelais's novel *Pantagruel* (1532): *"la moytié du monde ne sçait comment l'autre vit."* It has given rise to the figurative phrase *how the other half lives,* referring to a lifestyle very different from your own.

Variant of this proverb: half the world knows not how the other half lives.

one hand for yourself and one for the ship Do not neglect your own safety, security, or well-being for the sake of your work or your employers; also used literally as a safety maxim for those working at sea: *He gave the company everything he had for most of his working life, and what good did it do him? I'm determined not to follow in his footsteps—my motto is "One hand for yourself and one for the ship."* Of nautical origin, the proverb was first recorded in 1799.

one hand washes the other People cooperate and help one another, and expect favors to be reciprocated: *We were not surprised to learn that the maintenance contract for the party headquarters had been won by our rivals, who made such a generous contribution to the party's last election campaign—one hand washes the other.* First recorded in English in 1573, the proverb is of ancient origin, occurring in the works of the Greek poet Epicharmus (c. 540–450 B.C.).

Proverb expressing similar meaning: YOU SCRATCH MY BACK AND I'LL SCRATCH YOURS.

one hour's sleep before midnight is worth two after Those who go to bed early have a more refreshing night's sleep than those who rise late in the morning: *I was well aware of the saying "One hour's sleep before midnight is worth two after," but in my first year at college I never actually managed to put it to the test.* The proverb was first recorded in 1640 in George Herbert's *Outlandish Proverbs.*

Variant of this proverb: one hour's sleep before midnight is worth three after.

Proverb expressing similar meaning: EARLY TO BED AND EARLY TO RISE, MAKES A MAN HEALTHY, WEALTHY, AND WISE.

one law for the rich and another for the poor It sometimes seems that rich people are treated more leniently by the legal system than poor people: *"Now, if the husbands and fathers of these ladies,—those who have themselves enacted the laws,—wink at their infringement, why should not others do so? . . . There cannot be one law for the rich and another for the poor"* (Captain

Marryat, *The King's Own,* 1830). The quotation is the first recorded use of the proverb.

Variant of this proverb: there's one law for the rich and another for the poor.

one lie leads to another   Once you have told one lie, it is often necessary to continue lying to maintain the deception: *I had previously told them I wasn't married, so when my wife arrived I had to introduce her as my sister—one lie leads to another.* The proverb was first recorded in 1534.

Variants of this proverb: one lie begets another; one lie makes many; one seldom meets a lonely lie.

Proverb expressing similar meaning: WHAT A TANGLED WEB WE WEAVE WHEN FIRST WE PRACTICE TO DECEIVE.

one man's loss is another man's gain   People profit from the misfortunes of others; also used more literally: *One man's loss is another man's gain, and our takings doubled when the bar next door closed down.* The proverb was first recorded c. 1527 in the form "What one wins, another loses."

Proverb expressing similar meaning: IT'S AN ILL WIND THAT BLOWS NOBODY ANY GOOD.

one man's meat is another man's poison
What one person likes, another person dislikes: *The show had good reviews in the national press, but one man's meat is another man's poison, and I didn't enjoy it at all.* First recorded in English c. 1576, the proverb is of ancient origin: in his *De Rerum Natura* (first century B.C.), the Roman poet Lucretius wrote, "*quod ali cibus est aliis fuat acre venenum* [what is food to one person may be bitter poison to others]."

Proverbs expressing similar meaning: EVERY MAN TO HIS TASTE; TASTES DIFFER; THERE'S NO ACCOUNTING FOR TASTES.

one man's trash is another man's treasure   Many people prize things that others would not give houseroom to: *Nobody who has ever been to a yard sale or flea market can dispute the truth of the saying "One man's trash is another man's treasure."*

one might as well be hanged for a sheep as for a lamb   If you are going to suffer or be punished for something, you might as well get the maximum pleasure or benefit from it: *When the cakes arrived, she decided to ignore her diet and helped herself to a large cream puff, probably the most fattening item on the plate. "One might as well be hanged for a sheep as for a lamb," she said with a guilty smile.* The proverb was first recorded in 1678.

Proverb expressing similar meaning: IN FOR A PENNY, IN FOR A POUND.

one nail drives out another   One thing replaces another, or new ideas or customs cause old ones to fall into disuse: "As one nail by strength drives out another,/So the remembrance of my former love/Is by a newer object quite forgotten" (William Shakespeare, *The Two Gentlemen of Verona,* 1591). The proverb is of ancient origin, and was known to the Greek philosopher Aristotle in the fourth century B.C.

one of these days is none of these days   Somebody who says he or she will do something "one of these days"—that is, at some unspecified future time—will probably never do it; said in response to such a person: *"One of these days I must go through my wardrobe and get rid of all the* clothes I never wear." "One of these days is none of these days. If you don't get on and do it you'll have to buy a new wardrobe!" The proverb was first recorded in *Comes Facundus* (1658).

Proverb expressing similar meaning: TOMORROW NEVER COMES.

one picture is worth ten thousand words Visual images are often the most concise and effective means of expression: *They say that one picture is worth ten thousand words, and if you ask somebody to name a memorable news story from the past, the chances are that he or she will describe the photograph that accompanied it.* The proverb was first recorded in 1927 by Frederick R. Barnard in *Printers' Ink.*

Variant of this proverb: a picture is worth a thousand words.

one seldom meets a lonely lie *See* ONE LIE LEADS TO ANOTHER.

one step at a time Do not rush at things or try to do too much at once—if you proceed slowly and carefully, things will seem less daunting and you will be less likely to make mistakes: "I did not allow myself to think of ultimate escape. . . . One step at a time was enough" (John Buchan, *Mr. Standfast,* 1919). The proverb was first recorded in C. M. Yonge's *Heir of Redclyffe* (1853).

Proverb expressing similar meaning: LIFE IS HARD BY THE YARD, BUT BY THE INCH LIFE'S A CINCH.

one story is good till another is told People are happy to accept one idea until a new idea comes along to replace it: "A theory is not proved . . . because the evidence in its favour looks well at first

sight. . . . 'One story is good till another is told!'" (Thomas Babington Macaulay, in the *Edinburgh Review,* 1831). The proverb was first recorded in 1593 in the form "One tale is always good until another is heard."

one swallow does not make a summer You cannot generalize from a single occurrence: *One swallow does not make a summer, and the fact that she won the first race of the season does not prove that she is worthy of selection for the Olympic team.* The proverb is of ancient Greek and Latin origin in the form "One swallow does not make a spring."

Variant of this proverb: one swallow makes not a spring, nor one woodchuck a winter.

one sword keeps another in its scabbard Showing that you are ready and able to defend yourself is a good way of discouraging others from attacking you: "The proverb 'One sword drawn keeps the other in the scabbard' was verified, the hostile preparations led to negociations, and the question was settled without fighting" (Frederick Chamier, *Ben Brace,* 1836). The proverb was first recorded in 1640. The nuclear deterrent is a modern illustration of the sentiment it expresses.

Proverb expressing similar meaning: IF YOU WANT PEACE, PREPARE FOR WAR.

one thief robs another People who are dishonest will not scruple to steal from each other. The proverb was first recorded c. 1510 in A. Barclay's *Eclogues* in the form: "It is ill stealing from a thiefe."

one volunteer is worth two pressed men Those who volunteer for work or service are generally more efficient and reliable than those who are forced to do it against their will: *We never turn away anybody who offers to help, on the principle that one volunteer is worth two pressed men.* The proverb was first recorded in 1705 in T. Hearne's *Journal.*

Variant of this proverb: a volunteer is worth ten pressed men.

one wedding brings another The romantic atmosphere of a wedding may have an effect on unmarried guests, prompting other couples to get engaged or sparking off new relationships that will lead to the altar: *My son was a bit nervous when his new girlfriend invited him to her sister's wedding—one wedding brings another, and he doesn't want it to be his!* The proverb was first recorded in 1634, but with the implication that it was already in general use.

one year's seeding makes seven years' weeding If you allow weeds to seed themselves, it will take a long time to get rid of all the new plants they produce; also used figuratively of the need to eradicate something undesirable before it has a chance to spread, or to warn people that their actions can have lasting repercussions: *Weeds are not only unsightly, but also a potential source of trouble for the future—one year's seeding makes seven years' weeding.* The proverb was first recorded in 1866 in the form "One year's seeding may cost ten years' weeding."

the only difference between stumbling blocks and stepping-stones is the way you use them Be positive in your approach to obstacles that lie in your path, and try to turn them to your advan-

tage: *I firmly believe that the only difference between stumbling blocks and stepping-stones is the way you use them, and although my first few job applications were unsuccessful, they gave me the opportunity to hone my skills as an interviewee.* This proverb is recorded as a regional expression in the United States.

the only place where success comes before work is in a dictionary Nobody succeeds without first making an effort: *Remember that the only place where success comes before work is in a dictionary, and if you want to make a go of this business you need to focus all your time and attention on it.*

the only thing a heated argument ever produced is coolness An angry exchange of words resolves nothing and leads to a breakdown of friendly relations: *If you sit down and discuss your differences calmly and rationally, you may ultimately reach agreement, but the only thing a heated argument ever produced is coolness.* This proverb is recorded as a regional expression in the United States.

Variant of this proverb: heated arguments do not warm the fireside.

the only thing we have to fear is fear itself Negative feelings such as fear and doubt can do more harm than the things you are afraid of or uncertain about: *Once we have grasped the notion that the only thing we have to fear is fear itself, we can face the future with renewed courage, confidence, and optimism.* The proverb is associated with President Franklin D. Roosevelt, who used it in his first inaugural address in 1933, but it is probably of earlier origin.

Variant of this proverb: we have nothing to fear but fear itself.

only time will tell   See TIME WILL TELL.

open confession is good for the soul
See CONFESSION IS GOOD FOR THE SOUL.

an open door may tempt a saint   It is best not to put temptation in anybody's way—even the most honest and upright person might find it hard to resist: *She had never stolen a cent in her life before, but the sight of all that money lying there was too much for her—an open door may tempt a saint.* The proverb was first recorded in 1659 in James Howell's *Spanish Proverbs.*

Proverb expressing similar meaning: OPPORTUNITY MAKES A THIEF.

the opera ain't over till the fat lady sings   Wait until something finally comes to an end before you give up hope, celebrate your success, abandon your efforts, or make a judgment: "One day three years ago, Ralph Carpenter, who was then Texas Tech's sports information director, declared to the press box contingent in Austin, 'The rodeo ain't over till the bull riders ride.' Stirred to top that deep insight, San Antonio sports editor Dan Cook countered with, 'The opera ain't over till the fat lady sings'" (*Washington Post,* 1978). Current from at least the 1970s, the proverb has a possible origin in the southern U.S. saying, "Church ain't out till the fat lady sings."

Proverb expressing similar meaning: IT'S NOT OVER TILL IT'S OVER.

opportunities look for you when you are worth finding   Those who have good fortune are often those who best deserve it: *Don't just sit around complaining that you never get the breaks—people succeed on their own merits, not by luck, and opportunities look for you when you are worth finding.* The proverb is recorded as a regional expression in the United States.

Proverb expressing similar meaning: OPPORTUNITY NEVER KNOCKS FOR PERSONS NOT WORTH A RAP.

opportunity knocks but once   Take advantage of opportunities when they arise, because you may not get a second chance: "'Opportunity only knocks once in this world,' he would say. Major Major's father repeated this good joke at every opportunity" (Joseph Heller, *Catch-22,* 1961). The proverb was first recorded, with different wording, in 1567. Early examples of its use had *fortune* or *fate* in place of *opportunity.*

Variant of this proverb: opportunity never knocks twice at any man's door.

Proverb expressing similar meaning: HE THAT WILL NOT WHEN HE MAY, WHEN HE WILL HE MAY HAVE NAY.

opportunity makes a thief   Do not leave valuable things unsecured in a place where they could easily be stolen: *Opportunity makes a thief, and people who park their car on the street and leave the keys in the ignition should not be too surprised to find it gone when they return.* The proverb was first recorded in this form in 1387, but the sentiment it expresses is of earlier origin.

Proverbs expressing similar meaning: THE HOLE CALLS THE THIEF; AN OPEN DOOR MAY TEMPT A SAINT.

opportunity never knocks for persons not worth a rap   Worthless people are unlikely to enjoy good fortune: *She could have made something of herself if she had tried, but she was too idle and feckless to bother, and* *opportunity never knocks for persons not worth a rap.*

Proverb expressing similar meaning: OPPORTUNITIES LOOK FOR YOU WHEN YOU ARE WORTH FINDING.

opportunity never knocks twice at any man's door *See* OPPORTUNITY KNOCKS BUT ONCE.

opposites attract People who have nothing in common are often drawn together because they have qualities that complement each other: *They say that opposites attract, but a lasting friendship is more likely to be built on similarity than on difference.* The proverb was first recorded in 1918 in J. Watson and A. J. Rees's *Mystery of the Downs.*

Proverb expressing similar meaning: EXTREMES MEET.

Proverb expressing opposite meaning: LIKE ATTRACTS LIKE.

the optimist's cup is half full; the pessimist's cup is half empty *See* THE GLASS IS EITHER HALF EMPTY OR HALF FULL.

other times, other manners Customs and conventions change over the years, and we should not judge people or things of the past by modern standards, or vice versa; sometimes said to those who mock or criticize the behavior of members of a different generation: "Notwithstanding the favourite explanation of 'other times, other manners,' contemporary critics of Clarissa found very much the same fault with her history as people do to-day" (Austin Dobson, *Samuel Richardson,* 1902). The proverb was first recorded in English in 1576, in the form "Other times, other ways," but the sentiment it expresses is of ancient origin. It also occurs in the French form "*Autres temps, autres moeurs.*"

Variant of this proverb: other times, other customs.

an ounce of common sense is worth a pound of theory A practical common-sense approach is often far more effective than abstract theorizing: *Ms. Jackson and her helpers believe that an ounce of common sense is worth a pound of theory, and have worked wonders with some of the problem cases that the so-called experts gave up on long ago.*

Proverb expressing similar meaning: NEVER LET YOUR EDUCATION INTERFERE WITH YOUR INTELLIGENCE.

an ounce of discretion is worth a pound of wit Good judgment is often more valuable than knowledge or learning; also interpreted more literally as a warning to tactfully refrain from making jokes at another's expense: *At times like this it is wise to err on the side of caution, whatever the textbooks say—remember that an ounce of discretion is worth a pound of wit.* The proverb was first recorded in 1616 (T. Adams, *Sacrifice of Thankfulness*), with *learning* in place of *wit.*

an ounce of practice is worth a pound of precept The best way to teach is by example, and the best way to learn is by experience: "Remember that rigid probity, and the strictest punctuality . . . are the very soul of business, and that an ounce of practice is worth a pound of precept" (R. D. Blackmore, *Cradock Nowell,* 1866).

Proverbs expressing similar meaning: EXPERIENCE IS THE BEST TEACHER; AN OUNCE OF PRACTICE IS WORTH A POUND OF PRECEPT; YEARS KNOW MORE THAN BOOKS.

an ounce of prevention is worth a pound of cure   It often takes a lot of effort to put right something that could have been prevented with a little effort: "An ounce of prevention is worth a pound of cure. . . . All the old saws point up the value of heading off a problem before it reaches the pass" (*Washington Times,* 1997).

Proverbs expressing similar meaning: A STITCH IN TIME SAVES NINE; PREVENTION IS BETTER THAN CURE; WHO REPAIRS NOT HIS GUTTERS REPAIRS HIS WHOLE HOUSE.

out of debt, out of danger   Nobody who owes money can feel safe and secure: *I breathed a sigh of relief as I handed over the wad of bills—out of debt, out of danger.* The proverb was first recorded in 1639.

Proverb expressing similar meaning: A MAN IN DEBT IS CAUGHT IN A NET.

out of sight, out of mind   We tend to forget about people or things we have not seen for some time: "He did not actually suggest that she should come home. Evidently it was still necessary that she should remain out of sight and out of mind—a skeleton in a distant and well-locked cupboard" (George Orwell, *A Clergyman's Daughter,* 1935). The proverb was first recorded c. 1450, but the sentiment it expresses is of earlier origin.

Proverb expressing similar meaning: SELDOM SEEN, SOON FORGOTTEN.

Proverb expressing opposite meaning: ABSENCE MAKES THE HEART GROW FONDER.

out of the fullness of the heart the mouth speaks   People cannot avoid talking about what is on their mind; also used to imply that a person's true thoughts and feelings are revealed by what he or she says: *Out of the fullness of the heart the mouth speaks, and she was so angry and upset that she could restrain herself no longer.* The proverb is of biblical origin: "O generation of vipers, how can ye, being evil, speak good things? for out of the abundance of the heart the mouth speaketh" (Matthew 12:34).

Variant of this proverb: out of the abundance of the heart the mouth speaks.

out of the mouths of babes and sucklings come great truths   Children often make surprisingly pertinent remarks or profound observations by accident: *I asked Megan if she knew what divorce was, and she said, "It's when your dad doesn't live with you any more but buys you better birthday presents." Out of the mouths of babes and sucklings!* The proverb is of biblical origin: "Out of the mouth of babes and sucklings hath thou ordained strength" (Psalm 8:2), "Yea; have ye never read, Out of the mouth of babes and sucklings thou hast perfected praise?" (Matthew 21:16). It is often used in a shortened and allusive form, as in the example.

Variant of this proverb: from the mouths of babes come words of wisdom.

Proverb expressing similar meaning: CHILDREN AND FOOLS SPEAK THE TRUTH.

paddle your own canoe   Make your own way; rely upon your own resources: *He decided to go freelance and paddle his own canoe.* The proverb was first recorded in 1844, in Captain Frederick Marryat's *Settlers in Canada,* but became better known through a poem by Sarah Bolton, published in *Harper's Magazine* in May 1854: "Voyage upon life's sea,/To yourself be true,/And, whatever your lot may be,/Paddle your own canoe."

Proverbs expressing similar meaning: EVERY MAN IS THE ARCHITECT OF HIS OWN FORTUNE; IF YOU WANT A THING DONE WELL, DO IT YOURSELF; GOD HELPS THOSE WHO HELP THEMSELVES; LIFE IS WHAT YOU MAKE IT.

paper bleeds little   It is easy to do something in writing, without taking account of the human factors involved: *The conditions seemed reasonable and harmless enough on paper, but paper bleeds little, and nobody could have predicted how much suffering they would cause.* The proverb was first recorded in 1940, in Ernest Hemingway's novel *For Whom the Bell Tolls,* but with the implication that it was already in general use.

paper does not blush   It is possible to express in writing what you would be too ashamed or embarrassed to say: *I can't*

tell him face to face—I'll send him a letter. Paper does not blush. The proverb was first recorded in 1577 in John Grange's *The Golden Aphroditis.*

parents are patterns   Parents are role models for their children and should set a good example: *Parents are patterns, and with their father in prison and their mother funding her drug habit with prostitution, these children have little chance of remaining on the straight and narrow.* This proverb is recorded as a regional expression in the United States.

parsley seed goes nine times to the devil   Parsley is a difficult plant to grow, and the seeds take such a long time to germinate that it seems they have been down to hell several times before they sprout: *They say that parsley seed goes nine times to the devil, and in my experience some of it never comes back—I sowed a whole packet in that bed, and all I got was a few scrawny plants.* The proverb was first recorded in 1658, but with the implication that it was already in regional use in England.

past cure, past care   It is futile worrying about something when it is too late to do anything about it. The proverb was recorded in the works of Robert Greene in 1593: "Remember the old proverbe, past cure, past care." In 1594 William Shakespeare quoted the proverb in his play *Love's Labour's Lost* (5:2): "Great reason; for 'past cure is still past care.'"

the path of true love never runs smooth *See* THE COURSE OF TRUE LOVE NEVER DID RUN SMOOTH.

patience is a remedy for every sorrow In time grief will fade, ills will be cured, and problems will be solved, so all you can do is wait patiently: *Patience is a remedy for every sorrow, and in six months' time you'll probably have forgotten all about it.* The proverb was first recorded, with different wording, c. 1390. In modern usage the word *sorrow* may be replaced by *disease* or *trouble.*

Variant of this proverb: patience is a plaster for all sores.

Proverb expressing similar meaning: TIME IS A GREAT HEALER.

patience is a virtue It is good to be patient, but it is not easy: "patience is a virtue; and . . . you ought not to be in haste to take a first offer, for fear you should not have a second" (Samuel Richardson, *Sir Charles Grandison,* 1754). First recorded in English in the 14th century, the proverb is of ancient origin.

Variants of this proverb: patience is a virtue, catch it if you can: seldom in a woman and never in a man; patience is a virtue which few possess—some have a little, others have less.

patriotism is the last refuge of a scoundrel Those who have no better argument resort to appeals to patriotic sentiment: *The meeting split into those who believed it was right to fight to defend national interests and* *those who believed that such patriotism was the last refuge of scoundrels.* The proverb was first recorded as a quotation of Samuel Johnson in James Boswell's *Life of Johnson* (1791).

pay as you go and nothing you'll owe It is best to pay for everything when you receive it and not to get into debt: *In these days of credit cards and charge accounts, the saying "Pay as you go and nothing you'll owe" has a rather old-fashioned ring.* The proverb was first recorded in 1851 *Polly Peablossom's Wedding* (T. A. Burke, ed.).

pay beforehand was never well served People who are paid in advance for their services have little incentive to work hard or well: *Take my advice and don't hand over any money until the job is at least half done—pay beforehand was never well served.* The proverb was first recorded in 1591 in the form "He that pays aforehand has never his work well done."

pay what you owe and you'll know what you own Once you have paid in full for something, there can be no dispute about who owns it; also used with reference to the seizure of a debtor's property: *"Pay what you owe and you'll know what you own,"* *they say, so I guess the house and car aren't mine yet.* The proverb is first recorded in J. Stevens's *A New Spanish and English Dictionary* (1706).

peace makes plenty Peace brings prosperity: "Peace, Dear nurse of arts, plenties, and joyful births" (William Shakespeare, *Henry V*, 5:2). The proverb was first recorded in *Reliquae Antiquae* in the 15th century.

Variants of this proverb: peace maketh plenty; plenty maketh pride;

pride maketh war; war maketh poverty; poverty maketh peace.

the pen is mightier than the sword Writing can be more effective or persuasive than violence or aggression; also used to imply that words can be more dangerous than weapons: "Beneath the rule of men entirely great/The pen is mightier than the sword" (Edward George Bulwer-Lytton, *Richelieu*, 1838). The quotation is the first recorded use of the proverb in its current form, but the sentiment it expresses is of earlier origin.

Proverb expressing similar meaning: A GOOSE QUILL IS MORE DANGEROUS THAN A LION'S CLAW.

a penny saved is a penny earned It is wise to save money whenever you can, however small the amount: *This brand is not much cheaper, but a penny saved is a penny earned.* The proverb was first recorded in 1640 in the form "A penny spar'd is twice got," and the word *got* was used in place of *earned* in subsequent occurrences of the proverb up to the early 20th century.

Proverbs expressing similar meaning: SAVING IS GETTING; THRIFT IS A GREAT REVENUE.

penny wise and pound foolish By being too thrifty or frugal with small expenses you may incur a much larger expense; also used of those who combine parsimony with extravagance: "The problem in any police agency is that training assumes lower priority than putting people out on the street. In a lot of ways that's penny wise and pound foolish" (*New York Times*, 1987). The proverb was first recorded in 1607, in Edward Topsell's *History of*

Four-footed Beasts: "If by couetousnesse or negligence, one withdraw from them their ordinary foode, he shall be penny wise, and pound foolish."

Proverb expressing similar meaning: SPARE AT THE SPIGOT, AND LET OUT THE BUNGHOLE.

Proverb expressing opposite meaning: TAKE CARE OF THE PENCE AND THE POUNDS WILL TAKE CARE OF THEMSELVES.

people are more easily led than driven It is better to guide people by example than to force them to do as they are told: *You may find that a change of approach will work wonders—people are more easily led than driven, and nobody responds well to threats and coercion.* The proverb was first recorded in 1690 in *Winthrop Papers.*

people who live in glass houses shouldn't throw stones Do not criticize others if you have the same faults yourself and are therefore vulnerable to retaliation: "Granted, the present internal chaos and confusion of the Anglican churches in the Northern hemisphere forbids me to make merry at Rome's expense; people who live in glass houses should not throw stones; yet there is a difference here. The trouble with Western Anglicanism is that it has drifted from its Reformation roots in matters of mental method, and needs to return to those roots" (James I. Packer, "Assessing the Anglican-Roman Catholic Divide: An Anglican Perspective," *CRUX,* 1997). The proverb was first recorded in 1640, but the sentiment it expresses is of earlier origin: Chaucer's *Troilus and Criseyde* (c. 1385) contains a similar warning for "Who that hath an hed of verre [a head of glass]." A facetious variant is "People who live in glass houses should undress in the dark."

Proverb expressing similar meaning: JUDGE NOT, THAT YE BE NOT JUDGED.

physician, heal thyself Do not reproach another person for something that you are equally guilty of; also used to imply that you should solve your own problems before you try to deal with those of other people: "How can a man . . . teach sobriety or cleanliness, if he be himself drunken or foul? 'Physician, heal thyself,' is the answer of his neighbours" (Samuel Smiles, *Thrift,* 1875). The proverb is of biblical origin: "Ye will surely say unto me this proverb, Physician, heal thyself: whatsoever we have heard done in Capernaum, do also here in thy country" (Luke 4:23).

Proverb expressing similar meaning: SWEEP YOUR OWN DOORSTEP CLEAN.

a picture is worth a thousand words *See* ONE PICTURE IS WORTH TEN THOUSAND WORDS.

pigs are pigs All bad people or things are equally undesirable, regardless of where they come from: *Pigs are pigs, and this kind of behavior is no more acceptable in a college graduate than it is in an ignorant lout.* The proverb was first recorded in 1822, in a letter from Charles Lamb to Samuel Taylor Coleridge.

pigs may fly, but they are very unlikely birds *See* IF A PIG HAD WINGS, IT MIGHT FLY.

piss or get off the pot If you're not ready to take action or get on with what you have to do, then make way for somebody who is: *This is not the time for hesitation or indecision—piss or get off the pot!*

Variant of this proverb: shit or get off the pot.

Proverb expressing similar meaning: FISH OR CUT BAIT.

the pitcher will go to the well once too often Nothing can continue or be repeated indefinitely—a run of good fortune or success must come to an end, persistent cheats or swindlers will ultimately be caught out: *I decided not to push my luck by asking for yet another extension to the deadline—my publisher had accepted all the excuses I'd given so far, but the pitcher will go to the well once too often.* The proverb was first recorded in 1340.

Variant of this proverb: a pitcher that goes to the well too often is broken at last.

pity is akin to love Pity and love are related emotions: *She pitied him, and although pity is akin to love, it is not the best foundation for a lasting relationship.* The proverb was first recorded in 1696, but the sentiment it expresses is of earlier origin, occurring in Shakespeare's play *Twelfth Night* (3:1): "I pity you.—That's a degree to love."

a place for everything and everything in its place Everything belongs somewhere, and should be tidied away; often used to encourage orderliness or to describe an orderly place: "'I thought you were rather partial to anatomical specimens.' 'So I am, but not on the breakfast-table.' 'A place for everything and everything in its place,' as my grandmother used to say." (Dorothy L. Sayers, *Lord Peter Views Body,* 1928). The proverb was first recorded in 1640, with different wording, and occurs in guides to thrift and household management, notably that written by Mrs. Isabella Beeton (1836–65).

please your eye and plague your heart Those who choose their husbands, wives, or lovers on the basis of good looks alone may suffer for their choice: "'Please your eye and plague your heart' is an adage that want of beauty invented, I dare say, more than a thousand years ago" (William Cobbett, *Advice to Young Men,* 1829). The proverb was first recorded c. 1617.

pleasure first and business after *See* BUSINESS BEFORE PLEASURE.

plus ça change, plus c'est la même chose *See* THE MORE THINGS CHANGE, THE MORE THEY STAY THE SAME.

poets are born, not made The ability to write poetry is an innate quality and cannot be taught or learned: *She rejected the notion that poets are born, not made, and believed that everybody was capable of putting his or her thoughts into verse, with or without tuition.* The proverb is of ancient origin in its Latin form, *"Poeta nascitur, non fit."* It is sometimes applied to different skills or occupations by substituting another word for *poets,* as in "Salesmen are born, not made."

politeness costs nothing and gains everything *See* CIVILITY COSTS NOTHING.

politics makes strange bedfellows Politics tends to bring together those who would normally avoid each other's company, and unlikely alliances may be forged for political reasons: "For, if anything, Troy represented the earthy patriotism of New York's hard-hat voters, a fact which, according to Mankiewicz, 'made him a special hero to us.' Politics do indeed make strange bedfellows" (Victor Lasky, *It Didn't Start with Watergate,* 1977). The proverb was first recorded in 1839 in *Diary of Philip Hone.* The expression *strange bedfellows* derives from Shakespeare's *Tempest* (2:2; 1611): "Misery acquaints a man with strange bedfellows."

a poor excuse is better than none *See* A BAD EXCUSE IS BETTER THAN NONE.

possession is nine points of the law A person who actually has something in his or her possession is in a strong position for claiming legal ownership of or entitlement to it: "It is hard to reconcile this with Russia's dreadful example of looting masses of art, hiding it and then claiming that possession is 90 percent of the law" (*New York Times,* 1994). The proverb was first recorded in 1616 (T. Draxe, *Adages*). The *nine* in the proverb is nine out of ten parts. The "nine points" have been listed as (1) a good deal of money, (2) a good deal of patience, (3) a good case, (4) a good lawyer, (5) a good counsel, (6) good witnesses, (7) a good jury, (8) a good judge, and (9) good luck.

Variant of this proverb: possession is nine-tenths of the law.

a postern door makes a thief It is all too easy to rob a house that has a rear entrance through which people can slip in and out unnoticed: *They had fitted extra locks and bolts on the back door, on the basis of the saying "A postern door makes a thief," but unfortunately they had neglected to secure the windows.* The proverb was first recorded c. 1450 in the form "A back door makes a rich man poor."

Variant of this proverb: the back door robs the house.

the post of honor is the post of danger The most perilous positions in an administration or organization are those that have the highest prestige: *She had no ambitions to rise any further through the ranks, on the basis that the post of honor is the post of danger.* The proverb was first recorded in this form in 1832 in A. Henderson's *Scottish Proverbs* but the sentiment it expresses is of much earlier origin.

Proverbs expressing similar meaning: THE HIGHEST BRANCH IS NOT THE SAFEST ROOST; UNEASY LIES THE HEAD THAT WEARS A CROWN.

the pot calls the kettle black People criticize others for faults that they have themselves, or make accusations that are equally applicable to themselves: "But a very few weeks after Voltaire's arrival, little clouds of discord become visible on the horizon; and one can overhear the pot and the kettle . . . calling each other black" (Lytton Strachey, *Biographical Essays,* "Voltaire and Frederick the Great," 1949). The proverb was first recorded in this form in 1699, but the sentiment it expresses is of earlier origin. It alludes to the blackened bottoms of pots, pans, and kettles used on an open fire.

Proverb expressing similar meaning: THE BEST PLACE FOR CRITICISM IS IN FRONT OF YOUR MIRROR.

poverty comes from God, but not dirt Some people cannot avoid being poor, but nobody has any excuse for being dirty or for failing to keep his or her house clean: *"Poverty comes from God, but not dirt," my aunt used to say as she scrubbed the floor on her hands and knees.*

poverty is no crime *See* POVERTY IS NOT A CRIME.

poverty is no disgrace, but it's a great inconvenience Poor people have nothing to be ashamed of, but their situation is nonetheless undesirable: "'Poverty's no disgrace, but 'tis a great inconvenience' was a common saying among the Lark Rise people; but . . . their poverty was no less than a hampering drag upon them" (Flora Thompson, *Lark Rise to Candleford,* 1945). The proverb was first recorded in 1591 in the form "Poverty is no vice, though it be an inconvenience."

poverty is not a crime Poor people should not be treated like criminals: "It is easy enough to say that poverty is no crime. No; if it were men wouldn't be ashamed of it" (Jerome K. Jerome, *Idle Thoughts of an Idle Fellow,* 1889). The proverb was first recorded in 1591 in the form "Poverty is no vice."

Variants of this proverb: poverty is no crime; poverty is no sin.

poverty makes strange bedfellows *See* ADVERSITY MAKES STRANGE BEDFELLOWS.

power corrupts, and absolute power corrupts absolutely Power has an adverse effect on the integrity of those in authority, and the more power they have, the worse they become: *His impeccable record suggested that he would be a just and wise ruler, but power corrupts, and absolute power corrupts absolutely, and the people lived to regret their choice.* The proverb comes from a letter written by the English historian Lord Acton in 1887: "Power tends to corrupt, and absolute power corrupts absolutely. Great men are almost always bad men, even when they exercise influence and not authority." The sentiment expressed in the shorter form, "Power corrupts," is of earlier origin.

practice makes perfect The more often you do something, the better at it you become: "Young birds very frequently make their first flight when their parents are out of sight. Practice of course makes perfect and puts a polish on the somewhat awkward first performance; but there is no elaborate learning needed" (J. S. Huxley, *Man in the Modern World*, "The Intelligence of Birds," 1947). The proverb was first recorded in 1553 in T. Wilson's *Art of Rhetoric*.

practice what you preach Always follow the advice or instructions you give to others: *Practice what you preach—it's no use warning your children about the dangers of alcohol unless you are prepared to modify your own drinking habits.* The proverb is of ancient origin.

praise no man till he is dead Final judgments on a person's qualities can only become reliable after he or she is dead: *The revelation that their former boss had been swindling the corporation's pension fund made several employees wish they had observed the old proverb that warns against praising any man till he is dead.* The proverb was first recorded in R. Taverner, *Proverbs or Adages with New Additions, gathered out of the Chiliades of Erasmus* (1540).

Variant of this proverb: praise day at night.

praise the bridge that carries you over Do not criticize people or things that have helped you: *On the principle that you should always praise the bridge that carries you over, I spoke out in defense of the system that had enabled me to continue my education after the death of my parents.* The proverb was first recorded in 1678 in John Ray's *A Collection of English Proverbs*.

Variant of this proverb: everybody speaks well of the bridge that carries him over.

praise the child, and you make love to the mother Parents—especially mothers—are pleased and flattered by compliments paid to their children: *He struggled to think of something nice to say about her obnoxious son, anxious to win her favor and well aware that if you praise the child you make love to the mother.* The proverb was first recorded in 1829 (W. Cobbett, *Advice to Young Men*), but with the implication that it had long been in general use.

a preacher's son is often bad *See* CLERGYMEN'S SONS ALWAYS TURN OUT BADLY.

prejudice is being down on what we are not up on People automatically dislike or distrust anything they have no understanding of or familiarity with: *Disparaging and offensive remarks like these are just a sign of ignorance—prejudice is being down on what we are not up on.*

Proverb expressing similar meaning: PREJUDICE IS THE CHILD OF IGNORANCE.

prejudice is the child of ignorance Prejudice is caused by a lack of knowledge or understanding: *On the basis that prejudice is the child of ignorance, it is hoped that this new information campaign will pave the way for better race relations.* The proverb was first recorded in William Hazlitt's essay "On Prejudice" (c. 1821).

Proverb expressing similar meaning: PREJUDICE IS BEING DOWN ON WHAT WE ARE NOT UP ON.

Proverb expressing opposite meaning: ADMIRATION IS THE DAUGHTER OF IGNORANCE.

prevention is better than cure It is better to prevent something undesirable from happening than to have to fix it afterward: *The debate was evenly divided between those who favored abortion on demand and those who felt that free contraception should be available to all, on the basis that prevention is better than cure.* The proverb was first recorded in 1618, but the sentiment it expresses is of earlier origin.

Proverbs expressing similar meaning: AN OUNCE OF PREVENTION IS WORTH A POUND OF CURE; A STITCH IN TIME SAVES NINE; WHO REPAIRS NOT HIS GUTTERS REPAIRS HIS WHOLE HOUSE.

the price of liberty is eternal vigilance Freedom can only be preserved by keeping a watch on any threat to it: *The Treasury might wrangle over the cost of the nation's defense, but the price of liberty is eternal vigilance.* An Irish proverb first recorded by John Philpot Curran in 1790, it became a favorite maxim of U.S. reformer Wendell Phillips in the mid-19th century.

pride comes before a fall *See* PRIDE GOES BEFORE A FALL.

pride feels no pain People are able to endure or ignore the physical discomfort caused by smart or fashionable clothes, shoes, or jewelry; also used in other situations where people tolerate physical suffering in order not to lose face: *In those days women wore corsets that were sometimes so tightly laced as to cause internal injury, but pride feels no pain.* The proverb was first recorded in 1614.

Variant of this proverb: pride feels no cold.

pride goes before a fall Arrogance and overconfidence often lead to humiliation or disaster; often used as a warning: "'I suppose he thinks he'd be mayor himself,' said the people of Blackstable. They pursed their lips. 'Pride goeth before a fall'" (W. Somerset Maugham, *Cakes and Ale,* 1930). The proverb is of biblical origin—"Pride goeth before destruction, and an haughty spirit before a fall" (Proverbs 16:18)—and is sometimes regarded as a misquotation. The sentiment it expresses occurs in one of the fables of Aesop (sixth century B.C.), about a victorious fighting cock who flies up to a high place and crows in triumph, only to be carried off by a passing eagle.

Variant of this proverb: pride comes before a fall.

procrastination is the thief of time If you constantly put off doing things, you will only waste the time in which they could have been done and will ultimately run out of time in which to do them: "They were virtuous young men, and lost no opportunity that fell in their way to make their livelihood. Their motto was in these words, namely, 'Procrastination is the thief of time'" (Mark Twain, *The Innocents Abroad,* 1869). The proverb comes from Edward Young's poem *Night Thoughts* (1742): "Procrastination is the thief of time;/Year after year it steals, till all are fled." Other writers have different views on the subject: Oscar Wilde wrote, in *The Picture of Dorian Gray* (1891), "He was always late on principle, this principle being that punctuality is the thief of time," and according to Ogden Nash, in *The Primrose Path* (1935), "Far from being the thief of Time, procrastination is the king of it."

Proverbs expressing similar meaning: NEVER PUT OFF UNTIL TOMORROW

WHAT YOU CAN DO TODAY; THERE'S NO TIME LIKE THE PRESENT.

promises, like piecrust, are made to be broken People cannot be depended upon to keep their word: *She promised never to mention the incident again, but promises, like piecrust, are made to be broken, and she couldn't resist retelling the story—much to my embarrassment—at a dinner party the following week.* The proverb was first recorded in 1681, in the periodical *Heraclitus Ridens:* "He makes no more of breaking Acts of Parliaments, than if they were like Promises and Piecrust made to be broken."

Variant of this proverb: promises are like piecrust: easy made and easy broken.

Proverb expressing opposite meaning: A MAN'S WORD IS AS GOOD AS HIS BOND.

the proof of the pudding is in the eating Nothing can be properly judged until it is put to the test: *The car is very attractive in its new design, and the improved performance figures look good on paper, but the proof of the pudding is in the eating—let's go for a drive.* The proverb was first recorded in this form in the 17th century, but the sentiment it expresses is of earlier origin.

Variant of this proverb: the proof is in the pudding.

a prophet is not without honor, save in his own country People who give words of warning or wisdom are not heeded or appreciated by those closest to them: "In Florence the signori thought him an amusing fellow and his letters often made them laugh, but they had no great confidence in his judgment and never followed his advice. 'A prophet is not without honor save in his own coun-

try,' he sighed" (W. Somerset Maugham, *Then and Now,* 1946). The proverb is of biblical origin in its current form: "A prophet is not without honor, save in his own country, and in his own house" (Matthew 13:57).

Variant of this proverb: a prophet is without honor in his own country.

prosperity discovers vice; adversity, virtue Wealth or good fortune often brings out the worst in a person, whereas hardship or misfortune brings out the best: *The saying "Prosperity discovers vice; adversity, virtue" should not be used as an argument for withholding financial assistance from the needy.* The proverb was first recorded in 1732 in Thomas Fuller's *Gnomologia: Adagies and Proverbs.*

prosperity is just around the corner Things will improve in the near future: *Politicians are always telling us that prosperity is just around the corner—provided that we continue voting them into power—but over the past few years we seem to have done a complete tour of the block without tracking it down.* The proverb originated at the time of the Great Depression, during the administration of President Herbert Hoover (1929–33), with whom it is generally associated.

providence is always on the side of the big battalions Those with the greatest strength, power, or influence always seem to have luck on their side and inevitably win the day: *Not only do they outnumber us, but they also have better weapons at their disposal. Providence is always on the side of the big battalions, and I see no point in fighting a battle that we cannot possibly win.* The proverb has been attributed to various people, notably the French marshal Henri de Turenne (1611–75): "*la fortune est toujours, comme disait le pauvre M. de Turenne, pour les gros bataillons* [fortune is always, as poor Mr. de Turenne used to say, for the big battalions]" (Madame de Sévigné, letter dated December 22, 1673). The French writer Voltaire (1694–78) was of a different opinion: "*Dieu n'est pas pour les gros bataillons, mais pour ceux qui tirent le mieux* [God is on the side not of the big battalions, but of the best shots]."

Variant of this proverb: God is always on the side of the big battalions.

Proverbs expressing similar meaning: MIGHT MAKES RIGHT; THE WEAKEST GO TO THE WALL.

Proverb expressing opposite meaning: THE RACE IS NOT TO THE SWIFT, NOR THE BATTLE TO THE STRONG.

punctuality is the politeness of kings It is discourteous to be late, regardless of your rank or status: "Punctuality is the politeness of kings, and King Magnus is a model in that respect" (George Bernard Shaw, *The Apple Cart,* 1929). The proverb is attributed to King Louis XVIII (1755–1824) in its French form "*L'exactitude est la politesse des rois.*" It was first recorded in English in 1853, in the form "Punctuality is the virtue of princes."

Variant of this proverb: punctuality is the politeness of princes.

punctuality is the soul of business It is important to be on time for business appointments: *Punctuality is the soul of business, and most companies take a very dim view of job applicants who arrive late for their interviews.*

The proverb was first recorded in 1853 in T. C. Haliburton's *Sam Slick's Wise Saws.*

put first things first *See* FIRST THINGS FIRST.

put your best foot forward Always make the most of your strengths and abilities; also used to urge people to make their best effort or be on their best behavior: *Put your best foot forward, and try to make a good impression at the outset.* The proverb was first recorded in the 16th century. It occurs in Shakespeare's play *Titus Andronicus* (2:3), "Come on, my lords, the better foot before."

put your trust in God, and keep your powder dry Do not pin all your hopes on divine assistance or intervention—always be prepared to take action yourself if necessary: "Zwingli . . . believed in the necessity of war; while Luther put his sole trust in the Word of God. . . . Zwingli was a free republican; while Luther was a loyal monarchist. He belonged to the Cromwellian type of men who "trust in God and keep their powder dry" (Philip Schaff, *History of the Christian Church, 1883–1893*). The proverb is attributed to the English Civil War leader Oliver Cromwell (1599–1658), who is said to have given this advice to his troops at the battle of Edgehill in 1642. The word *powder* refers to gunpowder. The proverb has given rise to the cliché *to keep one's powder dry.*

Variant of this proverb: trust in God and keep your powder dry.

Proverb expressing similar meaning: HOPE FOR THE BEST AND PREPARE FOR THE WORST.

the quarrel of lovers is the renewal of love A loving relationship is often reestablished on a firmer footing after an argument: "The falling out of Lovers . . . is the renewal of Love. Are we not now better friends than if we had never differed?" (Samuel Richardson, *Sir Charles Grandison*, 1754). The proverb is of ancient origin, occurring in the Roman poet Terence's *Andria* (second century B.C.): "*Amantium irae amoris integratio est* [Lovers' quarrels are a strengthening of love]."

Variant of this proverb: the falling out of lovers is the renewing of love.

quickly come, quickly go Something that arises suddenly is likely to disappear just as suddenly; also used of something that is rapidly gained and lost: *It is an unpleasant illness, but rarely lasts more than a few days—quickly come, quickly go.* The proverb was first recorded in this form in 1869 in W. C. Hazlitt's *English Proverbs*.

Proverb expressing similar meaning: EASY COME, EASY GO.

quick ripe, quick rotten *See* SOON RIPE, SOON ROTTEN.

quit while you are ahead Give up doing something when you are in a good position rather than risk what you have already gained: *He was tempted to bet on one more game but remembered the adage "quit while you are ahead."* The proverb was first recorded c. 1350 in the *Douce MS*.

Variant of this proverb: leave off while the play is good.

the race is not to the swift, nor the battle to the strong Speed and power do not guarantee success—those who are slower and weaker may win through perseverance or tactics: "Amongst the wild tribes of the Malay Archipelago there is also a racing match; and it appears from M. Bourien's account, as Sir J. Lubbock remarks, that 'the race, "is not to the swift, nor the battle to the strong," but to the young man who has the good fortune to please his intended bride'" (Charles Darwin, *The Descent of Man,* 1871). The proverb is of biblical origin: "the race is not to the swift, nor the battle to the strong, neither yet bread to the wise, nor yet riches to men of understanding, nor yet favor to men of skill; but time and chance happeneth to them all" (Ecclesiastes 9:11).

Proverb expressing similar meaning: SLOW AND STEADY WINS THE RACE.

Proverbs expressing opposite meaning: PROVIDENCE IS ALWAYS ON THE SIDE OF THE BIG BATTALIONS; THE WEAKEST GO TO THE WALL.

rain before seven, fine before eleven Rain early in the morning often heralds a fine day; occasionally applied to other things that start in an unpromising way: *The weather forecast was not good, but my hopes were raised when I woke at dawn to the sound of rain beating on the window. Rain before seven, fine before eleven*—perhaps the *baseball game would not have to be canceled after all.* The proverb was first recorded in 1835, but with the implication that it was already in use among amateur weather forecasters.

Variant of this proverb: RAIN BEFORE SEVEN, CLEAR BEFORE ELEVEN.

rats desert a sinking ship People tend to leave an organization, pull out of a project, or abandon a cause when they become aware that it is heading for disaster; often used to imply disloyalty, or to predict the imminent failure of something: "What do you want HER to know how you are for? She don't want to see 'ee. She's the rat that forsook the sinking ship! . . . And I stuck to un—the more fool I! Have that strumpet in the house indeed!" (Thomas Hardy, *Jude the Obscure,* 1895). The proverb was first recorded in the 16th century, but a similar sentiment—referring to the notion that rats and mice always leave a house that is about to fall down—was expressed in the first century A.D. by the Roman scholar Pliny the Elder.

Variant of this proverb: rats abandon a sinking ship.

the receiver is as bad as the thief *See* IF THERE WERE NO RECEIVERS, THERE WOULD BE NO THIEVES.

red sky at night, sailor's delight; red sky in the morning, sailors take warning A red sky at sunset is a sign of fair weather the following day, but a red sky at sunrise means that bad weather is on the way: *A spectacular sunset on Saturday evening was followed by a glorious day for our outing on Sunday, fulfilling the promise of the old saying "Red sky at night, sailor's delight; red sky in the morning, sailors take warning."* The proverb is of biblical origin: "When it is evening, ye say, It will be fair weather: for the sky is red. And in the morning, It will be foul weather to day: for the sky is red and lowring" (Matthew 16:2–3).

Variant of this proverb: red sky at night, shepherd's delight; red sky in the morning, shepherd's warning.

a reed before the wind lives on, while mighty oaks do fall Those who are flexible and relatively insignificant can survive crises that bring down more prominent people who are unable or unwilling to yield or adapt: *Remembering the saying "A reed before the wind lives on while mighty oaks do fall," he managed to hold on to his job through successive administrations by keeping a low profile and adjusting his method of working in line with policy changes and prevailing trends.* The proverb was first recorded in Chaucer's *Troilus and Criseyde* (c. 1385): "And reed that boweth down for every blast,/Ful lightly, cesse wynd, it wol aryse;/ But so nyl nought an ook whan it is cast."

the remedy may be worse than the disease Action taken to put something right is often more unpleasant or damaging than the original problem: *"'But how much will it cost to win the day?' asked Mme. Sechard. 'Fees if you win, one thousand francs if we lose our case.' 'Oh, dear!' cried poor Eve, 'Why, the remedy is worse than the disease!'"* (Honoré de Balzac, *Eve and David,* 1841–43). The proverb was first recorded in 1582, but the sentiment it expresses is of ancient origin. It occurs in one of the fables of Aesop (sixth century B.C.), about a group of pigeons who ask a hawk to defend them against a kite: once inside their cote, the hawk kills more of them in a single day than the kite could have killed outside in a whole year.

Variant of this proverb: the cure may be worse than the disease.

render unto Caesar that which is Caesar's Give what you have to give to those who have a better claim to them: *He did not want to hand the extra money over to the taxman, but his accountant persuaded him to render unto Caesar what was Caesar's.* A biblical quotation from Matthew 22:21, the proverb has changed somewhat from its original meaning, which is evident from its fuller biblical form: "Then saith he unto them, Render therefore unto Caesar the things which are Caesar's; and unto God the things that are God's." An underlying message here is to keep worldly things separate from religion.

revenge is a dish best eaten cold Vengeance is often more satisfying if it is exacted some time after the original offense; said when a wrong cannot be immediately avenged, or used to discourage somebody from retaliating in the heat of the moment: *I'll get my own back one of* *these days, but I'm in no hurry—revenge is a dish best eaten cold.* The proverb was first recorded in 1885.

Variant of this proverb: revenge is a dish best served cold.

revenge is sweet It is very satisfying to retaliate or avenge a wrong: "I am the man from whom you ran, the man you sought to slay./That you may note and gaze and gloat, and say 'Revenge is sweet',/In the grit and grime of the river's slime I am rotting at your feet" (Robert Service, *Ballads of a Cheechako,* "The Ballad of One-Eyed Mike," 1909). The proverb was first recorded in 1566, in William Painter's *Palace of Pleasure:* "Vengeance is sweete vnto him, which in place of killing his enemy, giueth life to a perfect frende." In his poem *Paradise Lost* (1667), John Milton observed, "Revenge, at first, though sweet,/Bitter ere long, back on itself recoils."

revolutions are not made with rose water It is not possible to bring about drastic changes by pleasant, easy, or peaceful means, or without causing damage or suffering: "On either side harm must be done before good can accrue—revolutions are not to be made with rose water" (Lord Byron, letter dated October 3, 1819). The quotation is the first recorded use of the proverb in English. It comes from a rhetorical question posed by the French writer Nicolas (1741–94): "*Voulez-vous qu'on vous fasse des révolutions à l'eau rose* [Do you expect revolutions to be made with rose water]."

riches have wings Money is soon gone. The proverb is of biblical origin: "For riches taketh her to her wings, as an eagle, and flieth into the heaven" (Proverbs 23:5).

Proverb expressing similar meaning: MONEY IS ROUND AND RUNS AWAY.

the rich get richer and the poor get poorer Those who have money find it easy to make more, while those who have none sink further into debt; often applied to a specific economic period, climate, or policy that favors the rich and disadvantages the poor: *The most significant result of this method of taxation is that the rich get richer and the poor get poorer.* The proverb was popularized in the early 20th century as a line from the song "Ain't We Got Fun" (1921), by Gus Kahn and Raymond B. Egan, which also contains the facetious variant "The rich get rich and the poor get children."

the rich man has his ice in the summer and the poor man gets his in the winter It may seem that everybody, rich or poor, has an equal share of good fortune in life, but this is not so: "The rich get ice in the summer and the poor get it in the winter, so some people figure everyone gets an even break" (J. W. Rider, *Jersey Tomatoes,* 1986). The proverb was first recorded in 1921.

a rich man's joke is always funny Wealthy people are surrounded by those who hope to win their favor by flattery, such as, by laughing at all their jokes, whether they are funny or not: *He went on to tell an anecdote that was in rather poor taste, but his host—who had invited him with a view to securing a lucrative sponsorship deal—laughed appreciatively. A rich man's joke is always funny.* The proverb comes from the writings of the poet T. E. Brown (1830–97).

Proverb expressing similar meaning: He that has a full purse never wanted a friend.

a rising tide lifts all boats   Everybody benefits from an upward trend in a nation's prosperity or quality of life: "The country was in a sharp economic expansion coming out of '82. This made everybody look smart—you know, the rising tide lifts all boats" (*Washington Times*, 1990). The proverb is associated with President John F. Kennedy, who used it in a speech in 1963: "As they say on my own Cape Cod, a rising tide lifts all the boats."

the road to hell is paved with good intentions   Good intentions are of no value unless they are translated into action; also used when something done with good intentions has an undesirable or harmful effect: *To those who constantly make vague promises of future support for our charity, I have only this to say: "The road to hell is paved with good intentions."* The proverb was first recorded in English in 1574, in the form "Hell is full of good desires," but it is has been attributed to Saint Bernard (1091–1153).

Variants of this proverb: the streets of hell are paved with promises; hell is full of good meanings, but heaven is full of good works.

the robin and the wren are God's cock and hen   The robin and the wren are special birds in the eyes of heaven: *the robin and the wren are God's cock and hen: the martin and the swallow are God's mate and marrow.* The proverb appears in the *Poetical Description of Song Birds* (1787). The proverb reflects the time-honored superstition that it is unlucky to kill a robin or a wren. It may also have been influenced by the ancient misapprehension that the robin and the wren were the male and female of the same species.

Robin Hood could brave all weathers but a thaw wind   Of all kinds of weather, a raw wind after frost or snow is the most penetrating. The proverb appears in W. Neville, *The Life and Exploits of Robin Hood* (1855). In Yorkshire, England, where the historical Robin Hood may have lived, a cold wind from the north or east is called a "Robin Hood wind."

a rolling stone gathers no moss   People who spend their lives traveling or moving around tend to accumulate few responsibilities or personal attachments: "We keep repeating the silly proverb that rolling stones gather no moss, as if moss were a desirable parasite" (George Bernard Shaw, *Misalliance,* Preface, 1914). The proverb is probably of ancient origin: in his *Adagia* (1500) the Dutch humanist Desiderius Erasmus quotes Latin and Greek proverbs translated as "A rolling stone is not covered with moss" and "A rolling stone does not gather seaweed."

Rome was not built in a day   It takes a lot of time and effort to achieve great things; used to encourage patience and perseverance: "'These are early days, Trot,' she pursued, 'and Rome was not built in a day, nor in a year. You have chosen . . . a very pretty and a very affectionate creature. It will be your duty . . . to estimate her (as you chose her) by the qualities she has, and not by the qualities she may not have. The latter you must develop in her, if you can'" (Charles Dickens, *David Copperfield,* 1850). First recorded in English in 1545, the proverb is of ancient origin.

a rose by any other name would smell as sweet   It is the intrinsic qualities of people and things that matter, not what they are called—names have no bearing on character or nature: "Anne looked thoughtful. 'I read in a book once that a rose by any other name would smell as sweet, but I've never been able to believe it. I don't believe a rose WOULD be as nice if it was called a thistle or a skunk cabbage'" (Lucy Maud Montgomery, *Anne of Green Gables,* 1908). The proverb comes from Shakespeare's play *Romeo and Juliet* (2:2), "What's in a name? that which we call a rose/By any other name would smell as sweet."

Proverb expressing similar meaning: WHAT'S IN A NAME?

a rose is a rose is a rose is a rose Things and people are what they are—you cannot define them in any other way, or change their essential nature by giving them a different name: "A rose is a rose is a rose," said Jerome M. Becker . . . 'He committed the murder under the influence of

RUSSIAN PROVERBS

Many Russian proverbs are regional equivalents of others found in the English-speaking world, but others would appear to have arisen uniquely from the Russian experience of hardship and servitude over the centuries.

Ask a lot, but take what is offered

Better a bed of wood than a bier of gold

Don't praise your furnace when the house is cold

Eat until you are half full; drink until you are half drunk

An enemy will agree, but a friend will argue

Eternal peace lasts until the next war

Eternity makes room for a salty cucumber

Even in the ashes there will be a few sparks

He who offers his back should not complain if it is beaten

Honor goes to God; the priests get the bacon

The horses of hope gallop, but the asses of experience go slowly

If you don't have a hundred roubles, make sure you have a hundred friends

In Russia every day is of thirty hours

In the lake of lies there are many dead fish

No one is hanged who has money in his pocket

One cannot make a fur coat from a thank-you

Only chained bears dance

Thanks to one small candle the whole of Moscow burns

Vodka is the aunt of wine

Who lives in exile finds that spring has no charm

Who wants heat must endure the smoke

You can't sew buttons on your neighbor's mouth

Your body belongs to the Tsar, your soul to God, and your back to the squire cocaine and to me that's simple: It's murder and his conduct was depraved'" (*New York Times,* 1989). The proverb comes from the U.S. writer Gertrude Stein's *Sacred Emily* (1913).

the rotten apple spoils the barrel A single bad individual can have a corrupting influence on all those around him or her, or everybody with whom he or she comes into contact; also used to imply that one bad member of a group can create an unfavorable impression of the whole: *If we wish to retain our political neutrality, we must keep militants and activists out of the organization—the rotten apple spoils the barrel.* The proverb was first recorded, with different wording, in 1340.

Variants of this proverb: the rotten apple injures its neighbor; one bad apple spoils the lot.

rules are made to be broken People would not bother to make rules if they did not expect them to be broken every now and then; often used to justify some minor infringement, especially of a rule considered to be petty, unnecessary, or inappropriate: *I know we're not supposed to take food and drink into the library, but rules are made to be broken.* The proverb was first recorded in 1942 in F. Gruber's *Gift Horse.*

safe bind, safe find   If you fasten things securely before you leave, or lock somebody or something away, they will still be there when you return: "'I'll privately turn the key on her, in case she wakes before we come back. Safe bind, safe find—you know the proverb!'" (Wilkie Collins, *No Name,* 1862). The proverb was first recorded in 1546 in the form "Fast bind, fast find."

safety first   Safety issues should always be the first consideration: *This company has adopted a safety first policy.* This proverb dates back to 1929, when it appeared in W. R. Inge's *Assessment and Anticipation*: "'Safety first' is all very well when we are preparing to cross a street or board an omnibus."

Saturday's child works hard for its living Children born on a Saturday are supposed to be industrious and hardworking: *Both her sons were born on a Saturday, and neither of them has bothered to look for a job since leaving college. So much for the saying "Saturday's child works hard for its living"!* The proverb is the sixth line of a traditional rhyme beginning "Monday's child is fair of face." See entries at the days of the week for other proverbs from this rhyme.

save at the spigot and waste at the bung   *See* SPARE AT THE SPIGOT, AND LET OUT THE BUNGHOLE.

save something for a rainy day   It is sensible to put money aside in case it is needed in the future: *He remembered his grandmother's advice to save something for a rainy day.* The proverb was first recorded in 1583 in J. Stubbes's *Anatomie of Abuses.*

save us from our friends   Our friends can cause us far more harm or trouble than our enemies; usually—but not exclusively—applied to false, treacherous, or disloyal friends: *She says she felt compelled, as one of my oldest friends, to tell my employers about my alcohol problem. All I can say is, "Save us from our friends!"* The proverb was first recorded, with different wording, in 1477. Queen Elizabeth I is alleged to have said, in 1585, "There is an Italian proverb which saith, From my enemy let me defend myself; but from a pretensed friend, good Lord deliver me."

Variant of this proverb: God protect me from my friends—I can protect myself from my enemies.

Proverb expressing similar meaning: WITH FRIENDS LIKE THAT, WHO NEEDS ENEMIES?

SCANDINAVIAN PROVERBS

The proverbs of the Scandinavian countries provide a glimpse into the history of those nations, including as they do a fair number of pithy observations based on the experience of harsh weather and a seafaring tradition going back to the Vikings.

Ambition and revenge are always hungry

Ask for advice, then use your head

Better ice that melts than fire that extinguishes

Don't praise the bread that is not out of the oven

Don't sail out farther than you can row back

Even a small star shines in the dark

Fish bite best on a golden hook

Fresh air impoverishes doctors

Heaven dries what it has made wet

It is the great north wind that made the Vikings

It is too late to learn to swim when the water is up to your lips

Love has produced some heroes but many idiots too

A man without money is like a boat without sails

The most difficult mountain to cross is the threshold

No answer is also an answer

Nobody is too young to die tomorrow

Rain does not stay in the sky

A small cloud may hide both sun and moon

There is no wind that blows right for the sailor who does not know where the harbor is

The winter does not leave without a backward glance

saving is getting Money that is got through saving is as valuable as money that is earned. The proverb was first recorded in 1642 in G. Torriano's *Select Italian Proverbs*: "Saving is the first getting."

Proverb expressing similar meaning: A PENNY SAVED IS A PENNY EARNED.

scrambled eggs can't be unscrambled *See* YOU CAN'T UNSCRAMBLE EGGS.

scratch a Russian and you find a Tartar What a person claims to be may be different from what he or she actually is: "Until a short time ago the aphorism, 'Scratch a Russian and you find a Tartar,' was the sum of British comprehension of the Russian character" (*British Spectator*, 1911). Attributed to Napoleon Bonaparte (1769–1821), the proverb was first recorded in English in 1823, but with the implication that it was already in general use. Other words may be substituted for *Russian* and *Tartar*, as in the Republican slogan "Scratch a Democrat and you will find a rebel."

second thoughts are best Do not act on impulse: "Second thoughts, they say, are best:/I'll consider of it once again" (John Dryden, *The Spanish Friar*, 1681). The prov-

SCOTTISH PROVERBS

Scotland has a rich heritage in terms of proverbs, of which the following is merely a selection.

A bad wound may heal, but a bad name will kill

A blind man needs no looking glass

The devil's a busy bishop in his own diocese

A hungry man smells meat far

All that's said in the kitchen should not be told in the hall

Enough's as good as a feast

Every man to his taste, as the man said when he kissed his cow

From saving comes having

Get what you can and keep what you have; that's the way to get rich

Good company on a journey is worth a coach

If I had a dog as daft, I would shoot him

If you don't see the bottom, don't wade

Laws catch flies, but let hornets go free

A man cannot wive and thrive the same year

Many a mickle makes a muckle

A nod's as good as a wink to a blind horse

One whisky is all right; two is too much; three is too few

Penny wise and pound foolish

War makes thieves, and peace hangs them

A wise lawyer never goes to law himself

Ye may not sit in Rome and strive with the Pope

You will never know a man till you do business with him

erb is of ancient origin, occurring in Euripides' *Hippolytus* (fifth century B.C.): "The second thoughts are invariably wiser."

a secret is either too good to keep or too bad not to tell   It is very hard to keep a secret of any kind: *You'll never believe what Megan's planning to do to that guy who dumped her last week. It's a secret, of course, but you know what they say—a secret is either too good to keep or too bad not to tell.* The proverb is a regional expression in the United States.

a secret's a secret until it's told   When you pass on a secret to somebody else, it ceases to be a secret: *"Don't tell anybody else—it's a secret." "It can't be—a secret's a secret until it's told."*

Variant of this proverb: a secret shared is no secret.

see a pin and pick it up, all the day you'll have good luck; see a pin and let it lay, bad luck you'll have all the day   According to popular superstition, if you see a pin lying around, it is lucky to pick it up and unlucky not to; also used to encourage thriftiness: *See a pin and pick it up, all the day you'll have good luck—and you might also prevent somebody from getting a painful surprise if they kneel* down or walk around barefoot. The proverb was first recorded in 1843.

Variants of this proverb: find a penny, pick it up, all day long you'll have good luck; see a pin and pick it up, all the day you'll have good luck; see a pin and let it lie, you'll want a pin before you die.

seeing is believing People are often reluctant to believe something until they see it for themselves, but nobody doubts the evidence of his or her own eyes: "'if you had seen de great huge pieces of de plate so massive, Sir Arthur,—so fine fashion, Miss Wardour—and de silver cross dat we did find . . . you would have believed then.' 'Seeing is believing indeed'" (Sir Walter Scott, *The Antiquary*, 1816). The proverb was first recorded in 1609.

seek and you shall find You must make a personal effort to get what you want: "'What would you have me do?' said Fernand. 'How do I know? Is it my affair? I am not in love with Mademoiselle Mercedes; but for you—in the words of the gospel, seek, and you shall find'" (Alexandre Dumas, *The Count of Monte Cristo*, 1844–45). The proverb is of biblical origin: "Ask, and it shall be given you; seek, and ye shall find; knock, and it shall be opened unto you" (Matthew 7:7).

see no evil, hear no evil, speak no evil Ignore any wrongdoing, malice, or gossip that is going on around you, and do not get involved: *It's no use asking him about the latest office intrigue—his motto is "See no evil, hear no evil, speak no evil."* First recorded in 1926, the proverb is associated with a representation of three monkeys with their hands over their eyes, ears, and mouth, respectively.

seize the day Live for the present, and take full advantage of every moment: *Nobody knows what the future may hold, so seize the day.* The proverb comes from the writings of the Roman poet Horace (65–8 B.C.) and is often used in its original Latin form, "*Carpe diem.*" It was popularized in the late 20th century as the motto of the charismatic and unconventional English teacher John Keating, played by Robin Williams, in the movie *Dead Poets Society* (1989): "*Carpe diem*, lads! Seize the day! Make your lives extraordinary."

Variant of this proverb: seize the moment.

Proverbs expressing similar meaning: EAT, DRINK, AND BE MERRY, FOR TOMORROW WE DIE; GATHER YE ROSEBUDS WHILE YE MAY; LIFE IS SHORT AND TIME IS SWIFT; THE MILL CANNOT GRIND WITH THE WATER THAT IS PAST; TAKE TIME BY THE FORELOCK.

seldom seen, soon forgotten Persons or things rarely seen or mentioned are quickly forgotten: *At first he seemed quite upset about the break-up of their relationship, but after a few weeks it was a case of seldom seen, soon forgotten.* The proverb was first recorded c. 1350 in the *Douce MS*.

Proverb expressing similar meaning: OUT OF SIGHT, OUT OF MIND.

self-deceit is the easiest of any It is easy to convince yourself of something that you want to believe: *She has persuaded herself that she is innocent of the charge, but self-deceit is the easiest of any, and she will find it more difficult to persuade the judge and jury.* The proverb is recorded as a regional expression in the United States.

self-interest is the rule, self-sacrifice the exception People are far more concerned with looking after their own interests than with sacrificing their needs for the sake of others: *It was one of those rare occurrences, an act of pure altruism, in a world where self-interest is the rule and self-sacrifice the exception.* The proverb is recorded as a regional expression in the United States.

self-praise is no recommendation Boastful talk about your own abilities or achievements does not impress others, and may have the opposite effect—people often distrust those who have too high an opinion of themselves: "Self-praise is no recommendation, but I may say for myself that I am not so bad a man of business" (Charles Dickens, *Bleak House,* 1853). The proverb was first recorded in 1826, but the sentiment it expresses is of earlier origin.

Proverb expressing opposite meaning: TOOT YOUR OWN HORN LEST THE SAME BE NEVER TOOTED.

self-preservation is the first law of nature Survival is the primary natural instinct of all living things; used when people take action to protect themselves or their own interests: *The strike failed because not enough people were prepared to put their own jobs on the line for the sake of somebody else's—self-preservation is the first law of nature.* The proverb was first recorded in the English poet John Donne's *Biathanatos,* a defense of suicide, probably written c. 1610 but not published until 1646: "It is onley upon this reason, that selfe-preservation is of Naturall Law." The sentiment it expresses is of ancient origin, occurring in the writings of Cicero (106–43 B.C.): "*primamque ex natura hanc habere appetitionem, ut conservemus nosmet ipsos* [by nature our first impulse is to preserve ourselves]."

Proverb expressing similar meaning: EVERY MAN FOR HIMSELF AND THE DEVIL TAKE THE HINDMOST.

send a fool to market and a fool he'll return It is unrealistic to expect a fool to change into anything but a fool: "You may go back again, like a fool as you came" (Jonathan Swift, *Polite Conversation,* 1738). The proverb was first recorded in 1586 in G. Whitney's *Emblems.* Variants of this proverb have the fool being sent "to France" or simply "far."

set a beggar on horseback, and he'll ride to the devil People who suddenly acquire wealth or power are likely to be corrupted by it: "'Set a beggar on horseback, and he'll ride to the devil,' . . . some of these early manufacturers did ride to the devil in magnificent style" (Elizabeth Gaskell, *North and South,* 1855).

The proverb was first recorded in this form in 1669, but the sentiment it expresses is of earlier origin.

Proverb expressing similar meaning: GIVE A BEGGAR A HORSE AND HE'LL RIDE IT TO DEATH.

set a sprat to catch a mackerel See THROW OUT A SPRAT TO CATCH A MACKEREL.

set a thief to catch a thief A person who has been involved in wrongdoing—especially a reformed criminal—is good at catching others, because he or she can understand their thinking and anticipate their actions: "'Set a thief to catch a thief,' said Mr. Stryker, with his usual dry manner. 'I don't believe in the full success of your virtuous diplomatist. How is a man to know all the turnings and windings of the road that leads to treaties, unless he has gone over it himself?'" (Susan Fenimore Cooper, *Elinor Wyllys,* 1846). The proverb was first recorded in this form in 1665, but with the implication that it had long been in general use. The sentiment it expresses occurs in the writings of the poet Callimachus (third century B.C.): "being a thief myself I recognized the tracks of a thief."

Variant of this proverb: it takes a thief to catch a thief.

Proverbs expressing similar meaning: IT TAKES ONE TO KNOW ONE; AN OLD POACHER MAKES THE BEST GAMEKEEPER.

share and share alike Things must be shared equally and fairly among those who want or have a right to their part: "'Drink, Henry Fray—drink,' magnanimously said Jan Coggan, a person who held Saint-Simonian notions of share and share alike where liquor was concerned, as the vessel showed signs of approaching him in its gradual revolution among them. (Thomas Hardy, *Far from the Madding Crowd,* 1874). The proverb was first recorded c. 1564.

the sharper the storm, the sooner it's over The more unpleasant something is, the less time it lasts: *The unfortunate students who found themselves on the receiving end of his outbursts of rage used to console themselves with the saying "The sharper the storm, the sooner it's over."* The proverb was first recorded, in its variant form, in 1872. The sentiment it expresses, however, is of ancient origin: compare Seneca (c. 4 B.C.–A.D. 65), "*procellae, quanto plus habent virium, tanto minus temporis* [the harder storms are, the shorter they last]."

Variant of this proverb: the harder the storm, the sooner it's over.

the sheep that bleats loses a mouthful See A BLEATING SHEEP LOSES A BITE.

shit happens Sometimes you must resign yourself to the inevitability of bad things happening: *The detective shrugged. "I don't know why she died. She was just unlucky. Shit happens."* The proverb appears to be of late 20th-century U.S. origin.

shit or get off the pot See PISS OR GET OFF THE POT.

the shoe is on the other foot The situation has been reversed: *Now the shoe is on the other foot, and those responsible for laying off half the workforce are fighting to save their own jobs.* The proverb was first recorded in the 19th century in the form "The boot is on the other leg."

Variant of this proverb: the boot is on the other foot.

the shoemaker's child always goes barefoot People often fail to benefit from the professional skills of those closest to them: "My mother always used to say, 'The shoemaker's family goes barefoot.' Well . . . I married a plumber and every faucet in our house drips" (*Washington Times,* 1996). The proverb was first recorded, with different wording, in 1546. Other words may be substituted for *child,* such as *son, wife,* or *family,* as in the quotation.

Variant of this proverb: the cobbler's children go barefoot.

shoot first and ask questions afterward In certain circumstances—for example, when facing a potentially dangerous person or thing—it is safer not to lose time weighing up the situation before taking action; often used in contexts criticizing such hasty or arbitrary behavior: "It struck her, too, that war seemed to have made the people on that side of the ocean extremely ready with weapons. They would be quite likely to shoot first and ask questions afterward—which would be too late to be helpful" (Mary Roberts Rinehart, *The Amazing Interlude,* 1918).

Variant of this proverb: shoot first, ask questions later.

a short horse is soon curried A small task is soon done: *A short horse is soon curried—it won't take long to put the room back to rights.* The proverb was first recorded c. 1350 in *Douce MS 52.*

short reckonings make long friends If you want to keep your friends, and retain goodwill in business, always pay your debts and settle your accounts promptly: "'I will repay you in a minute,' returned Eugene. He unsealed one of the bags as he spoke, counted out a hundred and forty francs, and pushed them towards Mme. Vauquer. 'Short reckonings make good friends,' he added" (Honoré de Balzac, *Father Goriot,* 1835). The proverb was first recorded in this form in 1673 (J. Dare, *Counsellor Manners*) but the sentiment it expresses is of earlier origin.

short visits make long friends People are unlikely to establish lasting friendships with visitors who outstay their welcome: *The vicar did not appear to be familiar with the old saying "short visits make long friends," for he stayed for over an hour.* The proverb was first recorded in 1923 in *Folk-Lore.*

Proverb expressing similar meaning: FISH AND GUESTS STINK AFTER THREE DAYS.

show me a liar and I will show you a thief People who are prepared to tell lies are likely to be dishonest in other ways too. The proverb was first recorded in 1607 in R. West's *The Court of Conscience.*

Proverb expressing similar meaning: A LIAR IS WORSE THAN A THIEF.

the show must go on Things must continue as if nothing had happened; used when events or circumstances threaten to disrupt something planned: *The show must go on, as they say, and we cannot postpone the conference just because one of the delegates has been unfortunate enough to fall down the stairs and break his leg.* Of theatrical origin, the proverb was first recorded in 1867 in the *Dictionary of Americanisms.*

shrouds have no pockets Wealth and possessions are of no use to you after you are dead; often used to justify extravagant spending: *There's no point in hoarding money at your age—you have no children to leave it to, and shrouds have no pockets.* The proverb was first recorded, with different wording, in 1854.

Proverb expressing similar meaning: YOU CAN'T TAKE IT WITH YOU.

a shut mouth catches no flies It is often safest or wisest to say nothing: *To avoid the risk of incriminating myself, I remained silent—a shut mouth catches no flies.* The proverb was first recorded in 1599 in the form "In a closed up mouth a fly cannot get in."

Variant of this proverb: a closed mouth catches no flies.

Proverb expressing similar meaning: A STILL TONGUE MAKES A WISE HEAD.

silence gives consent Those who do not reply to a request or accusation, or who raise no objection to something said or done, are assumed to have acquiesced: "Of course I ought to have known that you could not care for a man like me, a stranger. Silence gives consent. Yes? Eh? I don't want any of that sort of consent. And unless some day you find you can speak . . . No! No! I shall never ask you" (Joseph Conrad, *Chance,* 1913). The proverb was first recorded, with different wording, c. 1380 by John Wycliffe.

Variant of this proverb: silence means consent.

silence is golden Silence is a quality of great value; often used as advice to say nothing, but also applied to a lack of environmental noise: "Silence is golden, as her father used to say when she used to fly into tempers and wanted to say nasty things to everybody within range" (Aldous Huxley, *Antic Hay,* 1923). The proverb was first recorded in 1865 (W. White, *Eastern England*), but with the implication that it was already in general use.

Proverbs expressing similar meaning: THERE IS A TIME TO SPEAK, AND A TIME TO BE SILENT; THINK BEFORE YOU SPEAK; A WORD SPOKEN IS PAST RECALLING.

silence is the fittest reply to folly The best way to respond to a foolish remark or action is to ignore it: *I treated her ill-informed and bigoted comments with the contempt they deserved and said nothing—silence is the fittest reply to folly.* The proverb was first recorded in 1948 in a U.S. proverb collection.

Variant of this proverb: silence is the best answer to the stupid.

silence means consent *See* SILENCE GIVES CONSENT.

silly question, silly answer *See* ASK A SILLY QUESTION AND YOU GET A SILLY ANSWER.

sin, sorrow, and work are the things that men can't shirk Nobody can lead a life that is utterly virtuous, happy, or idle: *I wish I could stay longer, but I must get back to the office—sin, sorrow, and work are the things that men can't shirk.* The proverb is recorded as a regional expression in the United States.

sing before breakfast, cry before night Those who wake up feeling happy and carefree often encounter sorrow or trouble before the end of the day: *There must be some truth in the saying "Sing before breakfast, cry before night"—I often find that my mood changes dramatically during the course of the day.* The proverb was first recorded, with different wording, in J. Palsgrave's *L'éclaircissement de la Langue Française* (1530).

Variants of this proverb: if you sing before breakfast, you'll cry before supper; laugh before breakfast, cry before sunset.

six hours' sleep for a man, seven for a woman, and eight for a fool Women need more sleep than men, but only fools sleep for eight hours or more: "John Wesley . . . considered that five hours' sleep was enough for him or any man. . . . The old English proverb, so often in the mouth of George III, was 'six hours for a man, seven for a woman, and eight for a fool'"

(J. H. Friswell, *The Gentle Life,* 1864). The quotation is the first recorded use of the proverb in this form, but the sentiment it expresses is of earlier origin. Variants of the proverb recommend five or seven hours' sleep for travelers, six or seven for students and scholars, eight for workmen, merchants, or children, and they say that only fools, knaves, or "lazy bodies" need more.

the sky's the limit   There is virtually no limit to what can be achieved, earned, or spent: "Teenoso was one colt who proved himself a dream horse by remaining in training after winning a Derby deemed of dubious quality; a year later he won the King George VI and Queen Elizabeth. 'The sky's the limit for a four-year-old, though the opportunities in the Pattern are not there for fillies,' Geoff Wragg, Teenoso's trainer, said" (*Independent,* 1989).

sleep is the brother of death   Sleep and death are related: "How wonderful is Death, Death his brother Sleep!" (Percy Bysshe Shelley, *Queen Mab,* 1813). The proverb is ultimately of Greek origin and appeared in the writings of Homer. Its earliest appearance in English dates from 1563, in *The Mirror of Magistrates.* The word *brother* is sometimes replaced by *cousin.*

a slice off a cut loaf isn't missed   You can get away with wrongdoing, such as adultery or petty theft, if you are not the first person to do it, or if the offended party is unlikely to notice the result: *He tried to justify his behavior with sayings of dubious morality, such as "A slice off a cut loaf isn't missed."* The proverb comes from Shakespeare's play *Titus Andronicus* (2:1;

1592): "What, man! more water glideth by the mill/Than wots the miller of; and easy it is/Of a cut loaf to steal a shive, we know."

Variant of this proverb: you never miss a slice from a cut loaf.

a slip of the lip will sink a ship   *See* LOOSE LIPS SINK SHIPS.

sloth is the mother of poverty   The less work you do, the less money you will earn. *If it were true that sloth is the mother of poverty, there would be no such thing as the idle rich.* The proverb was first recorded in 1669 in *Politeuphuia.*

Variant of this proverb: sloth is the key to poverty.

sloth makes all things difficult, but industry makes all things easy   *See* ALL THINGS ARE EASY TO INDUSTRY, ALL THINGS DIFFICULT TO SLOTH.

slow and steady wins the race   Those who work or proceed at a gentle steady pace are more likely to achieve success than those who rush: *We generally find that students of average ability who apply themselves diligently throughout the course do better in their final examinations than brighter students who leave all their studying to the last minute—slow and steady wins the race.* The proverb was first recorded in this form in Robert Lloyd's poem "The Hare and the Tortoise" (1762): "The bets were won, the Hare awake,/When thus the victor Tortoise spake./ . . . /You may deride my awkward pace/But slow and steady wins the race." The poem retells Aesop's fable of the same name, dating from the sixth century B.C., about a race between these two animals. The hare sets off at great speed, stops for a rest and falls asleep, and wakes up to find that the tortoise has plodded past it to the finishing line.

Variant of this proverb: slow but sure wins the race.

Proverbs expressing similar meaning: FAIR AND SOFTLY GOES FAR IN A DAY; MAKE HASTE SLOWLY; THE RACE IS NOT TO THE SWIFT, NOR THE BATTLE TO THE STRONG.

slow but sure Something that is done slowly and carefully is more likely to be done thoroughly and correctly than something that is done in haste: "But, the language of that country was quite gone from her, and she was forced to make signs. So she went on, getting better from day to day, slow, but sure, and trying to learn the names of common things" (Charles Dickens, *David Copperfield,* 1850). The proverb was first recorded in 1692. It has given rise to the adverbial phrase *slowly but surely.*

slow but sure wins the race *See* SLOW AND STEADY WINS THE RACE.

small choice in rotten apples When faced with two or more equally undesirable options, it matters little which one you choose: *"You can come shopping with me or you can stay at home and clean your room—which would you rather do?" "Small choice in rotten apples."* The proverb comes from Shakespeare's play *The Taming of the Shrew* (1:1; 1593).

a small gift usually gets small thanks If you give people less than they expect, they may be less grateful than you would like: *I was not surprised by her lukewarm response—a small gift gets small thanks, and*

she is probably accustomed to receiving much more generous tips from her clients.

small is beautiful Smallness can be an attractive and desirable quality: "In the 19th century, some classical composers forgot (if they had ever known) the principle that 'small is beautiful'" (*Washington Post,* 1991). The proverb was first used in 1973 as the title of a book by the German-born British economist E. F. Schumacher.

Proverbs expressing similar meaning: THE BEST THINGS COME IN SMALL PACKAGES; LITTLE FISH ARE SWEET.

Proverb expressing opposite meaning: BIG IS BEAUTIFUL.

small leaks sink big ships *See* LITTLE LEAKS SINK THE SHIP.

small sorrows speak; great ones are silent People are usually happy to talk about minor sorrows but tend to avoid discussing greater sadnesses: "The grief that does not speak whispers the o'er-fraught heart and bids it break" (William Shakespeare, *Macbeth*). The proverb was first recorded in English in 1587 in T. Hughes's *The Misfortunes of Arthur*, although it is ultimately of ancient origin, appearing in the writings of Seneca.

small things affect light minds *See* LITTLE THINGS PLEASE LITTLE MINDS.

soft and fair goes far Much can be achieved by adopting a calm and gentle approach: "Soft and fair, young lady. You that are going to be married think things can never be done too fast" (Oliver Goldsmith, *The Good-Natured Man,* 1768). The proverb was first recorded c. 1400 in *Beryn.*

Proverbs expressing similar meaning: THE MEEK SHALL INHERIT THE EARTH; SOFTLY, SOFTLY, CATCHEE MONKEY.

a soft answer turns away wrath   A gentle response will calm an angry person: "Speak briefly and to the point, and even if the call is a disagreeable one, follow the proverb that 'A soft answer turneth away wrath'" (Milla Alihan, *Corporate Etiquette,* 1974). The proverb is of biblical origin in its current form: "A soft answer turneth away wrath: but grievous words stir up anger" (Proverbs 15:1). A facetious extension of the proverb is "A soft answer turns away wrath but has little effect on a door-to-door salesman."

softly, softly, catchee monkey   A patient, careful, and gentle approach is best when trying to catch a wily or elusive person or thing, especially a criminal: *The operation must be carefully planned and followed through—softly, softly, catchee monkey.* The proverb was first recorded in 1907 in G. Benham's *Cassell's Book of Quotations.*

Proverbs expressing similar meaning: EASY DOES IT; SOFT AND FAIR GOES FAR.

so goes Maine, so goes the nation   *See* AS MAINE GOES, SO GOES THE NATION.

soldiers and travelers may lie in authority   *See* A TRAVELER MAY LIE WITH AUTHORITY.

so many countries, so many customs   Different nations and peoples have different ways of doing things, codes of behavior, and so on: *When traveling abroad, remember the saying "So many countries, so many customs"—what is considered a friendly* gesture in one place may be interpreted as an insult in another. The proverb was first recorded in this form in 1582, but the sentiment it expresses is of earlier origin, occurring in Chaucer's *Troilus and Criseyde* (c. 1385): "In sondry londes [lands], sondry ben usages."

Variant of this proverb: every country has its own customs.

Proverbs expressing similar meaning: EVERY LAND HAS ITS OWN LAW; WHEN IN ROME, DO AS THE ROMANS DO.

so many men, so many opinions   Everybody has his or her own way of thinking: *The saying "So many men, so many opinions" was amply illustrated by the lively discussion at yesterday's meeting, and it seems unlikely that agreement will ever be reached.* The proverb is of ancient origin, occurring in the Roman poet Terence's *Phormio* (second century B.C.): "*quot homines tot sententiae.*" It was first recorded in English in Chaucer's *Canterbury Tales* (c. 1390) in the form "As many heddes, as many wittes ther been."

Variant of this proverb: as many men, as many opinions.

some folks speak from experience; others, from experience, don't speak   People often learn from experience that there are times when it is better to say nothing: *There had been similar unrest at my previous workplace, and when I argued against the proposed strike—which subsequently failed—I was shouted down. So this time I kept my mouth shut—some folks speak from experience; others, from experience, don't speak.*

something is better than nothing   It is better to have or get less than we desire than nothing at all: *I gave her a couple of dollars—not much, I know, but something is better* *than nothing.* The proverb was first recorded in English in 1546, but a French equivalent was in use in the early 15th century.

Variant of this proverb: better something than nothing.

Proverb expressing similar meaning: HALF A LOAF IS BETTER THAN NO BREAD.

something is rotten in the state of Denmark There is something wrong, or something suspicious going on, in a place, organization, or system; often used to imply corruption: "To the Parisian common man, meanwhile, one thing remains inconceivable: that now when the Bastille is down, and French Liberty restored, grain should continue so dear. . . . Is it Aristocrat forestallers; a Court still bent on intrigues? Something is rotten, somewhere" (Thomas Carlyle, *The French Revolution,* 1837). The proverb comes from Shakespeare's play *Hamlet* (1:4; 1600–01). It is often used in a shortened and allusive form, as in the quotation, or with another name in place of *Denmark.*

a son is a son till he gets him a wife, a daughter's a daughter all of her life Men tend to neglect or lose contact with their parents after marriage, whereas women maintain the bonds of filial affection and loyalty throughout their lives: *I hardly ever see Frank and his family, though they live much closer than Annabel, who still comes to visit me once a month. I guess I shouldn't be surprised—a son is a son till he gets him a wife, a daughter's a daughter all of her life.* The proverb was first recorded in 1670 (John Ray, *A Collection of English Proverbs*).

Variant of this proverb: MY SON IS MY SON TILL HE GETS HIM A WIFE, BUT MY DAUGHTER'S MY DAUGHTER ALL THE DAYS OF HER LIFE.

the sooner begun, the sooner done The sooner you make a start on something—especially a difficult or unpleasant task—the sooner it will be finished: *I'm not looking forward to clearing out the attic, but the sooner begun, the sooner done.* The proverb was first recorded in 1578 in T. Garter's *Most Virtuous Susanna.*

sooner said than done *See* EASIER SAID THAN DONE.

soon ripe, soon rotten Precocious talent or premature success is often short-lived: "Very few prize boys and girls stand the test of wear. Prodigies are almost always uncertain; they illustrate the proverb of 'soon ripe, soon rotten'" (Samuel Smiles, *Life and Labour,* 1887). Of Latin origin, the proverb was first recorded in English, with different wording, in William Langland's *Piers Plowman* (c. 1377).

Variants of this proverb: EARLY RIPE, EARLY ROTTEN; QUICK RIPE, QUICK ROTTEN.

sorrow comes unsent for Sorrows will descend upon all individuals, however unwelcome they may be. The proverb was first recorded in 1579 in Edmund Spenser's *The Shepheardes Calendar*: "Sorrow, ne neede be hastened on:/For he will come without calling anon."

Variants of this proverb: sorrow and ill weather come uninvited; sorrow is soon enough when it comes.

sow dry and set wet Seeds should be sown in dry soil and seedlings should be planted in wet soil: *The old country saying "Sow dry and set wet" has a sound scientific basis—too much moisture will rot the seed*

SOUTH AMERICAN PROVERBS

The various peoples of South America share a large stock of proverbs covering most aspects of daily life. As well as succinct observations on everyday routine, these include a fair number of pithy sayings reflecting the region's strong religious traditions.

The baby who does not cry is not nursed

A dog that barks all the time gets little attention

A dog with many masters dies of starvation

Even the candle seller dies in the dark

For our sins God has created three enemies for us: mice in the house, the fox in the mountains, and a priest in our village

God is big, but the forest is bigger

God writes on crooked lines

Hands that give also receive

He who prays a lot is afraid of something

He who saves up for another day has no trust in God

If it were ever to rain soup, the poor would only have forks

If you have a tail of straw, then keep away from the fire

Laughing wife, crying purse

No one knows as much about the pot as does the spoon

A sleeping fox finds no meat

The one who loves you will also make you weep

That which is a sin in others is a virtue in ourselves

There is nothing hidden between heaven and earth

Tomorrow is as good as today

You make a road by walking on it

---

before it has a chance to germinate. The proverb was first recorded in 1660: S. Riders, *Riders: 1660 British Merlin.*

sow the wind and reap the whirlwind   *See* THEY THAT SOW THE WIND SHALL REAP THE WHIRLWIND.

spare and have is better than spend and crave   It is better to use your money wisely, keeping some in reserve, than to spend it all and find yourself in need: *I resisted the temptation to blow my winnings on an expensive vacation—spare and have*

is better than spend and crave. The proverb was first recorded in 1758, in Benjamin Franklin's *Poor Richard's Almanack.*

Proverb expressing similar meaning: SPARE WELL AND HAVE TO SPEND.

spare at the spigot, and let out the bunghole   Those who are reluctant to part with small sums of money are often careless or extravagant in their spending on other things; also used to warn against false economy: "People are often saving at the wrong place. . . . They spare at the spigot, and let all run away at the

249

SPANISH PROVERBS

As with many other countries, the proverbs of the Spanish reveal much about traditional national preoccupations. Among many other subjects may be found proverbs that relate to the family, music, prevarication, religion, and gossip.

Beware of women with beards and men without beards

Don't call me a little olive until you have picked me

A face that never laughs betrays an evil heart

God is good, but not crazy

The hand of the stranger is heavy

Her father's fortune will make the ugliest girl attractive

How beautiful it is to do nothing, and then rest afterward

I dance to the tune that is played

If I die, I forgive you; if I recover, we shall see

If you have nothing better to do, go to bed with your own wife

Insults should be well avenged or well endured

Italians talk to women, Frenchmen to the learned, and the Spaniard talks to God

The man deliberates, the woman decides

A mother-in-law made of sugar still tastes bitter

Only God helps the badly dressed

An ounce of mother is worth a ton of priest

Soup must be hot, insults cold

Spanish is the language of lovers, Italian is for the singer, French for diplomats, and German for horses

There is no woman who sleeps so deeply that the sound of a guitar will not bring her to the window

There was already twenty in the family, so my grandmother had a baby

Three Spaniards, four opinions

Tomorrow is often the busiest day of the week

Who gossips with you will gossip about you

bunghole" (E. J. Hardy, *How to Be Happy though Married,* 1885). The proverb was first recorded in 1642 in a collection of Italian proverbs.

Variant of this proverb: save at the spigot and waste at the bung.

Proverb expressing similar meaning: PENNY WISE AND POUND FOOLISH.

spare the rod and spoil the child Firm discipline is necessary for a good upbringing; used to justify the punishment of children when they misbehave, specifically to justify corporal punishment: "'I shall govern by affection, Mr. Harrison.' 'It won't do,' said Mr. Harrison, 'won't do at all, Anne. "Spare the rod and spoil the child."'" (Lucy Maud Montgomery, *Anne of Avonlea,* 1909). The proverb is of biblical origin: "He that spareth his rod hateth his son: but he that loveth him chasteneth him betimes" (Proverbs 13:24).

spare well and have to spend   If you do not waste money you will always be able to afford the things you need: *"Spare well and have to spend" was his motto, but he seemed to place far greater emphasis on the sparing than on the spending, and his reputation as a miser was not unjustified.* The proverb was first recorded in 1541.

Variant of this proverb: spare well and spend well.

Proverbs expressing similar meaning: SPARE AND HAVE IS BETTER THAN SPEND AND CRAVE; SPARE WHEN YOU'RE YOUNG AND SPEND WHEN YOU'RE OLD.

spare when you're young and spend when you're old   People who were thrifty in their youth can afford to be extravagant in their old age: *I'm paying as much as I can afford into a private pension plan, on the basis of the saying "Spare when you're young and spend when you're old."* The proverb was first recorded in 1721, in H. Bullinger's *Christian State of Matrimony.*

Proverb expressing similar meaning: SPARE WELL AND HAVE TO SPEND.

speak not of my debts unless you mean to pay them   It is considered rude or tactless to mention another person's debts: *I had heard rumors that his company was in severe financial trouble, so I tried to steer the conversation onto other matters, remembering the adage "Speak not of my debts unless you mean to pay them."* The proverb is first recorded in George Herbert's *Outlandish Proverbs* (1640).

speak of the devil and he always appears   People often appear unexpectedly when others are talking about them; said when such a coincidence occurs: *I hear Jack's found himself a job at last. . . . Ah, here he is, so he can tell us all about it. Speak of the devil and he's sure to appear!* The proverb was first recorded in 1666 in the form "Talk of the devil, and he's presently at your elbow." It is often used in the shortened and allusive form "Speak of the devil."

Variants of this proverb: talk of the devil and he's sure to appear; talk about the devil and his imps will appear.

speak softly and carry a big stick   Do not threaten violence or provoke aggression, but be prepared to use great force if the need arises: *Their policy of "Speak softly and carry a big stick" seems at last to have brought peace to the streets of the city.* The proverb was popularized in a speech made in 1901 by President Theodore Roosevelt: "There is a homely old adage which runs: 'Speak softly and carry a big stick; you will go far.' If the American nation will speak softly and yet build and keep at a pitch of the highest training a thoroughly efficient navy, the Monroe Doctrine will go far" (Speech at the Minnesota State Fair).

speak the truth and shame the devil   *See* TELL THE TRUTH AND SHAME THE DEVIL.

speak well of the dead   *See* NEVER SPEAK ILL OF THE DEAD.

speech is silver, but silence is golden   It is good to speak, but sometimes it is better still to say nothing: "She will give a pound note to the collection if I would cut my eloquence short, so in this case, though speech is silver, silence is certainly golden" (Winifred Holtby, *South Riding,* 1936). The proverb was first recorded in 1834, with the implication that it was of Swiss origin.

Proverbs expressing similar meaning: THERE IS A TIME TO SPEAK AND A TIME TO BE SILENT; THINK BEFORE YOU SPEAK; A WORD SPOKEN IS PAST RECALLING.

the spirit is willing but the flesh is weak People are often physically incapable of doing what they want to do, or what they know they ought to do; often used as an excuse: "Since then I have written many other books; and though ceasing my methodical study of the old masters (for though the spirit is willing, the flesh is weak), I have continued with increasing assiduity to try to write better" (W. Somerset Maugham, *The Summing Up,* 1938). The proverb is of biblical origin: "Watch and pray, that ye enter not into temptation: the spirit indeed is willing, but the flesh is weak" (Matthew 26:41).

the squeaky wheel gets the grease Those who complain the most loudly or persistently, or who make the most fuss, get what they want: "Do as others have done—put heat on your state legislature and urge your friends to do the same. The wheel that squeaks get the oil" (*Washington Post,* 1990). The proverb is attributed to the U.S. humorist Josh Billings, alias Henry Wheeler Shaw (1818–85), in the form "The wheel that squeaks the loudest is the one that gets the grease."

Variants of this proverb: the squeaky wheel gets the oil; the wheel that does the squeaking is the one that gets the grease.

stand on your own two feet Do not be dependent on others: *Stand on your own two feet—your parents will not be around forever, and you must learn to be more self-reliant.* The proverb was first recorded in L. Fioravanti's *Compendium of Rational Secrets* (1582).

step on a crack, break your mother's back It is unlucky to walk on the cracks between paving slabs on the sidewalk; a childish superstition, or used in a children's game: *"Look out!" cried my young nephew, as I was about to put my foot down, "Step on a crack, break your mother's back!"*

a stern chase is a long chase It takes a long time to catch up with something or somebody moving ahead of you in the same direction: "English poetry has had a start of some centuries, and a stern chase is proverbially a long one" (J. A. Bridges, *Victorian Recollections,* 1919). First recorded in 1823, the proverb is of nautical origin—a *stern chase* is a chase at sea in which one vessel follows in the wake of another.

sticks and stones may break my bones, but names will never hurt me Verbal abuse, malicious remarks, or defamatory statements do no physical harm; often said by children to those who call them names: *When the other kids teased me about the clothes my mother made me wear, I would reply, "Sticks and stones may break my bones, but names will never hurt me."* The proverb was first recorded in G. F. Northall's *Folk-Phrases* (1894).

Variant of this proverb: sticks and stones may break my bones, but words will never hurt me.

Proverb expressing similar meaning: HARD WORDS BREAK NO BONES.

Proverb expressing opposite meaning: THE TONGUE IS NOT STEEL, BUT IT CUTS.

stick to your guns Stand by your principles or convictions, assert your rights, and refuse to compromise: *Stick to your guns—to give way on this issue would be interpreted as a sign of weakness.* The proverb was first recorded, with different wording, in James Boswell's *The Life of Samuel Johnson* (1791): "Mrs. Thrale stood to her gun with great courage, in defence of amorous ditties."

a still tongue makes a wise head A wise person knows when it is best to keep silent; also used to imply that wisdom is gained by listening and thinking rather than talking all the time: *When people commented that her son was unusually quiet for a boy of his age, she would reply, "A still tongue makes a wise head."* The proverb was first recorded in 1562 in the *Works* of John Heywood.

Proverb expressing similar meaning: A SHUT MOUTH CATCHES NO FLIES.

still waters run deep People who are quiet and reserved often have a deeply passionate nature and may surprise others by doing something that is apparently out of character: "'Madame Odintsov is very charming, but she is so cold and reserved that . . .' 'Still waters run deep, you know,' interposed Bazarov. 'You say she is cold; that just adds to the flavor. You like ices, I expect' " (Ivan Turgenev, *Fathers and Sons,* 1862). The proverb was first recorded in English c. 1400 in the form "Where the flood is deepest the water stands stillest." It occurs in Shakespeare's play *Henry VI, Part 2* (3:1; 1592), "Smooth runs the water where the brook is deep, / And in his simple show he harbours treason."

Variant of this proverb: still water runs deep.

a stitch in time saves nine Prompt attention to minor problems will avoid major problems later: "'We could set it up

as good as new in a day. For I daresay your lot would turn to and give us a hand?' 'You see if we don't,' said Wicks. 'So be it, then,' concluded Trent. 'A stitch in time saves nine.'" (Robert Louis Stevenson, *The Wrecker,* 1892). The proverb was first recorded in 1732. It is believed that the number *nine* was chosen because it almost rhymes with *time.*

Proverbs expressing similar meaning: AN OUNCE OF PREVENTION IS WORTH A POUND OF CURE; PREVENTION IS BETTER THAN CURE; WHO REPAIRS NOT HIS GUTTERS REPAIRS HIS WHOLE HOUSE.

stolen fruit is sweet *See* FORBIDDEN FRUIT IS SWEET; STOLEN WATERS ARE SWEET.

stolen waters are sweet Illicit pleasures are often all the more enjoyable for this reason; also used of the pleasure derived from stolen goods or ill-gotten gains: *He reckons that no liquor tastes as good as the moonshine his uncle used to make, perhaps on the basis that stolen waters are sweet.* The proverb is of biblical origin: "Stolen waters are sweet, and bread eaten in secret is pleasant" (Proverbs 9:17).

Variants of this proverb: stolen fruit is sweet; stolen pleasures are sweetest.

Proverb expressing similar meaning: FORBIDDEN FRUIT IS SWEET.

stone-dead hath no fellow There is nothing so final as death; used by those in favor of capital punishment: "The execution of the death sentence had been postponed for a week, an unusual period in a country where the adage 'stone-dead hath no fellow' wins general support" (*London Times,* 1926). The proverb was first recorded c. 1633.

253

stone walls do not a prison make The mind and spirit are not imprisoned by merely physical restraints: "The poet assures us that—'Stone walls do not a prison make,' but a combination of the stone wall, the political parasite and the moral instructor is no garden of sweets" (Ambrose Bierce, *Devil's Dictionary*, 1911). The proverb comes from Richard Lovelace's poem "To Althea, From Prison" (1642): "Stone walls do not a prison make/Nor iron bars a cage."

straws show which way the wind blows Small things, such as apparently trivial details or insignificant events, can be useful indicators of what is going to happen in the future: *Journalists must learn to be highly observant, and not to dismiss any detail as insignificant—straws show which way the wind blows.* The proverb was first recorded in John Selden's *Table Talk* (c. 1654): "Take a straw and throw it up into the Air, you shall see by that which way the Wind is." It is probably of earlier origin, however, and is attributed to Francis Bacon (1561–1626) in Lord Byron's poem "Don Juan" (1819): "You know, or don't know, that great Bacon saith,/'Fling up a straw, 'twill show the way the wind blows.'" The proverb has given rise to the figurative phrases *a straw in the wind* and *to know* (or *see, find out,*) *which way the wind blows*.

Variant of this proverb: it's as well to know which way the wind blows.

a stream cannot rise above its source Nothing can be greater or better than what it comes from, or than the person who created it: "Just as it is true that a stream cannot rise above its source, so it is true that a national literature can-

not rise above the moral level of the social conditions of the people from whom it derives its inspiration" (James Connolly, *Labour in Irish History*, 1910). The proverb was first recorded in 1663.

Variant of this proverb: a stream never rises higher than its source.

the streets of hell are paved with promises *See* THE ROAD TO HELL IS PAVED WITH GOOD INTENTIONS.

stretch your arm no further than your sleeve will reach Do not try to live beyond your means, or to do more than you are capable of: *Stretch your arm no further than your sleeve will reach—you may be able to raise enough money to buy the boat, but can you afford all the running costs, mooring fees, and insurance?* The proverb was first recorded in 1541.

Proverbs expressing similar meaning: CUT YOUR COAT ACCORDING TO YOUR CLOTH; EVERYBODY STRETCHES HIS LEGS ACCORDING TO THE LENGTH OF HIS COVERLET.

strike while the iron is hot Take advantage of a favorable situation while it lasts: "Let George cut in directly and win her. . . . Strike while the iron's hot" (William Makepeace Thackeray, *Vanity Fair*, 1848). An allusion to the work of the blacksmith, the proverb was first recorded in English in Chaucer's *Canterbury Tales* (c. 1390): "Whil that iren is hoot, men sholden smyte." The sentiment it expresses, however, is of ancient origin. The English poet John Dryden expanded on the metaphor in "Aeneis" (1697), his translation of Virgil's *Aeneid*: "We must beat the iron while it is hot, but we may polish it at leisure." The U.S. writer Ambrose Bierce parodied the proverb in his *Devil's Dictionary* (1911): "Strike while your employer has a big contract."

Proverbs expressing similar meaning: HOIST YOUR SAIL WHEN THE WIND IS FAIR; MAKE HAY WHILE THE SUN SHINES.

strive not against the stream Do not struggle against things that cannot be overcome, or try to do the impossible; also used to encourage conformity: "Never strive against the stream, always drive the nail that will go" (Matthew Prior, *Four Dialogues of the Dead,* "The Vicar of Bray and Sir Thomas More," c. 1721). Of ancient origin, the proverb was first recorded in English c. 1300.

Variant of this proverb: it's ill striving against the stream.

stuff a cold and starve a fever *See* FEED A COLD AND STARVE A FEVER.

a stumble may prevent a fall A minor check may prevent greater disaster: *It was an unfortunate setback, but we must remember that a stumble may prevent a fall.* The proverb was first recorded in 1732 in Thomas Fuller's *Gnomologia.*

Variant of this proverb: it's a good horse that never stumbles.

the style is the man A person's style, especially in speaking and writing, is an indicator of his or her true nature: "'The style is the man.' This applies with peculiar force to Paul. His style has been called 'the most personal that ever existed.' It fitly represents the force and fire of his mind and the tender affections of his heart" (Philip Schaff, *History of the Christian Church,* 1883–93). First recorded in English in 1901, the proverb may be of

Latin or French origin: in his *Discours sur le style* (1753), the Comte de Buffon said, "*Ces choses sont hors de l'homme, le style est l'homme même* [These things are external to the man; style is the man]."

success breeds success One success leads to another: *Success breeds success, and within a few years she had a chain of health-food stores stretching from coast to coast.* The proverb was first recorded in 1927 in N. Martin's *Mosaic.*

Variants of this proverb: success begets success; success makes success as money makes money.

Proverb expressing similar meaning: NOTHING SUCCEEDS LIKE SUCCESS.

success has many fathers, while failure is an orphan Everybody want to take credit for success, but nobody will take responsibility for failure: "In the aftermath of the impeccably executed aerial attack that initiated the war with Iraq, the old saw that success has many fathers while failure is an orphan comes to mind" (*Washington Times,* 1991). The proverb may have originated in the diary of Mussolini's son-in-law, the Italian diplomat Count Galeazzo Ciano (1903–44): "*La vittoria trova cento padri, e nessuno vuole riconoscere l'insuccesso* [Victory has a hundred fathers, and nobody acknowledges a failure]."

Variant of this proverb: victory has a hundred fathers and defeat is an orphan.

success is never final You cannot afford to relax your efforts after a great achievement—you must keep working to maintain or improve your position: *History is littered with examples of those who forgot that success is never final in the world of politics.*

Variant of this proverb: success is never final and failure is never fatal.

success makes success as money makes money   *See* SUCCESS BREEDS SUCCESS.

sue a beggar and catch a louse   There is nothing to be gained by seeking legal redress from those who cannot afford to pay: *What is the point of entering into litigation with a company on the verge of bankruptcy? Sue a beggar and catch a louse.* The proverb was first recorded in 1639 in J. Clarke's *Paroemiologia Anglo-Latina.*

Variant of this proverb: sue a beggar and you'll get a louse.

sufficient unto the day is the evil thereof   There is quite enough to worry about at the present time, without anticipating future problems and troubles: "In the meanwhile there were no sense in worrying over schemes for a future, which we may not live to see. 'Sufficient for the day is the evil thereof'" (Jane Carlyle, letter dated April 1, 1836). The proverb is of biblical origin: "Take therefore no thought for the morrow: for the morrow shall take thought for the things of itself. Sufficient unto the day is the evil thereof" (Matthew 6:34).

Proverbs expressing similar meaning: DON'T CROSS THE BRIDGE TILL YOU COME TO IT; TAKE THINGS AS THEY COME.

the sun loses nothing by shining into a puddle   Those who are truly great cannot be corrupted by association with foul or wicked things or people: *As Chaucer said, the Bible is no less holy for describing the worst sins of humankind—the sun loses nothing by shining into a puddle.* The proverb was first recorded in English in 1303, but the sentiment it expresses is of ancient origin: the saying "the sun shines into dung but is not tainted" is attributed to the Greek philosopher Diogenes (c. 412–c. 323 B.C.).

Variant of this proverb: the sun is not less bright for shining on a dunghill.

Proverbs expressing opposite meaning: HE THAT TOUCHES PITCH SHALL BE DEFILED; IF YOU LIE DOWN WITH DOGS, YOU'LL GET UP WITH FLEAS.

sweep your own doorstep clean   Do not criticize others until you are beyond reproach yourself: *You have no right to accuse them of wasting public money, when your own department is squandering huge amounts on needless bureaucracy—sweep your own doorstep clean!* The proverb is first recorded in T. Adams's *Temple* (1624).

Proverbs expressing similar meaning: IF EVERY MAN WOULD SWEEP HIS OWN DOORSTEP THE CITY WOULD SOON BE CLEAN; PHYSICIAN, HEAL THYSELF.

the sweetest wine makes the sharpest vinegar   *See* FROM THE SWEETEST WINE, THE TARTEST VINEGAR.

_t_

the tailor makes the man A person's qualities may be judged by the clothes they wear: "Believe it, sir, that clothes do much upon the wit . . . and thence comes your proverb, the tailor makes the man" (Ben Jonson, _The Staple of News_, 1625). The proverb was first recorded in 1605 in William Shakespeare's _King Lear_.

Proverb expressing similar meaning: CLOTHES MAKE THE MAN.

take a hair of the dog that bit you Drinking more alcohol is supposed to be a cure for a hangover: "'Rouse yourself, lionheart. Ha ha! Put a good face upon it, and drink again. Another hair of the dog that bit you, captain! . . .' Mr Tappertit received these jovial promptings with a very bad grace, being much the worse, both in mind and body, for his two nights of debauch" (Charles Dickens, _Barnaby Rudge,_ 1841). The proverb was first recorded in 1546. It alludes to the former practice of treating a dog bite by putting a hair from the offending animal into the wound.

Variant of this proverb: the hair of the dog is good for the bite.

Proverb expressing similar meaning: LIKE CURES LIKE.

take care of number one Put your own interests before those of everybody else:

My motto is "Take care of number one," and I'm not going to risk losing my job for the sake of a hopeless cause. The proverb is first recorded in Maria Edgeworth, _The Parent's Assistant_ (1796): "I'm only talking of number one, you know. I must take care of that first."

Variant of this proverb: look out for number one.

take care of the pennies and the dollars will take care of themselves If you are careful with small sums of money, you will always have plenty—attend to the details of your financial affairs and do not worry about the larger picture. Its original form has _pence_ and _pounds_ in place of _pennies_ and _dollars_: "Take care of the pence and the pounds will take care of themselves is as true of personal habits as of money" (George Bernard Shaw, _Pygmalion,_ 1912). The proverb was first recorded in 1750 in a letter written by Lord Chesterfield, in which it is attributed to "Old Mr. Lowndes [William Lowndes (1652–1724)], the famous Secretary of the Treasury." In _Alice's Adventures in Wonderland_ (1865), Lewis Carroll punningly applied the proverb to language: "Take care of the sense, and the sounds will take care of themselves."

Variant of this proverb: look after the pennies and the dollars will look after themselves.

Proverb expressing similar meaning: LIGHT GAINS MAKE HEAVY PURSES.

Proverb expressing opposite meaning: PENNY WISE AND POUND FOOLISH.

take opportunity by the forelock *See* TAKE TIME BY THE FORELOCK.

take the goods the gods provide Make the most of anything you have or get by good fortune: *If you have a natural talent for music, you should not feel guilty about using it to make money—take the goods the gods provide.* In its current form, the proverb comes from John Dryden's poem "Alexander's Feast" (1697): "Lovely Thais sits beside thee, / Take the good the gods provide thee." The sentiment it expresses, however, occurs in the writings of the Roman dramatist Plautus (c. 250–184 B.C.): "*habeas quod di dant boni* [you may keep what good the gods give]."

take the will for the deed We must always give people credit for their good intentions, even if they fail to carry them through: *Take the will for the deed—she would have come to visit you at the hospital if there hadn't been a railroad strike.*

take things as they come Sometimes it is best to deal with possible problems only as they arise: *She decided to stop worrying about the future and just to take things as they came.* The proverb was first recorded in 1611 in J. Davies's *The Scourge of Folly.*

Variant of this proverb: take things as you find them.

Proverb expressing similar meaning: DON'T CROSS THE BRIDGE TILL YOU COME TO IT; DON'T MEET TROUBLES HALFWAY; SUFFICIENT UNTO THE DAY IS THE EVIL THEREOF.

take time by the forelock Take full advantage of the present, and do not waste time: "As his doing the one or the other was a mere question of time, he and Mrs. Pocket had taken Time by the forelock (when, to judge from its length, it would seem to have wanted cutting), and had married without the knowledge of the judicious parent" (Charles Dickens, *Great Expectations,* 1860–61). The proverb was first recorded in the 16th century. It alludes to a representation of Time as having a bald head with just a lock of hair at the front, so it can be seized as it arrives but not as it departs.

Variant of this proverb: take opportunity by the forelock.

Proverbs expressing similar meaning: THE MILL CANNOT GRIND WITH THE WATER THAT IS PAST; SEIZE THE DAY; THERE'S NO TIME LIKE THE PRESENT; TIME AND TIDE WAIT FOR NO MAN.

a tale never loses in the telling People are inclined to exaggerate, and anecdotes, gossip, or lies are embroidered by the teller each time they are retold: *A tale never loses in the telling—he is rumored to have inherited twenty million dollars, but if you knock a couple of zeros off the end of the figure, you will be a bit closer to the actual sum of money involved.* The proverb was first recorded in its current form in 1721, but the sentiment it expresses is of earlier origin.

Variant of this proverb: a tale grows better in the telling.

talk about the devil and his imps will appear *See* SPEAK OF THE DEVIL AND HE ALWAYS APPEARS.

talk is cheap It is easy to say that something can or will be done, but it takes money or effort to do it; often used when people make idle boasts or promises they are unlikely to keep: "'What can you do?' 'Go out to Montana, just as soon as the weather is fit, and relocate the mine. . . .' 'Talk is cheap, but it takes money to pay for railroad tickets,' went on Malone" (Horatio Alger, *Joe the Hotel Boy,* 1906). The proverb was first recorded in its current form in 1843 (T. C. Haliburton, *Attaché*), but the sentiment it expresses is of earlier origin.

Variants of this proverb: talk is cheap, but it takes money to buy land; talk is cheap, but it takes money to buy liquor.

talk of the devil and he's sure to appear   *See* SPEAK OF THE DEVIL AND HE ALWAYS APPEARS.

tastes differ   Different people like different things: "'I express my opinion,' retorted Neelie, chafing under the satirically indulgent tone in which the governess addressed her. 'It's a matter of taste, Miss Gwilt; and tastes differ'" (Wilkie Collins, *Armadale,* 1866). The proverb was first recorded in 1803.

Proverbs expressing similar meaning: EVERY MAN TO HIS TASTE; ONE MAN'S MEAT IS ANOTHER MAN'S POISON; THERE'S NO DISPUTING ABOUT TASTES.

tell it not in Gath   Be careful how much you tell your enemies: "The fact is—but tell it not in Gath—I was happier without them!" (Marie Corelli, *God's Good Man,* 1904). The proverb is biblical in origin, appearing at 2 Samuel 1:20, in which David hears of the death of Jonathan in battle with the Philistines: "Tell it not in Gath, publish it not in the streets of Askelon, lest the daughters of the Philistines rejoice."

tell not all you know, nor do all you can   It is good policy not to reveal the full extent of your knowledge or capabilities: *Sometimes it is wiser in business to tell not all you know, nor do all you can, but to keep something back for yourself.* The proverb was first recorded in 1739 in Benjamin Franklin's *Poor Richard's Almanack.*

tell the truth and shame the devil   It is always best to be honest, however great the temptation may be to lie: "I don't like the whole change that's come over you in the last year. I'm sorry if that hurts your feelings, but I've got to—tell the truth and shame the devil" (Thornton Wilder, *Our Town,* 1938). The proverb was first recorded in 1548. It occurs in Shakespeare's play *Henry IV, Part 1* (3:1): "And I can teach thee, coz, to shame the devil/By telling truth: tell truth and shame the devil."

Variant of this proverb: speak the truth and shame the devil.

that government is best which governs least   The best form of government is one that allows people the greatest freedom: "I heartily accept the motto, 'That government is best which governs least.' . . . Carried out, it finally amounts to this, which also I believe—'That government is best which governs not at all'" (Henry David Thoreau, *Civil Disobedience,* 1849). The proverb was first recorded in 1837, in John L. O'Sullivan's introduction to *The United States Magazine and Democratic Review:* "The best government is that which governs least." It is held to be one of the key principles of the Republican Party.

them as asks, gits; them as don't ask, don't git See ASK, AND IT SHALL BE GIVEN YOU; SEEK, AND YE SHALL FIND; KNOCK, AND IT SHALL BE OPENED UNTO YOU.

there are as good fish in the sea as ever came out of it See THERE ARE OTHER FISH IN THE SEA.

there are lies, damned lies, and statistics Statistics can be used to create a misleading impression: *"Statistically speaking, this is one of the safest forms of travel." "I don't believe it. Have you never heard the saying 'There are lies, damned lies, and statistics'?"* The proverb is attributed to the British statesman Benjamin Disraeli (1804–81) in Mark Twain's autobiography: "There are three kinds of lies: lies, damned lies and statistics."

there are more ways of killing a cat than choking it with cream If one method fails, there are plenty more to choose from: *Undeterred, we tried a more subtle approach—there are more ways of killing a cat than choking it with cream.* The proverb was first recorded in this form in 1855, in Charles Kingsley's novel *Westward Ho!,* but its variant forms are of earlier origin.

Variants of this proverb: there are more ways of killing a dog than choking it with butter; there are more ways of killing a dog than hanging it.

Proverbs expressing similar meaning: ALL ROADS LEAD TO ROME; THERE'S MORE THAN ONE WAY TO SKIN A CAT.

there are no birds in last year's nest Things are not as they were: *That may well have been the case when you were in office, but the circumstances are quite different now—there are no birds in last year's nest, as*

they say. The proverb was first recorded in 1620, in a translation of Cervantes' *Don Quixote.*

there are no gains without pains See NO PAIN, NO GAIN.

there are none so blind as those who will not see It is impossible to make people accept the evidence of their own eyes if they choose to ignore it or refuse to believe it: *"'None so blind as those that won't see.' . . . A single effort of the will was sufficient to exclude from his view whatever he judged hostile to his immediate purpose"* (Edward Fitzgerald, *Polonius,* 1852). The proverb was first recorded in 1546 in the form "Who is so deaf, or so blind, as is he that willfully will neither hear nor see."

Proverb expressing similar meaning: THERE ARE NONE SO DEAF AS THOSE WHO WILL NOT HEAR.

there are none so deaf as those who will not hear You cannot communicate with people who stubbornly refuse to listen: *I tried to warn her that her son was heading for trouble, but there are none so deaf as those who will not hear.* The proverb was first recorded in 1546, with different wording (see the preceding entry), but a French equivalent was in use 200 years earlier.

Proverb expressing similar meaning: THERE ARE NONE SO BLIND AS THOSE WHO WILL NOT SEE.

there are other fish in the sea Plenty more people, things, opportunities, or options are available; often used to console somebody whose relationship with a boyfriend or girlfriend has ended: "There's fish in the sea, no doubt of it,

As good as ever came out of it" (W. S. Gilbert, *Patience,* 1881). The proverb was first recorded, with different wording, c. 1573.

Variant of this proverb: there are as good fish in the sea as ever came out of it.

there are tricks in every trade People in every occupation have their own special—and often secret—ways of doing things that enable them to save time, effort, or money; often implying cleverness, craftiness, or deception: "'Where are you staying?' 'Mrs. May's boarding house.' 'I know her. What they tell is she fills you up with soup so you can't eat much meat.' 'I guess there are tricks to every trade,' said Adam" (John Steinbeck, *East of Eden,* 1952). The proverb was first recorded in 1632 in the form "Knavery in all trades." It has given rise to the figurative phrase *the tricks of the trade.*

there are two sides to every question Any issue can be looked at from two opposing viewpoints, both of which merit consideration: "Men of energy of character must have enemies: because there are two sides to every question, and . . . those who take the other will of course be hostile" (Thomas Jefferson, letter dated May 5, 1817). Of ancient origin, the proverb has been attributed to the Greek teacher Protagoras (c. 490–c. 420 B.C.). Other words may be used in place of *question,* such as *story, argument, coin,* or *fence.*

there goes more to marriage than four bare legs in a bed There is more to marriage than sex: *The most successful marriages are those where the husband and wife are intellectually as well as sexually compat-* *ible—there goes more to marriage than four bare legs in a bed.* The proverb was first recorded c. 1549 in John Heywood's *Dialogue of Proverbs.*

there'll be sleeping enough in the grave Life is too short to waste time having more sleep than you need: *She was one of those hearty outdoor types who insist on waking everybody up at the crack of dawn with a cry of "Rise and shine! There'll be sleeping enough in the grave."* The proverb was first recorded in 1741, in Benjamin Franklin's *Poor Richard's Almanack.*

there must be a first time for everything See THERE'S A FIRST TIME FOR EVERYTHING.

there's a black sheep in every flock In every family, community, organization, or profession there is at least one member who brings disgrace on the rest: "There are black sheep in nearly every large family . . . and these two one-idea'd curs were ready to tear any one to death that should interfere with that miserable inheritance which was their thought by day and their dream by night" (Charles Reade, *The Cloister and the Hearth,* 1861). The proverb was first recorded in 1816. Often reduced to the cliché *a black sheep,* or *the black sheep of the family,* it alludes to the undesirability of sheep with black wool that is difficult to dye.

Variant of this proverb: there's a black sheep in every family.

there's a first time for everything Everything must start somewhere, and the fact that something has not happened before does not mean that it will never happen; also used when somebody does something that he or she has never done before: *"It's perfectly safe—we've been doing it this way for the past ten years and we've never had an accident." "There's a first time for everything."* The proverb was first recorded in 1792 in A. Hamilton's *Papers*.

Variants of this proverb: there's always a first time; there must be a first time for everything.

there's a Jack for every Jill   *See* EVERY JACK HAS HIS JILL.

there's always a first time   *See* THERE'S A FIRST TIME FOR EVERYTHING.

there's always room at the top   Those who excel, or who are truly ambitious, will always succeed: *It's a competitive business, but there's always room at the top.* The proverb is attributed to the U.S. statesman Daniel Webster (1782–1852), who replied in this way to advise against joining the over-crowded legal profession. It was popular-ized in the mid-20th century by the British writer John Braine in his best-selling novel *Room at the Top* (1957) and its Academy Award–winning movie adaptation.

there's an exception to every rule   No rule applies in every single case: *This phenomenon, which appears to defy the laws of physics, demonstrates that there's an exception to every rule.* The proverb was first recorded in 1579 in the form "There is no rule so general that it admits not exception."

Proverb expressing similar meaning: THE EXCEPTION PROVES THE RULE.

there's a pot of gold at the end of the rainbow   Some things can never be achieved; used when people chase after ideals or ambitions that constantly elude

them: *There's a pot of gold at the end of the rainbow, and in this case the pot of gold is the crime-free society that no politician will ever be able to deliver.* The proverb alludes to the popular superstition, first recorded in 1836, that a pot of gold is to be found at the place where a rainbow touches the ground.

there's a remedy for everything except death   Death is final, irremediable, and inevitable; also used to imply that all other problems have a solution: "There is a remedy for everything except Death . . . so the bitterness of this disappoint-ment has long passed away" (Frederick Locker-Lampson, *My Confidences*, 1896). The proverb was first recorded in this form in 1573, but the sentiment it expresses is of earlier origin.

Variant of this proverb: there's a remedy for all things but death.

Proverb expressing similar meaning: DEATH DEFIES THE DOCTOR.

Proverb expressing opposite mean-ing: AVOIDANCE IS THE ONLY REMEDY.

there's a season and a time for every pur-pose under the heaven   *See* TO EVERY-THING THERE IS A SEASON.

there's a sin of omission as well as of commission   There are times when fail-ure to do what you should is as bad as doing what you should not do: *As he did nothing to prevent the burglars from entering the building, he was deemed to have helped them—there's a sin of omission as well as of commission.*

there's a skeleton in every closet   Every person, family, or organization has a shame-ful secret: *There's a skeleton in every closet, and he was one of those journalists who special-*

ize in flinging open the closet doors of the rich and famous and exposing their skeletons to the public eye. The proverb was first recorded in 1845 (in William Thackeray's *Punch in the East*) in the form "There is a skeleton in every house." It is often reduced to the cliché *a skeleton in the closet.*

Variant of this proverb: every family has a skeleton in the closet.

there's a sucker born every minute The world is full of gullible people: "'There's a sucker born every minute,'/P. T. Barnum declared,/And a con man is born every hour/To make sure no sucker is spared" (*Wall Street Journal,* 1994). The proverb is attributed to the U.S. showman Phineas T. Barnum (1810–91), but there is no evidence to support this attribution. It sometimes occurs in the allusive form "There's one born every minute," which is also applied more generally to fools.

there's a tide in the affairs of man In the ebb and flow of human existence, it is important to act at the most opportune or favorable time, and not to miss this moment when it comes: "'There is a tide in the affairs of men/Which, taken at the flood,'—you know the rest,/And most of us have found it now and then;/At least we think so, though but few have guess'd/The moment, till too late to come again (Lord Byron, "Don Juan," 1819). The proverb is a shortened and allusive form of a passage from Shakespeare's play *Julius Caesar* (4:3): "There is a time in the affairs of men/Which, taken at the flood, leads on to fortune; /Omitted, all the voyage of their life /Is bound in shallows and in miseries."

there's a time and place for everything Things should be done only at the

appropriate time and in the appropriate place: *There's a time and place for everything, and this is neither the time nor the place to be cracking jokes like that!* The proverb was first recorded in 1509 in A. Barclay, *Ship of Fools.*

Variant of this proverb: there's a time for everything.

Proverb expressing similar meaning: TO EVERYTHING THERE IS A SEASON.

there's a time to speak and a time to be silent Sometimes it is not appropriate to say anything: *She could have told him where he had gone wrong, but there is a time to speak, and a time to be silent.* The proverb is of biblical origin, appearing at Ecclesiastes 3:7.

Variant of this proverb: there's a time to wink as well as to see.

Proverbs expressing similar meaning: SILENCE IS GOLDEN; SPEECH IS SILVER, BUT SILENCE IS GOLDEN; THINK BEFORE YOU SPEAK; A WORD SPOKEN IS PAST RECALLING.

there's good and bad in everything Nothing is totally good or bad: *If you're hoping to find the perfect job, you're heading for disappointment—there's good and bad in everything.*

there's honor among thieves Criminals will not hurt or betray their fellow criminals, thus treating one another with more respect than their victims: *If it's true that there's honor among thieves, then why do the prisoners want to keep their personal possessions under lock and key?* The proverb was first recorded in this form in the early 19th century, but the sentiment it expresses is of earlier origin.

Proverbs expressing similar meaning: DOG DOES NOT EAT DOG; HAWKS WILL NOT PICK OUT HAWKS' EYES.

there's luck in leisure It is better not to act in haste; sometimes used to justify procrastination: *They say there's luck in leisure, so I decided to wait a little longer.* The proverb was first recorded in 1683 in G. Meriton's *Yorkshire Dialogue.*

Proverb expressing opposite meaning: DELAYS ARE DANGEROUS.

there's luck in odd numbers According to popular superstition, odd numbers are lucky; often said when somebody does something for the third, fifth, or seventh time: "'Now, Rory, leave off, sir: you'll hug me no more;/That's eight times to-day that you've kissed me before.'/'Then here goes another,' says he, 'to make sure,/For there's luck in odd numbers,' says Rory O'More" (Samuel Lover, "Rory O'More," 1836). The proverb was first recorded in Shakespeare's play *The Merry Wives of Windsor* (c. 1598). The sentiment it expresses, however, is of ancient origin, occurring in the writings of Virgil (70–19 B.C.): *numero deus impare gaudet* [the god delights in an uneven number]."

Proverb expressing similar meaning: THE THIRD TIME IS THE CHARM.

there's many a good cock come out of a tattered bag Do not be misled by external appearances—it is what is inside or what emerges from something that counts; also used to imply that people should not be judged by their parents, clothes, or background: *The classes take place in a dilapidated building on the wrong side of town, but they have produced some of the finest musicians in the county, proving that there's many a good cock come out of a tattered bag.* First recorded in 1883, the proverb comes from the sport of cockfighting.

Proverb expressing similar meaning: DON'T JUDGE A BOOK BY ITS COVER.

there's many a good tune played on an old fiddle Old people should not be dismissed as incapable: "Beyond a haricot vein in one of my legs I'm as young as ever I was. Old indeed! There's many a good tune played on an old fiddle" (Samuel Butler, *The Way of All Flesh,* 1903). The quotation is the first recorded use of the proverb.

there's many a slip between cup and lip Many things can go wrong in the process of putting a plan into action; often used to warn against overconfidence or overoptimism: *We can't be certain of success, and I won't be happy until I have the document in my hand—there's many a slip between cup and lip.* The proverb was first recorded in English in 1539, but the sentiment it expresses dates back to ancient times. It is said to have its origin in Greek mythology, in the story of a man who laughed at a prophecy that he would not live to drink the wine of his vineyard. As he raised the first glass to his lips he was told that a boar was destroying his vines; he put down the glass and rushed out, only to be killed by the boar.

Variant of this proverb: there's many a slip 'twixt cup and lip.

Proverb expressing similar meaning: DON'T COUNT YOUR CHICKENS BEFORE THEY ARE HATCHED.

there's many a true word said in jest *See* MANY A TRUE WORD IS SPOKEN IN JEST.

there's measure in all things Everything should be done in moderation: "'Why, carry out logically the theory you were advocating just now, and it follows that people may be killed.' 'Upon my word!' cried Luzhin. 'No, that's not so,' put in Zossimov. . . . 'There's a measure in all things,' Luzhin went on superciliously. 'Economic ideas are not an incitement to murder, and one has but to suppose'" (Fyodor Dostoevsky, *Crime and Punishment*, 1866). The proverb is of ancient origin, occurring in the writings of the Roman poet Horace (65–8 B.C.): "*est modus in rebus* [there is measure in things]." It was first recorded in English in Chaucer's *Troilus and Criseyde* (c. 1385): "In every thyng, I woot, there lith mesure."

Proverbs expressing similar meaning: ENOUGH IS AS GOOD AS A FEAST; ENOUGH IS ENOUGH; MODERATION IN ALL THINGS.

there's more than one way to skin a cat There are many different ways of doing something: *"The door's locked! Now what are we going to do?" "There's more than one way to skin a cat—let's see if we can find an open window."* The proverb is first recorded in John Ray's *A Collection of English Proverbs* (1670).

Proverbs expressing similar meaning: ALL ROADS LEAD TO ROME; THERE ARE MORE WAYS OF KILLING A CAT THAN CHOKING IT WITH CREAM.

there's no accounting for tastes Everybody likes different things; often said disparagingly of another person's choice, or predilection: *"'Shall we try another figure of the Lobster Quadrille?' the Gryphon went on. 'Or would you like the Mock Turtle to sing you a song?' 'Oh, a song, please, if the Mock Turtle would be so kind,' Alice replied, so eagerly that the Gryphon said, in a rather offended tone,*

'Hm! No accounting for tastes!'" (Lewis Carroll, *Alice's Adventures in Wonderland*, 1865). The proverb was first recorded in 1794.

Proverb expressing similar meaning: ONE MAN'S MEAT IS ANOTHER MAN'S POISON.

there's no disputing about tastes There is no point in arguing about what is good or bad, since everybody likes different things: *I tried to persuade her to choose a bolder color, but I soon realized I was wasting my breath. There's no disputing about tastes, and she likes pastel shades best.* Of ancient origin, the proverb is sometimes quoted in its Latin form, *"De gustibus non est disputandum."*

Proverb expressing similar meaning: TASTES DIFFER.

there's no fool like an old fool Foolish behavior in old people is often worse than that in the young: *"'You're an old woman, Emily, and there's no fool like an old fool. The man's twenty years younger than you, and don't fool yourself as to what he married you for. Money!"* (Agatha Christie, *The Mysterious Affair at Styles*, 1920). The proverb was first recorded in 1546 in John Heywood's *Dialogue of Proverbs*.

Variant of this proverb: an old fool is the worst fool.

Proverb expressing similar meaning: A FOOL AT FORTY IS A FOOL INDEED.

there's no great loss without some gain There is often a small advantage to be gained from an unfortunate or unpleasant occurrence: *My dreams of joining the diplomatic corps had been dashed, but there's no great loss without some gain, and I* had made a number of useful contacts along the way. The proverb dates from before 1641.

there's no little enemy Do no underestimate your enemies, all of whom are capable of great harm: "To be friendly with every one is another matter; we must remember that there is no little enemy" (Sir John Lubbock, *The Pleasures of Life,* 1887). The proverb was first recorded in 1659, but the sentiment it expresses is of ancient origin: compare Publilius Syrus (first century B.C.), "*Inimicum, quamvis humilem, docti est metuere* [It is a wise man who fears an enemy, however humble]."

there's no peace for the wicked Life is full of interruptions and disturbances; said by those who are bothered in this way, jocularly implying that they do not deserve to have any time to themselves: *The phone hasn't stopped ringing this evening—there's no peace for the wicked!* The proverb is of biblical origin: "There is no peace, saith the Lord, unto the wicked" (Isaiah 48:22).

Variant of this proverb: there's no rest for the wicked.

Proverb expressing similar meaning: THERE'S NO REST FOR THE WEARY.

there's no place like home Home is the place where people feel most comfortable and contented; often said by somebody on his or her return: "They . . . were only come now to stay a few weeks on account of their father's death; but they did so like Marsh End and Morton, and all these moors and hills about. They had been in London, and many other grand towns; but they always said there was no place like home" (Charlotte Brontë, *Jane Eyre,* 1847). The proverb is of ancient origin,

occurring in the Greek poet Hesiod's *Works and Days* (eighth century B.C.). It was popularized in the song "Home, Sweet Home" (1823) by J. H. Payne: "'Mid pleasures and palaces though we may roam,/Be it ever so humble, there's no place like home."

Proverbs expressing similar meaning: EAST, WEST, HOME'S BEST; HOME IS HOME, BE IT EVER SO HOMELY.

there's no pleasure without pain A happy or enjoyable experience is always accompanied by some sorrow or suffering: *There's no pleasure without pain, and the joy of our reunion was tempered by the knowledge that this was the last time the whole family would be together.* The first recorded use of this proverb is c. 1526: "Lyghtly there is no pleasure, but that vnto it some peyne is annexed" (*Dicta Sapientum*).

Proverbs expressing similar meaning: NO JOY WITHOUT ANNOY; THERE'S NO ROSE WITHOUT A THORN.

there's no putting old heads on young shoulders See YOU CAN'T PUT AN OLD HEAD ON YOUNG SHOULDERS.

there's no rest for the weary However hard you work, and however tired you are, there is always more to be done; said resignedly by somebody who suffers in this way: *I'd just sat down, for the first time all day, when my son called me into the kitchen to help him with a cake he was baking for his girlfriend—there's no rest for the weary!* The proverb was first recorded in B. Graeme's *Murder of Some Importance* (1931).

Variant of this proverb: there's no rest for the wicked.

Proverb expressing similar meaning: THERE'S NO PEACE FOR THE WICKED.

there's no rest for the wicked *See* THERE'S NO PEACE FOR THE WICKED; THERE'S NO REST FOR THE WEARY.

there's no rose without a thorn All good, beautiful, or pleasurable things have some drawback or unpleasant aspect: "'My pay is to be twenty-five louis a month, a good table, good lodging, etc., etc. . . . Do you think it is worth the trouble?' 'There's no rose without a thorn'" (Casanova, *Memoirs*, 1828–38). The proverb was first recorded c. 1435, but the sentiment it expresses is of ancient origin.

Variant of this proverb: every rose has a thorn.

Proverbs expressing similar meaning: NO JOY WITHOUT ALLOY; THERE'S NO PLEASURE WITHOUT PAIN; YOU HAVE TO TAKE THE BITTER WITH THE SWEET.

there's no royal road to learning Knowledge and skills can only be acquired by hard work—there are no short cuts: *There is no royal road to learning, but those who are prepared to put in the months of study required to master this subject will find their efforts well rewarded.* The proverb was first recorded in its current form in 1824. It comes from an anecdote about the Greek mathematician Euclid (fl. 300 B.C.), who allegedly replied, "There is no royal road to geometry," when asked by King Ptolemy I for an easier way to study the subject.

there's no smoke without fire Rumors usually have a factual basis, although they may present a misleading or exaggerated version of the truth: *The company has released a statement refuting the allegations of financial mismanagement made in* yesterday's newspapers, *but there's no smoke without fire, and its stockholders remain concerned.* The proverb was first recorded in this form in 1592, but the sentiment it expresses is of earlier origin. Compare the 13th-century French proverb "*Nul feu est sens fumee ne fumee sens feu* [No fire is without smoke, nor smoke without fire].

Variant of this proverb: where there's smoke, there's fire.

Proverbs expressing similar meaning: COMMON FAME IS SELDOM TO BLAME; WHAT EVERYBODY SAYS MUST BE TRUE.

Proverb expressing opposite meaning: MUCH SMOKE, LITTLE FIRE.

there's no such thing as a free lunch Everything must be paid for, sooner or later, directly or indirectly: "Europeans are now learning some hard facts of life about socialized medicine: There's no such thing as a free lunch" (*Washington Times*, 1996). The proverb was first recorded in 1966, in Robert Heinlein's *The Moon Is a Harsh Mistress*. It is associated with the U.S. economist Milton Friedman (1912–   ), who popularized it.

Variant of this proverb: there's no such thing as a free ride.

Proverb expressing similar meaning: YOU DON'T GET SOMETHING FOR NOTHING.

there's no such thing as bad weather, only the wrong clothes Any weather is tolerable if you are suitably dressed for it: *"There's no such thing as bad weather, only the wrong clothes,"she said as she put on her slicker, boots, and sou'wester and set off in the pouring rain for her daily walk with the dogs.* The proverb is of comparatively recent origin, and was first recorded in the *Washington Post* (Feb. 15, 1980).

Variant of this proverb: there's no such thing as bad weather, only bad clothes.

there's nothing constant but inconstancy

There will always be people and things that are unreliable or changeable: *There's nothing constant but inconstancy, and even our best friends may turn against us.* The proverb is recorded as a regional expression in the United States.

there's nothing lost by civility

Politeness does no harm, and may do a lot of good: *You could at least have apologized—there's nothing lost by civility.*

Proverb expressing similar meaning: CIVILITY COSTS NOTHING.

there's nothing new under the sun

What is thought to be a novelty is often shown to be nothing more than a revival or reintroduction of an old idea; also used as a comment on the changeless nature of things: "'They're after something quite new—something that's never been heard of before.' 'My dear fellow! There is nothing new under the sun'" (George Orwell, *Coming up for Air*, 1939). The proverb is of biblical origin: "The thing that hath been, it is that which shall be; and that which is done is that which shall be done: and there is no new thing under the sun" (Ecclesiastes 1:9).

Proverbs expressing similar meaning: EVERYTHING OLD IS NEW AGAIN; THE MORE THINGS CHANGE, THE MORE THEY STAY THE SAME.

there's nothing so good for the inside of a man as the outside of a horse

Riding is a healthy pastime: "The Squire will wind up . . . with an apocryphal saying which he attributes to Lord Palmerston—'There's nothing so good for the inside of a man as the outside of a horse'" (G. W. E. Russell, *Social Silhouettes*, 1906). The quotation is the first recorded use of the proverb.

there's no time like the present

Now is the best time to do something; used as encouragement to act without delay: "We must clear out the attic one of these days." "There's no time like the present—let's make a start on it straight away." The proverb was first recorded in this form in 1696, but the sentiment it expresses is of earlier origin.

Proverbs expressing similar meaning: TAKE TIME BY THE FORELOCK; PROCRASTINATION IS THE THIEF OF TIME.

there's nowt so queer as folk

People are uniquely unpredictable: *He shook his head when he heard the news and observed "There's nowt so queer as folk."* The proverb was first recorded in 1905 in the *English Dialect Dictionary*.

there's one law for the rich and another for the poor

See ONE LAW FOR THE RICH AND ANOTHER FOR THE POOR.

there's reason in all things

Everything is logical or done for a purpose: *They say there's reason in all things, but I have yet to understand the reason for this drastic change of plan.* The proverb was first recorded in 1602 in John Marston's *Antonio and Mellida*.

Proverb expressing similar meaning: EVERY WHY HATH ITS WHERFORE.

there's safety in numbers

It is preferable or advisable to face a dangerous or unpleasant situation in the company of others; also used more generally, to imply that many is better than a few, or to justify siding with the majority: *We always walk home from the* club together, *on the principle that there's safety in numbers*. The proverb is of biblical origin: "Where no counsel is, the people fall: but in the multitude of counselors there is safety" (Proverbs 11:14).

Proverb expressing similar meaning: EVERY WHY HAS ITS WHEREFORE.

there's truth in wine What people say when they are drunk is usually true: *There is truth in wine, and she had drunk the best part of a bottle of champagne, so I felt inclined to believe her.* Of ancient origin, the proverb is often used in its Latin form, "*In vino veritas*," as in the following quotation from Anthony Trollope's novel *Phineas Redux* (1873): "But he was flushed with much wine, and he was a man whose arrogance in that condition was apt to become extreme. 'In vino veritas!' The sober devil can hide his cloven hoof; but when the devil drinks he loses his cunning and grows honest."

Proverb expressing similar meaning: ALCOHOL WILL PRESERVE ANYTHING BUT A SECRET; DRUNKENNESS REVEALS WHAT SOBERNESS CONCEALS.

Variant of this proverb: in wine there is truth.

they also serve who only stand and wait You can be often be helpful without actively doing anything; also used to commend or encourage patience and endurance: "This man's life of patient suffering was not in vain, but a benediction to many who came in contact with it. 'Those also serve who only stand and wait'" (Philip Schaff, *History of the Christian Church, 1883–1893*). The proverb comes from John Milton's poem "On His Blindness" (c. 1650).

they that dance must pay the piper Those who gain pleasure or benefit from

something must be prepared to bear the costs or suffer the consequences: *He smoked and drank himself into an early grave—they that dance must pay the piper.* The proverb was first recorded in 1638 (J. Taylor, *Taylor's Feast*) in the form "Those that dance must pay the Musicke."

Variants of this proverb: he who dances must pay the fiddler; those who dance must pay the fiddler.

they that live longest see most Older people have more experience of life: *Many of her younger neighbors used to go to my grandmother for advice, on the basis of the saying "They that live longest see most."* The proverb was first recorded in English in 1620, in a translation of Cervantes's *Don Quixote,* but there is evidence of a French version in the early 14th century.

Proverb expressing similar meaning: DON'T TEACH YOUR GRANDMOTHER TO SUCK EGGS.

they that sow the wind shall reap the whirlwind People who provoke trouble or violence—or behave in a reckless manner—will suffer far worse consequences: ". . . the indiscriminate profusion that would glut avarice, or supply prodigality, neither does good, nor is rewarded by gratitude. It is sowing the wind to reap the whirlwind" (Sir Walter Scott, *The Black Dwarf,* 1816). The proverb is of biblical origin: "For they have sown the wind, and they shall reap the whirlwind" (Hosea 8:7).

Variant of this proverb: sow the wind and reap the whirlwind.

a thing of beauty is a joy forever Beautiful things bring lasting pleasure; often used to imply that the memory of something beautiful stays with you for a long time afterward: "I wished for a picture of her. A Madonna, whose face was a portrait of that beautiful Nazareth girl, would be a 'thing of beauty' and 'a joy forever'" (Mark Twain, *The Innocents Abroad*, 1869). The proverb comes from John Keats's poem "Endymion" (1818): "A thing of beauty is a joy for ever:/ Its loveliness increases; it will never/Pass into nothingness."

Proverb expressing opposite meaning: BEAUTY IS BUT A BLOSSOM.

things come in threes   According to popular superstition, two similar occurrences—bad or good—are inevitably followed by a third: *I fell down the steps this morning and trapped my finger in the door this afternoon, so if things come in threes—as people say they do—I'm in for another accident before long.* The proverb was first recorded in 1927.

Variants of this proverb: all good things come in threes; all bad things come in threes.

things past cannot be recalled   It is too late for regret after something is done; sometimes used to advise caution: *Many of us would do things differently if we had our lives to live over again, but things past cannot be recalled.* The proverb was first recorded in English in the 15th century, but there is evidence of a French version 100 years earlier.

Proverb expressing similar meaning: WHAT'S DONE CANNOT BE UNDONE.

a thing you don't want is dear at any price   Do not be tempted to buy something you do not need just because it is cheap: *When my mother came back from the sale laden with so-called bargains, I reminded her of the saying "A thing you don't want is dear at any price."*

think all you speak, but speak not all you think   Do not say anything that you do not believe, but never say everything that is in your mind: *I'm not asking you to lie, I'm just suggesting that it would be not be tactful to tell the whole truth—think all you speak, but speak not all you think.* The proverb is recorded as a regional expression in the United States.

think before you speak   Never express an opinion, make a remark, or answer a question until you have considered the possible effects of what you are going to say; also used to imply that careful thought beforehand leads to more eloquent speech: "A long article on airport-security tips for passengers ends with the advice: 'Think before you speak. Casual joking remarks may not be viewed as such by secret agents'" (*Boston Globe*, 1990). The proverb was first recorded in 1557 in the form "Think well and you will speak well."

Variants of this proverb: first think, and then speak; think first and speak afterward; think twice before you speak once.

Proverbs expressing similar meaning: THINK MUCH, SPEAK LITTLE, AND WRITE LESS; A WORD SPOKEN IS PAST RECALLING.

thinking is very far from knowing   Opinion and conjecture are not the same as knowledge and certainty: *"I think this is the right road." "Thinking is very far from knowing—let's look at the map!"* The proverb was first recorded in 1706 in J. Stevens, *A New Spanish and English Dictionary.*

think much, speak little, and write less It is best to think long and hard about something before expressing any thoughts about it. The proverb was first recorded c. 1430 in John Lydate's *Minor Poems* in the form: "Take no quarelle, thynk mekyl and say nought."

Proverb expressing similar meaning: THINK BEFORE YOU SPEAK.

think twice before you speak once *See* THINK BEFORE YOU SPEAK.

the third time is the charm According to popular superstition, success will come at the third attempt: *After two aborted missions, N.A.S.A. is hoping that the third time is the charm.* The proverb was first recorded in 1721 (James Kelly, *Scottish Proverbs*), but the sentiment it expresses is of earlier origin.

Variants of this proverb: third time lucky; the third time pays for all.

Proverbs expressing similar meaning: IF AT FIRST YOU DON'T SUCCEED, TRY, TRY AGAIN; THERE'S LUCK IN ODD NUMBERS.

this, too, shall pass Do not despair—an unpleasant situation or a difficult period will not last forever: *When things were going badly for me, in the early part of my career, my father consoled me with the saying "This, too, shall pass." He was right, of course, and soon the bad times were nothing more than a fading memory.* The proverb was first recorded in 1852. In a speech in 1859, Abraham Lincoln told a story about its origin: "It is said an Eastern monarch once charged his wise men to invent him a sentence . . . which should be true and appropriate in all times and situations. They presented him the words: 'And this, too, shall pass away.'" A

similar anecdote attributes the proverb to King Solomon.

Variant of this proverb: all things will pass.

those who can, do; those who can't, teach People who are incapable of putting their knowledge and skills to practical use go into education: *He graduated from law school in 1995 and went back there as a lecturer two years later, prompting his students to remark, "Those who can, do; those who can't, teach."* The proverb comes from George Bernard Shaw's *Man and Superman* (1903): "He who can does. He who cannot, teaches." Other words may be substituted for *teach*, as in "Those who can, do; those who can't, attend conferences."

those who cannot remember the past are condemned to repeat it Those who forget, are ignorant of, or fail to learn from the mistakes of earlier generations are likely to make the same mistakes themselves: *It is to be hoped that the study of modern history in our schools and colleges will prevent a recurrence of horrors such as the Holocaust of World War II—those who cannot remember the past are condemned to repeat it.* In its current form, the proverb comes from George Santayana's *The Life of Reason* (1905–06). The sentiment it expresses, however, is of ancient origin.

those who dance must pay the fiddler *See* THEY THAT DANCE MUST PAY THE PIPER.

those who hide can find The person who finds something is often the person who hid it in the first place: *The speed with which the discovery was made aroused suspicions that the police had planted the drugs on* the premises—*those who hide can find*. The proverb was first recorded c. 1400 in *Seven Sages of Rome*.

those who know don't speak; those who speak don't know   Those who talk the most volubly are usually those who know the least about the subject in question: *The more you say, the more you show your ignorance—have you never heard the proverb "Those who know don't speak and those who speak don't know"?* Of ancient Chinese origin, the proverb was first recorded in English in 1948.

   Proverb expressing similar meaning: WHO KNOWS MOST, SPEAKS LEAST.

those who play at bowls must look out for rubbers   It is foolish to embark on or participate in an enterprise without being aware of or taking account of the problems you may encounter: *"'And how if it fails?' said Darsie. 'Thereafter as it may be . . . those who play at bowls must meet with rubbers'"* (Sir Walter Scott, *Redgauntlet,* 1824). The proverb was first recorded in 1762. The word *rubbers* (or *rubs*) refers to the unevenness of the ground on which the game of bowls (or lawn bowling) is played.

those who please everybody please nobody   *See* YOU CAN'T PLEASE EVERYBODY.

thought is free   Anybody may think whatever he or she likes: *"'Ah, your Ursel was a jewel of worth,' said the girl earnestly. 'Would she were here.' 'Instead of her that is here?' 'I say not that,' and she blushed a little. 'You do but think it.' 'Thought is free'"* (Charles Reade, *The Cloister and the Hearth,* 1861). First

recorded c. 1390, the proverb occurs in Shakespeare's play *Twelfth Night* (1:3; 1601): *"'Fair lady, do you think you have fools in hand?' 'Now, sir, thought is free.'"*

the thread breaks where it is weakest   A weak point in a thread or anything else is likely to be the point where the whole thing fails: *He insisted upon changes in lower management, arguing that the thread breaks where it is weakest.* The proverb was first recorded in 1640 in George Herbert's *Outlandish Proverbs*.

   Proverb expressing similar meaning: A CHAIN IS NO STRONGER THAN ITS WEAKEST LINK.

threatened men live long   Threats are often not carried out, and people who have been warned are on their guard and therefore in less danger than others; sometimes said in defiant response to a threat or warning: *A succession of doctors had told him that if he didn't change his lifestyle, he wouldn't live to see his grandchildren, but threatened folks live long, and he proved them all wrong.* The proverb was first recorded in English in 1534 (Lady E. Wheathell, in M. St. C. Byrne, *Lisle Letters*), but with the implication that it was already an old saying, and a French equivalent was in use 200 years earlier.

   Variant of this proverb: threatened folks live the longest.

the three doctors Diet, Quiet, and Temperance are the best physicians   *See* THE BEST DOCTORS ARE DR. DIET, DR. QUIET, AND DR. MERRYMAN.

three may keep a secret, if two of them are dead   It is impossible for two or more people to keep a secret: *"Don't worry, your secret is safe with us." "I wish I could* believe you, but I've heard it said that three may keep a secret only if two of them are dead." The proverb was first recorded in 1546 in John Heywood, *Dialogue of Proverbs.*

Variant of this proverb: two can keep a secret if one is dead.

three moves are as bad as a fire The loss, damage, and stress involved in moving house three times is equivalent to that caused by a fire: *I can well believe that three moves are as bad as a fire—we have already moved house twice since we were married, and it was a major upheaval each time, so I hope we never have to do it again.* The proverb was first recorded in 1758, in Benjamin Franklin's *Poor Richard's Almanack.*

Variant of this proverb: moving three times is as bad as a fire.

three things are not to be trusted: a cow's horn, a dog's tooth, and a horse's hoof A cow is likely to gore you, a dog to bite you, and a horse to kick you, so treat all three with respect and caution: *Given that three things are not to be trusted—a cow's hoof, a dog's tooth, and a horse's hoof—is it any surprise that people prefer to live in cities and keep cats?* The proverb was first recorded in English c. 1383, with *woman's faith* as the third object of distrust, replacing *a cow's horn.* Other substitutes include *women's protestations, an Englishman's laugh,* and *a baby's bottom,* the last of these occurring in a 13th-century French version of the proverb.

three times a bridesmaid, never a bride *See* ALWAYS A BRIDESMAID, NEVER A BRIDE.

thrift is a great revenue Saving and frugality lead to financial gain: "Thrift

. . . is not only a great virtue but also 'a great revenue'" (*London Times,* 1930). The proverb was first recorded, with different wording, in 1659, but the sentiment it expresses is of ancient origin. Compare Cicero (106–43 B.C.): "*Non intelligunt homines quam magnum vectigal sit parsimonia* [Men do no realize how great a revenue thrift is]."

Proverbs expressing similar meaning: A PENNY SAVED IS A PENNY EARNED; SAVING IS GETTING.

throw dirt enough, and some will stick A reputation that is constantly attacked cannot remain undamaged—if false accusations or defamatory remarks are repeated often enough, people will begin to believe them: "Whatever harm a . . . venomous tongue could do them, he took care should be done. Only throw dirt enough and some of it is sure to stick" (Thomas Hughes, *Tom Brown's Schooldays,* 1857). The proverb was first recorded in 1656 in *Trepan.*

Variant of this proverb: fling dirt enough, and some will stick.

Proverb expressing similar meaning: GIVE A DOG A BAD NAME AND HANG HIM.

throw out a sprat to catch a mackerel It is worth making a small sacrifice to gain something of much greater value: *Loss leaders are goods offered for sale at below cost price to attract customers who will, it is hoped, make further purchases in the store—a modern illustration of the saying "Throw out a sprat to catch a mackerel."* The proverb was first recorded in 1810 in John Poole, *Hamlet Travestied.*

Variants of this proverb: you must lose a fly to catch a trout; set a sprat to catch a mackerel.

Thursday's child has far to go Children born on a Thursday are supposed to be destined to travel: *We were not surprised when Megan announced her intention to backpack around the world before going to college—she was born on a Thursday, and everybody knows that Thursday's child has far to go!* The proverb is the fourth line of a traditional rhyme. See entries at the days of the week for other proverbs from this rhyme.

time alone will tell See TIME WILL TELL.

time and tide wait for no man Nobody can afford to delay or be delayed: "'Annie, my dear,' said he, looking at his watch, and filling his glass, 'it is past your cousin Jack's time, and we must not detain him, since time and tide—both concerned in this case—wait for no man'" (Charles Dickens, *David Copperfield,* 1850). The proverb was first recorded in 1592 in a form referring to both time and tide, but the sentiment it expresses is of earlier origin.

Proverb expressing similar meaning: TAKE TIME BY THE FORELOCK.

time ends all things Everything must ultimately come to an end—nothing lasts forever: *Time ends all things, and the feuding families finally agreed to bury their differences.* The proverb is first recorded in N. Ames's *Almanacs* (1786).

Proverb expressing similar meaning: EVERYTHING HAS AN END.

time flies Time sometimes seems to pass with surprising rapidity: "'Time flies,' said Dick. 'George Thorne will be free before long, and he'll be coming out. I wonder if he'll stay here or try to take Mercedes away?'" (Zane Grey, *Desert Gold,*

1913). The proverb was first recorded in this form in 1639, but the sentiment it expresses is of ancient origin. It is sometimes found in its Latin form, *"Tempus fugit."* Extended forms of the proverb include "Time flies when you're having fun" and "Time flies when you're enjoying yourself," often used ironically.

time hangs heavy on idle hands Time seems to pass more slowly when we have little or nothing to do: *Business is sluggish at the moment, and the working day sometimes seems interminable—time hangs heavy on idle hands.* The proverb is recorded as a regional expression in the United States.

time is a great healer Grief, shock, wounded feelings, and so on will fade with time: *She thought she would never get over the death of her husband, but time is a great healer.* The proverb is of ancient origin, occurring in the writings of the Greek poet and dramatist Menander (c. 342–292 B.C.): "time is the healer of all necessary evils."

Variants of this proverb: time heals all wounds; time will heal.

Proverbs expressing similar meaning: PATIENCE IS A REMEDY FOR EVERY SORROW; TIME WORKS WONDERS.

time is money Nobody can afford to waste time that could be spent earning money: *"I'm only asking for ten minutes of your time—it won't cost you anything." "Yes it will—I'm self-employed, and time is money!"* The proverb was first recorded in this form in 1748, in Benjamin Franklin's *Advice to a Young Tradesman,* but the sentiment it expresses is of earlier origin.

time is the rider that breaks youth Young people become less wild and more sensible with age: *Most troublesome teenagers develop into responsible adults—time is the rider that breaks youth.* The proverb was first recorded in 1640, in George Herbert's *Outlandish Proverbs.*

Proverbs expressing similar meaning: WANTON KITTENS MAKE SOBER CATS; WITH AGE COMES WISDOM.

time lost cannot be recalled Time wasted cannot be reclaimed: "And time lost may well be repented, but never recalled" (John Lyly, *Euphues and his England*, 1580). The proverb was first recorded c. 1385 in Geoffrey Chaucer's *Troilus and Criseyde.*

Proverb expressing similar meaning: LOSE AN HOUR IN THE MORNING, CHASE IT ALL DAY; YESTERDAY WILL NOT BE CALLED AGAIN.

times change, and we with time Customs, values, and circumstances are constantly changing, and we must adapt ourselves accordingly: *When I first started work, nobody addressed their superiors or inferiors by their first names. But times change, and we with time—I don't even know the surnames of some of the people I work with today.* The proverb is of Latin origin: "*Tempora mutantur nos et mutamur in illis* [Times are changing and we with them]." It is often shortened to "Times change."

Variant of this proverb: times change, and we with them.

time will heal See TIME IS A GREAT HEALER.

time will tell Some things can only be judged or known after the passage of time: *I hope I have made the right decision, but only time will tell.* The proverb was

first recorded in its current form in the 20th century, earlier forms being "Time will show," "Time reveals all things," and "Time discloses all things." The sentiment it expresses is of ancient origin, occurring in the writings of the Greek poet and dramatist Menander (c. 342–292 B.C.): "time brings the truth to light."

Variants of this proverb: time alone will tell; only time will tell.

time works wonders Great things can be achieved in the course of time: *I thought she would never learn the job, but time works wonders, and now she is one of our best employees.* The proverb was first recorded in 1588 in A. Marten's *Exhortation to Defend Country.*

Proverb expressing similar meaning: TIME IS A GREAT HEALER.

timing is everything It is important to choose the right time to do something: *Timing is everything, and this is probably not the best moment to reopen the public debate about capital punishment.* The proverb comes from the Greek poet Hesiod's *Works and Days* (eighth century B.C.): "Observe due measure, for right timing is in all things the most important factor."

'tis better to have loved and lost, than never to have loved at all It is better to have experienced the joy of love, even if it ends in sorrow, than never to have had that experience: *I was devastated when my daughter died, but I cherish all my happy memories of her, and consider myself more blessed than some of my childless friends—'tis better to have loved and lost, than never to have loved at all.* In its current form, the proverb comes from Alfred, Lord Tennyson's poem "In Memoriam" (1850), but a similar sentiment was expressed by William Congreve 150 years earlier in his play *The Way of the World* (1700): "Say what you will, 'tis better to be left, than never to have been loved."

today is yesterday's tomorrow You cannot go on putting things off, because the future becomes the present: *"I'll quit smoking tomorrow." "You've said that before. Today is yesterday's tomorrow, so why not quit now?"* The proverb was first recorded in 1745 in Edward Young's *Night Thoughts.*

Proverb expressing similar meaning: NEVER PUT OFF UNTIL TOMORROW WHAT YOU CAN DO TODAY.

today you, tomorrow me What happens to one person one day could happen to another person the next day: "'Comrade,' I say to the dead man, but I say it calmly, 'Today you, tomorrow me'" (Erich Maria Remarque, *All Quiet on the Western Front,* 1929). The proverb is of Latin origin: "*Hodie mihi, cras tibi* [Today it is my turn, tomorrow yours]."

Variant of this proverb: I today, you tomorrow.

to each his own Everybody has his or her own tastes and idiosyncrasies: *Standing in the rain watching cars drive around a racetrack all afternoon is not my idea of fun, but to each his own.* The proverb was first recorded in 1713 in Wise, *Churches Quarrel Espoused.*

Proverb expressing similar meaning: EVERY MAN TO HIS TASTE.

to err is human, to forgive divine We all make mistakes, but not everybody is tolerant of the mistakes of others; sometimes used to ask for forgiveness, implying that it would be a magnanimous gesture: "The modern moralist pardons everything, because he is not certain of anything, except that to err is human" (*London Times Literary Supplement,* 1908). The first part of the proverb sometimes stands alone, as in the quotation, and is also found in the Latin form *"Humanum est errare."* In its current form, the proverb comes from Alexander Pope's *Essay on Criticism* (1711). Earlier versions do not mention forgiveness, but add that "to repent is divine" or "to persevere is diabolical." A modern facetious variant is "To err is human, but to really foul things up requires a computer."

Proverbs expressing similar meaning: HOMER SOMETIMES NODS; NOBODY IS INFALLIBLE.

to everything there is a season Everything has its own appropriate time: *Don't be too impatient to start a family—to everything there is a season.* The proverb is of biblical origin: "To everything there is a season, and a time to every purpose under the heaven" (Ecclesiastes 3:1). The passage goes on to list numerous examples: "A time to be born, and a time to die; . . . A time to kill, and a time to heal; . . . A time to weep, and a time to laugh; . . . A time to love, and a time to hate; a time of war, and a time of peace."

Variant of this proverb: there's a season and a time for every purpose under the heaven.

Proverb expressing similar meaning: THERE'S A TIME AND PLACE FOR EVERYTHING.

to forget a wrong is the best revenge *See* THE BEST WAY TO GET EVEN IS TO FORGET.

to know all is to forgive all The better you understand somebody's motives, the more likely you are to pardon him or her: *If only you would let me explain, you would see things in a different light—to know all is to forgive all.* First recorded in English in the mid-20th century, the proverb may be of French origin.

tomorrow is another day Don't worry about what has happened today—things may improve tomorrow; also used with reference to making a fresh start: *The search party has just returned, somewhat dispirited, but tomorrow is another day and they haven't given up hope of finding the child alive.* The proverb was first recorded, in its variant form, c. 1527. It was popularized as the closing line of Margaret Mitchell's novel *Gone with the Wind* (1936): "Tomorrow, I'll think of some way to get him back. After all, tomorrow is another day."

Variant of this proverb: tomorrow is a new day.

tomorrow never comes If you keep putting something off until tomorrow, it will never get done: "To-morrow, every Fault is to be amended; but that To-morrow never comes" (Benjamin Franklin, *Poor Richard's Almanack,* 1756). The proverb was first recorded, with different wording, in 1523 in Lord Berners's *Froissart.*

Proverb expressing similar meaning: ONE OF THESE DAYS IS NONE OF THESE DAYS.

the tongue always returns to the sore tooth People cannot help thinking or talking about what is bothering them most at a particular time: *I tried to bury myself in my work, but my mind kept going back to the argument I'd had with my husband the day before—the tongue always returns to the*

sore tooth. The proverb was first recorded, with different wording, in 1586.

Variant of this proverb: the tongue ever turns to the aching tooth.

the tongue is not steel, but it cuts Words can cause as much pain and damage as an edged tool or weapon: *The tongue is not steel, but it cuts, and the scars left by her cruel words took many months to heal.* The proverb was first recorded in this form in 1640, but the sentiment it expresses is of earlier origin.

Proverbs expressing opposite meaning: HARD WORDS BREAK NO BONES; STICKS AND STONES MAY BREAK MY BONES, BUT NAMES WILL NEVER HURT ME.

too many chiefs and not enough Indians There are too many people giving orders and not enough following them, or too many people in charge and not enough to do the work: *It was a classic case of too many chiefs and not enough Indians, with a top-heavy management structure and an overstretched labor force.* The proverb is thought to have originated in Australia about 1940.

Variants of this proverb: all chiefs and no Indians; too many chiefs and not enough braves.

too many cooks spoil the broth Too many people trying to help can be a hindrance; also used of too many people working on the same project, often pulling in different directions: *Some of the worst movies I've ever seen have a whole string of screenwriters in the credits, proving that too many cooks spoil the broth.* The proverb was first recorded in 1575 in the form "The more cooks the worse potage." Other words may be substituted for *broth,* such as *brew, stew,* or *pie.*

Proverb expressing opposite meaning: MANY HANDS MAKE LIGHT WORK.

too much of a good thing is worse than none at all *See* YOU CAN HAVE TOO MUCH OF A GOOD THING.

toot your own horn lest the same be never tooted Sing your own praises, in case nobody else does: *I think modesty is highly overrated as a virtue—my motto is "Toot your own horn lest the same be never tooted."* The proverb was first recorded c. 1776 in *Warren-Adams Letters.*

Variant of this proverb: if you don't toot your own horn, nobody else will.

Proverb expressing opposite meaning: SELF-PRAISE IS NO RECOMMENDATION.

to the pure all things are pure Virtuous people tend to be unaware of the wickedness or evil that is around them; sometimes used to imply naivety: *To the pure all things are pure, and it never occurred to her that he might have an ulterior motive in asking to see the picture that hung over her bed.* The proverb is of biblical origin: "Unto the pure all things are pure: but unto them that are defiled and unbelieving is nothing pure" (Titus 1:15).

to the victor belong the spoils The winner of a contest or battle gets everything that goes with victory: *The winner of the championship gets a lot more than a trophy—sponsorship deals, celebrity status—to the victor belong the spoils.* The proverb was first recorded in 1832, in a speech made by Senator William L. Marcy of New York. F. Scott Fitzgerald turned it around in his novel *The Beautiful and Damned* (1922): "The victor belongs to the spoils."

touch wood If nothing goes wrong, everything will turn out satisfactorily: *I expect the*

delivery to arrive in the morning, touch wood. This proverbial charm was first recorded in 1805 in R. Anderson's *Ballads in Cumberland Dialect* but may be much older. It refers to the ancient superstition (possibly rooted in pagan tree worship) that it is lucky to touch wood when you make a wish—and many people even today will seek to touch a piece of nearby wood as they say the charm.

Variant of this proverb: knock on wood; touch wood, it's sure to come good.

trade follows the flag One nation may colonize another for commercial purposes: "The removal of a million poor creatures to Canada and the establishment of them there . . . would probably have turned out . . . a profitable investment. Trade follows the flag" (J. A. Froude, *Fraser's Magazine,* 1870). The quotation is the first recorded use of the proverb.

travel broadens the mind People become more broad-minded and knowledgeable by visiting other countries and learning about the customs, culture, and lifestyle of those who live there: "He may be a trifle cracked . . . but that's only because his travels have been too much for his intellect. They say travel broadens the mind; but you must have the mind" (G. K. Chesterton, *The Poet and the Lunatics,* 1929). The quotation is the first recorded use of the proverb.

travel east and travel west, a man's own home is still the best *See* EAST, WEST, HOME'S BEST.

a traveler may lie with authority People who have traveled may boast of their experiences without fear of contradiction: *No* one believed the tale the stranger was spinning, but a traveller may lie with authority and no one could prove he was talking through the top of his hat. The proverb was first recorded c. 1362 in William Langland's *Piers Plowman*.

Variant of this proverb: soldiers and travelers may lie in authority.

the tree is known by its fruit   People should judged by what they do or produce—specifically, by their children—rather than by first impressions or outward appearance: "If then the tree may be known by the fruit, as the fruit by the tree, then, peremptorily I speak it, there is virtue in that Falstaff" (William Shakespeare, *Henry IV, Part I*, 1597–98). The proverb is of biblical origin: "Either make the tree good, and his fruit good; or else make the tree corrupt, and his fruit corrupt: for the tree is known by his fruit" (Matthew 12:33).

Proverb expressing similar meaning: HANDSOME IS AS HANDSOME DOES.

trifles make perfection, and perfection is no trifle   Perfection is a great thing, but not easy to achieve, and attention to detail is of the utmost importance: *She kept going back over her work, changing a comma here and a word there, until she was completely satisfied. It was a tiresome exercise, but trifles make perfection, and perfection is no trifle.* The proverb is attributed to the Italian artist Michelangelo (1475–1564), who is said to have made this remark to a friend after spending several days putting almost imperceptible finishing touches to a sculpture.

a trouble shared is a trouble halved   It often helps to discuss your problems with somebody else: *Advice columnists are inundated with letters from those how believe that a*

trouble shared is a trouble halved. The proverb was first recorded in 1931 in Dorothy L. Sayers's *Five Red Herrings*.

Proverb expressing similar meaning: MISERY LOVES COMPANY.

troubles never come singly   *See* MISFORTUNES NEVER COME SINGLY.

true blue will never stain   Persons of real integrity can never be corrupted. The proverb was first recorded c. 1630 in the *Roxburghe Ballads*: "You know true blew will never stain." One explanation of the proverb refers to the blue dye for which the city of Coventry, England, was known (and by which residents of the city might recognize each other), while another refers to the blue aprons of butchers, the dark color of which served to make bloodstains less obvious. There may also be a reference to the color blue as worn by the incorruptible Virgin Mary.

trust everybody, but cut the cards   Have faith in the honesty and integrity of those around you, but remain on your guard and take precautions in case you are wrong: *I have no reason to doubt his word, but I want to check out the story before taking any further action—trust everybody, but cut the cards.* First recorded in English in 1900, the proverb is of Russian origin: "Trust, but verify." It was popularized by President Ronald Reagan in the late 1980s.

trust in God and keep your powder dry   *See* PUT YOUR TRUST IN GOD, AND KEEP YOUR POWDER DRY.

trust not a new friend nor an old enemy   It is foolish to trust either a friend of short standing or someone else who may harbor hostile feelings: *She realized too late the truth of the old saw that you should never trust a new friend nor an old enemy.* The proverb was first recorded in a ballad of 1450.

Variant of this proverb: trust not the praise of a friend nor the contempt of an enemy.

trust not one night's ice Do not rely upon something that has yet to be tried and tested: *The general declined the offer of a royal audience, privately telling his advisers that he had learnt not to trust one night's ice.* The proverb was first recorded in 1651 in George Herbert's *Outlandish Proverbs.*

Proverb expressing similar meaning: FIRST TRY AND THEN TRUST.

trust not the praise of a friend nor the contempt of an enemy See TRUST NOT A NEW FRIEND NOR AN OLD ENEMY.

the truth hurts It is often unpleasant to learn the truth: "We want the truth. The President wants it. I want it. And the American people have a fundamental right to it. And if the truth hurts, so be it" (George Bush, *New York Times,* 1986). The first recorded use of this proverb is in Robert Browning's *Fifine at the Fair* (1872).

truth is stranger than fiction The truth is often far more unlikely than anything that can be dreamed up by the imagination: "He has based all his brilliancy and solidity upon the hackneyed, but yet forgotten, fact that truth is stranger than fiction. Truth, of course, must of necessity be stranger than fiction, for we have made fiction to suit ourselves" (G. K. Chesterton, *Heretics,* 1905). The proverb comes from Lord Byron's poem "Don Juan"

(1823): "'Tis strange—but true; for truth is always strange;/Stranger than fiction; if it could be told,/How much would novels gain by the exchange!"

Proverb expressing similar meaning: FACT IS STRANGER THAN FICTION.

truth is the first casualty of war When war breaks out, the truth quickly succumbs to propaganda and rumor. The proverb was first recorded in 1928 by A. Ponsonby in *Falsehood in Wartime*: "When war is declared, Truth is the first casualty."

truth is truth to the end of the reckoning The truth can never be changed: *If it was true then, it is must be true now—truth is truth to the end of the reckoning.* In its current form, the proverb comes from Shakespeare's play *Measure for Measure* (5:1; 1604), "Nay, it is ten times true; for truth is truth/To the end of reckoning." The sentiment it expresses, however, is of earlier origin.

truth lies at the bottom of a well It is often very difficult to discover the truth: *We will probably never know exactly what happened on that night—truth lies at the bottom of a well, and everybody I've interviewed so far has given me a different version of events.* The proverb is attributed to the Greek philosopher Democritus (c. 460–c. 370 B.C.): "we know nothing certainly, for truth lies in the deep."

Variant of this proverb: truth keeps to the bottom of her well.

Proverb expressing opposite meaning: TRUTH WILL OUT.

truth will out The truth cannot be concealed forever: "After all, the names of the principal characters will be quite as much disguised; for though in this history the chronicler would prefer to conceal the facts under a mass of contradictions, anachronisms, improbabilities, and absurdities, the truth will out in spite of him" (Honoré de Balzac, *The Collection of Antiquities*, 1839). First recorded in 1439, the proverb occurs in Shakespeare's play *The Merchant of Venice* (2:2), "Truth will come to light; murder cannot be hid long; a man's son may, but in the end truth will out."

Proverb expressing opposite meaning: TRUTH LIES AT THE BOTTOM OF A WELL.

try before you trust *See* FIRST TRY THEN TRUST.

Tuesday's child is full of grace Children born on a Tuesday are supposed to be graceful in movement and bearing; also interpreted in other senses of the word *grace: If it were true that Tuesday's child is full of grace, you might expect to find that a disproportionate number of ballet dancers and models were born on that day.* The proverb is the second line of a traditional rhyme. See entries at the days of the week for other proverbs from this rhyme.

TURKISH PROVERBS

Turkish proverbs cover many subjects, but they are perhaps at their most distinctive when discussing the facing of difficulty of one kind or another.

> Coffee should be black as hell, strong as death, and sweet as love
> The eagle does not feed on flies
> A friend is one soul in two bodies
> He who controls his tongue saves his head
> He who has no children has one sorrow, he who has children has a thousand sorrows
> A hungry dog will bring a lion down
> If you fall in a river hang on to a snake
> If you look for a faultless woman you will remain a bachelor
> In the company of the blind, close your eyes
> To live in peace one must be blind, deaf, and mute
> Measure a thousand times, cut once
> No matter how far down a wrong road you are, turn back
> One armpit cannot hold two watermelons
> One bad experience is worth more than a thousand threats
> One eats, another watches; that's how revolutions are born
> Profit is the brother of loss
> Sometimes you have to sacrifice your beard in order to save your head
> So the music, so the people
> When God wants to please a poor man, He lets him lose his donkey and then helps him find it again
> You don't wash blood away with blood but with water

turnabout is fair play   Taking turns to do something is the fairest way to proceed: *Come away from the computer and let your sister use it for a while—turnabout is fair play.* The proverb was first recorded in 1755.

two and two make four   Logic dictates that something must be so: *Two and two make four and the geologists were forced to admit that the signs of an impending earthquake were all there.* The proverb was first recorded in 1697 in Jeremy Collier's *Essays on Moral Subjects*.

Variant of this proverb: two and two do not make five.

two blacks don't make a white   *See* TWO WRONGS DON'T MAKE A RIGHT.

two boys are half a boy, and three boys are no boy at all   When two or more boys work together, they distract each other and do less work between them than a single boy working alone: *If the twins and their brother offer to help, I usually pick just one of them, on the principle that two boys are half a boy, and three boys are no boy at all.* The proverb was first recorded c. 1930 in F. Thompson's *Country Calendar*.

two can keep a secret if one is dead   *See* THREE MAY KEEP A SECRET, IF TWO OF THEM ARE DEAD.

two dogs fight over a bone while a third runs away with it   *See* WHILE TWO DOGS ARE FIGHTING FOR A BONE, A THIRD RUNS AWAY WITH IT.

two eyes see more than one   *See* FOUR EYES SEE MORE THAN TWO.

two heads are better than one   A problem is more quickly solved if two people put their minds to it: *Can you help me check these figures? There's an error in here somewhere, but I can't find it, and two heads are better than one.* The proverb was first recorded c. 1390 in John Gower, *Confessio Amantis* in the form "Tuo han more wit then on."

Proverb expressing similar meaning: FOUR EYES SEE MORE THAN TWO.

two is company but three is none   *See* TWO'S COMPANY, THREE'S A CROWD.

two of a trade never agree   Members of the same trade or profession often do not get on with one another, because of rivalry: *They say that two of a trade never agree, but my parents, both accountants, have been happily married for 30 years now.* The proverb was first recorded, with different wording, in 1630 by Thomas Dekker, *Honest Whore*, Part II.

Variant of this proverb: two of a trade seldom agree.

two's company, three's a crowd   Two people, especially friends or lovers, often regard a third as an unwelcome intruder: *Why does she always want to tag along with us? Has she never heard the saying "Two's company, three's a crowd"?* The proverb was first recorded in the mid-19th century, in the form "Two is company but three is none," (W. C. Hazlitt, *English Proverbs*) but the sentiment it expresses is of earlier origin.

Variants of this proverb: two is company but three is none; two's a couple, three's a crowd, four's too many, and five's not allowed.

two tailors go to a man   *See* NINE TAILORS MAKE A MAN.

two wrongs don't make a right   Wrongdoing is always unacceptable, even if another person has done the same thing; often used to discourage or condemn retaliation: "'Why didn't you just hit him over the head and take the bedsheet away from him?' Yossarian asked. . . . Milo shook his head. 'That would have been unjust,' he scolded firmly. 'Force is wrong, and two wrongs never make a right'" (Joseph Heller, *Catch-22*, 1961). The proverb was first recorded, in its variant form, in 1721. In *The Second Sin* (1773), Thomas Szasz mischievously argued that "Two wrongs don't make a right, but they make a good excuse."

Variant of this proverb: TWO BLACKS DON'T MAKE A WHITE.

uneasy lies the head that wears a crown Those in power are weighed down by responsibilities, feelings of insecurity, or fears of losing their position and can never rest easy: "'Uneasy lies the head that wears a crown!' Stepan Arkadyevich said playfully, hinting, evidently, not simply at the Princess's conversation, but at the cause of Levin's agitation, which he had noticed" (Leo Tolstoy, *Anna Karenina*, 1873–77). The proverb comes from Shakespeare's play *Henry IV, Part 2* (3:1; 1597), "Canst thou, O partial sleep, give thy repose/To the wet sea-boy in an hour so rude,/And in the calmest and most stillest night,/ . . . /Deny it to a king? Then happy low, lie down!/Uneasy lies the head that wears a crown."

Proverbs expressing similar meaning: THE HIGHEST BRANCH IS NOT THE SAFEST ROOST; THE POST OF HONOR IS THE POST OF DANGER.

Proverb expressing opposite meaning: BETTER BE FIRST IN A VILLAGE THAN SECOND AT ROME.

the unexpected always happens You can be always be sure that something unforeseen will happen for which you are not prepared: "Have nothing which in a case of emergency you cannot carry in your own hands. But remember that

the unexpected always happens" (Evelyn Waugh, *Scoop,* 1938). The proverb was first recorded in English in 1885, but the sentiment it expresses is of ancient origin, occurring in the writings of the Roman dramatist Plautus (c. 250–184 B.C.).

Variant of this proverb: it's always the unexpected that happens.

Proverb expressing similar meaning: NOTHING IS CERTAIN BUT THE UNFORESEEN.

union is strength People can achieve greater things by working together than by working alone: "Union is strength; union is also weakness. It is a good thing to harness two horses to a cart; but it is not a good thing to try and turn two hansom cabs into one four-wheeler" (G. K. Chesterton, *Heretics,* 1905). The proverb was first recorded in English in 1654 in the form "Union strengthens." The sentiment it expresses, however, is of ancient origin, occurring in Homer's *Iliad* (c. eighth century B.C.): "even weak men have strength in unity."

Variant of this proverb: in unity there is strength.

united we stand, divided we fall It is important that a group of people remain united in order to succeed; often used to discourage dissatisfied members from breaking away: *We must have the support of* the entire workforce in this protest—*united we stand, divided we fall*. The proverb comes from John Dickinson's "Liberty Song," published in the *Boston Gazette* in 1768: "Then join hand in hand, brave Americans all, / By uniting we stand, by dividing we fall." The sentiment it expresses, however, is of ancient origin, occurring in one of the fables of Aesop (sixth century B.C.), about a lion that persuades a group of bulls to separate and kills them one by one.

Proverbs expressing similar meaning: DIVIDE AND CONQUER; A HOUSE DIVIDED AGAINST ITSELF CANNOT STAND.

use brains not brawn   *See* WISDOM GOES BEYOND STRENGTH.

the used key is always bright   Activity, work, and exercise keep the mind and body in good form: *You must practice regularly to keep your skills up to scratch—the used key is always bright.* The proverb was first recorded, with different wording, in 1561 in *Kitt Hath Lost Key.*

Variant of this proverb: iron not used soon rusts.

use legs and have legs   The body, among other things, will continue to work properly only if kept in regular use: *When it comes to the maintenance of general fitness the old adage "use legs and have legs" still holds true.* First recorded in G. Harvey, *Marginalia* (c. 1582): "Use Legges, & have Legges: Use Law and Have Law. Use nether & have nether."

use your head and save your feet   *See* LET YOUR HEAD SAVE YOUR HEELS.

$\mathcal{V}$

variety is the spice of life Change and difference make life interesting: *People who never go to the same place twice on vacation fall into two groups—those who believe that variety is the spice of life and those who are constantly and vainly searching for the ideal spot.* The proverb comes from William Cowper's poem "The Task" (1785): "Variety's the very spice of life,/That gives it all its flavour."

Proverb expressing similar meaning:
A CHANGE IS AS GOOD AS A REST.

the vicar of Bray will be vicar of Bray still Some people doggedly cling to office or other privileges however much circumstances might change around them: *The chairman refused to resign after the vote, prompting one of his critics to observe "the vicar of Bray will be vicar of Bray still."* The proverb was recorded by Thomas Fuller in *The History of the Worthies of England* in 1662. It refers to an infamous vicar of Bray who during the reign of Henry VIII stubbornly held onto his post, first as a Catholic, then as a Protestant.

victory has a hundred fathers and defeat is an orphan *See* SUCCESS HAS MANY FATHERS, WHILE FAILURE IS AN ORPHAN.

virtue is its own reward The satisfaction of knowing you have done the right thing is all that is needed: *I know that virtue is its own reward, and I certainly didn't expect to be paid for my efforts, but she could at least have thanked me!* First recorded in English in 1509, in the form "Virtue has no reward," the proverb has been traced back to the works of the Roman poet Ovid (43 B.C.–A.D. 18).

the voice of the people is the voice of God The will of the people must be obeyed; also used to imply that the people are always right: "One Sansculottic bough that cannot fail to flourish is Journalism. The voice of the People being the voice of God, shall not such divine voice make itself heard? To the ends of France; and in as many dialects as when the first great Babel was to be built!" (Thomas Carlyle, *The French Revolution*, 1837). Of ancient origin, the proverb is sometimes used in its original Latin form, *"Vox populi, vox Dei."*

a volunteer is worth ten pressed men *See* ONE VOLUNTEER IS WORTH TWO PRESSED MEN.

uu

walls have ears What you say may be overheard; used as a warning: "In Paris, where walls have ears, where doors have tongues, and window bars have eyes, there are few things more dangerous than the practice of standing to chat in a gateway" (Honoré de Balzac, *Cousin Pons,* 1847–48). The proverb was first recorded in 1592.

Proverb expressing similar meaning: FIELDS HAVE EYES AND WOODS HAVE EARS.

walnuts and pears you plant for your heirs Walnut trees and pear trees take a long time to produce fruit: *A new fast-yielding variety has been developed, giving the lie to the old saying "Walnuts and pears you plant for your heirs."* The proverb was first recorded in 1732 in the form "He who plants a walnut tree expects not to eat of the fruit." The idea that trees of any kind are generally planted for the benefit of succeeding generations, however, is of ancient origin.

wanton kittens make sober cats People who live wildly or extravagantly in their youth usually develop into sensible and responsible adults: *I've heard that wanton kittens make sober cats, but it was hard to believe that the demure young woman who answered the door was the troublesome girl who had caused her parents so much anxiety*

several years earlier. The proverb was first recorded in 1732 in Thomas Fuller, *Gnomologia: Adagies and Proverbs.*

Proverb expressing similar meaning: TIME IS THE RIDER THAT BREAKS YOUTH.

war is hell War is a horrific experience and a terrible thing: "Let's not regard the Germans as enemies. War is never black or white: war is hell for all involved" (*Time,* 1994). The proverb is associated with General William T. Sherman, who used it in 1880: "There is many a boy here today who looks on war as all glory, but, boys, it is all hell." The sentiment it expresses, however, is of earlier origin.

war is too important to be left to the generals Those in authority cannot be relied on to do their job properly; applied to warfare, diplomacy, or government: *War is too important to be left to the generals, even in peacetime—the offensive action ordered by the police chiefs only heightened the tension and exacerbated the riot.* The proverb has been attributed to various people, notably the French politicians Charles-Maurice de Talleyrand (1754–1838) and Georges Clemenceau (1841–1929).

war will cease when men refuse to fight There will always be war while there are people who are prepared to serve in the armed forces; a pacifist slogan: *If it is true that war will cease when men refuse to fight, then the present military recruitment crisis should not be a cause for alarm.* The proverb is of 20th-century origin.

waste not, want not If you make full and careful use of your resources, you will never be in need; applied to everything from the eating up of leftover food to domestic and industrial recycling: "There were, besides, some little pleasures in the shape of helping her to vegetable she didn't want, and when it had nearly alighted on her plate taking across for his own use, on the plea of waste not, want not" (Thomas Hardy, *Under the Greenwood Tree,* 1872). The proverb was first recorded in this form in 1800 (in Maria Edgeworth, *Parent's Assistant*), but the sentiment it expresses is of earlier origin.

Proverb expressing similar meaning: WILLFUL WASTE MAKES WOEFUL WANT.

a watched pot never boils It seems that things take longer to happen when you watch or wait with impatience: "What's the use of watching? A watched pot never boils, and I see you are after watching that weather-cock. Why now, I try never to look at it, else I could do nought else" (Elizabeth Gaskell, *Mary Barton,* 1848). This quotation is the first recorded use of the proverb.

water finds its own level *See* WATER SEEKS ITS OWN LEVEL.

water is the only drink for a wise man Wise people avoid drinking alcohol: *He is strictly teetotal, never having* touched a drop in his life, believing that water is the only drink for a wise man. The proverb was first recorded in 1854, in Henry David Thoreau's *Walden.*

water seeks its own level People tend to be drawn toward, or to end up with, others of the same background, class, intelligence, or experience: *You can't go on pretending to be better than you are—water seeks its own level.* The proverb was first recorded in 1778 in *Public Papers of George Clinton, First Governor of New York.*

Variant of this proverb: water finds its own level.

the way to a man's heart is through his stomach The best way to please a man is by feeding him well: "'Well, you know, the way to a man's heart is through his stomach, Cornelia,' explained Captain Jim. 'I believe you—when he HAS a heart,' retorted Miss Cornelia. 'I suppose that's why so many women kill themselves cooking'" (Lucy Maud Montgomery, *Anne's House of Dreams,* 1917). The proverb was first recorded in 1814, in the form "The shortest road to men's hearts is down their throats," in a letter written by John Adams.

the way to be safe is never to feel secure *See* HE THAT IS TOO SECURE IS NOT SAFE.

the weakest go to the wall In any conflict or struggle, the weakest will always lose, be defeated, fail, or be ruined: *You have to be aggressive and self-assertive to survive in this industry, where the weakest go to the wall.* The proverb dates from before 1500, and occurs in Shakespeare's play *Romeo and Juliet* (1:1). It is said to have originally referred to seating installed around the walls of medieval churches, and has given rise to the figurative phrase *to go to the wall,* to be ruined; to fall or fail in a struggle.

Proverb expressing similar meaning: PROVIDENCE IS ALWAYS ON THE SIDE OF THE BIG BATTALIONS.

Proverb expressing opposite meaning: THE RACE IS NOT TO THE SWIFT, NOR THE BATTLE TO THE STRONG.

we all have our cross to bear Nobody is exempt from suffering—we all have our own problems and afflictions: *I know life is hard for him, but I wish he wouldn't complain so much—we all have our cross to bear.* The proverb is an allusion to the biblical quotation "And whosoever doth not bear his cross, and come after me, cannot be my disciple" (Luke 14:27).

wealth makes many friends Many people want to be the friend of a rich person: *Wealth makes many friends—but these so-called friends will lose interest in you when your money runs out.* The proverb is of biblical origin: "Wealth maketh many friends; but the poor is separated from his neighbor" (Proverbs 19:4).

Proverb expressing similar meaning: HE THAT HAS A FULL PURSE NEVER WANTED A FRIEND.

the wearer best knows where the shoe pinches Nobody can fully understand another person's hardship or suffering: *The wearer best knows where the shoe pinches, and charitable organizations must consult with those they are trying to help, so that the aid can be directed where it is most needed.* The proverb was first recorded in English in Chaucer's *Canterbury Tales* (c. 1390): "I

woot best where wryngeth me my sho." The sentiment it expresses, however, is of ancient origin, occurring in the writings of Plutarch (c. 46–c. A.D. 120).

wear your learning like your watch, in a private pocket Do not make a show of your knowledge or education: *She is one of those who believe that you should wear your learning like your watch, in a private pocket, and few people would guess that she is one of the country's leading astronomers.* The proverb comes from a letter written by Lord Chesterfield in 1748: "Wear your learning, like your watch in a private pocket: and do not merely pull it out and strike it; merely to show that you have one."

wedlock is a padlock Marriage brings with it many restrictions on personal freedom: *Wedlock is a padlock, and divorce lawyers make a comfortable income selling people the key.* The proverb was first recorded in 1678 in John Ray's *English Proverbs.*

Wednesday's child is full of woe Children born on a Wednesday are supposed to be miserable by nature: *My mother gave up trying to make Sam smile for the camera—he was born on a Wednesday, and seemed determined to prove that Wednesday's child is full of woe.* The proverb is the third line of a traditional rhyme. See entries at the days of the week for other proverbs from this rhyme.

we have nothing to fear but fear itself See THE ONLY THING WE HAVE TO FEAR IS FEAR ITSELF.

welcome is the best cheer Welcoming your guests with friendly hospitality is more important than giving them fine food and wine: *Tom is a kind, generous, and jovial* *host, which makes up for his shortcomings in the kitchen—as they say, welcome is the best cheer.* The proverb was first recorded c. 1550 in the form "Welcome is the best dish."

Variant of this proverb: welcome is the best dish on the table.

well begun is half done If you make a good start to a task, it will be quickly completed: *If you cut the pieces out carefully and accurately, you will have no difficulty fitting them together—well begun is half done.* The proverb was first recorded in English, with different wording, c. 1415. The sentiment it expresses, however, is of ancient origin, occurring in the writings of Plato and Horace.

Proverb expressing similar meaning: A GOOD BEGINNING IS HALF THE BATTLE.

we must eat a peck of dirt before we die Everybody must suffer a certain amount of unpleasantness during his or her lifetime; also used literally, as when eating unwashed food: *Whenever I came home from school with a tale of woe, my mother would console me with her favorite saying, "We must eat a peck of dirt before we die."* The proverb was first recorded in 1738, in Jonathan Swift's *Polite Conversation.*

Variant of this proverb: you have to eat a bushel of dirt before you die.

we must learn to walk before we can run It is necessary to learn the basics before progressing to more advanced things: "More fail from doing too much than too little. We must learn and be strong enough to walk before we can run" (James Platt, *Business,* 1875). The proverb was first recorded, with different wording, c. 1350. Early examples of its use had *creep* and *go* in place of *walk* and *run.*

Variant of this proverb: you have to learn to crawl before you can walk.

a wet May brings plenty of hay Wet weather in May means the hay harvest will be good later in the year: *As farmers everywhere will tell you, "a wet May brings plenty of hay."* The proverb was first recorded in 1846 in M. A. Denham's *A Collection of Proverbs . . . relating to the Weather.*

what a tangled web we weave when first we practice to deceive Once you have told one lie, you find yourself supporting it with other related lies, constructing an elaborate network of deceit from which it is not easy to escape: "People have pretty well forgotten my other mistakes. . . . But they'll never forget this. They will think I am not respectable. Oh, Marilla, 'what a tangled web we weave when first we practice to deceive.' That is poetry, but it is true." (Lucy Maud Montgomery, *Anne of Green Gables,* 1908). The proverb comes from Sir Walter Scott's poem *Marmion* (1808).

Proverb expressing similar meaning: ONE LIE LEADS TO ANOTHER.

what can't be cured must be endured If something cannot be put right, we must learn to put up with it: "'What cannot be cured must be endured,' the chained man says, trying to smile. But it comes out as a grimace" (*Washington Post,* 1997). The proverb was first recorded in 1579, but the sentiment it expresses is of earlier origin.

what can you expect from a pig but a grunt? Boorish or uncouth people cannot be expected to behave in any other way; used as an insult when such a person says or does something rude: *His remark was in very poor taste, but what can you expect from a pig but a grunt?* The proverb was first recorded, with different wording, in 1731.

whatever man has done, man may do If one person has succeeded in doing something, it should not be impossible for another person to do it too: "'Dark Deeds are written in an unknown tongue called "Lawyerish," where the sense is "as one grain of wheat in two bushels of chaff," pick it out if you can.' 'Whatever man has done man may do,' said Dr. Sampson stoutly. 'You have read it, and yet understood it: so why mayn't we, ye monster o' conceit?'" (Charles Reade, *Hard Cash,* 1863). The quotation is the first recorded use of the proverb.

Variant of this proverb: what man has done, man can do.

what everybody says must be true Public opinion is generally assumed to be accurate: "Everybody said so. Far be it from me to assert that what everybody says must be true. Everybody is, often, as likely to be wrong as right" (Charles Dickens, *The Haunted Man and the Ghost's Bargain,* 1848). The proverb was first recorded, with different wording, c. 1475.

Proverbs expressing similar meaning: COMMON FAME IS SELDOM TO BLAME; THERE'S NO SMOKE WITHOUT FIRE.

what goes around, comes around Those who say or do bad things to other people are likely to find themselves on the receiving end of similar criticism or treatment in the future; also used to imply that everybody eventually gets his or her just deserts: "No sooner had the

royal accusers sent Louis XVI and his queen to the guillotine, than they themselves were being hoist onto the tumbrels by men whose own heads would later drop into the basket. What goes around comes around" (*Washington Times,* 1989). Of U.S. origin, the proverb was first recorded in 1974.

Proverb expressing similar meaning: CURSES, LIKE CHICKENS, COME HOME TO ROOST.

what goes up must come down The law of gravity must be obeyed; also used figuratively of any rise and fall: *What goes up must come down, even on Wall Street, and you must sell your stocks at exactly the right moment to get the best return on your investment.* The proverb was first recorded in 1929 in F. A. Pottle's *Stretchers.*

what has happened once can happen again Something that has a precedent cannot be dismissed as impossible, and may recur: *What has happened once can happen again, but next time we will be better prepared to control the disease before it reaches epidemic proportions.* The proverb was first recorded in 1815 in *Journal of a Young Man of Massachusetts.*

what man has done, man can do *See* WHATEVER MAN HAS DONE, MAN MAY DO.

what must be, must be *See* WHAT WILL BE, WILL BE.

what's bred in the bone will come out in the flesh Inherited characteristics become evident in each new generation: *In his middle years he became an alcoholic, like his father and grandfather before him—what's bred in the bone will come out in the flesh.* Of medieval Latin origin, the proverb was first recorded in English in Sir Thomas Malory's *Le Morte d'Arthur* (c. 1470), in the form "Harde hit ys to take oute off the fleysshe that ys bredde in the bone." The current form of the proverb is a comparatively recent alteration of the original, "What's bred in the bone will not (come) out of the flesh," which has a slightly different meaning, implying that inherited characteristics cannot be eradicated: "Even Benjamin lost all patience with me this time. 'What is bred in the bone,' he said, quoting the old proverb, 'will never come out of the flesh. In years gone by, you were the most obstinate child that ever made a mess in a nursery'" (Wilkie Collins, *The Law and the Lady,* 1875).

Proverbs expressing similar meaning: BLOOD WILL TELL; NATURE PASSES NURTURE.

what's done cannot be undone   Once something has been done, it cannot be changed, no matter how much you regret having done it: "'I shouldn't have hurried on our affair, and brought you to a half-furnished hut before I was ready, if it had not been for the news you gave me, which made it necessary to save you, ready or no . . . Good God!' 'Don't take on, dear. What's done can't be undone'" (Thomas Hardy, *Jude the Obscure,* 1895). The proverb was first recorded in English c. 1450, but the sentiment it expresses is of ancient origin. It occurs in Shakespeare's play *Macbeth* (1605–06) in both its forms, "What's done is done" (3:2) and "What's done cannot be undone" (5:1).

Variant of this proverb: what's done is done.

Proverbs expressing similar meaning: IT'S NO USE CRYING OVER SPILLED MILK; THINGS PAST CANNOT BE RECALLED.

what's good for General Motors is good for America   Anything that benefits business and commerce is of benefit to the country as a whole: "You will never hear from me . . . that this country should do this or that simply because business wants it. What is good for General Motors may, or may not, be good for the country" (Arthur M. Schlesinger, Jr., *A Thousand Days,* 1965). In its current form, the proverb comes from testimony given in 1953 by Charles Erwin Wilson, president of General Motors, regarding his nomination as secretary of defense: "For many years I thought what was good for our country was good for General Motors, and vice versa." Other words may be substituted for *General Motors* and *America*.

what's got over the devil's back is spent under his belly   Money that is acquired by illicit or immoral means is spent in a similar manner: *They travel from one resort to the next, fleecing or robbing the tourists by day and squandering their ill-gotten gains in the bars and brothels by night—what's got over the devil's back is spent under his belly.* The proverb was first recorded in 1582 in S. Gosson's *Plays Confuted.*

Variant of this proverb: nothing goes over the back but that comes under the belly.

what's in a name?   The names borne by or given to people and things are not important: *What's in a name? Why pay $200 for a jacket with a designer label when you can buy one of the same—if not better—quality for half the price?* The proverb comes from

Shakespeare's play *Romeo and Juliet* (2:2), "What's in a name? that which we call a rose/By any other name would smell as sweet."

Proverb expressing similar meaning: A ROSE BY ANY OTHER NAME WOULD SMELL AS SWEET.

what's new cannot be true People are always skeptical about new ideas: *Throughout the ages, scientists and inventors have struggled against the popular misconception that what's new cannot be true.* The proverb was first recorded, with different wording, in 1639 in J. Clarke's *Parœmiologia Anglo-Latina.*

what's past is prologue Everything that has gone before is just the introduction to what is still to come: "A century and a quarter. A long time for any commercial entity, and something to take pride in. And we do, while bearing in mind that 'what's past is prologue.' It's the *next* 125 years that really count" (*New York Times,* 1991). The proverb comes from Shakespeare's play *The Tempest* (2:1; 1611), "We all were sea-swallow'd, though some cast again,/And by that destiny to perform an act/Whereof what's past is prologue, what to come/In yours and my discharge."

what's sauce for the goose is sauce for the gander What is appropriate for one person is equally appropriate for another person in a similar situation; sometimes used in the context of sexual equality: *If smoking is to be banned on the factory floor, then it should also be banned in the boardroom—what's sauce for the goose is sauce for the gander.* The proverb was first recorded in 1670 in John Ray's *English Proverbs.*

what's yours is mine, and what's mine is my own People often expect free use of what belongs to others while refusing to share their own property: *My husband's salary will be paid into our joint account, and I have set up a separate account for my own earnings. This is just to simplify my business affairs, as I'm self-employed—I have assured my husband that it is not a case of "What's yours is mine, and what's mine is my own"!* The proverb was first recorded in 1591. It is a facetious alteration of the less selfish notion "What's yours is mine, and what's mine is yours," associated with the sharing of money and possessions in marriage.

Variant of this proverb: what's yours is mine, and what's mine is mine.

what the eye doesn't see, the heart doesn't grieve over Nobody can be upset by something that he or she is unaware of: *He tried to exculpate himself by concealing all the evidence from his wife and saying, "What the eye doesn't see, the heart doesn't grieve over."* The proverb dates from before the 12th century, when it was used in a sermon by Saint Bernard: "*Quod non videt oculus cor non dolet* [What the eye sees not, the heart does not grieve at]."

Proverbs expressing similar meaning: ADMIRATION IS THE DAUGHTER OF IGNORANCE; WHAT YOU DON'T KNOW CAN'T HURT YOU.

what the soldier said isn't evidence Gossip, hearsay, and rumor are not reliable sources of the truth: *You need more than a secondhand account from an eyewitness to prove your case—what the soldier said isn't evidence.* The proverb was first recorded in 1837, in Charles Dickens's novel *The Pickwick Papers:* "'You must not tell us what the soldier, or any other man, said, sir,' interposed the judge; 'it's not evidence.'"

what will be, will be   What is destined to happen cannot be prevented: *There's no point in worrying about the future—what will be, will be.* The proverb was first recorded in Chaucer's *Canterbury Tales* (c. 1390): "Whan a thyng is shapen, it shal be." It is sometimes quoted in its Italian form, *"Che sarà, sarà,"* which was popularized in the mid-20th century as a line from the song "Whatever Will Be Will Be."

Variant of this proverb: what must be, must be.

what you don't know can't hurt you   It is often better to remain in ignorance of things that could distress you: *I decided that it would be wiser—and perhaps kinder—not to tell my parents the whole story of what happened that night, on the basis of the saying "What you don't know can't hurt you."* The proverb was first recorded in 1576 in G. Pettie's *Petit Palace.*

Proverbs expressing similar meaning: IGNORANCE IS BLISS; WHAT THE EYE DOESN'T SEE, THE HEART DOESN'T GRIEVE OVER.

what you lose on the swings you gain on the roundabouts   Gains and losses tend to balance one another overall: *Their delivery charges are higher, but their prices are lower—what you lose on the swings you gain on the roundabouts.* The proverb comes from Patrick Reginald Chalmers's poem "Roundabouts and Swings" (1912): "What's lost upon the roundabouts we pulls up on the swings!" It has given rise to the figurative phrase *swings and roundabouts.*

Variant of this proverb: what you gain on the swings you lose on the roundabouts.

what you put off and what you put on, never change till May be gone   See NE'ER CAST A CLOUT TILL MAY BE OUT.

what you see is what you get   Things or people are exactly as they seem; used to imply honesty, straightforwardness, etc.: "'My wife says I'm the most uncomplicated man in the world,' Dukakis admits. 'I guess I am.' Even his 83-year-old mother says of him, 'What you see is what you get'" (*Time,* 1987). First recorded in 1971, the proverb has acquired a specialized use (abbreviated to WYSIWYG) in the world of computing, where it means "What you see on the screen is exactly what you will get on the printout."

Proverb expressing opposite meaning: APPEARANCES ARE DECEIVING.

what you've never had you never miss   People do not feel the lack of something they have never possessed or enjoyed: "I castrate the male lambs . . . about an hour after they have been born. They say what you've never had, you never miss" (Ronald Blythe, *Akenfield,* 1969). The proverb was first recorded in 1912 in Jean Webster's *Daddy Long-Legs.*

Proverb expressing similar meaning: YOU CAN'T LOSE WHAT YOU NEVER HAD.

the wheel comes full circle   Things eventually reach a situation resembling that from which they began: *The word originally meant "foolish" or "ignorant," but over the centuries it lost its derogatory connotations and came to mean "amusing" or* "pleasant." However, the wheel comes full circle, and the word is now used as an expression of contempt. The proverb comes from Shakespeare's play *King Lear* (5:3; 1605), "The wheel is come full circle: I am here."

the wheel of fortune is forever in motion People's fortunes are constantly changing—somebody who has good luck one year may have bad luck the next, and vice versa: *It seemed that nothing could go wrong, but the wheel of fortune is forever in motion, and disaster struck the following day.* The proverb was first recorded in 1748 in *Papers of Benjamin Franklin.*

the wheel that does the squeaking is the one that gets the grease *See* THE SQUEAKY WHEEL GETS THE GREASE.

when Adam delved and Eve span, who was then the gentleman? The class system has not always existed and is therefore invalid or irrelevant: "'On what grounds do they hold us in vassalage? Do not we all come from the same father and mother, Adam and Eve?' The spirit of individual freedom breathed itself out in the effective rhyme, which ran like wildfire, 'When Adam delved and Eve span/Who was then the gentleman?'" (Philip Schaff, *History of the Christian Church,* 1883–1893). The proverb was first recorded c. 1340 in the form "When Adam delved and Eve span, where was then the pride of man?" (The word *delved* is archaic for "dug" and "span" the archaic past tense of *spin.*) It was associated with the period of social unrest in England that culminated in the Peasants' Revolt (1381).

Proverb expressing similar meaning: JACK'S AS GOOD AS HIS MASTER.

when a dog bites a man, that is not news; but when a man bites a dog, that is news The media are only interested in unusual or outrageous stories: *Needless to say, the photos that appeared in all the papers the following day were not of the president making his historic speech, but of him falling down the steps as he left the stage afterward. When a dog bites a man, that is not news; but when a man bites a dog, that is news.* The proverb was first recorded c. 1880, by John B. Bogart in *The New York Sun.*

when all fruit fails, welcome haws We must accept with gratitude whatever is available, even if it is not exactly what we want or need: "So even the excommunicated will do, when it's not easy to get anyone else. When all fruit fails, welcome haws" (Brendan Behan, *Borstal Boy,* 1958). The proverb was first recorded in 1721 in James Kelly, *Scottish Proverbs.* The haw is the berry of the hawthorn: When there is no fruit generally, even hawthorn berries are to be gladly received.

Proverb expressing similar meaning: BEGGARS CAN'T BE CHOOSERS.

when all you have is a hammer, everything looks like a nail People with a restricted range of knowledge or options often try to apply the same solution to every problem: "That kind of crude misapplication of PCs and PC software—the computer world's equivalent of the old saw that 'when all you have is a hammer, everything starts to look like a nail'—means death for productivity" (*PC Magazine,* 1989). The proverb was first recorded in 1981 in the *New York Times.*

when a man's single, his pockets will jingle
Unmarried men have more money than those who have a wife and family to support: *When a man's single, his pockets will jingle, but money isn't everything, and a bachelor's life can be a lonely one.*

when Greek meets Greek, then comes the tug of war
A contest or struggle between equally matched opponents is a long and fierce battle: *There is no prospect of an early end to the dispute, both sides having considerable support from different sectors of the general public—when Greek meets Greek, then comes the tug of war.* The proverb comes from Nathaniel Lee's play *The Rival Queens* (1477), about the latter years of Alexander the Great: "When Greeks joined Greeks, then was the tug of war!"

when house and land are gone and spent, then learning is most excellent
It is important to have a good education to fall back on if you lose or use up all your money and material assets: *My earnings as a child model had provided me with at very comfortable nest egg, but my parents urged me not to abandon my studies, on the principle that "When house and land are gone and spent, then learning is most excellent."* The proverb was first recorded in 1752 in S. Foote's *Taste.*

Proverb expressing similar meaning: LEARNING IS BETTER THAN HOUSE OR LAND.

when in doubt, do nothing
If you are unsure what to do, it is best to do nothing at all: *I thought I heard a scream, and wondered if I should call the police, go and investigate, or follow the age-old wisdom of "When in doubt, do nothing."* The proverb was first recorded in George John Whyte-Melville's novel *Uncle John* (1874): "When

in doubt what to do, he is a wise man who does nothing."

Variant of this proverb: when in doubt, leave it out.

Proverb expressing opposite meaning: BETWEEN TWO STOOLS ONE FALLS TO THE GROUND.

when in Rome, do as the Romans do
You should always follow the customs, rules, and laws of the place where you are: *I don't like kissing total strangers, but in this country it's considered impolite not to, and when in Rome we must do as the Romans do.* The proverb was first recorded c. 1475, but the sentiment it expresses is of much earlier origin, and has been attributed to Saint Ambrose (c. 339–A.D. 97).

Variant of this proverb: when you are at Rome, do as Rome does.

Proverb expressing similar meaning: SO MANY COUNTRIES, SO MANY CUSTOMS.

when one door closes, another one opens
Disappointment or failure is usually followed by a new opportunity: *I didn't get a part in the musical, but the next day's mail brought an offer of a recording contract—when one door closes, another one opens.* The proverb was first recorded in 1586 in D. Rowland's *Lazarillo.*

Variant of this proverb: WHEN ONE DOOR SHUTS, ANOTHER OPENS.

when poverty comes in at the door, love flies out of the window
Financial problems can cause the breakdown of a marriage or other loving relationship: *They lived together for five blissfully happy years, until their money ran out. Then they began to learn the truth of the proverb "When poverty comes in at the door, love flies out of the window."* The proverb was first recorded

in 1631, in R. Brathwait's *English Gentle-woman:* "It hath been an old Maxime: that as pouerty goes in at one doore, loue goes out at the other."

Variant of this proverb: when the wolf comes in at the door, love creeps out of the window.

when the cat's away, the mice will play People do as they please in the absence of those in authority: "Monsieur Grandet entered the room, threw his keen eye upon the table, upon Charles, and saw the whole thing. 'Ha! ha! so you have been making a feast for your nephew; very good, very good, very good indeed!' he said. . . . 'When the cat's away, the mice will play'" (Honoré de Balzac, *Eugenie Grandet,* 1833). The proverb was first recorded in 1607, but with the implication that it had long been in use. There is evidence of a French version, "*Ou chat na rat regne* [Where there is no cat, the rat reigns]," in the early 14th century.

when the going gets tough, the tough get going In times of crisis, those who are most resilient and determined take action and prove their worth: *You give up far too easily—have you never heard the saying "When the going gets tough, the tough get going"?* The proverb is attributed to the United States businessman and diplomat Joseph P. Kennedy (1888–1969), father of President John F. Kennedy. It is sometimes used facetiously to convey the opposite meaning, with *get going* in the sense of "run away."

Proverb expressing similar meaning: CALAMITY IS THE TOUCHSTONE OF A BRAVE MIND.

when the wind is in the east, 'tis neither good for man nor beast An easterly wind, which is often piercing and cold, is the worst of all: "When the wind's in the East, It's neither good for man nor beast . . . The East-wind with us is commonly very sharp, because it comes off the Continent" (John Ray, *A Collection of English Proverbs,* 1670). The proverb was first recorded in 1600 in R. Cawdrey's *Treasury of Similes.*

when the wine is in, the wit is out People say foolish things when they are drunk: *"You were talking nonsense at the dinner table last night." "Well, you know what they say—when the wine is in, the wit is out."* The proverb was first recorded c. 1390 in John Gower's *Confessio Amantis.*

when the wolf comes in at the door, love creeps out of the window See WHEN POVERTY COMES IN AT THE DOOR, LOVE FLIES OUT OF THE WINDOW.

when the worst comes, the worst is going See WHEN THINGS ARE AT THE WORST THEY BEGIN TO MEND.

when thieves fall out, honest men come by their own A dispute between criminals is to the advantage of their victims, either because they betray one another and reveal the truth, or because they are too busy arguing to commit the crime in the first place: *When thieves fall out, honest men come by their own—dissension within the gang led to one of their members making a full confession, and ultimately to the release of my brother, who had been wrongfully convicted of the crime.* The proverb was first recorded in 1546.

Variant of this proverb: when thieves fall out, honest men get their due.

when things are at the worst they begin to mend When things cannot get any worse, they begin to get better: "'I have heard about it, miss,' said Dolly, 'and it's very sad indeed, but when things are at the worst they are sure to mend.' 'But are you sure they are at the worst?' asked Emma with a smile. 'Why, I don't see how they can very well be more unpromising than they are; I really don't,' said Dolly" (Charles Dickens, *Barnaby Rudge*, 1841). The proverb was first recorded in 1582 in G. Whetstone's *Heptameron of Civil Discourses*.

Variant of this proverb: when the worst comes, the worst is going.

Proverbs expressing similar meaning: AFTER A STORM COMES A CALM; THE DARKEST HOUR IS JUST BEFORE DAWN.

when two ride one horse, one must sit behind *See* IF TWO RIDE ON A HORSE, ONE MUST RIDE BEHIND.

when you are at Rome, do as Rome does *See* WHEN IN ROME, DO AS THE ROMANS DO.

when you are in a hole, stop digging When you have landed yourself in trouble, such as through a foolish remark or action, do not say or do anything to make the situation worse: "Until now the president has ignored the first law of politics: When you get yourself in a hole, stop digging" (*Houston Chronicle*, 1993). First recorded in 1988, the proverb is attributed to the British politician Denis Healey (1917–).

when you argue with a fool, make sure he isn't similarly engaged Do not assume that you are more intelligent or knowledgeable than the person you are arguing with: *It is better not to enter into a dispute unless you are certain of the facts—remember* the saying *"When you argue with a fool, make sure he isn't similarly engaged."*

when you go to dance, take heed whom you take by the hand Beware of getting involved with dishonest or unscrupulous people: *It may sound like an unmissable business opportunity, but make sure this guy is on the level before you sign anything. As my grandmother used to say, "When you go to dance, take heed whom you take by the hand."* The proverb was first recorded in 1621 in Bartholomew Robinson's *Adagia in Latin and English*.

where bees are, there is honey Wherever there are industrious people, wealth is produced; also used of other types of people whose presence is indicative or suggestive of something: *The company has done well not through good fortune, but through the hard work of everybody involved—where bees are, there is honey.* The proverb was first recorded in 1616 in T. Draxe's *Adages*.

Variant of this proverb: where there are bees, there is honey.

where God builds a church, the devil will build a chapel Any force for good, such as progress or reform, is inevitably accompanied—or closely followed—by something bad; not exclusively used in religious contexts: "But, human sin and imperfection enter into all great movements of history. Wherever God builds a church, the Devil is sure to build a chapel close by" (Philip Schaff, *History of the Christian Church, 1883–1893*). The proverb was first recorded in 1560. In his satirical poem "The True-Born Englishman" (1701), Daniel Defoe wrote, "Wherever God erects a House of Prayer,/The Devil always builds a Chapel there:/And 'twill be found upon Examination,/The latter has the largest congregation."

Variant of this proverb: where God has a church, the devil has a chapel.

where ignorance is bliss, 'tis folly to be wise   *See* IGNORANCE IS BLISS.

where the carcass is, there will the eagles be gathered   People are drawn together, or to a particular place, when they think they will gain something to their advantage: "he explained his appearance at the inquest on the twin lines of busman's holiday and that where the carcass is there will the vultures be gathered together" (Christopher Bush, *The Perfect Murder Case,* 1929). The proverb is of biblical origin: "For wheresoever the carcase is, there will the eagles be gathered together" (Matthew 24:28). The word *eagles* is sometimes replaced by *vultures,* as in the quotation.

where there are bees, there is honey   *See* WHERE BEES ARE, THERE IS HONEY.

where there's a will there's a way   If you are sufficiently determined to achieve something, then you will find a way of doing so: *It won't be an easy task, but where there's a will there's a way.* The proverb was first recorded in 1640 in the form "To him that will, ways are not wanting." The U.S. writer Ambrose Bierce parodied the proverb in his *Devil's Dictionary* (1911): "Where there's a will there's a won't." Other facetious variants, punning on the word *will,* include "Where there's a will there's a lawsuit" and "Where there's a will there's a relatives."

Proverbs expressing similar meaning: HE WHO WILLS THE END, WILLS THE MEANS; NOTHING IS IMPOSSIBLE TO A WILLING HEART.

where there's life there's hope   *See* WHILE THERE'S LIFE THERE'S HOPE.

where there's muck there's brass   There is often money to be made wherever there is muck or dirt of some kind: *It may be surprising to many to learn that there are millionaires in the refuse-disposal business, but where there's muck there's brass.* The proverb was first recorded in 1678 in John Ray's *A Collection of English Proverbs.*

Variant of this proverb: where there's muck there's money.

where there's no vision, the people perish   People need hopes and dreams to sustain them: "I hope no one ever tries to raise a child without a vision. I hope nobody ever starts a business or plants a crop in the ground without a vision. For where there is no vision, the people perish" (Bill Clinton, *New York Times,* 1992). The proverb is of biblical origin: "Where there is no vision, the people perish: but he that keepeth the law, happy is he" (Proverbs 29:18).

where there's smoke, there's fire   *See* THERE'S NO SMOKE WITHOUT FIRE.

where the tree falls, there it shall lie   *See* AS A TREE FALLS, SO SHALL IT LIE.

which came first, the chicken or the egg?   It is sometimes difficult to distinguish between cause and effect: *Which came first, the chicken or the egg? Did the town develop because of the railroad, or was the railroad brought here because it was a developing town?*

while the grass grows, the steed starves   If somebody has to wait a long time for something, it may arrive too late to be of use: "I shall sell them next year fast enough, after my one-man-show; but while the grass grows the steed starves" (George Bernard Shaw, *The Doctor's Dilemma,* 1906). The proverb was first recorded c. 1350 in the form "While the grass grows, the good horse starves." It occurs in Shakespeare's play *Hamlet* (3:2; 1600–01), in an exchange between Hamlet and Rosencrantz: "'Sir, I lack advancement.' 'How can that be when you have the voice of the King himself for your succession in Denmark?' 'Ay, sir, but "While the grass grows . . ."'—the proverb is something musty.'"

Variant of this proverb: while the grass grows, the horse starves.

while there's life there's hope   Do not give up hope while there is the remotest possibility of survival, improvement, or success: "I will be pleasantly surprised if corporate America acts on your 'wake-up call'—but where there's life there's hope" (*Washington Times,* 1996). First recorded in English in 1539, the proverb is of ancient origin, occurring in the writings of Cicero (106–43 B.C.): "*dum anima est spes esse dicitur* [as the saying is, while there's life there's hope]."

Variant of this proverb: where there's life there's hope.

Proverb expressing similar meaning: NEVER SAY DIE.

while two dogs are fighting for a bone, a third runs away with it   When two parties are engaged in a dispute, their attention is distracted from what is going on around them, and both may end up as losers: *The larger suppliers were so busy trying to underbid each other for the contract, they failed to notice that their customer had entered into negotiations with another smaller company—while two dogs are fighting for a bone, a third runs away with it.* The proverb was first recorded in this form in 1639, but the sentiment it expresses is of earlier origin, occurring in Chaucer's *Canterbury Tales* (c. 1390).

Variant of this proverb: two dogs fight over a bone while a third runs away with it.

whiskey and gasoline don't mix   Do not drive an automobile after drinking alcohol: *The tables have been turned, and young people are now warning their parents that whiskey and gasoline don't mix.*

Variant of this proverb: gasoline and whiskey don't mix.

a whistling woman and a crowing hen are neither fit for God nor men   Females should not do things that are traditionally associated with males—it is men who whistle and cocks that crow, not women and hens; also interpreted more literally: *Whistling softly to herself as she went about her work, she became aware that her grandfather was looking at her with stern disapproval. "A whistling woman and a crowing hen are neither fit for God nor men," he snapped.* The proverb was first recorded in this form in 1850, but the sentiment it expresses is of earlier origin.

Variant of this proverb: a whistling girl and a crowing hen always come to the same bad end.

a white wall is the fool's writing paper   Only foolish people write on walls: *It is said that a white wall is the fool's writing paper, but there are occasional nug-*

gets of wisdom to be found in the graffiti that adorns the walls of the college lavatories. The proverb was first recorded in 1573 in James Sanford's *The Garden of Pleasure.*

who excuses himself accuses himself *See* HE WHO EXCUSES HIMSELF ACCUSES HIMSELF.

who has land has war There will always be disputes over the ownership of land; also used of larger territorial disputes: *The saying "Who has land has war" is quite true—I've lost thousands of dollars in legal battles since I bought this ranch.* The proverb was first recorded in 1579, but with the implication that it was already in common use.

who knows most, speaks least Wise or knowledgeable people say little: *Don't be misled by her reserved manner—who knows most, speaks least.* The proverb was first recorded in 1666, in an Italian proverb collection.

Proverb expressing similar meaning: THOSE WHO KNOW DON'T SPEAK; THOSE WHO SPEAK DON'T KNOW.

whom the gods love die young Premature death is a sign that somebody is worthy of divine favor because of great talent or virtue; also used to imply that it is better not to live long: "Thrice fortunate! who of that fragile mould,/The precious porcelain of human clay,/Break with the first fall . . ./'Whom the gods love die young,' was said of yore,/And many deaths do they escape by this:/The death of friends, and that which slays even more—/The death of friendship, love, youth, all that is" (Lord Byron, *Don*

Juan, 1819). The proverb is of ancient origin, occurring in the writings of the Greek poet and dramatist Menander (c. 342–292 B.C.).

Proverbs expressing similar meaning: GOD TAKES SOONEST THOSE HE LOVETH BEST; THE GOOD DIE YOUNG.

whom the gods would destroy, they first make mad Those who commit acts of great folly are heading for disaster, the implication being that such people lose their sanity or good sense because they are destined for this end: *The company's decision to pull out of such a lucrative market was nothing short of lunacy, but whom the gods would destroy they first make mad.* The sentiment expressed by the proverb is of ancient origin. The critic Cyril Connolly parodied the proverb in *Enemies of Promise* (1938): "Whom the gods wish to destroy they first call promising."

who repairs not his gutters repairs his whole house Those who neglect small repairs will find they have to make much bigger ones later: *It is easy to put aside routine maintenance jobs, but he who repairs not his gutters repairs his whole house.* The proverb was first recorded in 1849 in John Ruskin's *The Seven Lamps of Architecture.*

Variant of this proverb: he that repairs not a part, builds all.

Proverbs expressing similar meaning: AN OUNCE OF PREVENTION IS WORTH A POUND OF CURE; PREVENTION IS BETTER THAN CURE; A STITCH IN TIME SAVES NINE.

who says A must say B If you say or do one thing, you must be prepared to say or do what logically follows: "But who says 'A' must say 'B.' . . . You can't talk about victims and caring and knowing cows individually while, at the same time, you treat carrots as nobodies!" (*Washington Times,* 1988). The proverb was first recorded in 1838 in the form "If you say A, they'll make you say B."

Variant of this proverb: never say A without saying B.

whose bread I eat, his song I sing   People show loyalty to, or comply with the demands of, those who employ, pay, or feed them: *Unsurprisingly, her views on the subject are the same as those already expressed by her sponsors—whose bread I eat, his song I sing.*

Proverb expressing similar meaning: HE WHO PAYS THE PIPER CALLS THE TUNE.

whosoever draws his sword against the prince must throw the scabbard away   Those who overthrow a ruler or government must be constantly ready to defend themselves against a retaliatory or counterrevolutionary act: *The rebels will never be able to live in peace—whosoever draws his sword against the prince must throw the scabbard away.* The proverb was first recorded in 1604 in R. Dallington's *View of France.*

who won't be ruled by the rudder must be ruled by the rock   Those who refuse to be guided by reason, advice, or instructions are heading for disaster: *They ignored all our warnings, and now they must face the consequences—who won't be ruled by the rudder must be ruled by the rock.* The proverb was first recorded in 1666, in an Italian proverb collection.

why buy the cow when you can get the milk for free?   There is no point in taking on the expense and responsibility of a wife and family when you can fulfill your sexual and other needs through casual relationships; also used in other contexts: *Jack has no shortage of girlfriends, but he has no plans to marry any of them. As he says, "Why buy a cow when you can get the milk for free?"* The proverb was first recorded, with different wording, in 1659 in James Howell, *Proverbs.*

Variant of this proverb: why buy the cow when milk is so cheap?

why keep a dog and bark yourself?   If you employ somebody to do something for you, there is no point in doing it yourself: *I don't add up the figures—that's my accountant's job. Why keep a dog and bark yourself?* The proverb was first recorded in 1583 in B. Melbancke's *Philotimus.*

Proverb expressing opposite meaning: IF YOU WOULD BE WELL SERVED, SERVE YOURSELF.

why should the devil have all the best tunes?   Secular songs often have more catchy melodies than traditional religious music; used as justification for making hymn tunes more acceptable to popular taste: "The Primitive Methodists . . . acting upon the principle of 'Why should the devil have all the pretty tunes?' collect the airs which are sung at pot and public houses, and write their hymns to them" (William Chappell, *Popular Music of the Olden Time,* 1859). The quotation is the first recorded use of the proverb, which is attributed to the British evangelist Rowland Hill (1744–1833).

a willful man must have his way   Stubborn people will do as they please, so there is no point in arguing with them: *I have tried to persuade my father to come* *and live with us, but I seem to be wasting my breath—a willful man must have his way.* The proverb was first recorded in 1816, in Sir Walter Scott's novel *The Antiquary.*

willful waste makes woeful want Reckless extravagance leads to dire need: "Now young folks go off to Paris, and think nothing of the cost: and it's well if wilful waste don't make woeful want before they die" (Elizabeth Gaskell, *Wives and Daughters,* 1866). The proverb was first recorded in this form in 1721, but the sentiment it expresses is of earlier origin.

Proverb expressing similar meaning: WASTE NOT, WANT NOT.

the willing horse carries the load People tend to take advantage of those who never complain or refuse: *The willing horse carries the load, and she often finds herself working several hours a week longer than her less obliging colleagues.* The proverb was first recorded, with different wording, in 1546 in John Heywood's *Dialogue of Proverbs.*

Variant of this proverb: all lay loads on the willing horse.

wine has drowned more men than the sea Overindulgence in alcohol can be fatal: *If you must drink, do so in moderation—wine has drowned more men than the sea.* The proverb was first recorded in 1669 in *Politeuphuia.*

wink at small faults Let trivial offenses go unpunished. The proverb was first recorded c. 1598 in William Shakespeare's *Henry V* (2:2): "If little faults . . . shall not be wink'd at, how shall we stretch our eye when capital crimes . . . appear before us?"

a winner never quits, and a quitter never wins You need determination and perseverance if you want to succeed: *I urged her not to give up, reminding her of the saying "A winner never quits, and a quitter never wins."*

the winners laugh, the losers weep *See* LET THEM LAUGH THAT WIN.

winning isn't everything, it's the only thing In any competitive situation, winning is the only thing that matters; sometimes said in response to the remark "Winning isn't everything," or used to encourage single-mindedness in sportspeople: *She was one of those ambitious young lawyers for whom winning isn't everything, it's the only thing.* The proverb was first recorded in 1953. It is often attributed to the U.S. football coach Vince Lombardi, who made a similar remark in 1962.

Proverb expressing opposite meaning: IT'S NOT WHETHER YOU WIN OR LOSE, BUT HOW YOU PLAY THE GAME.

winter finds out what summer lays up When things go awry, that is the time when the extent of any resources is tested: "Winter draws out what summer laid in" (Thomas Fuller, *Gnomologia,* 1732). The proverb was first recorded c. 1460 in *Good Wyf wold a Pylgremage.*

wisdom goes beyond strength Intelligence always outmatches brute strength: *David's victory over Goliath merely illustrates the truth behind the maxim "wisdom goes beyond strength."* The proverb was first recorded in 1616 in T. Draxe's *Bibliotheca Scholastica.*

Variant of this proverb: use brains not brawn.

wisdom is better than rubies Wisdom is a highly desirable and very precious attribute, more valuable than riches: *My father was not a wealthy man, but he was very wise, and wisdom is better than rubies.* The proverb is of biblical origin: "For wisdom is better than rubies; and all the things that may be desired are not to be compared to it" (Proverbs 8:11).

Variant of this proverb: wisdom is better than wealth.

a wise lawyer never goes to law himself Those who practice the law and understand the costs involved know better than to rely upon it themselves. The proverb was first recorded in 1642 in G. Torriano's *Select Italian Proverbs.*

a wise man changes his mind, but a fool never does It is foolish to persist in the same opinion or course of action regardless of new information or different circumstances: *Accused of making a U-turn in policy, the mayor calmly replied, "A wise man changes his mind, but a fool never does."* The sentiment expressed by the proverb occurs in Chaucer's *Canterbury Tales* (c. 1390): "No folie to chaunge counseil whan the thyng is chaunged."

a wise man is never less alone than when alone An intelligent person has his or her own thoughts for company: *She did not worry about leaving the professor on his own, for he had often told her that a wise man is never less alone than when alone.* The proverb was first recorded in English in 1581 in George Pettie's *Guazzo's Civil Conversation* but is of much older, Roman origin and is sometimes attributed to Scipio Africanus the Elder or otherwise to Themistocles.

wise men learn by other men's mistakes, fools by their own *See* LEARN FROM THE MISTAKES OF OTHERS.

wishes won't wash dishes Merely wishing that something was done is not enough to get it done. The proverb appears to be a relatively recent U.S. introduction dating from the 20th century, although similar sentiments have been expressed in variant forms since the 17th century.

Variant of this proverb: wishes never can fill a sack.

Proverb expressing similar meaning: IF WISHES WERE HORSES, BEGGARS WOULD RIDE.

the wish is father to the thought Our beliefs and expectations are influenced by what we want or hope to be true: *I think she's looking better this morning, but perhaps the wish is father to the thought.* The proverb comes from Shakespeare's play *Henry IV, Part 2* (4:5), "Thy wish was father, Harry, to that thought."

with age comes wisdom People become more sensible and knowledgeable as they get older: *With age comes wisdom, which is perhaps why older drivers have few accidents.* The proverb was first recorded in 1523 in Erasmus's *Adagia.*

Proverbs expressing similar meaning: AN OLD FOX IS NOT EASILY SNARED; TIME IS THE RIDER THAT BREAKS YOUTH.

with friends like that, who needs enemies? Treacherous or disloyal friends are worse than enemies: *It was one of his so-called friends who reported him to the police—with friends like that, who needs enemies?* The proverb was dates from the early 20th century.

Variant of this proverb: with such friends, one hardly needs enemies.

Proverb expressing similar meaning: SAVE US FROM OUR FRIENDS.

a woman's work is never done The household tasks traditionally assigned to women—cooking, cleaning, and so on—seem endless because they are repeated day after day: *I was still ironing at midnight—a woman's work is never done!* The proverb was first recorded in Thomas Tusser's *Hundred Good Points of Husbandry* (1570) in the form "Some respite to husbands the weather doth send, but huswives affaires have never none ende."

Variant of this proverb: man's work lasts till set of sun, woman's work is never done.

a wonder lasts but nine days Sensational events are usually entirely forgotten after a short time: "These few days' wonder will be quickly worn" (William Shakespeare, *Henry VI (2:1)*). The proverb was first recorded c. 1374 in Geoffrey Chaucer's *Troilus and Criseyde*. The proverb is often referred to in the abbreviated form "a nine-day wonder."

wonders will never cease! Amazing things are constantly happening; often used ironically: *I hear she actually admitted that she had made a mistake—wonders will never cease!* The proverb was first recorded in 1776 in T. Boaden's *Private Correspondence of D. Garrick*.

Variant of this proverb: wonders never cease!

Proverb expressing opposite meaning: the age of miracles is past.

a word is enough to the wise *See* A WORD TO THE WISE IS SUFFICIENT.

a word spoken is past recalling You cannot take back what you have said, so think carefully before speaking: *I immediately regretted making such a hurtful remark, but a word spoken is past recalling.* The proverb was first recorded in 1509 in the form "A word once spoken cannot be revoked," but the sentiment it expresses is of ancient origin.

Variant of this proverb: words once spoken you can never recall. Proverb expressing similar meaning: THINK BEFORE YOU SPEAK.

a word to the wise is sufficient It is not necessary to explain things in detail to intelligent people; often used when dropping a subtle hint or making a cryptic remark: *He mentioned that four of the company's directors had just resigned, and a word to the wise is sufficient—I'm going to invest my money elsewhere.* The proverb is sometimes quoted in its Latin form, *"Verbum sapienti sat est,"* often shortened to *"verb. sap."* It was first recorded in English, with different wording, in 1570.

Variant of this proverb: a word is enough to the wise.

Proverb expressing similar meaning: A NOD'S AS GOOD AS A WINK TO A BLIND HORSE.

work before play Tasks and chores must be completed before we can relax and enjoy ourselves: *Work before play—you're not going anywhere until all these dishes are washed and dried!*

Proverb expressing similar meaning: BUSINESS BEFORE PLEASURE.

work expands so as to fill the time available for its completion Any task, however small, will use up all the time available for it, because it is done more slowly than necessary, or because it gives rise to extra work: *"I can't believe it took you all afternoon to write one letter." "Well, I didn't have anything else to do, and work expands to fill the time available."* The proverb is known as Parkinson's Law, named for the British historian C. Northcote Parkinson (1909–93), who coined it in 1955. A similar observation has been made about the tendency of objects to multiply until they occupy all the available space.

work never hurt anybody   Work will not do you any harm, and may do you some good; often said to those who are idle or lazy: *When I complained to my son's employer about the long hours he was expected to do, I got the curt reply, "Work never hurt anybody."* The proverb was first recorded in 1879 in Dinah Maria Mulock's *Young Mrs. Jardine.*

Variant of this proverb: hard work never hurt anybody.

the world is a stage and all the people in it actors   *See* ALL THE WORLD'S A STAGE.

the world runs on wheels   Daily events are unceasing and happen at a rapid pace: "The world runs all on wheels. All things therein move without intermission" (John Florio, translation of *Montaigne,* 1603). The proverb was first recorded in 1546 in John Heywood's *A Dialogue containing . . . the Proverbs in the English Tongue.*

the worm will turn   *See* EVEN A WORM WILL TURN.

worry is interest paid on trouble before it falls due   Do not add to the stress of everyday life by worrying about the future: *You won't catch me losing sleep over problems that may never happen—worry is interest paid on trouble before it falls due.* The proverb was first recorded in 1924 in *Judge Magazine.*

worry kills more men than work   *See* IT'S NOT WORK THAT KILLS, BUT WORRY.

worse things happen at sea   This present misfortune, though regrettable, could have been worse: *We shall have to give the show a miss, but never mind, worse things happen at sea.* The proverb was first recorded in 1869 in Charles Spurgeon's *John Ploughman's Talk.* The proverb has long since acquired the status of a cliché.

Proverbs expressing similar meaning: INTO EVERY LIFE A LITTLE RAIN MUST FALL; IT'S AN ILL WIND THAT BLOWS NOBODY ANY GOOD.

the worst is yet to come   Things are not as bad as they can and will be: *The mild weather we have been enjoying for the past few days does not mean winter is over—meteorologists are warning that the worst is yet to come.* The proverb was first recorded in Tennyson's poem "Sea Dreams" (1860): "His deeds yet live, the worst is yet to come. / Yet let your sleep for this one night be sound: / I do forgive him!"

Proverb expressing opposite meaning: THE BEST IS YET TO BE.

the worth of a thing is what it will bring   A thing is worth no more than somebody is willing to pay for it: *She claimed that the painting was worth $100,000, but the worth of a thing is what it will bring, and it has just been sold at auction*

for less than half that figure. The proverb is of Latin or French origin in the form "A thing is worth as much as it can be sold for." A rhyming version closer to the current form occurs in Samuel Butler's poem *Hudibras* (1664): "For what is worth in any thing,/But so much money as 'twill bring?"

years know more than books Experience is more valuable than academic education: *"Years know more than books,"* *said the old man, tapping the side of his nose.* The proverb was first recorded in George Herbert, *Outlandish Proverbs* (1640).

Proverb expressing similar meaning: EXPERIENCE IS THE BEST TEACHER; AN

YIDDISH PROVERBS

Yiddish proverbs rank among the most humorous and inventive anywhere in the world and have a unique worldly wise flavor. Typical subjects include food, health, money, and death.

A man should stay alive if only out of curiosity

An imaginary ailment is worse than a disease

Better ten times ill than one time dead

Better the best of the worst than the worst of the best

Better to hear curses than to be pitied

A clock that stands still is better than one that goes wrong

Every man knows that he must die, but no one believes it

Every pot will find its lid

Experience costs blood

God sends burdens, and shoulders

Health? Very nice! But where will we get potatoes?

He that lies on the ground cannot fall

He who has children will never die of starvation

If you eat your bagel you will have nothing in your pocket but the hole

If you stay at home you won't wear out your shoes

If you want your dreams to come true, don't sleep

Money buys everything but good sense

One does not live on joy or die of sorrow

Sleep faster—we need the pillows

When a thief kisses you, count your teeth

With money in your pocket, you are wise, handsome, and you sing well too

OUNCE OF PRACTICE IS WORTH A POUND OF PRECEPT.

yesterday will not be called again   It is impossible to relive the past: "Well, well (quoth she) what ever ye now saie, it is too late to call again yesterdaie" (J. Heywood, *A Dialogue containing . . . the Proverbs in the English Tongue*, 1546). The proverb was first recorded in John Skelton, *Magnyfycence* (1516).

Variant of this proverb: no man can call again yesterday.

Proverbs expressing similar meaning: THE MILL CANNOT GRIND WITH THE WATER THAT IS PAST; TIME LOST CANNOT BE RECALLED.

you are what you eat   Your diet affects your physical and mental well-being; often used to promote health food or to condemn junk food: "If you are what you eat, the survivor of tonight's world heavyweight championship fight will have been nourished either by sandwiches or seaweed" (*New York Times,* 1992). The proverb may be of German origin, but the sentiment it expresses occurs in the French gastronome Anthelme Brillat-Savarin's *Physiologie du Goût* (1825): "*Dis-moi ce que tu manges, je te dirai ce que tu es* [Tell me what you eat, and I will tell you what you are]."

you buy land, you buy stones; you buy meat, you buy bones   When you buy something, you must accept any undesirable elements that come with it: *In the past, customers did not object to paying for the lumps of earth that clung to the fresh vegetables sold on market stalls, on the principle that "You buy land, you buy stones; you buy meat, you buy bones."* The proverb was first

recorded in 1670 in John Ray's *A Collection of English Proverbs.*

you can catch more flies with honey than with vinegar   A polite or pleasant approach is more effective than rudeness or unpleasantness in dealing with people; sometimes used to recommend ingratiating behavior: "Ask his advice frequently, and thank him profusely for his wisdom and guidance. Remember that old adage 'You can catch more flies with honey than with vinegar'" (*Washington Post,* 1996). The proverb was first recorded in 1666 in G. Torriano's *Italian Proverbs.* The word *honey* is sometimes replaced by *sugar* or *molasses.*

Variant of this proverb: honey catches more flies than vinegar.

you can drive out nature with a pitchfork but she keeps on coming back   It is impossible to change your own or another person's character permanently, however hard you try; also used of attempts to change aspects of the natural world: *The saying "You can drive out nature with a pitchfork but she keeps on coming back" was never truer than in its horticultural sense, as any gardener who has done battle with a well-established weed will tell you.* The proverb originated in the writings of the Roman poet Horace (65–8 B.C.).

Variant of this proverb: drive nature out of the door and it will return by the window.

Proverb expressing similar meaning: THE LEOPARD CAN'T CHANGE ITS SPOTS.

you can fool some of the people all of the time, and all of the people some of the time, but you can't fool all of the people all of the time   It is impossible to maintain a deception that will convince everybody: *A few gullible people were taken in, but most soon realized that he was an impostor—you can fool some of the people all of the time, and all of the people some of the time, but you cannot fool all of the people all of the time.* The proverb is attributed to Abraham Lincoln in its current form, but the sentiment it expresses is of ancient origin.

you can have too much of a good thing An excess of anything, however desirable or beneficial it may be, is not good: "Modern liberals feel that a more tolerant society is a good thing, and they are right. Yet, it is possible to have too much of a good thing" (*Washington Post*, 1995). The proverb was first recorded in 1611, but the sentiment it expresses is of earlier origin. In Shakespeare's play *As You Like It* (4:1), Rosalind asks, "Why then, can one desire too much of a good thing?" The proverb is sometimes used in its opposite form, as in the following quotation from Casanova's *Memoirs* (1828–38): "I promised to tell my tale if he thought it would not weary him, warning him that it would take two hours. 'One could never have too much of a good thing,' he was kind enough to say."

Variant of this proverb: too much of a good thing is worse than none at all.

you can lead a horse to water, but you can't make him drink You can give somebody the opportunity to do something, but you cannot force him or her to do it: "If he is very strongly set against the work, perhaps it is better that he should take the opportunity there is now to break his articles . . . as you know you can take a horse to the water, but you can't make him drink" (W. Somerset Maugham, *Of Human Bondage,* 1915). The

proverb was first recorded c. 1175 in *Old English Homilies*. The journalist Dorothy Parker (1893–1967), asked to make up a sentence containing the word *horticulture,* is said to have punningly replied, "You can lead a horticulture, but you can't make her think."

Variant of this proverb: you can take a horse to the water, but you can't make him drink.

you can only die once Death may be a frightening and unpleasant prospect or experience, but we can console ourselves with the fact that it will never be repeated; a fatalistic attitude, as in a life-threatening situation: *I know it's a dangerous pastime, but you can only die once, and nothing can beat the thrill of hurtling down an almost vertical slope at more than 100 m.p.h.* The proverb was first recorded c. 1435. It occurs in Shakespeare's play *Henry IV, Part 2* (3:2; 1597) in the form "A man can die but once."

you can run, but you can't hide It is impossible to evade capture, or some other undesirable experience, forever: *They'll have to face the consequences of their actions sooner or later—you can run, but you can't hide.* The proverb is attributed to the U.S. boxer Joe Louis (1914–81), who is said to have remarked, with reference to the speed and agility of his opponent Billy Conn, "He can run, but he can't hide."

you can take a horse to the water, but you can't make him drink *See* YOU CAN LEAD A HORSE TO WATER, BUT YOU CAN'T MAKE HIM DRINK.

you can take the boy out of the country, but you can't take the country out of the boy People never lose inborn or ingrained characteristics, even after a change of environment or situation: "Back in the good old days, when eager young rubes were descending upon the great metropolises in search of fame and fortune, it used to be said that you can take the boy out of the country but you can't take the country out of the boy" (*Washington Post*, 1987). The proverb was first recorded in 1938. The words *boy* and *country* may be replaced by others, such as *girl* and *city*.

Proverb expressing similar meaning: NATURE PASSES NURTURE.

you can't argue with success Those who succeed must be doing things the right way: *It's a rather unconventional approach, but it works, and you can't argue with success.*

you can't be all things to all men It is impossible to do everything that everybody wants: *Politicians naturally want to win as many votes as possible, but you can't be all things to all men.* The proverb is of biblical origin: "To the weak became I as weak, that I might gain the weak: I am made all things to all men, that I might by all means save some" (1 Corinthians 9:22). It is also used in the form of the figurative phrase *to be all things to all men.*

Proverbs expressing similar meaning: A FRIEND TO ALL IS A FRIEND TO NONE; YOU CAN'T PLEASE EVERYBODY.

you can't beat a man at his own game Do not try to compete with or outdo somebody in his or her own field of activity, especially if you lack experience yourself: *They tried to outwit the fraudsters with trickery, but soon learned that you can't beat a man at his own game.* The proverb was first recorded in 1756. It is more frequently encountered in the form of the figurative phrase *to beat somebody at his or her own game.*

you can't beat somebody with nobody You cannot win, especially in politics, without support: *Both candidates have been canvassing hard, on the basis that you can't beat somebody with nobody.*

you can't be in two places at the same time *See* ONE CANNOT BE IN TWO PLACES AT ONCE.

you can't build a church with stumbling blocks Religion cannot be founded on doubt and uncertainty: *It was questions like these that caused the faith of early believers to waver—you can't build a church with stumbling blocks.*

you can't catch old birds with chaff Experienced people are not easily deceived: *You can't catch old birds with chaff—I've been in this job long enough to know when somebody is trying to pull a fast one.* The proverb was first recorded, with different wording, in 1481 in William Caxton, *Reynard the Fox.*

you can't eat your cake and have it too *See* YOU CAN'T HAVE YOUR CAKE AND EAT IT TOO.

you can't fight City Hall Members of the general public cannot hope to win a dispute or battle with officialdom or bureaucracy: *I thought of making a formal complaint, but there seemed little point—you can't fight City Hall.* The proverb dates from the late 17th century.

you can't fly with one wing *See* A BIRD NEVER FLEW ON ONE WING.

you can't get a quart into a pint pot You cannot fit something into too small a space; also used more generally of any attempt to do the impossible: *I would like to take more warm clothing, but you can't get a quart into a pint pot, and this is the largest suitcase I have.* The proverb was first recorded in 1896.

you can't get blood from a stone It is impossible to get money, help, information, or pity from somebody who is unwilling or unable to give it to you: "Blood cannot be obtained from a stone, neither can anything on account be obtained . . . from Mr. Micawber" (Charles Dickens, *David Copperfield,* 1850). The proverb was first recorded in 1666, in an Italian proverb collection.

Variant of this proverb: you can't get blood from a turnip.

you can't go home again You cannot return to the past as you remember it: *I have such happy memories of the time I spent there, but things are very different now, and you can't go home again.* The proverb was coined by the U.S. novelist Thomas Wolfe as the title of a book published posthumously in 1940.

you can't have it both ways You must choose between two mutually exclusive alternatives: "But you can't have it both ways. Either the much-vaunted 'caring society' is a myth, or a complete change in the value judgements of the people who govern television is needed" (*Glasgow Herald,* 1976). The proverb dates from the early 20th century.

Proverbs expressing similar meaning: A DOOR MUST BE EITHER SHUT OR OPEN; YOU CAN'T HAVE YOUR CAKE AND EAT IT TOO.

you can't have your cake and eat it too You cannot do two mutually incompatible things at the same time: *You can't have your cake and eat it too—if you want your children to lead happy, independent lives you must accept that they will not always be there when you need them.* The proverb was first recorded in 1546 in John Heywood's *Dialogue of Proverbs.*

Variant of this proverb: you can't eat your cake and have it too.

Proverb expressing similar meaning: YOU CAN'T HAVE IT BOTH WAYS.

you can't keep the birds from flying over your head, but you can keep them from building a nest in your hair When bad things happen—as they inevitably will—do not dwell on them or let them get to you: *It was a devastating blow, but I knew that I must pick up the pieces and carry on—you can't keep the birds from flying over your head, but you can keep them from building a nest in your hair.*

you can't lose what you never had Failure to get something you want is not a real loss; also used with reference to the loss of something that somebody only thinks he or she has: "'He has broke all; there's half a line and a good hook lost.' 'I, and a good Trout too.' 'Nay, the Trout is not lost, for . . . no man can lose what he never had'" (Izaak Walton, *The Compleat Angler,* 1676). The proverb was first recorded, with different wording, in Christopher Marlowe's poem *Hero and Leander,* published posthumously in 1598.

Variant of this proverb: you can't lose what you haven't got.

Proverb expressing similar meaning: WHAT YOU'VE NEVER HAD YOU NEVER MISS.

you can't make an omelette without breaking eggs Sacrifices have to be made in order to achieve a goal; often used to justify an act that causes loss, harm, or distress to others: "In war soldiers themselves sometimes cried, and their relations cried quite often. You can't make an omelette without breaking eggs" (L. P. Hartley, *The Hireling,* 1957). Of French origin, the proverb was first recorded in English in 1859.

you can't make a silk purse out of a sow's ear You cannot produce anything of good quality from poor raw material; often used of people: "The proverb says, 'You can't make a silk purse out of a sow's ear.' Well, I don't know about that. I rather think you may, if you begin early in life. She has made a home out of that old boat, sir, that stone and marble couldn't beat' (Charles Dickens, *David Copperfield,* 1850). The proverb was first recorded in 1518 in A. Barclay's *Eclogues:* "None can . . . make goodly silke of a gotes flece [goat's fleece]."

Proverb expressing similar meaning: GARBAGE IN, GARBAGE OUT.

you can't make bricks without straw You cannot produce anything without the necessary materials or resources: "You can only acquire really useful general ideas by first acquiring particular ideas, and putting those particular ideas together. You cannot make bricks without straw" (Arnold Bennett, *Literary Taste,* 1909). The proverb is of biblical origin: "Ye shall no more give the people straw to make brick, as heretofore: let them go and gather straw for themselves" (Exodus 5:7).

you can't mix business and pleasure *See* NEVER MIX BUSINESS WITH PLEASURE.

you can't please everybody It is impossible to do something that everybody will approve of: *If we reduce the fuel taxes we'll upset the environmentalist lobby, but you can't please everybody.* The proverb was first recorded in 1472 in E. Paston's *Letter,* but the sentiment it expresses is of ancient origin

Variants of this proverb: you can't please the whole world and his wife; those who please everybody please nobody.

Proverb expressing similar meaning: YOU CAN'T BE ALL THINGS TO ALL MEN.

you can't put an old head on young shoulders It is unreasonable to expect young people to be as sensible or knowledgeable as their elders: "'This boy will investigate and report to me.' . . . 'Aunt Rachel, you are certainly very eccentric.' 'I may be, but I am not often deceived.' 'Well, I hope you won't be this time. The boy seems to me a very good boy, but you can't put an old head on young shoulders'" (Horatio Alger, *Driven from Home,* 1889). The proverb was first recorded in 1591.

Variant of this proverb: there's no putting old heads on young shoulders.

you can't put a square peg in a round hole Do not give somebody a job for which he or she is unsuited or unqualified; also used of other situations in which a person is a misfit: *There's no point in asking Jack to take over responsibility for the company website—he has no aptitude for or interest in computing, and you can't put a square peg in a round hole.* The proverb was first recorded in the early 19th century. It is more frequently encountered in the form of the cliché *a square peg in a round hole* (or *a round peg in a square hole*).

Variant of this proverb: you can't put a round peg in a square hole.

you can't put new wine in old bottles The introduction of new methods, ideas, items, or components into something old and well established—or old and decrepit—can have disastrous consequences: *You can't put new wine in old bottles, and you can't expect today's software to run on a computer that's been gathering dust in the attic for the last 15 years.* The proverb is of biblical origin: "Neither do men put new wine into old bottles: else the bottles break, and the wine runneth out, and the bottles perish" (Matthew 9:17).

Variant of this proverb: don't put new wine in old bottles.

you can't run with the hare and hunt with the hounds You cannot support two opposing parties at the same time: "'You ought to know best,' he said, 'but if you want a divorce it's not very wise to go seeing her, is it? One can't run with the hare and hunt with the hounds'" (John Galsworthy, *The Forsyte Saga,* 1922). The proverb dates from before 1449. Until the late 19th century it was most frequently used in the form of the figurative phrase *to hold with the hare and run with the hound.*

Proverb expressing similar meaning: NO MAN CAN SERVE TWO MASTERS.

you can't serve God and mammon A devout or virtuous way of life is incompatible with the pursuit of material wealth and possessions: "'He hasn't many friends—been too busy all his life to make any. He's made heaps of money, though.' 'Well, he thought that since he couldn't serve God and Mammon he'd better stick to Mammon. . . . So he shouldn't complain

if he doesn't find Mammon very good company now'" (Lucy Maud Montgomery, *Anne's House of Dreams,* 1917). The proverb is of biblical origin: "No man can serve two masters. . . . Ye cannot serve God and mammon" (Matthew 6:24). *Mammon* means "material wealth or possessions."

Proverb expressing similar meaning: NO MAN CAN SERVE TWO MASTERS.

you can't shift an old tree without it dying Relocation is not good for old people: *We tried to persuade my mother to sell her house and move closer to us, but she refused. "You can't shift an old tree without it dying,"* she said. The proverb was first recorded, with different wording, c. 1518.

Variant of this proverb: old trees can't be transplanted.

you can't step twice into the same river Things are constantly changing: *Some people find change exciting and stimulating, while others find it unsettling and alarming, but the fact remains that you can't step twice into the same river.* The proverb is of ancient origin, occurring in the writings of the Greek philosopher Heraclitus (fifth century B.C.).

you can't take it with you You might as well spend your money while you are alive, because it can't be carried with you into the next world: *He decided to blow the remaining money on a world cruise, on the principle that you can't take it with you.* The proverb was first recorded in 1841.

Variant of this proverb: you can't take it with you when you go.

Proverb expressing similar meaning: SHROUDS HAVE NO POCKETS.

you can't teach an old dog new tricks Old people are often unwilling or unable to learn new skills or adopt new methods: "Since I'm 95 years old, it may be that 'you can't teach an old dog new tricks,' but I'm just not comfortable with new appliances. They make me nervous and . . . never work for me" (*New York Times,* 1989). The proverb was first recorded in 1636, but the sentiment it expresses is of earlier origin.

Variant of this proverb: an old dog will learn no tricks.

Proverb expressing opposite meaning: NEVER TOO OLD TO LEARN.

you can't tell a book by its cover   *See* DON'T JUDGE A BOOK BY ITS COVER.

you can't unscramble eggs   Damage cannot be undone, and changes cannot be reversed: *We must think very carefully before taking such a drastic step—the result could be disastrous, and you can't unscramble eggs.* The proverb is attributed to the U.S. financier and art collector J. Pierpont Morgan (1837–1913).

Variant of this proverb: scrambled eggs can't be unscrambled.

you can't win 'em all   Nobody can hope to succeed every time: *I thought she might be upset to learn that she hadn't got the job, but she just shrugged her shoulders and said, "You can't win 'em all."* The proverb dates from the mid-20th century.

Proverb expressing similar meaning: YOU WIN SOME, YOU LOSE SOME.

you don't get something for nothing   Everything has to be paid for, directly or indirectly, in money or in kind: *You don't get something for nothing—I'll expect you to return the favor one of these days.* The proverb was first recorded in Phineas T. Barnum's

Struggles and Triumphs (1870): "When people expect to get 'something for nothing' they are sure to be cheated." The sentiment it expresses, however is of earlier origin; in his novel *Sybil* (1845), Benjamin Disraeli wrote, "To do nothing and get something formed a boy's ideal of a manly career."

Proverbs expressing similar meaning: NOTHING FOR NOTHING; THERE'S NO SUCH THING AS A FREE LUNCH.

you get nothing for nothing   *See* NOTHING FOR NOTHING.

you get what you pay for   The quality of goods and services is reflected in their price—cheap things are usually inferior and expensive things are usually superior: *He charges more than my last barber, but you get what you pay for, and he cuts my hair well.*

you have to eat a bushel of dirt before you die   *See* WE MUST EAT A PECK OF DIRT BEFORE WE DIE.

you have to learn to crawl before you can walk   *See* WE MUST LEARN TO WALK BEFORE WE CAN RUN.

you have to take the bad with the good   *See* YOU HAVE TO TAKE THE BITTER WITH THE SWEET.

you have to take the bitter with the sweet   You must endure the bad times if you want to enjoy the good times: *In marriage, as in everything else, you have to take the bitter with the sweet.* The proverb was first recorded in 1546, but the sentiment it expresses is of earlier origin, occurring in Alexander Barclay's *The Ship of Fools* (1509): "Take ye in good worth the swetnes with the sour."

Variants of this proverb: always take the bitter with the better; you have to take the bad with the good.

Proverb expressing similar meaning: THERE'S NO ROSE WITHOUT A THORN.

you have to take the rough with the smooth Everything has pleasant and unpleasant—or difficult and easy—aspects: "'Every profession,' I said, 'has got its dirty jobs. . . .' 'And will have,' she said, 'so long as professional men consent to do the dirty work of their employers.' 'And where should I be, I should like to know,' I said, 'if I went on that lay? I've got to take the rough with the smooth.'" (John Galsworthy, *The Freelands*, 1915). The proverb was first recorded c. 1400.

Proverb expressing similar meaning: HE THAT WOULD HAVE EGGS MUST ENDURE THE CACKLING OF HENS.

you'll be damned if you do and damned if you don't In some situations it is impossible to do the right thing, because both of the options open to you will cause trouble or upset: "The toughest question I get is when people ask me what to do with policies of troubled companies. . . . Usually there's a surrender charge involved to get out of the policy, so you're damned if you do and damned if you don't" (*New York Times*, 1994). The proverb comes from Lorenzo Dow's *Reflections on the Love of God* (1836).

you must lose a fly to catch a trout *See* THROW OUT A SPRAT TO CATCH A MACKEREL.

you must take two bears to live with you—bear and forbear *See* BEAR AND FORBEAR.

you need more than dancing shoes to be a dancer Doing something well is not just a matter of having the right equipment: *Buying her a new piano is a waste of money—she has no talent, and you need more than dancing shoes to be a dancer.* The proverb is recorded as a regional expression in the United States.

you never accumulate if you don't speculate *See* IF YOU DON'T SPECULATE, YOU CAN'T ACCUMULATE.

you never get anything for nothing *See* NOTHING FOR NOTHING.

you never know a man until you live with him When you live with somebody you find out what he or she is really like: *She believes that all couples should cohabit before they marry, on the principle that you never know a man until you live with him.*

Variant of this proverb: you never know a man until you bed with him a winter and summer.

Proverb expressing similar meaning: COME LIVE WITH ME AND YOU'LL KNOW ME.

you never know what you can do until you try People are often surprised to discover what they are capable of when they make an effort: *I didn't think I could walk that far, but you never know what you can do till you try.* The proverb was first recorded in 1818 in William Cobbett's *Year's Residence in America.*

you never miss a slice from a cut loaf *See* A SLICE OFF A CUT LOAF ISN'T MISSED.

you never miss the water till the well runs dry We tend to take some things for granted, and become aware of their value only when they are no longer available: "Do not let your chances, like sunbeams pass you by;/For you never miss the water till the well runs dry" (Rowland Howard, *You Never Miss the Water,* 1876). The proverb dates from before 1628.

Proverbs expressing similar meaning: BLESSINGS BRIGHTEN AS THEY TAKE THEIR FLIGHT; THE COW KNOWS NOT THE VALUE OF HER TAIL TILL SHE HAS LOST IT.

a young barber and an old physician Youth is fine in a barber but undesirable in a doctor: *My aunt declined seeing the youthful locum on the grounds that "a young barber and an old physician" was best.* The proverb was first recorded in J. Sandford, *The Garden of Pleasure* (1573).

Variant of this proverb: a young physician fattens the churchyard.

the young cock crows as he heard the old one The young learn by the example of their elders. The proverb was first recorded in Alexander Barclay, *Ship of Fools* (1509): "The yonge cok lerneth to crowe hye of the olde."

Variant of this proverb: the young pig grunts like the old sow.

young folks think old folks to be fools, but old folks know young folks to be fools Young people think they are wiser than their elders, but the opposite is true: "'Young folks always think old ones fools, they say.' 'Finish the adage, Sir, that old folks know young ones to be so, and then agree with me that it is a saying founded on prejudice" (Francis Edward Smedley, *Frank Fairleigh,* 1850). The proverb was first recorded in 1577 in J. Grange's *Golden Aphroditis.*

a young man married is a young man marred It is not good to marry too young: "You may carve it on his tombstone, you may cut it on his card,/That a young man married is a young man marred!" (Rudyard Kipling, *The Story of the Gadsbys,* 1888). First recorded in 1589, with reference to young women rather than young men, the proverb occurs in Shakespeare's play *All's Well That Ends Well* (2:3; 1602): "A young man married is a man that's marr'd."

young men forgive, old men never *See* YOUTH AND OLD AGE WILL NEVER AGREE.

young men may die, but old men must die Death is a possibility at any age, but a certainty in old age: *I fought in two wars and survived, but nobody lives forever—young men may die, but old men must die.* The proverb was first recorded in this form in 1623, but the sentiment it expresses is of ancient origin, occurring in a story about a young Roman widow courted by an elderly man.

a young physician fattens the churchyard *See* A YOUNG BARBER AND AN OLD PHYSICIAN.

the young pig grunts like the old sow *See* THE YOUNG COCK CROWS AS HE HEARD THE OLD ONE.

young saint, old devil Those who behave best when they are young are often those who behave worst when they are old: *In later life he made up for the missed opportunities of his virtuous youth, indulging freely in all the excesses of the flesh—a classic illustration of the saying "Young saint, old devil."* The proverb was first recorded (*Middle English*

Sermons) c. 1400, but with the implication that it was already in common use.

Variant of this proverb: a young saint, an old sinner.

you pays your money and you takes your choice   It is up to you which item, course of action, or theory you choose; used when there is an element of chance involved, or when there is little difference between the options available: *Which of their stories is closest to the truth? You pays your money and you takes your choice.* The proverb was first recorded in 1846, as a cartoon caption in the British magazine *Punch.* It is sometimes occurs in the more grammatical form "You pay your money and you take your choice."

Variant of this proverb: you pays your money and you takes your chance.

you're only young once   Young people should take the opportunity to do all the things they will be unable to do when they're older: *He was in two minds about taking a year off to travel round the world, but I encouraged him, reminding him that you're only young once.* The proverbs first recorded use is P. Wentworth's *In the Balance* (1941).

you scratch my back, and I'll scratch yours   Favors will be reciprocated; often used to imply corruption, or a covert arrangement between the parties concerned: "In theory, racing's addiction to the thin drip of a levy on betting turnover should mean that bookmakers and the sport's administrators approach each other in a mutual spirit of: 'You scratch my back, and I'll scratch yours'" (*London Times,* 1998). The proverb was first recorded in 1704, in the form "Scratch

me and I'll scratch you," but the sentiment it expresses is of ancient origin.

Proverbs expressing similar meaning: ONE HAND WASHES THE OTHER; ONE GOOD TURN DESERVES ANOTHER.

you should know a man seven years before you stir his fire   You should not be too familiar with people, or interfere in their domestic affairs, until you have known them for some time: "Let me get you another drink. . . . I know one ought to know people seven years to poke their fires, but I believe it's less for cocktails" (Angela Thirkell, *Marling Hall,* 1942). The proverb was first recorded in 1803 in C. Dibdin's *Professional Life.*

you snooze, you lose   Those who fail to keep alert will lose out: "I felt sorry for his disappointment, but in this business it's a case of you snooze, you lose." The proverb appears to be of U.S. origin, dating from the late 20th century.

youth and old age will never agree   The young and the old see the world differently: "Youthe and elde is often at debaat" (Geoffrey Chaucer, *The Canterbury Tales,* c. 1387). It appears in William Shakespeare's *The Passionate Pilgrim* in the form "Crabbed age and youth cannot live together."

Variant of this proverb: young men forgive, old men never.

youth must be served   Young people should be allowed to have their own way, helped, or treated with forbearance: *Youth must be served, but we have to draw the line somewhere, and acts of wanton vandalism cannot be tolerated.* The proverb was first recorded in 1829 in P. Egan's *Boxiana.*

Variant of this proverb: youth will be served.

youth will have its fling Young people should be forgiven for their excesses or improprieties: "I pray you, pardon me, ex-Pirate King! / Peers will be peers, and youth will have its fling" (W. S. Gilbert and Arthur Sullivan, *The Pirates of Penzance,* 1879). The proverb was first recorded in 1562.

Variant of this proverb: youth will have its course.

you've made your bed, now lie in it *See* AS YOU MAKE YOUR BED, SO YOU MUST LIE IN-IT.

you win some, you lose some Successes and failures tend to balance one another overall; used to indicate or advocate a nonchalant attitude to defeat: *Hearing that he had not been successful in gaining the contract, he sighed with resignation, "You win some, you lose some. I guess there'll always be a next time."* The proverb was first recorded, in its variant form, in 1897, in Rudyard Kipling's *Captains Courageous.*

Variant of this proverb: you win a few, you lose a few.

Proverb expressing similar meaning: YOU CAN'T WIN 'EM ALL.

zeal without knowledge is a runaway horse Uninformed enthusiasm will only lead to disaster. The proverb is ultimately of biblical origin, appearing at Romans 10:2 in the form: "They have a zeal of God, but not according to knowledge."

Variant of this proverb: zeal without knowledge is the sister of folly.

Index by Key Word

The nouns, adjectives, and verbs of the proverbs are indexed under the base form (the singular noun or the infinitive of the verb), thus "Children should be seen and not heard" is indexed under *child, see,* and *hear,* and "Easier said than done" is indexed under *easy, say,* and *do.* The same principle applies to verb forms used as nouns and adjectives (such as those ending in *-ing* and *-ed*): for *blessing* and *blessed* look under *bless,* for *lining* look under *line,* for *willing* look under *will,* for *broke* look under *break,* and for *shorn* look under *shear.* Other derived forms, such as nouns ending in *-er* and adverbs ending in *-ly,* have their own keywords, for example, *loser* and *badly.* Note that common words such as *thing, man, all, have,* and *do* are not always indexed. Hyphenated forms and two-word compounds are indexed under their separate elements, thus "Beauty is only skin deep" is listed under *beauty, skin,* and *deep,* and "Don't jump from the frying pan into the fire" is under *jump, fry, pan,* and *fire.*

A   Who says A must say B

abandon   Rats abandon a sinking ship *See* rats desert a sinking ship

abhor   nature abhors a vacuum

above   Caesar's wife must be above suspicion

nobody is above the law

abroad   go abroad and you'll hear news of home

absence   absence is the mother of disillusion

absence makes the heart grow fonder

a little absence does much good

absent   he who is absent is always in the wrong

absolute   power corrupts, and absolute power corrupts absolutely

absolutely   power corrupts, and absolute power corrupts absolutely

abundance   out of the abundance of the heart the mouth speaks *See* out of the fullness of the heart the mouth speaks

accident   accidents will happen in the best-regulated families

account   there's no accounting for tastes

accumulate   if you don't speculate, you can't accumulate

accuse   accusing the times is but excusing ourselves

he who excuses himself accuses himself

never ask pardon before you are accused

accuse   *qui s'excuse, s'accuse See* he who excuses himself accuses himself

accuser   a guilty conscience needs no accuser

ache   the tongue ever turns to the aching tooth *See* the tongue always returns to the sore tooth

acorn   even a blind pig occasionally picks up an acorn

great oaks from little acorns grow

action   action is worry's worst enemy

actions speak louder than words

action without thought is like shooting without aim

a common danger causes common action

actor   the world is a stage and all the people in it actors *See* all the world's a stage

ad   big fleas have little fleas upon their backs to bite 'em, and little fleas have lesser fleas, and so ad infinitum

Adam   when Adam delved and Eve span, who was then the gentleman?

addle   as good be an addled egg as an idle bird

admire   admiration is the daughter of ignorance

advantage   the devil can quote scripture to his own advantage *See* the devil can cite scripture for his purpose

adventure   adventures are to the adventurous

adventurous   adventures are to the adventurous

adversity   adversity makes strange bedfellows

a dose of adversity is often as needful as a dose of medicine

prosperity discovers vice; adversity, virtue

advice   ask advice, but use your own common sense

nothing is given so freely as advice

affair   there's a tide in the affairs of man

affect   small things affect light minds *See* little things please little minds

afraid   he who rides a tiger is afraid to dismount

Africa   always something new out of Africa

aft   the best-laid schemes of mice and men gang aft a-gley

afterward   shoot first and ask questions afterward

again   what has happened once can happen again

yesterday will not be called again

against   strive not against the stream

Agamemnon   brave men lived before Agamemnon

age   age before beauty

the age of miracles is past

the golden age was never the present age

an idle youth, a needy age

with age comes wisdom

youth and old age will never agree

a-gley   the best-laid schemes of mice and men gang aft a-gley

agree   agree, for the law is costly

beauty and honesty seldom agree

birds in their little nests agree

history is a fable agreed upon

two of a trade never agree

youth and old age will never agree

agreement   an ill agreement is better than a good judgment

ahead   quit while you are ahead

aim   action without thought is like shooting without aim

air   don't air your dirty linen in public *See* don't wash your dirty linen in public

akin   cleanliness is akin to godliness *See* cleanliness is next to godliness

pity is akin to love

alcohol   alcohol will preserve anything but a secret

alibi   corruption will find a dozen alibis for its evil deeds

alike   great minds think alike
share and share alike
alive   if you want to live and thrive, let the spider run alive
all   all fish are not caught with flies
all's well that ends well
all things will pass *See* this, too, shall pass
the end crowns all *See* the end crowns the work
every man for himself and God for us all
a friend to all is a friend to none
hear all, see all, say nowt
it'll all be the same in a hundred years
it'll all come out in the wash
it's all grist for the mill *See* all is grist that comes to the mill
it's all in a day's work
it takes all kinds of people to make a world
a jack of all trades is master of none
mom is the measure of all things
tell not all you know, nor do all you can
the third time pays for all *See* the third time is the charm
to know all is to forgive all
you can fool some of the people all of the time, and all of the people some of the time, but you can't fool all of the people all of the time
you can't be all things to all men
you can't win 'em all
allow   every dog is allowed one bite
two's a couple, three's a crowd, four's too many, and five's not allowed *See* two's company, three's a crowd
alloy   no joy without alloy *See* no joy without annoy
alone   he travels fastest who travels alone
laugh and the world laughs with you, weep and you weep alone
leave well enough alone

misfortunes seldom come alone *See* misfortunes never come singly
a wise man is never less alone than when alone
alter   circumstances alter cases
always   always something new out of Africa
once a priest, always a priest
once a thief, always a thief
America   America is a tune: it must be sung together
the business of America is business
never sell America short
what's good for General Motors is good for America
American   good Americans, when they die, go to Paris
nobody ever went broke underestimating the intelligence of the American people
amor   *Amor vincit omnia See* love conquers all
an   if and an spoils many a good charter
if ifs and ans were pots and pans, there'd be no work for tinkers
ancestor   most people consider thrift a fine virtue in ancestors
angel   fools rush in where angels fear to tread
anger   anger improves nothing but the arch of a cat's back
anger without power is folly
never let the sun go down on your anger
angry   a hungry man is an angry man
animal   all animals are equal, but some are more equal than others
never work with children or animals
annoy   no joy without annoy
another   another day, another dollar
he who fights and runs away may live to fight another day
tomorrow is another day

answer ask a silly question and you get a silly answer

a civil question deserves a civil answer

fools ask questions that wise men cannot answer

silence is the best answer to the stupid *See* silence is the fittest reply to folly

a soft answer turns away wrath

anvil the church is an anvil which has worn out many hammers

anything if anything can go wrong, it will

you never get anything for nothing *See* nothing for nothing

apace ill news comes apace *See* bad news travels fast

ill weeds grow apace

ape an ape's an ape, a varlet's a varlet, though they be clad in silk or scarlet

old maids lead apes in hell

appear be what you appear to be *See* be what you would seem to be

speak of the devil and he always appears

appearance appearances are deceiving

judge not according to appearances

appetite appetite comes with eating

apple an apple a day keeps the doctor away

the apple never falls far from the tree

the rotten apple spoils the barrel

small choice in rotten apples

April April showers bring May flowers

arch anger improves nothing but the arch of a cat's back

architect every man is the architect of his own fortune

are *See* be

argue when you argue with a fool, make sure he isn't similarly engaged

you can't argue with success

argument the only thing a heated argument ever produced is coolness

arm kings have long arms

stretch your arm no further than your sleeve will reach

army an army marches on its stomach

around prosperity is just around the corner

what goes around, comes around

arrive it's better to travel hopefully than to arrive

ars *ars est celare artem See* the best art conceals art

ars longa, vita brevis See art is long and life is short

art all arts are brothers, each is a light to the other

art is long and life is short

art is power

the art of being a parent consists of sleeping when the baby isn't looking

the best art conceals art

artem *ars est celare artem See* the best art conceals art

ash beware of an oak, it draws the stroke; avoid an ash, it counts the flash; creep under the thorn, it can save you from harm

ask ask, and it shall be given you; seek, and ye shall find; knock, and it shall be opened unto you

ask advice, but use your own common sense

ask a silly question and you get a silly answer

ask me no questions and I'll tell you no lies

he that will thrive must first ask his wife

never ask pardon before you are accused

shoot first and ask questions afterward

ass better be the head of an ass than the tail of a horse *See* better be the head of a dog than the tail of a lion

astray the best-laid schemes of mice and men oft go astray *See* the best-laid schemes of mice and men gang aft a-gley

323

attack attack is the best form of defense *See* the best defense is a good offense

attract like attracts like

opposites attract

authority a traveler may lie with authority

autres autres temps, autres moeurs *See* other times, other manners

available work expands so as to fill the time available for its completion

avoid beware of an oak, it draws the stroke; avoid an ash, it counts the flash; creep under the thorn, it can save you from harm

criticism is something you can avoid by saying nothing, doing nothing, and being nothing

avoidance avoidance is the only remedy

away away goes the devil when he finds the door shut against him

blue are the hills that are far away

when the cat's away, the mice will play

aye marry in May, rue for aye

B who says A must say B

babe out of the mouths of babes and sucklings come great truths

baby the art of being a parent consists of sleeping when the baby isn't looking

don't throw out the baby with the bathwater

back anger improves nothing but the arch of a cat's back

the back door robs the house *See* a postern door makes a thief

big fleas have little fleas upon their backs to bite 'em, and little fleas have lesser fleas, and so ad infinitum

God makes the back to the burden

it's the last straw that breaks the camel's back

step on a crack, break your mother's back

what's got over the devil's back is spent under his belly

you scratch my back and I'll scratch yours

backyard a cock is mighty in his own backyard *See* every cock will crow upon his own dunghill

the grass is always greener in somebody else's backyard *See* the grass is always greener on the other side of the fence

bad all bad things come in threes *See* things come in threes

a bad excuse is better than none

a bad husband makes a bad wife *See* a good husband makes a good wife

bad money drives out good

bad news travels fast

a bad penny always turns up

a bad workman quarrels with his tools

don't throw good money after bad

fire is a good servant but a bad master

give a dog a bad name and hang him

a good horse cannot be of a bad color

good riddance to bad rubbish

the good seaman is known in bad weather

hard cases make bad law

he comes too early who brings bad news

hope is a good breakfast but a bad supper

nothing so bad but it might have been worse

one bad apple spoils the lot *See* the rotten apple spoils the barrel

a poor excuse is better than none *See* a bad excuse is better than none

a preacher's son is often bad *See* clergymen's sons always turn out badly

the receiver is as bad as the thief *See* if there were no receivers, there would be no thieves

a secret is either too good to keep or too bad not to tell

see a pin and pick it up, all the day you'll have good luck; see a pin and let it lay, bad luck you'll have all the day

there's good and bad in everything

there's no such thing as bad weather, only the wrong clothes

three moves are as bad as a fire

a whistling girl and a crowing hen always come to the same bad end *See* a whistling woman and a crowing hen are neither fit for God nor men

you have to take the bad with the good *See* you have to take the bitter with the sweet

badly clergymen's sons always turn out badly

bag an empty bag cannot stand *See* an empty sack cannot stand upright

there's many a good cock come out of a tattered bag

bait fish or cut bait

the hook without bait catches no fish

bake as you bake, so shall you brew

as you brew, so shall you bake *See* as you brew, so shall you drink

barber a young barber and an old physician

bare there goes more to marriage than four bare legs in a bed

barefoot he that waits for dead men's shoes may go a long time barefoot *See* it's ill waiting for dead men's shoes

the shoemaker's child always goes barefoot

bargain it takes two to make a bargain

bark a barking dog never bites

the dogs bark, but the caravan goes on

why keep a dog and bark yourself?

barn don't shut the barn door after the horse is stolen

a jackass can kick a barn door down, but it takes a carpenter to build one

barrel an empty barrel makes the most noise *See* empty vessels make the most sound

the rotten apple spoils the barrel

basket don't put all your eggs in one basket

bathwater don't throw out the baby with the bathwater

baton every soldier has the baton of a field-marshal in his knapsack

battalion providence is always on the side of the big battalions

battle a good beginning is half the battle

he who fights and runs away may live to fight another day, but he that is in battle slain will never rise to fight again *See* he who fights and runs away may live to fight another day

it's better to lose the battle and win the war

the race is not to the swift, nor the battle to the strong

bawl a bawling cow soon forgets her own calf *See* a bellowing cow soon forgets her calf

bayonet a bayonet is a weapon with a worker at each end

be the best is yet to be

be what you would seem to be

the future ain't what it used to be

what will be, will be

you are what you eat

bear (n.) you must take two bears to live with you—bear and forbear *See* bear and forbear

bear (v.) bear and forbear

beware of Greeks bearing gifts

a clear conscience can bear any trouble

we all have our cross to bear

beard it's merry in hall when beards wag all

beast music has charms to soothe the savage beast *See* music hath charms to soothe the savage breast

beat if you can't beat 'em, join 'em

it's easy to find a stick to beat a dog

might beats right *See* might makes right

you can't beat a man at his own game

you can't beat somebody with nobody

beautiful big is beautiful

small is beautiful

beauty age before beauty

beauty and honesty seldom agree

beauty draws with a single hair

beauty is a good letter of introduction

beauty is but a blossom

beauty is in the eye of the beholder

beauty is no inheritance

beauty is only skin deep

beauty is truth, truth beauty

fancy passes beauty

grace will last, beauty will blast

a thing of beauty is a joy forever

bed as you make your bed, so you must lie in it

early to bed and early to rise, makes a man healthy, wealthy, and wise

life is no bed of roses

there goes more to marriage than four bare legs in a bed

you never know a man until you bed with him a winter and summer *See* you never know a man until you live with him

bedfellow adversity makes strange bedfellows

politics makes strange bedfellows

bee where bees are, there is honey

beer he that drinks beer, thinks beer

life isn't all beer and skittles

before pride goes before a fall

beforehand pay beforehand was never well served

beg give a loaf and beg a slice

beget length begets loathing

like begets like *See* like breeds like

love begets love

money begets money

one business begets another

one lie begets another *See* one lie leads to another

success begets success *See* success breeds success

beggar beggars can't be choosers

give a beggar a horse and he'll ride it to death

if wishes were horses, beggars would ride

set a beggar on horseback, and he'll ride to the devil

sue a beggar and catch a louse

begin charity begins at home

equality begins in the grave

fish begin to stink at the head *See* a fish stinks from the head

a good beginning is half the battle

a good beginning makes a good ending

he that would the daughter win, must with the mother first begin

he who begins many things, finishes but few

he who would climb the ladder must begin at the bottom

an ill beginning makes an ill ending

a journey of a thousand miles begins with one step

life begins at forty

the sooner begun, the sooner done

well begun is half done

when things are at the worst they begin to mend

behind always in a hurry, always behind

behind every great man there is a great woman

if two ride on a horse, one must ride behind

beholder beauty is in the eye of the beholder

belfry the devil gets up to the belfry by the vicar's skirts

believe believe only half of what you see and nothing you hear

believing has a core of unbelieving

a liar is not believed when he tells the truth

seeing is believing

believer a believer is a songless bird in a cage

bellow a bellowing cow soon forgets her calf

belly the eye is bigger than the belly

a growing youth has a wolf in his belly See a growing youth has a wolf in his stomach

hungry bellies have no ears See a hungry stomach has no ears

what's got over the devil's back is spent under his belly

belong conscience gets a lot of credit that belongs to cold feet

to the victor belong the spoils

below no man is above the law, and no man is below it See nobody is above the law

bend as the twig is bent, so is the tree inclined

best accidents will happen in the best-regulated families

all's for the best in the best of all possible worlds

the best art conceals art

the best defense is a good offense

the best doctors are Dr. Diet, Dr. Quiet, and Dr. Merryman

the best is the enemy of the good

the best is yet to be

the best-laid schemes of mice and men gang aft a-gley

the best of friends must part

the best of men are but men at best

the best place for criticism is in front of your mirror

the best things come in small packages

the best things in life are free

the best way to get even is to forget

a dog is a man's best friend

don't shoot the pianist, he's doing his best

east, west, home's best

few words are best

God takes soonest those he loves best

a good example is the best sermon

the good is the enemy of the best

good to forgive, best to forget See forgive and forget

he laughs best who laughs last See he who laughs last, laughs longest

he lives longest who lives best See he lives long who lives well

he who laughs last, laughs best See he who laughs last, laughs longest

honesty is the best policy

hope for the best and prepare for the worst

hunger is the best sauce

it's best to be off with the old love before you are on with the new

it's best to be on the safe side See it's better to be on the safe side

laughter is the best medicine

a man's best reputation for the future is his record of the past

old friends and old wine are best

an old poacher makes the best gamekeeper

put your best foot forward

revenge is a dish best eaten cold

second thoughts are best

silence is the best answer to the stupid See silence is the fittest reply to folly

that government is best which governs least

welcome is the best cheer

the mother of mischief is no bigger than a midge's wing

providence is always on the side of the big battalions

small leaks sink big ships *See* little leaks sink the ship

speak softly and carry a big stick

billet   every bullet has its billet

bind   safe bind, safe find

bird   as good be an addled egg as an idle bird

a believer is a songless bird in a cage

a bird in the hand is worth two in the bush

a bird never flew on one wing

birds in their little nests agree

birds of a feather flock together

the early bird catches the worm

fine feathers make fine birds

an ill bird lays an ill egg

in vain the net is spread in the sight of the bird

it's an ill bird that fouls its own nest

little birds that can sing and won't sing must be made to sing

pigs may fly, but they are very unlikely birds *See* if a pig had wings, it might fly

there are no birds in last year's nest

you can't catch old birds with chaff

you can't keep the birds from flying over your head, but you can keep them from building a nest in your hair

birth   birth is much but breeding more

one for sorrow; two for mirth; three for a wedding; four for a birth

bis   *bis dat qui cito dat See* he gives twice who gives quickly

bishop   nobody is born learned; bishops are made of men

bit   the biter is sometimes bit

every little bit helps *See* every little helps

bitch   the hasty bitch bringeth forth blind whelps

life's a bitch, and then you die

bite   a barking dog never bites

big fleas have little fleas upon their backs to bite 'em, and little fleas have lesser fleas, and so ad infinitum

a bleating sheep loses a bite

dead men don't bite

don't bite off more than you can chew

don't bite the hand that feeds you

every dog is allowed one bite

if you can't bite, never show your teeth

once bitten, twice shy

take a hair of the dog that bit you

when a dog bites a man, that is not news; but when a man bites a dog, that is news

biter   the biter is sometimes bit

bitter   you have to take the bitter with the sweet

black   all cats are black at night *See* all cats are gray in the dark

the devil is not as black as he is painted

the pot calls the kettle black

there's a black sheep in every flock

two blacks don't make a white *See* two wrongs don't make a right

blame   a bad workman blames his tools *See* a bad workman quarrels with his tools

common fame is seldom to blame

blast   grace will last, beauty will blast

bleat   a bleating sheep loses a bite

bleed   paper bleeds little

bless   blessed are the dead that the rain rains on

blessed are they who expect nothing, for they shall not be disappointed

blessed is the bride that the sun shines on *See* happy is the bride that the sun shines on

blessings brighten as they take their flight

happy is the bride that the sun shines on, blessed is the corpse that the rain falls

the coward dies a thousand deaths, the brave but one *See* cowards die many times before their death

fortune favors the brave

none but the brave deserve the fair

Robin Hood could brave all weathers but a thaw wind

too many chiefs and not enough braves *See* too many chiefs and not enough Indians

Bray the vicar of Bray will be vicar of Bray still

bread bread always falls buttered side down

bread is the staff of life

half a loaf is better than no bread

man does not live by bread alone

whose bread I eat, his song I sing

break hard words break no bones

if it ain't broke, don't fix it

if it takes two to make a bargain, it takes two to break it *See* it takes two to make a bargain

if it were not for hope, the heart would break

ignorance of the law is no excuse for breaking it *See* ignorance of the law is no excuse

it's the last straw that breaks the camel's back

never give a sucker an even break

nobody ever went broke underestimating the intelligence of the American people

obey orders, if you break owners

a pitcher that goes to the well too often is broken at last *See* the pitcher will go to the well once too often

promises, like piecrust, are made to be broken

rules are made to be broken

step on a crack, break your mother's back

sticks and stones may break my bones, but words will never hurt me

the thread breaks where it is weakest

time is the rider that breaks youth

you can't make an omelette without breaking eggs

breakfast hope is a good breakfast but a bad supper

an hour before breakfast is worth two the rest of the day *See* an hour in the morning is worth two in the evening

sing before breakfast, cry before night

breast hope springs eternal in the human breast

music hath charms to soothe the savage breast

breed birth is much but breeding more

drought never bred dearth in England

familiarity breeds contempt

like breeds like

success breeds success

what's bred in the bone will come out in the flesh

brevis *ars longa, vita brevis See* art is long and life is short

brevity brevity is the soul of wit

brew as you bake, so shall you brew

as you brew, so shall you drink

bribe a bribe will enter without knocking

brick you can't make bricks without straw

bride always a bridesmaid, never a bride

happy is the bride that the sun shines on

bridesmaid always a bridesmaid, never a bride

bridge don't burn your bridges behind you

don't cross the bridge till you come to it

it's good to make a bridge of gold to a flying enemy

praise the bridge that carries you over

bridle a man without a religion is a horse without a bridle

bright always look on the bright side

the sun is not less bright for shining on a dunghill *See* the sun loses nothing by shining into a puddle

the used key is always bright

brighten blessings brighten as they take their flight

bring borrowing brings sorrowing *See* he that goes a-borrowing, goes a-sorrowing

he comes too early who brings bad news

night brings counsel

nothing can bring you peace but yourself

one wedding brings another

the worth of a thing is what it will bring

broaden travel broadens the mind

broke, broken *See* **break**

broom a new broom sweeps clean

broth every cook praises his own broth

too many cooks spoil the broth

brother all arts are brothers, each is a light to the other

sleep is the brother of death

build fools build houses and wise men live in them

it's easier to tear down than to build up

a jackass can kick a barn door down, but it takes a carpenter to build one

men build houses, women build homes *See* men make houses, women make homes

Rome was not built in a day

where God builds a church, the devil will build a chapel

you can't build a church with stumbling blocks

you can't keep the birds from flying over your head, but you can keep them from building a nest in your hair

bullet every bullet has its billet

bully a bully is always a coward

bump education doesn't come by bumping your head against the school house

if frogs had wings, they wouldn't bump their tails on rocks *See* if a pig had wings, it might fly

bundle a man wrapped up in himself makes a very small bundle

bung save at the spigot and waste at the bung *See* spare at the spigot, and let out the bunghole

bunghole spare at the spigot, and let out the bunghole

burden God makes the back to the burden

burn better a little fire to warm us than a big one to burn us

burn not your house to scare away the mice

a burnt child dreads the fire

don't burn your bridges behind you

if you play with fire, you get burned

money burns a hole in the pocket

Nero fiddled while Rome burned

once burned, twice shy

bury let the dead bury the dead

bush a bird in the hand is worth two in the bush

good wine needs no bush

bushel don't hide your light under a bushel

you have to eat a bushel of dirt before you die *See* we must eat a peck of dirt before we die

business business before pleasure

business is business

business is like a car, it will not run by itself except downhill

business neglected is business lost

the business of America is business

everybody's business is nobody's business

mind your own business

never mix business with pleasure

patience is a virtue, catch it if you can:
seldom in a woman and never in a man
See patience is a virtue

set a thief to catch a thief

a shut mouth catches no flies

softly, softly, catchee monkey

sue a beggar and catch a louse

throw out a sprat to catch a mackerel

you can catch more flies with honey than
with vinegar

you can't catch old birds with chaff

cattle   hurry no man's cattle

caught   *See* **catch**

cause   a man is a lion in his own cause

men are blind in their own cause

nobody should be judge in his own cause

caution   caution is the parent of safety

caveat   *caveat emptor See* let the buyer
beware

cease   war will cease when men refuse
to fight

wonders will never cease!

celare   *ars est celare artem See* the best art
conceals art

certain   children are certain cares, but
uncertain comforts

nothing is certain but death and taxes

nothing is certain but the unforeseen

chacun   *chacun à son goût See* every man
to his taste

chaff   you can't catch old birds with
chaff

chain   a chain is no stronger than its
weakest link

chance   blind chance sweeps the world
along

you pays your money and you takes your
chance *See* you pays your money and
you takes your choice

change   a change is as good as a rest

change not a clout till May be out *See*
ne'er cast a clout till May be out

don't change horses in the middle of
the stream *See* don't swap horses in
midstream

don't change the rules in the middle of
the game

honors change manners

the leopard can't change its spots

the more things change, the more they
stay the same

times change, and we with time

what you put off and what you put on,
never change till May be gone *See* ne'er
cast a clout till May be out

a wise man changes his mind, but a fool
never does

change   *plus ça change, plus c'est la même
chose See* the more things change, the
more they stay the same

channel   great minds run in the same
channels *See* great minds think alike

chapel   where God builds a church, the
devil will build a chapel

character   character is destiny

dreams retain the infirmities of our character

charity   charity begins at home

charity covers a multitude of sins

charity is not a bone you throw to a dog
but a bone you share with a dog

charm   music hath charms to soothe the
savage breast

the third time is the charm

if and an spoils many a good charter

chase   he who chases two hares catches
neither *See* if you run after two hares,
you will catch neither

a stern chase is a long chase

che   *che sarà, sarà See* what will be, will
be

cheap   buy in the cheapest market and
sell in the dearest

it's as cheap sitting as standing

talk is cheap

chooser beggars can't be choosers

chose *plus ça change, plus c'est la même chose See* the more things change, the more they stay the same

Christmas Christmas comes but once a year

the devil makes his Christmas pies of lawyers' tongues and clerks' fingers

church the blood of the martyrs is the seed of the church

the church is an anvil which has worn out many hammers

a church is God between four walls

the nearer the church, the farther from God

where God builds a church, the devil will build a chapel

you can't build a church with stumbling blocks

churchyard a green winter makes a fat churchyard

a young physician fattens the churchyard *See* a young barber, an old physician

cinch life is hard by the yard, but by the inch life's a cinch

circle the wheel comes full circle

circumstance circumstances alter cases

cite the devil can cite scripture for his purpose

cito *bis dat qui cito dat See* he gives twice who gives quickly

city a great city, a great solitude

if every man would sweep his own doorstep the city would soon be clean

you can't fight City Hall

civil a civil question deserves a civil answer

civility civility costs nothing

there's nothing lost by civility

clad an ape's an ape, a varlet's a varlet, though they be clad in silk or scarlet

claw a goose quill is more dangerous than a lion's claw

clean don't throw away your dirty water until you get clean

if every man would sweep his own doorstep the city would soon be clean

a new broom sweeps clean

sweep your own doorstep clean

cleanliness cleanliness is next to Godliness

clear a clear conscience can bear any trouble

rain before seven, clear before eleven *See* rain before seven, fine before eleven

clergyman clergymen's sons always turn out badly

clerk the clock goes as it pleases the clerk

the devil makes his Christmas pies of lawyers' tongues and clerks' fingers

client a man who is his own lawyer has a fool for his client

climb he that would eat the fruit must climb the tree

he who would climb the ladder must begin at the bottom

the higher the monkey climbs the more he shows his tail

climber hasty climbers have sudden falls

clock the clock goes as it pleases the clerk

clog from clogs to clogs is only three generations *See* from shirtsleeves to shirtsleeves is only three generations

close (adj.) the closer to the bone, the sweeter the meat *See* the nearer the bone, the sweeter the flesh

close sits my shirt, but closer my skin *See* near is my shirt, but nearer is my skin

little boats should stay close to shore

close (v.) a closed mouth catches no flies *See* a shut mouth catches no flies

love is blind; friendship closes its eyes

be the day weary or be the day long, at last it ringeth to evensong

the better the day, the better the deed

the child that is born on the Sabbath day is bonny and blithe and good and gay

the day is short and the work is long

every dog has his day

fair and softly goes far in a day

fish and guests stink after three days

from the day you were born till you ride in a hearse, there's nothing so bad but it might have been worse *See* nothing so bad but it might have been worse

give a man a fish, and you feed him for a day; show him how to fish, and you feed him for a lifetime

he who fights and runs away may live to fight another day

an hour before breakfast is worth two the rest of the day *See* an hour in the morning is worth two in the evening

it's all in a day's work

live every day as though it were your last

the longest day must have an end

my son is my son till he gets him a wife, but my daughter's my daughter all the days of her life *See* a son is a son till he gets him a wife, a daughter's a daughter all of her life

never is a long day *See* never is a long time

one of these days is none of these days

Rome was not built in a day

save something for a rainy day

see a pin and pick it up, all the day you'll have good luck; see a pin and let it lay, bad luck you'll have all the day

seize the day

sufficient unto the day is the evil thereof

tomorrow is another day

a wonder lasts but nine days

dead   be happy while you're living, for you're a long time dead

better be dead than out of fashion *See* better be out of the world than out of the fashion

blessed are the dead that the rain rains on

call no man happy till he is dead *See* call no man happy till he dies

dead men don't bite

dead men tell no tales

it's ill waiting for dead men's shoes

let the dead bury the dead

a live dog is better than a dead lion

never speak ill of the dead

praise no man till he is dead

stone-dead hath no fellow

three may keep a secret, if two of them are dead

deadly   the female of the species is deadlier than the male

deaf   a deaf husband and a blind wife are always a happy couple

there are none so deaf as those who will not hear

dear   buy in the cheapest market and sell in the dearest

experience keeps a dear school

far-fetched and dear-bought is good for ladies

gold may be bought too dear

a thing you don't want is dear at any price

dearth   drought never bred dearth in England

death   after death the doctor

better death than dishonor

cowards die many times before their death

death defies the doctor

death is the great leveler

death keeps no calendar

death pays all debts

a dry cough is the trumpeter of death

every door may be shut but death's door

give a beggar a horse and he'll ride it to death

medicine can prolong life, but death will seize the doctor, too

nothing is certain but death and taxes

sleep is the brother of death

there's a remedy for everything except death

debt   death pays all debts

a man in debt is caught in a net

out of debt, out of danger

speak not of my debts unless you mean to pay them

deceit   self-deceit is the easiest of any

deceive   appearances are deceiving

what a tangled web we weave when first we practice to deceive

deceptive   appearances are deceptive *See* appearances are deceiving

deed   the better the day, the better the deed

corruption will find a dozen alibis for its evil deeds

deeds, not words

deeds are fruits, words are but leaves

no good deed goes unpunished

take the will for the deed

deep   beauty is only skin deep

don't get into deep water until you learn how to swim *See* don't go near the water until you learn how to swim

no tree takes so deep a root as prejudice

still waters run deep

defeat   victory has a hundred fathers and defeat is an orphan *See* success has many fathers, while failure is an orphan

defense   the best defense is a good offense

defer   hope deferred makes the heart sick

defile   he that touches pitch shall be defiled

defy   death defies the doctor

dei   *vox populi, vox Dei See* the voice of the people is the voice of God

delay   delays are dangerous

desires are nourished by delays

delight   red sky at night, sailor's delight; red sky in the morning, sailors take warning

delve   when Adam delved and Eve span, who was then the gentleman?

Denmark   something is rotten in the state of Denmark

deny   deny self for self's sake

desert (n.)   desert and reward seldom keep company

desert (v.)   rats desert a sinking ship

deserve   a civil question deserves a civil answer

none but the brave deserve the fair

one good turn deserves another

desire   desires are nourished by delays

good health is more to be desired than wealth *See* health is wealth

humble hearts have humble desires

if you desire peace, prepare for war *See* if you want peace, prepare for war

desperate   desperate diseases must have desperate remedies

destiny   character is destiny

hanging and wiving go by destiny

destroy   whom the gods would destroy, they first make mad

detail   the devil is in the details

devil   away goes the devil when he finds the door shut against him

better the devil you know than the devil you don't know

cards are the devil's tools

the devil always leaves a stink behind him

the devil can cite scripture for his purpose

the devil dances in an empty pocket

the devil finds work for idle hands to do

the devil gets up to the belfry by the vicar's skirts

the devil is in the details

different different strokes for different folks

difficult all things are easy to industry, all things difficult to sloth

the difficult is done at once, the impossible takes a little longer

it's the first step that is difficult *See* the first step is the hardest

dig dig the well before you are thirsty

when you are in a hole, stop digging

digest cheese digests all things but itself

diligence diligence is the mother of good luck

dinner after dinner rest awhile, after supper walk a mile

better a dinner of herbs where love is than a stalled ox where hate is

dirt poverty comes from God, but not dirt

throw dirt enough, and some will stick

we must eat a peck of dirt before we die

dirty dirty water will quench fire

don't throw away your dirty water until you get clean

don't wash your dirty linen in public

disappoint blessed are they who expect nothing, for they shall not be disappointed

discover prosperity discovers vice; adversity, virtue

discretion discretion is the better part of valor

an ounce of discretion is worth a pound of wit

disease desperate diseases must have desperate remedies

the doctor is often more to be feared than the disease

the remedy may be worse than the disease

disgrace poverty is no disgrace, but it's a great inconvenience

dish revenge is a dish best eaten cold

welcome is the best dish on the table *See* welcome is the best cheer

wishes won't wash dishes

dishonor better death than dishonor

disillusion absence is the mother of disillusion

dismount he who rides a tiger is afraid to dismount

dispose man proposes, God disposes

disputandum *de gustibus non est disputandum* *See* there's no disputing about tastes

dispute there's no disputing about tastes

distance distance lends enchantment to the view

ditch if one sheep leaps over the ditch, all the rest will follow

if the blind lead the blind, both shall fall into the ditch

divide divide and conquer

a house divided against itself cannot stand

united we stand, divided we fall

dividend honesty is the best policy, though it may not pay the largest dividends *See* honesty is the best policy

divine to err is human, to forgive divine

do criticism is something you can avoid by saying nothing, doing nothing, and being nothing

do as I say, not as I do

do as you would be done by

do right and fear no man

do unto others as you would have them do unto you

do well and have well *See* never do things by halves

easier said than done

easy does it

everybody talks about the weather, but nobody does anything about it fools and children should never see half-done work

the good that men do lives after them

handsome is as handsome does

happy's the wooing that's not long a-doing

if a thing's worth doing, it's worth doing well

if you want a thing done well, do it yourself

it's dogged as does it

the king can do no wrong

a man's got to do what a man's got to do

monkey see, monkey do

the more said, the less done

nature does nothing in vain

never do evil that good may come of it

never do things by halves

never put off until tomorrow what you can do today

never send a boy to do a man's job

the sooner begun, the sooner done

tell not all you know, nor do all you can

those who can, do; those who can't, teach

well begun is half done

whatever man has done, man may do

what's done cannot be undone

when in doubt, do nothing

when in Rome, do as the Romans do

a woman's work is never done

you'll be damned if you do and damned if you don't

you never know what you can do until you try

doctor   after death the doctor

an apple a day keeps the doctor away

the best doctors are Dr. Diet, Dr. Quiet, and Dr. Merryman

death defies the doctor

diet cures more than doctors

the doctor is often more to be feared than the disease

medicine can prolong life, but death will seize the doctor, too

doer   evil doers are evil dreaders

dog   a barking dog never bites

better be the head of a dog than the tail of a lion

charity is not a bone you throw to a dog but a bone you share with a dog

a dead dog tells no tales *See* dead men tell no tales

the dog always returns to his vomit

dog does not eat dog

a dog is a man's best friend

the dogs bark, but the caravan goes on

a dog that will fetch a bone will carry a bone

every dog has his day

every dog is a lion at home *See* every cock will crow upon his own dunghill

every dog is allowed one bite

give a dog a bad name and hang him

a good dog deserves a good bone

he that would hang his dog gives out first that he is mad

if you can't run with the big dogs, stay under the porch

if you lie down with dogs, you'll get up with fleas

if you want something done, ask a busy person

it's a poor dog that's not worth whistling for

it's easy to find a stick to beat a dog

it's not the size of the dog in the fight, it's the size of the fight in the dog

let sleeping dogs lie

a live dog is better than a dead lion

love me, love my dog

take a hair of the dog that bit you

there are more ways of killing a dog than choking it with butter *See* there are more ways of killing a cat than choking it with cream there are more ways of killing a dog than hanging it *See* there are more ways of killing a cat than choking it with cream

three things are not to be trusted: a cow's horn, a dog's tooth, and a horse's hoof

when a dog bites a man, that is not news; but when a man bites a dog, that is news

while two dogs are fighting for a bone, a third runs away with it

why keep a dog and bark yourself?

you can't teach an old dog new tricks

dogged   it's dogged as does it

dollar   another day, another dollar

take care of the pennies and the dollars will take care of themselves

done   *See* **do**

door   away goes the devil when he finds the door shut against him

a creaking door hangs longest

don't shut the barn door after the horse is stolen

a door must be either shut or open

drive nature out of the door and it will return by the window *See* you can drive out nature with a pitchfork but she keeps on coming back

every door may be shut but death's door

a golden key can open any door

a jackass can kick a barn door down, but it takes a carpenter to build one

an open door may tempt a saint

opportunity never knocks twice at any man's door *See* opportunity knocks but once

a postern door makes a thief

when one door closes, another one opens

when poverty comes in at the door, love flies out of the window

doorstep   if every man would sweep his own doorstep the city would soon be clean

sweep your own doorstep clean

dose   a dose of adversity is often as needful as a dose of medicine

doubt   when in doubt, do nothing

down   don't hit a man when he's down

he that is down need fear no fall

prejudice is being down on what we are not up on

what goes up must come down

downhill   business is like a car, it will not run by itself except downhill

downward   the fish always stinks from the head downward *See* a fish stinks from the head

dozen   corruption will find a dozen alibis for its evil deeds

it's six of one and half a dozen of the other

draw   beauty draws with a single hair

beware of an oak, it draws the stroke; avoid an ash, it counts the flash; creep under the thorn, it can save you from harm

whosoever draws his sword against the prince must throw the scabbard away

dread   a burnt child dreads the fire

dreader   evil doers are evil dreaders

dream   dream of a funeral and you hear of a marriage

dreams go by contraries

dreams retain the infirmities of our character

morning dreams come true

drill   no names, no pack-drill

drink   as you brew, so shall you drink

eat, drink, and be merry, for tomorrow we die

he that drinks beer, thinks beer

water is the only drink for a wise man

you can lead a horse to water, but you can't make him drink

drip   constant dripping wears away a stone *See* constant dropping wears away a stone

easily he who has a mind to beat a dog will easily find a stick *See* it's easy to find a stick to beat a dog

an old fox is not easily snared

people are more easily led than driven

east east, west, home's best

East is East and West is West and never the twain shall meet

when the wind is in the east, 'tis neither good for man nor beast

easy all things are easy to industry, all things difficult to sloth

easier said than done

easy come, easy go

easy does it

it's easier to tear down than to build up

it's easy to be wise after the event

it's easy to find a stick to beat a dog

the least said is the easiest mended *See* least said, soonest mended

promises are like piecrust: easy made and easy broken *See* promises, like piecrust, are made to be broken

self-deceit is the easiest of any

eat appetite comes with eating

big fish eat little fish

the cat would eat fish, but would not wet her feet

dog does not eat dog

eat, drink, and be merry, for tomorrow we die

eat to live, do not live to eat

he that would eat the fruit must climb the tree

he who does not work, neither should he eat

the proof of the pudding is in the eating

revenge is a dish best eaten cold

we must eat a peck of dirt before we die

whose bread I eat, his song I sing

you are what you eat

you can't have your cake and eat it too

eavesdropper eavesdroppers hear no good of themselves *See* listeners never hear any good of themselves

edge it's ill jesting with edged tools

education education doesn't come by bumping your head against the school house

genius without education is like silver in the mine

never let your education interfere with your intelligence

egg as good be an addled egg as an idle bird

don't kill the goose that lays the golden eggs

don't put all your eggs in one basket

don't teach your grandmother to suck eggs

half an egg is better than an empty shell *See* half a loaf is better than no bread

he that would have eggs must endure the cackling of hens

all ill bird lays an ill egg

which came first, the chicken or the egg?

you can't make an omelette without breaking eggs

you can't unscramble eggs

eight six hours' sleep for a man, seven for a woman, and eight for a fool

elephant an elephant never forgets

eleven rain before seven, fine before eleven

ell give a man an inch and he'll take an ell *See* give a man an inch and he'll take a mile

elm every elm has its man

employee every employee tends to rise to his level of incompetence

emptor caveat emptor *See* let the buyer beware

empty the devil dances in an empty pocket

an empty sack cannot stand upright

empty vessels make the most sound

the glass is either half empty or half full

half an egg is better than an empty shell *See* half a loaf is better than no bread

enchantment distance lends enchantment to the view

end all good things must come to an end

all's well that ends well

a bayonet is a weapon with a worker at each end

charity begins at home but should not end there *See* charity begins at home

the end crowns the work

the end justifies the means

everything has an end

a good beginning makes a good ending

he who wills the end, wills the means

an ill beginning makes an ill ending

it's not the end of the world

it takes two to make a quarrel, but one can end it *See* it takes two to make a quarrel

the longest day must have an end

there's a pot of gold at the end of the rainbow

time ends all things

truth is truth to the end of the reckoning

a whistling girl and a crowing hen always come to the same bad end *See* a whistling woman and a crowing hen are neither fit for God nor men

endure all commend patience, but none can endure to suffer

he that would have eggs must endure the cackling of hens

what can't be cured must be endured

enemy action is worry's worst enemy

the best is the enemy of the good

the enemy of my enemy is my friend

every man is his own worst enemy

God protect me from my friends—I can protect myself from my enemies *See* save us from our friends

the good is the enemy of the best

it's good to make a bridge of gold to a flying enemy

lend money and you get an enemy *See* lend your money and lose your friend

love your enemy, but don't put a gun in his hand

one enemy is too much

there's no little enemy

trust not a new friend nor an old enemy

with friends like that, who needs enemies?

engage when you argue with a fool, make sure he isn't similarly engaged

England drought never bred dearth in England

English the English are a nation of shopkeepers

Englishman an Englishman's home is his castle *See* a man's home is his castle

enjoy gossip is vice enjoyed vicariously

if there were no clouds, we shouldn't enjoy the sun

enough enough is as good as a feast

enough is enough

too many chiefs and not enough Indians

a word is enough to the wise *See* a word to the wise is sufficient

enter a bribe will enter without knocking

envy better be envied than pitied

envy never dies

equal all animals are equal, but some are more equal than others

all men are created equal

equality equality begins in the grave

err to err is human, to forgive divine

errare *humanum est errare See* to err is human, to forgive divine

escape little thieves are hanged, but great ones escape

eternal hope springs eternal in the human breast

the price of liberty is eternal vigilance

Eve when Adam delved and Eve span, who was then the gentleman?

even the best way to get even is to forget

don't get mad, get even

never give a sucker an even break

evening an hour in the morning is worth two in the evening

evensong be the day weary or be the day long, at last it ringeth to evensong

event coming events cast their shadows before

it's easy to be wise after the event

everybody everybody's business is nobody's business

everybody's queer but you and me, and even you are a little queer

what everybody says must be true

you can't please everybody

everything everything has an end

everything is good in its season

money isn't everything

a place for everything and everything in its place

there's a first time for everything

there's a time and place for everything

timing is everything

to everything there is a season

winning isn't everything, it's the only thing

evidence what the soldier said isn't evidence

evil choose the lesser of two evils

corruption will find a dozen alibis for its evil deeds

evil be to him who thinks it

evil communications corrupt good manners

evil doers are evil dreaders

a great book is a great evil

idleness is the root of all evil

the love of money is the root of all evil

money is the root of all evil

never do evil that good may come of it

see no evil, hear no evil, speak no evil

sufficient unto the day is the evil thereof

ex *ex nihilo nihil fit* See nothing comes of nothing

example example is better than precept

a good example is the best sermon

exceedingly the mills of God grind slowly, yet they grind exceedingly small

excellent when house and land are gone and spent, then learning is most excellent

exception the exception proves the rule

self-interest is the rule, self-sacrifice the exception

there's an exception to every rule

exchange a fair exchange is no robbery

excuse the absent are never without fault nor the present without excuse *See* he who is absent is always in the wrong

accusing the times is but excusing ourselves

a bad excuse is better than none

he who excuses himself accuses himself

he who is good at making excuses is seldom good at anything else

ignorance of the law is no excuse

excuse *qui s'excuse, s'accuse See* he who excuses himself accuses himself

exist if God did not exist, it would be necessary to invent him

expand work expands so as to fill the time available for its completion

expect blessed are they who expect nothing, for they shall not be disappointed

what can you expect from a pig but a grunt?

experience experience is a comb that fate gives a man when his hair is all gone

experience is the best teacher

experience is the mother of wisdom

experience is the teacher of fools

experience keeps a dear school

some folks speak from experience; others, from experience, don't speak

extreme   extremes meet

extremity   man's extremity is God's opportunity

eye   beauty is in the eye of the beholder

the buyer needs a thousand eyes, the seller wants but one

an eye for an eye, and a tooth for a tooth

the eye is bigger than the belly

the eye of a master does more work than both his hands

the eyes are the mirrors of the soul

fields have eyes and woods have ears

four eyes see more than two

hawks will not pick out hawks' eyes

in the country of the blind, the one-eyed man is king

keep your eyes wide open before marriage, half shut afterward

keep your mouth shut and your eyes open

love is blind; friendship closes its eyes

please your eye and plague your heart

what the eye doesn't see, the heart doesn't grieve over

fable   history is a fable agreed upon

face   don't cut off your nose to spite your face

the face is the index of the mind See the eyes are the mirrors of the soul

a good face is a letter of recommendation

the joy of the heart makes the face fair See a merry heart makes a cheerful countenance

Monday's child is fair of face

fact   fact is stranger than fiction

facts are stubborn things

fail   when all fruit fails, welcome haws

failure   success has many fathers, while failure is an orphan

success is never final and failure is never fatal See success is never final

faint   faint heart never won fair lady

fair   all's fair in love and war

faint heart never won fair lady

fair and softly goes far in a day

a fair exchange is no robbery

fair feathers make fair fowl See fine feathers make fine birds

fair play's a jewel

fair words butter no cabbage See fine words butter no parsnips

give and take is fair play

hoist your sail when the wind is fair

it's always fair weather when good friends get together

the joy of the heart makes the face fair See a merry heart makes a cheerful countenance

Monday's child is fair of face

none but the brave deserve the fair

soft and fair goes far

turnabout is fair play

faith   faith will move mountains

fall   the apple never falls far from the tree

as a tree falls, so shall it lie

between two stools one falls to the ground

the bigger they are, the harder they fall

bread always falls buttered side down

a creaking door never falls from its hinges See a creaking door hangs longest

the falling out of lovers is the renewing of love See the quarrel of lovers is the renewal of love

happy is the bride that the sun shines on, blessed is the corpse that the rain falls on See happy is the bride that the sun shines on

hasty climbers have sudden falls

fear   courage is fear that has said its prayers

the doctor is often more to be feared than the disease

do right and fear no man

fear lends wings

fear the Greeks bearing gifts *See* beware of greeks bearing gifts

fools rush in where angels fear to tread

he that is down need fear no fall

the only thing we have to fear is fear itself

feast   the company makes the feast

a contented mind is a continual feast

enough is as good as a feast

feather   birds of a feather flock together

fine feathers make fine birds

feed   the appetite grows on what it feeds on *See* appetite comes with eating

don't bite the hand that feeds you

feed a cold and starve a fever

give a man a fish, and you feed him for a day; show him how to fish, and you feed him for a lifetime

God never sends a mouth but he feeds it *See* God never sends mouths but he sends meat

feel   a man is as old as he feels, and a woman as old as she looks

pride feels no pain

the way to be safe is never to feel secure *See* he that is too secure is not safe

feet   *See* **foot**

fell   little strokes fell great oaks

fellow   stone-dead hath no fellow

fellowship   a hedge between keeps fellowship green *See* a hedge between keeps friendship green

female   the female of the species is deadlier than the male

fence   don't take down a fence unless you are sure why it was put up

good fences make good neighbors

the grass is always greener on the other side of the fence

festina   *festina lente See* make haste slowly

fetch   a dog that will fetch a bone will carry a bone

far-fetched and dear-bought is good for ladies

fever   feed a cold and starve a fever

few   books and friends should be few and good

few words are best

he who begins many things, finishes but few

many are called, but few are chosen

patience is a virtue which few possess— some have a little, others have less *See* patience is a virtue

you win a few, you lose a few *See* you win some, you lose some

fiction   fact is stranger than fiction

truth is stranger than fiction

fiddle   Nero fiddled while Rome burned

there's many a good tune played on an old fiddle

fiddler   they that dance must pay the fiddler

field   fields have eyes and woods have ears

field-marshal   every soldier has the baton of a field-marshal in his knapsack

fierce   the lion is not so fierce as he is painted

fifteen   everybody has his fifteen minutes of fame

fight   councils of war never fight

fight fire with fire

he who fights and runs away may live to fight another day

it's not the size of the dog in the fight, it's the size of the fight in the dog

war will cease when men refuse to fight

while two dogs are fighting for a bone, a third runs away with it

you can't fight City Hall

fill   little and often fills the purse

work expands so as to fill the time available for its completion

final   success is never final

find   ask, and it shall be given you; seek, and ye shall find; knock, and it shall be opened unto you

the devil finds work for idle hands to do

find a penny, pick it up *See* see a pin and pick it up

finding is keeping

a good man is hard to find *See* good men are scarce

the husband is always the last to find out *See* the husband is always the last to know

it's easy to find a stick to beat a dog

keep a thing seven years and you'll find a use for it

love will find a way

opportunities look for you when you are worth finding

safe bind, safe find

scratch a Russian and you find a Tartar

seek and you shall find

those who hide can find

water finds its own level *See* water seeks its own level

winter finds out what summer lays up

finder   finders keepers, losers weepers

fine   fine feathers make fine birds

fine words butter no parsnips

the mills of God grind slowly, but they grind exceedingly fine *See* the mills of God grind slowly, yet they grind exceedingly small

most people consider thrift a fine virtue in ancestors

rain before seven, fine before eleven

finger   the devil makes his Christmas pies of lawyers' tongues and clerks' fingers

fingers were made before forks

finish   don't start anything you can't finish

he who begins many things, finishes but few

nice guys finish last

fire   better a little fire to warm us than a big one to burn us

a burnt child dreads the fire

dirty water will quench fire

don't jump from the frying pan into the fire

fight fire with fire

fire is a good servant but a bad master

if you play with fire, you get burned

much smoke, little fire

there's no smoke without fire

three moves are as bad as a fire

you should know a man seven years before you stir his fire

fireside   heated arguments do not warm the fireside *See* the only thing a heated argument ever produced is coolness

first   better be first in a village than second at Rome

first catch your hare

first come, first served

the first duty of a soldier is obedience

the first hundred years are the hardest

first impressions are the most lasting

the first seven years are the hardest

the first step is the hardest

first things first

first think, and then speak *See* think before you speak

first thrive and then wive

first try and then trust

if at first you don't succeed, try, try again

let him who is without sin cast the first stone

pleasure first and business after *See* business before pleasure

safety first

self-preservation is the first law of nature

shoot first and ask questions afterward

there's a first time for everything

think first and speak afterward *See* think before you speak

truth is the first casualty of war

which came first, the chicken or the egg?

whom the gods would destroy, they first make mad

fish   all fish are not caught with flies

all is fish that comes to the net

better a big fish in a little pond than a little fish in a big pond

big fish eat little fish

the cat would eat fish, but would not wet her feet

fish and guests stink after three days

fish or cut bait

a fish stinks from the head

fish where the fish are

give a man a fish, and you feed him for a day; show him how to fish, and you feed him for a lifetime

the hook without bait catches no fish

it's good fishing in troubled waters

little fish are sweet

there are other fish in the sea

fit   God fits the back to the burden *See* God makes the back to the burden

if the shoe fits, wear it

silence is the fittest reply to folly

a whistling woman and a crowing hen are neither fit for God nor men

fit   *ex nihilo nihil fit See* nothing comes of nothing

five   two's a couple, three's a crowd, four's too many, and five's not allowed *See* two's company, three's a crowd

fix   if it ain't broke, don't fix it

flag   trade follows the flag

flash   beware of an oak, it draws the stroke; avoid an ash, it counts the flash; creep under the thorn, it can save you from harm

flattery   flattery, like perfume, should be smelled but not swallowed

imitation is the sincerest form of flattery

flaunt   if you've got it, flaunt it

flea   big fleas have little fleas upon their backs to bite 'em, and little fleas have lesser fleas, and so ad infinitum

if you lie down with dogs, you'll get up with fleas

nothing should be done in haste but gripping a flea

flesh   the nearer the bone, the sweeter the flesh

the spirit is willing but the flesh is weak

what's bred in the bone will come out in the flesh

flew   *See* fly (v.)

flight   blessings brighten as they take their flight

one courageous thought will put to flight a host of troubles

fling   fling dirt enough, and some will stick *See* throw dirt enough, and some will stick

youth will have its fling

flock   birds of a feather flock together

there's a black sheep in every flock

flower   April showers bring May flowers

flowers leave fragrance in the hand that bestows them

fly (n.)   all fish are not caught with flies

eagles don't catch flies

a shut mouth catches no flies

you can catch more flies with honey than with vinegar

you must lose a fly to catch a trout *See* throw out a sprat to catch a mackerel

fly (v.) a bird in the hand is worth a hundred flying *See* a bird in the hand is worth two in the bush

a bird never flew on one wing

birds of a feather fly together *See* birds of a feather flock together

if a pig had wings, it might fly

it's good to make a bridge of gold to a flying enemy

time flies

when poverty comes in at the door, love flies out of the window

you can't keep the birds from flying over your head, but you can keep them from building a nest in your hair

folk busy folks are always meddling

different strokes for different folks

some folks speak from experience; others, from experience, don't speak

there's nowt so queer as folk

threatened folks live the longest *See* threatened men live long

young folks think old folks to be fools, but old folks know young folks to be fools

follow if one sheep leaps over the ditch, all the rest will follow

trade follows the flag

follower a good leader is also a good follower

folly anger without power is folly

silence is the fittest reply to folly

where ignorance is bliss, 'tis folly to be wise *See* ignorance is bliss

fond absence makes the heart grow fonder

food food without hospitality is medicine

more die of food than famine

fool children and fools speak the truth

experience is the teacher of fools

experience keeps a dear school, but fools will learn in no other *See* experience keeps a dear school

a fool and his money are soon parted

a fool at forty is a fool indeed

a fool may give a wise man counsel

fool me once, shame on you; fool me twice, shame on me

fools and children should never see half-done work

fools ask questions that wise men cannot answer

a fool's bolt is soon shot

fools build houses and wise men live in them

fools rush in where angels fear to tread

fortune favors fools

a man who is his own lawyer has a fool for his client

send a fool to market and a fool he'll return

six hours' sleep for a man, seven for a woman, and eight for a fool

there's no fool like an old fool

when you argue with a fool, make sure he isn't similarly engaged

a white wall is the fool's writing paper

a wise man changes his mind, but a fool never does

wise men learn by other men's mistakes, fools by their own *See* learn from the mistakes of others

you can fool some of the people all of the time, and all of the people some of the time, but you can't fool all of the people all of the time

young folks think old folks to be fools, but old folks know young folks to be fools

foolish a foolish consistency is the hobgoblin of little minds

it's a foolish sheep that makes the wolf his confessor

penny wise and pound foolish

foot the cat would eat fish, but would not wet her feet

gang the best-laid schemes of mice and men gang aft a-gley

garbage garbage in, garbage out

garden a book is like a garden carried in the pocket

if you would be happy for a week take a wife; if you would be happy for a month kill a pig; but if you would be happy all your life plant a garden

gasoline whiskey and gasoline don't mix

gate a creaking gate hangs longest *See* a creaking door hangs longest

Gath tell it not in Gath

gather gather ye rosebuds while ye may

a rolling stone gathers no moss

where the carcass is, there will the eagles be gathered

gay the child that is born on the Sabbath day is bonny and blithe and good and gay

geese *See* **goose**

general war is too important to be left to the generals

what's good for General Motors is good for America

generation from shirtsleeves to shirtsleeves is only three generations

it takes three generations to make a gentleman

generous be just before you're generous

genius genius is an infinite capacity for taking pains

genius is one percent inspiration and ninety-nine percent perspiration

genius without education is like silver in the mine

gentleman a gentleman's word is his bond *See* a man's word is as good as his bond

it takes three generations to make a gentleman

when Adam delved and Eve span, who was then the gentleman?

gently drive gently over the stones

gently does it *See* easy does it

get the best way to get even is to forget

don't get mad, get even

don't wish too hard; you might just get what you wished for

ill-gotten goods never thrive

money gets money *See* money begets money

the more you get, the more you want

piss or get off the pot

saving is getting

what's got over the devil's back is spent under his belly

what you see is what you get

when the going gets tough, the tough get going

you can't get blood from a stone

you don't get something for nothing

you get nothing for nothing *See* nothing for nothing

you get what you pay for

you never get anything for nothing *See* nothing for nothing

giant a dwarf on a giant's shoulders sees further of the two

gift beware of Greeks bearing gifts

never look a gift horse in the mouth

a small gift usually gets small thanks

gill every herring must hang by its own gill

girl boys seldom make passes at girls who wear glasses

one for sorrow, two for joy, three for a girl, and four for a boy *See* one for sorrow; two for mirth; three for a wedding; four for a birth

a whistling girl and a crowing hen always come to the same bad end *See* a whistling woman and a crowing hen are neither fit for God nor men

git them as asks, gits

them as don't ask, don't git *See* ask, and it shall be given you; seek, and ye shall find; knock, and it shall be opened unto you

give ask, and it shall be given you; seek, and ye shall find; knock, and it shall be opened unto you

don't give up the ship

everybody to whom much is given, of him will much be required

Friday's child is loving and giving

give a beggar a horse and he'll ride it to death

give a civil answer to a civil question *See* a civil question deserves a civil answer

give a loaf and beg a slice

give a dog a bad name and hang him

give a man a fish, and you feed him for a day; show him how to fish, and you feed him for a lifetime

give a man an inch and he'll take a mile

give a man enough rope and he'll hang himself

give and take is fair play

give a thing, and take a thing, to wear the devil's gold ring

give credit where credit is due

give me a child for the first seven years and he is mine for life

give the devil his due

he gives twice who gives quickly

it's better to give than to receive

the Lord gives and the Lord takes away

neither give nor take offense

never give a sucker an even break

nothing is given so freely as advice

glass the glass is either half empty or half full

people who live in glass houses shouldn't throw stones

glasses boys seldom make passes at girls who wear glasses

glitter all that glitters is not gold

glove a cat in gloves catches no mice

gluttony gluttony kills more than the sword

go as Maine goes, so goes the nation

the best-laid schemes of mice and men oft go astray *See* the best-laid schemes of mice and men gang aft a-gley

the clock goes as it pleases the clerk

don't go near the water until you learn how to swim

easy come, easy go

fair and softly goes far in a day

go abroad and you'll hear news of home

go farther and fare worse

good Americans, when they die, go to Paris

he that goes a-borrowing, goes a-sorrowing

he that would go to sea for pleasure would go to hell for a pastime

he that would learn to pray, let him go to sea

he who has a tiger by the tail dare not let go *See* he who rides a tiger is afraid to dismount

if anything can go wrong, it will

if the mountain will not come to Mohammed, Mohammed must go to the mountain

laws go as kings like

a lie can go around the world and back again while the truth is lacing up its boots

love makes the world go round

many go out for wool and come home shorn

March comes in like a lion, and goes out like a lamb

money makes the mare go

money makes the world go round

much water goes by the mill that the miller knows not of

never let the sun go down on your anger

nothing goes over the back but that comes under the belly *See* what's got over the devil's back is spent under his belly

pay as you go and nothing you'll owe

the pitcher will go to the well once too often

pride goes before a fall

quickly come, quickly go

the show must go on

Thursday's child has far to go

two tailors go to a man *See* nine tailors make a man

what goes around, comes around

what goes up must come down

when house and land are gone and spent, then learning is most excellent

when the going gets tough, the tough get going

when the worst comes, the worst is going *See* when things are at the worst they begin to mend

when you go to dance, take heed whom you take by the hand

wisdom goes beyond strength

you can't go home again

you can't take it with you when you go *See* you can't take it with you

God, god all things are possible with God

a church is God between four walls

every man for himself and God for us all

God helps those who help themselves

God is always on the side of the big battalions *See* providence is always on the side of the big battalions

God is in the details *See* the devil is in the details

God made the country and man made the town

God makes the back to the burden

God moves in mysterious ways

God never sends mouths but he sends meat

God protect me from my friends—I can protect myself from my enemies *See* save us from our friends

God sends meat, but the devil sends cooks

God's in his heaven; all's right with the world

the gods send nuts to those who have no teeth

God takes soonest those he loves best

God tempers the wind to the shorn lamb

if God did not exist, it would be necessary to invent him

man proposes, God disposes

man's extremity is God's opportunity

the mills of God grind slowly, yet they grind exceedingly small

the nearer the church, the farther from God

poverty comes from God, but not dirt

put your trust in God, and keep your powder dry

the robin and the wren are God's cock and hen

take the goods the gods provide

the voice of the people is the voice of God

where God builds a church, the devil will build a chapel

a whistling woman and a crowing hen are neither fit for God nor men

whom the gods love die young

whom the gods would destroy, they first make mad

you can't serve God and mammon

godliness cleanliness is next to godliness

gold all that glitters is not gold

give a thing, and take a thing, to wear the devil's gold ring

gold may be bought too dear

an ill agreement is better than a good
judgment

it's a good horse that never stumbles *See* a
stumble may prevent a fall

it's always fair weather when good friends
get together

it's an ill wind that blows nobody any
good

it's good fishing in troubled waters

it's good to make a bridge of gold to a
flying enemy

Jack's as good as his master

leave off while the play is good *See* quit
while you are ahead

a liar should have a good memory

listeners never hear any good of themselves

a little absence does much good

a little of what you fancy does you good

a man's word is as good as his bond

a miss is as good as a mile

never do evil that good may come of it

nobody forgets a good teacher

a nod's as good as a wink to a blind horse

no good deed goes unpunished

no news is good news

one good turn deserves another

one story is good till another is told

the road to hell is paved with good intentions

a secret is either too good to keep or too
bad not to tell

see a pin and pick it up, all the day you'll
have good luck; see a pin and let it lay,
bad luck you'll have all the day

there are as good fish in the sea as ever
came out of it *See* there are other fish
in the sea

there's good and bad in everything

there's many a good cock come out of a
tattered bag

there's many a good tune played on an
old fiddle

there's nothing so good for the inside of a
man as the outside of a horse

what's good for General Motors is good
for America

you can have too much of a good thing

you have to take the bad with the good
See you have to take the bitter with
the sweet

goodness   beauty is only skin-deep, but
goodness goes to the bone *See* beauty is
only skin-deep

goods   ill-gotten goods never thrive

take the goods the gods provide

goose   don't kill the goose that lays the
golden eggs

every man thinks his own geese swans

a goose quill is more dangerous than a
lion's claw

what's sauce for the goose is sauce for
the gander

gossip   gossip is the lifeblood of society

gossip is vice enjoyed vicariously

got, gotten   *See* get

goût   *chacun à son goût See* every man to
his taste

govern   that government is best which
governs least

government   governments have long
arms *See* kings have long arms

that government is best which governs
least

grace   blushing is a sign of grace

grace will last, beauty will blast

Tuesday's child is full of grace

grain   little drops of water, little grains
of sand, make a mighty ocean and a
pleasant land

grandmother   don't teach your grandmother to suck eggs

grasp   grasp no more than the hand
will hold

grass   the grass is always greener on the
other side of the fence

while the grass grows, the steed starves

gratitude don't overload gratitude; if you do, she'll kick

grave equality begins in the grave

there'll be sleeping enough in the grave

gray all cats are gray in the dark

the gray mare is the better horse

grease the squeaky wheel gets the grease

great behind every great man there is a great woman

death is the great leveler

great boats may venture more, but little boats should keep near shore *See* little boats should stay close to shore

a great book is a great evil

a great city, a great solitude

great cry but little wool *See* much cry and little wool

the greater the truth, the greater the libel

great men have great faults

great minds think alike

great oaks from little acorns grow

great trees keep down little ones

a half-truth is often a great lie *See* half the truth is often a whole lie

little strokes fell great oaks

little thieves are hanged, but great ones escape

out of the mouths of babes and sucklings come great truths

poverty is no disgrace, but it's a great inconvenience

small sorrows speak; great ones are silent

there's no great loss without some gain

thrift is a great revenue

time is a great healer

Greek beware of Greeks bearing gifts

when Greek meets Greek, then comes the tug of war

green far away the hills are green *See* blue are the hills that are far away

the grass is always greener on the other side of the fence

a green winter makes a fat churchyard

a hedge between keeps friendship green

grieve what the eye doesn't see, the heart doesn't grieve over

grind the mill cannot grind with the water that is past

the mills of God grind slowly, yet they grind exceedingly small

grip nothing should be done in haste but gripping a flea

grist all is grist that comes to the mill

ground between two stools one falls to the ground

grow absence makes the heart grow fonder

the appetite grows on what it feeds on *See* appetite comes with eating

as the twig is bent, the child will grow *See* as the twig is bent, so is the tree inclined

great oaks from little acorns grow

a growing youth has a wolf in his stomach

ill weeds grow apace

laugh and grow fat

money doesn't grow on trees

one for the mouse, one for the crow, one to rot, one to grow

a tale grows better in the telling *See* a tale never loses in the telling

while the grass grows, the steed starves

grunt what can you expect from a pig but a grunt?

guard don't let the fox guard the henhouse

guest a constant guest is never welcome

fish and guests stink after three days

guilty a guilty conscience needs no accuser

a man is innocent until proven guilty

listeners never hear any good of themselves

see no evil, hear no evil, speak no evil

there are none so deaf as those who will not hear

the young cock crows as he heard the old one

hearse from the day you were born till you ride in a hearse, there's nothing so bad but it might have been worse *See* nothing so bad but it might have been worse

heart absence makes the heart grow fonder

cold hands, warm heart

faint heart never won fair lady

a heavy purse makes a light heart

home is where the heart is

hope deferred makes the heart sick

humble hearts have humble desires

if it were not for hope, the heart would break

it's a poor heart that never rejoices

kind hearts are more than coronets

the larger the body, the bigger the heart

a light purse makes a heavy heart

a merry heart makes a cheerful countenance

nothing is impossible to a willing heart

out of the fullness of the heart the mouth speaks

please your eye and plague your heart

the way to a man's heart is through his stomach

what the eye doesn't see, the heart doesn't grieve over

heat if you can't stand the heat, get out of the kitchen

the only thing a heated argument ever produced is coolness

heaven crosses are ladders that lead to heaven

God's in his heaven; all's right with the world

heaven helps those who help themselves *See* God helps those who help themselves

heaven protects children, sailors, and drunken men

hell is full of good meanings, but heaven is full of good works *See* the road to hell is paved with good intentions

marriages are made in heaven

there's a season and a time for every purpose under the heaven *See* to everything there is a season

heavy every horse thinks its own pack heaviest

a heavy purse makes a light heart

light gains make heavy purses

a light purse makes a heavy heart

time hangs heavy on idle hands

hedge a hedge between keeps friendship green

heed when you go to dance, take heed whom you take by the hand

heel let your head save your heels

heir walnuts and pears you plant for your heirs

hell hell hath no fury like a woman scorned

he that would go to sea for pleasure would go to hell for a pastime

old maids lead apes in hell

the road to hell is paved with good intentions

war is hell

help every little helps

God helps those who help themselves

help you to salt, help you to sorrow

a mouse may help a lion

hen he that would have eggs must endure the cackling of hens

it's a sad house where the hen crows louder than the cock

the robin and the wren are God's cock and hen

a whistling woman and a crowing hen are neither fit for God nor men

hence it'll all be the same a hundred years hence *See* it'll all be the same in a hundred years

henhouse don't let the fox guard the henhouse

herb better a dinner of herbs where love is than a stalled ox where hate is

hero no man is a hero to his valet

herring every herring must hang by its own gill

hesitate he who hesitates is lost

hide don't hide your light under a bushel

love and a cough cannot be hid

those who hide can find

you can run, but you can't hide

high the higher the monkey climbs the more he shows his tail

the higher the tree, the sweeter the plum

the highest branch is not the safest roost

imitation is the highest form of flattery *See* imitation is the sincerest form of flattery

a stream never rises higher than its source *See* a stream cannot rise above its source

hill blue are the hills that are far away

himself every man for himself and God for us all

every man for himself and the devil take the hindmost

hinder meat and mass never hindered man

hindmost every man for himself and the devil take the hindmost

hinge a creaking door never falls from its hinges *See* a creaking door hangs longest

hire the laborer is worthy of his hire

historian history doesn't repeat itself— historians do *See* history repeats itself

history happy is the country that has no history

history is a fable agreed upon

history repeats itself

hit don't hit a man when he's down

hitch hitch your wagon to a star

hobgoblin a foolish consistency is the hobgoblin of little minds

hoist hoist your sail when the wind is fair

hold grasp no more than the hand will hold

hole the fox preys furthest from his hole

the hole calls the thief

if wind blows on you through a hole, say your prayers and mind your soul

money burns a hole in the pocket

the mouse that has but one hole is quickly taken

when you are in a hole, stop digging

you can't put a square peg in a round hole

home charity begins at home

curses, like chickens, come home to roost

east, west, home's best

every dog is a lion at home *See* every cock will crow upon his own dunghill

go abroad and you'll hear news of home

home is home, be it ever so homely

home is where the heart is

home is where you hang your hat

it takes a heap of living to make a house a home

the longest way around is the shortest way home

a man's home is his castle

many go out for wool and come home shorn

men make houses, women make homes

there's no place like home

you can't go home again

homely home is home, be it ever so homely

Homer Homer sometimes nods

honest an honest look covereth many faults

an honest man's word is as good as his bond *See* a man's word is as good as his bond

honest men marry quickly, wise men not at all

when thieves fall out, honest men come by their own

honesty beauty and honesty seldom agree

honesty is more praised than practiced

honesty is the best policy

honesty pays

honey where bees are, there is honey

you can catch more flies with honey than with vinegar

honor honors change manners

the post of honor is the post of danger

a prophet is not without honor, save in his own country

there's honor among thieves

hoof three things are not to be trusted: a cow's horn, a dog's tooth, and a horse's hoof

hook the hook without bait catches no fish

hope he that lives in hope dances to an ill tune

he that lives on hope will die fasting

hope and have

hope deferred makes the heart sick

hope for the best and prepare for the worst

hope is a good breakfast but a bad supper

hope springs eternal in the human breast

if it were not for hope, the heart would break

while there's life there's hope

hopefully it's better to travel hopefully than to arrive

horn three things are not to be trusted: a cow's horn, a dog's tooth, and a horse's hoof

toot your own horn lest the same be never tooted

horse better be the head of an ass than the tail of a horse *See* better be the head of a dog than the tail of a lion

don't put the cart before the horse

don't shut the barn door after the horse is stolen

don't swap horses in midstream

every horse thinks its own pack heaviest

for want of a nail the shoe was lost, for want of a shoe the horse was lost, and for want of a horse the rider was lost

give a beggar a horse and he'll ride it to death

a good horse cannot be of a bad color

the gray mare is the better horse

a horse can't pull while kicking

horses for courses

if two ride on a horse, one must ride behind

if wishes were horses, beggars would ride

it's a good horse that never stumbles *See* a stumble may prevent a fall

the man who is born in a stable is not a horse

a man without a religion is a horse without a bridle

never look a gift horse in the mouth

a nod's as good as a wink to a blind horse

a short horse is soon curried

there's nothing so good for the inside of a man as the outside of a horse

three things are not to be trusted: a cow's horn, a dog's tooth, and a horse's hoof

while the grass grows, the horse starves *See* while the grass grows, the steed starves the willing horse carries the load

you can lead a horse to water, but you can't make him drink

zeal without knowledge is a runaway horse

horseback set a beggar on horseback, and he'll ride to the devil

hospitality food without hospitality is medicine

host one courageous thought will put to flight a host of troubles

hostage he that has a wife and children has given hostages to fortune

hot hot love is soon cold

a little pot is soon hot

strike while the iron is hot

hound you can't run with the hare and hunt with the hounds

hour better three hours too soon than a minute too late *See* it's better to be an hour too early than a minute too late

the darkest hour is just before dawn

a fool can ask more questions in an hour than a wise man can answer in seven years *See* fools ask questions that wise men cannot answer

an hour in the morning is worth two in the evening

it's better to be an hour too early than a minute too late

lose an hour in the morning, chase it all day

one hour's sleep before midnight is worth two after

six hours' sleep for a man, seven for a woman, and eight for a fool

house the back door robs the house *See* a postern door makes a thief

better one house spoiled than two

burn not your house to scare away the mice

education doesn't come by bumping your head against the school house

fools build houses and wise men live in them

a house divided against itself cannot stand

the house shows the owner

a house without books is like a room without windows

it's a sad house where the hen crows louder than the cock

it takes a heap of living to make a house a home

learning is better than house or land

men make houses, women make homes

never speak of rope in the house of a man who has been hanged

people who live in glass houses shouldn't throw stones

when house and land are gone and spent, then learning is most excellent

who repairs not his gutters repairs his whole house

how it's not what you say, but how you say it

human hope springs eternal in the human breast

to err is human, to forgive divine

humanum humanum est errare *See* to err is human, to forgive divine

humble humble hearts have humble desires

hundred a bird in the hand is worth a hundred flying *See* a bird in the hand is worth two in the bush

the buyer has need of a hundred eyes, the seller of but one *See* the buyer needs a thousand eyes, the seller wants but one

the first hundred years are the hardest

it'll all be the same in a hundred years

victory has a hundred fathers and defeat is an orphan *See* success has many fathers, while failure is an orphan

hunger hunger drives the wolf out of the wood

hunger is the best sauce

hungry a hungry man is an angry man

a hungry stomach has no ears

hunt go hunting where the ducks are

you can't run with the hare and hunt with the hounds

hurry always in a hurry, always behind

hurry no man's cattle

hurt don't cry before you're hurt

sticks and stones may break my bones, but words will never hurt me

the truth hurts

what you don't know can't hurt you

work never hurt anybody

husband a deaf husband and a blind wife are always a happy couple

a good husband makes a good wife

the husband is always the last to know

I I today, you tomorrow *See* today you, tomorrow me

ice the rich man has his ice in the summer and the poor man gets his in the winter

trust not one night's ice

idea all words are pegs to hang ideas on

idle as good be an addled egg as an idle bird

the devil finds work for idle hands to do

an idle brain is the devil's workshop

idle people have the least leisure

an idle youth, a needy age

it's idle to swallow the cow and choke on the tail

time hangs heavy on idle hands

idleness idleness is the root of all evil

if if and an spoils many a good charter

if ifs and ans were pots and pans, there'd be no work for tinkers

ignorance admiration is the daughter of ignorance

ignorance is a voluntary misfortune

ignorance is bliss

ignorance of the law is no excuse

prejudice is the child of ignorance

ill he that has an ill name is half hanged *See* give a dog a bad name and hang him

he that lives in hope dances to an ill tune

an ill agreement is better than a good judgment

an ill beginning makes an ill ending

an ill bird lays an ill egg

ill doers are ill dreaders *See* evil doers are evil dreaders

ill-gotten goods never thrive

an ill master makes an ill servant *See* like master, like man

ill news comes apace *See* bad news travels fast

ill weeds grow apace

it's an ill bird that fouls its own nest

it's an ill wind that blows nobody any good

it's ill jesting with edged tools

it's ill sitting at Rome and striving with the Pope

it's ill speaking between a full man and a fasting

it's ill striving against the stream *See* strive not against the stream

it's ill waiting for dead men's shoes

never speak ill of the dead

imitation imitation is the sincerest form of flattery

imp talk about the devil and his imps will appear *See* talk of the devil and he's sure to appear

important war is too important to be left to the generals

impossible the difficult is done at once, the impossible takes a little longer

nothing is impossible to a willing heart

impression first impressions are the most lasting

improve anger improves nothing but the arch of a cat's back

in garbage in, garbage out

jester   jesters do oft prove prophets

jewel   fair play's a jewel

Jill   every Jack has his Jill

a good Jack makes a good Jill

jingle   when a man's single, his pockets will jingle

job   if a job's worth doing, it's worth doing well *See* if a thing's worth doing, it's worth doing well

never send a boy to do a man's job

join   if you can't beat 'em, join 'em

joke   a rich man's joke is always funny

journey   a journey of a thousand miles begins with one step

Jove   Jove but laughs at lover's perjury

joy   the joy of the heart makes the face fair *See* a merry heart makes a cheerful countenance

no joy without annoy

one for sorrow, two for joy, three for a girl, and four for a boy *See* one for sorrow; two for mirth; three for a wedding; four for a birth

a thing of beauty is a joy forever

judge   don't judge a book by its cover

don't judge a man until you have walked a mile in his boots

judge not according to appearances

judge not, that ye be not judged

nobody should be judge in his own cause

judgment   an ill agreement is better than a good judgment

jump   don't jump from the frying pan into the fire

June   a dripping June sets all in tune

just   be just before you're generous

justice   justice is blind

justify   the end justifies the means

keep   death keeps no calendar

finding is keeping

great boats may venture more, but little boats should keep near shore *See* little boats should stay close to shore

great trees keep down little ones

hope keeps the heart from breaking *See* if it were not for hope, the heart would break

keep a thing seven years and you'll find a use for it

keep no more cats than will catch mice

keep your eyes wide open before marriage, half shut afterward

keep your mouth shut and your eyes open

keep your shop and your shop will keep you

a man is known by the company he keeps

one sword keeps another in its scabbard

put your trust in God, and keep your powder dry

a secret is either too good to keep or too bad not to tell

truth keeps to the bottom of her well *See* truth lies at the bottom of a well

why keep a dog and bark yourself?

you can't keep the birds from flying over your head, but you can keep them from building a nest in your hair

keeper   finders keepers, losers weepers

kernel   he that would eat the kernel must crack the nut *See* he that would eat the fruit must climb the tree

kettle   the pot calls the kettle black

key   a golden key can open any door

sloth is the key to poverty *See* sloth is the mother of poverty

the used key is always bright

kick   don't overload gratitude; if you do, she'll kick

a horse can't pull while kicking

a jackass can kick a barn door down, but it takes a carpenter to build one

kill   care killed the cat

curiosity killed the cat

don't kill the goose that lays the golden eggs

gluttony kills more than the sword

if you would be happy for a week take a wife; if you would be happy for a month kill a pig; but if you would be happy all your life plant a garden

it's not work that kills, but worry

it's the pace that kills

killing no murder

neglect will kill an injury sooner than revenge

there are more ways of killing a cat than choking it with cream

kind (adj.) be kind to your friends; if it weren't for them, you would be a total stranger

kind hearts are more than coronets

kind (n.) better a good cow than a cow of a good kind

it takes all kinds of people to make a world

king a cat can look at a king

in the country of the blind, the one-eyed man is king

the king can do no wrong

kings have long arms

laws go as kings like

punctuality is the politeness of kings

kingdom content is more than a kingdom

for want of a nail the kingdom was lost *See* for want of a nail the shoe was lost, for want of a shoe the horse was lost, and for want of a horse the rider was lost

kirtle near is my kirtle, but nearer is my smock *See* near is my shirt, but nearer is my skin

kiss kissing goes by favor

many kiss the hand they wish to see cut off

kitchen a fat kitchen makes a lean will

if you can't stand the heat, get out of the kitchen

kitten wanton kittens make sober cats

knapsack every soldier has the baton of a field-marshal in his knapsack

knee it's better to die on your feet than live on your knees

knife fingers were made before knives and forks *See* fingers were made before forks

knock a bribe will enter without knocking

ask, and it shall be given you; seek, and ye shall find; knock, and it shall be opened unto you

opportunity knocks but once

opportunity never knocks for persons not worth a rap

know better the devil you know than the devil you don't know

by learning to obey, you will know how to command *See* he that cannot obey cannot command

come live with me and you'll know me

the good seaman is known in bad weather

the husband is always the last to know

it's a wise child that knows its own father

it's not what you know, but who you know

it takes one to know one

know thyself

a man is known by the company he keeps

necessity knows no law

a new broom sweeps clean, but an old broom knows all the corners *See* a new broom sweeps clean

one half of the world doesn't know how the other half lives

pay what you owe and you'll know what you own

tell not all you know, nor do all you can

thinking is very far from knowing

those who know don't speak; those who speak don't know

to know all is to forgive all

the tree is known by its fruit

the wearer best knows where the shoe pinches

what you don't know can't hurt you

who knows most, speaks least

years know more than books

you never know a man until you live with him

you never know what you can do until you try

young folks think old folks to be fools, but old folks know young folks to be fools

you should know a man seven years before you stir his fire

knowledge   experience is the mother of knowledge *See* experience is the mother of wisdom

knowledge and timber shouldn't be much used until they are seasoned

knowledge and wisdom are far from being one

knowledge is power

a little knowledge is a dangerous thing

zeal without knowledge is a runaway horse

known   *See* **know**

laborat   *qui non laborat non manducet See* he who does not work, neither should he eat

laborer   the laborer is worthy of his hire

lace   a lie can go around the world and back again while the truth is lacing up its boots

ladder   crosses are ladders that lead to heaven

he who would climb the ladder must begin at the bottom

lady   faint heart never won fair lady

far-fetched and dear-bought is good for ladies

the opera ain't over till the fat lady sings

laid   *See* **lay**

laird   new lairds make new laws *See* new lords, new laws

lamb   God tempers the wind to the shorn lamb

March comes in like a lion and goes out like a lamb

one might as well be hanged for a sheep as for a lamb

land   every land has its own law

in the land of the blind, the one-eyed are kings *See* in the country of the blind, the one-eyed man is king

learning is better than house or land

little drops of water, little grains of sand, make a mighty ocean and a pleasant land

talk is cheap, but it takes money to buy land *See* talk is cheap

when house and land are gone and spent, then learning is most excellent

who has land has war

you buy land, you buy stones; you buy meat, you buy bones

lane   it's a long lane that has no turning *See* it's a long road that has no turning

large   honesty is the best policy, though it may not pay the largest dividends *See* honesty is the best policy

the larger the body, the bigger the heart

lark   if the sky falls, we shall catch larks

last (adj.)   he who laughs last, laughs longest

the husband is always the last to know

it's the last straw that breaks the camel's back

last but not least

the last drop makes the cup run over

live every day as though it were your last

nice guys finish last

patriotism is the last refuge of a scoundrel

a pitcher that goes to the well too often is broken at last *See* the pitcher will go to the well once too often there are no birds in last year's nest

last (n.)   let the cobbler stick to his last

last (v.)   first impressions are the most lasting

grace will last, beauty will blast

hoist up the sail while the gale does last *See* hoist your sail when the wind is fair

long foretold, long last; short notice, soon past

man's work lasts till set of sun; woman's work is never done *See* a woman's work is never done

a wonder lasts but nine days

late   better late than never

the early man never borrows from the late man

it's better to be an hour too early than a minute too late

it's never too late to learn

it's never too late to mend

it's too late to shut the stable door after the horse has bolted *See* don't shut the barn door after the horse is stolen

late children, early orphans

shoot first, ask questions later *See* shoot first and ask questions afterward

laugh   he who laughs last, laughs longest

it's better to laugh than to cry

Jove but laughs at lover's perjury

laugh and grow fat

laugh and the world laughs with you, weep and you weep alone

laugh before breakfast, cry before sunset *See* sing before breakfast, cry before night

let them laugh that win

love laughs at locksmiths

laughter   laughter is the best medicine

law   agree, for the law is costly

every land has its own law

hard cases make bad law

ignorance of the law is no excuse

laws go as kings like

necessity knows no law

new lords, new laws

nobody is above the law

one law for the rich and another for the poor

possession is nine points of the law

self-preservation is the first law of nature

a wise lawyer never goes to law himself

lawbreaker   lawmakers should not be lawbreakers

lawmaker   lawmakers should not be lawbreakers

lawyer   the devil makes his Christmas pies of lawyers' tongues and clerks' fingers

a man who is his own lawyer has a fool for his client

a wise lawyer never goes to law himself

lay   all lay loads on the willing horse *See* the willing horse carries the load

the best-laid schemes of mice and men gang aft a-gley

don't kill the goose that lays the golden eggs

see a pin and pick it up, all the day you'll have good luck; see a pin and let it lay, bad luck you'll have all the day

lead   all roads lead to Rome

crosses are ladders that lead to heaven

if the blind lead the blind, both shall fall into the ditch

old maids lead apes in hell

one lie leads to another

people are more easily led than driven

you can lead a horse to water, but you can't make him drink

leader   a good leader is also a good follower

leaf   deeds are fruits, words are but leaves

leak   little leaks sink the ship

lean   a fat kitchen makes a lean will

leap   if one sheep leaps over the ditch, all the rest will follow

look before you leap

learn   by learning to obey, you will know how to command *See* he that cannot obey cannot command

don't go near the water until you learn how to swim

experience keeps a dear school, but fools will learn in no other *See* experience keeps a dear school

he that would learn to pray, let him go to sea

in politics a man must learn to rise above principle

it's never too late to learn

learn from the mistakes of others

learning is better than house or land

a little learning is a dangerous thing *See* a little knowledge is a dangerous thing

live and learn

nobody is born learned; bishops are made of men

an old dog will learn no tricks *See* you can't teach an old dog new tricks

there's no royal road to learning

wear your learning like your watch, in a private pocket

we must learn to walk before we can run

when house and land are gone and spent, then learning is most excellent

least   idle people have the least leisure

last but not least

least said, soonest mended

that government is best which governs least

who knows most, speaks least

leave   the devil always leaves a stink behind him

leave no stone unturned

leave off while the play is good *See* quit while you are ahead

leave well enough alone

war is too important to be left to the generals

when in doubt, leave it out *See* when in doubt, do nothing

led   *See* **lead**

left   *See* **leave**

leg   everybody stretches his legs according to the length of his coverlet

there goes more to marriage than four bare legs in a bed

use legs and have legs

legem   necessitas non habet legem *See* necessity knows no law

leisure   the busiest men have the most leisure

idle people have the least leisure

marry in haste, repent at leisure

there's luck in leisure

lend   distance lends enchantment to the view

fear lends wings

lend your money and lose your friend

lender   neither a borrower nor a lender be

length   everybody stretches his legs according to the length of his coverlet

length begets loathing

lengthen   as the day lengthens, so the cold strengthens

lente   festina lente *See* make haste slowly

leopard   the leopard can't change its spots

less   less is more

more haste, less speed

the more said, the less done

of two evils choose the less *See* choose the lesser of two evils

patience is a virtue which few possess— some have a little, others have less *See* patience is a virtue

lesser   big fleas have little fleas upon their backs to bite 'em, and little fleas have lesser fleas, and so ad infinitum

choose the lesser of two evils

lift   a rising tide lifts all boats

light (adj.)   a heavy purse makes a light heart

light come, light go *See* easy come, easy go

light gains make heavy purses

a light purse makes a heavy heart

many hands make light work

small things affect light minds *See* little things please little minds

light (n.)   all arts are brothers, each is a light to the other

don't hide your light under a bushel

light (v.)   it's better to light one candle than curse the darkness

lightly   in the spring a young man's fancy lightly turns to thoughts of love

lightning   lightning never strikes twice in the same place

like (adj.)   like attracts like

like breeds like

like cures like

like father, like son

like master, like man

like mother, like daughter

like people, like priest

like (v.)   if you don't like it, you can lump it

if you don't like the heat, get out of the kitchen *See* if you can't stand the heat, get out of the kitchen

limit   the sky's the limit

line   every cloud has a silver lining

linen   don't wash your dirty linen in public

never choose your women or linen by candlelight

link   a chain is no stronger than its weakest link

linstock   the cobbler to his last and the gunner to his linstock *See* let the cobbler stick to his last

lion   better be the head of a dog than the tail of a lion

every dog is a lion at home *See* every cock will crow upon his own dunghill

a goose quill is more dangerous than a lion's claw

the lion is not so fierce as he is painted

a live dog is better than a dead lion

a man is a lion in his own cause

march comes in like a lion, and goes out like a lamb

a mouse may help a lion

lip   loose lips sink ships

there's many a slip between cup and lip

liquor   talk is cheap, but it takes money to buy liquor *See* talk is cheap

listener   listeners never hear any good of themselves

little   better a big fish in a little pond than a little fish in a big pond

better a little fire to warm us than a big one to burn us

big fish eat little fish

big fleas have little fleas upon their backs to bite 'em, and little fleas have lesser fleas, and so ad infinitum

birds in their little nests agree

everybody's queer but you and me, and even you are a little queer

every little helps

a foolish consistency is the hobgoblin of little minds

great oaks from little acorns grow

great trees keep down little ones

into every life a little rain must fall

it's better to light one little candle than curse the darkness *See* it's better to light one candle than curse the darkness

life is too short to be little *See* life is too short

a little absence does much good

little and often fills the purse

little birds that can sing and won't sing must be made to sing little boats should stay close to shore

little drops of water, little grains of sand, make a mighty ocean and a pleasant land

little fish are sweet

a little knowledge is a dangerous thing

little leaks sink the ship

a little of what you fancy does you good

little pitchers have big ears

a little pot is soon hot

little strokes fell great oaks

little thieves are hanged, but great ones escape

little things please little minds

love me little, love me long

many a little makes a mickle

much cry and little wool

much smoke, little fire

paper bleeds little

patience is a virtue which few possess— some have a little, others have less *See* patience is a virtue

there's no little enemy

live (adj.) a live dog is better than a dead lion

live (v.) be happy while you're living, for you're a long time dead

brave men lived before Agamemnon

can't live with 'em, can't live without 'em

come live with me and you'll know me

eat to live, do not live to eat

fools build houses and wise men live in them

the good that men do lives after them

he lives long who lives well

he that lives in hope dances to an ill tune

he that lives on hope will die fasting

he who fights and runs away may live to fight another day

he who lives by the sword dies by the sword

if you want to live and thrive, let the spider run alive

it's better to die on your feet than live on your knees

it's hard to live in Rome and strive against the Pope *See* it's ill sitting at Rome and striving with the Pope

it takes a heap of living to make a house a home

live and learn

live and let live

live every day as though it were your last

a living dog is better than a dead lion *See* a live dog is better than a dead lion

man does not live by bread alone

one half of the world doesn't know how the other half lives

people who live in glass houses shouldn't throw stones

a reed before the wind lives on, while mighty oaks do fall

saturday's child works hard for its living

they that live longest see most

threatened men live long

you must take two bears to live with you—bear and forbear *See* bear and forbear

you never know a man until you live with him

load the willing horse carries the load

loaf give a loaf and beg a slice

half a loaf is better than no bread

a slice off a cut loaf isn't missed

loathe length begets loathing

location location, location, location

locksmith love laughs at locksmiths

lonely one seldom meets a lonely lie *See* one lie leads to another

long art is long and life is short

be happy while you're living, for you're a long time dead

be not idle and you shall not be longing *See* an idle youth, a needy age

be the day weary or be the day long, at last it ringeth to evensong

a creaking door hangs longest

the day is short and the work is long

the difficult is done at once, the impossible takes a little longer

happy's the wooing that's not long a-doing

he lives long who lives well

he that waits for dead men's shoes may go a long time barefoot *See* it's ill waiting for dead men's shoes

he who laughs last, laughs longest

he who sups with the devil should have a long spoon

it's a long road that has no turning

kings have long arms

the longest day must have an end

the longest journey begins with a single step *See* a journey of a thousand miles begins with one step

the longest way around is the shortest way home

long foretold, long last; short notice, soon past

love me little, love me long

never is a long time

old sins cast long shadows

short reckonings make long friends

short visits make long friends

a stern chase is a long chase

they that live longest see most

threatened men live long

longa *ars longa, vita brevis See* art is long and life is short

look always look on the bright side

the art of being a parent consists of sleeping when the baby isn't looking

a cat can look at a king

the devil looks after his own

an honest look covereth many faults

if it looks like a duck, walks like a duck, and quacks like a duck, it's a duck

look out for number one *See* take care of number one

look after the pennies and the dollars will look after themselves *See* take care of the pennies and the dollars will take care of themselves

look before you leap

a man is as old as he feels, and a woman as old as she looks

never look a gift horse in the mouth

opportunities look for you when you are worth finding

when all you have is a hammer, everything looks like a nail

looker lookers-on see most of the game

loose loose lips sink ships

lord everybody loves a lord

the Lord gives and the Lord takes away

the Lord moves in mysterious ways *See* God moves in mysterious ways

new lords, new laws

lordship lordships change manners *See* honors change manners

lose a bleating sheep loses a bite

business neglected is business lost

catch not at shadows and lose the substance

the cow knows not the value of her tail till she has lost it

for want of a nail the shoe was lost, for want of a shoe the horse was lost, and for want of a horse the rider was lost

a good name is sooner lost than won

heads I win, tails you lose

he who hesitates is lost

it's better to lose the battle and win the war

it's not whether you win or lose, but how you play the game

lend your money and lose your friend

lose an hour in the morning, chase it all day

the sun loses nothing by shining into a puddle

a tale never loses in the telling

there's nothing lost by civility

time lost cannot be recalled

'tis better to have loved and lost, than never to have loved at all

what you lose on the swings you gain on the roundabouts

you can't lose what you never had

you must lose a fly to catch a trout *See* throw out a sprat to catch a mackerel

you snooze, you lose

you win some, you lose some

loser finders keepers, losers weepers

the winners laugh, the losers weep *See* let them laugh that win

loss one man's loss is another man's gain

there's no great loss without some gain

lost *See* **lose**

lot one bad apple spoils the lot *See* the rotten apple spoils the barrel

lottery marriage is a lottery

loud actions speak louder than words

the more you stir a stink, the louder it smells *See* the more you stir it, the worse it stinks

louse sue a beggar and catch a louse

love all's fair in love and war

better a dinner of herbs where love is than a stalled ox where hate is

the course of true love never did run smooth

everybody loves a lord

faults are thick where love is thin

Friday's child is loving and giving

God takes soonest those he loves best

hot love is soon cold

in the spring a young man's fancy lightly turns to thoughts of love

it's best to be off with the old love before you are on with the new

love and a cough cannot be hid

love begets love

love conquers all

love is blind; friendship closes its eyes

love is free

love laughs at locksmiths

love makes the world go round

love me little, love me long

love me, love my dog

the love of money is the root of all evil

love will find a way

love your enemy, but don't put a gun in his hand

love your neighbor as yourself

lucky at cards, unlucky in love

misery loves company

money loves company *See* money begets money

one cannot love and be wise

pity is akin to love

praise the child, and you make love to the mother

the quarrel of lovers is the renewal of love

'tis better to have loved and lost, than never to have loved at all

when poverty comes in at the door, love flies out of the window

whom the gods love die young

lover Jove but laughs at lover's perjury

the quarrel of lovers is the renewal of love

luck better luck next time

the devil's children have the devil's luck

diligence is the mother of good luck

see a pin and pick it up, all the day you'll have good luck; see a pin and let it lay, bad luck you'll have all the day

there's luck in leisure

there's luck in odd numbers

lucky it's better to be born lucky than rich

lucky at cards, unlucky in love

third time lucky *See* the third time is the charm

lump   if you don't like it, you can lump it

lunch   there's no such thing as a free lunch

mackerel   throw out a sprat to catch a mackerel

mad   don't get mad, get even

he that would hang his dog gives out first that he is mad

whom the gods would destroy, they first make mad

made   see **make**

maid   old maids lead apes in hell

Maine   as Maine goes, so goes the nation

majority   it's better to be right than in the majority

make   as you make your bed, so you must lie in it

clothes don't make the man

clothes make the man

the company makes the feast

conscience does make cowards of us all

the cowl does not make the monk

don't make the same mistake twice

fingers were made before forks

first catch your rabbit and then make your stew *See* first catch your hare

from nothing, nothing is made *See* nothing comes of nothing

haste makes waste

he who is good at making excuses is seldom good at anything else

if you don't make mistakes you don't make anything

it takes all kinds of people to make a world

it takes money to make money

it takes two to make a bargain

it takes two to make a quarrel

life is what you make it

little birds that can sing and won't sing must be made to sing

love makes the world go round

make haste slowly

make hay while the sun shines

manners make the man

marriages are made in heaven

men make houses, women make homes

might makes right

money makes a man

money makes money *See* money begets money

money makes the mare go

money makes the world go round

neither take offense nor make offense *See* neither give nor take offense

nine tailors make a man

one lie makes many *See* one lie leads to another

one swallow does not make a summer

opportunity makes a thief

peace makes plenty

poets are born, not made

a postern door makes a thief

practice makes perfect

praise the child, and you make love to the mother

promises are like piecrust: easy made and easy broken *See* promises, like piecrust, are made to be broken

revolutions are not made with rose water

rules are made to be broken

short visits make long friends

success makes success as money makes money *See* success breeds success

the tailor makes the man

two and two and makes four

two wrongs don't make a right

you can lead a horse to water, but you can't make him drink

you can't make an omelette without breaking eggs

you can't make a silk purse out of a sow's ear

you can't make bricks without straw

male   the female of the species is deadlier than the male

mammon   you can't serve God and mammon

man   all men are created equal

behind every great man there is a great woman

the best-laid schemes of mice and men gang aft a-gley

the best of men are but men at best

better be an old man's darling than a young man's slave

a blind man's wife needs no paint

brave men lived before Agamemnon

the busiest men have the most leisure

call a man a thief and he will steal

call no man happy till he dies

the child is father of the man

clothes don't make the man

clothes make the man

dead men don't bite

dead men tell no tales

a dog is a man's best friend

don't hit a man when he's down

don't judge a man until you have walked a mile in his boots

do right and fear no man

a drowning man will catch at a straw

the early man never borrows from the late man

early to bed and early to rise, makes a man healthy, wealthy, and wise

every elm has its man

every man after his fashion

every man for himself and God for us all

every man for himself and the devil take the hindmost

every man has his price

every man is his own worst enemy

every man is the architect of his own fortune

every man must skin his own skunk

every man thinks his own geese swans

every man to his taste

every man to his trade

a fool may give a wise man counsel

fools ask questions that wise men cannot answer

give a man a fish, and you feed him for a day; show him how to fish, and you feed him for a lifetime

give a man an inch and he'll take a mile

give a man enough rope and he'll hang himself

God made the country and man made the town

good men are scarce

the good that men do lives after them

great men have great faults

haste makes waste, and waste makes want, and want makes strife between a good man and his wife *See* haste makes waste

a hungry man is an angry man

hurry no man's cattle

in politics a man must learn to rise above principle

in the country of the blind, the one-eyed man is king

in the spring a young man's fancy lightly turns to thoughts of love

it's ill speaking between a full man and a fasting

it's ill waiting for dead men's shoes

like master, like man

a man can only die once

man does not live by bread alone

a man in debt is caught in a net

a man is a lion in his own cause

a man is as old as he feels, and a woman as old as she looks

a man is innocent until proven guilty

a man is known by the company he keeps

man is the measure of all things

manners make the man

man proposes, God disposes

a man's best reputation for the future is his record of the past

man's extremity is God's opportunity

a man's got to do what a man's got to do

a man's home is his castle

a man's word is as good as his bond

man's work lasts till set of sun; woman's work is never done *See* a woman's work is never done

the man who is born in a stable is not a horse

a man who is his own lawyer has a fool for his client

a man without a religion is a horse without a bridle

a man wrapped up in himself makes a very small bundle

meat and mass never hindered man

men are blind in their own cause

men are from Mars, women are from Venus

men make houses, women make homes

money makes a man

never send a boy to do a man's job

never speak of rope in the house of a man who has been hanged

nine tailors make a man

nobody is born learned; bishops are made of men

no man can call again yesterday *See* yesterday will not be called again

no man can serve two masters

no man is above the law, and no man is below it *See* nobody is above the law

no man is a hero to his valet

no man is an island

no man is necessary *See* nobody is indispensable

no moon, no man

one man's loss is another man's gain

one man's meat is another man's poison

one man's trash is another man's treasure

one volunteer is worth two pressed men

patience is a virtue, catch it if you can: seldom in a woman and never in a man *See* patience is a virtue

praise no man till he is dead

the rich man has his ice in the summer and the poor man gets his in the winter

a rich man's joke is always funny

six hours' sleep for a man, seven for a woman, and eight for a fool

so many men, so many opinions

the style is the man

the tailor makes the man

there's a tide in the affairs of man

there's nothing so good for the inside of a man as the outside of a horse

threatened men live long

time and tide wait for no man

war will cease when men refuse to fight

the way to a man's heart is through his stomach

whatever man has done, man may do

when a dog bites a man, that is not news; but when a man bites a dog, that is news

when a man's single, his pockets will jingle

a whistling woman and a crowing hen are neither fit for God nor men

a willful man must have his way

a wise man changes his mind, but a fool never does

a wise man is never less alone than when alone

wise men learn by other men's mistakes, fools by their own *See* learn from the mistakes of others

you can't be all things to all men

you can't beat a man at his own game

you never know a man until you live with him

young men may die, but old men must die

May   April showers bring May flowers

marry in May, rue for aye

May chickens come cheeping

ne'er cast a clout till May be out

a wet May brings plenty of hay

me   today you, tomorrow me

mean   hell is full of good meanings, but heaven is full of good works *See* the road to hell is paved with good intentions

silence means consent *See* silence gives consent

speak not of my debts unless you mean to pay them

means   the end justifies the means

he who wills the end, wills the means

measure   man is the measure of all things

there's measure in all things

meat   the closer to the bone, the sweeter the meat *See* the nearer the bone, the sweeter the flesh

God never sends mouths but he sends meat

God sends meat, but the devil sends cooks

meat and mass never hindered man

one man's meat is another man's poison

you buy land, you buy stones; you buy meat, you buy bones

meddle   busy folks are always meddling

medicine   a dose of adversity is often as needful as a dose of medicine

food without hospitality is medicine

laughter is the best medicine

medicine can prolong life, but death will seize the doctor, too

meek   the meek shall inherit the earth

meet   be nice to people on your way up because you'll meet them on your way down

don't meet troubles halfway

East is East and West is West and never the twain shall meet

extremes meet

one seldom meets a lonely lie *See* one lie leads to another

when Greek meets Greek, then comes the tug of war

même   *plus ça change, plus c'est la même chose See* the more things change, the more they stay the same

memory   a liar should have a good memory

men   *See* **man**

mend   it's never too late to mend

least said, soonest mended

when things are at the worst they begin to mend

mention   never mention a rope in the house of a man who has been hanged *See* Never speak of rope in the house of a man who has been hanged

merry   eat, drink, and be merry, for tomorrow we die

it's merry in hall when beards wag all

a merry heart makes a cheerful countenance

the more the merrier

merryman   the best doctors are Dr. Diet, Dr. Quiet, and Dr. Merryman

messenger   don't shoot the messenger

mice   *See* **mouse**

mickle   many a little makes a mickle

middle   don't change horses in the middle of the stream *See* don't swap horses in midstream

don't change the rules in the middle of the game

midge   the mother of mischief is no bigger than a midge's wing

midnight   one hour's sleep before midnight is worth two after

if you don't make mistakes you don't make anything

learn from the mistakes of others

mix   never mix business with pleasure

oil and water do not mix

whiskey and gasoline don't mix

moderation   moderation in all things

moeurs   *autres temps, autres moeurs See* other times, other manners

Mohammed   if the mountain will not come to Mohammed, Mohammed must go to the mountain

moment   seize the moment *See* seize the day

Monday   Monday's child is fair of face

money   bad money drives out good

both poverty and prosperity come from spending money—prosperity from spending it wisely

don't throw good money after bad

a fool and his money are soon parted

a good reputation is more valuable than money

it takes money to make money

lend your money and lose your friend

the love of money is the root of all evil

money begets money

money burns a hole in the pocket

money can't buy happiness

money doesn't grow on trees

money has no smell

money isn't everything

money is power

money is round and rolls away

money is the root of all evil

money makes a man

money makes the mare go

money makes the world go round

money talks

never marry for money, but marry where money is

success makes success as money makes money *See* success breeds success

talk is cheap, but it takes money to buy land *See* talk is cheap

talk is cheap, but it takes money to buy liquor *See* talk is cheap

time is money

you pays your money and you takes your choice

monk   the cowl does not make the monk

monkey   the higher the monkey climbs the more he shows his tail

if you pay peanuts, you get monkeys

monkey see, monkey do

softly, softly, catchee monkey

month   if you would be happy for a week take a wife; if you would be happy for a month kill a pig; but if you would be happy all your life plant a garden

moon   no moon, no man

more   content is more than a kingdom

grasp no more than the hand will hold

half is more than the whole *See* the half is better than the whole

less is more

more haste, less speed

the more said, the less done

the more the merrier

the more things change, the more they stay the same

the more you get, the more you want

the more you stir it, the worse it stinks

much would have more

there are more ways of killing a cat than choking it with cream

there's more than one way to skin a cat

years know more than books

morning   an hour in the morning is worth two in the evening

lose an hour in the morning, chase it all day

morning dreams come true

red sky at night, sailor's delight; red sky in the morning, sailors take warning

mortuis *de mortuis nil nisi bonum* See never speak ill of the dead

moss a rolling stone gathers no moss

most they that live longest see most

who knows most, speaks least

mother absence is the mother of disillusion

diligence is the mother of good luck

experience is the mother of wisdom

he that would the daughter win, must with the mother first begin

idleness is the mother of all the vices See idleness is the root of all evil

like mother, like daughter

a mother can take care of ten children, but sometimes ten children can't take care of one mother

the mother of mischief is no bigger than a midge's wing

necessity is the mother of invention

praise the child, and you make love to the mother

sloth is the mother of poverty

step on a crack, break your mother's back

motion the wheel of fortune is forever in motion

motor what's good for General Motors is good for America

mountain faith will move mountains

if the mountain will not come to Mohammed, Mohammed must go to the mountain

mouse the best-laid schemes of mice and men gang aft a-gley

burn not your house to scare away the mice

a cat in gloves catches no mice

keep no more cats than will catch mice

a mouse may help a lion

the mouse that has but one hole is quickly taken

one for the mouse, one for the crow, one to rot, one to grow

when the cat's away, the mice will play

mouth God never sends mouths but he sends meat

keep your mouth shut and your eyes open

never look a gift horse in the mouth

out of the fullness of the heart the mouth speaks

out of the mouths of babes and sucklings come great truths

a shut mouth catches no flies

mouthful the sheep that bleats loses a mouthful See a bleating sheep loses a bite

move faith will move mountains

god moves in a mysterious way

three moves are as bad as a fire

much birth is much but breeding more

everybody to whom much is given, of him will much be required

much coin, much care

much cry and little wool

much smoke, little fire

much water goes by the mill that the miller knows not of

much would have more

one enemy is too much

you can have too much of a good thing

muck where there's muck there's brass

muckle many a mickle makes a muckle See many a little makes a mickle

multitude charity covers a multitude of sins

murder killing no murder

murder will out

music he that lives in hope dances without music See he that lives in hope dances to an ill tune

music hath charms to soothe the savage breast

must needs must when the devil drives

what must be, must be See what will be, will be

young men may die, but old men must die

mysterious   God moves in mysterious ways

nail   for want of a nail the shoe was lost, for want of a shoe the horse was lost, and for want of a horse the rider was lost

one nail drives out another

when all you have is a hammer, everything looks like a nail

name   give a dog a bad name and hang him

a good name is better than precious ointment

a good name is sooner lost than won

no names, no pack-drill

a rose by any other name would smell as sweet

sticks and stones may break my bones, but names will never hurt me

what's in a name?

nation   as Maine goes, so goes the nation

the English are a nation of shopkeepers

nature   nature abhors a vacuum

nature does nothing in vain

nature passes nurture

nature will have its course

nurture passes nature

self-preservation is the first law of nature

you can drive out nature with a pitchfork but she keeps on coming back

nay   he that will not when he may, when he will he may have nay

near   the farthest way about is the nearest way home See the longest way around is the shortest way home

great boats may venture more, but little boats should keep near shore See little boats should stay close to shore

the nearer the bone, the sweeter the flesh

the nearer the church, the farther from God

near is my shirt, but nearer is my skin

necessary   if God did not exist, it would be necessary to invent him

no man is necessary See nobody is indispensable

necessitas   necessitas non habet legem See necessity knows no law

necessity   make a virtue of necessity

necessity is the mother of invention

necessity knows no law

necessity sharpens industry

needs must when necessity drives See needs must when the devil drives

need   a blind man's wife needs no paint

the buyer needs a thousand eyes, the seller wants but one

a friend in need is a friend indeed

a full cup needs a steady hand See full cup, steady hand

good wine needs no bush

a guilty conscience needs no accuser

need makes the old wife trot

needs must when the devil drives

with friends like that, who needs enemies?

you need more than dancing shoes to be a dancer

needful   a dose of adversity is often as needful as a dose of medicine

needy   an idle youth, a needy age

neglect   business neglected is business lost

neglect will kill an injury sooner than revenge

neighbor   good fences make good neighbors

love your neighbor as yourself

the rotten apple injures its neighbor See the rotten apple spoils the barrel

Nero   Nero fiddled while Rome burned

nest   birds in their little nests agree

it's an ill bird that fouls its own nest

there are no birds in last year's nest

you can't keep the birds from flying over your head, but you can keep them from building a nest in your hair

net   all is fish that comes to the net

in vain the net is spread in the sight of the bird

a man in debt is caught in a net

never   better late than never

envy never dies

never do things by halves

never is a long time

never say die

never say never

never trouble trouble till trouble troubles you

never work with children or animals

nought is never in danger

tomorrow never comes

true blue will never stain

what you've never had you never miss

wonders will never cease!

you can't lose what you never had

youth and old age will never agree

new   always something new out of Africa

everything old is new again

it's best to be off with the old love before you are on with the new

a new broom sweeps clean

a new day, a new dollar *See* another day, another dollar

new lords, new laws

there's nothing new under the sun

tomorrow is a new day *See* tomorrow is another day

trust not a new friend nor an old enemy

what's new cannot be true

you can't put new wine in old bottles

you can't teach an old dog new tricks

news   bad news travels fast

go abroad and you'll hear news of home

he comes too early who brings bad news

no news is good news

when a dog bites a man, that is not news; but when a man bites a dog, that is news

nice   be nice to people on your way up because you'll meet them on your way down

nice guys finish last

night   all cats are black at night *See* all cats are gray in the dark

at night all cats are gray *See* all cats are gray in the dark

the longest night will have an end *See* the longest day must have an end

night brings counsel

red sky at night, sailor's delight; red sky in the morning, sailors take warning

sing before breakfast, cry before night

trust not one night's ice

nihil   *ex nihilo nihil fit See* nothing comes of nothing

nihilo   *ex nihilo nihil fit See* nothing comes of nothing

nil   *de mortuis nil nisi bonum See* never speak ill of the dead

nine   a cat has nine lives

nine tailors make a man

parsley seed goes nine times to the devil

possession is nine points of the law

a stitch in time saves nine

a wonder lasts but nine days

ninety-nine   genius is one percent inspiration and ninety-nine percent perspiration

nisi   *de mortuis nil nisi bonum See* never speak ill of the dead

no   beauty is no inheritance

leave no stone unturned

no joy without annoy

no man can call again yesterday *See* yesterday will not be called again

no moon, no man

no names, no pack-drill

there's luck in odd numbers

there's safety in numbers

nurture   nature passes nurture

nurture passes nature

nut   the gods send nuts to those who have no teeth

he that would eat the kernel must crack the nut *See* he that would eat the fruit must climb the tree

oak   beware of an oak, it draws the stroke; avoid an ash, it counts the flash; creep under the thorn, it can save you from harm

great oaks from little acorns grow

little strokes fell great oaks

a reed before the wind lives on, while mighty oaks do fall

obedience   the first duty of a soldier is obedience

obey   he that cannot obey cannot command

obey orders, if you break owners

obvious   the obvious choice is usually a quick regret

ocean   little drops of water, little grains of sand, make a mighty ocean and a pleasant land

odd   there's luck in odd numbers

odious   comparisons are odious

off   it's best to be off with the old love before you are on with the new

offender   offenders never pardon

offense   the best defense is a good offense

neither give nor take offense

often   little and often fills the purse

the pitcher will go to the well once too often

oil   oil and water do not mix

the squeaky wheel gets the oil *See* the squeaky wheel gets the grease

ointment   a good name is better than precious ointment

old   better be an old man's darling than a young man's slave

everything old is new again

it's best to be off with the old love before you are on with the new

a man is as old as he feels, and a woman as old as she looks

need makes the old wife trot

never too old to learn *See* it's never too late to learn

a new broom sweeps clean, but an old broom knows all the corners *See* a new broom sweeps clean

an old fox is not easily snared

old friends and old wine are best

old habits die hard

old maids lead apes in hell

an old poacher makes the best gamekeeper

old sins cast long shadows

old soldiers never die

spare when you're young and spend when you're old

there's many a good tune played on an old fiddle

there's no fool like an old fool

trust not a new friend nor an old enemy

you can't catch old birds with chaff

you can't put an old head on young shoulders

you can't put new wine in old bottles

you can't shift an old tree without it dying

you can't teach an old dog new tricks

a young barber and an old physician

the young cock crows as he heard the old one

young folks think old folks to be fools, but old folks know young folks to be fools

young men forgive, old men never *See* youth and old age will never agree

young men may die, but old men must die

young saint, old devil

youth and old age will never agree

older   the older the wiser

olet   *non olet* *See* money has no smell

omelette   you can't make an omelette without breaking eggs

omission   there's a sin of omission as well as of commission

omnia   *amor vincit omnia* *See* love conquers all

on   it's best to be off with the old love before you are on with the new

once   Christmas comes but once a year

the difficult is done at once, the impossible takes a little longer

fool me once, shame on you; fool me twice, shame on me

a man can only die once

once a priest, always a priest

once a thief, always a thief

once bitten, twice shy

once burned, twice shy

one cannot be in two places at once

opportunity knocks but once

the pitcher will go to the well once too often

what has happened once can happen again

you can only die once

you're only young once

one   all arts are one, all branches on one tree *See* all arts are brothers, each is a light to the other

better one house spoiled than two

a bird never flew on one wing

the buyer needs a thousand eyes, the seller wants but one

the coward dies a thousand deaths, the brave but one *See* cowards die many times before their death

every dog is allowed one bite

every one after his fashion *See* every man after his fashion

from the sublime to the ridiculous is only one step

genius is one percent inspiration and ninety-nine percent perspiration

if one sheep leaps over the ditch, all the rest will follow

if two ride on a horse, one must ride behind

in the country of the blind, the one-eyed man is king

it's six of one and half a dozen of the other

it takes one to know one

it takes two to make a quarrel, but one can end it *See* it takes two to make a quarrel

a journey of a thousand miles begins with one step

knowledge and wisdom are far from being one

the mouse that has but one hole is quickly taken

one bad apple spoils the lot *See* the rotten apple spoils the barrel

one business begets another

one enemy is too much

one for sorrow; two for mirth; three for a wedding; four for a birth

one for the mouse, one for the crow, one to rot, one to grow

one funeral makes many

one good turn deserves another

one hand for yourself and one for the ship

one hand washes the other

one hour's sleep before midnight is worth two after

one law for the rich and another for the poor

one lie leads to another

one man's loss is another man's gain

one man's meat is another man's poison

one man's trash is another man's treasure

one nail drives out another

one of these days is none of these days

one picture is worth ten thousand words

one step at a time

you get what you pay for

you pays your money and you takes your choice

peace   if you want peace, prepare for war

nothing can bring you peace but yourself

peace makes plenty

there's no peace for the wicked

peanut   if you pay peanuts, you get monkeys

pear   walnuts and pears you plant for your heirs

pearl   don't cast your pearls before swine

peck   we must eat a peck of dirt before we die

peg   all words are pegs to hang ideas on

you can't put a square peg in a round hole

pen   the pen is mightier than the sword

penny   a bad penny always turns up

don't spoil the ship for half a penny's worth of tar

find a penny, pick it up *See* see a pin and pick it up

in for a penny, in for a pound

no penny, no paternoster

a penny saved is a penny earned

penny wise and pound foolish

take care of the pennies and the dollars will take care of themselves

people   be nice to people on your way up because you'll meet them on your way down

idle people have the least leisure

it takes all kinds of people to make a world

like people, like priest

like priest, like people *See* like people, like priest

most people consider thrift a fine virtue in ancestors

nobody ever went broke underestimating the intelligence of the American people

people are more easily led than driven

people who live in glass houses shouldn't throw stones

the voice of the people is the voice of God

where there's no vision, the people perish

the world is a stage and all the people in it actors *See* all the world's a stage

you can fool some of the people all of the time, and all of the people some of the time, but you can't fool all of the people all of the time

percent   genius is one percent inspiration and ninety-nine percent perspiration

perfect   nobody is perfect

practice makes perfect

perfection   trifles make perfection, and perfection is no trifle

perfume   flattery, like perfume, should be smelled but not swallowed

perish   he who lives by the sword shall perish by the sword *See* he who lives by the sword dies by the sword

where there's no vision, the people perish

perjury   Jove but laughs at lover's perjury

perpetual   a contented mind is a perpetual feast *See* a contented mind is a continual feast

person   if you want something done, ask a busy person

opportunity never knocks for persons not worth a rap

pessimist   the optimist's cup is half full; the pessimist's cup is half empty *See* the glass is either half empty or half full

physician   physician, heal thyself

the three doctors Diet, Quiet, and Temperance are the best physicians *See* the best doctors are Dr. Diet, Dr. Quiet, and Dr. Merryman a young barber and an old physician

pianist   don't shoot the pianist, he's doing his best

pick   even a blind pig occasionally picks up an acorn

hawks will not pick out hawks' eyes

see a pin and pick it up, all the day you'll have good luck; see a pin and let it lay, bad luck you'll have all the day

pickle   hunger is the best pickle *See* hunger is the best sauce

picture   every picture tells a story

one picture is worth ten thousand words

pie   the devil makes his Christmas pies of lawyers' tongues and clerks' fingers

piecrust   promises, like piecrust, are made to be broken

pig   even a blind pig occasionally picks up an acorn

if a pig had wings, it might fly

if you would be happy for a week take a wife; if you would be happy for a month kill a pig; but if you would be happy all your life plant a garden

pigs are pigs

what can you expect from a pig but a grunt?

the young pig grunts like the old sow *See* the young cock crows as he heard the old one

pilot   in a calm sea every man is a pilot

pin   it's a sin to steal a pin

see a pin and pick it up, all the day you'll have good luck; see a pin and let it lay, bad luck you'll have all the day

pinch   the wearer best knows where the shoe pinches

pint   you can't get a quart into a pint pot

piper   he who pays the piper calls the tune *See* they that dance must pay the piper

they that dance must pay the piper

piss   piss or get off the pot

pitch   he that touches pitch shall be defiled

pitcher   little pitchers have big ears

the pitcher will go to the well once too often

pitchfork   you can drive out nature with a pitchfork but she keeps on coming back

pity   better be envied than pitied

pity is akin to love

place   the best place for criticism is in front of your mirror

lightning never strikes twice in the same place

one cannot be in two places at once

the only place where success comes before work is in a dictionary

a place for everything and everything in its place

there's a time and place for everything

there's no place like home

plague   please your eye and plague your heart

plant   if you would be happy for a week take a wife; if you would be happy for a month kill a pig; but if you would be happy all your life plant a garden

it's not spring until you can plant your foot upon twelve daisies

walnuts and pears you plant for your heirs

plaster   patience is a plaster for all sores *See* patience is a remedy for every sorrow

play   all work and no play makes Jack a dull boy

don't play with edged tools *See* it's ill jesting with edged tools

fair play's a jewel

give and take is fair play

if you play with fire, you get burned

it's not whether you win or lose, but how you play the game

leave off while the play is good *See* quite while you are ahead

there's many a good tune played on an old fiddle

those who play at bowls must look out for rubbers

turnabout is fair play

when the cat's away, the mice will play

work before play

player   lookers-on see more than players *See* lookers-on see most of the game

pleasant   little drops of water, little grains of sand, make a mighty ocean and a pleasant land

please   the clock goes as it pleases the clerk

little things please little minds

please your eye and plague your heart

you can't please everybody

pleasure   business before pleasure

he that would go to sea for pleasure would go to hell for a pastime

never mix business with pleasure

stolen pleasures are sweetest *See* stolen waters are sweet

there's no pleasure without pain

plenty   peace makes plenty

a wet May brings plenty of hay

plum   the higher the tree, the sweeter the plum

plus   *plus ça change, plus c'est la même chose See* the more things change, the more they stay the same

poacher   an old poacher makes the best gamekeeper

pocket   a book is like a garden carried in the pocket

the devil dances in an empty pocket

money burns a hole in the pocket

shrouds have no pockets

wear your learning like your watch, in a private pocket

when a man's single, his pockets will jingle

poet   poets are born, not made

point   possession is nine points of the law

poison   one man's meat is another man's poison

policy   honesty is the best policy

polish   look on the bright side, or polish up the dark one *See* always look on the bright side

politeness   politeness costs nothing and gains everything *See* civility costs nothing

punctuality is the politeness of kings

politics   in politics a man must learn to rise above principle

politics makes strange bedfellows

pond   better a big fish in a little pond than a little fish in a big pond

poor   better be a poor man's darling than a rich man's slave *See* better be an old man's darling than a young man's slave

it's a poor dog that's not worth whistling for

it's a poor heart that never rejoices

one law for the rich and another for the poor

the rich get richer and the poor get poorer

the rich man has his ice in the summer and the poor man gets his in the winter

pope   it's ill sitting at Rome and striving with the Pope

populi   *vox populi, vox Dei See* the voice of the people is the voice of God

porch   if you can't run with the big dogs, stay under the porch

port   any port in a storm

possess   patience is a virtue which few possess—some have a little, others have less *See* patience is a virtue

possession   possession is nine points of the law

prepare hope for the best and prepare for the worst

if you want peace, prepare for war

present the absent are never without fault nor the present without excuse *See* he who is absent is always in the wrong

the golden age was never the present age

there's no time like the present

preservation self-preservation is the first law of nature

preserve alcohol will preserve anything but a secret

press one volunteer is worth two pressed men

prevent a stumble may prevent a fall

prevention an ounce of prevention is worth a pound of cure

prevention is better than cure

prey the fox preys furthest from his hole

price every man has his price

the price of liberty is eternal vigilance

a thing you don't want is dear at any price

pride pride feels no pain

pride goes before a fall

priest like people, like priest

once a priest, always a priest

prince punctuality is the politeness of princes *See* punctuality is the politeness of kings

whosoever draws his sword against the prince must throw the scabbard away

principle in politics a man must learn to rise above principle

prison stone walls do not a prison make

private wear your learning like your watch, in a private pocket

problem if you're not part of the solution, you're part of the problem

procrastination procrastination is the thief of time

produce the only thing a heated argument ever produced is coolness

prologue what's past is prologue

prolong medicine can prolong life, but death will seize the doctor, too

promise promises, like piecrust, are made to be broken

the streets of hell are paved with promises *See* the road to hell is paved with good intentions

proof the proof of the pudding is in the eating

prophet jesters do oft prove prophets

a prophet is not without honor, save in his own country

propose man proposes, God disposes

prosper cheaters never prosper

ill-gotten goods seldom prosper *See* ill-gotten goods never thrive

prosperity both poverty and prosperity come from spending money—prosperity from spending it wisely

prosperity discovers vice; adversity, virtue

prosperity is just around the corner

protect God protect me from my friends—I can protect myself from my enemies *See* save us from our friends

heaven protects children, sailors, and drunken men

prove the exception proves the rule

jesters do oft prove prophets

a man is innocent until proven guilty

provide take the goods the gods provide

providence providence is always on the side of the big battalions

public don't wash your dirty linen in public

publicity any publicity is good publicity

pudding the proof of the pudding is in the eating

repeat   history repeats itself

those who cannot remember the past are condemned to repeat it

repent   marry in haste, repent at leisure

reply   silence is the fittest reply to folly

reputation   a good reputation is more valuable than money

a man's best reputation for the future is his record of the past

require   everybody to whom much is given, of him will much be required

respond   many are called, but few respond *See* many are called, but few are chosen

rest   after dinner rest awhile, after supper walk a mile

a change is as good as a rest

there's no rest for the weary

there's no rest for the wicked *See* there's no peace for the wicked

retain   dreams retain the infirmities of our character

return   the dog always returns to his vomit

drive nature out of the door and it will return by the window *See* you can drive out nature with a pitchfork but she keeps on coming back

send a fool to market and a fool he'll return

the tongue always returns to the sore tooth

reveal   drunkenness reveals what soberness conceals

revenge   neglect will kill an injury sooner than revenge

revenge is a dish best eaten cold

revenge is sweet

revenue   thrift is a great revenue

review   he who would write and can't write can surely review

revolution   revolutions are not made with rose water

reward   desert and reward seldom keep company

virtue is its own reward

rich   better be a poor man's darling than a rich man's slave *See* better be an old man's darling than a young man's slave

it's better to be born lucky than rich

one law for the rich and another for the poor

riches have wings

the rich get richer and the poor get poorer

the rich man has his ice in the summer and the poor man gets his in the winter

a rich man's joke is always funny

riddance   good riddance to bad rubbish

ride   from the day you were born till you ride in a hearse, there's nothing so bad but it might have been worse *See* nothing so bad but it might have been worse

give a beggar a horse and he'll ride it to death

he who rides a tiger is afraid to dismount

if two ride on a horse, one must ride behind

if wishes were horses, beggars would ride

set a beggar on horseback, and he'll ride to the devil

there's no such thing as a free ride *See* there's no such thing as a free lunch

rider   for want of a nail the shoe was lost, for want of a shoe the horse was lost, and for want of a horse the rider was lost

time is the rider that breaks youth

ridiculous   from the sublime to the ridiculous is only one step

right   the customer is always right

do right and fear no man

sad   it's a sad heart that never rejoices
See it's a poor heart that never rejoices
it's a sad house where the hen crows louder than the cock

safe   better safe than sorry
he that is too secure is not safe
the highest branch is not the safest roost
it's better to be on the safe side
safe bind, safe find

safety   caution is the parent of safety
safety first
there's safety in numbers

said   *See* say

sail   hoist your sail when the wind is fair

sailor   heaven protects children, sailors, and drunken men
red sky at night, sailor's delight; red sky in the morning, sailors take warning

saint   the devil was sick, the devil a saint would be; the devil was well, the devil a saint was he
an open door may tempt a saint
young saint, old devil

sake   deny self for self's sake

salt   help you to salt, help you to sorrow

same   don't make the same mistake twice
great minds run in the same channels *See* great minds think alike
it'll all be the same in a hundred years
lightning never strikes twice in the same place
the more things change, the more they stay the same
toot your own horn lest the same be never tooted
you can't be in two places at the same time *See* one cannot be in two places at once
you can't step twice into the same river

sand   footprints on the sands of time are not made by sitting down
little drops of water, little grains of sand, make a mighty ocean and a pleasant land

sapienti   *verbum sapienti sat est See* a word to the wise is sufficient

sarà   *che sarà, sarà See* what will be, will be

sat   *verbum sapienti sat est See* a word to the wise is sufficient

Saturday   Saturday's child works hard for its living

sauce   hunger is the best sauce
what's sauce for the goose is sauce for the gander

savage   music hath charms to soothe the savage breast

save   beware of an oak, it draws the stroke; avoid an ash, it counts the flash; creep under the thorn, it can save you from harm
let your head save your heels
a penny saved is a penny earned
save at the spigot and waste at the bung *See* spare at the spigot, and let out the bunghole
save something for a rainy day
save us from our friends
saving is getting
a stitch in time saves nine

say   courage is fear that has said its prayers
criticism is something you can avoid by saying nothing, doing nothing, and being nothing
do as I say, not as I do
easier said than done
if wind blows on you through a hole, say your prayers and mind your soul
it's not what you say, but how you say it
least said, soonest mended
the more said, the less done

never say die

never say never

there's many a true word said in jest *See* many a true word is spoken in jest

what everybody says must be true

what the soldier said isn't evidence

who says A must say B

scabbard one sword keeps another in its scabbard

whosoever draws his sword against the prince must throw the scabbard away

scarce good men are scarce

scare burn not your house to scare away the mice

scarlet an ape's an ape, a varlet's a varlet, though they be clad in silk or scarlet

scheme the best-laid schemes of mice and men gang aft a-gley

school education doesn't come by bumping your head against the school house

experience keeps a dear school

never tell tales out of school

scorn hell hath no fury like a woman scorned

scoundrel patriotism is the last refuge of a scoundrel

scramble scrambled eggs can't be unscrambled *See* you can't unscramble eggs

scratch scratch a Russian and you find a Tartar

you scratch my back and I'll scratch yours

scripture the devil can cite scripture for his purpose

sea he that would go to sea for pleasure would go to hell for a pastime

he that would learn to pray, let him go to sea

in a calm sea every man is a pilot

there are other fish in the sea

wine has drowned more men than the sea

worse things happen at sea

seaman the good seaman is known in bad weather

season everything is good in its season

knowledge and timber shouldn't be much used until they are seasoned

to everything there is a season

second better be first in a village than second at Rome

second thoughts are best

secret alcohol will preserve anything but a secret

a secret is either too good to keep or too bad not to tell

a secret's a secret until it's told

three may keep a secret, if two of them are dead

secure he that is too secure is not safe

see believe only half of what you see and nothing you hear

children should be seen and not heard

a dwarf on a giant's shoulders sees further of the two

four eyes see more than two

hear all, see all, say nowt

lookers-on see most of the game

many kiss the hand they wish to see cut off

monkey see, monkey do

see a pin and pick it up, all the day you'll have good luck; see a pin and let it lay, bad luck you'll have all the day

seeing is believing

see no evil, hear no evil, speak no evil

seldom seen, soon forgotten

there are none so blind as those who will not see

they that live longest see most

what the eye doesn't see, the heart doesn't grieve over

what you see is what you get

seed the blood of the martyrs is the seed of the church

good seed makes a good crop

one year's seeding makes seven years' weeding

parsley seed goes nine times to the devil

seek ask, and it shall be given you; seek, and ye shall find; knock, and it shall be opened unto you

seek and you shall find

water seeks its own level

seem be what you would seem to be

seen See **see**

seize medicine can prolong life, but death will seize the doctor, too

seize the day

self deny self for self's sake

self-deceit is the easiest of any

self-interest is the rule, self-sacrifice the exception

self-praise is no recommendation

self-preservation is the first law of nature

sell buy in the cheapest market and sell in the dearest

never sell America short

seller the buyer needs a thousand eyes, the seller wants but one

send God never sends mouths but he sends meat

God sends meat, but the devil sends cooks

the gods send nuts to those who have no teeth

never send a boy to do a man's job

send a fool to market and a fool he'll return

sense ask advice, but use your own common sense

an ounce of common sense is worth a pound of theory

sermon a good example is the best sermon

servant fire is a good servant but a bad master

serve any stick will serve to beat a dog with See it's easy to find a stick to beat a dog

first come, first served

if you would be well served, serve yourself

no man can serve two masters

pay beforehand was never well served

revenge is a dish best served cold See revenge is a dish best eaten cold

they also serve who only stand and wait

you can't serve God and mammon

youth must be served

set don't set a wolf to watch the sheep See don't let the fox guard the henhouse

a dripping June sets all in tune

man's work lasts till set of sun; woman's work is never done See a woman's work is never done

set a beggar on horseback, and he'll ride to the devil

set a thief to catch a thief

sow dry and set wet

seven the first seven years are the hardest

a fool can ask more questions in an hour than a wise man can answer in seven years See fools ask questions that wise men cannot answer

give me a child for the first seven years and he is mine for life

keep a thing seven years and you'll find a use for it

one year's seeding makes seven years' weeding

rain before seven, fine before eleven

six hours' sleep for a man, seven for a woman, and eight for a fool

you should know a man seven years before you stir his fire

a fool's bolt is soon shot

shoot first and ask questions afterward

shop keep your shop and your shop will keep you

shopkeeper the English are a nation of shopkeepers

shore little boats should stay close to shore

shorn *See* **shear**

short art is long and life is short

the day is short and the work is long

good company on the road is the shortest cut

life is short and sweet

life is short and time is swift

life is too short

the longest way around is the shortest way home

long foretold, long last; short notice, soon past

never sell America short

a short horse is soon curried

short reckonings make long friends

short visits make long friends

shorten cheerful company shortens the miles *See* good company on the road is the shortest cut

shoulder a dwarf on a giant's shoulders sees further of the two

you can't put an old head on young shoulders

shout don't shout until you are out of the woods

show give a man a fish, and you feed him for a day; show him how to fish, and you feed him for a lifetime

the higher the monkey climbs the more he shows his tail

the house shows the owner

if you can't bite, never show your teeth

show me a liar and I will show you a thief

the show must go on

straws show which way the wind blows

shower April showers bring May flowers

shroud shrouds have no pockets

shut away goes the devil when he finds the door shut against him

don't shut the barn door after the horse is stolen

a door must be either shut or open

every door may be shut but death's door

keep your eyes wide open before marriage, half shut afterward

keep your mouth shut and your eyes open

a shut mouth catches no flies

when one door shuts, another opens *See* when one door closes, another one opens

shy once bitten, twice shy

once burned, twice shy

sick the devil was sick, the devil a saint would be; the devil was well, the devil a saint was he

hope deferred makes the heart sick

sickness health is not valued till sickness comes

side always look on the bright side

bread always falls buttered side down

the grass is always greener on the other side of the fence

it's better to be on the safe side

providence is always on the side of the big battalions

there are two sides to every question

sight in vain the net is spread in the sight of the bird

out of sight, out of mind

sign blushing is a sign of grace

silence silence gives consent

silence is golden

silence is the fittest reply to folly

speech is silver, but silence is golden

silent small sorrows speak; great ones are silent

there's a time to speak and a time to be silent

silk   an ape's an ape, a varlet's a varlet, though they be clad in silk or scarlet

you can't make a silk purse out of a sow's ear

silly   ask a silly question and you get a silly answer

silver   every cloud has a silver lining

genius without education is like silver in the mine

speech is silver, but silence is golden

similarly   when you argue with a fool, make sure he isn't similarly engaged

similia   *similia similibus curantur See* like cures like

similibus   *similia similibus curantur See* like cures like

sin   charity covers a multitude of sins

it's a sin to steal a pin

let him who is without sin cast the first stone

old sins cast long shadows

sin, sorrow, and work are the things that men can't shirk

there's a sin of omission as well as of commission

sincere   imitation is the sincerest form of flattery

sing   America is a tune: it must be sung together

little birds that can sing and won't sing must be made to sing

the opera ain't over till the fat lady sings

sing before breakfast, cry before night

whose bread I eat, his song I sing

single   beauty draws with a single hair

the longest journey begins with a single step *See* a journey of a thousand miles begins with one step

when a man's single, his pockets will jingle

singly   misfortunes never come singly

sink   little leaks sink the ship

loose lips sink ships

rats desert a sinking ship

sinner   a young saint, an old sinner *See* young saint, old devil

sit   after dinner sit awhile, after supper walk a mile *See* after dinner rest awhile, after supper walk a mile

close sits my shirt, but closer my skin *See* near is my shirt, but nearer is my skin

footprints on the sands of time are not made by sitting down

it's as cheap sitting as standing

it's ill sitting at Rome and striving with the Pope

when two ride one horse, one must sit behind *See* if two ride on a horse, one must ride behind

six   it's six of one and half a dozen of the other

six hours' sleep for a man, seven for a woman, and eight for a fool

size   it's not the size of the dog in the fight, it's the size of the fight in the dog

skeleton   there's a skeleton in every closet

skin   beauty is only skin deep

every man must skin his own skunk

near is my shirt, but nearer is my skin

there's more than one way to skin a cat

skirts   the devil gets up to the belfry by the vicar's skirts

skittle   life isn't all beer and skittles

skunk   every man must skin his own skunk

sky   if the sky falls, we shall catch larks

red sky at night, sailor's delight; red sky in the morning, sailors take warning

the sky's the limit

slain   *See* **slay**

slave better be an old man's darling than a young man's slave

slay he who fights and runs away may live to fight another day, but he that is in battle slain will never rise to fight again *See* he who fights and runs away may live to fight another day

sleep the art of being a parent consists of sleeping when the baby isn't looking

let sleeping dogs lie

one hour's sleep before midnight is worth two after

six hours' sleep for a man, seven for a woman, and eight for a fool

sleep is the brother of death

there'll be sleeping enough in the grave

sleeve stretch your arm no further than your sleeve will reach

slender he that lives on hope has a slender diet *See* he that lives on hope will die fasting

slice give a loaf and beg a slice

a slice off a cut loaf isn't missed

slip a slip of the lip will sink a ship *See* loose lips sink ships

there's many a slip between cup and lip

sloth all things are easy to industry, all things difficult to sloth

sloth is the mother of poverty

slow slow and steady wins the race

slow but sure

slowly make haste slowly

the mills of God grind slowly, yet they grind exceedingly small

small the best things come in small packages

it's a small world

a man wrapped up in himself makes a very small bundle

the mills of God grind slowly, yet they grind exceedingly small

small choice in rotten apples

a small gift usually gets small thanks

small is beautiful

small leaks sink big ships *See* little leaks sink the ship

small sorrows speak; great ones are silent

small things affect light minds *See* little things please little minds

wink at small faults

smell fish and visitors smell in three days *See* fish and guests stink after three days

flattery, like perfume, should be smelled but not swallowed

money has no smell

a rose by any other name would smell as sweet

smock near is my kirtle, but nearer is my smock *See* near is my shirt, but nearer is my skin

smoke love and smoke cannot be hidden *See* love and a cough cannot be hid

much smoke, little fire

there's no smoke without fire

smooth the course of true love never did run smooth

you have to take the rough with the smooth

snare an old fox is not easily snared

snooze you snooze, you lose

snow the north wind doth blow and we shall have snow

so so many countries, so many customs

so many men, so many opinions

sober wanton kittens make sober cats

soberness drunkenness reveals what soberness conceals

society gossip is the lifeblood of society

soft soft and fair goes far

a soft answer turns away wrath

softly fair and softly goes far in a day

softly, softly, catchee monkey

speak softly and carry a big stick

soldier   every soldier has the baton of a field-marshal in his knapsack

the first duty of a soldier is obedience

old soldiers never die

soldiers and travelers may lie in authority *See* a traveler may lie with authority

what the soldier said isn't evidence

solitude   a great city, a great solitude

solution   if you're not part of the solution, you're part of the problem

some   you can fool some of the people all of the time, and all of the people some of the time, but you can't fool all of the people all of the time

you win some, you lose some

somebody   you can't beat somebody with nobody

something   gambling is getting nothing for something

save something for a rainy day

something is better than nothing

something is rotten in the state of Denmark

you don't get something for nothing

son   clergymen's sons always turn out badly

like father, like son

a son is a son till he gets him a wife, a daughter's a daughter all of her life

song   whose bread I eat, his song I sing

songless   a believer is a songless bird in a cage

soon   bad news always comes too soon *See* he comes too early who brings bad news

better three hours too soon than a minute too late *See* it's better to be an hour too early than a minute too late

God takes soonest those he loves best

least said, soonest mended

seldom seen, soon forgotten

the sharper the storm, the sooner it's over

the sooner begun, the sooner done

sooner said than done *See* easier said than done

soon ripe, soon rotten

soothe   music hath charms to soothe the savage breast

sore   patience is a plaster for all sores *See* patience is a remedy for every sorrow

the tongue always returns to the sore tooth

sorrow   help you to salt, help you to sorrow

he that goes a-borrowing, goes a-sorrowing

one for sorrow; two for mirth; three for a wedding; four for a birth

patience is a remedy for every sorrow

sin, sorrow, and work are the things that men can't shirk

small sorrows speak; great ones are silent

sorrow comes unsent for

sorry   better safe than sorry

happy is the bride that the sun shines on, sorry is the bride that the rain rains on *See* happy is the bride that the sun shines on

sort   it takes all sorts to make a world *See* it takes all kinds of people to make a world

soul   brevity is the soul of wit

confession is good for the soul

corporations have neither bodies to be punished nor souls to be damned

the eyes are the mirrors of the soul

if wind blows on you through a hole, say your prayers and mind your soul

punctuality is the soul of business

sound   empty vessels make the most sound

source   a stream cannot rise above its source

sow (n.)   you can't make a silk purse out of a sow's ear

stern a stern chase is a long chase

stew first catch your rabbit and then make your stew *See* first catch your hare

stick (n.) it's easy to find a stick to beat a dog

speak softly and carry a big stick

sticks and stones may break my bones, but names will never hurt me

stick (v.) let the cobbler stick to his last

stick to your guns

throw dirt enough, and some will stick

still a still tongue makes a wise head

still waters run deep

the vicar of Bray will be vicar of Bray still

stink (n.) the devil always leaves a stink behind him

stink (v.) fish and guests stink after three days

a fish stinks from the head

the more you stir it, the worse it stinks

stir the more you stir it, the worse it stinks

you should know a man seven years before you stir his fire

stitch a stitch in time saves nine

stolen *See* **steal**

stomach an army marches on its stomach

a growing youth has a wolf in his stomach

a hungry stomach has no ears

the way to a man's heart is through his stomach

stone constant dropping wears away a stone

drive gently over the stones

leave no stone unturned

let him who is without sin cast the first stone

the only difference between stumbling blocks and stepping-stones is the way you use them

people who live in glass houses shouldn't throw stones

a rolling stone gathers no moss

sticks and stones may break my bones, but words will never hurt me

stone-dead hath no fellow

stone walls do not a prison make

you buy land, you buy stones; you buy meat, you buy bones

you can't get blood from a stone

stool between two stools one falls to the ground

stop when you are in a hole, stop digging

storm after a storm comes a calm

any port in a storm

the sharper the storm, the sooner it's over

story every picture tells a story

one story is good till another is told

strange adversity makes strange bedfellows

fact is stranger than fiction

politics makes strange bedfellows

truth is stranger than fiction

stranger be kind to your friends; if it weren't for them, you would be a total stranger

straw a drowning man will catch at a straw

it's the last straw that breaks the camel's back

straws show which way the wind blows

you can't make bricks without straw

stream cross the stream where it is shallowest

don't change horses in the middle of the stream *See* don't swap horses in midstream

a stream cannot rise above its source

strive not against the stream

street the streets of hell are paved with promises *See* the road to hell is paved with good intentions

if there were no clouds, we shouldn't enjoy the sun

make hay while the sun shines

man's work lasts till set of sun; woman's work is never done *See* a woman's work is never done

never let the sun go down on your anger

the sun loses nothing by shining into a puddle

there's nothing new under the sun

sung *See* **sing**

sunset laugh before breakfast, cry before sunset *See* sing before breakfast, cry before night

sup he who sups with the devil should have a long spoon

supper after dinner rest awhile, after supper walk a mile

hope is a good breakfast but a bad supper

if you sing before breakfast, you'll cry before supper *See* sing before breakfast, cry before night

sure slow but sure

slow but sure wins the race *See* slow and steady wins the race

talk of the devil and he's sure to appear

suspicion Caesar's wife must be above suspicion

swallow (n.) one swallow does not make a summer

swallow (v.) flattery, like perfume, should be smelled but not swallowed

it's idle to swallow the cow and choke on the tail

swan every man thinks his own geese swans

swap don't swap horses in midstream

sweat no sweat, no sweet *See* no pain, no gain

sweep blind chance sweeps the world along

if every man would sweep his own doorstep the city would soon be clean

a new broom sweeps clean

sweep your own doorstep clean

sweet forbidden fruit is sweet

from the sweetest wine, the tartest vinegar

the higher the tree, the sweeter the plum

life is short and sweet

little fish are sweet

the nearer the bone, the sweeter the flesh

no sweat, no sweet *See* no pain, no gain

revenge is sweet

a rose by any other name would smell as sweet

stolen waters are sweet

you have to take the bitter with the sweet

swift life is short and time is swift

the race is not to the swift, nor the battle to the strong

swim don't go near the water until you learn how to swim

swine don't cast your pearls before swine

swing what you lose on the swings you gain on the roundabouts

sword gluttony kills more than the sword

he who lives by the sword dies by the sword

one sword keeps another in its scabbard

the pen is mightier than the sword

whosoever draws his sword against the prince must throw the scabbard away

table welcome is the best dish on the table *See* welcome is the best cheer

tail better be the head of a dog than the tail of a lion

the cow knows not the value of her tail till she has lost it

heads I win, tails you lose

he who has a tiger by the tail dare not let go *See* he who rides a tiger is afraid to dismount the higher the monkey climbs the more he shows his tail

if frogs had wings, they wouldn't bump their tails on rocks *See* if a pig had wings, it might fly

it's idle to swallow the cow and choke on the tail

tailor nine tailors make a man

the tailor makes the man

take blessings brighten as they take their flight

the devil takes care of his own *See* the devil looks after his own

don't take down a fence unless you are sure why it was put up

every man for himself and the devil take the hindmost

genius is an infinite capacity for taking pains

give and take is fair play

give a thing, and take a thing, to wear the devil's gold ring

God takes soonest those he loves best

it takes a heap of living to make a house a home

it takes all kinds of people to make a world

it takes a thief to catch a thief *See* set a thief to catch a thief

it takes a village to raise a child

it takes money to make money

it takes one to know one

it takes three generations to make a gentleman

it takes two to make a bargain

it takes two to make a quarrel

it takes two to tango

the Lord gives and the Lord takes away

a mother can take care of ten children, but sometimes ten children can't take care of one mother

the mouse that has but one hole is quickly taken

neither give nor take offense

take care of number one

take care of the pennies and the dollars will take care of themselves

take the goods the gods provide

take the will for the deed

take things as they come

take time by the forelock

when you go to dance, take heed whom you take by the hand

you can take a horse to the water, but you can't make him drink *See* you can lead a horse to water, but you can't make him drink

you can take the boy out of the country but you can't take the country out of the boy

you can't take it with you

you have to take the bitter with the sweet

you have to take the rough with the smooth

you must take two bears to live with you—bear and forbear *See* bear and forbear

you pays your money and you takes your choice

tale dead men tell no tales

a good tale is not the worse for being told twice

never tell tales out of school

a tale never loses in the telling

talk don't talk the talk if you can't walk the walk

everybody talks about the weather, but nobody does anything about it

money talks

talk is cheap

talk of the devil and he's sure to appear *See* speak of the devil and he always appears

tangle what a tangled web we weave when first we practice to deceive

tango it takes two to tango

tar don't spoil the ship for half a penny's worth of tar

tart from the sweetest wine, the tartest vinegar

Tartar scratch a Russian and you find a Tartar

taste every man to his taste

tastes differ

there's no accounting for tastes

there's no disputing about tastes

tatter there's many a good cock come out of a tattered bag

tax nothing is certain but death and taxes

teach don't teach your grandmother to suck eggs

those who can, do; those who can't, teach

you can't teach an old dog new tricks

teacher experience is the best teacher

experience is the teacher of fools

nobody forgets a good teacher

tear don't tear down a wall unless you are sure why it was put up *See* don't take down a fence unless you are sure why it was put up

it's easier to tear down than to build up

teeth *See* **tooth**

tell ask me no questions and I'll tell you no lies

blood will tell

dead men tell no tales

a good tale is not the worse for being told twice

a liar is not believed when he tells the truth

never tell tales out of school

one story is good till another is told

a secret is either too good to keep or too bad not to tell

a secret's a secret until it's told

a tale never loses in the telling

tell it not in Gath

tell not all you know, nor do all you can

tell the truth and shame the devil

time will tell

you can't tell a book by its cover *See* don't judge a book by its cover

temper God tempers the wind to the shorn lamb

temperance the three doctors Diet, Quiet, and Temperance are the best physicians *See* the best doctors are Dr. Diet, Dr. Quiet, and Dr. Merryman

temps *autres temps, autres moeurs* *See* other times, other manners

tempt an open door may tempt a saint

tempus *tempus fugit* *See* time flies

ten genius is ten percent inspiration and ninety percent perspiration *See* genius is one percent inspiration and ninety-nine percent perspiration

a mother can take care of ten children, but sometimes ten children can't take care of one mother

one picture is worth ten thousand words

a volunteer is worth ten pressed men *See* one volunteer is worth two pressed men

tenth possession is nine-tenths of the law *See* possession is nine points of the law

terrible a mind is a terrible thing to waste

thanks a small gift usually gets small thanks

thaw Robin Hood could brave all weathers but a thaw wind

themselves God helps those who help themselves

theory an ounce of common sense is worth a pound of theory

thereof sufficient unto the day is the evil thereof

thick blood is thicker than water

faults are thick where love is thin

thief call a man a thief and he will steal

the hole calls the thief

if there were no receivers, there would be no thieves

one courageous thought will put to flight a host of troubles

second thoughts are best

thought is free

the wish is father to the thought

thousand the buyer needs a thousand eyes, the seller wants but one

the coward dies a thousand deaths, the brave but one *See* cowards die many times before their death

a journey of a thousand miles begins with one step

one picture is worth ten thousand words

thread the thread breaks where it is weakest

threaten threatened men live long

three better three hours too soon than a minute too late *See* it's better to be an hour too early than a minute too late

fish and guests stink after three days

from shirtsleeves to shirtsleeves is only three generations

it takes three generations to make a gentleman

one for sorrow; two for mirth; three for a wedding; four for a birth

one hour's sleep before midnight is worth three after *See* one hour's sleep before midnight is worth two after

things come in threes

the three doctors Diet, Quiet, and Temperance are the best physicians *See* the best doctors are Dr. Diet, Dr. Quiet, and Dr. Merryman

three may keep a secret, if two of them are dead

three moves are as bad as a fire

three things are not to be trusted: a cow's horn, a dog's tooth, and a horse's hoof

three times a bridesmaid, never a bride *See* always a bridesmaid, never a bride

two boys are half a boy, and three boys are no boy at all

two's company, three's a crowd

thrift most people consider thrift a fine virtue in ancestors

thrift is a great revenue

thrive first thrive and then wive

he that will thrive must first ask his wife

if you want to live and thrive, let the spider run alive

ill-gotten goods never thrive

throw charity is not a bone you throw to a dog but a bone you share with a dog

don't throw away your dirty water until you get clean

don't throw good money after bad

don't throw out the baby with the bathwater

don't throw pearls to swine *See* don't cast your pearls before swine

people who live in glass houses shouldn't throw stones

throw dirt enough, and some will stick

throw out a sprat to catch a mackerel

whosoever draws his sword against the prince must throw the scabbard away

Thursday Thursday's child has far to go

thyself know thyself

physician, heal thyself

tide a rising tide lifts all boats

there's a tide in the affairs of man

time and tide wait for no man

tiger he who rides a tiger is afraid to dismount

timber knowledge and timber shouldn't be much used until they are seasoned

time accusing the times is but excusing ourselves

be happy while you're living, for you're a long time dead

better luck next time

cowards die many times before their death

footprints on the sands of time are not made by sitting down

he that waits for dead men's shoes may go a long time barefoot *See* it's ill waiting for dead men's shoes

four eyes see more than two

an hour in the morning is worth two in the evening

if two ride on a horse, one must ride behind

if you run after two hares, you will catch neither

it takes two to make a bargain

it takes two to make a quarrel

no man can serve two masters

one cannot be in two places at once

one for sorrow; two for mirth; three for a wedding; four for a birth

one hour's sleep before midnight is worth two after

stand on your own two feet

there are two sides to every question

three may keep a secret, if two of them are dead

two and two make four

two boys are half a boy, and three boys are no boy at all

two heads are better than one

two of a trade never agree

two's company, three's a crowd

two tailors go to a man *See* nine tailors make a man

two wrongs don't make a right

while two dogs are fighting for a bone, a third runs away with it

you must take two bears to live with you—bear and forbear *See* bear and forbear

it takes two to tango

one volunteer is worth two pressed men

unbelieving believing has a core of unbelieving

uncertain children are certain cares, but uncertain comforts

underestimate nobody ever went broke underestimating the intelligence of the American people

undo what's done cannot be undone

uneasy uneasy lies the head that wears a crown

unemployed mind unemployed is mind unenjoyed

unenjoyed mind unemployed is mind unenjoyed

unexpected the unexpected always happens

unforeseen nothing is certain but the unforeseen

union union is strength

unite united we stand, divided we fall

unity in unity there is strength *See* union is strength

unlikely pigs may fly, but they are very unlikely birds *See* if a pig had wings, it might fly

unlucky lucky at cards, unlucky in love

unpunished no good deed goes unpunished

unscramble you can't unscramble eggs

unsent sorrow comes unsent for

unto do unto others as you would have them do unto you

render unto Caesar that which is Caesar's

up prejudice is being down on what we are not up on

what goes up must come down

upright an empty sack cannot stand upright

use ask advice, but use your own common sense

it's no use crying over spilled milk

keep a thing seven years and you'll find a use for it

knowledge and timber shouldn't be much used until they are seasoned

the only difference between stumbling blocks and stepping-stones is the way you use them

use brains not brawn *See* wisdom goes beyond strength

the used key is always bright

use legs and have legs

use your head and save your feet *See* let your head save your heels

vacuum nature abhors a vacuum

vain in vain the net is spread in the sight of the bird

nature does nothing in vain

valet no man is a hero to his valet

valor discretion is the better part of valor

valuable a good reputation is more valuable than money

value the cow knows not the value of her tail till she has lost it

health is not valued till sickness comes

variety variety is the spice of life

varlet an ape's an ape, a varlet's a varlet, though they be clad in silk or scarlet

venture great boats may venture more, but little boats should keep near shore *See* little boats should stay close to shore

nothing ventured, nothing gained

Venus men are from Mars, women are from Venus

verbum *verbum sapienti sat est See* a word to the wise is sufficient

veritas *in vino veritas See* there's truth in wine

vessel empty vessels make the most sound

vicar the devil gets up to the belfry by the vicar's skirts

the vicar of Bray will be vicar of Bray still

vicariously gossip is vice enjoyed vicariously

vice gossip is vice enjoyed vicariously

idleness is the mother of all the vices *See* idleness is the root of all evil

prosperity discovers vice; adversity, virtue

victor to the victor belong the spoils

victory in war there is no substitute for victory

victory has a hundred fathers and defeat is an orphan *See* success has many fathers, while failure is an orphan

view distance lends enchantment to the view

vigilance the price of liberty is eternal vigilance

village better be first in a village than second at Rome

it takes a village to raise a child

vincit *amor vincit omnia See* love conquers all

vinegar from the sweetest wine, the tartest vinegar

oil and vinegar will not mix *See* oil and water do not mix

you can catch more flies with honey than with vinegar

vino *in vino veritas See* there's truth in wine

virtue make a virtue of necessity

most people consider thrift a fine virtue in ancestors

patience is a virtue

prosperity discovers vice; adversity, virtue

virtue is its own reward

vision where there's no vision, the people perish

visit short visits make long friends

visitor fish and visitors smell in three days *See* fish and guests stink after three days

vita *ars longa, vita brevis See* art is long and life is short

voice the voice of the people is the voice of God

voluntary ignorance is a voluntary misfortune

volunteer one volunteer is worth two pressed men

vomit the dog always returns to his vomit

vox *vox populi, vox Dei See* the voice of the people is the voice of God

wag it's merry in hall when beards wag all

wagon hitch your wagon to a star

few words are best

fine words butter no parsnips

from the mouths of babes come words of wisdom *See* out of the mouths of babes and sucklings come great truths

hard words break no bones

a man's word is as good as his bond

many a true word is spoken in jest

one picture is worth ten thousand words

sticks and stones may break my bones, but words will never hurt me *See* sticks and stones may break my bones but names will never hurt me

a word spoken is past recalling

a word to the wise is sufficient

work all work and no play makes Jack a dull boy

a change of work is a rest *See* a change is as good as a rest

the day is short and the work is long

the devil finds work for idle hands to do

the end crowns the work

the eye of a master does more work than both his hands

fools and children should never see half-done work

hell is full of good meanings, but heaven is full of good works *See* the road to hell is paved with good intentions

he who does not work, neither should he eat

if ifs and ans were pots and pans, there'd be no work for tinkers

it's all in a day's work

it's not work that kills, but worry

many hands make light work

never work with children or animals

the only place where success comes before work is in a dictionary

Saturday's child works hard for its living

sin, sorrow, and work are the things that men can't shirk

time works wonders

a woman's work is never done

work before play

work expands so as to fill the time available for its completion

work never hurt anybody

worker a bayonet is a weapon with a worker at each end

workman a bad workman quarrels with his tools

workshop an idle brain is the devil's workshop

world all's for the best in the best of all possible worlds

all the world's a stage

better be out of the world than out of the fashion

blind chance sweeps the world along

God's in his heaven; all's right with the world

the hand that rocks the cradle rules the world

it's a small world

it's not the end of the world

it takes all kinds of people to make a world

laugh and the world laughs with you, weep and you weep alone

a lie can go around the world and back again while the truth is lacing up its boots

love makes the world go round

money makes the world go round

one half of the world doesn't know how the other half lives

the world runs on wheels

you can't please the whole world and his wife *See* you can't please everybody

worm the early bird catches the worm

even a worm will turn

worn *See* **wear**

worry action is worry's worst enemy

don't swallow the cow and worry with the tail *See* it's idle to swallow the cow and choke on the tail it's not work that kills, but worry

worry is interest paid on trouble before it falls due

worse go farther and fare worse

a liar is worse than a thief

more haste, worse speed *See* more haste, less speed

the more you stir it, the worse it stinks

nothing so bad but it might have been worse

the remedy may be worse than the disease

too much of a good thing is worse than none at all *See* you can have too much of a good thing

worse things happen at sea

worst action is worry's worst enemy

every man is his own worst enemy

hope for the best and prepare for the worst

an old fool is the worst fool *See* there's no fool like an old fool

when things are at the worst they begin to mend

the worst is yet to come

worth a bird in the hand is worth two in the bush

don't spoil the ship for half a penny's worth of tar

the game is not worth the candle

an hour in the morning is worth two in the evening

if a thing's worth doing, it's worth doing well

it's a poor dog that's not worth whistling for

one picture is worth ten thousand words

one volunteer is worth two pressed men

opportunities look for you when you are worth finding

opportunity never knocks for persons not worth a rap

the worth of a thing is what it will bring

worthy the laborer is worthy of his hire

wound time heals all wounds *See* time is a great healer

wrap a man wrapped up in himself makes a very small bundle

wrath hell knows no wrath like a woman scorned *See* hell hath no fury like a woman scorned

let not the sun go down on your wrath *See* never let the sun go down on your anger

a soft answer turns away wrath

wren the robin and the wren are God's cock and hen

write he who would write and can't write can surely review

think much, speak little, and write less

a white wall is the fool's writing paper

wrong he who is absent is always in the wrong

if anything can go wrong, it will

the king can do no wrong

there's no such thing as bad weather, only the wrong clothes

two wrongs don't make a right

yard life is hard by the yard, but by the inch life's a cinch

year Christmas comes but once a year

the first hundred years are the hardest

the first seven years are the hardest

a fool can ask more questions in an hour than a wise man can answer in seven years *See* fools ask questions that wise men cannot answer

it'll all be the same in a hundred years

keep a thing seven years and you'll find a use for it

one year's seeding makes seven years' weeding

there are no birds in last year's nest

years know more than books

you should know a man seven years before you stir his fire

yesterday today is yesterday's tomorrow

yesterday will not be called again

Index by Theme

In this index the proverbs are grouped together under thematic headings. Note that these headings relate to the meaning of the proverb, not the words it contains. "Give a dog a bad name and hang him" is not about dogs, so it is not listed under animals, but under its metaphorical themes of **defamation** and **reputation.** Similarly, "It never rains but it pours" is under **misfortune,** not **weather.** The themes are listed at the beginning for quick reference.

see most; time is the rider that breaks youth; wanton kittens make sober cats; with age comes wisdom; you can't catch old birds with chaff; you can't put an old head on young shoulders; you can't shift an old tree without it dying; you can't teach an old dog new tricks; a young barber and an old physician; young folks think old folks to be fools, but old folks know young folks to be fools; young men may die, but old men must die; young saint, old devil; you're only young once; youth and old age will never agree; youth must be served; youth will have its fling

aggression
the best defense is a good offense; a bully is always a coward; if you can't bite, never show your teeth

agriculture See **gardening**

alcohol See **drinking**

ambition
every soldier has the baton of a field-marshal in his knapsack; hasty climbers have sudden falls; he who would climb the ladder must begin at the bottom; the higher the monkey climbs the more he shows his tail; the higher the tree, the sweeter the plum; hitch your wagon to a star; humble hearts have humble desires; many go out for wool and come home shorn; the sky's the limit; there's always room at the top

America
America is a tune: it must be sung together; the business of America is business; good Americans, when they die, go to Paris; never sell America short; nobody ever went broke underestimating

the intelligence of the American people; what's good for General Motors is good for America

anger
anger improves nothing but the arch of a cat's back; anger without power is folly; don't get mad, get even; hell hath no fury like a woman scorned; a hungry man is an angry man; a little pot is soon hot; never let the sun go down on your anger; the only thing a heated argument ever produced is coolness; a soft answer turns away wrath

animals
a cat has nine lives; a dog is a man's best friend; an elephant never forgets; if you want to live and thrive, let the spider run alive; never work with children or animals; one for sorrow; two for mirth; three for a wedding; four for a birth; the robin and the wren are God's cock and hen; there's nothing so good for the inside of a man as the outside of a horse; three things are not to be trusted: a cow's horn, a dog's tooth, and a horse's hoof

anticipation
don't count your chickens before they are hatched; don't cross the bridge till you come to it; don't cry before you're hurt; don't meet troubles halfway; don't shout until you are out of the woods; don't throw away your dirty water until you get clean; first catch your hare; it's not over till it's over; let them laugh that win; never trouble trouble till trouble troubles you; the opera ain't over till the fat lady sings; sufficient unto the day is the evil thereof; worry is interest paid on trouble before it falls due

anxiety See **worry**

apology

he who excuses himself accuses himself; never ask pardon before you are accused

appearance

all that glitters is not gold; an ape's an ape, a varlet's a varlet, though they be clad in silk or scarlet; appearances are deceiving; beauty and honesty seldom agree; beauty is only skin-deep; the best art conceals art; be what you would seem to be; a blind man's wife needs no paint; blushing is a sign of grace; clothes don't make the man; clothes make the man; the cowl does not make the monk; don't judge a book by its cover; fancy passes beauty; fine feathers make fine birds; a good face is a letter of recommendation; a good horse cannot be of a bad color; handsome is as handsome does; an honest look covereth many faults; if it looks like a duck, walks like a duck, and quacks like a duck, it's a duck; judge not according to appearances; the lion is not so fierce as he is painted; a man is as old as he feels, and a woman as old as she looks; a merry heart makes a cheerful countenance; never choose your women or linen by candlelight; the proof of the pudding is in the eating; there's many a good cock come out of a tattered bag; the tree is known by its fruit; what you see is what you get

appreciation

blessings brighten as they take their flight; the cow knows not the value of her tail till she has lost it; don't cast your pearls before swine; health is not valued till sickness comes; if there were no clouds, we shouldn't enjoy the sun; you never miss the water till the well runs dry

arguing   See **conflict**

armed forces

an army marches on its stomach; every soldier has the baton of a field-marshal in his knapsack; the first duty of a soldier is obedience; old soldiers never die; war will cease when men refuse to fight

arts

all arts are brothers, each is a light to the other; art is long and life is short; art is power; the best art conceals art

associates

adversity makes strange bedfellows; birds of a feather flock together; Caesar's wife must be above suspicion; evil communications corrupt good manners; he that touches pitch shall be defiled; he who sups with the devil should have a long spoon; hitch your wagon to a star; if you lie down with dogs, you'll get up with fleas; it's not what you know, but who you know; like attracts like; love me, love my dog; a man is known by the company he keeps; politics makes strange bedfellows; the rotten apple spoils the barrel; the sun loses nothing by shining into a puddle; water seeks its own level; when you go to dance, take heed whom you take by the hand

authority   (*See also* **power**)

divide and conquer; kings have long arms; that government is best which governs least; too many chiefs and not enough Indians; when the cat's away, the mice will play; you can't fight City Hall

bad people   (*See also* **wrongdoing**)

a bad penny always turns up; the devil can cite scripture for his purpose; the devil looks after his own; the devil's children have the devil's luck; don't let the fox guard the henhouse; an ill bird lays an ill egg; there's a black sheep in every flock; when you go to dance, take heed whom you take by the hand

bad things   (*See also* **good and bad**)
cards are the devil's tools; choose the lesser of two evils; the devil always leaves a stink behind him; evil be to him who thinks it; he that touches pitch shall be defiled; ill weeds grow apace; the love of money is the root of all evil; money is the root of all evil; one year's seeding makes seven years' weeding; pigs are pigs; the rotten apple spoils the barrel; the sharper the storm, the sooner it's over; shit happens; small choice in rotten apples; there's a skeleton in every closet; you can't keep the birds from flying over your head, but you can keep them from building a nest in your hair

barriers
don't take down a fence unless you are sure why it was put up; good fences make good neighbors; a hedge between keeps friendship green

beauty
age before beauty; beauty and honesty seldom agree; beauty draws with a single hair; beauty is a good letter of introduction; beauty is but a blossom; beauty is in the eye of the beholder; beauty is no inheritance; beauty is only skin-deep; beauty is truth, truth beauty; boys seldom make passes at girls who wear glasses; fancy passes beauty; grace will last, beauty will blast; Monday's child is fair of face; please your eye and plague your heart; small is beautiful; a thing of beauty is a joy forever

beginning   (*See also* **raw material**)
the first step is the hardest; a good beginning is half the battle; a good beginning makes a good ending; great oaks from little acorns grow; he who begins many things, finishes but few; he who would climb the ladder must begin at the bottom; hope is a good breakfast but a bad supper; an ill beginning makes an ill ending; a journey of a thousand miles begins with one step; the mother of mischief is no bigger than a midge's wing; the sooner begun, the sooner done; a stream cannot rise above its source; there's a first time for everything; well begun is half done; what's past is prologue

behavior
as you sow, so shall you reap; boys will be boys; Caesar's wife must be above suspicion; handsome is as handsome does; honors change manners; if it looks like a duck, walks like a duck, and quacks like a duck, it's a duck; what can you expect from a pig but a grunt?; when in Rome, do as the Romans do; young saint, old devil

belief
believe only half of what you see and nothing you hear; a believer is a songless bird in a cage; believing has a core of unbelieving; the danger past and God forgotten; faith will move mountains; seeing is believing

betrayal
dead men tell no tales; little birds that can sing and won't sing must be made to sing; never tell tales out of school; no names, no pack-drill

birds   See **animals**

birthplace

the man who is born in a stable is not a horse; you can take the boy out of the country but you can't take the country out of the boy

bluntness

call a spade a spade; children and fools speak the truth; hard words break no bones; out of the mouths of babes and sucklings come great truths; tell the truth and shame the devil; truth will out

boasting

don't hide your light under a bushel; don't talk the talk if you can't walk the walk; every cook praises his own broth; if you've got it, flaunt it; much cry and little wool; self-praise is no recommendation; toot your own horn lest the same be never tooted

boldness   (*See also* **courage**)

adventures are to the adventurous; a cat in gloves catches no mice; faint heart never won fair lady; nothing so bold as a blind mare; nothing ventured, nothing gained

books

a book is like a garden carried in the pocket; books and friends should be few and good; a great book is a great evil; a house without books is like a room without windows

borrowing   (*See also* **debt**)

the early man never borrows from the late man; he that goes a-borrowing, goes a-sorrowing; neither a borrower nor a lender be

bribery

a bribe will enter without knocking; every man has his price; a golden key can open any door

business

business before pleasure; business is business; business is like a car, it will not run by itself except downhill; business neglected is business lost; the business of America is business; buy in the cheapest market and sell in the dearest; corporations have neither bodies to be punished nor souls to be damned ; the customer is always right; from shirtsleeves to shirtsleeves is only three generations; if you don't speculate, you can't accumulate; keep your shop and your shop will keep you; let the buyer beware; never mix business with pleasure; no penny, no paternoster; one business begets another; pay beforehand was never well served; punctuality is the soul of business; there are tricks in every trade; there's no such thing as a free lunch; trade follows the flag; what's good for General Motors is good for America

buying and selling

the buyer needs a thousand eyes, the seller wants but one; buy in the cheapest market and sell in the dearest; the customer is always right; let the buyer beware; location, location, location; a thing you don't want is dear at any price; the worth of a thing is what it will bring; you buy land, you buy stones; you buy meat, you buy bones; you get what you pay for

calendar

a dripping June sets all in tune; as the day lengthens, so the cold strengthens; in the spring a young man's fancy lightly turns to thoughts of love; it's not spring until you can plant your foot upon twelve daisies; March comes in like a lion, and goes out like a lamb; marry in May, rue for aye; may chickens come cheeping;

ne'er cast a clout till May be out; no moon, no man

calm
after a storm comes a calm; in a calm sea every man is a pilot; music hath charms to soothe the savage breast; nothing can bring you peace but yourself

capture
catching's before hanging; in vain the net is spread in the sight of the bird; an old poacher makes the best gamekeeper; set a thief to catch a thief; softly, softly, catchee monkey

carefulness
fair and softly goes far in a day; haste makes waste; the longest way around is the shortest way home; make haste slowly; more haste, less speed; one step at a time; slow and steady wins the race; slow but sure

caution
better safe than sorry; beware of Greeks bearing gifts; caution is the parent of safety; discretion is the better part of valor; don't burn your bridges behind you; don't go near the water until you learn how to swim; don't put all your eggs in one basket; easy does it; first try and then trust; a fool's bolt is soon shot; full cup, steady hand; he who fights and runs away may live to fight another day; he who sups with the devil should have a long spoon; if and an spoils many a good charter; if you can't be good, be careful; it's better to be on the safe side; let the buyer beware; little boats should stay close to shore; a live dog is better than a dead lion; look before you leap; love your enemy, but don't put a gun in

his hand; once bitten, twice shy; once burned, twice shy; put your trust in God, and keep your powder dry; safe bind, safe find; second thoughts are best; safety first; save something for a rainy day; three things are not to be trusted: a cow's horn, a dog's tooth, and a horse's hoof; trust everybody, but cut the cards; trust not a new friend nor an old enemy; trust not one night's ice; when you go to dance, take heed whom you take by the hand

certainty   See uncertainty

chance
accidents will happen in the best-regulated families; blind chance sweeps the world along; even a blind pig occasionally picks up an acorn; lightning never strikes twice in the same place; marriage is a lottery; you pays your money and you takes your choice

change   (*See also* reform)
a change is as good as a rest; don't change the rules in the middle of the game; don't jump from the frying pan into the fire; don't swap horses in midstream; from the sweetest wine, the tartest vinegar; the more things change, the more they stay the same; a new broom sweeps clean; new lords, new laws; one nail drives out another; other times, other manners; the shoe is on the other foot; there are no birds in last year's nest; there's nothing constant but inconstancy; times change, and we with time; variety is the spice of life; the wheel of fortune is forever in motion; a wise man changes his mind, but a fool never does; the world runs on wheels; you can't step twice into the same river; young saint, old devil

changelessness

as a tree falls, so shall it lie; the more things change, the more they stay the same; once a priest, always a priest; once a thief, always a thief; there's nothing constant but inconstancy; there's nothing new under the sun; what's done cannot be undone; you can drive out nature with a pitchfork but she keeps on coming back; you can take the boy out of the country but you can't take the country out of the boy; you can't unscramble eggs

character

an ape's an ape, a varlet's a varlet, though they be clad in silk or scarlet; the apple never falls far from the tree; as the twig is bent, so is the tree inclined; beauty is only skin-deep; better a good cow than a cow of a good kind; be what you would seem to be; character is destiny; the child is father of the man; great men have great faults; the higher the monkey climbs the more he shows his tail; if it looks like a duck, walks like a duck, and quacks like a duck, it's a duck; it takes one to know one; kind hearts are more than coronets; the leopard can't change its spots; like father, like son; like mother, like daughter; the man who is born in a stable is not a horse; nature passes nurture; once a thief, always a thief; the proof of the pudding is in the eating; a rose by any other name would smell as sweet; a rose is a rose is a rose; scratch a Russian and you find a Tartar; still waters run deep; the style is the man; there's many a good cock come out of a tattered bag; there's nowt so queer as folk; what can you expect from a pig but a grunt?; what's bred in the bone will come out in the flesh; you can drive out nature with a pitchfork but she keeps on coming back; you can take the boy out of

the country but you can't take the country out of the boy

charity

charity begins at home; charity covers a multitude of sins; charity is not a bone you throw to a dog but a bone you share with a dog; give a man a fish, and you feed him for a day; show him how to fish, and you feed him for a lifetime

cheerfulness

it's better to laugh than to cry; laugh and grow fat; laugh and the world laughs with you, weep and you weep alone; laughter is the best medicine; a merry heart makes a cheerful countenance; sing before breakfast, cry before night

children (*See also* **parents and children**)

boys will be boys; children and fools speak the truth; children are certain cares, but uncertain comforts; children should be seen and not heard; the child that is born on the Sabbath day is bonny and blithe and good and gay; Friday's child is loving and giving; late children, early orphans; little pitchers have big ears; May chickens come cheeping; Monday's child is fair of face; never work with children or animals; no moon, no man; out of the mouths of babes and sucklings come great truths; praise the child, and you make love to the mother; Saturday's child works hard for its living; spare the rod and spoil the child; Thursday's child has far to go; Tuesday's child is full of grace; Wednesday's child is full of woe

choice (*See also* **indecision**)

choose the lesser of two evils; a door must be either shut or open; fish or cut bait; he that has a choice has trouble; no man can serve two masters; the obvious choice is usually a quick regret; one cannot be in two places at once; piss or get off the pot; small choice in rotten apples; you can't have it both ways; you can't have your cake and eat it too; you can't run with the hare and hunt with the hounds; you can't serve God and mammon; you'll be damned if you do and damned if you don't; you pays your money and you takes your choice

Christianity   See **religion**

church   See **religion**

circumstance
circumstances alter cases; cut your coat according to your cloth; everybody stretches his legs according to the length of his coverlet; the shoe is on the other foot; stretch your arm no further than your sleeve will reach; the vicar of Bray will be vicar of Bray still

class
fine feathers make fine birds; it takes three generations to make a gentleman; one half of the world doesn't know how the other half lives; when Adam delved and Eve span, who was then the gentleman?

clothes   See **dress**

coercion
he that complies against his will is of his own opinion still; little birds that can sing and won't sing must be made to sing; one volunteer is worth two pressed men; people are more easily led than driven; you can lead a horse to water, but you can't make him drink

coincidence
great minds think alike; it's a small world; jesters do oft prove prophets; speak of the devil and he always appears

commerce   See **business**

common sense
ask advice, but use your own common sense; never let your education interfere with your intelligence; one cannot love and be wise; an ounce of common sense is worth a pound of theory; an ounce of discretion is worth a pound of wit

company   (*See also* **associates**)
the company makes the feast; good company on the road is the shortest cut; laugh and the world laughs with you, weep and you weep alone; misery loves company; the more the merrier; there's safety in numbers; two's company, three's a crowd

complaining
everybody talks about the weather, but nobody does anything about it; every horse thinks its own pack heaviest; it's better to light one candle than curse the darkness; the squeaky wheel gets the grease

compromise
agree, for the law is costly; give and take is fair play; an ill agreement is better than a good judgment; it's better to lose the battle and win the war

concealment
the best art conceals art; crime must be concealed by crime; an honest look covereth many faults; murder will out; those who hide can find; truth will out; you can run, but you can't hide

457

conciseness

brevity is the soul of wit; few words are best; few words are best; a great book is a great evil; length begets loathing

confession

confess and be hanged; confession is good for the soul; a fault confessed is half redressed; he who excuses himself accuses himself

conflict

all's fair in love and war; it's ill sitting at Rome and striving with the Pope; it takes two to make a quarrel; the only thing a heated argument ever produced is coolness; the quarrel of lovers is the renewal of love; two of a trade never agree; when Greek meets Greek, then comes the tug of war; when thieves fall out, honest men come by their own; when you argue with a fool, make sure he isn't similarly engaged; while two dogs are fighting for a bone, a third runs away with it; who has land has war; you can't fight City Hall

conformity

don't rock the boat ; if you can't beat 'em, join 'em; it's better to be right than in the majority; strive not against the stream; when in Rome, do as the Romans do

conscience

a dear conscience can bear any trouble; conscience does make cowards of us all; conscience gets a lot of credit that belongs to cold feet; do right and fear no man; evil doers are evil dreaders; a guilty conscience needs no accuser; let him who is without sin cast the first stone

consequence

as you bake, so shall you brew; as you brew, so shall you drink; as you make your bed, so you must lie in it; as you sow, so shall you reap; for want of a nail the shoe was lost, for want of a shoe the horse was lost, and for want of a horse the rider was lost; garbage in, garbage out; good seed makes a good crop; he that drinks beer, thinks beer; if you play with fire, you get burned; let the chips fall where they may; nothing comes of nothing; one lie leads to another; one year's seeding makes seven years' weeding; they that dance must pay the piper; they that sow the wind shall reap the whirlwind; who says A must say B; who won't be ruled by the rudder must be ruled by the rock

contentment   (*See also* **happiness; satisfaction**)

be happy while you're living, for you're a long time dead; a contented mind is a continual feast; content is more than a kingdom; God's in his heaven; all's right with the world; what you've never had you never miss

conviviality

the company makes the feast; good company on the road is the shortest cut; it's always fair weather when good friends get together; it's merry in hall when beards wag all; the more the merrier

cooperation

a chain is no stronger than its weakest link; a common danger causes common action; a dwarf on a giant's shoulders sees further of the two; it takes two to make a bargain; it takes two to tango; one hand washes the other; union is strength; united we stand, divided we fall; you scratch my back and I'll scratch yours

corruption   (*See also* **bribery**)

corruption will find a dozen alibis for its evil deeds; evil communications corrupt good manners; a fish stinks from the head; he that touches pitch shall be defiled; kissing goes by favor; the more you stir it, the worse it stinks; power corrupts, and absolute power corrupts absolutely; the rotten apple spoils the barrel; set a beggar on horseback, and he'll ride to the devil; something is rotten in the state of Denmark

courage

brave men lived before Agamemnon; courage is fear that has said its prayers; faint heart never won fair lady; fortune favors the brave; none but the brave deserve the fair; one courageous thought will put to flight a host of troubles; the only thing we have to fear is fear itself

courtesy

be nice to people on your way up because you'll meet them on your way down; civility costs nothing; a civil question deserves a civil answer; courtesy is contagious; honors change manners; manners make the man; nice guys finish last; punctuality is the politeness of kings; there's nothing lost by civility; you can catch more flies with honey than with vinegar

courtship

faint heart never won fair lady; happy's the wooing that's not long a-doing; he that would the daughter win, must with the mother first begin; marry in haste, repent at leisure; none but the brave deserve the fair

cowardice

a bully is always a coward; conscience does make cowards of us all; conscience gets a lot of credit that belongs to cold feet; cowards die many times before their death

credit

give credit where credit is due; give the devil his due; success has many fathers, while failure is an orphan

crime   See **wrongdoing**

crisis

calamity is the touchstone of a brave mind; Nero fiddled while Rome burned; when the going gets tough, the tough get going

criticism

the best place for criticism is in front of your mirror; the biter is sometimes bit; criticism is something you can avoid by saying nothing, doing nothing, and being nothing; don't judge a man until you have walked a mile in his boots; don't shoot the pianist, he's doing his best; faults are thick where love is thin; he who is absent is always in the wrong; he who would write and can't write can surely review; if every man would sweep his own doorstep the city would soon be clean; if the shoe fits, wear it; judge not, that ye be not judged; let him who is without sin cast the first stone; people who live in glass houses shouldn't throw stones; physician, heal thyself; the pot calls the kettle black; sweep your own doorstep clean

curiosity   See **questions**

customs

every land has its own law; other times, other manners; so many countries, so many customs; when in Rome, do as the Romans do

danger   (*See also* **risk**)

a common danger causes common action; fire is a good servant but a bad master; he that is too secure is not safe; he that would learn to pray, let him go to sea; he who rides a tiger is afraid to dismount; the highest branch is not the safest roost; if you play with fire, you get burned; it's ill jesting with edged tools; the post of honor is the post of danger; uneasy lies the head that wears a crown

days
the better the day, the better the deed; the child that is born on the Sabbath day is bonny and blithe and good and gay; Friday's child is loving and giving; Monday's child is fair of face; Saturday's child works hard for its living; Thursday's child has far to go; Tuesday's child is full of grace; Wednesday's child is full of woe

death   (*See also* **premature death**)
as a tree falls, so shall it lie ; better death than dishonor; blessed are the dead that the rain rains on; dead men don't bite; dead men tell no tales; death defies the doctor; death is the great leveler; death keeps no calendar; death pays all debts; equality begins in the grave; every bullet has its billet; every door may be shut but death's door; good Americans, when they die, go to Paris; the good that men do lives after them; if you're born to be hanged, then you'll never be drowned; it's better to die on your feet than live on your knees; it's ill waiting for dead men's shoes; let the dead bury the dead; a live dog is better than a dead lion; a man can only die once; medicine can prolong life, but death will seize the doctor, too; never speak ill of the dead; one funeral makes many; shrouds have no pockets; stone-dead hath no fellow; there's a remedy for everything except death; wine has drowned more

men than the sea; you can only die once; you can't take it with you; young men may die, but old men must die

debt   (*See also* **borrowing**)
be just before you're generous; death pays all debts; a man in debt is caught in a net; out of debt, out of danger; pay as you go and nothing you'll owe; short reckonings make long friends; speak not of my debts unless you mean to pay them

deceit   See **lies**

deception
fool me once, shame on you; fool me twice, shame on me; there are tricks in every trade; you can fool some of the people all of the time, and all of the people some of the time, but you can't fool all of the people all of the time; you can't catch old birds with chaff

defamation
call a man a thief and he will steal; give a dog a bad name and hang him; he that would hang his dog gives out first that he is mad; never speak ill of the dead; throw dirt enough, and some will stick

delay   (*See also* **lateness; procrastination**)
delays are dangerous; desires are nourished by delays; he who hesitates is lost; hope deferred makes the heart sick; revenge is a dish best eaten cold; there's luck in leisure; while the grass grows, the steed starves

desire   (*See also* **getting what you want**)
appetite comes with eating; desires are nourished by delays; don't wish too hard; humble hearts have humble desires; you might just get what you wished for; if wishes were horses, beggars would ride;

wishes won't wash dishes; the wish is father to the thought

despair
the darkest hour is just before dawn; if it were not for hope, the heart would break

destiny
character is destiny; every bullet has its billet; God moves in mysterious ways; hanging and wiving go by destiny; if you're born to be hanged, then you'll never be drowned; man proposes, God disposes; marriages are made in heaven; what goes up must come down; what will be, will be; whom the gods would destroy, they first make mad

destruction
it's easier to tear down than to build up; a jackass can kick a barn door down, but it takes a carpenter to build one; whom the gods would destroy, they first make mad

deterioration
don't jump from the frying pan into the fire; rats desert a sinking ship; when you are in a hole, stop digging; the worst is yet to come

determination
he who wills the end, wills the means; it's dogged as does it; it's not the size of the dog in the fight, it's the size of the fight in the dog; nothing is impossible to a willing heart; the show must go on; when the going gets tough, the tough get going; where there's a will there's a way; a willful man must have his way

difference
different strokes for different folks; East is East and West is West and never the twain shall meet; every land has its own law; extremes meet; horses for courses; it takes all kinds of people to make a world; oil and water do not mix; opposites attract; so many countries, so many customs; so many men, so many opinions; tastes differ; variety is the spice of life

difficulty
all things are easy to industry, all things difficult to sloth ; the difficult is done at once, the impossible takes a little longer; easier said than done; the first hundred years are the hardest; life is hard by the yard, but by the inch life's a cinch

diligence   See **industry**

discipline
spare the rod and spoil the child; when the cat's away, the mice will play; who won't be ruled by the rudder must be ruled by the rock

discontent
go farther and fare worse; the golden age was never the present age; the grass is always greener on the other side of the fence

discretion   (*See also* **tact**)
don't wash your dirty linen in public; fields have eyes and woods have ears; hear all, see all, say nowt; loose lips sink ships; never tell tales out of school; no names, no pack-drill; tell it not in Gath; tell not all you know, nor do all you can; think all you speak, but speak not all you think; think before you speak; walls have ears

disgrace
better death than dishonor; it's an ill bird that fouls its own nest; poverty is no

disgrace, but it's a great inconvenience; there's a black sheep in every flock; there's a skeleton in every closet

disillusion
absence is the mother of disillusion; blessed are they who expect nothing, for they shall not be disappointed

disloyalty
rats desert a sinking ship; save us from our friends; with friends like that, who needs enemies?

disobedience
forbidden fruit is sweet; rules are made to be broken

disrespect   See respect

distance
blue are the hills that are far away; distance lends enchantment to the view

disunity
divide and conquer; a house divided against itself cannot stand; united we stand, divided we fall

downfall
be nice to people on your way up because you'll meet them on your way down; the bigger they are, the harder they fall; from the sublime to the ridiculous is only one step; give a man enough rope and he'll hang himself; hasty climbers have sudden falls; he that is down need fear no fall; pride goes before a fall; what goes up must come down

drawbacks   (See also good and bad)
the cat would eat fish, but would not wet her feet; he that would have eggs

must endure the cackling of hens; no joy without annoy; no pain, no gain; there's no pleasure without pain; there's no rose without a thorn; you have to take the bitter with the sweet; you have to take the rough with the smooth

dreams
dream of a funeral and you hear of a marriage; dreams go by contraries; dreams retain the infirmities of our character; morning dreams come true

dress
an ape's an ape, a varlet's a varlet, though they be clad in silk or scarlet; better be out of the world than out of the fashion; clothes don't make the man; clothes make the man; fine feathers make fine birds; ne'er cast a clout till May be out; nine tailors make a man; pride feels no pain; the tailor makes the man; there's no such thing as bad weather, only the wrong clothes

drinking
alcohol will preserve anything but a secret; drunkenness reveals what soberness conceals; he that drinks beer, thinks beer; take a hair of the dog that bit you; there's truth in wine; water is the only drink for a wise man; when the wine is in, the wit is out; whiskey and gasoline don't mix; wine has drowned more men than the sea

earliness   (See also promptness)
the early bird catches the worm; the early man never borrows from the late man; early to bed and early to rise, makes a man healthy, wealthy, and wise; first come, first served; an hour in the morning is worth two in the evening; it's better to be an hour too early than a minute too late;

one hour's sleep before midnight is worth two after; soon ripe, soon rotten

easiness
all things are easy to industry, all things difficult to sloth; cross the stream where it is shallowest; easy come, easy go; life is hard by the yard, but by the inch life's a cinch

eating
after dinner rest awhile, after supper walk a mile; an apple a day keeps the doctor away; an army marches on its stomach; the best doctors are Dr. Diet, Dr. Quiet, and Dr. Merryman; bread is the staff of life; cheese digests all things but itself; diet cures more than doctors; eat to live, do not live to eat; a fat kitchen makes a lean will; feed a cold and starve a fever; fingers were made before forks; food without hospitality is medicine; gluttony kills more than the sword; God never sends mouths but he sends meat; God sends meat, but the devil sends cooks; help you to salt, help you to sorrow; hunger is the best sauce; a hungry stomach has no ears; man does not live by bread alone; meat and mass never hindered man; more die of food than famine; the way to a man's heart is through his stomach; welcome is the best cheer; you are what you eat

eavesdropping
walls have ears; fields have eyes and woods have ears; listeners never hear any good of themselves; little pitchers have big ears

education
education doesn't come by bumping your head against the schoolhouse; genius without education is like silver in the mine; give a man a fish, and you feed him for a day; give me a child for the first seven years and he is mine for life; show him how to fish, and you feed him for a lifetime; it's never too late to learn; learning is better than house or land; never let your education interfere with your intelligence; nobody is born learned; nobody forgets a good teacher; an ounce of practice is worth a pound of precept; there's no royal road to learning; those who can, do; those who can't, teach; wear your learning like your watch, in a private pocket; when house and land are gone and spent, then learning is most excellent

efficiency
he travels fastest who travels alone; an hour in the morning is worth two in the evening; if you want something done, ask a busy person; keep no more cats than will catch mice; let your head save your heels; time is money

effort
he that would eat the fruit must climb the tree; if a thing's worth doing, it's worth doing well; no pain, no gain; the only place where success comes before work is in a dictionary; put your best foot forward; you never know what you can do until you try

embarrassment
blushing is a sign of grace; paper does not blush

ending
all good things must come to an end; all's well that ends well; the best of friends must part; be the day weary or be the day long, at last it ringeth to evensong; the end crowns the work; everything has an end; a good beginning makes a good ending;

exchange

a fair exchange is no robbery; give and take is fair play

excuses

a bad excuse is better than none; a bad workman quarrels with his tools; accusing the times is but excusing ourselves; corruption will find a dozen alibis for its evil deeds; he who excuses himself accuses himself; he who is good at making excuses is seldom good at anything else; ignorance of the law is no excuse; it's easy to find a stick to beat a dog; killing no murder

exercise

after dinner rest awhile, after supper walk a mile; there's nothing so good for the inside of a man as the outside of a horse

expectation

blessed are they who expect nothing, for they shall not be disappointed; everybody to whom much is given, of him will much be required; it's better to travel hopefully than to arrive; it's ill waiting for dead men's shoes

expediency

the end justifies the means; if you can't beat 'em, join 'em; it's better to lose the battle and win the war; it's good to make a bridge of gold to a flying enemy; killing no murder; make a virtue of necessity

experience

a burnt child dreads the fire; don't judge a man until you have walked a mile in his boots; don't make the same mistake twice; don't teach your grandmother to suck eggs; experience is a comb that fate gives a man when his hair is all gone; experience is the best teacher; experience is the mother of wisdom; experience is the teacher of fools; experience keeps a dear school; learn from the mistakes of others; live and learn; the older the wiser; an old fox is not easily snared; an old poacher makes the best gamekeeper; once bitten, twice shy; once burned, twice shy; an ounce of practice is worth a pound of precept; practice makes perfect; set a thief to catch a thief; some folks speak from experience; others, from experience, don't speak; they that live longest see most; those who cannot remember the past are condemned to repeat it; a traveler may lie with authority; years know more than books; you can't catch old birds with chaff

expertise

every man to his trade; the good seaman is known in bad weather; horses for courses; a jack of all trades is master of none; let the cobbler stick to his last; never send a boy to do a man's job; you can't beat a man at his own game; you need more than dancing shoes to be a dancer

exploitation

don't overload gratitude; if you do, she'll kick; give a man an inch and he'll take a mile; it's good fishing in troubled waters; nobody ever went broke underestimating the intelligence of the American people; the willing horse carries the load

extravagance   (*See also* **spending**)

Christmas comes but once a year; penny wise and pound foolish; spare at the spigot, and let out the bunghole; willful waste makes woeful want

extremes

East is East and West is West and never the twain shall meet; extremes meet; from the sweetest wine, the tartest vinegar; opposites attract

failure

if anything can go wrong, it will; an ill beginning makes an ill ending; a miss is as good as a mile; rats desert a sinking ship; success has many fathers, while failure is an orphan; when one door closes, another one opens

fairness

all's fair in love and war; be just before you're generous; a fair exchange is no robbery; fair play's a jewel; give and take is fair play; give credit where credit is due; give the devil his due; never give a sucker an even break; share and share alike; there are two sides to every question; turnabout is fair play; what's sauce for the goose is sauce for the gander

fame

brave men lived before Agamemnon; everybody has his fifteen minutes of fame; every dog has his day

familiarity

better the devil you know than the devil you don't know; come live with me and you'll know me; familiarity breeds contempt; no man is a hero to his valet; a prophet is not without honor, save in his own country; you never know a man until you live with him; you should know a man seven years before you stir his fire

family (*See also* **heredity; parents and children**)

better a good cow than a cow of a good kind; blood is thicker than water; charity begins at home; the family that prays together stays together; from shirtsleeves to shirtsleeves is only three generations; he that has a wife and children has given hostages to fortune; he travels fastest who travels alone; love me, love my dog; a mother can take care of ten children, but sometimes ten children can't take care of one mother; near is my shirt, but nearer is my skin; the shoemaker's child always goes barefoot; there's a black sheep in every flock; there's a skeleton in every closet

fate   See **destiny**

fear

courage is fear that has said its prayers; fear lends wings; the only thing we have to fear is fear itself

feelings

the eyes are the mirrors of the soul; out of the fullness of the heart the mouth speaks

festivals

the better the day, the better the deed; Christmas comes but once a year

fiction

fact is stranger than fiction; history is a fable agreed upon; truth is stranger than fiction

finding

finders keepers, losers weepers; finding is keeping

first impressions

beauty is a good letter of introduction; first impressions are the most lasting

flattery

flattery, like perfume, should be smelled but not swallowed; imitation is the sincerest form of flattery; praise the child, and you make love to the mother; a rich man's joke is always funny; you can catch more flies with honey than with vinegar

food   See **eating**

foolishness
ask a silly question and you get a silly answer; children and fools speak the truth; empty vessels make the most sound; experience is the teacher of fools; a fool and his money are soon parted; a fool at forty is a fool indeed; fools ask questions that wise men cannot answer; fools rush in where angels fear to tread; fortune favors fools; little things please little minds; monkey see, monkey do; never give a sucker an even break; send a fool to market and a fool he'll return; silence is the fittest reply to folly; six hours' sleep for a man, seven for a woman, and eight for a fool; there's no fool like an old fool; when the wine is in, the wit is out; when you argue with a fool, make sure he isn't similarly engaged; a white wall is the fool's writing paper; whom the gods would destroy, they first make mad; a wise man changes his mind, but a fool never does; young folks think old folks to be fools, but old folks know young folks to be fools

foresight
nothing is certain but the unforeseen; an ounce of prevention is worth a pound of cure; prevention is better than cure; a stitch in time saves nine; the unexpected always happens; who repairs not his gutters repairs his whole house

forethought
action without thought is like shooting without aim; let your head save your heels;

look before you leap; think before you speak; a word spoken is past recalling

forgetting
a bellowing cow soon forgets her calf; the best way to get even is to forget; an elephant never forgets; forgive and forget; out of sight, out of mind; seldom seen, soon forgotten

forgiveness
charity covers a multitude of sins; every dog is allowed one bite; forgive and forget; let bygones be bygones; never let the sun go down on your anger; offenders never pardon; to err is human, to forgive divine; to know all is to forgive all; wink at small faults

freedom
give a man enough rope and he'll hang himself; liberty is not licence; the price of liberty is eternal vigilance; stone walls do not a prison make; that government is best which governs least

friends
be kind to your friends; books and friends should be few and good; a friend to all is a friend to none; if it weren't for them, you would be a total stranger; the best of friends must part; a dog is a man's best friend; a friend in need is a friend indeed; a hedge between keeps friendship green; he that has a full purse never wanted a friend; it's always fair weather when good friends get together; lend your money and lose your friend; love is blind; friendship closes its eyes; old friends and old wine are best; save us from our friends; short reckonings make long friends; short visits make long friends; trust not a new friend nor an old enemy; wealth makes many

God (*See also* **providence; religion**)
all things are possible with God; every man for himself and God for us all; God helps those who help themselves; God makes the back to the burden; God moves in mysterious ways; God never sends mouths but he sends meat; God tempers the wind to the shorn lamb; the Lord gives and the Lord takes away; man proposes, God disposes ; man's extremity is God's opportunity; put your trust in God, and keep your powder dry

good and bad (*See also* **drawbacks**)
April showers bring May flowers; bad money drives out good; every cloud has a silver lining; if there were no clouds, we shouldn't enjoy the sun; there's good and bad in everything; there's no rose without a thorn; where God builds a church, the devil will build a chapel; you buy land, you buy stones; you buy meat, you buy bones; you have to take the bitter with the sweet; you have to take the rough with the smooth

good intentions
never do evil that good may come of it; the road to hell is paved with good intentions; take the will for the deed

good things (*See also* **good and bad**)
the age of miracles is past; all good things must come to an end; the best things in life are free; a little of what you fancy does you good; what's good for General Motors is good for America; you can have too much of a good thing

gossip (*See also* **rumors**)
bad news travels fast; a dog that will fetch a bone will carry a bone; gossip is the lifeblood of society; gossip is vice enjoyed vicariously; never tell tales out of school; see no evil, hear no evil, speak no evil; a tale never loses in the telling; what the soldier said isn't evidence

gratitude
beggars can't be choosers; don't bite the hand that feeds you; don't overload gratitude; if you do, she'll kick; never look a gift horse in the mouth; praise the bridge that carries you over; a small gift usually gets small thanks

great and small (*See also* **greatness; size; small things**)
better a big fish in a little pond than a little fish in a big pond; better be the head of a dog than the tail of a lion; big fish eat little fish; big fleas have little fleas upon their backs to bite 'em, and little fleas have lesser fleas, and so ad infinitum; big is beautiful; the dogs bark, but the caravan goes on; eagles don't catch flies; great trees keep down little ones; if you can't run with the big dogs, stay under the porch; little thieves are hanged, but great ones escape; a mouse may help a lion; a reed before the wind lives on, while mighty oaks do fall; too many chiefs and not enough Indians; when the cat's away, the mice will play

greatness
behind every great man there is a great woman; calamity is the touchstone of a brave mind; eagles don't catch flies; from the sublime to the ridiculous is only one step; full cup, steady hand; great men have great faults; the highest branch is not the safest roost; the post of honor is the post of danger; the sun loses nothing by shining into a puddle

the doctor; diet cures more than doctors; the doctor is often more to be feared than the disease; early to bed and early to rise, makes a man healthy, wealthy, and wise; feed a cold and starve a fever; gluttony kills more than the sword; health is not valued till sickness comes; health is wealth; if wind blows on you through a hole, say your prayers and mind your soul; laugh and grow fat; laughter is the best medicine; a little of what you fancy does you good; one funeral makes many; there's nothing so good for the inside of a man as the outside of a horse; use legs and have legs

help
four eyes see more than two; if you're not part of the solution, you're part of the problem; many hands make light work; a mouse may help a lion; praise the bridge that carries you over; they also serve who only stand and wait; too many cooks spoil the broth; two boys are half a boy, and three boys are no boy at all; two heads are better than one; you can't beat somebody with nobody

heredity
the apple never falls far from the tree; beauty is no inheritance; birth is much but breeding more; blood will tell; like father, like son; like mother, like daughter; nature passes nurture; what's bred in the bone will come out in the flesh

hesitation   See **delay**

hierarchy
big fleas have little fleas upon their backs to bite 'em, and little fleas have lesser fleas, and so ad infinitum; if two ride on a horse, one must ride behind; in the country of the blind, the one-eyed man is king

hindsight
blessings brighten as they take their flight; the cow knows not the value of her tail till she has lost it; don't shut the barn door after the horse is stolen; health is not valued till sickness comes; it's easy to be wise after the event; you never miss the water till the well runs dry

hints
a nod's as good as a wink to a blind horse; straws show which way the wind blows; a word to the wise is sufficient

history
happy is the country that has no history; history is a fable agreed upon; history repeats itself

home
east, west, home's best; every cock will crow upon his own dunghill; home is home, be it ever so homely; home is where the heart is; home is where you hang your hat; the house shows the owner; it takes a heap of living to make a house a home; a man's home is his castle; men make houses, women make homes; there's no place like home

honesty   (*See also* **truth**)
beauty and honesty seldom agree; cheaters never prosper; children and fools speak the truth; confession is good for the soul; honesty is more praised than practiced; honesty is the best policy; honesty pays; a liar is not believed when he tells the truth; tell the truth and shame the devil; there's truth in wine

hope   (*See also* **optimism**)
a drowning man will catch at a straw; he that lives in hope dances to an ill tune; he

that lives on hope will die fasting; hope and have; hope deferred makes the heart sick; hope is a good breakfast but a bad supper; if it were not for hope, the heart would break; it's better to travel hopefully than to arrive; it's not over till it's over; never say die; the opera ain't over till the fat lady sings; where there's no vision, the people perish; while there's life there's hope; the wish is father to the thought

hospitality See **entertaining**

human nature
the best of men are but men at best; hope springs eternal in the human breast; self-preservation is the first law of nature; sin, sorrow, and work are the things that men can't shirk; to err is human, to forgive divine

humility (*See also* **meekness**)
the meek shall inherit the earth; soft and fair goes far; softly, softly, catchee monkee

hunger
an empty sack cannot stand upright; a growing youth has a wolf in his stomach; hunger drives the wolf out of the wood; hunger is the best sauce; a hungry man is an angry man; a hungry stomach has no ears; it's ill speaking between a full man and a fasting; more die of food than famine

hygiene
cleanliness is next to godliness; poverty comes from God, but not dirt; we must eat a peck of dirt before we die

hypocrisy
the devil was sick, the devil a saint would be; the devil was well, the devil a saint was he; do as I say, not as I do; many kiss the hand they wish to see cut off; the nearer the church, the farther from God

ideas
all words are pegs to hang ideas on; one story is good till another is told; an ounce of common sense is worth a pound of theory; thinking is very far from knowing

idleness
all things are easy to industry, all things difficult to sloth; as good be an addled egg as an idle bird; better to wear out than to rust out; the devil finds work for idle hands to do; footprints on the sands of time are not made by sitting down; he who does not work, neither should he eat; an idle brain is the devil's workshop; idleness is the root of all evil; idle people have the least leisure; an idle youth, a needy age; mind unemployed is mind unenjoyed; sloth is the mother of poverty; time hangs heavy on idle hands; you snooze, you lose

ignorance
admiration is the daughter of ignorance; the husband is always the last to know; if the blind lead the blind, both shall fall into the ditch; ignorance is a voluntary misfortune; ignorance is bliss; ignorance of the law is no excuse; much water goes by the mill that the miller knows not of; nothing so bold as a blind mare; one half of the world doesn't know how the other half lives; prejudice is being down on what we are not up on; prejudice is the child of ignorance; a slice off a cut loaf isn't missed; those who know don't speak; those who speak don't know; what the eye doesn't see, the heart doesn't grieve over; what you don't know can't

hurt you; zeal without knowledge is a runaway horse

illusion

admiration is the daughter of ignorance; blue are the hills that are far away; catch not at the shadow and lose the substance; distance lends enchantment to the view; the golden age was never the present age; self-deceit is the easiest of any; there's a pot of gold at the end of the rainbow

imitation

as Maine goes, so goes the nation; imitation is the sincerest form of flattery; like breeds like; like master, like man; like people, like priest; monkey see, monkey do

impatience   See **patience**

imperfection

nobody is perfect; there's good and bad in everything

impossibility

the difficult is done at once, the impossible takes a little longer; there's a pot of gold at the end of the rainbow; you can't get a quart into a pint pot; you can't get blood from a stone; you can't make a silk purse out of a sow's ear; you can't make bricks without straw; you can't put a square peg in a round hole; you can't unscramble eggs

improbability

the age of miracles is past; if a pig had wings, it might fly; if ifs and ans were pots and pans, there'd be no work for tinkers; if the sky falls, we shall catch larks; if wishes were horses, beggars would ride

improvement

after a storm comes a calm; the best is yet to be; better luck next time; the darkest hour is just before dawn; everybody talks about the weather, but nobody does anything about it; it's a long road that has no turning; it's never too late to mend; prosperity is just around the corner; a rising tide lifts all boats; when things are at the worst they begin to mend

inaction

care is no cure; councils of war never fight; lookers-on see most of the game; they also serve who only stand and wait; when in doubt, do nothing

incompetence

a bad workman quarrels with his tools; every employee tends to rise to his level of incompetence; he who would write and can't write can surely review; if you pay peanuts, you get monkeys; those who can, do; those who can't, teach; war is too important to be left to the generals

incompleteness

a bird never flew on one wing; fools and children should never see half-done work

indecision   (*See also* **choice**)

between two stools one falls to the ground; councils of war never fight; he who hesitates is lost; if you run after two hares, you will catch neither; when in doubt, do nothing

independence   See **self-reliance**

industry

all things are easy to industry, all things difficult to sloth; the busiest men have the most leisure; diligence is the mother of good luck; footprints on the sands of time are not made by sitting down; genius is an infinite capacity for taking pains; if you want something done, ask a busy person; necessity sharpens industry; where bees are, there is honey; where there's muck there's brass

inefficiency
always in a hurry, always behind; a horse can't pull while kicking; more haste, less speed

inflexibility
a foolish consistency is the hobgoblin of little minds; a wise man changes his mind, but a fool never does

influence
art is power; as Maine goes, so goes the nation; beauty draws with a single hair; behind every great man there is a great woman; give me a child for the first seven years and he is mine for life; a golden key can open any door; the hand that rocks the cradle rules the world; hitch your wagon to a star; it's not what you know, but who you know; money talks

inheritance
a fat kitchen makes a lean will; most people consider thrift a fine virtue in ancestors

innovation
everything old is new again; there's nothing new under the sun; what's new cannot be true; you can't put new wine in old bottles

integrity
it's better to be right than in the majority; a man's word is as good as his bond; think all you speak, but speak not all you think; true blue will never stain

intellect
genius is an infinite capacity for taking pains; genius is one percent inspiration and ninety-nine percent perspiration; genius without education is like silver in the mine; a mind is a terrible thing to waste; mind unemployed is mind unenjoyed

interference
busy folks are always meddling; the more you stir it, the worse it stinks; you should know a man seven years before you stir his fire

jocularity
it's better to laugh than to cry; jesters do oft prove prophets; many a true word is spoken in jest; an ounce of discretion is worth a pound of wit

judgment
comparisons are odious; don't judge a man until you have walked a mile in his boots; judge not, that ye be not judged; the proof of the pudding is in the eating; there's good and bad in everything

kindness
be nice to people on your way up because you'll meet them on your way down; cold hands, warm heart; don't hit a man when he's down; God tempers the wind to the shorn lamb; kind hearts are more than coronets; the larger the body, the bigger the heart; nice guys finish last

knowledge
knowledge and timber shouldn't be much used until they are seasoned; knowledge

and wisdom are far from being one; knowledge is power; let the cobbler stick to his last; little birds that can sing and won't sing must be made to sing; a little knowledge is a dangerous thing; an ounce of discretion is worth a pound of wit; thinking is very far from knowing; those who know don't speak; those who speak don't know; who knows most, speaks least; you can't put an old head on young shoulders

lateness

after death the doctor; better late than never; don't shut the barn door after the horse is stolen; experience is a comb that fate gives a man when his hair is all gone; it's better to be an hour too early than a minute too late; while the grass grows, the steed starves

laughter See **cheerfulness; jocularity**

law

agree, for the law is costly; the devil makes his Christmas pies of lawyers' tongues and clerks' fingers; every land has its own law; hard cases make bad law; ignorance of the law is no excuse; an ill agreement is better than a good judgment; justice is blind; the king can do no wrong; lawmakers should not be lawbreakers; laws go as kings like; a man is innocent until proven guilty; a man who is his own lawyer has a fool for his client; new lords, new laws; nobody is above the law; one law for the rich and another for the poor; possession is nine points of the law; sue a beggar and catch a louse; when in Rome, do as the Romans do; a wise lawyer never goes to law himself

laziness See **idleness**

leadership

a fish stinks from the head; a good leader is also a good follower; he that cannot obey cannot command; if one sheep leaps over the ditch, all the rest will follow; war is too important to be left to the generals

learning See **education; knowledge**

lending

lend your money and lose your friend; neither a borrower nor a lender be

lies

ask me no questions and I'll tell you no lies; half the truth is often a whole lie; jove but laughs at lover's perjury; a liar is not believed when he tells the truth; a liar is worse than a thief; a liar should have a good memory; a lie can go around the world and back again while the truth is lacing up its boots; one lie leads to another; show me a liar and I will show you a thief; there are lies, damned lies, and statistics; what a tangled web we weave when first we practice to deceive

life

all the world's a stage; the first hundred years are the hardest; he lives long who lives well; life begins at forty; life is hard by the yard, but by the inch life's a cinch; life is just a bowl of cherries; life is no bed of roses; life isn't all beer and skittles; life is short and sweet; life is short and time is swift; life is too short; life is what you make it; life's a bitch, and then you die; a live dog is better than a dead lion; man does not live by bread alone; while there's life there's hope; the world runs on wheels

living within your means

cut your coat according to your cloth; everybody stretches his legs according to the length of his coverlet; stretch your arm no further than your sleeve will reach

logic

every why hath its wherefore; there's reason in all things; two and two make four; who says A must say B

loss See also winning and losing

blessings brighten as they take their flight; the cow knows not the value of her tail till she has lost it; don't throw good money after bad; easy come, easy go; finders keepers, losers weepers; good riddance to bad rubbish; the Lord gives and the Lord takes away; quickly come, quickly go; a slice off a cut loaf isn't missed; there are other fish in the sea; 'tis better to have loved and lost, than never to have loved at all; what you've never had you never miss; you can't lose what you never had; you never miss the water till the well runs dry

love

absence makes the heart grow fonder; all's fair in love and war; better a dinner of herbs where love is than a stalled ox where hate is; cold hands, warm heart; the course of true love never did run smooth; Friday's child is loving and giving; home is where the heart is; hot love is soon cold; in the spring a young man's fancy lightly turns to thoughts of love; it's best to be off with the old love before you are on with the new; jove but laughs at lover's perjury; love and a cough cannot be hid; love begets love; love conquers all; love is blind; love is blind; friendship closes its eyes; love is free; love laughs at locksmiths; love makes the world go round; love me little, love me long; love me, love my dog; love will find a way; lucky

at cards, unlucky in love; one cannot love and be wise; pity is akin to love; the quarrel of lovers is the renewal of love; there are other fish in the sea; 'tis better to have loved and lost, than never to have loved at all; when poverty comes in at the door, love flies out of the window

loyalty

dog does not eat dog; a dog is a man's best friend; hawks will not pick out hawks' eyes; it's an ill bird that fouls its own nest; no man can serve two masters; there's honor among thieves; whose bread I eat, his song I sing; you can't run with the hare and hunt with the hounds

luck

better luck next time; a cat has nine lives; the devil looks after his own; the devil's children have the devil's luck; diligence is the mother of good luck; every dog has his day; fortune favors fools; fortune favors the brave; it's better to be born lucky than rich; lucky at cards, unlucky in love; opportunities look for you when you are worth finding; opportunity never knocks for persons not worth a rap; providence is always on the side of the big battalions; see a pin and pick it up, all the day you'll have good luck; see a pin and let it lay, bad luck you'll have all the day; take the goods the gods provide; there's luck in odd numbers; the third time is the charm; touch wood; the wheel of fortune is forever in motion

lying See lies

marriage

always a bridesmaid, never a bride; better be an old man's darling than a young man's slave; better one house spoiled than two; a deaf husband and a blind wife are always a happy couple; every Jack has his Jill; first thrive and then wive; a good husband makes a good wife; a good Jack makes a good Jill; the gray mare is the better horse; hanging and wiving go by destiny; happy is the bride that the sun shines on; happy's the wooing that's not long a-doing; he that has a wife and children has given hostages to fortune; he that will thrive must first ask his wife; honest men marry quickly, wise men not at all; the husband is always the last to know; keep your eyes wide open before marriage, half shut afterward; marriage is a lottery; marriages are made in heaven; marry in haste, repent at leisure; marry in May, rue for aye; never marry for money, but marry where money is; old maids lead apes in hell; one wedding brings another; there goes more to marriage than four bare legs in a bed; wedlock is a padlock; when a man's single, his pockets will jingle; why buy the cow when you can get the milk for free?; a young man married is a young man marred

meaning
every picture tells a story; one picture is worth ten thousand words

mediocrity
in the country of the blind, the one-eyed man is king; a jack of all trades is master of none

meekness (*See also* **humility**)
even a worm will turn; the meek shall inherit the earth

memory
an elephant never forgets; a liar should have a good memory

men (*See also* **men and women**)
boys will be boys; the way to a man's heart is through his stomach

men and women (*See also* **men; women**)
behind every great man there is a great woman; can't live with 'em, can't live without 'em; every Jack has his Jill; the female of the species is deadlier than the male; a good husband makes a good wife; a good Jack makes a good Jill; the gray mare is the better horse; it's a sad house where the hen crows louder than the cock; a man is as old as he feels, and a woman as old as she looks; men are from Mars, women are from Venus; men make houses, women make homes; six hours' sleep for a man, seven for a woman, and eight for a fool; a son is a son till he gets him a wife, a daughter's a daughter all of her life

merit
desert and reward seldom keep company; give credit where credit is due; it's a poor dog that's not worth whistling for; opportunities look for you when you are worth finding

merrymaking
the company makes the feast; eat, drink, and be merry, for tomorrow we die; it's merry in hall when beards wag all; laugh and grow fat; the more the merrier

misfortune
accidents will happen in the best-regulated families; bad news travels fast; the best-laid schemes of mice and men gang aft a-gley; bread always falls buttered side down; help you to salt, help you to sorrow; if anything can go wrong, it will; into every life a little rain must fall; it never rains but it pours;

it's an ill wind that blows nobody any good; it's no use crying over spilled milk; lightning never strikes twice in the same place; many go out for wool and come home shorn; marry in May, rue for aye; misfortunes never come singly; one man's loss is another man's gain; shit happens; worse things happen at sea

mistakes

accidents will happen in the best-regulated families; don't make the same mistake twice; Homer sometimes nods; if you don't make mistakes you don't make anything; learn from the mistakes of others; a miss is as good as a mile; nobody is infallible; a stumble may prevent a fall; there's many a slip between cup and lip; those who cannot remember the past are condemned to repeat it; to err is human, to forgive divine

moderation

enough is as good as a feast; enough is enough; the half is better than the whole; less is more; love me little, love me long; moderation in all things; tell not all you know, nor do all you can; there's measure in all things

modesty

don't hide your light under a bushel; it's all in a day's work; wear your learning like your watch, in a private pocket

money (*See also* **payment; spending; wealth**)

another day, another dollar; bad money drives out good; the best things in life are free; don't throw good money after bad; a fool and his money are soon parted; a golden key can open any door; a heavy purse makes a light heart; it takes money to make money; a light purse makes a

heavy heart; little and often fills the purse; the love of money is the root of all evil; money begets money; money can't buy happiness; money doesn't grow on trees; money has no smell; money isn't everything; money is power; money is round and rolls away; money is the root of all evil; money makes the mare go; money makes the world go round; money talks; never marry for money, but marry where money is; riches have wings; save something for a rainy day; saving is getting; shrouds have no pockets; take care of the pennies and the dollars will take care of themselves; time is money; where there's muck there's brass; you can't serve God and mammon; you can't take it with you

months   See **calendar**

mortality

art is long and life is short; be happy while you're living, for you're a long time dead; eat, drink, and be merry, for tomorrow we die; every door may be shut but death's door; gather ye rosebuds while ye may; life is short and sweet; life is short and time is swift; life is too short; life's a bitch, and then you die; live every day as though it were your last; medicine can prolong life, but death will seize the doctor, too; old soldiers never die; young men may die, but old men must die

music

music hath charms to soothe the savage breast; why should the devil have all the best tunes?

names

a rose by any other name would smell as sweet; a rose is a rose is a rose is a rose; what's in a name?

nature   (*See also* **human nature**)
God made the country and man made the town; it's not spring until you can plant your foot upon twelve daisies; nature abhors a vacuum; nature does nothing in vain; nature will have its course; self-preservation is the first law of nature; you can drive out nature with a pitchfork but she keeps on coming back

necessity
any port in a storm; beggars can't be choosers; desperate diseases must have desperate remedies; dirty water will quench fire; hunger drives the wolf out of the wood; if the mountain will not come to Mohammed, Mohammed must go to the mountain; make a virtue of necessity; a man's got to do what a man's got to do; necessity is the mother of invention; necessity knows no law; necessity sharpens industry; need makes the old wife trot; needs must when the devil drives; when all fruit fails, welcome haws; when all you have is a hammer, everything looks like a nail; you can't make an omelette without breaking eggs

neglect
a mother can take care of ten children, but sometimes ten children can't take care of one mother; one year's seeding makes seven years' weeding; the shoemaker's child always goes barefoot; there's a sin of omission as well as of commission

news
bad news travels fast; don't shoot the messenger; go abroad and you'll hear news of home; he comes too early who brings bad news ; no news is good news; when a dog bites a man, that is not news; but when a man bites a dog, that is news

nobility
everybody loves a lord; it takes three generations to make a gentleman; kind hearts are more than coronets; when Adam delved and Eve span, who was then the gentleman?

noise
a bellowing cow soon forgets her calf; much cry and little wool; the squeaky wheel gets the grease

noninterference
don't rock the boat; if it ain't broke, don't fix it; leave well enough alone; let sleeping dogs lie; let the cobbler stick to his last; mind your own business; never trouble trouble till trouble troubles you; when in doubt, do nothing

numbers
there's luck in odd numbers; things come in threes; the third time is the charm

obedience
the first duty of a soldier is obedience; a good leader is also a good follower; he that cannot obey cannot command; obey orders, if you break owners

objectivity
justice is blind; lookers-on see most of the game

observation
the eye of a master does more work than both his hands; four eyes see more than two; keep your mouth shut and your eyes open; lookers-on see most of the game; seeing is believing

obstinacy
little birds that can sing and won't sing must be made to sing; stick to your guns;

there are none so blind as those who will not see; there are none so deaf as those who will not hear; a willful man must have his way; you can lead a horse to water, but you can't make him drink; you can't get blood from a stone

offense

the greater the truth, the greater the libel; hell hath no fury like a woman scorned; neither give nor take offense

old age   See **age**

opinion

he that complies against his will is of his own opinion still; so many men, so many opinions; thinking is very far from knowing; thought is free; a wise man changes his mind, but a fool never does

opportunity

all is fish that comes to the net; all is grist that comes to the mill; a bleating sheep loses a bite; business neglected is business lost; Christmas comes but once a year; eat, drink, and be merry, for tomorrow we die; every dog has his day; gather ye rosebuds while ye may; the gods send nuts to those who have no teeth; he that will not when he may, when he will he may have nay; hoist your sail when the wind is fair; the hole calls the thief; it's good fishing in troubled waters; life is short and time is swift; make hay while the sun shines; the mill cannot grind with the water that is past; opportunities look for you when you are worth finding; opportunity knocks but once; opportunity never knocks for persons not worth a rap; peace makes plenty; a postern door makes a thief; seize the day; strike while the iron is hot; take the goods the gods provide; take time by the forelock; there

are other fish in the sea; there's a tide in the affairs of man; there's no time like the present; time and tide wait for no man; when one door closes, another one opens; when the cat's away, the mice will play; while two dogs are fighting for a bone, a third runs away with it; you can lead a horse to water, but you can't make him drink; you're only young once

oppression

the blood of the martyrs is the seed of the church; it's better to die on your feet than live on your knees

optimism   (*See also* **hope**)

all's for the best in the best of all possible worlds; always look on the bright side; another day, another dollar; April showers bring May flowers; the best is yet to be; the darkest hour is just before dawn; don't count your chickens before they are hatched; every cloud has a silver lining; the glass is either half empty or half full; God's in his heaven; all's right with the world; hope for the best and prepare for the worst; hope springs eternal in the human breast; it's an ill wind that blows nobody any good; nothing so bad but it might have been worse ; prosperity is just around the corner; there's no great loss without some gain; tomorrow is another day

options

don't put all your eggs in one basket; the mouse that has but one hole is quickly taken; there are other fish in the sea

order

don't put the cart before the horse; first catch your hare; first things first; last but not least; which came first, the chicken or the egg?

overambitiousness

cut your coat according to your cloth; don't bite off more than you can chew; don't go near the water until you learn how to swim; don't start anything you can't finish; everybody stretches his legs according to the length of his coverlet; grasp no more than the hand will hold; he who begins many things, finishes but few; stretch your arm no further than your sleeve will reach

overconfidence

don't count your chickens before they are hatched; don't shout until you are out of the woods; he that is too secure is not safe; let them laugh that win; a little knowledge is a dangerous thing; there's many a slip between cup and lip

overreaction

burn not your house to scare away the mice; don't throw out the baby with the bathwater

parents and children   (*See also* **children; family; heredity**)

the art of being a parent consists of sleeping when the baby isn't looking; children are certain cares, but uncertain comforts; happy is he that is happy in his children; he that has a wife and children has given hostages to fortune; he that would the daughter win, must with the mother first begin; it's a wise child that knows its own father; late children, early orphans; a mother can take care of ten children, but sometimes ten children can't take care of one mother; parents are patterns; praise the child, and you make love to the mother; a son is a son till he gets him a wife, a daughter's a daughter all of her life; the tree is known by its fruit

past   (*See also* **history**)

the future ain't what it used to be; the golden age was never the present age; it's no use crying over spilled milk; let bygones be bygones; let the dead bury the dead; the mill cannot grind with the water that is past; old sins cast long shadows; other times, other manners; there are no birds in last year's nest; things past cannot be recalled; those who cannot remember the past are condemned to repeat it; what's done cannot be undone; what's past is prologue; yesterday will not be called again; you can't go home again

patience

all commend patience, but none can endure to suffer; all things come to those who wait; bear and forbear; desires are nourished by delays; first things first; hurry no man's cattle; the longest way around is the shortest way home; nothing should be done in haste but gripping a flea; one step at a time; patience is a remedy for every sorrow; patience is a virtue; revenge is a dish best eaten cold; Rome was not built in a day; slow and steady wins the race; softly, softly, catchee monkey; there's luck in leisure; they also serve who only stand and wait; a watched pot never boils; we must learn to walk before we can run

patriotism

patriotism is the last refuge of a scoundrel

payment

he who pays the piper calls the tune; if you pay peanuts, you get monkeys; the laborer is worthy of his hire; no penny, no paternoster; nothing for nothing; pay as you go and nothing you'll owe; pay beforehand was never well served; pay what you owe and you'll know what you own; render unto Caesar that which is Caesar's; there's no such thing as a free lunch; they that dance must pay the piper; whose bread I eat, his song I sing; you don't get something for nothing; you get what you pay for

peace

if you want peace, prepare for war; one sword keeps another in its scabbard; peace makes plenty; war will cease when men refuse to fight

perfection

the best is the enemy of the good; God's in his heaven; all's right with the world; trifles make perfection, and perfection is no trifle

perseverance

if at first you don't succeed, try, try again; it's dogged as does it; it's idle to swallow the cow and choke on the tail; the race is not to the swift, nor the battle to the strong; Rome was not built in a day; a stern chase is a long chase; the third time is the charm; the vicar of Bray will be vicar of Bray still; a winner never quits, and a quitter never wins

persistence

constant dropping wears away a stone; don't give up the ship; little strokes fell great oaks; never say die; the pitcher will go to the well once too often; the squeaky wheel gets the grease; the tongue always returns to the sore tooth

pessimism

the glass is either half empty or half full; the worst is yet to come

pity See **sympathy**

plans

the best-laid schemes of mice and men gang aft a-gley; man proposes, God disposes

pleasing people

you can't be all things to all men; you can't please everybody; you'll be damned if you do and damned if you don't

pleasure

forbidden fruit is sweet; stolen waters are sweet; there's no pleasure without pain; they that dance must pay the piper

politics

in politics a man must learn to rise above principle; politics makes strange bedfellows

positive thinking

it's better to laugh than to cry; the only difference between stumbling blocks and stepping-stones is the way you use them

possession

a bird in the hand is worth two in the bush; finders keepers, losers weepers; finding is keeping; nought is never in danger; pay what you owe and you'll know what you own; possession is nine points of the law; what you've never had you never miss; you can't lose what you never had

possibility

all things are possible with God; nothing is impossible to a willing heart; whatever man has done, man may do; what has happened once can happen again

poverty

better a dinner of herbs where love is than a stalled ox where hate is; both poverty and prosperity come from spending money—prosperity from spending it wisely; an empty sack cannot stand upright; from shirtsleeves to shirtsleeves is only three generations; a light purse makes a heavy heart; one law for the rich and another for the poor; poverty comes from God, but not dirt; poverty is no disgrace, but it's a great inconvenience; poverty is not a crime; the rich get richer and the poor get poorer; the rich man has his ice in the summer and the poor man gets his in the winter; sloth is the mother of poverty; sue a beggar and catch a louse; when poverty comes in at the door, love flies out of the window; willful waste makes woeful want

power

anger without power is folly; better be first in a village than second at Rome; big fish eat little fish; he who pays the piper calls the tune; the highest branch is not the safest roost; in the country of the blind, the one-eyed man is king; it's ill sitting at Rome and striving with the Pope; kings have long arms; knowledge is power; love conquers all; a man's home is his castle; might makes right; money is power; power corrupts, and absolute power corrupts absolutely; providence is always on the side of the big battalions; uneasy lies the head that wears a crown

praise

give credit where credit is due; imitation is the sincerest form of flattery; praise the bridge that carries you over

prediction

coming events cast their shadows before; jesters do oft prove prophets; long fore-told, long last; short notice, soon past; nothing is certain but the unforeseen; one swallow does not make a summer; straws show which way the wind blows; the unexpected always happens

prejudice

no tree takes so deep a root as prejudice; prejudice is being down on what we are not up on; prejudice is the child of ignorance

premature death

God takes soonest those he loves best; the good die young; whom the gods love die young; young men may die, but old men must die

preparation

dig the well before you are thirsty; don't go near the water until you learn how to swim; the early man never borrows from the late man; forewarned is forearmed; hope for the best and prepare for the worst; if you want peace, prepare for war; nothing is certain but the unforeseen; one sword keeps another in its scabbard; put your trust in God, and keep your powder dry; speak softly and carry a big stick

present

eat, drink, and be merry, for tomorrow we die; gather ye rosebuds while ye may; the golden age was never the present age; jam tomorrow and jam yesterday, but never jam today; seize the day; there's no time like the present; today is yesterday's tomorrow

pride

nobody is indispensable; pride feels no pain; pride goes before a fall

publicity

any publicity is good publicity; good wine needs no bush

punctuality   See **promptness**

punishment

catching's before hanging; confess and be hanged; crime doesn't pay; kings have long arms; little thieves are hanged, but great ones escape; no names, no pack-drill; spare the rod and spoil the child

quarreling   See **conflict**

questions

ask a silly question and you get a silly answer; ask me no questions and I'll tell you no lies; a civil question deserves a civil answer; curiosity killed the cat; fools ask questions that wise men cannot answer

raw material

garbage in, garbage out; good seed makes a good crop; an ill bird lays an ill egg; you can't make a silk purse out of a sow's ear; you can't make bricks without straw

reciprocity

do as you would be done by; dog does not eat dog; do unto others as you would have them do unto you; hawks will not pick out hawks' eyes; love begets love; one good turn deserves another; one hand washes the other; you don't get something for nothing; you scratch my back and I'll scratch yours

reconciliation

never let the sun go down on your anger; the quarrel of lovers is the renewal of love

recreation

all work and no play makes Jack a dull boy; the best doctors are Dr. Diet, Dr. Quiet, and Dr. Merryman; business before pleasure; never mix business with pleasure; work before play

reform

it's never too late to mend; the leopard can't change its spots; an old poacher makes the best gamekeeper

regret

marry in haste, repent at leisure; the obvious choice is usually a quick regret; things past cannot be recalled; what's done cannot be undone

religion   (*See also* **God**)

a believer is a songless bird in a cage; the better the day, the better the deed; the blood of the martyrs is the seed of the church; the church is an anvil which has worn out many hammers; a church is God between four walls; clergymen's sons always turn out badly; courage is fear that has said its prayers; the danger past and God forgotten; the devil can cite scripture for his purpose; the devil gets up to the belfry by the vicar's skirts; faith will move mountains; the family that prays together stays together; if God did not exist, it would be necessary to invent him; like people, like priest; man's extremity is God's opportunity; a man without a religion is a horse without a bridle; meat and mass never hindered man; the nearer the church, the farther from God; no penny, no paternoster; why should the devil have all the best tunes?; you can't build a church with stumbling blocks; you can't serve God and mammon

rest

the best doctors are Dr. Diet, Dr. Quiet, and Dr. Merryman; a change is as good as a rest; it's as cheap sitting as standing; there's no peace for the wicked; there's no rest for the weary

retaliation   (*See also* **revenge**)

the biter is sometimes bit; even a worm will turn; an eye for an eye, and a tooth for a tooth; he who laughs last, laughs longest; judge not, that ye be not judged; people who live in glass houses shouldn't throw stones; two wrongs don't make a right; whosoever draws his sword against the prince must throw the scabbard away

retribution

curses, like chickens, come home to roost; ill-gotten goods never thrive; the mills of God grind slowly, yet they grind exceedingly small; what goes around, comes around

revenge   (*See also* **retaliation**)

the best way to get even is to forget; blood will have blood; don't cut off your nose to spite your face; don't get mad, get even; hell hath no fury like a woman scorned; neglect will kill an injury sooner than revenge; revenge is a dish best eaten cold; revenge is sweet

revolution

revolutions are not made with rose water; whosoever draws his sword against the prince must throw the scabbard away

reward

desert and reward seldom keep company; good Americans, when they die, go to Paris; a good dog deserves a good bone; the higher the tree, the sweeter the plum; if you pay peanuts, you get monkeys; the laborer is worthy of his hire; the meek shall inherit the earth; no good deed goes unpunished; none but the brave deserve the fair; virtue is its own reward

risk   (*See also* **danger**)

adventures are to the adventurous; a bird in the hand is worth two in the bush; don't go near the water until you learn how to swim; don't put all your eggs in one basket; the game is not worth the candle; if you don't speculate, you can't accumulate; little boats should stay close to shore; nothing ventured, nothing gained; nought is never in danger

rulers

Caesar's wife must be above suspicion; the king can do no wrong; kings have long arms; Nero fiddled while Rome burned; uneasy lies the head that wears a crown; whosoever draws his sword against the prince must throw the scabbard away

rules

every land has its own law; the exception proves the rule; necessity knows no law; new lords, new laws; rules are made to be broken; there's an exception to every rule; when in Rome, do as the Romans do

rumors   (*See also* **gossip**)

common fame is seldom to blame; a lie can go around the world and back again while the truth is lacing up its boots; there's no smoke without fire; what everybody says must be true; what the soldier said isn't evidence

ruthlessness

a cat in gloves catches no mice; nice guys finish last; you can't make an omelette without breaking eggs

487

sacrifice

gold may be bought too dear; throw out a sprat to catch a mackerel; you can't make an omelette without breaking eggs

safety See security

sailing

the good seaman is known in bad weather; he that would go to sea for pleasure would go to hell for a pastime; he that would learn to pray, let him go to sea; one hand for yourself and one for the ship

satisfaction

the best is the enemy of the good; enough is as good as a feast; go farther and fare worse; the good is the enemy of the best; half a loaf is better than no bread; if it ain't broke, don't fix it; leave well enough alone; something is better than nothing

saying and doing

actions speak louder than words; all commend patience, but none can endure to suffer; a barking dog never bites; deeds, not words; deeds are fruits, words are but leaves; do as I say, not as I do; don't talk the talk if you can't walk the walk; easier said than done; example is better than precept; fine words butter no parsnips; honesty is more praised than practiced; the more said, the less done; much cry and little wool; much smoke, little fire; practice what you preach; the road to hell is paved with good intentions; talk is cheap; threatened men live long

seasons See calendar

secrecy

alcohol will preserve anything but a secret; fields have eyes and woods have ears; little birds that can sing and won't sing must be made to sing; love and a cough cannot be hid; never tell tales out of school; no names, no pack-drill; a secret is either too good to keep or too bad not to tell; a secret's a secret until it's told; there's a skeleton in every closet; three may keep a secret, if two of them are dead; walls have ears

security

caution is the parent of safety; don't put all your eggs in one basket; he that is too secure is not safe; the mouse that has but one hole is quickly taken; one hand for yourself and one for the ship; safe bind, safe find; safety first; there's safety in numbers

self-centeredness

every horse thinks its own pack heaviest; a man wrapped up in himself makes a very small bundle

self-harm

don't cut off your nose to spite your face; every man is his own worst enemy

self-help

every man is the architect of his own fortune; God helps those who help themselves; if you want a thing done well, do it yourself; if you would be well served, serve yourself; life is what you make it; put your trust in God, and keep your powder dry

self-interest

every man for himself and the devil take the hindmost; interest will not lie; a man is a lion in his own cause; near is my shirt, but nearer is my skin; self-interest is the rule, self-sacrifice the exception; take care of number one

selfishness   See **self-interest**

self-knowledge
the best place for criticism is in front of your mirror; it takes one to know one; know thyself; physician, heal thyself; the pot calls the kettle black; sweep your own doorstep clean; the wearer best knows where the shoe pinches; a wise man is never less alone than when alone

selflessness
deny self for self's sake; self-interest is the rule, self-sacrifice the exception

self-preservation
every man for himself and God for us all; every man for himself and the devil take the hindmost; one hand for yourself and one for the ship; self-preservation is the first law of nature

self-reliance
every man must skin his own skunk; every tub must stand on its own bottom; God helps those who help themselves; he travels fastest who travels alone; nothing can bring you peace but yourself; paddle your own canoe; stand on your own two feet

selling   See **buying and selling**

sharing
share and share alike; turnabout is fair play; what's yours is mine, and what's mine is my own

sickness
a creaking door hangs longest; the doctor is often more to be feared than the disease; a dry cough is the trumpeter of death; feed a cold and starve a fever; a green winter makes a fat churchyard; love

and a cough cannot be hid; may chickens come cheeping

silence
children should be seen and not heard; keep your mouth shut and your eyes open; least said, soonest mended; little birds that can sing and won't sing must be made to sing; no news is good news; a shut mouth catches no flies; silence gives consent; silence is golden; silence is the fittest reply to folly; speech is silver, but silence is golden; a still tongue makes a wise head; still waters run deep; there is a time to speak and a time to be silent; think before you speak; those who know don't speak; those who speak don't know; who knows most, speaks least; a word spoken is past recalling

similarity
all cats are gray in the dark; the apple never falls far from the tree; birds of a feather flock together; diamond cuts diamond; the enemy of my enemy is my friend; extremes meet; fight fire with fire; great minds think alike; it's six of one and half a dozen of the other; like attracts like; like breeds like; like cures like; like father, like son; like mother, like daughter; pigs are pigs; take a hair of the dog that bit you; water seeks its own level; the wheel comes full circle; when Greek meets Greek, then comes the tug of war

size   (*See also* **great and small; small things**)
better a little fire to warm us than a big one to burn us; big fish eat little fish; the bigger they are, the harder they fall; big is beautiful; great oaks from little acorns grow; it's not the size of the dog in the fight, it's the size of the fight in the dog;

the larger the body, the bigger the heart; a little pot is soon hot; the nearer the bone, the sweeter the flesh; providence is always on the side of the big battalions; the weakest go to the wall; you can't get a quart into a pint pot

skepticism
believe only half of what you see and nothing you hear; believing has a core of unbelieving; seeing is believing; what's new cannot be true

sleep
early to bed and early to rise, makes a man healthy, wealthy, and wise; night brings counsel; one hour's sleep before midnight is worth two after; six hours' sleep for a man, seven for a woman, and eight for a fool; sleep is the brother of death; there'll be sleeping enough in the grave

slowness
fair and softly goes far in a day; life is hard by the yard, but by the inch life's a cinch; make haste slowly; the mills of God grind slowly, yet they grind exceedingly small; one step at a time; slow and steady wins the race; slow but sure

small things (*See also* **great and small; size**)
the best things come in small packages; the devil is in the details; a drowning man will catch at a straw; every little helps; for want of a nail the shoe was lost, for want of a shoe the horse was lost, and for want of a horse the rider was lost; it's a sin to steal a pin; it's better to light one candle than curse the darkness; little and often fills the purse; little boats should stay close to shore; little drops of water, little grains of sand,

make a mighty ocean and a pleasant land; little fish are sweet; little leaks sink the ship; little strokes fell great oaks; many a little makes a mickle; the mother of mischief is no bigger than a midge's wing; a short horse is soon curried; a small gift usually gets small thanks; small is beautiful; straws show which way the wind blows; trifles make perfection, and perfection is no trifle

social interaction
be nice to people on your way up because you'll meet them on your way down; different strokes for different folks; do as you would be done by; dog does not eat dog; do unto others as you would have them do unto you; fair and softly goes far in a day; gossip is the lifeblood of society; hawks will not pick out hawks' eyes; love your neighbor as yourself; two's company, three's a crowd; you can catch more flies with honey than with vinegar

society
if every man would sweep his own doorstep the city would soon be clean; it takes a village to raise a child; love makes the world go round; no man is an island; one half of the world doesn't know how the other half lives

soldiers   See **armed forces**

solitude
a great city, a great solitude; he travels fastest who travels alone; laugh and the world laughs with you, weep and you weep alone; no man is an island

sorrow
a bellowing cow soon forgets her calf; it's a poor heart that never rejoices; laugh and the

world laughs with you, weep and you weep alone; a light purse makes a heavy heart; misery loves company; no joy without annoy; patience is a remedy for every sorrow; sin, sorrow, and work are the things that men can't shirk; sing before breakfast, cry before night; small sorrows speak; great ones are silent; sorrow comes unsent for; Wednesday's child is full of woe

spare time
the busiest men have the most leisure; idle people have the least leisure

speech   See **talking**

spending   (*See also* **extravagance**)
both poverty and prosperity come from spending money—prosperity from spending it wisely; don't throw good money after bad; easy come, easy go; a fool and his money are soon parted; money burns a hole in the pocket; money is round and rolls away; riches have wings; spare and have is better than spend and crave; spare well and have to spend; spare when you're young and spend when you're old

sportsmanship
it's not whether you win or lose, but how you play the game; don't hit a man when he's down; fair play's a jewel

storytelling
a good tale is not the worse for being told twice; a tale never loses in the telling

strangeness
everybody's queer but you and me, and even you are a little queer; fact is stranger than fiction; truth is stranger than fiction

strength
a chain is no stronger than its weakest link; might makes right; providence is always on the side of the big battalions; the race is not to the swift, nor the battle to the strong; the weakest go to the wall; wisdom goes beyond strength

stress   (*See also* **worry**)
care killed the cat; if you can't stand the heat, get out of the kitchen; it's not work that kills, but worry; it's the pace that kills; when the going gets tough, the tough get going

style
it's not what you say, but how you say it; the style is the man

subjectivity
beauty is in the eye of the beholder; every man thinks his own geese swans; love is blind; love is blind; friendship closes its eyes; a man who is his own lawyer has a fool for his client; men are blind in their own cause; nobody should be judge in his own cause

success
every dog has his day; a good beginning makes a good ending; he that will thrive must first ask his wife; it's better to travel hopefully than to arrive; let them laugh that win; nothing succeeds like success; one business begets another; the only place where success comes before work is in a dictionary; success breeds success; success has many fathers, while failure is an orphan; success is never final; you can't argue with success

suffering
crosses are ladders that lead to heaven; no pain, no gain; pride feels no pain; the sharper the storm, the sooner it's over; there's no pleasure without pain; we all

have our cross to bear; the wearer best knows where the shoe pinches

suitability

every Jack has his Jill; horses for courses; if the shoe fits, wear it; never send a boy to do a man's job; there's a time and place for everything; to everything there is a season; what's sauce for the goose is sauce for the gander; you can't put a square peg in a round hole

superstition

dream of a funeral and you hear of a marriage; help you to salt, help you to sorrow; if you want to live and thrive, let the spider run alive; marry in May, rue for aye; morning dreams come true; no moon, no man; one for sorrow; two for mirth; three for a wedding; four for a birth; see a pin and pick it up, all the day you'll have good luck; see a pin and let it lay, bad luck you'll have all the day; step on a crack, break your mother's back; there's luck in odd numbers; things come in threes; the third time is the charm; touch wood; a wet May brings plenty of hay

surprise

nothing is certain but the unforeseen; the unexpected always happens; wonders will never cease!

surrender   See **giving up**

sycophancy

everybody loves a lord; he that has a full purse never wanted a friend; a rich man's joke is always funny; wealth makes many friends

sympathy

better be envied than pitied; misery loves company; pity is akin to love; a trouble shared is a trouble halved

tact   (*See also* **discretion**)

least said, soonest mended; never speak of rope in the house of a man who has been hanged; an ounce of discretion is worth a pound of wit; a soft answer turns away wrath; speak not of my debts unless you mean to pay them; there's a time to speak and a time to be silent; think all you speak, but speak not all you think; think before you speak; think much, speak little, and write less

tactics

all fish are not caught with flies; the fox preys furthest from his hole; he who fights and runs away may live to fight another day; quit while you are ahead; soft and fair goes far; softly, softly, catchee monkey; take things as they come

taking no notice

a deaf husband and a blind wife are always a happy couple; the dogs bark, but the caravan goes on; a hungry stomach has no ears; love is blind; friendship closes its eyes; Nero fiddled while Rome burned; see no evil, hear no evil, speak no evil; there are none so blind as those who will not see; there are none so deaf as those who will not hear

talent

everybody to whom much is given, of him will much be required; good men are scarce; poets are born, not made

talking   (*See also* **saying and doing; words**)

a bleating sheep loses a bite; empty vessels make the most sound; it's merry in hall when beards wag all; loose lips sink ships; out of the fullness of the heart the mouth speaks; some folks speak from experience;

others, from experience, don't speak; speech is silver, but silence is golden; think before you speak; those who know don't speak; those who speak don't know; a word spoken is past recalling

taste
every man after his fashion; every man to his taste; far-fetched and dear-bought is good for ladies; one man's meat is another man's poison; one man's trash is another man's treasure; tastes differ; there's no accounting for tastes; there's no disputing about tastes; to each his own

temptation
away goes the devil when he finds the door shut against him; the devil dances in an empty pocket; don't let the fox guard the henhouse; forbidden fruit is sweet; the hole calls the thief; the hook without bait catches no fish; an open door may tempt a saint; opportunity makes a thief; stolen waters are sweet

thoroughness
don't spoil the ship for half a penny's worth of tar; in for a penny, in for a pound; it's idle to swallow the cow and choke on the tail; leave no stone unturned; the longest way around is the shortest way home; never do things by halves; one might as well be hanged for a sheep as for a lamb

threats
a barking dog never bites; if you can't bite, never show your teeth; speak softly and carry a big stick; threatened men live long

thrift   (*See also* **frugality**)
keep a thing seven years and you'll find a use for it; most people consider thrift

a fine virtue in ancestors; a penny saved is a penny earned; saving is getting; see a pin and pick it up, all the day you'll have good luck; see a pin and let it lay, bad luck you'll have all the day; spare and have is better than spend and crave; spare well and have to spend; spare when you're young and spend when you're old; take care of the pennies and the dollars will take care of themselves; thrift is a great revenue; waste not, want not

tidiness
the house shows the owner; a place for everything and everything in its place; see a pin and pick it up, all the day you'll have good luck; see a pin and let it lay, bad luck you'll have all the day

time
the clock goes as it pleases the clerk; the day is short and the work is long; life is short and time is swift; lose an hour in the morning, chase it all day; patience is a remedy for every sorrow; take time by the forelock; time flies; time hangs heavy on idle hands; time is a great healer; time is money; time lost cannot be recalled; time works wonders; work expands so as to fill the time available for its completion; yesterday will not be called again

timeliness
everything is good in its season; there's a time and place for everything; timing is everything; to everything there is a season; who repairs not his gutters repairs his whole house

tolerance
bear and forbear; give and take is fair play; it takes all kinds of people to make a world; judge not, that ye be not judged;

upbringing

as the twig is bent, so is the tree inclined; birth is much but breeding more; it takes a village to raise a child; nature passes nurture; nurture passes nature; spare the rod and spoil the child

usefulness

all is fish that comes to the net; all is grist that comes to the mill; fire is a good servant but a bad master; keep a thing seven years and you'll find a use for it

value

bad money drives out good; it's a poor dog that's not worth whistling for; one man's trash is another man's treasure; a thing you don't want is dear at any price; the worth of a thing is what it will bring; you get what you pay for

vice

gossip is vice enjoyed vicariously; prosperity discovers vice; adversity, virtue

victory (*See also* **winning and losing**)

divide and conquer; he who laughs last, laughs longest; in war there is no substitute for victory; it's better to lose the battle and win the war; let them laugh that win; the race is not to the swift, nor the battle to the strong; slow and steady wins the race; to the victor belong the spoils; winning isn't everything, it's the only thing

violence

he who lives by the sword dies by the sword; revolutions are not made with rose water

virtue

do right and fear no man; the good die young; good men are scarce; the good

that men do lives after them; he lives long who lives well; if you can't be good, be careful; let him who is without sin cast the first stone; nobody is perfect; prosperity discovers vice; adversity, virtue; to the pure all things are pure; virtue is its own reward

waiting

it's ill waiting for dead men's shoes; they also serve who only stand and wait; while the grass grows, the steed starves

war

a bayonet is a weapon with a worker at each end; truth is the first casualty of war; war is hell; war is too important to be left to the generals; war will cease when men refuse to fight

warning

coming events cast their shadows before; the dogs bark, but the caravan goes on; forewarned is forearmed; a prophet is not without honor, save in his own country; threatened men live long

waste

don't cast your pearls before swine; don't throw good money after bad; haste makes waste; a mind is a terrible thing to waste; mind unemployed is mind unenjoyed; waste not, want not; willful waste makes woeful want

ways and means

all roads lead to Rome; easy does it; fish where the fish are; give a man enough rope and he'll hang himself; go hunting where the ducks are; he who wills the end, wills the means; set a thief to catch a thief; softly, softly, catchee monkey;

there are more ways of killing a cat than choking it with cream; there's more than one way to skin a cat; throw out a sprat to catch a mackerel; where there's a will there's a way; you can catch more flies with honey than with vinegar

weakness

a chain is no stronger than its weakest link; if you can't run with the big dogs, stay under the porch; if you can't stand the heat, get out of the kitchen; the spirit is willing but the flesh is weak; the thread breaks where it is weakest; the weakest go to the wall

wealth   (*See also* **money**)

better a dinner of herbs where love is than a stalled ox where hate is; both poverty and prosperity come from spending money—prosperity from spending it wisely; early to bed and early to rise, makes a man healthy, wealthy, and wise; give a beggar a horse and he'll ride it to death; gold may be bought too dear; a heavy purse makes a light heart; he that has a full purse never wanted a friend; if you don't speculate, you can't accumulate; it's better to be born lucky than rich; light gains make heavy purses; money is power; money makes a man; money talks; much coin, much care; never marry for money, but marry where money is; one law for the rich and another for the poor; prosperity discovers vice; adversity, virtue; the rich get richer and the poor get poorer; the rich man has his ice in the summer and the poor man gets his in the winter; a rich man's joke is always funny; set a beggar on horseback, and he'll ride to the devil; wealth makes many friends; when a man's single, his pockets will jingle; where bees are, there is honey

weather

as the day lengthens, so the cold strengthens; avoid an ash, it counts the flash; beware of an oak, it draws the stroke; blessed are the dead that the rain rains on; creep under the thorn, it can save you from harm; a dripping June sets all in tune; drought never bred dearth in England; a green winter makes a fat churchyard; happy is the bride that the sun shines on; long foretold, long last; March comes in like a lion, and goes out like a lamb; ne'er cast a clout till May be out; the north wind doth blow and we shall have snow; rain before seven, fine before eleven; red sky at night, sailor's delight; red sky in the morning, sailors take warning; Robin Hood could brave all weathers but a thaw wind; short notice, soon past; there's no such thing as bad weather, only the wrong clothes; a wet May brings plenty of hay; when the wind is in the east, 'tis neither good for man nor beast; winter finds out what summer lays up

willingness

one volunteer is worth two pressed men; the spirit is willing but the flesh is weak; the willing horse carries the load

winning and losing   (*See also* **victory; loss**)

heads I win, tails you lose; it's an ill wind that blows nobody any good; it's not whether you win or lose, but how you play the game; nice guys finish last; one man's loss is another man's gain; there's no great loss without some gain; what you lose on the swings you gain on the roundabouts; a winner never quits, and a quitter never wins; winning isn't everything, it's the only thing; you can't beat a man at his own game; you can't beat somebody with nobody; you can't win 'em all; you win some, you lose some

wisdom
early to bed and early to rise, makes a man healthy, wealthy, and wise; experience is the mother of wisdom; it's better to be happy than wise; knowledge and wisdom are far from being one; the older the wiser; an old fox is not easily snared; out of the mouths of babes and sucklings come great truths; a still tongue makes a wise head; wisdom goes beyond strength; wisdom is better than rubies; a wise man changes his mind, but a fool never does; with age comes wisdom; you can't put an old head on young shoulders

wishes   See **desire**

women   (*See also* **men and women**)
behind every great man there is a great woman; far-fetched and dear-bought is good for ladies; the female of the species is deadlier than the male; the gray mare is the better horse; the hand that rocks the cradle rules the world; hell hath no fury like a woman scorned; he that will thrive must first ask his wife; he that would the daughter win, must with the mother first begin; a whistling woman and a crowing hen are neither fit for God nor men; a woman's work is never done

words   (*See also* **talking; writing**)
all words are pegs to hang ideas on; hard words break no bones; it's not what you say, but how you say it; one picture is worth ten thousand words; sticks and stones may break my bones, but names will never hurt me; the tongue is not steel, but it cuts

work   (*See also* **industry**)
all work and no play makes Jack a dull boy; another day, another dollar; better to wear out than to rust out; business before pleasure; first thrive and then wive; fools and children should never see half-done work; genius is one percent inspiration and ninety-nine percent perspiration; he who does not work, neither should he eat; it's all in a day's work; it's not work that kills, but worry; many hands make light work; Saturday's child works hard for its living; a short horse is soon curried; sin, sorrow, and work are the things that men can't shirk; a woman's work is never done; work before play; work expands so as to fill the time available for its completion; work never hurt anybody

workers
a bad workman quarrels with his tools; a bayonet is a weapon with a worker at each end; every employee tends to rise to his level of incompetence; if you pay peanuts, you get monkeys; if you want a thing done well, do it yourself; if you would be well served, serve yourself; keep no more cats than will catch mice; the laborer is worthy of his hire; like master, like man; pay beforehand was never well served; too many chiefs and not enough Indians; two boys are half a boy, and three boys are no boy at all; why keep a dog and bark yourself?

worry
action is worry's worst enemy; care is no cure; care killed the cat; don't meet troubles halfway; it'll all be the same in a hundred years; it's not work that kills, but worry; one courageous thought will put to flight a host of troubles; past cure, past care; sufficient unto the day is the evil thereof; worry is interest paid on trouble before it falls due

worthlessness
garbage in, garbage out; good riddance to bad rubbish; ill weeds grow apace; it's a

poor dog that's not worth whistling for; opportunity never knocks for persons not worth a rap; you can't make a silk purse out of a sow's ear

writing

a goose quill is more dangerous than a lion's claw; he who would write and can't write can surely review; paper bleeds little; paper does not blush; the pen is mightier than the sword; poets are born, not made; a white wall is the fool's writing paper

wrongdoing

catching's before hanging; charity covers a multitude of sins; cheaters never prosper; crime doesn't pay; crime must be concealed by crime; curses, like chickens, come home to roost; the devil dances in an empty pocket; the devil finds work for idle hands to do; the devil gets up to the belfry by the vicar's skirts; the dog always returns to his vomit; every dog is allowed one bite; evil doers are evil dreaders; the fox preys furthest from his hole; the hole calls the thief; an idle brain is the devil's workshop; idleness is the root of all evil; if there were no receivers, there would be no thieves; ill-gotten goods never thrive; it's a sin to steal a pin; lawmakers should not be lawbreakers; little thieves are hanged, but great ones escape; a man is innocent until proven guilty; murder will out; never ask pardon before you are accused; never do evil that good may come of it; offenders never pardon; an old poacher makes the best gamekeeper; old sins cast long shadows; once a thief, always a thief; one thief robs another; a postern door makes a thief; set a thief to catch a thief; sin, sorrow, and work are the things that men can't shirk; a slice off a cut loaf isn't missed; stolen waters are sweet; there's a sin of omission as well as of commission; there's honor among thieves; two wrongs don't make a right; what's got over the devil's back is spent under his belly; when thieves fall out, honest men come by their own

youth See **age; children; premature death**

Bibliography

Bertram, A., and R. A. Spears, eds. *NTC's Dictionary of Proverbs and Clichés.* Lincolnwood, Ill.: NTC Publishing Group, 1993.

Fergusson, R., and J. Law. *The Penguin Dictionary of Proverbs.* 2nd edition. London: Penguin Books, 2000.

Flavell, L., and R. Flavell. *Dictionary of Proverbs and Their Origins.* London: Kyle Cathie, 2004.

Knowles, E. *The Oxford Dictionary of Phrase, Saying, and Quotation.* Oxford: Oxford University Press, 1997.

Mieder, W., S. A. Kingsbury, and K. B. Harder, eds. *A Dictionary of American Proverbs.* New York: Oxford University Press, 1997.

Oxford English Dictionary. 2nd edition. Oxford: Oxford University Press, 1989.

Pickering, D. *Cassell's Dictionary of Proverbs.* 2nd edition. London: Cassell, 2001.

Ridout, R., and C. Witting. *English Proverbs Explained.* London: Pan Books, 1995.

Simpson, J., and J. Speake. *The Oxford Dictionary of Proverbs.* 5th edition. Oxford: Oxford University Press, 2004.

Titelman, G. *Random House Dictionary of America's Popular Proverbs and Sayings.* 2nd edition. New York: Random House, 2000.

Wilson, F. P. *The Oxford Dictionary of English Proverbs.* 3rd edition. Oxford: Oxford University Press, 1970.